Unexceptional

To: Jenna

Best Wishes !

Marc O'Reilly

Unexceptional

America's Empire in the Persian Gulf, 1941–2007

MARC J. O'REILLY

LEXINGTON BOOKS

A division of
ROWMAN & LITTLEFIELD PUBLISHERS, INC.
Lanham • Boulder • New York • Toronto • Plymouth, UK

LEXINGTON BOOKS

A division of Rowman & Littlefield Publishers, Inc.
A wholly owned subsidiary of The Rowman & Littlefield Publishing Group, Inc.
4501 Forbes Boulevard, Suite 200
Lanham, MD 20706

Estover Road
Plymouth PL6 7PY
United Kingdom

British Library Cataloguing in Publication Information Available

Library of Congress Cataloging-in-Publication Data

O'Reilly, Marc J., 1969–
  Unexceptional : America's empire in the Persian Gulf, 1941–2007 / Marc J. O'Reilly.
     p. cm.
  Includes bibliographical references and index.
  ISBN-13: 978-0-7391-0590-0 (cloth : alk. paper)
  ISBN-10: 0-7391-0590-6 (cloth : alk. paper)
  1. Persian Gulf Region—Foreign relations—United States. 2. United States—Foreign
relations—Persian Gulf Region. I. Title.
  DS326.O74 2008
  327.73053609'045—dc22

                                                          2007045659

Printed in the United States of America

♾ ™ The paper used in this publication meets the minimum requirements of American
National Standard for Information Sciences—Permanence of Paper for Printed Library
Materials, ANSI/NISO Z39.48–1992.

To my family

Contents

Tables

Preface

Many commentators, mainly scholars and journalists, now consider the United States the heir—rightful or not—to Rome.[1] They write of an American empire. Some point out its similarities to previous imperia, while others tout its exceptional features.[2] A few discuss its genesis and historical raison d'être—economic necessity (i.e., the need for export markets) and ideological fervor (i.e., the impulse to instill U.S. republican values in foreign societies).[3] Many claim that the first term of President George W. Bush ushered in a *new* American empire, one that so-called neo-conservatives cheered and critics derided.[4]

Periodically (for example, during the so-called imperial era following the Spanish-American War), analysts as well as politicians have examined the issue of U.S. empire. During the Vietnam War, critics associated with the New Left in American politics repeatedly accused Washington of prosecuting an imperial foreign policy. Following the end of the Cold War, however, few observers—usually critics of U.S. efforts at economic globalization—addressed the matter. Only in the aftermath of the September 11, 2001, terrorist attacks did commentators and policy advocates, especially conservative ones, return in earnest to the theme of American empire. "[A] left-wing accusation," wrote *The New Yorker*'s Joshua Marshall, "became a right-wing aspiration: conservatives increasingly began to espouse a world view that was unapologetically imperialist."[5]

Despite the conviction of some who spoke of an unmistakable American empire, others thought the evidence inconclusive, insufficient, or non-existent. Professor John Gray, for example, opined that "[t]he truth is that America lacks most of the attributes that make an imperial power."[6] For his part, political economist Robert Skidelsky asserted that "illuminating though it is, the attempt to fit the United States into historical patterns of empire is ultimately misguided."[7] Rather than settle the matter, however, this kind of skepticism only intensified the scholarly and policy debate regarding empires and whether the United States qualified as some type of imperium. Linda Colley, an authority on British imperialism, insightfully observed that, unlike the study of past imperia, "investigating current versions of empire is bound to be far more difficult and controversial; but it is vital."[8] Epistemological disagreements, in other words, will continue to shape thinking on the subject.

That varying definitions of empire preoccupy scholars and policymakers to such an extent today serves as a testament to the durability of the concept and the passions it continues to stir. As scholar Stephen Howe notes, empire "has had a complicated history and many different, fiercely contested meanings."[9] Still, I consider Stephen Peter Rosen's explication useful. "Empire," this professor argues, "is the rule exercised by one nation over others both to regulate their *external* behavior and to ensure minimally acceptable forms of *internal* behavior within the subordinate states."[10] To that definition I would add that for a country to possess an empire, it should have a physical presence in the influenced region (bases, advisors, entrepreneurs, corporations, etc.), establish decision-making parameters for subordinate states (i.e., restrict foreign-policy choices), and have access to different levers of power (political, economic, diplomatic, military, socio-cultural, psychological) to exercise influence and compel other countries to comply with its wishes.

Though many analysts depict America as an empire, some scholars prefer to think of the United States as merely a hegemonic power.[11] Like empire, however, the term "hegemony" connotes different types of American behavior.[12] For some observers, Washington exercises benign and helpful political leadership within the international community.[13] Others confine hegemony to the economic realm.[14] Finally, some use empire and hegemony synonymously.[15]

As with many contentious issues in political science, specifically within the subfield of international relations, ill-defined and/or disputed terminology often only confuses readers. Despite this concern, I consider empire an enduring and still relevant concept, notwithstanding its mostly negative connotation in the post-colonial era.[16] Although some scholars and other analysts denounce empire while others celebrate it, I consider this controversial entity capable of effecting both positive (e.g., economic growth, an end to ethnic bloodshed and tyranny) and negative outcomes (e.g., foreign oppression, exploitation, cultural insensitivity).[17]

By comparing the United States to previous imperia such as Athens, another maritime empire, one can certainly pinpoint similarities while appreciating differences.[18] Scholars can make these comparisons if they assume empire a dynamic, rather than static, construct. Given that, historically, empires have evolved to adjust to changing local, regional, and international contexts, analysts should admit to the possibility that America constitutes an empire of some kind[19]—liberal,[20] hybrid (liberal-classical, for example), or otherwise. Some scholars, however, consider any discussion of an American empire inappropriate as well as intellectually and ideologically repugnant.[21]

This belated or latest realization that U.S. policy shares much in common with past overlords and colossi occurred as President George W. Bush pondered, in 2002 and early 2003, invading and occupying a sovereign country, Iraq, whose leader, Saddam Hussein, continued to vex Washington. The possibility of American colonialism in the Middle East, considered anathema by many analysts who believed decolonization forever ruled out a renewal of this imperial remedy to disorder, disconcerted many observers who could not fathom why the United States would adopt such a discredited strategy.

Analysts missed the point, however. America had already evolved an "informal" empire in the Persian Gulf—one that married coercion, co-optation, and occasional violence but eschewed occupation, the hallmark of "formal" empire. Starting in World War II, U.S. policymakers crafted a variety of imperial responses that enabled the country to extend and preserve its interests in this region, deemed critical to American security due to the Gulf's plentiful hydrocarbons that powered Western economies. Like many imperial powers, Washington built up its Gulf empire fitfully. Early postwar successes augmented U.S. prestige and clout. But setbacks in the 1970s eroded American credibility and jeopardized the viability of this vital U.S. sphere of influence until victories in consecutive Persian Gulf wars elevated American power in this area to its apex. Victory in Iraq proved Pyrrhic, however, as the U.S. occupation has weakened its Gulf juggernaut considerably.

Washington's post-World War II Gulf empire waxed until 1958, waned until 1981, ascended until 2003, and has declined since the summer of that year. On a graph, high and low points in this "peak and valley" pattern corresponded to the aftermath of the 1956 Suez crisis, the 1979–81 Iranian revolution and hostage crisis, and the post-1991 Gulf War era. Whether the current U.S. predicament in Iraq constitutes a low point in the sequence will only be determined in hindsight. Notwithstanding such temporary imprecision, the U.S. empire in the Gulf is not simply "rising and falling." Such an oversimplification omits the iteration endemic to empires, which tend to wax and wane continuously over decades, if not centuries, without disappearing. Thus, better to think of the U.S. empire in the Gulf as emulating the zigzag lines on a seismogram. Analytically, this geology metaphor allows for contingency, whether in the form of regional upheaval, strong leadership, government ineptitude, fortuitousness, or bad luck.[22]

Although the U.S. empire in the Persian Gulf might qualify as sui generis, given America's obsession with Middle Eastern oil, in fact Washington's imperium in the Gulf resembles past and present U.S. spheres of influence in Latin America, East Asia, and Western Europe. Currently, though, the United States seems particularly fixated on the Gulf. Yet, despite this heightened concern, intense American involvement in this region occurred only intermittently—not unexpected in an informal empire—until 1991. Previous to *Operation Desert Shield/Storm*, Washington typically partook in contingent or situational imperialism rather than consistent or sustained imperialism. This imperial style meshed with America's professed anti-imperialism and exceptionalism.[23] Most of its citizens, including policymakers, oppose colonialism (political and military imperialism), but do not consider U.S. commercial endeavors imperial. Hence, Americans tend to balk at formal empire.[24]

Until the 2003 invasion and occupation of Iraq, the U.S. variant of empire in the Persian Gulf emphasized mostly cooperative diplomatic and other ventures with willing partners and allies—who, admittedly, did not necessarily incarnate majority sentiment in their countries, as evidenced, for example, in the 1953 American-supported coup d'état in Iran. Typically, Washington sought not to impose its will militarily unless unavoidable. Its reluctance to assume responsibility for governance enabled area governments to fashion authoritarian societies without constant U.S. interference. Unfortunately, such a policy ensured occasional discord with friends who sought to exercise their independence from America, and, more seriously, a U.S. inability to master certain situations. By providing Gulf elites with a stake in an oil-centered[25] American corporatist system that yielded financial and other rewards, Washington tried to maintain its position via co-optation rather than simply violence or the threat of military intervention.[26]

This modern empire, not unlike the United Kingdom's informal imperium to which it is often compared,[27] could adjust to altered circumstances more readily and more easily than other imperia (e.g., the Soviet Empire), whose rigid command structures and inflexible ideologies prevented opportune retrenchment, worthwhile expansion, or a recognition of the value and stability of the status quo.[28] Such superiority did not translate, however, into omnipotence or infallibility. The United States may have improved the odds of its empire in the Persian Gulf surviving, but its perpetuation hinged on—and continues to hinge on—unknowable systemic, regional, governmental, and individual factors.

Using empire as its analytical framework, this book examines U.S. policy in the Persian Gulf since the Second World War. In particular, it underscores the *creation and evolution* of an *informal* American empire in the Gulf. Although currently preponderant in this region, Washington should not be jubilant; its postwar experience in this remote part of the world, which most Americans barely know and continue to misunderstand,[29] has proven bittersweet. Like Great Powers before it, the United States has sought to improve its geopolitical and economic position in the Gulf to stave off for as long as possible (assuming Americans remain in the area indefinitely) the demise that will eventually occur—or so the story of empires has taught—unless U.S. exceptionalism, in the form of a continuously successful imperial model, can somehow prevent such an historical inevitability.[30]

Notes

1. See, for example, Adam Goodheart, "Wrapped in the Star-Spangled Toga," *New York Times*, 1 July 2007, http://www.nytimes.com.

2. See, for example, Daniel H. Nexon and Thomas Wright, "What's at Stake in the American Empire Debate," *American Political Science Review* 101, no. 2 (May 2007): 253–71; Christopher Layne and Bradley A. Thayer, *American Empire: A Debate* (New York: Routledge, 2007); Charles W. Kegley and Gregory A. Raymond, *After Iraq: The Imperiled American Imperium* (New York: Oxford University Press, 2007); Charles S. Maier, *Among Empires: American Ascendancy and Its Predecessors* (Cambridge, MA: Harvard University Press, 2006); Bernard Porter, *Empire and Superempire: Britain, America and the World* (New Haven, CT: Yale University Press, 2006); Robert D. Kaplan, *Imperial Grunts: The American Military on the Ground* (New York: Random House, 2005); Chalmers Johnson, *The Sorrows of Empire: Militarism, Secrecy, and the End of the Republic* (New York: Owl Books, 2004); Tony Judt, "Dreams of Empire," *New York Review of Books*, 4 November 2004, 38–41; Michael Cox, "Empire, Imperialism, and the Bush Doctrine," *Review of International Studies* 30, no. 4 (October 2004): 585–608; G. John Ikenberry, "Liberalism and Empire: Logics of Order in the American Unipolar Age," *Review of International Studies* 30, no. 4 (October 2004): 609–30; Niall Ferguson, *Colossus: The Price of America's Empire* (New York: Penguin Press, 2004); G. John Ikenberry, "Illusions of Empire: Defining the New American Order," *Foreign Affairs* 83, no. 2 (March/April 2004): 144–54; Amy Kaplan, "Violent Belongings and the Question of Empire Today: Presidential Address to the American Studies Association, 17 October 2003," *American Quarterly* 56, no. 1 (March 2004): 1–18; Edward W. Said,

"Preface to the Twenty-Fifth Anniversary Edition," *Orientalism* (New York: Vintage Books, 1979), xv–xxx; Michael Cox, "The Empire's Back in Town: Or America's Imperial Temptation—Again" (paper presented at the annual conference of the International Studies Association, Montreal, Canada, 17–20 March 2004); Andrew J. Bacevich, ed., *The Imperial Tense: Prospects and Problems of American Empire* (Chicago: Ivan R. Dee, 2003); Dimitri K. Simes, "America's Imperial Dilemma," *Foreign Affairs* 82, no. 6 (November/December 2003): 91–102; Michael Elliott, "Why Empires Strike Out," *Time*, 12 May 2003, 45; Peter Bender, "America: The New Roman Empire?" *Orbis* 47, no. 1 (Winter 2003): 145–59; Jay Tolson, "The New American Empire?" *U.S. News & World Report*, 13 January 2003, 35–40; Michael Ignatieff, "The Burden," *New York Times Magazine*, 5 January 2003, http://www.nytimes.com; Michael Elliott, "The Trouble with Saving the World," *Time*, 30 December 2002–6 January 2003, 90–93; Charles S. Maier, "An American Empire?" *Harvard Magazine*, November–December 2002, http://www.harvardmagazine.com; Michael C. Hudson, "Imperial Headaches: Managing Unruly Regions in an Age of Globalization," *Middle East Policy* 9, no. 4 (December 2002): 61–74; Fareed Zakaria, "Our Way," *New Yorker*, 14 October, 2002, http://www.newyorker.com; Mark Danner, "The Struggles of Democracy and Empire," *New York Times*, 9 October, 2002, http://www.nytimes.com; G. John Ikenberry, "America's Imperial Ambition," *Foreign Affairs* 81, no. 5 (September/October 2002): 44–60; Michael Hirsh, "Bush and the World," *Foreign Affairs* 81, no. 5 (September/October 2002): 18–43; Philip S. Golub, "Westward the Course of Empire," translated by Harry Forster, *Le Monde Diplomatique*, September 2002, http://mondediplo.com; Michael Elliott, "The Lessons of Empire," *Time*, 29 September 2002, http://www.time.com; Paul Krugman, "White Man's Burden," *New York Times*, 24 September 2002, http://www.nytimes.com; Bill Emmott, "Present at the Creation: A Survey of America's World Role," *Economist*, 29 June 2002, www.economist.com; Sebastian Mallaby, "The Reluctant Imperialist," *Foreign Affairs* 81, no. 2 (March/April 2002): 2–7; and Michael Cox, "The New Liberal Empire: US Power in the Twenty-First Century," *Irish Studies in International Affairs* 12 (2001): 39–56.

3. Mary Ann Heiss, "The Evolution of the Imperial Idea and U.S. National Identity," *Diplomatic History* 26, no. 4 (Fall 2002): 511–40; Andrew Bacevich, *American Empire: The Realities & Consequences of U.S. Diplomacy* (Cambridge, MA: Harvard University Press, 2002); Bruce Cumings, "Is America an Imperial Power?" *Current History* (November 2003): 355–60; and John Lewis Gaddis, *Surprise, Security, and the American Experience* (Cambridge, MA: Harvard University Press, 2004), 106–10.

4. See, for example, Joshua Micah Marshall, "Power Rangers: Did the Bush Administration Create a New American Empire—or Weaken the Old One?" *New Yorker*, 2 February 2004, http://www.newyorker.com; Max Boot, "Neither New nor Nefarious: The Liberal Empire Strikes Back," *Current History* (November 2003): 361–66; Max Boot, "The Sun Never Sets . . . ," *Weekly Standard*, 4 November 2002, 26–29; Max Boot, "The Case for American Empire," *Weekly Standard*, 15 October 2001, 27–30; Michael Mann, "The First Failed Empire of the 21st Century," *Review of International Studies* 30, no. 4 (October 2004): 631–53; and Lloyd C. Gardner and Marilyn B. Young, eds., *The New American Empire: A 21st Century Teach-In on U.S. Foreign Policy* (New York: New Press, 2005).

5. On the return of the U.S. empire debate, see Michael Cox, "Forum on the American Empire: Introduction: A New American Empire?" *Review of International Studies* 30, no. 4 (October 2004): 583. For the Marshall quote, see Marshall, "Power Rangers."

6. John Gray, "The Mirage of Empire," *New York Review of Books*, 12 January 2006, 4.

7. Robert Skidelsky, "Hot, Cold & Imperial," *New York Review of Books*, 13 July 2006, 55.

8. Linda Colley, "Imperial Trauma: The Powerlessness of the Powerful, Part 1," *Common Knowledge* 11, no. 2 (Spring 2005): 213.

9. Stephen Howe, *Empire: A Very Short Introduction* (Oxford: Oxford University Press, 2002), 9.

10. Stephen Peter Rosen, "An Empire, If You Can Keep It," *National Interest*, no. 71 (Spring 2003): 51. Italics in original.

11. See, for example, Alexander J. Motyl, "Empire Falls: Washington May Be Imperious, but It Is Not Imperial," *Foreign Affairs* 85, no. 4 (July/August 2006): 190–94; and Ikenberry, "Illusions of Empire."

12. See John Agnew, "American Hegemony Into American Empire? Lessons from the Invasion of Iraq," *Antipode* 35, no. 5 (November 2003): 871–85; and Elke Krahmann, "American Hegemony or Global Governance? Competing Visions of International Security," *International Studies Review* 7, no. 4 (December 2005): 531–45.

13. See, for example, Philip Zelikow, "The Transformation of National Security: Five Redefinitions," *National Interest*, no. 71 (Spring 2003): 17–28.

14. See, for example, Robert O. Keohane, "The United States and the Postwar Order: Empire or Hegemony?" *Journal of Peace Research* 28, no. 4 (1991): 437–38.

15. See, for example, Michael Cox, "September 11th and U.S. Hegemony—Or Will the 21st Century Be American Too?" *International Studies Perspectives* 3, no. 1 (February 2002): 53–70; Cox, "The New Liberal Empire"; Henry Kissinger, *Does America Need a Foreign Policy? Toward a Diplomacy for the 21st Century* (New York: Simon & Schuster, 2001); and Christopher Layne, "Offshore Balancing Revisited," *Washington Quarterly* 25, no. 2 (Spring 2002): 233–48. Layne writes (233) that "[h]egemony is the term political scientists use to denote the overwhelming military, economic, and diplomatic preponderance of a single great power in international politics."

16. See Sumit Ganguly, "Imperial Nostalgia," *Current History* (November 2003): 394–95.

17. See Judt, "Dreams of Empire," 38.

18. See, for example, Victor Davis Hanson, *A War Like No Other: How the Athenians and Spartans Fought the Peloponnesian War* (New York: Random House, 2005); and Martin Walker, "An Empire Unlike Any Other," in Bacevich, ed., *The Imperial Tense*, 145.

19. See Niall Ferguson, "Hegemony or Empire?" *Foreign Affairs* 82, no. 5 (September/October 2003): 154–61.

20. See Tony Smith, *The Pattern of Imperialism: The United States, Great Britain, and the Late Industrializing World since 1815* (New York: Cambridge University Press, 1981); Cox, "The New Liberal Empire;" and Boot, "Neither New nor Nefarious."

21. See, for example, Zelikow, "The Transformation of National Security," 18–19.

22. On the importance of contingency, see John Lewis Gaddis, *The Landscape of History: How Historians Map the Past* (New York: Oxford University Press, 2002). My thanks to Professor Amy Berger, Heidelberg College's geologist, for her expertise.

23. For a recent analysis of U.S. exceptionalism, see Anatol Lieven, *America Right or Wrong: An Anatomy of American Nationalism* (New York: Oxford University Press, 2004).

24. See Joseph S. Nye, "Ill-Suited for Empire," *Washington Post*, 25 May 2003, http://www.washingtonpost.com.

25. See Nathan J. Citino, *From Arab Nationalism to OPEC: Eisenhower, King Saud, and the Making of U.S.-Saudi Relations* (Bloomington, IN: Indiana University Press, 2002).

26. See, for example, Fareed Mohamedi and Yahya Sadowski, "The Decline (But Not Fall) of US Hegemony in the Middle East," *Middle East Report*, no. 220 (Fall 2001): 12–22.

27. See Ferguson, "Hegemony or Empire?"

28. See Jack Snyder, "Imperial Temptations," *National Interest*, no. 71 (Spring 2003): 29–40.

29. See Douglas Little, *American Orientalism: The United States and the Middle East Since 1945* (Chapel Hill, NC: University of North Carolina Press, 2004); and Shibley Telhami, *The Stakes: America and the Middle East: The Consequences of Power and the Choice for Peace* (Boulder, CO: Westview Press, 2002).

30. See Parag Khanna, "The Counsel of Geopolitics," *Current History* (November 2003): 388–93.

Acknowledgments

Many individuals and several institutions made this book possible. I would like to thank as many as I can.

Thanks to Lexington Books for publishing this manuscript. Special thanks to Martin Hayward for his initial interest in this work, encouragement, and assistance.

Thanks to Julie, my spouse, known at Heidelberg College as *The* Dr. O'Reilly. She provided love and support throughout this lengthy project, from dissertation to book, and helped with editing and preparing the manuscript.

Thanks to Garry Clifford, my Ph.D. advisor and mentor, who contributed his usual expertise on U.S. foreign policy, considerable editorial skills, and friendship. Thanks to Betty Hanson, Jeff Lefebvre, Richard Vengroff, Jennifer Sterling-Folker, Wes Renfro, Srdjan Vucetic, John Miglietta, and my brother, Alex O'Reilly, all of whom made numerous helpful suggestions that improved the manuscript. Thanks to Robert Schuettinger and Wayne Lesperance for their comments on the U.S. variant of empire. And thanks to Andrew Bacevich and Gregory Gause for reading the manuscript and contributing blurbs.

Thanks to those individuals who served as discussants, chairs, presenters, and audience members on panels where I presented my work on U.S. empire in the Persian Gulf. Those panels occurred at the annual conference of the International Studies Association (ISA) 2000–2003 and 2005, the ISA-Northeast conference in 2000, the ISA-Midwest conference in 2005 and 2006, and the New England Political Science Association conference in 2000 and 2001.

Thanks to Julie Hada and Greg Trumble, students of mine in 2006–07, for their assistance in preparing the final manuscript. Thanks to Greg as well for this insight: While the aircraft carrier number 66 on the book cover was originally intended to underscore the extent (66 years) of the U.S. experience in the Persian Gulf, CV-66 was appropriately the USS *America*, a Cold-War carrier decommissioned in 1996.

Thanks to Frank Cucciarre for the attractive cover art. Thanks to Karen "Mickey" Malmisur for making the index and proofreading the manuscript.

Thanks to Doug Little, who kindly confirmed the appropriateness of the topic studied in this book while awaiting the start of a foreign-policy talk at the University of Rhode Island in the spring of 1998.

Thanks to the archival staffs at the John F. Kennedy Library in Boston and the Public Record Office (PRO) in Surrey, England. And thanks to Huron University in London, especially Alan Hertz, for providing me with comfortable and very affordable housing in Central London while I researched at the PRO in June 2002.

Thanks to the Oxford Study Abroad Programme, Chris Marsh at Baylor University, Matt Bloom at Bowling Green State University, Andrew Richter at the University of Windsor, and Bruce Bigelow at Butler University for inviting me to lecture on U.S. policy in the Persian Gulf/Middle East in January 2002, March 2003, January 2005, March 2005, and April 2007. And thanks to the Indiana Consortium for International Programs for inviting me to speak on U.S.-Iranian relations at an October 2006 conference on Iran held at Marian College in Indianapolis. I also benefited from presentations I made on America's Gulf policy at St. Lawrence University in December 2006 and Murray State University in January 2007.

Thanks to John Gaddis for having provided me (and several others) with a first-class education at Ohio University. Thanks also to the following OU faculty for their tutelage and encouragement: Kathy Lambert, Michael Mumper, Sung-Ho Kim, David Williams, Patricia Weitsman, Harold (Spike) Molineu, and Chester Pach.

Thanks to Mark Boyer and Tom Paterson, each of whom taught me at the University of Connecticut, and to John Rourke, who as chair of UConn's Department of Political Science provided me with much needed financial and other support. Thanks also to the University of Connecticut Graduate School and the UConn Foundation for their generous financial support. Thanks to Sue Durdan and Maria Niles, former administrative assistants in UConn's Political Science Department, for their help and patience. And thanks to my colleagues at UConn-Avery Point, a seaside campus that will always hold special memories.

Thanks to Heidelberg College, where I teach, for its financial support of my research (including a 2006 Summer Research Grant) and for allowing me, via its annual Faculty Research Conference, opportunities in February 2003 and 2006 to present my work on American policy in the Persian Gulf. Thanks to my chair, John Bing, and two former Heidelberg colleagues, Skip Oliver and Josie Setzler, for their thoughts on my research. Thanks, as well, to Kim Chhay, my colleague in International Programs who survived the Cambodian genocide and thus always inspires me. And thanks to many other Heidelberg colleagues, past and present, who have made working there a very rewarding experience.

Thanks to Patrick James, who taught me at McGill University when I was an undergraduate and recently co-edited a book with Nelson Michaud and me on Canadian foreign policy, for his long-time friendship and continual encouragement. Thanks also to Marijke Breuning, a more recent friend who, like Patrick, always offers generous support to me and other younger scholars.

Thanks to my friends from graduate school who made the experience worthwhile: Charley Jacobs, Chris Marsh, Kim Slusarski, Erin Carrière, James Allan, Mary Caprioli, Doug Becker, Neal Coates, Richard Cole, John Burns, Ray Haberski, Marc Selverstone, and Molly Smith.

Thanks to other good friends and their families for their encouragement over the years: Marcel Martin, Marc Fust, Donald Bisson, Philippe Miquelon, Martin Boyer, Stéphane Ethier, Luc Drouin, the Nathans, Barb and Norm Hawkins, John Egazarian, Bob Monterio, Mike Burch, Paul Hunt, Pastor Val Roberts-Toler, Paul and Heather Grover, Cathy Willoughby, and Pastor Greg Sellers. Thanks as well to Chief Abel Bosum and the Oujé-Bougoumou Cree First Nation for allowing me to work for and with them in the early 1990s. I learned many important life lessons while living in northern Québec.

Thanks to my students at Ohio University, the University of Connecticut, and Heidelberg College. They have made teaching rewarding. I especially thank my fall 2002, 2004, 2005, 2006, and 2007 POL 409 students at Heidelberg for their comments on American foreign policy and U.S. empire. As well, I thank the students who took a spring 2006 Honors course with me on empires. That seminar helped me rethink a number of issues and consider others.

The May 2006 trip to Italy, Vatican City, and Greece that served as an addendum to that class provided incredible insight into what makes an empire. Visiting the Vatican and the remnants of imperial Rome and Athens, as well as Pompeii and Delphi, awed me, just as my visits to London and Paris had. "This is empire," I told my brother in July 2002, as our eyes took in Trafalgar Square and followed Whitehall Street to Westminster. The same thought entered my mind as I viewed the magnificent Champs Elysées for the first time in August of that year. A March 2007 visit to Spain only added to the sensory delight while confirming the impact of empire on a variety of civilizations. As Julie and I toured the Catedral and Real Alcázar in Sevilla, the amazing Alhambra in Granada, and the Mezquita in Córdoba, we witnessed the intersection of Moorish/Islamic and Hispanic/Catholic empires. At the Palacio Real in Madrid, we took in the grandeur of a Spanish empire whose influence, both uplifting and crushing, still pervades the so-called New World.

While those travels added to my knowledge of empires, my identity and experiences have enabled me to grapple with this controversial matter without flinching. As a French and Irish Canadian from Montréal, I hail from a culture forged by empire, both French and British. Growing up in Québec, moreover, I experienced the American empire constantly via U.S. popular culture—my spouse's academic specialty, coincidentally. Annual O'Reilly vacations to Higgins Beach, Maine, only enhanced my familiarity with the United States.

On the subject of kin, I owe heartfelt thanks to my family (O'Reilly, Gendron, and Stevenson), to whom this book is dedicated. My family's love, encouragement, support, and patience made this study possible. My parents, Jim and Michèle, deserve special kudos. This book encapsulates everything they have taught me.

Finally, with this book, I celebrate two individuals. First, I honor the memory of my great-uncle Paul Morisset, a Jesuit priest who passed away in spring 2006. He was the kindest, gentlest man I have ever known. His education made him a very learned man, but his patience with my many questions about life and faith made him the wisest man I have ever known. Second, I toast my niece, Anne-Elizabeth Desjardins, born on this day to my sister, Julie, and brother-in-law, Stéphane.

Merci à tous. Thanks to all.

Marc J. O'Reilly
Tiffin, OH
January 7, 2008

Chapter 1

Not So Innocents Abroad: America, the Persian Gulf, and Empire

We [Americans] have transformed our imperial way of life from a culture that we built and benefited from into an abstract self-evident Law of Nature that we must now re-examine in light of its costs and consequences. It is, we shrug, simply the way of the world. Empire is freedom. Empire is liberty. Empire is security.

—William Appleman Williams (1980)[1]

The shocking events of September 11, 2001, flummoxed the United States—as well as much of the world. As with the Japanese devastation of Pearl Harbor in December 1941, the destruction of New York City's World Trade Center and the attack on the Pentagon incensed a nation previously insulated from most of the globe's perils. The horror of 9/11 prompted many Americans to reconsider why certain foreigners (in this case, al-Qaeda terrorists under the direction of Osama bin Laden) so profoundly disliked the United States—its capitalism, culture, foreign and military policy—that they hijacked U.S. commercial aircraft to realize their apocalyptic dream of Islamic revenge and salvation. While America's grasp of development issues in the Middle East and elsewhere has often lacked sophistication and, at times, certainly hindered rather than helped post-colonial societies, the wanton killing of thousands of innocent civilians—from many countries and religious traditions—seemed utterly out of proportion with whatever travesty Washington may have committed in Saudi Arabia or elsewhere.[2]

Al-Qaeda's incredible audacity jolted the White House, which responded in fall 2001 with a war on that organization and its most visible sponsor, Afghanistan's repressive Taliban government. *Operation Enduring Freedom* enabled the United States to avenge the lives lost in New York and Washington; it also confirmed the American ability to project substantial political, economic, and military power into the most remote regions of the world. While impressive, U.S. prowess could not defeat al-Qaeda and Taliban forces without local Afghan sol-

1

diers from the Northern and Eastern Alliance. These U.S. proxies achieved success despite an initial lack of confidence in their ability to evict the enemy from
its fortified positions.[3]

The American military victory in Afghanistan allowed Hamid Karzai, a perceived moderate in Afghan politics and member of the majority Pashtun tribe, to
assume the leadership of that ravaged country. Washington's renewed commitment to Afghanistan, after a decade or so of neglect following the Soviet defeat,
promised years of sustained involvement to repair this so-called failed state and
prevent it from again sheltering anti-American terrorists. To improve its geopolitical position in Central Asia, the White House acquired base rights in several
area nations. This extension of U.S. influence to a region adjacent to the Persian
Gulf, the fulcrum of American power in the Middle East, resembled imperial
deeds once carried out by the British and Russians.[4]

With the Afghan phase of America's war on international terrorism see-
mingly completed, Washington sought to undermine Iraq, a member of President
George W. Bush's "Axis of Evil" supposedly armed with weapons of mass destruction (WMD) and in cahoots with terrorists that threatened the United States.
After failing to persuade much of the world community as to the necessity of
attacking Iraq, the White House ordered an invasion to rid that country of its
WMD—considered an imminent, rather than a potential, threat to America.
Some U.S. officials, including President Bush, also spoke of democratizing Iraq
and remaking the Middle East, which boiled throughout much of the 20th century as a result of Western imperialism, into a more U.S. friendly region.[5]

In a matter of weeks in spring 2003, U.S. armed forces (with British, Australian, and Polish assistance) overthrew, as part of *Operation Iraqi Freedom*,
Iraq's despised president, Saddam Hussein, whose brutal regime Washington
had once supported. Occupation followed invasion. In the wake of a tumultuous
and violent summer and fall where insurgents attacked American soldiers, United Nations personnel, and perceived Iraqi collaborators, a beleaguered Bush
administration agreed in November to restore Iraqi sovereignty by the following
summer—which it did, albeit with coalition forces remaining to assist the interim
Iraqi government with security and reconstruction. Though U.S. experts found
no WMD, in December 2003, American Special Forces nabbed the man who
might know the location of such weapons—Saddam Hussein. His capture
seemed to vindicate White House policy and warned other regional despots (e.g.,
in Iran and Syria) that the United States could remove them should they hinder
U.S. plans for the Middle East, especially the Persian Gulf, an area of paramount
strategic value for Washington.

Great Powers in the Gulf: Present and Past

That the United States could reconfigure the Persian Gulf's balance of power underscored its evolution since World War II into the area's de facto arbiter.
In the past half millennium, the British, Ottomans, Persian Safavids, and Portuguese, all acknowledged empires, held comparable clout and played a similar
role. Until *Operation Iraqi Freedom*, however, many scholars denied the exis-

tence of a U.S. empire in the Gulf. They preferred the term *hegemony*. Yet Washington's modus operandi resembled that of London and Istanbul when they ruled over the region.

Although the comparisons can be useful—they underline, for example, the crucial importance of tribal politics in the Gulf and the ability of sheiks to manipulate their patrons—distinctions should be kept in mind. When the Ottomans tried to annex the Arabian Peninsula to their empire in the late nineteenth century, they already exhibited telltale signs of imminent decline. They possessed a centralized empire, whose bankruptcy kept expenditures in the Persian Gulf to a minimum. Inadequate communications networks, corruption within the local bureaucracy, administrative incompetence, lack of military preparedness, inability to ward off pirates and marauding tribesmen, untrustworthy proxies, and the Sublime Porte's indecision condemned the Ottomans to failure in the Gulf. Cognizant of Turkish weakness, European Great Powers pressed it for territorial and other concessions while often defeating the Ottomans on the battlefield.[6]

While Istanbul, home to the Muslim Caliphate, struggled to assert its authority in the Persian Gulf and elsewhere, the British basked in the glory of empire. London served as the financial capital of the world, the Royal Navy ruled the seas, UK trade flourished, and every Great Power respected British might. In the Gulf, the United Kingdom pursued a strategy of "informal" empire whereby it secured the coastline for British trade by eliminating pirates and slavery, established protectorates over Trucial Oman, Bahrain, and Kuwait, and undermined Ottoman interests whenever possible. After World War II, however, His Majesty's Government could not sustain its Gulf and global position due to financial constraints and decolonization. As with the Ottomans, the British scaled back many of their commitments in the Gulf and eventually watched as another Great Power supplanted them.[7]

Washington officially took the baton from London in a period (1968–71) characterized by cold war and waning American influence worldwide. The country's bitter Vietnam debacle and its aftermath humbled the White House—Reagan administration rhetoric notwithstanding—until the end of the Cold War left a resurgent America as the "sole superpower." Today, despite the widespread unpopularity abroad of many of the Bush administration's policies, the United States continues to occupy the pantheon of global politics. In the Persian Gulf, Washington exercises significant, albeit contested, authority despite its preference for an empire more informal than Britain's.[8]

The Rise of American Power

To understand America's contemporary as well as historic experience in the Gulf, students of U.S. foreign policy must keep in mind why Great Powers expand. Expansion occurs for a variety of reasons. Analysts invoke economic imperatives, strategic necessity, diplomatic opportunity, power asymmetries, political requirements, social learning, and civilizational hubris to explain the empowerment of empires, hegemons, and superpowers. Great Powers take advantage of or seize upon the weaknesses of other, lesser powers to organize parts or all of the international community. The strong rule by virtue of their capacity to influence, if not determine, outcomes. They restrict the choices of others so that events mesh with their interests. Lesser powers matter, but their opinions and desires count for less. Whether as unsophisticated bullies, benevolent patrons, or despicable overlords, Great Powers strive to shape the world so that it serves them first and foremost. With or without malice, they seek to maximize their security while trying to prevent their own demise.[9]

Much scholarship on Great Powers spotlights decline rather than rise. Political scientists and historians dwell on imperial mistakes, setbacks, defeats, and collapses. Consequently, they devote less attention to the initial phase when a Great Power extends its political, economic, military, and cultural influence beyond its borders.[10]

Although its impressive post-Civil War economic performance ranked it as one of the world's most prosperous countries, the United States expanded slowly by Great-Power standards until victory in World War II turned it into a superpower with global interests. Thereafter, the Cold War ensured Washington would not retreat to a comfortable isolationism. From the Truman administration until the fall of the Berlin Wall, American liberal democracy and capitalism clashed with Soviet communism. This ideological duel yielded U.S. commitments in every region. In the Middle East, the United States waded into the morass of the Arab-Israeli conflict while trying to tap the Persian Gulf's oil reserves, the world's most abundant.[11]

The U.S. experience in the Persian Gulf started in the nineteenth century as merely an exercise in economic diplomacy. American merchants explored the area in search of commerce only. Consistent with its historic "Open Door" policy, Washington sought trade opportunities worldwide without assuming political and diplomatic responsibilities. As the new Phoenicians, Americans recoiled from Europe's *Realpolitik*, which resulted in imperial rivalries in the Middle East and elsewhere in Asia, as well as in Africa. With no Middle Eastern Great Power to prevent unwanted encroachments, European imperialists divided the region into spheres of influence. Thus, while Russia and Great Britain resolutely played the "Great Game," the United States eschewed the so-called Eastern Question in favor of continental expansion and hemispheric domination. The Atlantic Ocean supposedly provided "free security," thereby insulating America from the perceived impurities of the Old World—its wars, colonialism, and pervasive immorality—and allowing Americans to pursue their Manifest Destiny while strenuously denying their own brand of empire.[12]

Washington's post-World War II superpower status and support for Israel complicated U.S. relations with Gulf states, whose petroleum Western countries needed to power their economies. Successive administrations sought policies that could please, or at least placate, both sides while advancing American interests in the Middle East. Influential domestic constituencies, such as the Israeli and oil lobbies, as well as electoral concerns, made it impossible for the White House to dismiss either Tel Aviv or the Arab world.[13]

While many scholars have focused on America's postwar role in the Holy Land, the Persian Gulf has remained critical to U.S. national security. Most studies of Washington's Gulf policy have spotlighted bilateral ties, particularly with

Iran and Saudi Arabia. Only a few have examined the history of American aggrandizement in the region comprehensively. Unlike those latter works, which typically avoid explicit analytical frameworks or else merely highlight American benevolence, this book asserts that empire and imperialism can explain the U.S. rise to prominence in the Gulf since 1941 as well as the evolution of American policy and strategy in that region.[14]

Empires

Although empire and imperialism have existed for millennia, defining each remains controversial. Regarding the former, Bradley Thayer provides an orthodox explication. "An empire," he writes, "is a state that surpasses all others in capabilities and sense of mission. An empire usually exceeds others in capabilities such as the size of its territory and material resources. Its capabilities are much greater than the average or norm prevailing in the international system." As well, he notes, "an empire has worldwide interests. Its interests are coterminous with boundaries of the system itself, and the interests are defended directly by the imperial states or by client states." Finally, "empires always have a mission they seek to accomplish—this is usually creating, and then maintaining, a world order."[15]

As Stephen Rosen observes, an empire will establish parameters to achieve its ultimate objective. It delineates either broadly or narrowly what states within its sphere of influence can do internally, regionally, and globally. An empire therefore decides what is permissible within its confines. Adjustments will be necessary, but every empire must discover what will enable it to excel within its distinctive circumstances. Imperatives explain imperial choices; abilities determine outcomes. Since superior capabilities usually distinguish imperia from non-imperial entities, an empire will often seek to expand. According to George Liska, it can do so "because of a spontaneous drive for sustenance, booty, or other assets located outside its existing boundary of control; it can be driven into expansion from within by factional or other conflict for power; and it can be drawn into expansion by contests among third powers or by contest with another power over a stake located between them."[16]

So-called classic empires, whether of the ancient or nineteenth century variety, typically sought conquest and colonialism. As a result, they achieved territorial expansion and economic exploitation, while oppressing those societies they conquered. Land and sea empires may have differed somewhat in terms of their genesis and modus operandi, but their objectives endured—e.g., to gain materially at the expense of others, to inculcate the conquered with political and other values, to achieve status and glory. Regardless of what civilization imperialists promoted (whether Egyptian, Spartan, Persian, Roman, Chinese, Aztec, French, or otherwise), and regardless of what notion (e.g., Athenian democracy, Christianity, or Islam) they sought to impose, empires transformed societies, their own as well as those they encountered, both positively and negatively. While death, destruction, and slavery (physical and emotional) characterized the imperial experience, empires also became known for their beneficial political, economic, and cultural achievements. Despite their success, which typically favored small elites, empires could not overcome inherent weaknesses. Success generated hubris and complacency, asymmetries of power fostered jealousies and resentments, and enemies from adjacent lands coveted imperial spoils. In the twentieth century, a political revolution (the call for self-determination) and consecutive major wars (World War I and II) doomed Europe's already weakened overseas empires and seemed the death knell of imperialism.[17]

This form of world order survived the end of European colonial rule, however, and not just in Eastern Europe, home to the Soviet Empire. Imperialism, Raymond Aron wrote in his mid-1970s book *The Imperial Republic*, "in the form of behavior calculated to construct an empire in the classic and political sense has receded from the foreground, while imperialism in the form of a non-egalitarian relationship between states and a great power's will to influence the domestic life and foreign conduct of a small power has, like Descartes' common sense, never been so widespread as it is in our own time." Imperialism implies a degree of domination, which in Klaus Knorr's view "rests on power," whereby one country exercises some kind of influence over another. The ability to coerce and/or co-opt other nations allows an imperial state to evolve some type of empire, which Michael Doyle describes as a "system of interaction between two political entities, one of which, the dominant metropole, exerts political control over the internal and external policy—the effective sovereignty—of the other, the subordinate periphery." Doyle considers imperialism "the process of establishing and maintaining an empire" and notes that throughout history "merchants, monopolists, and war machines have clamored for expansion; changing interstate balances called for compensation; frontiers were occasionally expansive, and trade could be imperializing in unstable peripheries."[18]

According to Doyle, imperialism falls into three categories: metrocentric, pericentric, and systemic. Thinkers who have espoused the metrocentric view include John Hobson, Vladimir Lenin, and Joseph Schumpeter. These individuals, notes Doyle, rely on a "dispositional [i.e., reductionist] analysis: they see the roots of empire in imperialism, a force emanating from the metropole like radio waves from a transmitter." Contrary to the Hobson-Schumpeter school, Ronald Robinson and John Gallagher believe that peripheries explain imperialism. Since resources Great Powers rely upon to ensure economic success can be found in these parts of the world, metropoles must integrate peripheries into their political-economic systems—hence Robinson and Gallagher's reference to the "imperialism of free trade." As for systemic imperialism, Kenneth Waltz and other so-called structural realists opine that a state's position within an anarchical, self-help international system can allow it to exercise "imperial control" if the distribution of power favors it.[19]

Doyle defines an empire as "effective control, whether formal or informal, of a subordinated society by an imperial society." This outcome occurs as a result of "force," "political collaboration," and "economic, social, or cultural dependence." Two kinds of empire exist: formal and informal. In a formal empire, the "social, economic, and cultural environments of the metropole penetrate those of the periphery through metropolitan forces and actors—missionaries, merchants, soldiers, bureaucrats." "These actors," Doyle asserts, "shape peripheral demands or tastes and influence the content of domestic coalitions, classes, factions, and parties in the periphery." An informal empire strives for *indirect*, as opposed to direct, control over a foreign society. This more subtle method involves the "collaboration of a legally independent (but actually subordinate) government in the periphery." As Doyle points out, "[t]he closer the control over actual decisions, the more efficient will foreign penetration be; alternatively, the further from the decision point that one attempts to exert influence over the decision, the larger will be the range of factors that must be controlled." While peripheries often suffer (although they sometimes flourish) within an imperium, they can, as Doyle stresses, "exert return influence on the metropole." Peripheral collaboration with imperial authorities thus implies some degree of mutual dependency, an insight some scholars neglect or deny. Alexander Motyl, for example, insists that a "dictatorial" relationship must exist between center and periphery.[20]

Beyond typologies and the nature of influence, any scholar interested in empire must satisfy Doyle's criteria. One must therefore "demonstrate the existence of control," "explain why one party expands and establishes such control," and, finally, "explain why the other party submits or fails to resist effectively." For Doyle, imperialism relies on four variables: "the metropolitan regime, its capacities and interests; the peripheral political society, its interests and weakness; the transnational system and its needs; and the international context and the incentives it creates."[21]

Like Doyle, other scholars have explored the complicated issues of empire, imperialism, and imperial control. For Geir Lundestad, an empire denotes "a hierarchical system of political relationships with one power clearly being much stronger than any other." According to Thomas Paterson, an imperium can be "invited, consensual, imposed, coerced, predatory, resisted, benevolent, informal, formal, open, or closed." For Daniel Nexon and Thomas Wright, "[e]mpires, like all political systems, are based on bargains that specify rights and obligations." They add, however, that "cores develop distinctive bargains with each periphery under their control." Imperialism, argues Tony Smith, occurs as a result of the intersection of "three analytically distinct, although historically interrelated, forces: the particularistic demands of private interest groups in the dominant countries; the perspective of the dominant states with respect to general concerns of national interest; and the strength and stability of political organization on the periphery." Regarding imperial control, John Vloyantes refers to "hard" and "soft" spheres of influence. In the first case, a Great Power will be "more often prone to open and direct intervention." In the second, countries within the soft sphere can exercise their independence "without the threat of interference or dictation [although] the paramount power continues to claim a stake in the area and exercises a constant concern for what is done or not done."[22]

To preserve their power and interests, imperial nations adopt a variety of time-honored strategies. For example, they tend to counter states that threaten their regional or international position, rather than fend off the most powerful countries in the international system, as balance-of-power theory stipulates. Threats can be military, political, economic, ideological, and psychological. This recourse to what Stephen Walt calls a policy of "balance of threat" can secure unilateral advantage, but gains can be shared with others if a Great Power elects to pursue a strategy of guardianship.[23]

By creating protectorates or some equivalent, an imperial power can extend its influence into a strategic region more easily and quickly. Guardianship also implies political leadership, which a country can exercise via alliances and clients. Mark Gasiorowski insists that "cliency relationships . . . involve reciprocal exchanges of goods and services that are intended to enhance the security of the patron and the client and generally cannot be obtained by them from other sources." He adds that the "importance of these goods and services to the security of the two countries binds their governments together in a cooperative, mutually beneficial relationship." A guardian can impose its own domestic preferences upon another state, or it can allow its friends to formulate whatever domestic policy they prefer provided that it meshes with the Great Power's overall objectives—to oppose communism, fascism, or fundamentalism, for example.[24]

American Empire

Just as definitions and explanations of empire and imperialism differ, so do assessments of U.S. imperialism and empire. Among those analysts who consider America an imperium, Michael Hardt and Antonio Negri note that the "U.S. Constitution, as [Thomas] Jefferson said, is the one best calibrated for extensive Empire." Congruent with that assessment, George Liska observes that "[l]ike Rome from the Seven Hills, the United States was driven by the competitive dynamic of particular interests from its parochial base in the thirteen states into continental and overseas expansion before it grew strong enough to be authentically drawn into global commitments of an unmistakably imperial nature." After the Civil War, America tentatively started to expand beyond its continental boundaries while its industrial economy outperformed everyone. At the turn of the twentieth century, it officially joined the imperial ranks as a result of its victory in the Spanish-American War.[25]

Although Theodore Roosevelt and, before him, Jefferson touted the benefits of U.S. empire, most Americans have professed an aversion to such an anti-republican creation. Yet, despite its rhetoric, the United States has applied its anti-imperial mantra selectively. As Mary Ann Heiss writes, "[i]f ideals dovetailed with concrete national need, then a happy confluence developed between the nation's stance on the imperial idea and its professed principles. If the two diverged, however, need routinely prevailed over ideals, so that the nation's empire/imperial stance did not directly square with the ideals for which it supposedly stood." The need for security motivated U.S. expansion. Opines James Chace, "the growth of the American empire [came] about not so much through a search for economic well-being as through a quest for absolute security, that is to say, invulnerability."[26]

Compared to the British, notes Geir Lundestad, American behavior could be "just as striking as in some of the more directly ruled parts of the British Empire." "On the whole," he adds, "Britain possessed a formal empire, but few imperial institutions. The United States had no formal empire, but more developed institutions—in the form of alliances, security treaties and partly also economic arrangements—than the British." Lundestad thus deems the U.S. empire "an informal hierarchical structure" and argues that "states within this empire were generally politically independent; many, if not most of them, were political democracies, but they were still tied to America through important military, political, and economic arrangements." Unlike with typical empires, countries often asked Washington for assistance, which Lundestad calls "empire by invitation." Finally, he observes that U.S. influence was "more pronounced in shaping the overall structure . . . than in forcing individual countries to make specific policy choices they would not otherwise have made."[27]

In their experiences with "weak" societies, opines Tony Smith, Washington and London promoted a "framework for world order through defending certain basic principles designed to regulate conduct among the great powers as well as between the strong and the weak." Furthermore, Smith asserts, "the dominant and preferred policy of each country was to foster a liberal 'antiimperialism' [sic] based on respect for the integrity of self-government . . . and a corresponding opposition to the extension of rival great power spheres of influence." Political anti-imperialism mixed with American and British business interests to form a liberal economic order. This melding of political and economic philosophies often resulted in "liberal imperialism." As Smith points out, "the fragility or malleability of southern [i.e., developing countries'] social and political systems confronted by the power of Western expansion sometimes made the contact imperialist even when this was not the intention of London and Washington."[28]

For some scholars, observes Raymond Aron, an American empire existed "with neither frontiers nor sovereignty, invisible and ubiquitous." In reaction to this benign view, a school of thought pioneered by William Appleman Williams contested the well-accepted post-World War II notion that the United States constituted, in Jerome Slater's words, "a defensive, status-quo power seeking to contain the revolutionary or simply imperialist expansionism of Soviet-led communism." Revisionist works considered Washington's policy imperialist; in short, "a deliberate, planned, and generally quite successful effort at world domination under the pretext of the 'containment' of a largely nonexistent military or political threat." America's empire thrived on commercial expansion secured via the Open Door. This emphasis on "neoimperialism" often overstated the U.S. impact upon complex events and usually implied nefarious intentions on Washington's part. Although critics of revisionism spotlighted its twin methodological shortcomings of ethnocentrism and, more seriously, economic determinism, Slater notes that mainstream scholars validated the New Left's contention that the United States should be considered an authentic empire.[29]

Several analysts contend, however, that America should be thought of as "imperial," not "imperialist." This correction may only confuse, yet, in the end, the argument over semantics hinges on motivation; on whether a country pursues empire or achieves it "accidentally," to quote Ronald Steel, as a result of its role in international politics. While revisionists such as Williams emphasize human agency, the adherents of the "imperial" school underline structure as the key variable. According to this view, America's preponderant position in the world explains why the history of U.S. foreign relations can be compared to that of the Roman Empire and other imperia.[30]

From a military point of view, the United States surpassed Rome in its ability to inflict devastation upon enemies and intimidate potential foes. By the end of World War II, writes Michael Sherry, American policymakers "sought to disseminate an ideology of preparedness, to forge a permanent military-industrial-scientific establishment, to reorganize the armed forces, to institute a permanent system of universal training, to acquire far-flung bases, to occupy defeated enemies with American forces, to retain a monopoly of atomic weapons, and to create a high-tech Pax Aeronautica." The competition between America and the Soviet Union resembled that between the Romans and Carthaginians. The outcome in the first case resulted in the capitulation of Washington's main adversary; in the second, the elimination of Rome's despised rival.[31]

Today, with the Cold War "won" (or at least settled in their favor), Americans emulate the ancient Romans as they overshadow everyone else with their military supremacy. As Gregg Easterbrook notes, the country possesses the "sole military whose primary mission is not defense. Practically the entire U.S. military is an expeditionary force, designed not to guard borders . . . but to 'project power' elsewhere in the world." This ability allows the United States to claim "only superpower" status, rely reflexively on its military to cope with, if not pacify, troublesome frontiers, and qualify, in Chalmers Johnson's words, as an "empire of bases." In 2004, Washington possessed "full-scale bases" in approximately 40 countries and military installations in some 130. Regarding these bases, Johnson observes that "[t]hese installations form a more or less secret global network many parts of which once may have had temporary strategic uses but have long since evolved into permanent outposts." He adds that "[w]hatever the original reason the United States entered a country and set up a base, it remains there for imperial reasons—regional and global hegemony, denial of territory to rivals, providing access for American companies, maintenance of 'stability' or 'credibility' as a military force, and simple inertia."[32]

America's military strength and prowess enabled it to join the ranks of empires, yet, as Sherry states, "understandably, empire was as hard to recognize as militarization. After all, America's postwar empire rested little on territorial acquisition, plunder, or brute force, although more than most Americans cared to admit." "Instead," Sherry underscores, "it was maintained through consensual arrangements with allies and clients that often prodded the United States to exercise more power and sometimes defied that power." As well, Sherry observes that "[a]bove all, measured against crude Soviet aggression, American policy seemed reactive and American ideals lofty."[33]

Many scholars, most of them American, prefer this more positive explanation of U.S. imperialism. They emphasize the *primus inter pares* (i.e., first among equals) quality of American leadership, which resulted in many consensus decisions within U.S.-led alliances and institutions. Robert McMahon thus concludes that Washington established a "defensive empire," noting that it evolved as a result of "America's fears [of Soviet and Chinese communism as well as local nationalisms] rather than its greed." Robert Kagan writes of a "benevolent empire"—without true enemy from the end of the Cold War until the 9/11 attacks. Andrew Bacevich asserts that "[a]s befits a nation founded on the conviction of its own uniqueness, the American empire is like no other in history. Indeed, the peculiar American approach to empire offers a striking affirmation of American exceptionalism. . . . We [Americans] prefer access and influence to ownership." Sharing such felicitous views, Michael Mandelbaum opines that "[i]n contrast with empires of the past . . . the United States does not control, or aspire to control, directly or indirectly, the politics and economics of other societies." Unlike Bacevich, who would staunchly oppose the Bush administration's invasion and occupation of Iraq, and Kagan, Mandelbaum authored his congratulatory essay in an era of virulent anti-Americanism, which he dismissed as the world's "inevitable ingratitude" rather than as a response to the missteps and excesses of U.S. foreign policy. Like Mandelbaum, Bradley Thayer emphasizes the exceptional quality and nature of America's empire, dubbing it "the most singular of all empires," despite world opinion to the contrary. For Thayer and others who tout U.S. exceptionalism, Washington's good intentions, selflessness, and willingness to cooperate internationally define the country's imperial experience. For them, the United States seeks ideological conversion, an objective that requires submission to American values, not acquisition of territory. Without colonies and spheres of influence, America therefore lacks the typical geography of empire.[34]

Imbued with such thinking, many policymakers have justified, both artfully and clumsily, U.S. interventions. Yet, despite Washington's habitual protestations, such incursions call to mind the achievements—proud and awful—of past imperialists. Thus, Sherry remarks that "in the riches generated for the imperial center, in the universalist claims for American ideals, in the racial or gendered language used to describe nonwhite peoples, in the resentments it aroused, and above all in the reach of its military power, the United States after World War II achieved much of the reality and many of the trappings of empire. Precisely how much seems a matter only for quibbling."[35]

The existence and extent of U.S. imperialism may not be easily determined, but its effects seem undeniable. Still, as professed anti-imperialists, Americans do not usually refer to their country's foreign policy as imperialistic even when that term should apply. They prefer an alternative lexicon that describes the United States as friendly, even altruistic. This American pretense seems to validate the International Relations (IR) theory of constructivism, whereby states and their citizens subjectively create their own reality rather than submit to the predetermined laws of world politics touted by so-called IR realists.[36]

Although most Americans rarely admit to the existence of U.S. imperialism and tend not to use the vocabulary of empire, Klaus Knorr writes of a postwar America in pursuit of an informal empire "compatible with the interests of the advanced capitalist societies." He dubs such an effort "a kind of neoimperialism." In his opinion, Washington "aimed not at territorial acquisition but at building a huge conglomerate of patron-client relationships, within which clients were often able to exploit the patron." This "reverse donor dependency" or "tyranny of the weak" may have empowered some Third-World leaders such as South Korea's Syngman Rhee, yet, as Scott Bills observes, many countries that achieved independence soon after World War II perceived the United States as the "last avatar of the imperial ethos."[37]

Fouad Ajami admits that the United States may qualify as a "modern imperium," but points out that, contrary to past imperialists, it has exhibited "the greatest of reluctance" to intervene abroad. A disastrous war in Indochina effected this trepidation, a national obsession known as the "Vietnam syndrome." But prior to 1965, the year President Lyndon B. Johnson dramatically escalated U.S. involvement in Southeast Asia, Washington pursued its post-World War II interests rather vigorously. Superpower standing bestowed increased international responsibilities upon America and invited European-style imperial behavior in the name of anti-communism, the *mission civilisatrice* of that era. Similarly, the current U.S. War on Terror has provided Washington with a renewed pretext to intervene whenever and wherever it sees fit.[38]

In his review of the U.S. Cold-War experience, Garry Wills rejects comparisons to Europe's brand of imperialism. The United States, he argues, "wanted a network of perches for military action against the Soviet Union. It did not want to annex the countries but to use them—call it 'security imperialism.'" For his part, John Lewis Gaddis juxtaposes the flexibility of Washington's "democratic empire" with Moscow's ossified imperium and stresses the reactive quality of U.S. policy. Thomas Paterson inverses Gaddis' argument, however, by underlining the offensive, as opposed to defensive, character of U.S. expansionism. Paterson faults American policymakers for their constant exaggeration of so-called Communist threats, a ploy that rallied domestic opinion and enabled America to inject itself into numerous foreign disputes.[39]

While Wills, Gaddis, and Paterson dwell on political and military strategies, other analysts spotlight economic and cultural issues. Andrew Bacevich writes of contemporary America's "commitment to global openness—removing barriers that inhibit the movement of goods, capital, ideas, and people." To achieve that goal, he argues, Washington seeks "an open and integrated international order based on the principles of democratic capitalism, with the United States as the ultimate guarantor of order and enforcer of norms." As the leading proponent and embodiment of "globalization" (often thought of as the Americanization of the world), Uncle Sam "colonizes minds, not territory," in the words of Mark Hertsgaard, by relentlessly marketing U.S. brands such as McDonald's and Coca-Cola in every continent. The unbridled promotion of American goods and services, combined with Washington's clout within the International Monetary Fund (IMF), the World Bank, and the World Trade Organization (WTO), homogenizes global tastes, undermines cultural diversity, and subjects the world's most destitute to the imperatives of U.S. capitalism, with its emphasis on market efficiencies rather than individual or collective sufficiency and well-being. As a result of Wall Street's greed and the secretive ways of the democracy-deficient IMF, World Bank, and WTO, Samuel Huntington points out that many countries, not to mention anti-globalization protesters, accuse the United States of "financial imperialism" and "intellectual colonialism." While these critics assail America for its callous economic and cultural imperialism, they tend to ignore the benefits of U.S. innovation and productivity (i.e., impressive economic growth in the world economy in the past century and significant improvements in the global standard of living) and hesitate or refuse to acknowledge—despite ample evidence to the contrary—that not all foreigners dislike American products.[40]

The U.S. ability to export economic and cultural values so successfully contributes to the country's imperial distinctiveness. Asserts Michael Ignatieff, "America's empire is not like empires of times past, built on colonies, conquest and the white man's burden." He argues that "[t]he 21st century imperium is a new invention in the annals of political science, an empire lite, a global hegemony whose grace notes are free markets, human rights and democracy, enforced by the most awesome military power the world has ever known." This creation, he notes, "is an empire without consciousness of itself as such, constantly shocked that its good intentions arouse resentment abroad."[41]

Americans may not fully understand why a foreign leader, invoking cultural distinctiveness or "relativism" to justify repression, publicly associates Washington's human-rights agenda with "western moral imperialism." But they should not be surprised that their country's policies sometimes earn it international disdain. Subjects of imperial Rome frequently displayed similar ingratitude vis-à-vis their ruler while partaking in the benefits of empire. Such hypocrisy stems from animosity toward the powerful, especially those sans peer who seek order, whether regional or global, on their own terms. Comparing Rome to the United States, Peter Bender observes that "[w]orld powers without rivals are a class unto themselves. They do not accept anyone as an equal, and are quick to call loyal followers friends, or *amicus populi Romani*. They no longer know any foes, just rebels, terrorists, and rogue states. They no longer fight, merely punish. They no longer wage wars but merely create peace." Harold James calls this "the Roman predicament." If überpowers want to thrive, they must take exception to the rules they have invented and enforced; violating their own norms, in turn, invites hostility, opposition, and resistance.[42]

Such a conundrum can enervate an empire, even a "superempire" (to use Bernard Porter's term) such as the United States, and possibly destroy it. With that in mind, scholars such as John Ikenberry, ex-Clinton official Joseph Nye, and conservative economist Clyde Prestowitz acknowledge U.S. imperial capabilities but deem Washington incapable of staying its mostly unilateral course and unwise to pretend otherwise. Ikenberry opines that "America's nascent neoimperial grand strategy threatens to rend the fabric of the international community and political partnerships precisely at a time when that community and those partnerships are urgently needed. It is an approach fraught with peril and likely to fail." He adds that "[i]t is not only politically unsustainable but diplomatically harmful. And if history is a guide, it will trigger antagonism and resistance that will leave America in a more hostile and divided world." To convey the error in U.S. ways, Prestowitz quotes former American Ambassador to Saudi Arabia Chas Freeman vividly, if not amusingly, amending John Winthrop's famous phrase: "the United States is a City on a Hill," Freeman said, "but it is increasingly fogged in." The ever optimistic Ronald Reagan, who adopted Winthrop's Puritan slogan as his own, would no doubt have objected to this characterization of his country, but an assessment of global trends leaves Nye unpersuaded of America's unrivaled strength. Despite ample "soft power" (i.e., the global appeal of its culture as well as its political and societal values) and overwhelming military capacity, the United States must cope with economic multipolarity (i.e., the European Union, Japan, and the People's Republic of China) and complex transnational relations—involving myriad non-governmental organizations (NGOs)—that complicate U.S. foreign policy and render it less effective.[43]

Unlike Ikenberry, Nye, and Prestowitz, Niall Ferguson argues in favor of the U.S. imperium (i.e., the "empire in denial") and compares it favorably to Pax Britannica, yet also questions whether the United States can sustain its imperial creation. His analysis spotlights, however, U.S. domestic shortcomings—the country's "attention, man-power, and economic deficits"—rather than external resistance to Washington's preferred modus operandi. While urging the White House to reprise Great Britain's nineteenth century role in the world, Ferguson bemoans Americans' lack of enthusiasm for empire. Even federal politicians must attend primarily to parochial constituent needs rather than ponder the nuances of U.S. geopolitics. The American body politic does not care much, moreover, for foreign ventures that drag on. Eager for quick, decisive victories, Americans often display impatience whenever their government struggles to achieve its stated objectives expeditiously due to, for example, bureaucratic wrangling, diplomatic and military incompetence, or unforeseen problems. Given the U.S. electoral cycle, politicians, especially presidents, cannot countenance stalemate abroad, never mind defeat, lest voters vent their frustration by turning out incumbents—even though members of Congress infrequently lose their seats. American fickleness, combined with a typical incuriosity about the world beyond U.S. shores, makes the United States a less than ideal candidate for sustained empire.[44]

Ferguson also notes the absence of an imperial mentality among the country's young elite, who prefer the lure of Wall Street's millions to the considerable challenge of refashioning Middle Eastern and foreign societies to suit U.S. interests. Oxbridge men of yore may have opted for service in Asia and Africa in the name of God and empire, but most well-educated American men and women aspire to much more pedestrian and predictable careers. Most do not yearn to serve their country as soldiers either, though the recent "revolution in military affairs," which Ferguson omits in his analysis, allows U.S. armed forces (who number only approximately 1.4 million, a small number given Washington's extensive global commitments) to rely more on technology and effective tactics and less on the size of America's army, navy, air force, or marine corps. Unfortunately for the White House and U.S. soldiers, terrorists, insurgents, and militiamen who oppose American occupation policies in Iraq and Afghanistan also possess better equipment and lethal modus operandi, such as suicide-homicide bombings.[45]

In addition to public indifference and a dearth of enlisted personnel (who do not typically relish "nation-building" duty abroad), Ferguson points out that the United States cannot afford an extended empire given its significant budget deficit ($260 billion for fiscal year 2006) and worrisome external debt ($8.8 trillion, as of June 2005) as well as Washington's commitment to very expensive social-welfare programs such as Social Security and Medicare. Although in the 1990s the country rectified similar fiscal imbalances inherited from the Reagan years, the Bush administration's election-year promise in 2004 to halve the budget deficit within five years hinged on uncertain U.S. economic growth and could not account for the likely exorbitant costs of America's War on Terror, whose end no one could foresee.[46]

While Ferguson underlines psychological and economic dimensions of the American empire, Amy Kaplan examines lexical and other cultural manifestations of this creation. She assesses the "dominant narratives" associated with contemporary U.S. imperialism: the "coming-out narrative" espoused by the so-called neo-conservatives, several of whom have advised President Bush, and the "reluctant imperialist" narrative preferred by so-called liberal interventionists such as Clinton Secretary of State Madeleine Albright and former Harvard professor Michael Ignatieff. The "coming-out" school, in Kaplan's words, "aggressively celebrates the United States as finally revealing its true essence—its manifest destiny—on a global stage." Conversely, the "reluctant" group claims that the country "never sought an empire and may even be constitutionally unsuited to rule one, but it had the burden thrust upon it by the fall of earlier empires and the failures of modern states, which abuse the human rights of their own people and spawn terrorism."[47]

While the neo-conservatives invoke America's right and duty to crush enemies (i.e., rogue countries and individuals alike) and envision a perpetual empire, they fear and thus desperately seek to prevent imperial decline, the destiny of all previous empires. Writes Kaplan, "[i]n this hypermasculine narrative there's a paradoxical sense of invincibility and unparalleled power and at the same time utter and incomprehensible vulnerability. . . ." For liberal interventionists who prize international moral rectitude, Kaplan points out that "[b]enevolence and self-interest merge . . . ; backed by unparalleled force, the United States can save the people of the world from their own anarchy, their descent into an uncivilized state." Neo-conservative and liberal interventionist thinking invariably connote a racial view of the world, a hallmark of empire, prompting Kaplan to comment: "The images of an unruly world, of anarchy and chaos, of failed modernity, recycle stereotypes of racial inferiority from earlier colonial discourses about races who are incapable of governing themselves."[48]

On race and other matters of U.S. empire, the "dominant narratives" intersect. In Kaplan's view, "[t]hey take American exceptionalism to new heights: its paradoxical claim to uniqueness and universality at the same time. They share a teleological narrative of inevitability, that America is the apotheosis of history, the embodiment of universal values of human rights, liberalism, and democracy, the 'indispensable nation,' in Madeleine Albright's words." Kaplan adds that the country "claims the authority to 'make sovereign judgments on what is right and what is wrong' for everyone else and 'to exempt itself with an absolutely clear conscience from all the rules that it proclaims and applies to others.' Absolutely protective of its own sovereignty, it upholds a doctrine of limited sovereignty for others and thus deems the entire world a potential site for intervention." Deductively, Kaplan concludes: "If in these narratives imperial power is deemed the solution to a broken world, then they preempt any counternarratives that claim U.S. imperial actions, past and present, may have something to do with the world's problems. According to this logic, resistance to empire can never be opposition to the imposition of foreign rule; rather, resistance means irrational opposition to modernity and universal human values."[49]

Kaplan's uncompromising critique of the American variant of empire, like Edward Said's trenchant criticisms of U.S. imperial policy in the Middle East and elsewhere, calls out for the elimination of such a wicked form of *raison d'état*. After all, empire harms most citizens of the imperium, whether American or foreign. The loss in treasure, civil liberties, and life (of both civilians in terrorist attacks and military personnel on the battlefield) often seems inversely proportional to the level of American security. Higher costs translate into greater U.S. insecurity, in other words, or so Americans and others may perceive the War on Terror and other imperial tasks. Yet, despite the "security dilemma" currently afflicting the United States (i.e., violent efforts to maximize U.S. safety invite violent reprisals; by repeating itself, this tit-for-tat pattern results in a so-called spiral of insecurity), can an entity other than an empire guarantee security *both* for itself and others? The United Nations provides many benefits to the global community—its agencies, in conjunction with NGOs, care for the world's impoverished and sick (especially women, children, and the elderly)—but currently only an empire such as the United States can seemingly marshal the resources and political will to fulfil a "human security" agenda (with its emphasis on humanitarian issues such as disease, migration, anti-personnel land mines, and the environment) *and* a "national security" agenda (with its emphasis on political-military issues such as the proliferation of weapons of mass destruction).

Consistent with this view, several scholars underscore the advantages of a U.S. imperium while acknowledging its deficiencies. Michael Cox remarks that "in a fragmenting, postmodern world, where small bands of fanatics based in crumbling polities could cause havoc and mayhem elsewhere, imperialism with American characteristics was the only real answer to the kind of dangers that now threatened the peace." Before the U.S.-led occupation of Iraq (conceived beforehand as "temporary territorial imperialism," in the words of Michael Mann) alerted the White House to the perils of empire, Washington typically resisted such overt manifestations of authority. Thus, Tony Judt opines that "[w]hereas the British were constrained (after some initial reluctance) to exercise formal—and costly—*imperium* over whole subcontinents, the US has hitherto perfected the art of controlling foreign countries and their resources without going to the expense of actually owning them or ruling their subjects."[50]

Judt notes, however, that various intersecting trends hobble the world's only "imperial democracy." Those include a postcolonial international context often characterized by virulent and armed ethnic nationalism; a contentious, divided American body politic generally averse to foreign aid and other costs of empire; Washington's uncouth ties, past and present, with unsavory autocrats; and the U.S. historical opposition to democratically elected governments (e.g., in Guatemala, Chile, Algeria, and Venezuela). As well, unlike previous imperia, the United States must administer its empire before an always and instantly informed global television viewership typically eager to condemn American imperial efforts, as well as inaction—such as in Rwanda in 1994 and in Darfur, Sudan, most recently. Finally, Judt ominously asserts that the United States "cannot be an effective empire precisely because it comes in the wake of all other empires before it and must pay the price for their missteps as well as its own."[51]

Michael Mann reinforces Judt's assertion by juxtaposing America's current imperial efforts with nineteenth century European imperialism, which occurred during the so-called Age of Empire. "Britain and France were not go-it alone imperialists," Mann writes. "Despite fighting wars against each other, they were partners in a much broader so-called 'civilising mission' launched first by Europe, then by the West, on the rest of the world." "This Western imperialism," he adds, "was much more formidable than the US is today, militarily, politically, economically, and especially ideologically. From the point of view of the rest of the world, Britain, France, Belgium, Russia, the United States and so on, all looked culturally the same. When viewed collectively, there was simply no escaping their power." For Mann, the twenty-first century—with its post-imperial ethos, assertive nationalisms, interconnected societies, and interdependent economies—diminishes America's advantages, while exacerbating its shortcomings. That reality thwarts Washington's imperial aspirations. Consequently, he opines: "[t]he US is a military giant, an economic back-seat driver, a political schizophrenic and an ideological phantom. The result is a mess of contradictions, at first an incoherent empire—then a failed one."[52]

Despite such impediments to Washington's imperial policies and pessimism regarding their likelihood of success, William Odom and Robert Dujarric note that "[t]he American empire incurs much lower transaction costs because its Liberal institutions allow member states to prosper while affording them diplomatic and informal political influence on US foreign, economic, and military policy. The incentives for voluntary compliance, therefore, greatly reduce the need for coercive measures." As John Gaddis points out, the velvet or consensual quality of America's imperium enables the country to contrast its rule with some worse alternative: fascism, communism, or Islamic fundamentalism. Such comparisons do not preclude or necessarily justify, however, Washington's habitual use of violence to secure its interests—inflicted militarily, but also politically, economically, culturally, and psychologically. The iron-fist or martial component of U.S. imperialism, in combination with unilateralist attitudes and reflexes, may result in the mandatory elimination of enemies, but it could likewise ensure the implosion of the American empire. Though commentators will continue to forecast such an eventual outcome, a banal prediction given the apparent inevitability of the imperial trajectory (i.e., empires rise, thrive, stagnate, decline, and fall—though they can rise, thrive, stagnate, and decline repeatedly without collapsing), the U.S. imperium, like the Roman version, could endure, *in one form or another*, for hundreds of years.[53]

For now, America's *preferred* variant of empire is an *informal* one, whereby, according to John Gray, Washington seeks to achieve its objectives in its various spheres of influence, such as the Persian Gulf, and then leave. President George W. Bush's Iraq policy in 2003 aimed to do exactly that. In Gray's opinion, the United States resorts to empire simply out of practicality, not to uphold an imperial ideology. Unlike nineteenth century European empires, what matters to Washington is the outcome of its policy, not the accoutrements of imperialism. For Gray, such a modus operandi undercuts any imperial pretensions the country might have and makes for an ineffective empire. In the event, however, the United States has remained involved in regions, such as western Europe, for many years despite having secured favorable results warranting at least a U.S. military withdrawal. The American occupation of Iraq, now in its fifth year, illustrates the perils of *formal* empire, the difficulty imperia can encounter when trying to convert from formal to informal empire, and how arduous it can be for an imperium to exit a country, never mind a region.[54]

Despite hardships in Iraq, the United States, like previous empires, all of which experienced various setbacks and fiascoes, will continue its quest, quixotic though it may be, for a better imperium. In the Bush administration's perilous post-9/11 world, which necessitates an expansionist foreign policy, the U.S. empire confirms what William Appleman Williams noted in 1980: "Empire is freedom. Empire is liberty. Empire is security." As the most sophisticated air-naval empire ever, America relies on its state-of-the-art war planes and ships, and their formidable arsenals, to impose its will. So armed, Washington frequently opts for a classic imperial strategy. "Rather than operate within multilateral frameworks," notes John Ikenberry, "the United States forges a hub and spoke array of 'special relationships' around the world. Countries that cooperate with the United States and accept its leadership receive special bilateral security and economic favors." This familiar way to proceed has allowed Washington to achieve a post-World War II tour de force, especially when combined with regional organizations such as the North Atlantic Treaty Organization and assistance programs such as the Marshall Plan. Such imperial success did not occur without significant incompetence and expenditure, both in treasure and lives (American and other), but the outcome, measured by imperial standards, remained impressive, albeit not necessarily satisfactory, especially to critics of U.S. foreign policy.[55]

Often with such criticism in mind, Washington has experimented with differing imperial strategies. By forging a *hybrid* empire, one with *both liberal and classic features*, America has adopted many of the best attributes of each type. As a liberal empire, the United States affords its "subjects" much political and economic leeway and rarely oppresses them bitterly, the hallmark of many empires. As Charles Maier observes, America "is prepared to exert imperial control over relatively small states that compose its 'frontiers,' but it depends on consensual acquiescence and common elite interests within its spheres of influence." Ikenberry adds that such countries "are given 'voice opportunities,' that is, they are given informal access to the policymaking process of the United States and the wider array of intergovernmental institutions that constitute the system." Due to the informal character of that liberal empire, members can contravene the United States intermittently to assert independent policies and/or achieve domestic political victories. Given America's penchant for selective punishment, occasional affronts to U.S. prerogative only infrequently result in sustained American hostility. With the White House often fixated upon antithetical ideologies such as Soviet communism and Islamic radicalism, U.S. partners, whether autocratic or democratic, have periodically behaved insubordinately without serious repercussion. Typically, only revolt within the empire, such as in Cuba following the

Castro revolution and in Iran under Ayatollah Khomeini, will ensure Washington's continuous enmity and wrath.[56]

As a classic empire, America can administer severe political, economic, and military blows when required, without much concern or pity for those it attacks and hurts. As Ikenberry notes, "[t]he United States is an unrivalled military power and this does lead Washington to pursue old-style imperial policies. The other major powers have no control over American imperial impulses." This ability to inflict physical, emotional, and material injury so that it can achieve its way endows the United States with the ruthlessness imperial purpose demands. Not surprisingly, American and foreign critics of such recourse consider Washington hypocritical for carrying out such violence while promoting itself as an exceptional country that rhetorically strives to improve the world *peacefully*. Such duplicity is not unprecedented, however; previous empires relied on such tactics to justify their expansion and rule to their citizens as well as to the world.[57]

Despite such similarities with past imperia, Gray and other analysts do not consider America much of an imperium. Opines Ikenberry, "the neo-conservatives in Washington do offer an imperial vision of international order . . . . But this neo-conservative vision is built on illusions about American power . . . . The American people are not seized with the desire to run colonies or a global empire. So even in a unipolar era, there are limits on American imperial pretensions." Domestic opposition to empire is not uniquely American, however. While many Europeans celebrated imperial achievements, anti-imperialists protested Europe's autocratic empires, which ministers, mandarins, and other elites administered.[58]

Although useful, comparing imperia is not easy, especially given the widely differing regional and global contexts spanning several millennia. Even if one tries to evaluate empires via a chart, graph, or continuum, the exercise will likely be vexing and unsatisfactory. Assessing various imperial dimensions (e.g., political, economic, military, and social-cultural) involves objectivity. Yet subjective judgments will also be necessary. While scholars can quantify wealth and military prowess, ascertaining influence and impact requires a sophisticated, and likely biased, model of empire that can account for evolving political systems and behavioral norms, as well as technological innovation. A wax-and-wane graph, such as the one proposed in the Preface, may serve a heuristic or illustrative purpose, but it should not be considered scientific. How effectively, then, can any analyst compare an American empire, a twenty-first century entity in a democratic, capitalist, post-colonial, transnational, interdependent, human-rights era, with the Roman Empire, an ancient imperium that excelled in a time of despotism, slavery, and sanctioned brutality? Although each empire achieved preponderant, sometimes overwhelming, power over others, any comparison beyond that will likely be subject to appreciable methodological bias. Nevertheless, such taxonomical issues will continue to interest students of empire, who seek to identify patterns of imperial behavior and, based on those, divine the future of the U.S. imperium.[59]

For political scientists, matters of epistemology (e.g., how does one define empire?), "operationalization" (e.g., what criteria make for empire?), and "falsification" (e.g., when is a Great Power not an empire?) only complicate the study of empire, especially the American variant. Quantifying empire, as mentioned, remains elusive. Scholars can count military personnel, expenditures, and hardware (e.g., guns, tanks, ships, planes, and missiles), but how should they assess imperial ideology and influence? Models account well for the material, not so well the ideational. Semantically, empire may be synonymous with superpower and other names that connote superiority within the international system. But empire's longevity as a term and concept gives it "value-added." Since many empires have existed, U.S. foreign policy can be subjected to rigorous analysis. The post-World War II U.S. empire in the Persian Gulf can be compared, for example, to the seventh century Islamic empire in the same region that also ruled informally. Each empire relied on *amirs* (Gulf monarchs in the twentieth century, provincial governors in the seventh), eschewed imposing its own culture, and stationed its soldiers apart from local populations. Such an historical comparison may be imperfect, but it serves an instrumental purpose: it explains behaviors in specific contexts and highlights similarities as well as differences. Comparing empires may or may not offer lessons, but it prevents easy or reflexive recourse to exceptionalism. America may possess an exceptional empire. But without comparison to other imperia, an analyst cannot know. With comparison, she or he can. That may not satisfy political scientists who adhere to the social scientific method. But comparison precludes the fallacy of ahistorical analysis by making history relevant to the U.S. experience. In the words of Michael Cox, "[i]f nothing else, the idea of Empire drags the United States back into the historical mainstream where it should be, and hopefully will remain."[60]

Currently, consistent with the country's so-called argument culture, the issue of American empire continues to generate lively discussion in both the academy and policy circles. Historically, the debate has raged *intermittently* rather than whenever the United States has invaded another country and/or overthrown its leadership, either overtly or covertly. The Spanish-American War and its aftermath of U.S. expansion in the Caribbean and Pacific ushered in an imperial era in American history, pitting imperialists such as Theodore Roosevelt versus anti-imperialists such as William Jennings Bryan. The Vietnam War stirred similar passions. The on-going U.S.-led occupation of Iraq exercises opponents of empire as well as proponents. Once *Operation Iraqi Freedom* ends, however, the debate over empire will likely subside, save for a few analysts who will continue to study the topic without attracting much media, policy, or scholarly attention. The cycle ought to resume if and when Americans have to cope with the consequences of yet another controversial, drawn-out intervention abroad.[61]

Hegemony, Not Empire

While many observers, both American and foreign, exchange views regarding the U.S. imperium, its features, and its future, some analysts consider the designation inappropriate. Alexander Motyl, for example, opines that "[t]he United States and its institutions, political and cultural, certainly have an overbearing influence on the world today, but why should that influence be termed 'imperial,' as opposed to 'hegemonic' or just 'exceptionally powerful'?" He further notes that "[w]hat has caused the empire vogue recently has not been the sudden appearance of imperially structured US power, but the seemingly arbitrary use of that power." For his part, Michael Hirsh asserts that "[i]t is simply not in America's national DNA to impose a pax Romana. We [Americans] are a nation whose reason for existence is to maximize freedom. We cannot be, in any traditional sense, an empire." Unlike Hirsh, whose thinking mirrors that of former U.S. Secretary of Defense Donald Rumsfeld (who said of his fellow countrymen and women, "[w]e don't do empire"), Leon Hadar equates the contemporary use of the term empire with globalization, the ubiquitous word of the 1990s, and thus considers the former "an intellectual fad produced by pundits searching for catchy phrases and colorful metaphors to explain complex reality."[62]

Regardless of what the term *du jour* may be, Philip Zelikow states unequivocally that, without colonies, America will never qualify as an empire. Also denying the existence of an American imperium, Victor Davis Hanson waxes sarcastic that "[s]hould the day come when Washington charges all host countries for our [U.S.] troops and appropriates Persian Gulf oil fields, and when epic poems about noble missions of the 101st Airborne replace pop music on our radio stations, then perhaps we should worry about the rise of empire and imperial culture." While eschewing Zelikow's uncompromising words and Hanson's dismissive prose, Fareed Zakaria argues that political and other inadequacies disqualify the country as an imperial power. Not surprisingly, then, Zakaria has repeatedly criticized American blunders in occupied Iraq as well as other U.S. imperial preoccupations. In a February 2004 *Newsweek* editorial, for example, he writes that "[w]hile Washington worries about traditional problems of empire—disorder on the periphery—there is a new globalizing world slowly taking shape, in search of leadership." Similarly, John Ikenberry notes that "[t]he American system has features that it shares with past great empires. But ultimately the term 'empire' is misleading and misses the distinctive aspects of the global political order. Today's US-centred political formation requires new ways of thinking about liberalism, power, and international order rather than the rehabilitation of the evocative—but ultimately ill-fitting—notion of empire." In a similar vein, Robert Skidelsky asserts that "[t]he United States is not in transition from hegemony to empire. The world is in transition to new forms of political organization, whose outlines can be dimly perceived, but whose frontiers cannot yet be fixed."[63]

Analysts who doubt that an American empire exists, or dislike the term, often refer to U.S. hegemony or primacy, which they characterize as preponderance of power and influence combined with mostly benevolent international political leadership. Donald Nuechterlein prefers hegemony "because it implies less direct control over the decisions of other states, even though the outcome in terms of their policies [empire and hegemony] may be similar." Although some scholars conflate hegemony and empire, or consider the former a facet of the latter, Ikenberry argues that "[t]he key difference between empire and hegemony is that in an empire, the lead state operates unilaterally and outside the order, whereas in a hegemonic order, the lead establishes multilateral rules and institutions that it itself operates within. They are different types of domination." For Michael Hunt, "empire does not suffice . . . [since it] fails to fully capture the impressive reach of the United States in its post-1945 ascendancy." Hence, he opines, "[i]f ever the term 'hegemony' was appropriately applied, it is to what the United States became in the latter half of the twentieth century and now remains. To equate 'hegemony' with 'empire' or use them interchangeably is to obscure the significance of this recent unprecedented, pervasive U.S. role all around the world."[64]

Although, for Hunt, hegemony connotes supra-empire, a heterodox point of view among scholars, a more specific definition is often used. According to one International Relations (IR) school of thought, hegemony underscores economic relationships between countries, markets, and classes. Whenever this kind of hegemony occurs, one state underpins the world capitalist economy. As a buyer or lender of last resort, this supreme economic power can prevent a systemic collapse that could result in a global economic slump akin to the Great Depression. Studies spotlight Great Britain in the nineteenth century and the United States in the twentieth as countries that have stabilized the international economic system.[65]

Other scholars dismiss, however, this positive (or liberal) assessment of hegemony. Immanuel Wallerstein, for example, examines the origins of a world capitalist economy made up of "core," "semiperipheral," and "peripheral" countries. In this system, strong economies, such as England in the sixteenth century, press their competitive advantages (political, social, demographic, and geographic) as they exploit a disadvantaged nation's resources and weakened position to improve their overall economic performance. Other writers push this analysis further, highlighting the developing world's "dependence" upon advanced economies and the resulting widespread inequality and injustice.[66]

Validation of this globalist argument can be found in the realist analysis of Robert Gilpin, who notes that "[a]s the power of a state increases, it seeks to extend its territorial control, its political influence, and/or its domination of the international economy." "Reciprocally," he adds, "these developments tend to increase the power of the state as more and more resources are made available to it and it is advantaged by economies of scale. The territorial, political, and economic expansion of a state increases the availability of economic surplus required to exercise dominion over the system." As a result of this need to improve upon their status, Gilpin emphatically asserts that historically states and empires have "sought to expand and extend their dominance over their neighbors in order to increase their share of the economic surplus."[67]

Concurring with Gilpin, Robert Keohane points out that the United States achieved hegemony, not empire, following the Second World War and the establishment of the Bretton Woods system. By virtue of America's atypical Great-Power expansion, any reference to U.S. imperialism seems inappropriate. "It is not clear," Keohane writes, "how the appellation, 'empire' assists in understanding the dynamics of hegemony in a world economy, and world politics, characterized by both sovereignty and interdependence." Like Keohane, Thomas McCormick details Washington's maturation into a hegemon. Both note, however, that U.S. hegemony started to decline steadily only two decades after the American victory in World War II.[68]

Keohane's "after hegemony" thesis seemed to explain America's post-Vietnam troubles, but the end of the Cold War returned the country to its former glory. As the United States struck a pose reminiscent of V-J Day in the Bush *père* and Clinton years, it resumed its hegemonic ways by bailing out Mexico in 1994, and eventually stabilizing the international economy following the Asian panic of 1997–98. At the same time, Washington punished Iraq on an almost daily basis with its sophisticated and unmatched arsenal. These attacks killed innocent Iraqis and begged the following question: Why would a hegemon employ what could only be construed as imperial methods?

Contingent Imperialism in a Zone of Conflict

John Ikenberry provides an initial answer to this paradox. Having evolved a "protean order," the United States relies on *both hegemony and empire* to achieve its objective: an international community supportive of U.S. values and interests. Washington thus opts for either a hegemonic tactic, liberalism, or an imperial one, militarism, to realize its strategic goal of sustaining or expanding the American world order. In North America, most of Europe, and parts of Asia, hegemonic policies suffice for capitalism and democracy to thrive. In regions such as the Middle East, however, the United States must pursue imperial policies to assure itself at least the benefits of capitalism, Washington's primary concern. In the Persian Gulf, plentiful, accessible, and affordable oil matters more than representative government, notwithstanding the current Bush administration's commitment to democracy throughout the Middle East.[69]

This duality in the American world order, which, as Ikenberry notes, most analysts of U.S. empire overlook, mirrors the current division of the globe into zones of peace and conflict. This dichotomy corresponds to the liberal and realist worlds of IR theory. Where war does not occur and is considered obsolete, such as in the European Union, institutions, rules, and norms regulate and constrain state behavior, including America's. Each country seeks maximum economic performance consistent with governmental and societal preferences. Robert Cooper refers to this type of so-called postmodern imperialism as "the voluntary imperialism of the global economy"—a U.S.-led liberal imperialism, or "market empire," which Daniel Vernet considers "essentially ideological." Where military clashes remain pervasive or likely, however, Hobbesian rather than Kantian solutions continue to prevail. Regional context, economic imperative, and strategic necessity therefore explain the existence of a U.S. empire in the Persian Gulf. This regional imperium, part of America's global empire, serves mostly as a "soft" sphere of influence, to use Vloyantes' term, that seeks to benefit, expand, consolidate, or preserve American hegemony and security in the Gulf, as well as worldwide. Yet, given Washington's often intermittent, as opposed to sustained, involvement in the region since 1941, the concept of U.S. imperialism must be refined, hence the notion of *contingent imperialism*—which could also be dubbed selective or "situational" imperialism.[70]

Contingent imperialism occurs whenever an imperial Great Power responds to a perceived external threat by resorting to political, economic, or military re-

medies to secure its hegemonic (i.e., financial and commercial) and other strategic interests in a foreign country or region. Remedies include coercive diplomacy,
sanctions, and force. As an avowed reluctant interventionist, one presupposes
that the United States intervenes selectively, mainly in favorable regional and
international contexts, and usually in response to certain types of threats. Consequently, one would expect Washington to rely on contingent imperialism rather
than reflexive imperialism, whereby an imperial Great Power intervenes continuously. But what if a situation calls for imperialism and America does not act?
Intuitively, one would think that either global circumstances and/or decision-
maker personality traits could explain such an unwillingness or inability.[71]

To understand if, when, why, and in what form contingent imperialism occurs, one must examine four factors: level of threat, regional constraints, domestic reaction, and bureaucratic impediments. Threats to U.S. hegemony, which
presidents *perceive* as well as assess objectively, can be international or regional.
They may be characterized as significant or minor. Significant threats can potentially result in diminished access to important resources such as oil. Minor
threats should be considered irritants that may involve temporary loss of credibility but will not harm American strategic interests. Regional constraints, such
as the state of the Arab-Israeli contest or ideological cleavages within the Persian
Gulf or Middle East, can limit or rule out Washington's involvement in certain
disputes, especially if international clashes, such as the Cold War, impact regional developments. The same can be said for U.S. public opinion, which includes the media and influential interest groups eager to promote their own business and political agendas. Finally, institutional rivalries within the executive
and between the various branches of government can circumscribe U.S. decision-making.

While any, or a combination, of these factors may preclude recourse to contingent imperialism, in favorable circumstances the United States can choose
from three variants of this response: unilateral, alliance, and proxy. Each variant
seeks to deter or remove threats, whether significant or minor, to American hegemony and security. Unilateral contingent imperialism occurs whenever Washington can act alone or cannot recruit allies or friends. Such a strategy typically
involves preponderant American political, economic, and military contributions
and influence. For example, Washington may prop up an unpopular regime, provide a country with timely financial aid, or send soldiers to expel invaders from a
friendly country. For unilateral contingent imperialism to apply, the United
States must rely on itself, not anyone else. With the second variant, allies agree
to join a U.S.-led venture or vice-versa. In this case, Washington forges some
kind of partnership, whether equal or not. As such, America can lead or follow.
What matters is that the United States proceeds in tandem with others, rather
than strictly on its own. Examples of this variant would be Washington providing
military assistance while another country contributes money, or an administration securing diplomatic sanction while another country helps a Gulf state deter
an invasion by a neighbor. As for proxy contingent imperialism, Washington
opts for this variant whenever it asks surrogates to carry out U.S. policy. Proxies
provide material, political, or psychological support in situations when the Unit-

ed States cannot due to preoccupation with more urgent matters, lack of resources, or some other reason.

With the previous discussion in mind, one can posit five propositions (P):

P1: The United States will exercise unilateral contingent imperialism whenever a significant threat to American hegemony and security occurs, Washington can act alone or cannot rely on anyone else to secure its interests and can overcome any regional constraints, consensus exists within the executive, and no majority in Congress or critical segment of domestic opinion strongly opposes White House action.

P2: The United States will exercise alliance contingent imperialism whenever a significant threat to American hegemony and security occurs, allies agree to join a U.S.-led venture or vice-versa, Washington can overcome any regional constraints, consensus exists within the executive, and no majority in Congress or critical segment of domestic opinion strongly opposes White House action.

P3: The United States will exercise proxy contingent imperialism whenever a significant or minor threat to American hegemony and security occurs, surrogates can preserve U.S. interests, Washington cannot overcome regional constraints, consensus may not exist within the executive, and a majority of Congress or critical segment of domestic opinion strongly opposes direct White House involvement.

P4: Even in the event of a significant threat to American hegemony and security, the United States will not exercise any type of contingent imperialism if it cannot overcome regional constraints, no consensus within the executive exists, and either a majority of Congress or critical segment of domestic opinion (or both) strongly opposes White House action or involvement.

P5: The United States will not exercise any type of contingent imperialism if no threat to American hegemony and security exists.

To evaluate those propositions, this book examines the U.S. experience in the Persian Gulf since World War II in the context of the *creation and evolution* of an *informal* American empire in the Gulf. Washington has greatly valued, and continues to value, that region's oil, one of the keys to America's postwar political and economic success. Due, then, to the Gulf's strategic and commercial importance, contingent imperialism should be most applicable.

Given that it covers sixty-six years, this case study relies on *selected* episodes and issues. A methodology of "structured, focused comparison" spotlights important events and divides the case into six *stages* (1941–47, 1948–58, 1959–72, 1973–89, 1990–2000, 2001–07), each corresponding to an era in U.S. policymaking vis-à-vis the Middle East. Each of these six chapters provides a summary of the global and regional (i.e., Mideast) context before spotlighting key events and decisions that pertain to American policy in the Persian Gulf. At the end of each stage, empire and contingent imperialism are assessed over time and in different contexts.[72]

Contingent imperialism can help explain the American rise in the Persian Gulf since 1941 as well as illustrate the country's reliance on imperial techniques to expand and maintain the U.S. hegemonic and security position in the area. In short, contingent imperialism can explicate why and how Washington created a mostly *informal* empire in the Gulf that mixed co-optation with coercion. Parts of that imperium currently thrive (Kuwait and Qatar), while others convulse (Iraq). Unfortunately for the United States, today's bittersweet experience resembles past U.S. involvement in the region and, worse, may presage the future. Americans, who know the Middle East somewhat better than Mark Twain's travelers in *Innocents Abroad*, though stereotypes and misunderstandings persist, may not care for that kind of prediction. But empires seemingly always generate sorrow—both in the metropole and periphery—no matter the geopolitical and other success they achieve.[73]

Above all else, this study seeks to answer one question: Is the American empire in the Persian Gulf exceptional? In other words, is American behavior different from that of previous Gulf imperialists? If Bradley Thayer is indeed correct and the United States constitutes "the most singular of all empires," then one expects the following account and analysis to highlight consistent achievement, rather than the archetypal pattern of success and failure characteristic of all imperia. Or one anticipates an analytical narrative that spotlights how Washington has overcome temporary failure by employing *novel* ways that have ensured, and will continue to ensure, the perpetuation of its Gulf empire. If the story told in the following pages merely confirms America's banal imperial experience, then the relevance of imperial history in the Gulf, whether British, Ottoman, Persian, Portuguese, Islamic, or otherwise, will be obvious. While analogies tell cautionary tales, scenarios vary based on era. The context in the Gulf today may remind observers of various historical episodes, but important distinctions invalidate certain comparisons or render them meaningless. Still, certain axioms of empire apply in the twenty-first century, just as they did in the seventh, sixteenth, nineteenth, and twentieth centuries. One—that every imperium engenders resistance to it—not only imperils the U.S. position in the Gulf, but threatens to weaken, if not undermine Washington's global empire.

Despite its current Gulf woes, the United States retains impressive power and influence in the region, a fact befitting its recent success there. One achievement that should elude it, however, pertains to the name of the region where so many American soldiers serve as part of *Operation Iraqi Freedom*. While U.S. sailors may think of the Persian Gulf as America's *mare nostrum*, Arabs, unsurprisingly, call that body of water and adjacent area the Arab Gulf. Simply out of convenience, however, reference throughout this study will be made to the Persian Gulf (a more widely used designation) instead of the Persian/Arab Gulf. Also, the Near and Middle East should be considered the same region: east from Egypt to Iran, north to Turkey, and south to the Arabian Peninsula. The Gulf region includes Iran, Iraq, Kuwait, Bahrain, Qatar, Saudi Arabia, the United Arab Emirates, and Oman.

Some events (e.g., the Suez crisis) in Egypt, the Levant, Israel/Palestine, Yemen, and elsewhere in the Middle East discussed herein did not necessarily affect Gulf states directly or significantly, but their impact on the region and U.S. policy makes them worthy of inclusion. In other words, the Persian Gulf should be considered a subsystem (or subregion) of the Greater Middle East, which extends to North Africa, the Horn of Africa, Pakistan, the Caucasus, and Central Asia. Typically, subsystems accommodate themselves to the dynamics of a so-called major system, such as U.S.-Soviet bipolarity during the Cold War. Yet, in the case of the Persian Gulf since World War II, an inverse relationship can often be observed: events in that region compel Great Powers, especially imperial ones, to partake in and adjust to the complex interactions of the subsystem.[74]

Notes

1. William Appleman Williams, *Empire As A Way of Life* (Brooklyn, NY: Ig Publishing, 2007), 20.

2. See Strobe Talbott and Nayan Chanda, eds., *The Age of Terror: America and the World After September 11* (New York: Basic Books, 2001); and Mark Danner, "The Battlefield in the American Mind," *New York Times*, 16 October 2001, http://www.nytimes.com. On foreign attitudes vis-à-vis the United States, see Mark Hertsgaard, *The Eagle's Shadow: Why America Fascinates and Infuriates the World* (New York: Picador, 2002). On U.S.-Third World relations, see David D. Newsom, *The Imperial Mantle: The United States, Decolonization, and the Third World* (Bloomington, IN: Indiana University Press, 2001).

3. Robert F. Worth, "A Nation Defined by Its Enemies," *New York Times*, 24 February 2002, http://www.nytimes.com; and R.C. Longworth, "'Bush Doctrine' Arises from Ashes of Sept. 11," *Chicago Tribune*, 7 March 2002, http://www.chicagotribune.com.

4. David Wood, "U.S. Garrisons Rising Across Asia," *The Plain Dealer* (Cleveland), 15 February 2002, http://www.cleveland.com/plaindealer; and Albert Legault, "L'Empire Tentaculaire [i.e., The Octopus Empire]," *Le Devoir* (Montréal), 16 February 2002, http://www.ledevoir.com.

5. On Western imperialism in the Middle East, see Rashid Khalidi, *Resurrecting Empire: Western Footprints and America's Perilous Path in the Middle East* (Boston: Beacon Press, 2004).

6. See Frederick F. Anscombe, *The Ottoman Gulf: The Creation of Kuwait, Saudi Arabia, and Qatar* (New York: Columbia University Press, 1997).

7. See Uzi Rabi, "Britain's 'Special Position' in the Gulf: Its Origins, Dynamics and Legacy," *Middle Eastern Studies* 42, no. 3 (May 2006): 351–64; and F. Gregory Gause, III, "The Approaching Turning Point: The Future of U.S. Relations with the Gulf States," *Brookings Project on U.S. Policy Towards the Islamic World*, Analysis Paper Number Two (May 2003), 5.

8. For samples of foreign opinion, see Pew Research Center for the People & the Press, "Pew Global Attitudes Project: 13 June 2006, Survey: America's Image Slips, But Allies Share U.S. Concerns Over Iran, Hamas"; "Pew Global Attitudes Project: 23 June 2005, Survey: U.S. Image Up Slightly, But Still Negative"; and "Pew Global Attitudes Project: 16 March 2004, Survey: A Year After Iraq War," http://people-press.org/reports.

9. Paul Kennedy, *The Rise and Fall of the Great Powers: Economic Change and Military Conflict from 1500 to 2000* (London: Fontana Press, 1989); Robert Gilpin, *War and Change in World Politics* (Cambridge: Cambridge University Press, 1981); Fareed

Zakaria, *From Wealth to Power: The Unusual Origins of America's World Role* (Princeton, NJ: Princeton University Press, 1998), 13–43; Richard Rosecrance, *The Rise of the Trading State: Commerce and Conquest in the Modern World* (New York: Basic Books, 1986); and Samuel P. Huntington, "The Clash of Civilizations?" *Foreign Affairs* 72, no. 3 (Summer 1993): 22–49.

10. See, for example, Kennedy, *The Rise and Fall of the Great Powers*; Jack Snyder, *Myths of Empire: Domestic Politics and International Ambition* (Ithaca, NY: Cornell University Press, 1991); Charles A. Kupchan, *The Vulnerability of Empire* (Ithaca, NY: Cornell University Press, 1994); William H. McNeill, "The Fall of Great Powers: Peace, Stability and Legitimacy," unpublished paper, April 1993; and "The Receding Influence of Empires," *New York Times*, 22 December 1999, http://www.nytimes.com.

11. Zakaria, *From Wealth to Power*; Sean Lynn-Jones, "Realism and America's Rise," *International Security* 23, no. 2 (Fall 1998): 157–82; "The American Century: A Roundtable (Part 1)," *Diplomatic History* 23, no. 2 (Spring 1999):157–370; Kennedy, *Rise and Fall of the Great Powers*, 665–92; Robert Gilpin, *The Political Economy of International Relations* (Princeton, NJ: Princeton University Press, 1987); and Joseph S. Nye, Jr., *Bound to Lead: The Changing Nature of American Power* (New York: Basic Books, 1990). Although many historians and political scientists characterize U.S. foreign policy as either isolationist or internationalist, one scholar, Walter Russell Mead, refers to the following strands: Hamiltonian, Jeffersonian, Wilsonian, and Jacksonian. Hamiltonians seek to ensure U.S. economic success. Jeffersonians think the United States should lead by example rather than, in John Quincy Adams' famous words, scour the world "in search of monsters to destroy." Wilsonians seek to export American democracy. Finally, Jacksonians seek military victory by whatever means necessary whenever the United States must fight. Walter Russell Mead, *Special Providence: American Foreign Policy and How It Changed the World* (New York: Knopf, 2001). See also James P. Rubin, "Santayana Syndrome," *New Republic*, 18 March 2002, 29–33.

12. Michael A. Palmer, *Guardians of the Gulf: A History of America's Expanding Role in the Persian Gulf, 1833–1992* (New York: Free Press, 1992), 1–19; Ian S. Lustick, "The Absence of Middle Eastern Great Powers: Political 'Backwardness' in Historical Perspective," *International Organization* 51, no. 4 (Autumn 1997): 653–83; and Michael H. Hunt, *Ideology and U.S. Foreign Policy* (New Haven, CT: Yale University Press, 1987). On the Eastern Question, see L. Carl Brown, *International Politics and the Middle East: Old Rules, Dangerous Game* (Princeton, NJ: Princeton University Press, 1984). For an overview of twentieth century Gulf history, see J.E. Peterson, "The Arabian Peninsula in Modern Times: A Historiographical Survey," *American Historical Review* 96, no. 5 (December 1991): 1435–49.

13. Douglas Little, *American Orientalism: The United States and the Middle East since 1945* (Chapel Hill, NC: University of North Carolina Press, 2004); George Lenczowski, *American Presidents and the Middle East* (Durham, NC: Duke University Press, 1990); William B. Quandt, *Peace Process: American Diplomacy and the Arab-Israeli Conflict since 1967* (Washington, DC, and Berkeley, CA: The Brookings Institution and University of California Press, 1993); and Daniel Yergin, *The Prize: The Epic Quest for Oil, Money & Power* (New York: Simon & Schuster, 1991). For a perceptive, yet distinctly "orientalist," analysis of recent Middle Eastern history, see Bernard Lewis, *The Shaping of the Modern Middle East* (New York: Oxford University Press, 1994). For a discussion of "orientalism," see Edward W. Said, *Orientalism* (New York: Vintage Books, 1979). For a history of the United States and the Middle East since the American Revolution, see Michael B. Oren, *Power, Faith, and Fantasy: America in the Middle East, 1776 to the Present* (New York: W.W. Norton, 2007).

14. Douglas Little, "Gideon's Band: America and the Middle East since 1945," *Diplomatic History* 18, no. 4 (Fall 1994): 513–40; and Palmer, *Guardians of the Gulf*. Lit-

tle's excellent *American Orientalism* serves as an exception. A recent book on the United States and the Persian Gulf is Robert J. Pauly, Jr.'s *US Foreign Policy and the Persian Gulf: Safeguarding American Interests through Selective Multilateralism* (Aldershot, England: Ashgate, 2005). Pauly spotlights U.S. policies since 1989.

15. Bradley A. Thayer, "The Case for the American Empire," in Christopher Layne and Bradley A. Thayer, *American Empire: A Debate* (New York: Routledge, 2007), 3. Similar to Thayer, Deepak Lal writes that "the major argument in favor of empires is that they provide the most basic of public goods – order – in an anarchical international society of states." Deepak Lal, "In Defense of Empires," in Andrew J. Bacevich, ed., *The Imperial Tense: Prospects and Problems of American Empire* (Chicago: Ivan R. Dee, 2003), 29. For definitional problems with empire, imperialism, and associated phenomena, such as colonialism, see, for example, Charles S. Maier, *Among Empires: American Ascendancy and Its Predecessors* (Cambridge, MA: Harvard University Press, 2006); Stephen Howe, *Empire: A Very Short Introduction* (Oxford: Oxford University Press, 2002); and Dominic Lieven, *Empire: The Russian Empire and Its Rivals* (New Haven, CT: Yale University Press, 2000).

16. Stephen Peter Rosen, "An Empire, If You Can Keep It," *National Interest*, no. 71 (Spring 2003): 51; and George Liska, *Imperial America: The International Politics of Primacy* (Baltimore: Johns Hopkins Press, 1967), 19.

17. For excellent documentaries on the Egyptian, Athenian, Roman, Islamic, British, French, and other imperia, see the Public Broadcasting Service (PBS) series, *Empires*.

18. Raymond Aron, *The Imperial Republic: The United States and the World 1945–1973*, translated by Frank Jellinek (Cambridge, MA: Winthrop Publishers, 1974), 259; Klaus Knorr, *The Power of Nations: The Political Economy of International Relations* (New York: Basic Books, 1975), 240; and Michael W. Doyle, *Empires* (Ithaca, NY: Cornell University Press, 1986), 12, 19, 28.

19. Doyle, *Empires*, 25, 27.

20. Doyle, *Empires*, 30, 37–38, 45; and Alexander J. Motyl, "Thinking about Empire," in *After Empire: Multiethnic Societies and Nation-Building*, eds. Karen Barkey and Mark von Hagen (Boulder, CO: Westview Press, 1997), 20–25.

21. Doyle, *Empires*, 45–46.

22. Geir Lundestad, *The American "Empire" and Other Studies of US Foreign Policy in a Comparative Perspective* [hereafter *The American "Empire"*] (New York: Oxford University Press, 1990), 23; Thomas G. Paterson, "Cold War Revisionism: A Practitioner's Perspective," *Diplomatic History* 31, no. 3 (June 2007): 391; Daniel H. Nexon and Thomas Wright, "What's at Stake in the American Empire Debate," *American Political Science Review* 101, no. 2 (May 2007): 259; Tony Smith, *The Pattern of Imperialism: The United States, Great Britain, and the Late Industrializing World since 1815* (New York: Cambridge University Press, 1981), 3–4; and John P. Vloyantes, *Silk Glove Hegemony: Finnish-Soviet Relations, 1944–1974: A Case Study of the Theory of the Soft Sphere of Influence* (Kent, OH: Kent State University Press, 1975), 21–22.

23. Thucydides, *History of the Peloponnesian War*, translated by Rex Warner (New York: Penguin Books, 1972), 400–8; Hans J. Morgenthau and Kenneth W. Thompson, *Politics Among Nations: The Struggle for Power and Peace*, 6th ed. (New York: Alfred A. Knopf, 1985), 3–17; Kenneth N. Waltz, *Theory of International Politics* (New York: Random House, 1979); Kenneth N. Waltz, *Man, the State and War: A Theoretical Analysis* (New York: Columbia University Press, 1954); and Stephen M. Walt, *The Origins of Alliances* (Ithaca, NY: Cornell University Press, 1987), 21–22.

24. Palmer, *Guardians of the Gulf*, 243–49; and Mark J. Gasiorowski, *U.S. Foreign Policy and the Shah: Building a Client State in Iran* (Ithaca, NY: Cornell University Press, 1991), 2. See also John Lewis Gaddis, *We Now Know: Rethinking Cold War History* (New York: Clarendon Press, 1997), 26–84, 152–220.

25. Michael Hardt and Antonio Negri, *Empire* (Cambridge, MA: Harvard University Press, 2000), 182; Liska, *Imperial America*, 23; and Zakaria, *From Wealth to Power*, 44–192. For a book on the American empire debate, see Bacevich, ed., *The Imperial Tense*.

26. Mary Ann Heiss, "The Evolution of the Imperial Idea and U.S. National Identity," *Diplomatic History* 26, no. 4 (Fall 2002): 511–40, quote can be found on 512; and James Chace, "In Search of Absolute Security," in Bacevich, ed., *The Imperial Tense*, 119–33, quote can be found on 121.

27. Lundestad, *The American "Empire,"* 38–39, 104. For analysis of the British Empire, see Bernard Porter, *Empire and Superempire: Britain, America and the World* (New Haven, CT: Yale University Press, 2006); and Niall Ferguson, *Empire: The Rise and Demise of the British World Order and the Lessons for Global Power* (New York: Basic Books, 2002).

28. Smith, *The Pattern of Imperialism*, 1, 3.

29. Aron, *The Imperial Republic*, 279; and Jerome Slater, "Is United States Foreign Policy 'Imperialist' or 'Imperial'?" *Political Science Quarterly* 91, no. 1 (Spring 1976): 63–65. On Williams' thinking, see Andrew J. Bacevich, *American Empire: The Realities & Consequences of U.S. Diplomacy* (Cambridge, MA: Harvard University Press, 2002), 23–31.

30. Ronald Steel, *Pax Americana* (New York: Viking Press, 1967), 15–27. Hardt and Negri note that the U.S. Constitution is imperial, not imperialist, "because (in contrast to imperialism's project always to spread its power linearly in closed spaces and invade, destroy, and subsume subject countries within its sovereignty) the U.S. constitutional project is constructed on the model of rearticulating an open space and reinventing incessantly diverse and singular relations in networks across an unbounded terrain." Hardt and Negri, *Empire*, 182.

31. Michael S. Sherry, *In the Shadow of War: The United States since the 1930s* (New Haven, CT: Yale University Press, 1995), 125.

32. Gregg Easterbrook, "Apocryphal Now," *The New Republic*, September 11, 2000, 24; and Chalmers Johnson, *The Sorrows of Empire: Militarism, Secrecy, and the End of the Republic* (New York: Owl Books, 2004), 25–26. See also Andrew J. Bacevich, *The New American Militarism: How Americans Are Seduced by War* (New York: Oxford University Press, 2005); Robert D. Kaplan, *Imperial Grunts: The American Military on the Ground* (New York: Random House, 2005); and Steven Erlanger, "Military Gulf Separates U.S. and European Allies," *New York Times*, 16 March 2002, http://www.nytimes.com. Statistics on U.S. overseas bases can be found in Michael Mann, "The First Failed Empire of the 21st Century," *Review of International Studies* 30, no. 4 (October 2004): 639–40. Given America's hundreds of bases worldwide, maps similar to the well-known, popular ones of the British Empire, with British imperial possessions (both colonies and members of the Commonwealth) typically colored red, could be made and hung in classrooms, government offices, and businesses throughout the United States. That such a development will likely never occur speaks to important ideological differences between Americans, anti-imperialists at heart, and Britons, once proud imperialists.

33. Sherry, *In the Shadow of War*, 125.

34. Robert J. McMahon, *The Limits of Empire: The United States and Southeast Asia since World War II* (New York: Columbia University Press, 1999), 221; Robert Kagan, "The Benevolent Empire," *Foreign Policy*, no. 111 (Summer 1998): 24–35; Andrew J. Bacevich, "New Rome, New Jerusalem," in Bacevich, ed., *The Imperial Tense*, 93–101, quote can be found on 94; Michael Mandelbaum, "David's Friend Goliath," *Foreign Policy*, no. 152 (January/February 2006): 50–56, quotes can be found on 52, 55; and Thayer, "The Case for the American Empire," 1–7, quote can be found on 5. On

Bacevich's opposition to Bush's Iraq policy, see Andrew J. Bacevich, "I Lost My Son to a War I Oppose. We Were Both Doing Our Duty," *Washington Post*, 27 May 2007, http://www.washingtonpost.com.

35. Sherry, *In the Shadow of War*, 126.

36. For overviews of constructivism, see Jack Snyder, "One World, Rival Theories," *Foreign Policy*, no. 145 (November/December 2004): 59–61; and Stephen M. Walt, "International Relations: One World, Many Theories," *Foreign Policy*, no. 110 (Spring 1998): 40–41. On the U.S. aversion to empire, see Michael Wines, "A World Seeking Security Is Told There's Just One Shield," *New York Times*, 22 July 2001, http://www.nytimes.com.

37. Knorr, *The Power of Nations*, 306–7; Yong S. Lee, "Master and Servants: U.S.-East Asian Relations and the Tyranny of the Weak" (M.A. Thesis, Ohio University, June 1995); and Scott L. Bills, *Empire and Cold War: The Roots of U.S.-Third World Antagonism, 1945–47* (New York: St. Martin's Press, 1990), 210. On "reverse donor dependency," see Jeffrey A. Lefebvre, *Arms for the Horn: U.S. Security Policy in Ethiopia and Somalia 1953–1991* (Pittsburgh, PA: University of Pittsburgh Press, 1991).

38. Fouad Ajami, "National Lampoon," *New Republic*, 20 March 2000, 6; Yuen Foong Khong, *Analogies at War: Korea, Munich, Dien Bien Phu, and the Vietnam Decisions of 1965* (Princeton, NJ: Princeton University Press, 1992); and H.W. Brands, *The Devil We Knew: Americans and the Cold War* (New York: Oxford University Press, 1993). On the so-called post-Vietnam malaise and its impact on U.S. policy, see, for example, Henry A. Kissinger, "The Long Shadow of Vietnam," *Newsweek*, 1 May 2000, 47–50; and Walter A. McDougall, "Who Were We in Vietnam?" *New York Times*, 26 April 2000, A27. On the Bush administration's intervention doctrine, see George W. Bush, "The National Security Strategy of the United States of America," September 2002, http://www.whitehouse.gov/nsc/nss.pdf.

39. Garry Wills, "Bully of the Free World," *Foreign Affairs* 78, no. 2 (March/April 1999): 52; Gaddis, *We Now Know*, 26–84; John Lewis Gaddis, *Surprise, Security, and the American Experience* (Cambridge, MA: Harvard University Press, 2004), 106–10; and Thomas G. Paterson, *On Every Front: The Making and Unmaking of the Cold War*, Revised Edition (New York: W.W. Norton, 1992), 41–118.

40. Bacevich, *American Empire*, 3; Hertsgaard, *The Eagle's Shadow*, 175–95, quote can be found on 183; and Samuel P. Huntington, "The Lonely Superpower," *Foreign Affairs* 78, no. 2 (March/April 1999): 43. In response to anti-globalization protests, which began in earnest in 1999 in Seattle, the IMF, World Bank, and WTO have made their proceedings more transparent in an effort to lessen public scrutiny of their policies. For contrasting analyses of globalization, see Eduardo Galeano, *Upside Down: A Primer for the Looking-Glass World*, translated by Mark Fried (New York: Picador USA, 2000); and Thomas L. Friedman, *The World Is Flat: A Brief History of The Twenty-First Century* (New York: Farrar, Straus & Giroux, 2005). Galeano is very critical of globalization and its consequences, especially for the developing world and its many impoverished citizens. Friedman, on the other hand, touts the benefits of globalization, both for the developed and developing world.

41. Michael Ignatieff, "The Burden," *New York Times Magazine*, 5 January 2003, http://www.nytimes.com.

42. Michael Ignatieff, "The Attack on Human Rights," *Foreign Affairs* 80, no. 6 (November-December 2001): 102–16; Peter Bender, "America: The New Roman Empire?" *Orbis* 47, no. 1 (Winter 2003): 155; and Harold James, *The Roman Predicament: How the Rules of International Order Create the Politics of Empire* (Princeton, NJ: Princeton University Press, 2006).

43. Porter, *Empire and Superempire*; G. John Ikenberry, "America's Imperial Ambition," *Foreign Affairs* 81, no. 5 (September/October 2002): 44–60, quote can be found

on 45; Clyde Prestowitz, *Rogue Nation: American Unilateralism and the Failure of Good Intentions* (New York: Basic Books, 2003), quote can be found on 49; and Joseph S. Nye, Jr., *The Paradox of American Power: Why the World's Only Superpower Can't Go It Alone* (New York: Oxford University Press, 2002), especially 39.

44. Niall Ferguson, *Colossus: The Price of America's Empire* (New York: Penguin Press, 2004), 1–26, 290–95.

45. Ferguson, *Colossus*, 204–13. Michael Mann writes that "a second 'revolution in military affairs' has turned the tide of pacification technology against imperialism. Guerilla fighters are now better-equipped, especially in urban warfare, than their historical predecessors. The Kalashnikov assault rifle, the shoulder-held anti-tank missile, Semtech, ammonium nitrate, cellphone-activated bombs and so on, are freely available globally, ideal weapons to take out small numbers of Great Power troops and helicopters, as seen today in Chechnya, Afghanistan and Iraq." See Mann, "The First Failed Empire of the 21st Century," 641.

46. Ferguson, *Colossus*, 267–85; Reuters, "CBO Sees Rising Fiscal 2007 U.S. Budget Deficit," 17 August 2006, http://today.reuters.com; and Central Intelligence Agency, "CIA World Factbook," https://www.cia.gov/cia/publications/factbook/. Although the FY 2006 deficit, as forecast by the Congressional Budget Office, was quite a bit less than FY 2004 ($412.5 billion, 3.6 percent of the country's Gross Domestic Product), the external debt was up significantly from January 2004 ($3 trillion). See Reuters, "U.S. Budget Deficit Expands to $412.5 Billion," *MSNBC.com*, 14 October 2004, http://www.msnbc.msn.com; Elizabeth Becker and Edmund L. Andrews "I.M.F. Says U.S. Debts Threaten World Economy," *New York Times*, 8 January 2004, http://www.nytimes.com; and Nick Beams, "IMF Delivers Strong Warning on Growth of US Debt," *World Socialist Web Site*, 12 January 2004, http://www.wsws.org. See also Bradley Graham, "Military Spending Sparks Warnings," *Washington Post*, 8 March 2004, http://www.washingtonpost.com.

47. Amy Kaplan, "Violent Belongings and the Question of Empire Today: Presidential Address to the American Studies Association, October 17, 2003," *American Quarterly* 56, no. 1 (March 2004): 4.

48. Kaplan, "Violent Belongings and the Question of Empire Today," 4–5.

49. Kaplan, "Violent Belongings and the Question of Empire Today," 5. Another student of U.S. imperial rhetoric, Marilyn Young, writes that "[o]ne must distinguish, I think, between the language of imperialism and the language of empire. The language of imperialism, of the act of creating and sustaining empire, is immediate, direct, often monosyllabic, given to slang but not to euphemism. Its dominant tense is the imperative. The language of empire is benign, nurturing, polysyllabic; its preferred tense is the future conditional. The language of empire reassures." Marilyn B. Young, "Imperial Language," in *The New American Empire: A 21st Century Teach-In on U.S. Foreign Policy*, eds. Lloyd C. Gardner and Marilyn B. Young (New York: New Press, 2005), 32. For a detailed account of America's capricious, unilateral ways, see Prestowitz, *Rogue Nation*.

50. Michael Cox, "Empire, Imperialism, and the Bush Doctrine," *Review of International Studies* 30, no. 4 (October 2004): 590; Mann, "The First Failed Empire of the 21st Century," 634; and Tony Judt, "Dreams of Empire," *New York Review of Books*, 4 November 2004, 38–39.

51. Judt, "Dreams of Empire," 38–39. Michael Mann observes that "[t]oday, 'weapons of mass communication' have also levelled the playing field, communicating such values as nationalism, anti-imperialism, racial equality and human rights across the South of the world. Literacy and the media are global. . . . Such weapons are no longer controlled by the imperialists." Mann, "The First Failed Empire of the 21st Century," 648.

52. Mann, "The First Failed Empire of the 21st Century," 647, 650.

53. William E. Odom and Robert Dujarric, *America's Inadvertent Empire* (New Haven, CT: Yale University Press, 2004), 36–63, quote can be found on 60; Gaddis, *Surprise, Security, and the American Experience*, 117. Gaddis writes (117) that "[t]he essence of responsibility . . . is remembering what the ancients taught us about the sin of pride. Which is to say that we badly need mirrors. Which is to say that you can't sustain hegemony without consent. Which is to say that consent requires the existence of an alternative more frightening than your own hegemony. Which is to say that that was how American global leadership came about in the twentieth century: it was partly skill and partly luck, but always the fact that there was something worse."

54. John Gray, "The Mirage of Empire," *New York Review of Books*, 12 January 2006, 4. On the problems of U.S. empire, see also Charles W. Kegley and Gregory A. Raymond, *After Iraq: The Imperiled American Imperium* (New York: Oxford University Press, 2007).

55. G. John Ikenberry, "Liberalism and Empire: Logics of Order in the American Unipolar Age," *Review of International Studies* 30, no. 4 (October 2004): 628. During the twentieth century, the British had their own version of an air-naval empire in the Persian Gulf. See James A. Russell, "Whither Regional Security in a World Turned Upside Down?" *Middle East Policy* 14, no. 2 (Summer 2007): 142–43.

56. Maier, *Among Empires*, 67; and Ikenberry, "Liberalism and Empire," 628.

57. Ikenberry, "Liberalism and Empire," 630. On American exceptionalism, see Anatol Lieven, *America Right or Wrong: An Anatomy of American Nationalism* (New York: Oxford University Press, 2004).

58. Ikenberry, "Liberalism and Empire," 630.

59. Students in my Spring 2006 Heidelberg College Honors course on empires and I attempted to compare the imperia we studied (Egypt, Islam, Athens, Sparta, Rome, France, Britain, and the United States) using a spectrum. After a frustrating effort to compare the various empires using different dimensions (political, economic, military, and social-cultural), the students gave up. One particularly exasperated student exclaimed: "It's all semantics." For a taxonomy comparing the U.S. empire to "traditional" imperia, see Thayer, "The Case for the American Empire," 6.

60. Michael Cox, "The Empire's Back in Town: Or America's Imperial Temptation—Again" (paper presented at the annual conference of the International Studies Association, Montreal, Canada, 17–20 March 2004), 30. On the seventh century Islamic empire, see Reza Aslan, *No god but God: The Origins, Evolution, and Future of Islam* (New York: Random House, 2006), 122–23.

61. Deborah Tannen, *The Argument Culture: Stopping America's War of Words* (New York: Ballantine Books, 1999). Scholar Walter Hixson points out that diplomatic historians have been studying U.S. empire since "at least" 1960. Walter L. Hixson, "Empire as a Way of Life," *Diplomatic History* 31, no. 2 (April 2007): 332–33.

62. Alexander J. Motyl, "Empire Falls: Washington May Be Imperious, but It Is Not Imperial," *Foreign Affairs* 85, no. 4 (July/August 2006): 192, 194; Michael Hirsh, *At War with Ourselves: Why America Is Squandering Its Chance to Build a Better World* (New York: Oxford University Press, 2003), 238; and Leon Hadar, "U.S. Empire? Let's Get Real," *Los Angeles Times*, 2 July 2002, http://www.latimes.com.

63. Philip Zelikow, "The Transformation of National Security: Five Redefinitions," *The National Interest*, no. 71 (Spring 2003): 17–28; Victor Davis Hanson, "What Empire?" in Andrew J. Bacevich, ed., *The Imperial Tense*, 146–55, quote can be found on 154; Fareed Zakaria, "Our Way," *New Yorker*, 14 October 2002, http://www.newyorker.com; Fareed Zakaria, "The One-Note Superpower," *Newsweek*, 2 February 2004, 41; Ikenberry, "Liberalism and Empire," 630; and Robert Skidelsky, "Hot, Cold & Imperial," *New York Review of Books*, 13 July 2006, 55. The Rumsfeld

quote can be found in Roger Cohen, "Strange Bedfellows: 'Imperial America' Retreats From Iraq," *New York Times*, 4 July 2004, http://www.nytimes.com.

64. On hegemony as preponderance and benevolent political leadership, see Nye, *The Paradox of American Power*; and Zelikow, "The Transformation of National Security: Five Redefinitions." For the Nuechterlein quote, see Donald E. Nuechterlein, *Defiant Superpower: The New American Hegemony* (Washington, DC: Potomac Books, 2005), 19. Those who use hegemony and empire synonymously include Michael Cox, "September 11th and U.S. Hegemony—Or Will the 21st Century Be American Too?" *International Studies Perspectives* 3, no. 1 (February 2002): 53–70; Michael Cox, "The New Liberal Empire: US Power in the Twenty-First Century," *Irish Studies in International Affairs* 12 (2001): 39–56; Henry Kissinger, *Does America Need a Foreign Policy? Toward a Diplomacy for the 21st Century* (New York: Simon & Schuster, 2001); and Christopher Layne, "Offshore Balancing Revisited," *Washington Quarterly* 25, no. 2 (Spring 2002): 233–48. For the Ikenberry quote, see Ikenberry, "Liberalism and Empire," 615. For the Hunt quote, see Michael H. Hunt, *The American Ascendancy: How the United States Gained and Wielded Global Dominance* (Chapel Hill, NC: University of North Carolina Press, 2007), 311, 314. For an excellent discussion of hegemony versus empire, see John Agnew, "American Hegemony Into American Empire? Lessons from the Invasion of Iraq," *Antipode* 35, no. 5 (November 2003): 871–85. On hegemony and international security, see Elke Krahmann, "American Hegemony or Global Governance? Competing Visions of International Security," *International Studies Review* 7, no. 4 (December 2005): 531–45. Nexon and Wright discuss unipolar, hegemonic, and imperial orders. See Nexon and Wright, "What's at Stake in the American Empire Debate," 256–66.

65. See Helen V. Milner, "International Political Economy: Beyond Hegemonic Stability," *Foreign Policy*, no. 110 (Spring 1998): 112–15; Charles P. Kindleberger, "Dominance and Leadership in the International Economy," *International Studies Quarterly* 25, no. 2 (June 1981): 242–54; Timothy J. McKeown, "Hegemonic Stability Theory and 19th Century Tariff Levels in Europe," *International Organization* 37, no. 1 (Winter 1983): 73–91; Gilpin, *The Political Economy of International Relations*; Robert O. Keohane, *After Hegemony: Cooperation and Discord in the World Political Economy* (Princeton, NJ: Princeton University Press, 1984), 31–46; and John Gerard Ruggie, "International Regimes, Transactions, and Change: Embedded Liberalism in the Postwar Economic Order," in *International Regimes*, ed. Stephen D. Krasner (Ithaca, NY: Cornell University Press, 1983), 195–231. For a primer on economic thought, see Robert L. Heilbroner, *The Worldly Philosophers: The Lives, Times and Ideas of the Great Economic Thinkers* (New York: Simon & Schuster, 1992).

66. Immanuel Wallerstein, *The Capitalist World-Economy: Essays by Immanuel Wallerstein* (Cambridge: Cambridge University Press, 1979), 37–48; Immanuel Wallerstein, "The Three Instances of Hegemony in the History of the Capitalist World-Economy," in *The Theoretical Evolution of IPE: A Reader*, eds. George T. Crane and Abla Amawi (New York: Oxford University Press, 1991), 236–44; Robert A. Denemark, "World System History: From Traditional International Politics to the Study of Global Relations," *International Studies Review* 1, no. 2 (Summer 1999): 43–75; Thomas J. McCormick, *America's Half-Century: United States Foreign Policy during the Cold War* (Baltimore: Johns Hopkins University Press, 1989), 1–16; and Theotonio dos Santos, "The Structure of Dependence," *American Economic Review* 60, no. 2 (May 1970): 231–36.

67. Gilpin, *War and Change in World Politics*, 106–8.

68. Robert O. Keohane, "The United States and the Postwar Order: Empire or Hegemony?" *Journal of Peace Research* 28, no. 4 (1991): 437–38; and McCormick, *America's Half-Century*, 17–243.

69. G. John Ikenberry, "Illusions of Empire: Defining the New American Order," *Foreign Affairs* 83, no. 2 (March/April 2004): 144–54. For Ikenberry, "[t]he American order is hierarchical and ultimately sustained by economic and military power. But it is order infused with liberal characteristics and put at the service of supporting an expanding system of democracy and capitalism." See Ikenberry, "Liberalism and Empire," 620. He adds (624) that "[w]hen [the United States] acts as a liberal hegemon, it is seeking to lead or manage the global system of rules and institutions; when it is acting as a nationalist great power, it is seeking to advance domestic interests and its relative power position. Today, these two roles—liberal hegemon and nationalist great power—are increasingly in conflict." Scholars Charles Kegley and Gregory Raymond propose the term "imperium" in lieu of either empire or hegemony. For them, "An imperium is an imposed order that arises when the preponderant state in a unipolar distribution of international power functions as the supreme normative agent, establishing and maintaining rules of conduct by making pronouncements and applying sanctions, rather than by engaging in multilateral negotiation and working through consensual institutions. To speak of an American Imperium is not to rule out a transition to true empire. An imperium becomes an imperial power when it projects its unrivaled military might without apology, claiming to be pursing a moral mission." Yet, by that definition, given the U.S. Cold War mission (i.e., to counter Soviet communism) and the American mission in Iraq (i.e., to democratize that country as well as the region), the United States already constitutes an imperial power. Kegley and Raymond, *After Iraq*, 37.

70. Ikenberry, "Illusions of Empire"; Robert Cooper, "The New Liberal Imperialism," *Observer*, 7 April 2002, http://observer.guardian.co.uk; and Daniel Vernet, "Postmodern Imperialism," *Le Monde*, 24 April 2003, accessed via Google search engine. On "market empire," see Michael H. Hunt, "Conquest American Style," *Diplomatic History* 31, no. 2 (April 2007): 325–29. On the liberal versus realist dichotomy from a theoretical and policy standpoint, see James M. Goldgeier and Michael McFaul, "A Tale of Two Worlds: Core and Periphery in the Post-Cold War Era," *International Organization* 46, no. 2 (Spring 1992): 467–91; and Robert Kagan, *Of Paradise and Power: America and Europe in the New World Order* (New York: Alfred A. Knopf, 2003). For overviews of IR theory, see Snyder, "One World, Rival Theories," 53–62; Walt, "International Relations," 29–46. For a critical assessment, see John Lewis Gaddis, "International Relations Theory and the End of the Cold War," *International Security* 17, no. 3 (Winter 1992/93): 5–58. Finally, thanks to Professor Wayne Lesperance for coining the term "situational" imperialism.

71. John O'Sullivan opines that "America acts in an imperial way, it seems, in a very limited set of circumstances." John O'Sullivan, "The Reluctant Empire," *National Review*, 19 May 2003, 43–45.

72. Alexander L. George, "Case Studies and Theory Development: The Method of Structured, Focused Comparison," in *Diplomacy: New Approaches in History, Theory, and Policy*, ed. Paul Gordon Lauren (New York: Free Press, 1979), 43–68.

73. Mark Twain, *The Innocents Abroad* (New York: Signet Classic, 1966). On American perceptions of the Middle East, see Little, *American Orientalism*, 1–42; and Shibley Telhami, *The Stakes: America and the Middle East: The Consequences of Power and the Choice for Peace* (Boulder, CO: Westview Press, 2002). On empires and sorrow, see Johnson, *The Sorrows of Empire*. Finally, Michael Oren notes that "the United States can be expected to pursue the traditional patterns of its Middle East involvement. Policymakers will press on with their civic mission as mediators and liberators in the area and strive for a *pax Americana*. American churches and evangelist groups will still seek to save the region spiritually. And the producers of films about the mysterious, menacing Orient will never lack for audiences. The themes that evolved over the course of more than two centuries of America's interaction with the Middle East will continue to distin-

guish those ties, binding and animating them for generations." Oren, *Power, Faith, and Fantasy*, 594.

74. On subsystems, see Leonard Binder, "The Middle East as a Subordinate International System," *World Politics* 10, no. 3 (April 1958): 408–29.

Chapter 2

Initiation: 1941–47

In the *first* stage (1941–47) of its post-World War II expansion in the Persian Gulf, America underwent a prickly apprenticeship. Prior to the war, it displayed only minimal political interest in the region. During the conflagration, Washington familiarized itself with the area as it participated in the resupply of the Soviet Union. After the war, U.S. involvement in the Gulf and its adjacent lands ushered in a new era of increased American stakes. Although in 1947 most of its citizens knew nothing about Muslims who lived thousands of miles from New York or San Francisco, the United States elevated the Middle East to the rank of strategic priority. For a country formerly bent on preserving Fortress America, this startling development symbolized the climax of a journey from relative "isolationism" to fully-fledged "internationalism" that started when Nazi Germany defeated France in June 1940 and continued when the Japanese rudely awakened a nation mostly oblivious to the world's concerns.

In his famous February 1941 essay in *Life*, Henry R. Luce urged his fellow Americans to shed their reflexive timidity in matters international in favor of an assertive foreign policy consonant with the United States' rank as the world's foremost economic, political, and military power. The publisher exhorted Americans "to exert upon the world the full impact of our influence, for such purposes as we see fit and by such means as we see fit." Luce's hyperbolic vision of an "American century" did not resonate with a typically isolationist America until, paradoxically, Japanese bombers destroyed much of the U.S. Pacific fleet at Pearl Harbor on December 7 of that year. That "day of infamy" jolted a country previously smugly secure in its distant proximity to the world's terror. Tokyo's treacherous attack infused the United States with a hardy martial spirit. Immediately, the "arsenal of democracy" sent its soldiers to avenge a national humiliation. World War II beckoned.[1]

That conflict scattered Americans to every corner of the world. Previously content to assist the British, who bravely resisted Nazi Germany's assault on the UK isles, Washington now prepared for multi-front warfare with Japan, Germany, and Italy. A renewed opportunity, or "second chance," to establish a Wilsonian international political system devoid of European-style rivalries underlay the White House's quest to defeat the fascist conquerors of Europe and Asia.

Unlike the Great War, however, in this military clash the United States joined an alliance on the defensive and without prospects for swift victory. President Franklin D. Roosevelt (FDR) could not rely, moreover, on well-prepared armed forces.[2]

The tonic of war sparked the listless American economy. After a decade of Great Depression, U.S. productivity finally recovered. Factories turned out a steady supply of matériel. While "Rosie the Riveter" and her fellow workers manufactured countless guns, tanks, ships, and planes, American troops confronted tenacious enemies in the Pacific, North Africa, and Western Europe. The 1942 U.S. naval victory at Midway served as an initial step on the way to V-J Day, but years of fierce combat and the possibility of considerable casualties in a final assault on the Japanese home islands led the United States to develop and use the atomic bomb, a weapon that revolutionized warfare. The destruction of Hiroshima and Nagasaki in August 1945 ended the Pacific War and followed Germany's unconditional surrender in May.[3]

World War II shattered the myth that the United States could isolate itself politically, diplomatically, and militarily from the rest of the world. FDR preached internationalism to prevent a recurrence of the disasters that ravaged many countries in the first half of the twentieth century. With the Axis powers defeated, Americans encountered an international landscape utterly transformed. The United States occupied center stage. Its robust economy and military prowess awed and intimidated World War II's victors and vanquished. Washington could now craft a Wilsonian peace. Yet its Grand Alliance partners opposed such a plan. The British wanted to sustain their empire, a violation of Woodrow Wilson's principle of self-determination. The Soviets sought a buffer zone to prevent replays of the two previous World Wars, when Germany devastated their country and killed millions. At the Yalta conference in February 1945, President Roosevelt compromised Wilson's legacy when he, British Prime Minister Winston S. Churchill, and Soviet head of state Joseph Stalin ratified a new division of the world into spheres of influence. FDR could not proceed otherwise. He could not deny his allies their security needs. Ironically, the president died before he could assess the consequences of his diplomacy.[4]

In contrast to FDR, the Truman administration mistrusted Stalin. When in 1946 Churchill spoke of a Soviet "Iron Curtain" in Europe, President Harry S. Truman and most of his advisors agreed with the ex-prime minister. They disapproved of the Kremlin's postwar foreign policy, perceiving its modus operandi as aggressive. Meanwhile, Washington considered its own international behavior merely reactive.[5]

Postwar Soviet moves in Eastern Europe destroyed American faith in Wendell Willkie's "One World." Everywhere, Moscow's intentions seemed hostile. The Truman administration subscribed to diplomat George F. Kennan's recommendation: the United States would seek to curb Soviet influence via a concerted policy of "containment." According to historian Melvyn Leffler, this grand strategy called for "strength at the center; strength at the periphery; the retraction of Soviet power and a change in the Soviet system. . . . By containing Communist gains and Soviet expansion, American officials hoped to perpetuate American preponderance." Alarmed by American insensitivity toward Soviet interests, the

Kremlin reciprocated with policies it considered defensive. This "security di-lemma" acidified U.S.-Soviet relations and complicated postwar issues. A Cold War began.[6]

Each side possessed certain advantages. America's arsenal included atomic weapons. Its wealth and political clout enabled it to fashion the Bretton Woods economic system, which applied American capitalism to the world economy. While Washington sought to prevent a return to the disastrous economic natio-nalism of the 1930s, it could not immediately alleviate war-induced deprivation in Europe and elsewhere. The Truman administration announced the Marshall Plan in 1947, but not before many hungry and desperate Europeans, in France and Italy for example, had embraced communism as an economic and political panacea. The Soviets welcomed these developments, as they rebuilt their tattered infrastructure. At the same time, Moscow spied on its Grand Alliance partners to keep pace with Anglo-American military technology.[7]

In the Near East, Washington's postwar plans originally called for the Unit-ed Kingdom to continue its indirect management of the region. American in-volvement would be limited to the petroleum industry. Soviet moves in the area alarmed the White House, however. The Truman administration worried whether the British could defend Western interests. London had overexerted itself in the struggle to defeat the Axis powers; this Herculean effort sapped Great Britain's strength and caused its position in various corners of the empire to recede. In 1947, Whitehall gave up its mandate in Palestine, a decision that led to the parti-tion of the Holy Land, Israeli independence, and Truman's recognition of the Jewish state. Anguished to see its Anglo ally so enfeebled and concerned about Soviet intentions, the United States stepped up its involvement in the Near East.[8]

In 1941, however, Germany, not the Soviet Union, threatened U.S. strategic and commercial interests in the Persian Gulf. If the Nazis seized control of the area, then they might cut UK imperial lines and isolate the Soviets, possibly knocking Moscow out of World War II. These gloomy scenarios preoccupied the Roosevelt administration.

Innocents Abroad: The Second World War

After Pearl Harbor, America's war planners informed FDR that the U.S. Army and Navy required vast quantities of petroleum for their equipment. North American reserves could satisfy this demand in the short term, but other sources would be needed beyond that. Policymakers thought that the recent discovery of significant oil deposits in Persia (i.e., Iran), Iraq, and the Arabian Peninsula could make up for any shortfall, provided that the United States and its allies, Great Britain most obviously, could prevent an Axis takeover of Middle Eastern fields. Such prescription endowed the Persian Gulf region with new strategic importance. Coupled with London's concern for imperial communications link-ing British India to Europe, Washington's heightened interest in the intersection between East and West ensured prominence for Muslim leaders in the region.

America's knowledge of the Near East, though scanty, owed much to busi-ness ventures and missionary work. Ever since the War for American Independence, U.S. merchants had plied the major international trade routes in search of merchandise and profit. Historian Michael Palmer remarks that, "[w]hile many people in the United States considered those of the Islamic world heathen barbarians living in darkness, the Americans who rounded the Cape of Good Hope found the Arabs to be shrewd businessmen whose societies were generally well ordered and civil." In the years following World War I, representatives from the "majors," the wealthiest and most powerful U.S. oil companies, flocked to Arabian sands in search of extractable petroleum deposits that could be refined in commercial quantity. They convinced Abdul Aziz ibn Abdul Rahman al Saud (i.e., Ibn Saud), the Saudi Arabian king, and other Persian Gulf monarchs to grant them concessions. American oilmen rewarded their bosses with numerous discoveries that promised millions in revenue for the majors and the region's autocrats. Unfortunately, their religious counterparts encountered Muslims mostly uninterested in, and even hostile to, Christianity. Despite such setbacks, these missionaries managed to disseminate American ideals and savoir-faire via the many schools and hospitals they established throughout the region.[9]

Evangelism in the remote deserts of Arabia and Persia concerned next to no one in wartime Washington, however, as U.S. officials joined their UK counterparts in organizing a desperate military crusade. In various plans, countries such as Iran, Iraq, and Saudi Arabia, situated at a vital intersection that linked the Soviet Union to British-controlled seas, became critical to any Allied victory over the Axis. Aid to the Soviet Red Army would be transported through this vital corridor. Allied reliance upon petroleum for its ships, tanks, and planes also warranted a serious effort to thwart any German foray into this oil-rich area. Yet success would not come easily, as several regional leaders preferred the European fascists to anyone associated with Great Britain, whose imperialism many Middle Easterners detested.

Veterans of the Great Game, the British intently pursued an "Arab policy" consistent with their traditional prerequisite of preserving ties to India. In contrast to its Victorian-era heyday, London opted for proxy rule, a variant that enabled it to reduce substantially its expenditures in the Middle East. Increased outlays, courtesy of the war and geopolitical overextension, necessitated such a reorientation. This imperial style in no way lessened Whitehall's commitment to the British Empire. Still, Prime Minister Churchill and other UK decision makers recognized that only American economic assistance to British clients, such as Ibn Saud, could preserve their country's influence in the area.[10]

London's insistence on U.S. involvement in Saudi Arabia contravened Washington's Lend-Lease priorities. When the British asked the rich but inexperienced Americans to subsidize Ibn Saud, Secretary of State Cordell Hull explained that the United States could not fund everyone. But Alexander Kirk, the American minister responsible for Saudi Arabia, worried that his nation's refusal would convince Arabs of the White House's subservience to Whitehall. U.S. representatives in the region frequently argued that if America continuously deferred to Great Britain, then the Saudis and their neighbors would turn exclusively to the British on political and commercial matters. Arab disdain for UK rule required, moreover, anti-imperial Washington to set a contrary example. To that end, the State Department favored extending political influence to the region as a complement to American economic interests.[11]

Wartime exigencies precluded such a preference, in the short term. Thus, in August 1942, FDR and Hull endorsed the United Kingdom as the area's "senior military partner." This acquiescence surely reassured Whitehall, but British policymakers nonetheless urged increased American participation in the region. Without it, Great Britain could not sustain its position as the Middle East's ultimate political authority. Yet, in the case of Saudi Arabia, many U.S. diplomats and oilmen yearned to exclude their ally.[12]

In Iran, the United States sought the opposite, inclusion in a British-Soviet zone of contention. As an outsider with a solid reputation among Persians, Washington could only interpose itself between its Grand Alliance partners, each of which occupied one section of the country starting in August 1941. The Soviets ruled over the northern part of Persia, while the British watched over their oil fields in the south. This division of the country into zones of occupation satisfied a primary Allied military objective, to prevent unwanted German encroachment, yet it also restored Great-Power boundaries established in the 1907 Anglo-Russia Convention.[13]

That agreement confirmed Iran's continued inability to ward off outside powers coveting its resources. Although the British and Russians allowed for a "neutral sphere" in central Persia and vowed to respect Iranian sovereignty, each Great Power could not resist meddling in Iran's affairs. An expansionist Kremlin treated northern Persia as an adjunct to its empire in the Caucasus. Moscow's envy of its neighbor's warm-water ports, a luxury consistently denied to Russia, guaranteed Tehran no respite from Russian pressure for territorial and other concessions. Meanwhile, London eyed Iranian oil deposits that promised energy and profits. The discovery of petroleum in the buffer zone in 1908 had prompted British authorities to sign the Secret Treaty of 1915 with the Russians. This instance of stealth diplomacy secured Whitehall's access to Persia's precious minerals in that nation's subterranean heartland. Shared control over Iran ensured a standoff that Great Britain and tsarist Russia could tolerate until the October Revolution of 1917 invalidated this arrangement. Despite its withdrawal from World War I, Moscow returned to its imperial ways when it seized Gilan province in Persia's Azerbaijan region in 1920. A year later, however, Soviet leader Vladimir I. Lenin ordered support for the Soviet Republic of Gilan to cease.[14]

In the inter-war period, Reza Shah Pahlavi ascended the Peacock throne via a series of political and military moves that either removed, co-opted, or neutralized most of his opponents. His efforts to reform Iran, while probably well-intentioned, failed to rid the country of its susceptibility to Great-Power intrigue. Instead of ruling over a united Persia, he presided over an entity loyal to many masters, foreign and domestic.[15]

As Moscow and London resumed in the 1920s their pre-war rivalry in Iran, Reza Shah turned to Germany and the United States as "counterweights." His decisions mirrored past Iranian policy and aimed to outwit the Soviet and British interventionists, who consistently interfered in Persia's domestic arena. The Shah invited Arthur Millspaugh and other American experts, as part of the Millspaugh Mission of 1922–27, to identify remedies to his country's many chronic econom-

ic shortcomings. In Millspaugh's mind, Tehran wanted "to use America as a political balancer and an economic Santa Claus." The completion of the Trans-
Iranian Railway in 1938 allowed Iran to overcome its communication and transportation conundrum. Paradoxically, this technological marvel increased Iran's
vulnerability. In the event of a major European war, Great Powers would undoubtedly make use of the valuable track to move supplies to distant battlefields.[16]

Just such an occasion arose once the Germans initiated Operation Barbaros-
sa in June 1941. In response to the *Wermacht*'s invasion of the Soviet Union, the
British devised plans to resupply the battered and retreating Red Army by using
the Trans-Iranian Railway. Iran's neutrality temporarily checked London's policy, as Reza Shah vetoed any transit of Allied soldiers through his country. Pro-
German sentiment in Tehran and other Persian cities alarmed the Soviets and
especially the British, who suspected expatriate Germans in Iran of undermining
Allied interests. In response to the *Wermacht* threat, Stalin and Churchill ordered
that Iran be occupied. Stripped of authority over his own citizens, Reza Shah
turned power over to his son, Mohammed Reza Pahlavi. The Allies, including
the Americans, approved of the new leader provided that he supported their war
requirements.[17]

Until the Soviets repulsed the Germans in 1943 at the Battle of Stalingrad,
the need for Allied solidarity muted most Anglo and Soviet rivalry in Iran. With
the new shah and his people wary of their former oppressors, Secretary of State
Hull insisted that London and Moscow commit to Atlantic Charter principles by
guaranteeing Persian territorial integrity. In January 1942, the United Kingdom,
Soviet Union, and Iran thus signed the Tripartite Treaty of Alliance.[18]

Distrustful of its official partners, Tehran resurrected its "third-power strategy" by asking the United States to commit itself to Iranian independence. Washington refused, confident that neither the British nor the Soviets coveted Persia.
The Kurdish rebellion of 1942 in the Soviet sector accelerated American involvement. While the Kremlin wanted to exclude the Iranians from Azerbaijan,
wartime necessity compelled it to cooperate with Persian authorities. Critical
Lend-Lease supplies (approved in March 1942) passed through the Persian Corridor, with the U.S. Persian Gulf Command (made up of 30,000 servicemen)
responsible for their delivery to the Soviets. This lifeline contributed to the Red
Army's victory at Stalingrad, a triumph that altered the course of World War II.
With the Nazis in retreat, Allied interactions in Persia underwent a transformation. Without a common objective (i.e., the supply of the Soviet Union), the British and Soviets resumed their competition and violated the Tripartite Treaty.
Moscow, in particular, disregarded Iranian prerogative.[19]

Despite the United States' increased knowledge of the region (via the Office
of Strategic Services and U.S. involvement in the British-supervised Middle East
Supply Centre), American policy in Iran resembled the U.S. stance elsewhere.
FDR's preference for bold statements that promised salvation for all only served
to confuse those individuals responsible for translating American rhetoric into
deeds. U.S. inexperience with Near Eastern affairs compounded this problem of
how to reconcile means and ends. In the spring of 1943, for example, General
Patrick J. Hurley provided the president with an analysis of Persia after a short

visit to the Middle East. Hurley underlined the Anglo-Soviet rivalry in Iran and opined that the United States should jump into the controversy either unilaterally or in partnership with the enervated British. He also supported an American trusteeship for Persia, a solution Roosevelt would tout repeatedly in front of Churchill and Stalin.[20]

Hurley's impractical recommendations conflicted with Soviet geopolitical imperatives. With the Germans turning back, Moscow pressed the Iranians for economic favors that Tehran could not easily deny. The Kremlin also sought to undermine Mohammed Reza Shah via the Tudeh Party, a Soviet-sponsored opposition group made up mostly of workers. As a result of Soviet coercion and propaganda in northern Iran, Allied unity fractured. The Great Game resumed. The Americans sided with the British, whose stated objectives meshed better with Washington's particular vision for Persia.[21]

Though many U.S. officials suspected Moscow of wanting to annex its zone of occupation, some of them mistrusted the British as well. Louis Dreyfus, the American minister in Iran, John Jernegan, Iranian desk officer in the Division of Near Eastern Affairs (NEA) at the Department of State, and Wallace Murray, the official in charge at NEA, sought to deter the Anglo-Soviet juggernaut and preserve Persian autonomy. Their resentment vis-à-vis the predatory ways of the other Great Powers in the region confirmed the naïveté of U.S. policy. With only "vaguely defined" interests in Iran, Washington could scold and patronize its rivals with impunity. In a January 1943 memorandum, Jernegan summarized the historic Russo-British stalemate. While critical of both countries, he characterized Russian policy as "fundamentally aggressive" as opposed to the United Kingdom's "fundamentally defensive" posture. Jernegan underscored his juxtaposition by spotlighting conspiratorial Soviet activities in Azerbaijan. Yet he refused to exonerate the British, whose "blunt, uncompromising attitude" promised continued upheaval in Iran.[22]

Jernegan's disapproval of Moscow's and London's imperial techniques stemmed from the State Department's desire to replace European imperialism with an international doctrine of collective security. This brand of internationalism, the cornerstone of postwar plans for a United Nations organization, required concrete results, not simply eloquent speeches. To avoid a repeat of the inter-war years, moreover, Washington would have to involve itself. Coveted by two Great Powers, Iran, in Jernegan's view, constituted "a test case for the good faith of the United Nations and their ability to work out among themselves an adjustment of ambitions, rights and interests which will be fair not only to the Great Powers of our coalition but also to the small nations associated with us or brought into our sphere by circumstances."[23]

Naïvely, American officials presumed that their balm would cure an aching Iran. In his summary of Jernegan's January 1943 memorandum, Murray stated that postwar events could render Persia a "danger point" and that only the United States could "render effective assistance to Iran without rousing the fears and opposition of Great Britain or Russia, or of the Iranians themselves." Jernegan argued that his country "alone" could "build up Iran to the point [where] it will stand in need of neither British nor Russian assistance to maintain order in its own house."[24]

Oblivious to past U.S. colonial experiences in the Philippines and Caribbean, Jernegan thought that if Washington followed through on a commitment to Iran, then "we [i.e., America] can hope to remove any excuse for a post-war occupation, partition, or tutelage of Iran." "Disinterested" American advisors would ensure that Iran metamorphosed into a "self-reliant and prosperous" state that traded with everyone and threatened no one. In return for such bliss, the United States would demand no compensation or favors.[25]

Surmising that neither the Soviet Union nor Great Britain could withdraw from Iran lest the other occupy and exploit the entire country, Jernegan postulated that "a third, disinterested, power should be called in to eliminate the dispute." Preposterously, he claimed that "it seems hardly possible that either could suspect the United States of having imperialistic designs in a country so far removed from us and where we could never hope to employ military force against an adjacent Great Power." Obviously intoxicated with a sense of Messianism, Jernegan's exhortations epitomized one type of U.S. policy, one that smacked of the idealism that George Kennan and other realists would later vehemently condemn.[26]

Such hyperbole extended to other American policymakers. Dreyfus and Secretary of State Hull concurred with Wallace's and Jernegan's facile views and called for the United States to pursue a more vigorous policy in Iran. Mindful of their commitment to the Atlantic Charter and its principle of self-determination, U.S. officials rejected any kind of imposition upon the Iranians. The war's end removed any justification for continued occupation of Persia. By refusing to endorse the Kremlin's and London's methods, Washington made explicit its disapproval of European Machiavellism.[27]

Sympathy for an oppressed society meshed with America's Open Door policy. Without entry into "closed" markets such as Iran and Iraq, the United States could not expand its commerce. Economic success often translated, moreover, into political influence, an outcome Washington clearly desired despite its professed reluctance to meddle in Middle Eastern affairs. James S. Landis, who in 1943 assumed the directorship of the American Economic Mission to the Middle East, emphasized that his country could not divorce political and economic goals. U.S. trade could not thrive in a mercantile context—the UK sterling bloc, for example—that excluded American businessmen. To avoid such an outcome, the U.S. government would have to ensure, secure, and sometimes underwrite the independence of its more vulnerable economic partners. Yet once American policy threatened to undermine the British system of preferences, tensions with the United States' most important political and military ally strained the Washington-London relationship, as the Culbertson Mission of 1944–45 so illustrated.[28]

The high-minded rhetoric of the State Department notwithstanding, the burgeoning American interest in Persian Gulf oil fueled typical Great-Power incentive. "[A]ltruism now coincided nicely with self-interest," writes historian Bruce Kuniholm, as Washington promoted a sovereign Iran that could shield U.S. assets in Saudi Arabia. Such selflessness advantaged the British, whose interests mostly meshed with Washington's, but irritated the Soviets, who coveted Iranian resources and considered the Atlantic Charter detrimental to their goals. Even though it failed to do so, the Kremlin could have called into question American self-righteousness by pointing out that U.S. economic doctrine, the Open Door, qualified as "a form of imperialism," owing to America's competitive superiority. Scholar Mark Lytle remarks, "Could anyone realistically expect the United States to make a substantial commitment to Iran without a tangible stake in that nation? And as American interests grew, would not Iran then move into the kind of neocolonial system the United States maintained in Latin America?" Logically, he adds, "[a]ny policy that proposed to eliminate Russian and British influence would realistically have to anticipate a far greater American presence. Iran would remain within some sphere of influence or balance of power system, the very mechanisms of political order that Jernegan, like Cordell Hull, had rejected as inherently unstable."[29]

Big Three acrimony and suspicion vis-à-vis one another's long-term objectives in Iran dissipated briefly as the Allies agreed to the Tehran Declaration of December 1943. A vacuous reaffirmation of Iran's status as a valuable and independent ally, FDR secured this quixotic pronouncement by raising with Stalin the issue of a future Persian Gulf trusteeship, which the Soviet leader desired. Unlike the mustachioed comrade, Roosevelt believed that wartime principles could translate into satisfactory arrangements once peace returned. According to historian Bruce Kuniholm, the American president "thought of Iran as something of a clinic for his postwar policies, one aspect of which was to develop and stabilize backward areas." Hurley also believed that his country's relations with Iran could serve as a precedent. Yet it was hard to tell "where ideals left off and practical interests began." As rhetorical purity clashed with impure economic wants, the United States tried to marry its democratic instincts with its capitalist habits.[30]

This effort ran afoul of Soviet preferences in Iran. Unlike Stalin, FDR and Hull refused to patronize Tehran. They insisted America refrain from such callousness. Others disagreed. Though neither grasped or admitted to the complexities of Iranian politics, Hurley and Millspaugh (who returned to Iran for a second financial mission in 1943) advocated overlord status for the United States in Persia so that the Iranians could recover economically. Such forthrightness troubled U.S. official Harold Minor, who realized that "[i]mperialism can be, especially in the beginning, benevolent and well-intentioned." Few Americans could recognize this red flag; most were blind to any notion of a budding U.S. sphere of influence.[31]

The keen American interest in Saudi and Iranian oil reserves belied such confidence in Washington's moral superiority. For decades, U.S. companies had traveled to the region in search of "black gold." Government interest in a Middle Eastern supply of petroleum burgeoned once the First World War underscored the critical importance of this fuel. Without it, a country could not prosecute a mechanized war. State Department officials worried that their country's reserves could be depleted in the near term and thus scrambled for an alternative. Still, they refused to sanction state ownership of concessions in the Near East or anywhere else. Instead, they encouraged the American majors to take part in joint ventures with their European counterparts, which benefited from generous government support.[32]

The intense competition between U.S. corporations and Great Britain in the 1920s over the Middle East's precious resource resulted in the creation of a multinational consortium that evolved, in 1929, into the Iraq Petroleum Company (IPC). Members of IPC adhered to the so-called Red Line Agreement, a cooperative scheme that sought efficient exploitation of area reserves and production levels in pace with global demand for oil. This search for steady profits yielded partnerships that surveyed and exploited promising fields in Bahrain, Saudi Arabia, Kuwait, and elsewhere on the Arabian Peninsula. Standard Oil of California (SOCAL) and Texas Oil Company, which eventually formed Cal-Tex, established the Bahrain Petroleum Company and the California Arabian Standard Oil Company (CASOC), the predecessor to the Arab American Oil Company (ARAMCO). Gulf Oil Company and Anglo-Persian Oil Company (APOC) worked in tandem to develop the Kuwaiti oil industry.[33]

To fulfil private needs for industry regulation, U.S. companies cooperated with New Dealers intent on monitoring the domestic and foreign oil business. This corporate style of management presaged Cold-War era arrangements. As World War II dawned, however, the Great Depression, renewed hostilities among Europe's Great Powers, and the threat of nationalizations à la Mexico, sundered the initial "Anglo-American petroleum order."[34]

The war disabled Saudi production and incapacitated Ibn Saud's government. Unable to provide relief for his people, the king, deprived of lucrative revenue from annual pilgrimages to the holy city of Mecca, asked the American majors and Whitehall for advance payment on Saudi oil. Cal-Tex worried that if it could not bail out a desperate Saud, he would award concessions to the British. The American oil men asked Washington to preserve their advantage. Fortunately for them, Secretary of the Interior Harold Ickes, whose duties included that of petroleum administrator for war, recognized the pressing Allied demand for a steady supply of oil, both domestic and foreign. Saudi Arabia's abundant resources promised security and riches for anyone who could offer Saud short-term aid. Aware of the Saudi leader's predicament and the diminished American oil capacity both in the near and long term, Ickes convinced FDR to extend Lend-Lease to Saudi Arabia in February 1943.[35]

The prospect of an unbridled competition over petroleum prompted U.S. and British officials to seek accommodation, albeit on unequal terms. Washington wanted to solidify its position in the Middle East and prevent UK discrimination against American companies in the region. London could cede political and economic ground to its ascendant ally provided that it could hold on to its imperial privileges in the area. In August 1944, the two wartime partners reached an agreement that clearly favored the Americans. U.S. domestic producers opposed the deal, claiming that inexpensive oil imports would ruin them. Without support from this well-connected lobby, the treaty could not pass in the Senate. Whitehall and the White House therefore revised the document the following year, signing it in September 1945. Once again key U.S. opponents of an Anglo-American oil agreement accused Washington of dirigisme, a charge the Truman administration could not dismiss or overcome. As a result of such opposition, the State Department considered alternatives that could guarantee U.S. access to crucial oil reserves abroad.[36]

In southern Iran, the United States competed with the British for concessions. In the north, the Soviets replicated tsarist methods by insulating their zone from Anglo-American influence. According to scholar David Painter, "America would be the referee between its two allies and defend the rights and interests of the local people." As U.S. desire for Middle Eastern oil intensified, Washington conceived of Iranian territory as a "strategic buffer," with the Soviet Union on one side and American petroleum interests on the other. Secretary of State Hull told FDR that "it is to our interest that no great power be established on the Persian Gulf opposite the important American petroleum development in Saudi Arabia." Although the 1943 Tehran Declaration safeguarded Iranian independence, the United States undermined its own political initiative by frenetically prospecting for oil, much to Soviet consternation. Excluded from the Anglo-American petroleum talks, in September 1944 the Kremlin pressured the Iranian government, via the so-called Kavtaradze mission, into granting the Soviet Union exclusive concessions in its zone of occupation.[37]

The *Majlis*, Iran's parliament, countered Soviet insistence by postponing all decisions on oil concessions until after the war. Iranian Bolsheviks published canards accusing Tehran of reactionary policies. An insulted Moscow authorized the Communist Tudeh Party to remonstrate the Iranian government's biased (i.e., pro-British and U.S.) policy. Washington warned Moscow by reiterating the Big Three's promise to uphold Persian independence. Yet some American officials blamed their own government for the incident. Kennan noted that Anglo-American commercial advances in Iran potentially jeopardized the security of the Soviet Union's southern frontier and, hence, irked a nervous Kremlin. With its own reserves of black gold nearby (in the Baku oil fields), Soviet leaders feared any British or U.S. move that threatened one of the Soviet Union's most important resources and could undermine Soviet prestige in the region.[38]

Each Great Power relied on varying tactics in Iran. "[T]he Americans appealed to principle, the British used the velvet glove, and the Soviets the bludgeon," in scholar Bruce Kuniholm's words. The Iranians complicated matters by striving for what politician Mohammed Mossadeq called "negative equilibrium." They pitted allies against one another, a favorite ploy of weaker states. All interested parties reached for the same objective: the pursuit of national interest. With the war nearly won and FDR mostly uninterested in Iran, the State Department and Whitehall turned blunt.[39]

They construed Soviet policy as provocative, not defensive, thereby belittling Moscow's insecurities. The Kavtaradze mission smacked of "Red Fascism," U.S. analogical thinking that paired Soviet communism with German Nazism. With appeasement out of vogue, America reflexively termed the exercise of Kremlin self-interest a menace to the Western way of life. "What might have been a limited, albeit threatening, Soviet response to a specific provocation," historian Mark Lytle writes, "was perceived by many officials in Washington and some in London as the first step in a Soviet global offensive." Ironically, such reasoning set in motion an American policy of expansion. Soviet malevolency soon justified, moreover, Anglo-American intervention in Iranian politics to "bolster" the Persian regime.[40]

Capitalizing on resurgent American anti-Communist sentiment, London tried to forge a senior-junior partnership with its North American ally, so that British interests could be protected from the Red Army as well as angry nationalists, who wanted UK agents expelled from the Middle East. The United States preferred, however, to pursue a "unilateral security sphere," a wish shared by the Soviets, who, unlike the Americans, explicitly favored "exclusive spheres." These wartime fulminations over Iran previewed Cold-War animosities. As Sir Claremont Skrine, the British wartime consul in Iran, noted, "it was the vigorous American intervention, the financial, military, and gendarmerie missions, the apparent drive by the US to capture the Persian market, and above all, the efforts [of American and UK companies] to secure oil prospecting rights that changed the Russians in Persia from hot-war allies into cold war rivals." To be sure, Stalin's ruthlessness and sense of entitlement also fanned the flames. It would take two swords, one Soviet and one Anglo-American, for a postwar clash to occur.[41]

On the Arabian Peninsula, Washington tussled with the British rather than the Soviets. Alexander Kirk, the U.S. minister in Cairo, spoke of an Anglo-American rift in Saudi Arabia emanating from divergent goals: "the British . . . aimed to make countries in which they are interested dependent on the Empire, [while the Americans intended] to help backward countries to help themselves in order that they may lay the foundations for real self-dependence." The British welcomed U.S. involvement in the Middle East, albeit with some trepidation. Each side thought the other insincere, and neither wished to see an economic competitor impose its will upon the region.[42]

Though it failed to buy Saudi oil and muster adequate support for a pipeline project in the Kingdom, Washington continued to aid Saudi Arabia. Thanks in part to Lend-Lease supplies, Ibn Saud's government survived 1943. Hull pushed FDR to consider providing 50 percent of the monarch's subsidy to counter British leverage. Whitehall, hitherto responsible for the king's wartime solvency, objected to American aspirations in Saudi Arabia but shied away from a public dispute with the White House. Dwindling finances hamstrung the overburdened British, whose overexertion in the Battle of Britain saved their country yet rendered their empire vulnerable. UK officials assured their U.S. counterparts that the United Kingdom would not stand in the way of American commercial ambition in Saudi Arabia. NEA distrusted London, expecting it to reassert its primacy regarding Saudi matters once the Allies had defeated the Axis powers.[43]

Various American bureaucrats confirmed the importance of Saudi Arabia to U.S. commercial expansion and security. The State Department considered the Kingdom "an American national interest, basically strategic in character." William Eddy, American representative in Saudi Arabia, urged his government in September 1944 to extend a $55 million loan program to the Saudis so that they could sustain their economy and build an infrastructure. Eddy also lobbied to provide the Kingdom with airfields, roads, and military aid. The U.S. Army wanted a base to serve as a stopover for planes on their way to Japan from points west. NEA pushed for Saudi aid as a preventive measure, in case FDR favored the Zionists on the contentious Palestine issue. Thus, in 1945, in the waning months of the war, a U.S. commitment to Saudi Arabia seemed unavoidable, especially considering the crucial postwar need for oil and the British inability to fund Saud at previous levels, epitomized by the UK decision to halve its previous year's subsidy to Saud.[44]

From a military standpoint, the Dhahran Airfield in the eastern part of the Kingdom emerged as a priority. Washington authorized the construction of that installation to satisfy an Army requirement for a transit facility that could carry soldiers and supplies from Cairo to the Asian theater. An ancillary benefit motivated the Americans, notes diplomat-scholar Parker Hart: "Dhahran promised to be the hub of a rapidly growing oil community." The Saudi king hesitated when asked to approve the project, turning to his principal benefactor, the United Kingdom, for guidance and balance. The British advised Saud to reject the American offer, whereupon the State Department reminded London that a confrontation over Dhahran could jeopardize postwar British interests in the Middle East. Deterred, London acquiesced in the American desire to build an air base in a prized British sphere of influence. As apparent victory in World War II effaced the War Department's rationale for a base, President Truman designated the project essential to his country's national security in the summer of 1945. Although the not yet completed airfield reverted to Saudi ownership upon the Japanese surrender in September, America retained a "three-year right of occupancy and use, intended for wide-ranging military postwar cleanup and repatriation of personnel and equipment." The completion of the work in May 1946 provided the United States with a platform from which it could deliver supplies, military and otherwise, and strike at opponents that threatened U.S. interests in the area.[45]

Previous to this cooperative venture, in February 1945, FDR and Saud exchanged views and pleasantries aboard the USS *Quincy*, upon the president's return from the Yalta conference. With only weeks to live, Roosevelt dazzled his Arab guest with the same charm that won him four national elections. FDR even offered his spare wheelchair to the king, a fellow infirm, as a gift. The warm rapport that evolved between the heads of state during the meetings pleased the Saudi, who received personal assurances from his American counterpart that their countries' nascent relationship mattered to Washington and that the United States would pay special attention to Saudi Arabia's economic and political needs. The king's esteem for his American friend would benefit Truman, who found himself an unprepared president upon Roosevelt's death in April 1945.[46]

Taking Sides: The 1946 Iran Crisis

Within months, as they celebrated a smashing victory over the Axis, the prominent members of the Grand Alliance considered their next moves. At this point, the United States revised its political calculations. Whereas the genial FDR had baffled State Department bureaucrats with his juggling act, Truman sought organizational coherence when it came to foreign policy. While Roosevelt kept state-to-state relations within White House circles, the former senator from Missouri consulted with his diplomats and asked for their advice. These anti-Soviet policymakers, who behind closed doors criticized America's so-called concessions at the Yalta conference of February 1945, came forward to provide the new commander-in-chief with a mantra—stand up to the Soviets—

antithetical to FDR's conciliatory instincts. At the Potsdam conference, in July 1945, Truman experienced Soviet intransigence and pettiness for himself. As Moscow bullied Eastern European countries, the president vowed to contest Soviet moves elsewhere. On the issue of Iran, for example, Stalin refused to commit to an evacuation of troops, as called for in the Tripartite Treaty. This violation bothered the Americans, many of whom believed the Soviets would exploit any opportunity to extend their control.[47]

The American tack away from Rooseveltian accommodation manifested itself in a reevaluation of the country's Middle Eastern policy. In a November 10, 1945, letter to Brigadier General H.H. Vaughan, military aide to President Truman, Loy W. Henderson, NEA's director, outlined the U.S. transition from a "passive spectator" to a "more active" participant. He stressed that for his country to fulfil its objectives, "the countries of the Near East which have already attained their independence should continue to be entirely independent." Those states should copy the Western model of political, economic, and social development rather than imitate authoritarian and totalitarian states. Failure or refusal to do so "would render sympathetic understanding and cooperation between that part of the world and the United States more difficult." Finally, he reaffirmed the American commitment to the Open Door: "We believe that the policy of the open door is beneficial to us in our commercial relations and in the end will be beneficial to world peace."[48]

In their meeting with Truman on November 10, the American chiefs of mission in the Middle East (S. Pinkney Tuck, William Eddy, George Wadsworth, and Lowell C. Pinkerton) provided a *tour d'horizon* of the region. They spoke of an Arab world "in ferment" and "on the threshold of a new renaissance." Each country "wants forthrightly to run its own show . . . without imperialistic interference, be it British or French, in their internal affairs." They extolled American "moral leadership" and asserted that Middle Eastern states "want most of all to know whether we are going to implement that leadership, whether we are going to follow through after our great victory or leave the field, as we did at the end of the last war, to others." They underscored the area's wariness of renewed British and French tutelage by saying that locals "look especially to us to support them in their efforts to block any such development. . . . If the United States fails them, they will turn to Russia [i.e., Soviet Union] and will be lost to our civilization; of that we feel certain." They added, "[o]n the other hand, there need be no conflict between us and Russia in that area. On the contrary, Russian policy has thus far closely paralleled our own. . . . We venture to suggest that if you are looking for a field in which our policy and that of Russia can be made to dovetail with minimum friction, there is none better."[49]

This call for increased involvement and cooperation with the Soviets swayed the president, who assented to most of the suggestions made by his *chefs de mission*. Contrary to the country's previous policy and despite isolationist inclinations within Congress, Truman agreed that the United States should enter into treaties of friendship with Middle Eastern states that espoused similar or identical views to Washington's. He concurred that American financial, agricultural, and military experts should be sent to the region. Truman equivocated on one issue: Zionism. His representatives wanted him to clarify the U.S. position.

The president eschewed any promise other than to confirm that his administration would honor FDR's pledge to consult with Arab leaders prior to any decision on a possible Jewish homeland. He asked the envoys to explain to their accredited governments the implications of this thorny matter for U.S. domestic politics and its possible impact on the 1946 and 1948 elections. With respect to the Soviet Union, Truman concurred that his country could and should cooperate with Moscow on Near Eastern issues.[50]

Analyses of Soviet motives in Iran tempered such optimism. Unable to dismiss the possibility of intervention by the Red Army, the State Department canvassed its experts for informed views. Ambassador Wallace Murray cabled from Tehran that a restive Soviet Union, unlike a weakened Great Britain, menaced Iran, where "[i]nternal political, economic and social conditions are deplorable and [the] present ruling class shows little evidence of either will or ability to improve them." According to Murray, Moscow sought to carve out a "buffer zone in Iran as protection against attack from [the] south." The Kremlin could be counted on to install a compliant regime similar in outlook to the one in Romania. This Soviet preference for subservient clients jeopardized U.S. aviation and commercial interests in Persia. Most seriously, a Communist incursion into Iran "would mean extension of Soviet influence to [the] shores of [the] Persian Gulf creating [a] potential threat to [the United States'] immensely rich oil holdings in Saudi Arabia, Bahrein [sic], and Kuwait." If Stalin exposed America's geopolitical flank in the Near East, Washington would have to shore up its position by way of an increased military presence or else retrench. Neither option appealed to Washington. It still preferred a Soviet-Anglo-American condominium or the United Nations to nurse Iran's collapsed economy.[51]

Moscow thought otherwise. With the Soviet Union's productive capacity depleted and its citizens weary after five years of supreme sacrifice, high-level Communist policymakers affirmed the "primacy of Soviet security interests," endorsed continued trilateral cooperation, and promoted "a great power concert based upon some kind of a division of the world into spheres of influence." Soviet documents suggest that the Kremlin wanted to "[keep] Germany and Japan *down*, [keep] the Soviet Union *in* the big council of the world [i.e., the United Nations Security Council], and [legitimize] the USSR's post-war borders and sphere of influence." In internal discussions, however, opinions varied as to how Moscow could best achieve its objectives. Some officials vaunted the benefits of closer ties with London and Washington, insisting, in typical Leninist fashion, that Anglo-American dissension would inevitably occur as a result of "capitalist contradictions." The British-U.S. rivalry would thus redound to Soviet advantage.[52]

Unfortunately for these optimists, Stalin's distrust of the Western powers undermined any Soviet enthusiasm for strategic (as opposed to tactical) collaboration with the Kremlin's ideological foes. The death of his "dream partner" FDR and the explosion of nuclear weapons in August 1945 heightened the marshal's sense of vulnerability. Stalin's disrespect for Truman fueled his implacability vis-à-vis Western aspirations, whereas the American capacity to strike Soviet targets with atomic bombs pushed him to achieve a "security belt of friendly regimes around the Soviet Union." This *cordon sanitaire* would retard the arrival of U.S. B-29s, or any other aircraft that could deliver a nuclear device, thus providing Moscow with extra time to absorb the blow and carry out countermeasures.[53]

In Iran, the Soviet Union sought to maintain its pervasive influence over the northern section of the country, much to the dismay of the United States and Great Britain. With the Red Army ensconced on Iranian soil, contra the 1942 Tripartite Treaty, the Soviets obviously considered themselves entitled to a major presence in an area contiguous with their territory. They even incited rebellions in Azerbaijan and Kurdistan, in line with Stalin's renewed enthusiasm for revolutionary movements. This interference upset Tehran; it disconcerted London and Washington.[54]

In response, the Truman administration proposed to step up its involvement in Iran. It soon advocated multilateral assistance programs that included the Soviets and tackled the twin irritants of Iranian separatism and factionalism. Yet American recommendations seemed quixotic. Policymakers could not run roughshod over Iranian, Soviet, and British concerns if they expected to secure U.S. objectives. With insufficient regard for the possible consequences, the United States, in the words of historian Mark Lytle, "embarked on a major extension of the Monroe Doctrine in an area that would soon supersede the Balkans as the world's most explosive powderkeg." The State Department upbraided the Soviets for their imperial conduct in Iran, unaware, or unwilling to admit, that some facets of U.S. policy resembled Moscow's.[55]

In 1946, the Grand Alliance dissipated. In his famous "Long Telegram," an exposé on the Soviet mindset that crystallized American thought on U.S.-Soviet relations, Russian expert George Kennan argued that "[w]here individual governments stand in the path of Soviet purposes pressure will be brought for their removal from office. This can happen [in Turkey and Iran,] where governments oppose Soviet foreign policy aims." In May, with the matter before the United Nations (UN), the Soviet Union begrudgingly vacated Iran two months past the March 2 deadline, in exchange for an oil concession. Despite the Red Army's exit, the United States monitored Soviet machinations in northern Iran, where Moscow-sponsored separatists and radicals taunted Iranian Prime Minister Ahmad Qavam with their calls for an independent Azerbaijan.[56]

The Kremlin's involvement in Iran unnerved suspicious American officials, who believed in and continuously promoted the ideals of the UN Charter. U.S. policy called for Iranian independence. Washington aimed "to create a condition of internal security, and thus prevent a situation which might invite foreign intervention." Secondly, it should "encourage democratic institutions and processes, and thus prevent the growth of a dictatorial regime which might either oppose or limit friendly intercourse with other nations." In the short term, the Department of State sought to dissuade Tehran from fraternizing "exclusively" with Moscow. But without American succor, a destitute Iran might succumb to Soviet slogans denouncing the so-called fascist authorities in the Iranian capital.[57]

Washington promised economic support but could not deliver supplies on the scale asked for by Tehran. This fact limited Prime Minister Qavam's options. In the previous year, Iran's Azeri and Kurdish provinces had achieved semi-autonomous status courtesy of the Red Army, which barred Iranian soldiers from reestablishing national authority. This development frightened the White House and seemed to confirm that the Kremlin craved proxies. For their part, the British prodded the Americans to inject themselves into the controversy for the sake of Western interests.[58]

Civil unrest in southern Iran involving the Qashqai and Bakhtiari tribes, possibly incited (though vehemently denied) by the British, convulsed the Iranian polity. With a possible revolt underway, Qavam hesitated to expulse the three Tudeh members of his cabinet lest the Soviets retaliate by intensifying their anti-Tehran efforts in Azerbaijan. As the political vise tightened, the Iranian leader implored Washington to provide assistance. He claimed that only with U.S. assent "could he prevent Iran from falling under domination of either foreign powers or subversive elements." Sincere or not, Qavam's plea failed to sway American policymakers. Yet the prime minister believed that Moscow preferred access to his country's oil over independence for Azeris. He guessed correctly. Soviet archival materials indicate that the Kremlin sought not direct control but to "participate on a par [sic] in the postwar competition of great powers for the right to possess the new oil fields in the Middle East."[59]

The Soviet quest to exploit Iran's impressive petroleum reserves alarmed the U.S. Joint Chiefs of Staff (JCS), who deemed the country "of major strategic interest to the United States." They pointed out that "[f]rom the standpoint of defensive purposes the area offers opportunities to conduct delaying operations and/or operations to protect United States-controlled oil resources in Saudi Arabia." If Iran fell to the Soviets, the Anglo-American position in the Middle East might founder. In juxtaposition to this so-called domino thinking, the JCS noted that "[a]s to counteroffensive operations, the proximity of important Soviet industries, [sic] makes the importance of holding the Eastern Mediterranean-Middle East area obvious." Scarcity of petroleum would cripple any war effort, thus Washington could not allow the Kremlin to secure subsoil rights in Iran or anywhere else in the region. "Our best estimates indicate that the USSR does not derive sufficient oil from sources within her borders to support a major war," the JCS explained. Conversely, "[U.S.] [l]oss of the Iraq and Saudi Arabia sources . . . would mean that in the case of war [America] would fight an oil-starved war." A concerned JCS considered the "military implications" in Iran analogous to those in Turkey, where the Soviets were pushing for navigation privileges.[60]

NEA added its concerns. "[T]he Iranian question," it argued, "transcends the mere bilateral relations between Iran and the United States. Politically, it involves our policy of supporting the independence of small countries in the spirit of the United Nations." Even more, "[s]trategically, it involves the defense of our military interests in the entire Near and Middle Eastern area, having particular relevance to the position we have taken with regard to Turkey." NEA recommended that Washington provide "positive encouragement and assistance to Iran in an endeavor to *save* it from falling completely under Soviet domination and to *rescue* it if possible from its present state of partial subservience to the Soviet Union." As NEA Director Loy Henderson put it in Manichean terms, "unless [the United States] show[s] by concrete acts that [it is] seriously interested in carrying out [its] various assurances to Iran, the Iranian Government and people will eventually become so discouraged that they will no longer be able to resist

Soviet pressure." Deeds would "save" and "rescue" Iran, not rhetorical references to UN principles.[61]

In a daring move, Qavam ousted the three Communist politicians from Iran's executive. U.S. Ambassador to Iran George V. Allen praised the *coup de tonnerre* and advocated commercial credits. Without them, Iran could not invigorate its economy. Absent economic modernization, the Iranian government could not expect to outwit with impunity the Soviets and their lackeys whenever societal displeasure threatened to fracture the country. Allen urged his superiors to seize the "psychological moment." With parliamentary elections impending, timely aid could possibly ensure an anti-Soviet *Majlis*.[62]

The Truman administration preferred that Qavam postpone the vote until Iranian soldiers could reassert control over the renegade provinces of Azerbaijan and Kurdistan, both Soviet-supported. The election seemed of secondary importance to Allen, who wrote that the exercise "will be [a] farce." Still, he believed Washington should not contravene Tehran's wish. With the UN Security Council debating Soviet interference in Iran and with Qavam tarred in the Soviet press, Allen emphasized that the Shah "has reserved his power for future use." Prime ministers could be replaced, the U.S. ambassador intimated, but if the United States aspired to a meaningful role in Iran, then Mohammed Reza Pahlavi could serve as Washington's loyal ally.[63]

While the immodest young Shah inspired American confidence, State Department policymakers mistrusted the wily Qavam and questioned whether his government represented the "true interests" of Iranians. These doubts notwithstanding, Assistant Secretary of State Dean Acheson informed Allen that the United States intended to carry out "appropriate acts," in the form of military and economic assistance, in support of Iran's independence. This support hinged, however, on the reestablishment of Iranian authority over renegade Azerbaijan.[64]

Qavam vacillated. He promised to order troops into the region and keep the Security Council abreast of events. The prime minister expected that august body, responsible for international security, to condemn any encroachments upon the sovereignty of one of its member states. The inviolability of that concept trumped any Soviet veto, or so Qavam presumably reasoned. Most importantly, the United States preached respect for that sacred UN commandment. With America on its side, the Iranian Army could venture northward to reassert national authority in Azerbaijan, a move the Soviet Union objected to stridently. Moscow's ambassador warned that Iran could suffer the consequences should events imperil the Soviet position in the south Caucasus. An irate Kremlin might reintroduce the Red Army into Iran.[65]

American diplomats eyed Tehran's quandary with trepidation. Yet they urged Qavam to defy the Soviets and reaffirmed the U.S. commitment to the Iranian cause. They even counseled the prime minister on how to present Iran's case before the Security Council. With American prestige underpinning his policy, Qavam submitted a brief. His complaint spotlighted Soviet truculence: Moscow's threats, if realized, could undermine the *Majlis* elections. Qavam's recourse to the United Nations failed to impress the Kremlin. The Soviet ambassador reiterated his country's displeasure regarding this most serious issue and asked the Iranian leader to reconsider his views. The prime minister refused. In his various explanations, Qavam singled out Iranian public opinion, which endorsed his militancy, as his motive for authorizing the repossession of Iranian territory. In the end, his revanchism, justified and enjoying American backing, overwhelmed the brittle vanguard that presided over Azeri (and Kurdish) affairs for some twelve months. This overthrow surely affronted Moscow and probably exacerbated Stalin's paranoia regarding so-called secure borders. After two twentieth-century German invasions, he constantly worried about Great Powers encircling his country and threatening it with incursion. To counter this menace and insulate the Soviet Union, he atavistically sought a ring of buffer zones around the Fatherland. But the United Nations' first cause célèbre prevented the creation of such an area in Azerbaijan.[66]

Ostensibly, the Soviets had abandoned their Azeri lackeys in return for parliamentary approval of an oil concession. With World War II ended, the *Majlis* could legally consider Moscow's wartime agreement with Tehran. Qavam outfoxed his Soviet opponents a second time when elections in early 1947 returned a majority of deputies opposed to the petroleum deal. In due course, Iranian legislators refused to ratify Soviet commercial ambition, leaving the Kremlin further humiliated and without access to precious Iranian oil. Nationalist deputies, such as Mossadeq, exclaimed that only Iran could develop its oil industry and, therefore, foreigners should be kept out or, in the case of the British, expelled.[67]

Washington ignored the hint that Iranians might someday expropriate British and American petroleum assets and instead interpreted the dénouement as vindication of a firm policy toward the Soviet Union. Stalin considered Iran expendable; he backed off in Iran and elsewhere in 1946 to avoid a "premature confrontation" with the British and Americans. He wanted to minimize friction with his former allies so that he could revitalize Soviet military might. Nevertheless, Stalin's clumsy diplomacy yielded an unsatisfactory outcome: Qavam duped him. Evidence from the Soviet archives points to a distracted Stalin, whose obsession with the critical issues discussed at the various Council of Foreign Ministers talks in 1945–46 caused him to stumble over Iran. As scholar Vladimir Pechatnov writes, "how could [Stalin] alone watch over everything, if everybody else counted on his wisdom and omniscience?" Basically left to its own devices, the Soviet Ministry of Foreign Affairs erred in Iran, much to the annoyance of the enraged despot.[68]

Despite its satisfaction with the result of the Azeri crisis, the United States, consistent with its promotion of equal economic opportunity for all nations, did not oppose Soviet petroleum exploration in Iran. Excessive quantities of oil on the international market quelled the need for American concessions in Iran in the short term. Still, Washington insisted that Qavam institute reforms so that Persians could prosper. Communists and their sympathizers would mold opinions and command allegiance if Iranians could not overcome scarcity. This U.S. political orthodoxy called for Iran to modernize. Yet, as subsequent events would demonstrate, the Western model of political and economic development risked destabilizing Iranian society and offending Persian cultural sensitivities.[69]

The events of 1946 in Iran and Turkey foreshadowed the Truman Doctrine. Soviet probes in the Near East convinced the president and his advisors that the

United States had to preserve its core values of democracy and capitalism, as well as Western security assets, by contesting Soviet power at various "pressure" points throughout the world. The White House's international policy of anti-communism took shape once the British informed the president that they could not fund Turkey and Greece, countries threatened with Communist takeovers. In March 1947, Truman informed the Congress of his intention to proffer aid to those two "Northern Tier" countries as well as to support any state opposed to Stalinism. Prime Minister Qavam and the Shah wondered, however, why the United States would not commit to defending Iran and refused to provide free assistance. Surely, Iran deserved similar treatment to Turkey, Tehran claimed. When the "Pentagon Talks" confirmed the Middle East as an intrinsic component of Anglo-American postwar strategy, Iran became a frontline bulwark in Washington's global competition with the Soviet Union.[70]

As subsequent events would show, the United States stamped Iran and Saudi Arabia as countries of primary importance in the Cold War. These key friends would facilitate the projection of American power into the Persian Gulf region. Hitherto a peripheral area for Washington, the Gulf turned into a hot spot in the 1941–47 period. With this designation came political, economic, and military expansion befitting a Great Power. As British influence waned (despite London's preeminent role in the Arabian emirates) and a Soviet menace emerged, the United States, the superpower with atomic weapons and the most productive economy in the world, officially joined the Great Game.[71]

Assessment

From 1941 to 1947, the United States underwent a rather taxing initiation when it came to the Persian Gulf. Substantial American effort enabled the Grand Alliance to resupply the Soviet Union at a critical juncture. That contribution helped the Allies win the Second World War. Afterward, with oil a strategic commodity and considerable U.S. petroleum interests in Saudi Arabia, Iraq, and Kuwait, Washington's postwar objectives impelled it to stay involved in the region. America thus familiarized itself with an area of undeniable geopolitical importance for the West and Moscow. As U.S.-Soviet relations soured in 1946–47, the Truman administration's harsh rhetoric, which differed markedly from FDR's optimism, sought to prevent Communist inroads.

With respect to this *first* stage (1941–47) of U.S. expansion in the Persian Gulf, the following case can be made for American imperialism. To defeat Germany in World War II, Washington joined London and Moscow in an alliance of convenience that sought to break the Nazi stranglehold on Europe. Just as with Napoleonic France, a formidable concert of Great Powers halted the country trying to unify the Old Continent under its despotic rule. A few years after the Third Reich's disintegration, however, America identified a renewed threat from Soviet communism. British imperialism certainly worried American policymakers, but most of them preferred to vilify the Soviet Union, a nation whose wartime death toll approximated twenty million and whose infrastructure the ruthless Germans decimated. Though the Soviets lacked the wealth and international clout of the British, the White House aligned itself with the United Kingdom for ideological reasons.

While the United States sought to counter Great-Power threats, a favorite imperial tactic, it befriended the Saudis and Iranians. As a result, one can apply Michael Doyle's imperialism criteria to this period. On Doyle's first point ("demonstrate the existence of control"), Washington persuaded the Iranians and Saudis to heed American advice. On the second ("explain why one party expands and establishes such control"), the United States eventually asserted itself in Iran to thwart Soviet advances into the Northern Tier and fortify its position of economic primacy in Saudi Arabia. On the third ("explain why the other party submits or fails to resist effectively"), the Iranians requested U.S. involvement in their country's politics consistent with their traditional "third-power" policy, a ploy that enabled them to offset the various Soviet and British violations of their sovereignty. As in Europe, America received an invitation to bolster the Saudi and Iranian regimes.

Why Ibn Saud and Mohammed Reza Shah trusted the White House not to subjugate or overwhelm their polities cannot be simply chalked up to American wartime pronouncements. The Atlantic Charter may have endowed the United States with moral rectitude, but luckily for Uncle Sam, lack of familiarity with U.S. heavy-handedness in Latin America (i.e., Yankee imperialism) probably minimized Arab and Persian concerns when it came to Washington's motives in the Gulf. Also, American inexperience with the Byzantine politics of Iran and the tribal loyalties of the Saudi sheiks may have convinced regional leaders that, in contrast to the all too familiar British and Soviets, they could manipulate more easily the newest participant in the Great Game. This so-called reverse leverage could possibly extract U.S. commitments, yet keep America at arm's length.[72]

As the Second World War moved to a climax, Washington abandoned its timid ways in favor of a vigorous policy that led to a semi-entrenched position by 1947. With Whitehall relegated to a secondary role on many important issues, the United States invested in an informal empire, or "soft" sphere, that would come to rely on oilmen, Central Intelligence Agency operatives, and aircraft carriers. Formal control would prove unnecessary and illogical while the United States sanctioned worldwide decolonization. Yet U.S. efforts could be construed as either "liberal imperialism" or "security imperialism."

Untainted by colonialism, or so administrations claimed, the White House condemned European practices of exploitation and promoted Third-World nationalism unless it clashed with American geopolitical and economic interests. The United States favored conservative leaders who could uphold the status quo, in harmony with American strategic objectives. Still, U.S. leaders could not overcome a basic contradiction. They spoke the words of Woodrow Wilson, promoting self-determination, but carried out policies reminiscent of Theodore Roosevelt and Wilson himself. While they believed in U.S. "exceptionalism," they behaved as imperialists. Winston Churchill remarked that, in its rhetoric, the United States disdained "power politics," yet its policies resembled those of any European Great Power. In the Middle East, Washington initially secured its economic interests, then inherited British political and diplomatic duties in the wake of World War II. America also built up its armed forces in the area, starting with the Dhahran air base. This three-step process replicated the British experience in the region. Each power opted to rule informally rather than exercise complete control over entire societies. This kind of influence suited the Americans, whose previous experiences with formal imperial rule (in the Philippines, for example) had proved frustrating.[73]

While, at first, the United States did not intend to organize the Persian Gulf as an explicitly American sphere of influence, it increased its level of commitment steadily in the years 1941–47. The objectives of U.S. policy—unfettered access to Gulf oil and the warding off of any enemy—called for resolute, unilateral policies. Without them, the Soviet Union might try to establish a regional imperium, a development that could undermine the American position in the world. Instead of proceeding alone, the United States implemented its Gulf agenda with the collaboration of Ibn Saud and Mohammed Reza Shah. These conservative authoritarians, as well as Ahmad Qavam and other Iranian prime ministers, invited Americans into their countries to counter British and Soviet meddling. Scholar Mark Lytle notes that, in the case of Persia, America "did not simply assume neocolonial domination over Iran. It was the Iranians, not the Americans, who urged the creation of economic and political instruments—oil concessions, advisory mission, and commercial agreements—that traditionally were the devices of imperialist penetration." In this era, Saudi and Iranian leaders prodded Washington to redouble its efforts, much to their own benefit. By 1947, U.S. assertiveness had replaced the previous deference accorded London on political and military matters. This new policy aimed to achieve not only economic goals, but also political and military ones.[74]

As Washington organized the Bretton Woods economic system, private U.S. businesses sought commercial opportunities in the Persian Gulf. In Saudi Arabia, the majors exploited the country's most precious resource in a concessions-for-royalties transaction that promised untold riches for American oil companies and the Saudi monarchy. While company men made profitable deals, Washington craved petroleum so that its armed forces could fight America's postwar enemies. Iran's proximity to Saudi fields thus heightened U.S. interest in the 1945–46 Soviet-Iranian confrontation.

While Gulf oil served a critical military purpose, it also improved the United States' hegemonic position in the international economy. America could not continue to prosper, however, without access to Saudi, Iraqi, Kuwaiti, and eventually Iranian oil. An industrial economy weaned on petroleum products since the turn of the century, and a post-World War II net importer of oil, could not afford to see the Soviet Union or any potential rival seize and hoard critical Gulf supplies. To preserve its core nation status, the United States started enforcing its doctrine of "containment," a quarantine policy that aimed to keep the Soviets away from American strategic resources.

As the U.S. role in the region intensified, Washington relied on contingent imperialism. With respect to World War II, proposition P2 (The United States will exercise alliance contingent imperialism whenever a significant threat to American hegemony and security occurs, allies agree to join a U.S.-led venture or vice-versa, Washington can overcome any regional constraints, consensus exists within the executive, and no majority in Congress or critical segment of domestic opinion strongly opposes White House action) seems confirmed. U.S. soldiers occupied Iran so that Washington could aid London in supplying the Soviets with vital matériel. Big Three cooperation prevented a German victory in Europe and a possible take-over of the Persian Gulf area. In the case of the 1946 Iran crisis, proposition P3 (The United States will exercise proxy contingent imperialism whenever a significant or minor threat to American hegemony and security occurs, surrogates can preserve U.S. interests, Washington cannot overcome regional constraints, consensus may not exist within the executive, and a majority of Congress or critical segment of domestic opinion strongly opposes direct White House involvement) seems correct. In that instance, Tehran outmaneuvered the Soviets, who desisted. Washington supported the Iranians, but essentially watched events unfold.

Via alliance and proxy imperialism, American expansion in the 1941–47 era conformed to previous Great-Power aggrandizement: the United States coveted resources, sought military advantages, and urged Gulf countries to emulate its political example. At the same time, America confounded expectations by earnestly trying to accommodate Saudi and Iranian needs. The intersection of patron-client interests may have explained American adaptability, in contrast with Soviet intractability in the region, but subsequent events would test this contention.

Notes

1. Henry R. Luce, "The American Century," *Life*, 17 February 1941, reprinted in "The American Century: A Roundtable (Part 1)," *Diplomatic History* 23, no. 2 (Spring 1999): 159–71; Robert Dallek, *Franklin D. Roosevelt and American Foreign Policy, 1932–1945* (New York: Oxford University Press, 1979), 171–313; J. Garry Clifford, "Both Ends of the Telescope: New Perspectives on FDR and American Entry into World War II," *Diplomatic History* 13, no. 2 (Spring 1989): 213–30; Warren F. Kimball, *The Juggler: Franklin Roosevelt as Wartime Statesman* (Princeton, NJ: Princeton University Press, 1991); Michael S. Sherry, *In the Shadow of War: The United States since the 1930s* (New Haven, CT: Yale University Press, 1995), 65–122; John Lewis Gaddis, *The United States and the Origins of the Cold War, 1941–1947* (New York: Columbia University Press, 1972), 1–94; Robert A. Divine, *Roosevelt & World War II* (New York: Penguin Books, 1969); Robert Dallek, *The American Style of Foreign Policy: Cultural Politics and Foreign Affairs* (New York: Oxford University Press, 1983), 123–53; and Mark A. Stoler, "A Half Century of Conflict: Interpretations of U.S. World War II Diplomacy," *Diplomatic History* 18, no. 3 (Summer 1994): 375–403.

2. On Woodrow Wilson and his foreign-policy ideas and legacy, see N. Gordon Levin, Jr., *Woodrow Wilson and World Politics: America's Response to War and Revolution* (New York: Oxford University Press, 1968); Arthur S. Link, *Woodrow Wilson: Revolution, War, and Peace* (Arlington Heights, IL: Harlan Davidson, 1979); and Tony Smith, *America's Mission: The United States and the Worldwide Struggle for Democracy in the Twentieth Century* (Princeton, NJ: Princeton University Press, 1994), 84–109.

3. Dallek, *Franklin D. Roosevelt and American Foreign Policy*, 317–528; John W. Dower, *War without Mercy: Race & Power in the Pacific War* (New York: Pantheon Books, 1986); Michael J. Hogan, ed., *Hiroshima in History and Memory* (Cambridge: Cambridge University Press, 1996); and Richard Overy, *Why the Allies Won* (New York: W.W. Norton, 1995), 1–24, 314–30.

4. Thomas G. Paterson, *On Every Front: The Making and Unmaking of the Cold War*, Revised Edition (New York: W.W. Norton, 1992), 3–69.

5. Gaddis, *The United States and the Origins of the Cold War*, 198–361. See also the 1998–99 Cable News Network (CNN) series, "Cold War": episode 2, "Iron Curtain."

6. Melvyn P. Leffler, *A Preponderance of Power: National Security, the Truman Administration, and the Cold War* (Stanford, CA: Stanford University Press, 1992), quote can be found on 18; John Lewis Gaddis, *Strategies of Containment: A Critical Appraisal of Postwar American National Security Policy* (New York: Oxford University Press, 1982), 25–88; George F. Kennan, *Memoirs 1925–1950* (Boston: Little, Brown, 1967), 271–97, 547–59; Wilson D. Miscamble, *George F. Kennan and the Making of American Foreign Policy, 1947–1950* (Princeton, NJ: Princeton University Press, 1992), 25–28; Melvyn P. Leffler, *The Specter of Communism: The United States and the Origins of the Cold War, 1917–1953* (New York: Hill & Wang, 1994); Gaddis, *The United States and the Origins of the Cold War*, 282–315; Warren I. Cohen, *America in the Age of Soviet Power, 1945–1991*, in *Cambridge History of American Foreign Relations*, 4, ed. Warren I. Cohen (Cambridge: Cambridge University Press, 1993), 3–57; and David S. Painter, "Cold War," in *Encyclopedia of U.S. Foreign Relations*, 1, eds. Bruce W. Jentleson and Thomas G. Paterson (New York: Oxford University Press, 1997), 273–81. On the "security dilemma" and the psychology of threats in international politics, see Robert Jervis, "Cooperation Under the Security Dilemma," *World Politics* 30, no. 2 (January 1978): 186–214; and Robert Jervis, "Perceiving and Coping with Threat," in *Psychology and Deterrence*, eds. Robert Jervis, Richard Ned Lebow, and Janice Gross Stein (Baltimore: Johns Hopkins University Press, 1985), 13–33. On their relevance to the Cold War, see Cohen, *America in the Age of Soviet Power, 1945–1991*.

7. Thomas J. McCormick, *America's Half-Century: United States Foreign Policy during the Cold War* (Baltimore: Johns Hopkins University Press, 1989), 17–71; John Lewis Gaddis, *The Long Peace: Inquiries into the History of the Cold War* (New York: Oxford University Press, 1987), 40–43, 56; Michael J. Hogan, *The Marshall Plan: America, Britain, and the Reconstruction of Western Europe, 1947–1952* (Cambridge: Cambridge University Press, 1987); Paterson, *On Every Front*, 79; and John Lewis Gaddis, *We Now Know: Rethinking Cold War History* (New York: Clarendon Press, 1997), 92–95, 224–25. See also the CNN series, "Cold War": episode 3, "Marshall Plan."

8. On Palestine, see George Lenczowski, *American Presidents and the Middle East* (Durham, NC: Duke University Press, 1990), 21–30.

9. Michael A. Palmer, *Guardians of the Gulf: A History of America's Expanding Role in the Persian Gulf, 1833–1992* (New York: Free Press, 1992), 1–19, quote can be found on 3; and Robert D. Kaplan, *The Arabists: The Romance of an American Elite* (New York: Free Press, 1993), 13–43. Unlike most European imperialists, Americans tended to encounter foreigners as a result of economic and cultural, rather than political-military, expansion. See Emily S. Rosenberg, *Spreading the American Dream: American Economic and Cultural Expansion, 1890–1945* (New York: Hill & Wang, 1982). Nathan Godfried writes that "[t]he State and Commerce departments . . . actively promoted American oil interests in the Middle East during the 1920s. Government officials ignored, however, the region's development, living standards and meagre attempts to industrialize." Nathan Godfried, "Economic Development and Regionalism: United States Foreign Relations in the Middle East, 1942–5," *Journal of Contemporary History* 22, no. 3 (1987): 482. For a portrait of Ibn Saud, see Parker T. Hart, *Saudi Arabia and the United States: Birth of a Security Partnership* (Bloomington, IN: Indiana University Press, 1998), 1–9. On U.S. economic expansion, see Thomas G. Paterson, J. Garry Clifford, and Kenneth J. Hagan, *American Foreign Relations: A History–To 1920* (Boston: Houghton Mifflin, 2000); and Walter LaFeber, *The American Search for Opportunity, 1865–1913*,

in *Cambridge History of American Foreign Relations*, 2, ed. Warren I. Cohen (Cambridge: Cambridge University Press, 1993).

10. Michael W. Doyle, *Empires* (Ithaca, NY: Cornell University Press, 1986), 38; and L. Carl Brown, *International Politics and the Middle East: Old Rules, Dangerous Game* (Princeton, NJ: Princeton University Press, 1984), 107–35.

11. Barry Rubin, *The Great Powers in the Middle East 1941–1947* (London: Frank Cass, 1980), 34–37.

12. Rubin, *The Great Powers in the Middle East 1941–1947*, 38–47. Quote can be found on 38.

13. Bruce Robellet Kuniholm, *The Origins of the Cold War in the Near East: Great Power Conflict and Diplomacy in Iran, Turkey, and Greece* (Princeton, NJ: Princeton University Press, 1980), 130–31. Historian James Bill notes that from 1883, when the United States sent representatives to Iran and vice-versa, until World War II, America "developed a positive, benevolent image in the eyes of the Iranian people, who increasingly resented British and Russian intervention." James A. Bill, *The Eagle and the Lion: The Tragedy of American-Iranian Relations* (New Haven, CT: Yale University Press, 1988), 16.

14. Kuniholm, *The Origins of the Cold War in the Near East*, 130–33. On World War I, see A.J.P. Taylor, *The First World War: An Illustrated History* (London: Penguin Books, 1966).

15. Kuniholm, *The Origins of the Cold War in the Near East*, 134–35. For a fascinating perspective on life in Persia under Reza Shah, see Shusha Guppy, *The Blindfold Horse: Memories of a Persian Childhood* (Boston: Beacon Press, 1988).

16. Bill, *The Eagle and the Lion*, 5; Kuniholm, *The Origins of the Cold War in the Near East*, 136–38; and Rouhollah K. Ramazani, *Iran's Foreign Policy 1941–1973: A Study of Foreign Policy in Modernizing Nations* (Charlottesville, VA: University Press of Virginia, 1975), 39, 70. Quote can be found in Bill, *The Eagle and the Lion*, 5.

17. Kuniholm, *The Origins of the Cold War in the Near East*, 138–42.

18. Kuniholm, *The Origins of the Cold War in the Near East*, 142–43; and Rubin, *The Great Powers and the Middle East 1941–1947*, 76–77.

19. Ramazani, *Iran's Foreign Policy 1941–1973*, 25–44, 70–108; Kuniholm, *The Origins of the Cold War in the Near East*, 143–48; Godfried, "Economic Development and Regionalism," 482; and Bill, *The Eagle and the Lion*, 18–20.

20. Bill, *The Eagle and the Lion*, 20; Kuniholm, *The Origins of the Cold War in the Near East*, 148–50; and Godfried, "Economic Development and Regionalism," 482. According to historian Barry Rubin, FDR promoted a U.S. mission to Iran that, in the president's mind, combined "[the] 'open door,' anti-imperialism, great-power cooperation, and a certain amount of altruism." Rubin, *The Great Powers and the Middle East 1941–1947*, 90. For examples of American officials working at cross purposes, see Bill, *The Eagle and the Lion*, 18–25.

21. Kuniholm, *The Origins of the Cold War in the Near East*, 151–55.

22. Rubin, *The Great Powers and the Middle East 1941–1947*, 90–91; Kuniholm, *The Origins of the Cold War in the Near East*, 155–57. First quote can be found on 157; Mark Hamilton Lytle, *The Origins of the Iranian-American Alliance: 1941–1953* (New York: Holmes & Meier, 1987), 36–41; and "American Policy in Iran," Memorandum by Mr. John D. Jernegan of the Division of Near Eastern Affairs, 23 January 1943, *Foreign Relations of the United States* [hereafter *FRUS*], 1943, 4, *The Near East and Africa* (Washington, DC: Government Printing Office, 1964), 331–36. Second and third quotes can be found on 332. Final quote can be found on 333.

23. "American Policy in Iran," 331–36. Quote can be found on 331.

24. Memorandum by the Adviser on Political Relations (Murray), *FRUS*, 1943, 4: 330; and "American Policy in Iran," 334.

25. "American Policy in Iran," 335.

26. "American Policy in Iran," 335; and George F. Kennan, *American Diplomacy* (Chicago: University of Chicago Press, 1984). For a trenchant analysis of the Jernegan memorandum, see Lytle, *The Origins of the Iranian-American Alliance*, 41–46.

27. James A. Thorpe, "The United States and the 1940–1941 Anglo-Iraqi Crisis: American Policy in Transition," *Middle East Journal* 25, no. 1 (Winter 1971): 79–89. In national radio broadcasts in 1942 and 1943, Secretary Hull reiterated the hallmarks of American foreign policy ("nondiscrimination in economic opportunity" and "cooperation between nations in the spirit of good neighbors, founded on the principles of liberty, equality, justice, morality, and law") and sketched out a postwar vision for peaceful international relations ("The pledge of the Atlantic Charter is of a system which will give every nation, large or small, a greater assurance of stable peace, greater opportunity for the realization of its aspirations to freedom, and greater facilities for material advancement. But that pledge implies an obligation for each nation to demonstrate its capacity for stable and progressive government, to fulfill scrupulously its established duties to other nations, to settle its international differences and disputes by none but peaceful methods, and to make its full contribution to the maintenance of enduring peace"). "The War and Human Freedom," Cordell Hull Address, 23 July 1942, reprinted in *Department of State Bulletin*, 25 July 1942, 7, no. 161, 639–47, quote can be found on 644; and "Our Foreign Policy in the Framework of Our National Interests," Cordell Hull Address, 12 September 1943, reprinted in *Department of State Bulletin*, 18 September 1943, 9, no. 221, 173–79, quote can be found on 176.

28. Alfred E. Eckes. Jr., "Open Door Expansionism Reconsidered: The World War II Experience," *Journal of American History* 59, no. 4 (March 1973): 909–24; Godfried, "Economic Development and Regionalism," 481–500; and John A. DeNovo, "The Culbertson Economic Mission and Anglo-American Tensions in the Middle East, 1944–1945," *Journal of American History* 63, no. 4 (March 1977): 913–36.

29. Kuniholm, *The Origins of the Cold War in the Near East,* 158–63, first and second quotes can be found on 160, 163; and Lytle, *The Origins of the Iranian-American Alliance*, 43–44. Third quote can be found on 43. Fourth quote can be found on 43–44.

30. Kuniholm, *The Origins of the Cold War in the Near East*, 166–68. Quotes can be found on 168.

31. Kuniholm, *The Origins of the Cold War in the Near East*, 174–78. Quote can be found on 175. On Iran's domestic situation in the 1940s, see Bill, *The Eagle and the Lion*, 23–27.

32. David S. Painter, *Oil and the American Century: The Political Economy of U.S. Foreign Oil Policy, 1941–1954* (Baltimore: Johns Hopkins University Press, 1986), 14. On U.S. oil policy after World War I, see John A. DeNovo, "The Movement for an Aggressive American Oil Policy Abroad, 1918–1920," *American Historical Review* 61, no. 3 (April 1956). 854–76.

33. Painter, *Oil and the American Century,* 3–8, 14; and Kuniholm, *The Origins of the Cold War in the Near East,* 178–80. Discoveries forced the majors to grapple with the knotty problem of how to tap Middle Eastern crude without glutting the market.

34. Painter, *Oil and the American Century,* 6–9.

35. Painter, *Oil and the American Century,* 34–37; and Kuniholm, *The Origins of the Cold War in the Near East,* 181–82.

36. Painter, *Oil and the American Century,* 50–51, 59–74; Cordell Hull, *Memoirs of Cordell Hull,* 2 (New York: Macmillan, 1948), 1511–27; John A. Loftus, "Petroleum in International Relations," *Department of State Bulletin,* 5 August 1945, 13, no. 319, 173–75; and "Anglo-American Petroleum Agreement," *Department of State Bulletin,* 30 September 1945, 13, no. 327, 481–83.

37. Ramazani, *Iran's Foreign Policy 1941–1973,* 92–96; Rubin, *The Great Powers in the Middle East 1941–1947*, 145; Lytle, *The Origins of the Iranian-American Alliance,* 86–89; Kuniholm, *The Origins of the Cold War in the Near East*, 185–86, 189–200; and Painter, *Oil and the American Century*, 75–81. Quotes can be found on 77.

38. Painter, *Oil and the American Century*, 78–81; Ramazani, *Iran's Foreign Policy 1941–1973*, 96–108; Lytle, *The Origins of the Iranian-American Alliance*, 89–90, 124; and Kuniholm, *The Origins of the Cold War in the Near East*, 200–201.

39. Kuniholm, *The Origins of the Cold War in the Near East*, 203–8, quote can be found on 203; Lytle, *The Origins of the Iranian-American Alliance*, 101, n50, 126–27. FDR fixated upon Saudi Arabia, whose leader, Ibn Saud, in contrast to Shah Mohammed Reza Pahlavi, "he made far more of an effort to woo." With respect to Iran, "[m]ost likely," Lytle argues, the president "believed that a concession to Stalin on what was to him [FDR] a peripheral matter would help establish the basis for a lasting peace." Lytle, *The Origins of the Iranian–American Alliance*, 127.

40. Lytle, *The Origins of the Iranian-American Alliance*, 90–93. Quote can be found on 91. For information on "Red Fascism," see Thomas G. Paterson, J. Garry Clifford, and Kenneth J. Hagan, *American Foreign Relations: A History–since 1895* (Boston: Houghton Mifflin, 2000), 232, 234. For an explication of "bolstering," see Douglas J. Macdonald, *Adventures in Chaos: American Intervention for Reform in the Third World* (Cambridge, MA: Harvard University Press, 1992), 11–15.

41. Lytle, *The Origins of the Iranian-American Alliance*, 93–99, 120–35. Quote can be found on 98. On "exclusive spheres," see Paterson, *On Every Front*, 41–69.

42. Simon Davis, "Keeping the Americans in Line? Britain, the United States and Saudi Arabia, 1939–45: Inter-Allied Rivalry in the Middle East Revisited," *Diplomacy & Statecraft* 8, no. 1 (March 1997): 96–136. Quote can be found on 99; and Barry Rubin, "Anglo-American Relations in Saudi Arabia, 1941–1945," *Journal of Contemporary History* 14, no. 2 (1979): 253–67, especially 255–56.

43. Painter, *Oil and the American Century*, 42–47, 52–59, 85–86. For his part, Saud "sought to avoid the ire of either party [British or American], as he struggled to keep his country's independence." The king feared the British, whose clients included the Hashemite rulers in Iraq and Jordan—old foes of the king. His Majesty's Government also held sway over the emirates that bordered Saudi Arabia in the east and south. Hart, *Saudi Arabia and the United States*, 13.

44. Painter, *Oil and the American Century*, 86–95.

45. Hart, *Saudi Arabia and the United States*, 14–21. In Hart's opinion (21), "The airfield, more than any other tangible achievement in US-Saudi relations, was, and remained for fifteen years, a touchstone of the quality and durability of the US connection—a concrete symbol of official US interest in Saudi security. To obtain this relationship the United States planned and executed a variety of projects of assistance intended to show good-will, to protect the US-based oil concession, and to raise the level of personal cordiality between the two heads of state and their peoples."

46. William A. Eddy, *F.D.R. Meets Ibn Saud* (New York: American Friends of the Middle East, 1954); and Memorandum of Conversation between the King of Saudi Arabia (Abdul Aziz Al Saud) and President Roosevelt, 14 February 1945, Aboard the U.S.S. "Quincy," *FRUS*, 1945, 8, *The Near East and Africa* (Washington, DC: Government Printing Office, 1969), 2–3.

47. Dallek, *Franklin D. Roosevelt and American Foreign Policy;* Lytle, *The Origins of the Iranian-American Alliance*, 130–33; and Gaddis, *The United States and the Origins of the Cold War*, 198–243.

48. NEA Director Loy Henderson to Brigadier General H.H. Vaughan, Military Aide to President Truman, 10 November 1945, *FRUS*, 1945, 8: 10–11.

49. Summary of Remarks Made by Mr. Wadsworth to President Truman on 10 November on Behalf of Himself and of Mr. Tuck, Colonel Eddy and Mr. Pinkerton, Annex 1, in Loy Henderson to Secretary of State James F. Byrnes, 13 November 1945, *FRUS,* 1945, 8: 13–15.

50. Replies of the President, Annex 2, *FRUS,* 1945, 8: 15–18.

51. "United States Policy Toward Iran," Henderson to Secretary of State Byrnes, 23 August 1945, *FRUS,* 1945, 8: 393–400; and Wallace Murray, Ambassador in Iran, to Byrnes, 25 September 1945, *FRUS,* 1945, 8: 417–19. Quotes can be found on 418–19.

52. Vladimir O. Pechatnov, "The Big Three after World War II: New Documents on Soviet Thinking about Post War Relations with the United States and Great Britain," *Cold War International History Project (CWIHP),* Working Paper no. 13 (July 1995), 1–26. Quotes can be found on 16, 17, and 18. Italics in original.

53. Vladislav Zubok and Constantine Pleshakov, *Inside the Kremlin's Cold War: From Stalin to Khrushchev* (Cambridge, MA: Harvard University Press, 1996), 36–46, quotes can be found on 39, 43; and Vladimir O. Pechatnov, "'The Allies Are Pressing on You to Break Your Will . . .': Foreign Policy Correspondence between Stalin and Molotov and Other Politburo Members, September 1945-December 1946," *CWIHP,* Working Paper no. 26 (September 1999), 8.

54. Natalia I. Yegorova, "The 'Iran Crisis' of 1945–1946: A View from the Russian Archives," *CWIHP,* Working Paper no. 15 (May 1996), 12; Pechatnov, "The Big Three after World War II," 22. For Soviet thinking on Iran, see 3. Assistant People's Commissar for Foreign Affairs Ivan M. Maisky opined that the Soviet Union should "build up [its] economic, cultural and political presence in the northern part of the country." Quoted on 3. On Soviet involvement in northern Iran and the Red Army's refusal to withdraw, see Ramazani, *Iran's Foreign Policy 1941–1973,* 111–26.

55. Lytle, *The Origins of the Iranian-American Alliance,* 133–35. Quote can be found on 134.

56. Kennan, *Memoirs 1925–1950,* 556. See also Miscamble, *George F. Kennan and the Making of American Foreign Policy,* 25. Stalin stated that his soldiers could not remain in Iran lest they "undercut the basis of our liberationist policies in Europe and Asia." Quoted in Zubok and Pleshakov, *Inside the Kremlin's Cold War,* 45.

57. "Current US Policy Toward Iran," Policy and Information Statement on Iran Prepared in the Department of State, 15 July 1946, *FRUS,* 1946, 7, *The Near East and Africa* (Washington, DC: Government Printing Office, 1969), 507–9. First and second quotes can be found on 507. Third quote can be found on 508; and George V. Allen, Ambassador to Iran, to Byrnes, 31 July, 1946, *FRUS,* 1946, 7: 509. In the 20th century, the United States reflexively promoted democracy throughout the world, regardless of whether or not foreign polities could assimilate democratic norms and construct sturdy democratic institutions. See Smith, *America's Mission.* Ironically, Washington would come to underwrite autocracy in the Middle East, prizing stability rather than participation. See "Democracy and the West," *Middle East International,* 1 October 1999, 3.

58. Lytle, *The Origins of the Iranian-American Alliance,* 138–52; and Wm. Roger Louis, *The British Empire in the Middle East 1945–1951: Arab Nationalism, the United States, and Postwar Imperialism* (Oxford: Clarendon Press, 1984), 53–73. A crisis in Turkey started in August 1946, making the Middle East the first battleground of a nascent postwar Soviet-American antagonism. On the Turkish crisis, see Eduard Mark, "The War Scare of 1946 and Its Consequences," *Diplomatic History* 21, no. 3 (Summer 1997): 383–415.

59. Allen to Byrnes, 6 September 1946, *FRUS,* 1946, 7: 514–15; William L. Clayton, Acting Secretary of State, to Byrnes, 27 September 1946, *FRUS,* 1946, 7: 516–17; Allen to Byrnes, 30 September 1946, *FRUS,* 1946, 7: 518–20. First quote can be found on 520. And Dean Acheson, Acting Secretary of State, to Byrnes, 1 October 1946,

FRUS, 1946, 7: 520. Second quote can be found in Yegorova, "The 'Iran Crisis' of 1945–1946," 3–4.

60. "SWN-4818," Memorandum by the State-War-Navy Coordinating Committee to Major General John H. Hilldring, 12 October 1946, *FRUS*, 1946, 7: 529–32. Every quote except the last one can be found on 530. The last quote can be found on 532. The Soviets wanted unfettered access to the Turkish Straits so that their Navy could sail to and from the Mediterranean. On the issue of the domino theory and its relevance to American foreign policy, see Frank Ninkovich, *Modernity and Power: A History of the Domino Theory in the Twentieth Century* (Chicago: University of Chicago Press, 1994), xi–xviii.

61. "Implementation of United States Policy toward Iran," Memorandum Prepared in the Office of Near Eastern and African Affairs, 18 October 1946, *FRUS*, 1946, 7: 535–36. First three quotes can be found on 535, italics added; and Henderson to Under Secretary of State Acheson, 18 October 1946, *FRUS*, 1946, 7: 533–34. Last quote can be found on 534. For a discussion of American encirclement of the Soviet Union and the U.S. propensity to "exaggerate" the Soviet threat, see Paterson, *On Every Front*.

62. Allen to Byrnes, 19 October 1946, *FRUS*, 1946, 7: 536–37; Allen to Byrnes, 22 October 1946, *FRUS*, 1946, 7: 539–40, quote can be found on 539; Ramazani, *Iran's Foreign Policy 1941–1973*, 147–51; and Lytle, *The Origins of the Iranian-American Alliance*, 174–79. The Shah claimed vaingloriously that he deserved the kudos for the removal of the Tudeh officials. See Allen to Byrnes, 20 October 1946, *FRUS*, 1946, 7: 537–39. Scholar Rouhollah Ramazani credits Qavam for the tour de force, but underscores the Shah's helpfulness. Ramazani, *Iran's Foreign Policy 1941–1973*, 150. Qavam's moxie enraged the Soviets, who immediately pilloried him.

63. Byrnes to Allen, 30 October 1946, *FRUS*, 1946, 7: 540–41; Acting Secretary of State Acheson to Allen, 11 October 1946, *FRUS*, 1946, 7: 529; Allen to Byrnes, 2 November 1946, *FRUS*, 1946, 7: 541–43. First quote can be found on 543. Second quote can be found on 541; and Lytle, *The Origins of the Iranian-American Alliance*, 179.

64. Acting Secretary of State Acheson to Allen, 22 November 1946, *FRUS*, 1946, 7: 546–47. First quote can be found on 547. Second quote can be found on 546; Allen to Byrnes, 8 November 1946, *FRUS*, 1946, 7: 545; and Allen to Byrnes, 2 November 1946, *FRUS*, 1946, 7: 544–45.

65. Allen to Byrnes, 24 November 1946, *FRUS*, 1946, 7: 547–48 (including footnote on 547); Allen to Byrnes, 27 November 1946, *FRUS*, 1946, 7: 548–49; Allen to Byrnes, 29 November 1946, *FRUS*, 1946, 7: 549–50; Ramazani, *Iran's Foreign Policy 1941–1973*, 116–43; and Zubok and Pleshakov, *Inside the Kremlin's Cold War*, 45. On U.S. support for the United Nations in the immediate postwar years, see Stanley Michalak's review of Gary B. Ostrower, *The United Nations and the United States* (New York: Twayne, 1998) on H-Diplo (h-diplo@h-net.msu.edu).

66. Ramazani, *Iran's Foreign Policy 1941–1973*, 143–53; Lytle, *The Origins of the Iranian-American Alliance*, 179–80; Allen to Byrnes, 1 December 1946, *FRUS*, 1946, 7: 550–51; Acting Secretary of State Acheson to Allen, 2 December 1946, *FRUS*, 1946, 7: 551–52; Allen to Byrnes, 3 December 1946, *FRUS*, 1946, 7: 553–54; Acting Secretary of State Acheson to Allen, 6 December 1946, *FRUS*, 1946, 7: 554–55; Henderson Memorandum of Telephone Conversation, 7 December 1946, *FRUS*, 1946, 7: 556–58; Allen to Byrnes, 11 December 1946, *FRUS*, 1946, 7: 559–60; Allen to Byrnes, 12 December 1946, *FRUS*, 1946, 7: 560–61; Consul at Tabriz (Sutton) to Byrnes, 12 December 1946, *FRUS*, 1946, 7: 561–62; Allen to Byrnes, 17 December 1946, *FRUS*, 1946, 7: 562–63; Byrnes to Allen, 20 December 1946, *FRUS*, 1946, 7: 563; Allen to Byrnes, 23 December 1946, *FRUS*, 1946, 7: 564–65; and Ambassador to the Soviet Union Walter Bedell Smith to Byrnes, 27 December 1946, *FRUS*, 1946, 7: 566–67.

67. *FRUS*, 1946, 7: 564n; Yegorova, "The 'Iran Crisis' of 1945–1946," 22; Ramazani, *Iran's Foreign Policy 1941–1973*, 108; and Lytle, *The Origins of the Iranian-American Alliance*, 184–88.

68. Dean Acheson, *Present at the Creation: My Years in the State Department* (New York: W.W. Norton, 1969), 196–98; Yegorova, "The 'Iran Crisis' of 1945–1946," 20–21, 23–24; Zubok and Pleshakov, *Inside the Kremlin's Cold War*, 47. First quote can be found on 47; and Pechatnov, "'The Allies Are Pressing on You to Break Your Will . . . ,'" 1–25, especially 20. Second quote can be found on 20.

69. Allen to Byrnes, 3 December 1946, *FRUS*, 1946, 7: 554; Byrnes to Allen, 20 December 1946, *FRUS*, 1946, 7: 563; Byrnes to Allen, 20 December 1946, *FRUS*, 1946, 7: 564; and Lytle, *The Origins of the Iranian-American Alliance*, 180–84. For additional overviews of the Iran crisis, see Gary R. Hess, "The Iranian Crisis of 1945–46 and the Cold War," *Political Science Quarterly* 89, no. 1 (March 1974): 117–46; and Richard Pfau, "Containment in Iran, 1946: The Shift to an Active Policy," *Diplomatic History* 1, no. 4 (Fall 1977): 359–72. Hess concludes (145–46) that the United States won in 1946—in the sense that the Americans denied the Soviets a keen objective of theirs, an oil concession. He ascribes American motivation to the "vivid memory of Munich"—in other words, to the intolerance of any kind of appeasement. Quote can be found on 146. Pfau writes (372) that the United States aspired to "the negative goal of keeping Iran out of Soviet hands, thus to contain what Washington policymakers construed as Soviet expansion." On post-World War II American "modernization theory" in the context of the Middle East, see Daniel Lerner, *The Passing of Traditional Society: Modernizing the Middle East* (New York: Free Press, 1958), 43–75.

70. As an "orthodox" historian (i.e., someone who blames the Soviet Union for the outbreak of the Cold War), Bruce Kuniholm argues that the "American interpretation of what clearly was a Soviet threat [in Iran] was not exaggerated, and America's response was not aggressive." Kuniholm, *The Origins of the Cold War in the Near East*, 381. Whereas Mark Lytle, à la Thomas Paterson, offers the following "revisionist" interpretation of U.S. involvement in the Iran crisis: "American policymakers had exaggerated both the nature and the strength of Soviet ambitions." Lytle, *The Origins of the Iranian-American Alliance*, 188. On the Truman Doctrine, see Gaddis, *The United States and the Origins of the Cold War*, 316–52; Paterson, *On Every Front*, 70–78; Leffler, *A Preponderance of Power*, 141–81; Allen to Secretary of State George Marshall, 27 March 1947, *FRUS*, 1947, 5, *The Near East and Africa* (Washington, DC: Government Printing Office, 1971), 901–2; and Allen to Marshall, 16 June 1947, *FRUS*, 1947, 5: 914–16. On the "Pentagon Talks," see "The British and American Positions," Memorandum Prepared in the Department of State, undated, *FRUS*, 1947, 5: 511–21.

71. The emirates included Kuwait, Bahrain, Qatar, the Trucials, today's United Arab Emirates, and Muscat and Oman, currently the Sultanate of Oman.

72. On U.S. imperialism in Latin America, see, for example, Louis A. Pérez, "Intervention, Hegemony, and Dependency: The United States in the circum-Caribbean, 1898–1980," *Pacific Historical Review* 51, no. 2 (May 1982): 165–94.

73. Michael Hudson, "To Play the Hegemon: Fifty Years of US Policy Toward the Middle East," *Middle East Journal* 50, no. 3 (Summer 1996): 329–43. On the importance of Third-World regime type for U.S. foreign policy, see Robert S. Snyder, "The U.S. and Third World Revolutionary States: Understanding the Breakdown in Relations," *International Studies Quarterly* 43, no. 2 (June 1999): 265–90.

74. Lytle, *The Origins of the Iranian-American Alliance*, xviii.

Chapter 3

Confrontations: 1948–58

In the *second* stage (1948–58) of its post-World War II encounter with the Persian Gulf, the United States asserted itself politically and economically. To achieve its goals in the region, Washington sometimes assisted, other times angered, the United Kingdom, its most important ally. While the White House defied Iranian and other nationalists, U.S. oil companies placated them. As a result of its increased involvement, America expanded its influence in the area and throughout the Middle East.

In the previous stage (1941–47), the United States underwent an initiation in the clever and calculated ways of Gulf politics, which Westerners derisively referred to as emotional and Byzantine. Washington deferred to British experience and presumed wisdom in most situations until Whitehall's post-World War II political and economic vulnerabilities left the White House with a stark choice. It could retreat from the region, possibly inviting a Soviet takeover, or assist His Majesty's Government, a policy that could entangle America in an anti-colonial backlash. President Franklin D. Roosevelt and his surprise successor, Harry S. Truman, opted to underwrite British policy in Saudi Arabia and Persia to help relieve the Exchequer from its acute balance-of-payments problems. In 1946, however, events in Iran ushered in a new era of Great-Power crisis. This preview of the Cold War warned the U.S. administration that the Soviet Union might press forward whenever possible.

By 1948, with the Truman Doctrine serving as the rationale for postwar American security policy, Washington had acknowledged UK geopolitical weakness and vowed to prevent any debacle that could redound to Moscow's presumed advantage. But the Palestine issue polarized the U.S. executive, as President Truman recognized Israel over the objections of the State Department and Pentagon. Whereas the Missourian mixed moral conviction with electoral concerns, his country's Arabists worried that Saudi King Abdul Aziz ibn Abdul Rahman al Saud (i.e., Ibn Saud) and other Muslim leaders would resent American support for Israel. The bureaucracy's concern would not be misplaced. Truman's decision would greatly complicate U.S. policy vis-à-vis the Middle East. Notes historian Salim Yaqub: "[d]ecades of philanthropy and political disinterestedness had given the United States a relatively benign reputation in the Arab world. U.S. support for Israel's creation turned much of that goodwill into bitter resentment. For decades to come, such resentment would be an inescapable fact of life in Arab politics." In the 1940s, however, the Arab-Israeli feud preoccupied only a handful of irritated U.S. area experts.[1]

Meanwhile, the Truman administration spotlighted Cold-War flashpoints: the Czech coup of 1948, same year elections in France and Italy that could have resulted in Communist triumphs, the 1948–49 Soviet blockade of Berlin, the Chinese Communist Party's victory over the Kuomintang in China's civil war in 1949, and the outbreak of war in Korea in June 1950. A reeling White House responded with the Marshall Plan, Central Intelligence Agency (CIA) involvement in Western Europe to shore up Christian Democratic parties, acquiescence in the creation of the North Atlantic Treaty Organization (NATO) in 1949, and a revision of America's international policy, a process that resulted in the adoption of National Security Council (NSC) document sixty-eight. NSC 68 militarized U.S. foreign policy and enshrined resistance to the Soviet Union, described as an implacable foe that the United States would resist and defeat no matter the cost to the American taxpayer.[2]

Amidst charges of disloyalty and espionage within government, President Truman and his advisors sought to oppose every perceived Soviet violation of Western interests. This tit-for-tat version of U.S. containment policy, dubbed "symmetrical" by historian John Lewis Gaddis, relied on conventional weaponry rather than nuclear weapons. The United States downplayed its anti-communism, however, when it forthrightly criticized the anachronistic colonial policies of Great Britain and France, NATO partners. This liberal stance, which favored American interests in the Middle East, pleased countries in the throes of nationalist upheavals—Iran, for example. By pushing for decolonization, Washington clashed with London, the protector of the Persian Gulf emirates.[3]

This worrisome situation troubled the winner of the 1952 presidential election, Dwight D. Eisenhower, the war hero who remained fond of the British and indifferent toward Israel. Ike differed from Truman on several other counts. The Republican and his secretary of state, John Foster Dulles, disapproved of the alleged extravagance displayed by the Democrats. Eisenhower's concern for fiscal responsibility ruled out the level of military spending explicit in NSC 68. Washington, he explained, would not retaliate with expensive conventional forces every time the Kremlin infringed upon Western assets, especially in Asia. America would act independently and with impressive firepower (via so-called Massive Retaliation, which could involve nuclear weapons) or it would forge alliances that lessened U.S. security burdens. In theory, this "asymmetrical" variant of containment promised thrift and no repeat of the stalemated war in Korea. This restrained policy also relied on covert intervention, inexpensive CIA operations that could topple unfriendly governments, either Communist or sympathetic to Moscow.[4]

American objectives revolved around trade and anti-communism. The United States pursued hegemony via extensive commercial networks. Eisenhower utilized America's status as an economic Leviathan to counter or thwart communism whenever and wherever it threatened U.S. interests. In the Middle East, this quest to halt and overturn Communist advances united Washington and London on some issues, the nationalization of Iranian oil for example, yet opposed them on others, the attack on Suez most prominently.[5]

To carry out its "Outer Ring" strategy, a type of Anglo-American perimeter defense that stretched from the Taurus (Turkish) mountains in the west to the Zagros (Iranian) mountains in the east, Washington sought Strategic Air Command bases in Turkey and Egypt (from where it could launch nuclear attacks upon the nearby Soviet Union) and continued access to Persian Gulf oil. According to scholar Irene Gendzier, "[U.S.] economic and strategic considerations were integrally related, movements for social and political reform were suspect and consistently subordinated, and cooperation and competition with Great Britain were based on political calculations." Although often oblivious to local developments, U.S. policymakers tried throughout the decade to adapt to nascent inter-Arab and other rivalries and to the region's noticeable tilt toward a more assertive kind of nationalism, one that promised to transform or even remake entire societies. Meanwhile, Gulf and other Middle Eastern nations adjusted to British decline and a fundamental shift in the area's balance of power. Regional upheaval thus intersected with Great-Power competition to reward some while punishing others.[6]

The Art of the Possible:
The Fifty-Fifty Agreement with Saudi Arabia

President Truman's controversial decision in 1948 to recognize Israeli statehood upset the Middle East's Muslim leaders, who expected the United States to woo rather than infuriate them. Ibn Saud rued Truman's diplomacy, but remained in business with the Americans for obvious reasons. Only Washington could subsidize the monarch's regime, prevent a feared Hashemite encroachment from either Iraq or Jordan, stave off any Soviet move against the Kingdom, and pressure concessions from the Arab-American Oil Company (ARAMCO), whose royalty payments provided Saudi Arabia with its primary source of revenue. The Americans gained from a geopolitical and economic standpoint, yet this convenient exchange failed to salve Saudi bitterness over Palestine or remedy typical U.S. indifference to the plight of far away Arab tribesmen. As a result, the Saudis and Americans remained less than fully committed to one another. This type of Great Power-small power dynamic empowered Riyadh. Unfortunately for the frustrated Americans, this so-called tyranny of the weak characterized many U.S. relationships during the Cold War.[7]

Saud tempered his animosity, however, mindful that Washington could provide the protection and succor his Kingdom desperately needed. The monarch and his countrymen liked the Americans, whose technology they considered superior and commercial practices they welcomed. The Saudis' Islamic worldview, *Dar al-Islam* (followers of the Prophet Mohammed) versus *Dar al-Harb* (non believers), confirmed their moral superiority, thus diminishing their wariness of Western imperialism. Ironically, Saud mistrusted Muslims, the Iraqis and Jordanians specifically, whom he suspected of revanchism ever since they lost the Hijaz, with its holy cities of Mecca and Medina, to the Saudis earlier in the century. Truman's willingness to aid Saudi Arabia, a country Americans knew somewhat well and considered friendly, comforted the monarch, who counted on steady increases in revenue to keep his subjects satiated. Unless Saud could command loyalty, he risked tribal rivalries that could unravel his elaborate patronage networks and result in the country's dissolution. Aware of the king's problems, the White House searched for solutions that melded with the administration's "containment" grand strategy.[8]

Washington prized Saudi Arabia's vast quantities of petroleum reserves and the base at Dhahran. Each asset enhanced the United States' economic and military position vis-à-vis the Soviet Union. The U.S. Navy counted on Saudi fuel and oil products. To assure an uninterrupted Gulf supply to American warships, Admiral Richard Conolly established a command structure in 1948, renamed the Middle East Force (MIDEASTFOR) in August 1949 and headquartered in Bahrain, a UK protectorate just off the Saudi coast. Although small, MIDEASTFOR symbolized a more serious postwar U.S. commitment to the region and its fortunes.[9]

The American naval presence shielded ARAMCO, whose concession in Saudi Arabia yielded healthy company profits but also enriched the U.S. Treasury. The consortium's corporate taxes exceeded the royalties, $0.33 per barrel, remitted to the Saudis, an injustice Ibn Saud vowed to rectify. The king asked ARAMCO for an arrangement that divided benefits equally. Precedent for this type of profit sharing existed. In 1948, the Venezuelan government approved a law stipulating that it would collect half of the country's oil profits. In 1950, the same year it completed the trans-Arab pipeline known as TAPLINE, ARAMCO signed a Fifty-Fifty Agreement with the Saudis on December 30. The State Department nurtured and applauded this development. Throughout the negotiations, it urged ARAMCO to accommodate Ibn Saud's wishes so that expropriation à la Mexico (which occurred in 1938) could be averted. Company executives made their decision confident that they would deduct their royalty payments from taxes owed the Internal Revenue Service (IRS). Eventually, the IRS granted such permission. Washington thus absorbed the loss of ARAMCO profits by subsidizing Riyadh.[10]

The Fifty-Fifty Agreement preserved ARAMCO's concession, the cornerstone of the U.S. economic position in the Gulf. Saudi Arabia's oil rents may have increased, but Anglo-American companies still retained their oligopoly. While the "majors" fixed prices and monitored distribution, developed countries purchased greater quantities of petroleum products. These commercial arrangements buttressed U.S. global hegemony, hence Washington approved of them.

While the opulent Americans could rationalize an equitable settlement over Saudi oil profits as enlightened Cold-War policy and a check on Saudi nationalism, the British disapproved of such a fair arrangement, even though Kuwait and Iraq soon asked for and received similar treatment from U.S. and UK companies. Cursed with inadequate currency reserves and too many expenditures, London could not be as charitable. Neither could the Anglo-Iranian Oil Company (AIOC), whose stingy and arrogant "petro-colonialism" balked at any fifty-fifty deal with Iran.[11]

Adventures in Nationalism:
Iranian Oil, Mossadeq, and TPAJAX

The AIOC's monopoly over Iran's petroleum, courtesy of William Knox D'Arcy's 1901 concession, corrupted it in the eyes of Mohammed Mossadeq and other Iranian nationalists, who resented the British company's exploitation of their country's most valuable natural resource. In 1932, Reza Shah Pahlavi had revoked UK rights only to renew his nation's subservience to the AIOC a year later. A 1947 *Majlis* law barred future oil development by non-Iranian companies and instructed Tehran to negotiate a more satisfactory contract with the AIOC. Yet unless Mossadeq, who pushed for these measures, achieved the prime ministership, AIOC officers could count on unwavering support from a pro-British Iranian executive. Significantly, Shah Mohammed Reza Pahlavi, Reza's son, fully endorsed this tilt toward London.[12]

Events in the early 1950s disabused Iran's cabinet and monarch of their naïve belief that they could tame nationalist aspirations. Mossadeq and his followers wanted to wrest Iranian oil from the so-called evil British imperialists, a point of view not shared by the AIOC or London, which owned half of the company. Nationalization would spell the probable demise of the AIOC and potentially devastate Whitehall financially. Whether or not Iran could operate a petroleum industry efficiently remained unknown. The British scoffed at such a possibility. Their condescension vis-à-vis Muslims, inferior in every way, informed their skepticism. They mocked perceived Iranian incompetence, certain that the locals could not master the complexities of the international oil business.[13]

The Truman administration played no favorites. It dared not risk losing the confidence of either side. Division over Iranian oil could embolden the Soviets, probably still smarting over the Azeri humiliation and the concession rebuff. Still, Washington pressed the British. Whitehall should soften its uncompromising stance, the Americans complained. London said no.[14]

UK intransigence hampered Iran, whose precarious financial situation jeopardized its ambitious Seven-Year Plan. Although U.S. officials criticized British obstinacy and avarice, they denied Tehran's request for American military and economic assistance. Washington urged Iranian Prime Minister Mohammad Sa'ed to allocate his country's still considerable petroleum revenues intelligently. Without largesse from the British, Iran might become insolvent. Fortunately, the 1949 Supplemental Oil Agreement promised a reprieve, if the AIOC honored it.[15]

The National Front, an informal group of Iranians resentful of British hegemony, opposed that petroleum settlement. It wanted economic sovereignty for Iran. Mossadeq's views typified those of this hodgepodge of reformers. As the most visible and noteworthy member of this motley crew, the colorful septuagenarian, who perplexed Westerners with his personality and dress, commanded attention whenever he spoke or acted. His calculated displays of emotion and preference for pajamas over formal attire endeared him to most Iranians, but his Persian eccentricities unnerved most British and Americans who encountered him. They labeled him effeminate. Yet his sensitivity and bizarre fashion belied a shrewd politician, who seized upon widespread Iranian frustration with the AIOC and its imperious practices to promote his nationalist agenda.[16]

Two prominent institutions within Iran opposed Mossadeq and objected to nationalization of the oil industry, the Aladdin's lamp expected to carry the country into an era of self-reliance. The Communist Tudeh party, with ties to the Soviet Union, and the conservative Senate, whose wealthy and aristocratic elite tended toward the British point of view on most issues, dismissed Mossadeq's plan as contrary to their own, not the country's, best interests. In Mossadeq's and the National Front's popularity, however, Prime Minister Sa'ed and the Shah recognized an opportunity to press the AIOC for extra benefits. Without them, the *Majlis* would surely reject the Supplemental Oil Agreement.[17]

The possibility of a legislative setback failed to intimidate the British, who downplayed the likely results. Unlike London, Washington fretted that, with nationalist aspirations unmet, Iranians would oust the Sa'ed regime and trust Mossadeq to lead the country. This scenario could invite Soviet influence and deprive the West of a vital source of energy. Despite such trepidations, American decision-makers continued to support Great Britain, still considered the premier Great-Power authority in Iran and the Near East. In deference to Whitehall, the U.S. Government turned down Iranian pleas for mediation.[18]

Although the Iranian economy started to falter noticeably under successive centrist governments, UK obstinacy never wavered. Exasperated, Prime Minister Ali Razmara faulted the British for their shortsightedness. Invigorated, the National Front devised a way to dispense with the Supplemental Oil Agreement. With five of its seven parliamentary representatives named to the influential *Majlis* Oil Commission, the organization set out to achieve a legal victory for Iranian self-determination. Predictably, the Mossadeq-led commission targeted the provisions in the agreement detrimental to Iran. Still, the veteran politician could not persuade his fellow commissioners to recommend nationalization as the only option for the country. Instead, they merely dismissed the AIOC's handiwork as discriminatory, hence unacceptable. This decision convinced Washington that the National Front would insist on a fifty-fifty deal for the AIOC. The British recoiled whenever such talk arose.[19]

U.S. officials fumed. Preoccupation with Cold-War events in Western Europe and Korea hindered Washington's policy toward Iran. Saddled with costly overseas commitments, the State Department remained an ineffective third party to the Anglo-Iranian dispute. In early 1951, it advocated a compromise. Meanwhile, the AIOC and the National Front continued to press their maximum positions. On March 7, 1951, a pro-nationalization Islamist assassinated General Razmara, whose conservative views the British and Americans approved. Mossadeq came to power following a brief, tumultuous interlude with Hossein Ala as prime minister. As expected, Mossadeq proclaimed Iran's petroleum industry nationalized, a heterodox move (from the UK standpoint) that threatened to undermine America's anti-Soviet policy.[20]

Mossadeq's strident ways alienated the White House, prompting the Truman administration to reconcile with the British. Like London, Washington harbored ill will toward the National Front. The State Department concurred with Foreign

Office opinion that someone partial to Anglo-American wishes should replace Mossadeq.[21]

More so than Harry Truman, General Dwight Eisenhower endorsed the clandestine aspect of the Cold War. Without hesitation, the newly inaugurated president, a World War II expert on every type of warfare, authorized CIA extralegal activity in March 1953 that sought to topple Mossadeq's increasingly unfriendly regime. Ike particularly disliked Tehran's close ties to the Communist Tudeh.[22]

Operation TPAJAX aimed to remove the Iranian prime minister. An ex post facto CIA analysis explained the rationale for this initial American Cold-War coup:

> By the end of 1952, it had become clear that the Mossadeq government in Iran was incapable of reaching an oil settlement with interested Western countries; was reaching a dangerous and advanced stage of illegal, deficit financing; was disregarding the Iranian constitution in prolonging Premier Mohammed Mossadeq's tenure of office; was motivated mainly by Mossadeq's desire for personal power; was governed by irresponsible policies based on emotion; had weakened the Shah and the Iranian Army to a dangerous degree; and had cooperated closely with the Tudeh (Communist) Party of Iran.

The report also identified the objectives of TPAJAX:

> [T]o cause the fall of the Mossadeq government; to reestablish the prestige and power of the Shah; and to replace the Mossadeq government with one which would govern Iran according to constructive policies. Specifically, the aim was to bring to power a government which would reach an equitable oil settlement, enabling Iran to become economically sound and financially solvent, and which would vigorously prosecute the dangerously strong Communist Party.

The CIA selected General Fazlollah Zahedi to succeed one of the West's most visible Third-World irritants. The agency regarded the former Mossadeq cabinet member "as the most suitable successor to the Premier since he stood out as the only person of stature who had consistently been openly in opposition to Mossadeq and who claimed any significant following." America's violation of the United Nations Charter, which prohibited interference in a country's internal politics, was to be carried out in conjunction with the British Secret Intelligence Service (SIS).[23]

In August 1953, Iranians (mainly from the military and clergy) inimical to Mossadeq sought to overthrow the prime minister in an unchoreographed scene that left the CIA and the SIS convinced of the coup's imminent failure. Mossadeq's supporters celebrated victory prematurely, however. On August 19, following publication of the Shah's decrees, General Zahedi assumed Iran's premiership, two days after claiming it. Five days after TPAJAX had commenced, the White House exhaled. Zahedi proved a compliant leader, who satisfied the Americans and British both politically and economically. The 1954 Oil Agreement upheld nationalization, but allowed the U.S. majors into Persia and kept Iranians subservient to the whims of the international petroleum industry. This breakthrough extended American hegemonic interests into a country with vast oil reserves that could power Western economies for many years. To safeguard these assets, the Eisenhower administration turned to the Shah, providing him with substantial military and economic aid.[24]

Although U.S. decision-makers rejoiced at the removal of Mossadeq, a familiar problem persisted at the time in a desolate corner of southeastern Arabia. The contest over ownership of the Buraimi Oasis pitted yet another key American client, in this case Saudi Arabia, versus the United Kingdom. As with Iranian nationalization, the United States initially relied on diplomatic finesse and political dexterity to alleviate the problem.

Lines in the Sand: The Buraimi Oasis

The intense scramble for petroleum reserves not only involved the Great Powers. In the early 1950s, it galvanized the Saudi monarchy. With the extra revenue of the Fifty-Fifty Agreement in mind, Ibn Saud and his entourage surveyed their country in search of additional supplies of "black gold." The king recognized that whoever occupied a remote area of the Arabian Peninsula known as the Buraimi Oasis might strike oil. The Trucial state of Abu Dhabi and the Sultanate of Muscat and Oman abutted this abode and claimed ownership. Yet on August 31, 1952, Saudi Arabia seized this coveted desert refuge with the help of ARAMCO equipment.[25]

London bristled. As the overlord for the Trucials and Muscat and Oman, it condemned the rash Saudi move to occupy disputed territory. Already in a tizzy over the nationalization of AIOC assets in Iran, Whitehall would not tolerate any encroachment upon its protectorates' economic rights. Conversely, the United States sided with its valued regional partner, Saudi Arabia. This quasi-betrayal irked the British, who patronizingly dismissed their rival's diplomatic talents: "American impulsiveness and inexperience in dealing with Arabs may sometimes lead them to act injudiciously, but we must endeavor to persuade them and guide them on the right lines and be patient with their mistakes." The White House could not risk UK infuriation over Buraimi, lest Her Majesty's Government withdraw its support for America's Cold-War policy. Yet, notes historian Nathan Citino, "[i]ntent on improving relations with the Arab states and preventing expansion of Soviet influence in the Middle East, the Americans were wary of appearing to be accomplices to British imperialism. At the same time," he adds, "the sterling oil of the Gulf was essential to economic policy in Europe and to British participation in the free-trading, multilateral economy so cherished by American policy makers." As such, he opines, "U.S. policy on Buraymī [sic] sought Anglo-Saudi compromise, but a strong British presence in the region remained the overriding American priority." In a replay of the Iranian quandary, then, Washington yearned for a Solomonic judgment to which each side would adhere submissively and without rancor. Unfortunately, the possibility of a quick and amicable settlement vanished into the Arabian night.[26]

Tensions mounted. An Omani countermove would have occurred if not for British intercession. In October 1952, London and Riyadh devised the "Standstill Agreement," an ephemeral entente that froze current positions until the protagonists could devise a permanent solution. Saudi Arabia asked that a plebiscite settle the issue. Inhabitants of Buraimi would state their affinity: for or against Riyadh. To eliminate the possibility of Saudi bribery in a referendum, a tactic likely to carry the House of Saud to victory, Great Britain called for arbitration of the dispute. Although Washington preferred the Saudi approach and Secretary of State Dulles bemoaned British quaintness, U.S. policymakers refrained from interfering in the matter. The British ordered the encirclement of the Saudi occupation force commanded by Amir Turki Ibn Ataishan, to isolate it from oasis residents and possibly effect starvation. Once Whitehall realized that it could not alter Buraimi affection for the Saudis, it pushed for an all-party retreat from the oasis.[27]

The contest over oil prevented an expeditious resolution to the crisis. ARAMCO wanted access to Buraimi, a goal shared by British-owned AIOC and the Iraq Petroleum Company (IPC). In January 1954, UK Foreign Minister Anthony Eden suggested a new oil consortium for the oasis similar to the one under discussion in Iran. If ARAMCO, AIOC, and IPC collaborated, then a rational allocation of resources would be possible and competition unnecessary.[28]

Such a rosy scenario ignored the wants of King Saud, Ibn Saud's son and heir. The new monarch would not yield on Buraimi. ARAMCO's vice president, James Terry Duce, thus claimed that his company served only as a messenger, not an interested party, when it denied other petroleum multinationals the right to exploit the oasis' reserves. This supposed coincidence of interests between Riyadh and ARAMCO preserved the latter's lucrative concession, one that covered a wide expanse of Saudi desert. ARAMCO vetoed any consortium scheme in Buraimi as unpalatable. Such a precedent might hurt the company's long-term profitability.[29]

For London, the issues at stake in southeastern Arabia intersected with others in Iran and Egypt, where the Free Officers' regime sought to expel the British from the key Suez base. With the Americans pressuring them to relent on AIOC compensation in Iran, but not on military arrangements in Egypt, the British resisted U.S. prodding on Buraimi. Sadly for UK Prime Minister Winston S. Churchill, his country's impuissance in the Middle East and elsewhere hindered the Foreign Office's many efforts to impose its will in this case.[30]

While the British sulked, ARAMCO officials resolved in May 1954 that some of its men should burst into the oasis to stake the company's claim. Washington warned London not to interfere. When ARAMCO arrived at Buraimi, Her Majesty's Government prepared for a stout reprisal. Churchill counseled restraint, and the American multinational hesitated. British power sufficiently impressed the company to recall its personnel in June. ARAMCO eschewed responsibility for the crisis, however, insisting that the Saudis should be held accountable for the standoff. Later that month, an Anglo-American summit ended with the Declaration of Washington, a proclamation of transatlantic solidarity that confined the Buraimi matter to the diplomatic realm.[31]

With UK and U.S. oil companies absent from the table, British-Saudi negotiations resulted in an agreement to arbitrate the dispute. In the meantime, London and Riyadh withdrew all but fifteen of their soldiers and established a neutral zone. The Saudis kept a secret infrastructure in place, however, which worked to discredit the British and win over Buraimi opinion.[32]

This violation contradicted U.S. policy. Many other such instances of Saudi defiance occurred in these years. Riyadh objected to the Baghdad Pact, a Turkish-Iraqi creation that Washington touted as its so-called Northern Tier solution to possible Soviet infringement in the Middle East; opposed American intercessions in the Arab-Israeli conflict; and financed Egypt and Syria, two countries inimical to the United States. As with many other U.S. clients, Saudi Arabia exercised remarkable independence and stubbornness vis-à-vis its major benefactor, behavior that Washington could not tame despite its provision of substantial economic, political, and military largesse to the Saudis. To emphasize his displeasure with the Americans over the Buraimi matter, King Saud said that hereafter his country would refuse Point IV military assistance, a step that anguished U.S. officials, who feared Riyadh might terminate the soon-to-expire Dhahran Airfield Agreement. As Saudi assertiveness continued, only convergence on the oil issue and the desire to trump the British seemed to keep American relations with Saudi Arabia tolerable.[33]

The animosity between London and Riyadh over Buraimi climaxed in October 1955. With arbitration a memory due to Saudi mischief, Whitehall answered its opponent's illicit activities by expelling the Saudis from the oasis and affirming a return to the *status quo ante bellum*. The British carried out their military ouster without providing the United States with advance notice. Still, the Eisenhower administration reluctantly acquiesced. The securing of UK oil in the Persian Gulf remained critical to Western European economic success, an ultimate White House priority given the Cold War. This proclivity to exclude the United States from decisions relevant to American foreign policy, not to mention London's disregard for Arab nationalism, was to manifest itself again in the fall of 1956. Unlike Buraimi, the Suez crisis promised a sharper U.S. response to UK unilateralism. Before that debacle, however, Washington tried to rally Middle Eastern states to its supreme task: keeping the Soviets out of Western areas of influence.[34]

Diplomacy of Indecision: The Baghdad Pact

Post-World War II American familiarity with Iraq owed much to British tutorials. As with other Persian Gulf countries, the United States sought to assist in the preservation of UK influence in the former Mesopotamia. London's steadfast support for the conservative clique that ruled in Baghdad outraged many local opponents of an oligarchy that offended and often oppressed most Iraqi denizens.[35]

As Whitehall's colonial authority continued to ebb throughout the Middle East, Iraq's Hashemite monarchy contended with a fierce storm that could bury it: Arab nationalism. Active since the Great War, when Arabs expulsed the Sublime Porte (i.e., the Ottomans) from their lands, this movement yearned to restore Arab pride by expunging the nation of all foreign influence. This desire for self-determination called for the overthrow of any regime in cahoots with European imperialists. Baghdad's extensive ties with and reliance upon the British exposed it to continual harangues from nationalist opponents. Other Iraqis joined in these denunciations to vent their economic and cultural frustrations.[36]

Gamal Abdel Nasser's ascent to the Egyptian premiership in 1954 ensured that Iraq's royals would endure harsh criticism from the region's arch nationalist and exponent of Third-World neutralism. To prevent a Nasserite takeover, Nuri al-Said rallied Iraqi conservatives. These monarchists continued to rely on the United Kingdom, their benefactor and protector, for advice and aid. The juxtaposition of earlier liberal measures (such as the authorization of political parties in 1945) with renewed ties to the detested British overlord (specifically the 1948 Portsmouth Treaty, which replaced the 1930 Anglo-Iraqi Treaty) nullified any conservative hope of mollifying the regime's critics. For most Iraqis, the partition of Palestine in 1947, the end of the UK mandate in 1948, the creation of Israel the same year, and the first Arab-Israeli war (1948–49) confirmed British indifference to Arab aspirations.[37]

The United States stayed on the sidelines until the onset of the Korean War. Despite the uproar (known as the "*wathbah*" or "uprising") over the Portsmouth Treaty and its subsequent rejection, Washington either misunderstood or overlooked Iraq's serious internal problems, an unfortunate habit that would continue to hamper America's postwar Middle East policy. The Truman White House deferred to British expertise on Iraqi domestic matters. Meanwhile, as in Egypt and elsewhere in the region, it focused on strategic threats that could harm the Western position in Iraq. American officials believed that if the Palestine issue could be resolved, then U.S.-Iraqi relations would improve.[38]

Unlike its predecessor, the Eisenhower administration initially assigned the Arab-Israeli conflict a lower rank in terms of U.S. priorities. Secretary of State John Foster Dulles obsessed over the so-called Northern Tier states—Turkey, Iraq, Iran, and Pakistan—that bordered the Soviet Union. A May 1953 Middle East tour strengthened his belief that Soviet communism must not corrupt the region. He cared not that Iraqis opposed security measures that perpetuated the Western presence in their country. The secretary wanted a line of defense that kept Soviet expansion in check, even though, paradoxically, the Kremlin could not prevent the marginalization and persecution of the region's various Communist parties. Dulles also dismissed the notion that past Russian and Soviet incursions into the Northern Tier had sealed Arab, Persian, Turkish, and Pakistani mistrust of Moscow. Just as in Eastern Europe, the Republican lawyer expected the Soviets to rely on force in the Near East to overcome any inconveniences, such as historical animosity and ideological incompatibility. Yet, due to London's poor reputation in the area and Egyptian recalcitrance, Dulles considered a British-led Middle East Defence Organization headquartered in Cairo unworkable. He urged regional leaders to create an alternative institution that could thrive without conspicuous UK input. Prime Minister Nuri and his followers accommodated him, although such a move further alienated Iraqis weary of that clique's outdated views.[39]

The American push for a regional organization that could fend off the Soviets resulted in a symbolically important bilateral accord between Turkey and Pakistan in February 1954, a U.S.-Iraqi military assistance "understanding" in

April, and Baghdad's rapprochement with Ankara in 1955, another move that contravened Iraqi popular sentiment. Iraq wanted American help so that it could modernize its infrastructure, a policy that promised widespread unrest. Iraqi leaders needed weapons to ensure internal stability. Fearful that the Iraqis would use these arms against Israel, Washington would extend an offer of military supplies only if Iraq joined an anti-Communist coalition. When, in February 1955, Nuri obliged (with significant Turkish encouragement), a surprised United States refused membership in what became known as the Baghdad Pact under the pretext that such a step would offend the Israelis as well as Nasser. A vociferous critic of Nuri's diplomatic handiwork, the Egyptian prime minister ordered the Cairo-based Voice of the Arabs to pillory his ideological rival. With regional supremacy at stake, Nasser sought to discredit his opponent in Arab eyes.[40]

As Egypt bashed Iraq in the Middle Eastern media, America withheld its approval of Nuri in the hope that, via project Alpha, it could persuade Nasser to endorse a resolution to the Arab-Israeli dispute, by now the administration's foremost concern. The Dulles plan to incorporate the Northern Tier countries into a bulwark thus occurred without formal U.S. participation. Instead, the United Kingdom joined the Baghdad Pact as the sole Western member. Washington retained an essential role within the organization, sending representatives to important committee meetings. But the White House's tepid support for its previous institution of choice diminished American credibility with Middle Eastern governments favorably disposed toward the United States.[41]

While Washington dithered, Arab states divided into camps that presaged the so-called Arab Cold War. Iraq formed the Arab Union with Jordan in early 1956 to counter the Egyptian-Syrian tandem, a precursor to the United Arab Republic, founded in 1958. More seriously, Whitehall moved boldly to recover its eminent status within the region. American policymakers continued to criticize their British counterparts, yet rarely refuted UK initiatives. Without a U.S. veto to prevent a risky and covert démarche, London blundered terribly in the fall of 1956. British irresponsibility at Suez infuriated Washington, which rued its erstwhile endorsement of UK leadership in the Middle East, and rendered the Baghdad Pact useless. American inability to reform Anglo thinking resulted in events inimical to U.S. interests and a reconfiguration of area dynamics to the advantage of the Soviet Union, precisely the outcome the United States wanted to avoid when Dulles set out on his mission to enhance Western security in the Near East. Ironically, American indecisiveness turned to resoluteness only when Great Britain, France, and Israel, all friendly to the United States and supportive of U.S. aims in the region, invaded Egypt, a country opposed to the Baghdad Pact.

The Lion Overruled: Suez

In July 1956, Secretary Dulles finally withdrew the U.S. offer to finance the construction of the Aswan dam in Egypt to satisfy members of Congress and, according to historian Robert Dallek, "humiliate" the Soviet Union, which had recently cozied up to Cairo. In reaction to the Dulles announcement, Nasser nationalized the Suez Canal. France and Great Britain, both with century-old political and financial ties to the canal, scorned Nasser's seizure of the waterway and vowed to counter the Egyptian's audacious move with a clever trick of their own. Without direct access to markets east of Suez, these Western European countries, whose tankers transported vast quantities of oil from Saudi Arabia and Iran to the Mediterranean Sea via the canal, could not power their economies. Nor could they prosper, unlike the United States, which relied on TAPLINE and other pipelines.[42]

Provoked by Nasser and his defiant neutralism, London and Paris sought to eliminate the popular nationalist, whose bombastic rhetoric routinely whipped Arab crowds into an anti-Western frenzy. The French despised the Egyptian, now president of his country. By arming Algerian rebels intent on overthrowing French rule in Northern Africa, Nasser had positioned himself to incur France's wrath. With the British upset over Egypt's 1955 purchase of Czech weapons and Cairo's efforts to undermine the Baghdad Pact, the cornerstone of UK policy in the Middle East, Paris knew that it could recruit its former imperial adversary and plot Nasser's demise.[43]

In the fall of 1956, with the canal issue still unresolved, British and French leaders colluded with the Israelis, whose antipathy for Nasser exceeded that of the French. The resulting Sèvres Protocol called for Israel to attack its Arab enemy in late October 1956. France and the United Kingdom intended to use a Suez war as a pretext to intervene in Egypt and resolve the crisis in their favor. They aimed to depose Nasser, reestablish the West's control over the canal, and internationalize that commercial hub linking Western Europe and the area east of Suez.[44]

On October 29, 1956, Israeli Army planes dropped paratroopers at the Mitla Pass, near the Suez Canal. Such a move confused Egypt's High Command; no Egyptian troops patrolled that area of the Sinai Peninsula. Convinced that Tel Aviv's plan called for an initial feinting maneuver, military leaders in Cairo expected Israel to probe other Egyptian positions in the Sinai desert. To counter the Israeli flanking strategy, Nasser ordered his forces to cross the canal. He directed them to attack the Israelis in the northern part of the peninsula, southwest of the Gaza Strip.[45]

With another Middle Eastern war brewing, the Eisenhower administration strove to uphold the 1950 Tripartite Declaration, expecting that the United Kingdom and France would join Washington in preserving an Arab-Israeli truce. But when the United States (and the Soviet Union) rushed to the United Nations (UN) Security Council, accused Israel of violating the 1949 Armistice Agreement, and urged a return to the *status quo ante bellum*, London and Paris refused to censure Israel. The French and British thus betrayed their anti-Nasser intentions.[46]

In Tel Aviv, Prime Minister David Ben-Gurion turned down President Eisenhower's request not to take any "forceful initiative." The Israeli authorized retaliatory measures designed to cripple the Egyptian-supported *fedayeen*, Palestinian paramilitary groups responsible for the deaths of many Israelis. Saying that he wanted to "eliminate the Egyptian fedayeen bases in the Sinai Peninsula,"

Ben-Gurion invoked self-defense to justify Israel's attacks. The United States expressed concern; Israeli reprisals only agitated Arabs.[47]

Distracted by the upcoming presidential election and preoccupied with the concurrent Hungarian crisis, Ike warned of "risks of new Koreas." His administration would "use [the] full moral power of America" to prevent an escalation of hostilities into a regional war. *The New York Times* editorialized that "[t]he situation is of immense concern to the United States as well as to Britain and France because they are pledged to maintain the peace in the Middle East."[48]

The newspaper also reminded its readers of Washington's, London's, and Paris' "unilateral opposition to the use of force or threat of force between states in that area." But the United Kingdom and France refused to invoke the Tripartite Declaration. On October 30, 1956, Egypt and Israel received an Anglo-French ultimatum demanding that Egyptian and Israeli soldiers retire to positions ten miles from the Suez Canal Zone.[49]

Egypt's provocation, Israel's response, the British-French demand, and U.S. dismay seemed to signal yet another Cold-War crisis. Out of desperation, Cairo turned to Moscow to fend off the invaders. Opposed to Soviet intervention and Victorian-era bravado (especially in an era of decolonization), a peeved White House denounced the Franco-British secret plan to overthrow Nasser. In the words of Dulles, "this was the blackest day which has occurred in many years in the relations between England and France and the United States." He wondered "how the former relationship of trust and confidence could possibly be restored in view of these developments."[50]

His Middle East "strategy of delay" in shambles, President Eisenhower protested the UK-French coup de théâtre and asked London and Paris to "reconsider." According to biographer Stephen Ambrose, "[the president's] immediate decision, from which he never retreated one inch, was that the cabal could not be allowed to succeed." Ike cabled British Prime Minister Anthony Eden and French Premier Guy Mollet that "peaceful processes can and should prevail." Eden replied that "this is to be a temporary measure pending a settlement of all these [Near Eastern] problems."[51]

An incredulous Dulles dismissed such British nonsense. He would not endorse such an ill-conceived plot to unseat Nasser and take over the Suez Canal, not when the United States could expose dissent within the Soviet bloc. The U.S. secretary of state considered it "a great tragedy, when the world stands shocked at Soviet brutality in Hungary, that the world should also be confronted by similar action on the part of the British and French in Egypt." Under Anglo-French cover, the Soviet Union could attend to its security problems in Budapest. Powerless to respond without introducing the possibility of a Soviet-American nuclear war, the White House could only voice concern and spotlight the Red Army's sinister friendship doctrine—obey or be crushed.[52]

Much to Washington's consternation, any criticism of Soviet policy could now only smack of hypocrisy. British and French intervention, pathetically masked as lawful, would not convince Arab and Asian neutrals that Moscow stooped lower than its adversaries in preserving its interests. The Eisenhower administration recognized, moreover, that the confrontation between Nasser and the trio of Ben-Gurion, Mollet, and Eden intoxicated anti-colonial states seeking political independence after centuries of Western imperialism.

To pick up the pieces and extend U.S. influence in the Middle East, the White House would have to tread very carefully. It would need British advice on how to organize the region, hence it could not alienate London. Neither could it risk offending the Arab-Asian voting bloc in the United Nations. That would set American policy back and allow the Soviets to score a political victory while shoring up their East-European empire. President Eisenhower and his advisors would try, therefore, to overrule the French and British, as well as minimize a possible Third-World backlash that could hurt both short- and long-term U.S. interests.

Henry Cabot Lodge, America's UN representative, introduced a resolution at the Security Council on October 30 calling on Israel to remove its soldiers from Egyptian soil. Although the Latin American states praised U.S. efforts, France and Great Britain, whose support the United States needed to pressure the Soviets on Hungary, vetoed the measure. Eden characterized the American condemnation of the Jewish state as "a harsh demand." The U.S. resolution, he pointed out, offered no security guarantees to Israel.[53]

The French and British veto in the Security Council portended grave consequences for the Atlantic Alliance. The United States could not support France's and Great Britain's Near East policies. An irate Eisenhower remarked that "France and Britain have made a terrible mistake. Because they had such a poor case, they have isolated themselves from the good opinion of the world and it will take them many years to recover." In Ike's opinion, Paris and London failed to realize that "Nasser embodie[d] the emotional demands of the people of the area for independence and for 'slapping the white Man down.'"[54]

Soviet policies only compounded the president's diplomatic problems. Unable to control puppet governments in Poland and Hungary, the Soviet Union said it could tolerate independent Communist leaderships in each country if the Poles and Hungarians continued to adhere to Warsaw Treaty Organization directives (i.e., remained part of the Soviet sphere of influence). Poland acceded to Soviet security demands, but Hungary refused to give in. Defying Moscow, President Imre Nagy declared Hungary neutral. The Kremlin rebuffed Nagy. Without the political-military arrangements instituted by Joseph Stalin, the Soviet buffer zone in East-Central Europe could disappear. Moscow also knew that, if it accepted Hungarian neutrality, such a precedent could undermine, and perhaps Balkanize, the entire Soviet Empire.[55]

Events in Egypt provided Soviet leaders with an unexpected boon. The Suez crisis simplified their task of disciplining Hungary. In the Security Council, the Soviet Union and the United States said "Yes" to a resolution condemning Israel; the United Kingdom and France voted "No." With the Western alliance bickering over the Near East, Red Army tanks, artillery, and infantry could be moved into Budapest, and Soviet overlordship reconfirmed. Policymakers in Washington could not be pleased; they never expected the Anglo-French policy plunge into Suez to drown out their rhetorical calls for the "liberation" of Eastern Europe's "captive nations."

On October 31, the British and French bombed Egyptian airfields, as called for in *Musketeer Revise*, the military plan London and Paris devised in the fall of 1956. Since supporting his erstwhile friends could undermine American credibility worldwide, Eisenhower frowned upon UK-French strategy. The president could not support neo-colonialist tactics without incensing Arabs and Asians, hostile to any form of Western subjugation. The United States could only condemn London and Paris up to a point, however. Beyond that, the Soviet Union would benefit from serious NATO schisms.[56]

An outraged Eisenhower berated Anglo-French misdeeds and deplored Anglo-French disrespect for the Tripartite Declaration. The president even surmised that those states would try for a fait accompli. Once Ike had vented his frustration, he reconsidered. As a peace candidate in the 1952 election, Eisenhower had delivered on his promise to end America's painful ordeal in Korea. Three years removed from the Panmunjom truce talks, Eisenhower's second presidential campaign stressed the peacemaker theme once more. True to his rhetoric, Ike directed Dulles to explore measures that the United States could present at the United Nations. Unwilling to resort to war, Eisenhower and Dulles would try their luck in New York.[57]

In the Security Council, the Yugoslav delegation called for a special meeting of the UN General Assembly. Yugoslavia's draft resolution referred to the hitherto unused "Uniting for Peace" procedure. France and Great Britain questioned the proviso's legality and eventually opposed the UN proposal. The resolution passed nonetheless, thereby empowering the General Assembly to pass Security Council-like resolutions to prevent a worse calamity.[58]

That night, October 31, in a television and radio address to the American people, President Eisenhower proclaimed that Britain and France "were in error." He labeled the United Nations an appropriate forum for conflict resolution and concluded that "[t]he peace we seek and need means much more than mere absence of war. It means the acceptance of law, and the fostering of justice, in all the world." Ike's speech confirmed White House thinking: the United States would not declare war.[59]

On November 1, 1956, with unrest in Budapest and the Suez Canal a war zone, the world political situation seemed poised to explode into an East-West confrontation. An unsavory UN solution to the Suez crisis, Ike thought, could whittle away Washington's political, economic, and strategic advantages. The president told Dulles that the United States could not insert itself into the diplomatic crossfire. Expecting the Soviet Union to exploit the situation in the Middle East, Eisenhower emphasized that America "must lead" at the United Nations to prevent the Soviets "from seizing a mantle of world leadership through a false but convincing exhibition of concern for smaller nations."[60]

In conjunction with the Canadians, the Americans pushed for a UN solution. But the British and French would not end their invasion of Egypt, the victim in U.S. eyes. In response to intolerable UK defiance, the Eisenhower administration (sans Dulles, who fell ill) applied a financial squeeze to the vulnerable British. The president calculated that Whitehall would curtail its ill-considered cloak-and-dagger tactics once the Exchequer acknowledged that hostile U.S. economic diplomacy could bankrupt the UK treasury.[61]

As Ike expected, Chancellor of the Exchequer Harold Macmillan told Eden's cabinet on November 5, 1956, that a run on the pound and a lack of petroleum reserves precluded continued British involvement in the Suez War. Once a vociferous proponent of a military *face-à-face* with Nasser, Macmillan now recommended capitulation. The Americans would not provide Her Majesty's Government with a parachute made of dollars while UK paratroopers tried a pincer movement in the Nile Delta. The White House decreed instead that U.S. petrol sanctions be imposed on Great Britain and asked that International Monetary Fund credits be denied to London. With his country's currency and oil supply thus exposed, and with no other recourse than to cave in to economic coercion, the British prime minister surrendered to the United Nations.[62]

Eden's resignation in the wake of his titanic folly at Suez allowed for a U.S.-UK rapprochement. But Ike's victory would be merely Pyrrhic if he could not reverse the West's tattered reputation in the Middle East. With the British Empire in irreversible decline, only Washington could prop up pro-Western regimes in the region. Without staunch American support, the administration reasoned, the Soviet cordon sanitaire might expand southward. To prevent such a geopolitical disaster, the president and his secretary of state created the Eisenhower Doctrine as a complement to the Baghdad Pact.[63]

A New Course: The Eisenhower Doctrine

Ike could not support Britain and France's neo-colonial policy. It contradicted U.S. objectives outlined in NSC 5428 and could have prevented future American "containment" of the Soviet Union in the Middle East. Eisenhower defused the Suez crisis promptly so that world opinion could turn its attention back to Soviet brutalities in Hungary. His policy of compellence thereby ensured that U.S. Cold-War ideological imperatives would eclipse Anglo-French imperialism.

Following Suez, the United States stepped up its involvement in the region, yet, according to historian John Lewis Gaddis, "lost influence." As a beneficiary of the aborted plan to crush Nasser, the Soviet Union increased its power in the area and improved its reputation. This development alarmed Washington. U.S. Deputy Under Secretary of State Robert Murphy stated that "[i]t has become apparent that the achievement of a just and lasting peace in the Middle East would run counter to Soviet objectives. The Soviets are clearly planning a procession of events starting from reduction of Western influence and proceeding to the eventual incorporation of the nations of the area into the Soviet orbit." President Eisenhower worried that Moscow would undermine Middle Eastern regimes, even though several area governments (in Lebanon, Turkey, Iraq, Iran, and Israel) criticized Soviet support for radical Arab demands. The White House preferred to back these conservative, pro-West executives, since they could assure a regional equilibrium favorable to U.S. interests, or so Washington thought.[64]

With Great Britain and France incapable of resisting Soviet power, the United States would have to carry out policies that minimized the Kremlin's influence in the Middle East. In a January 1, 1957, meeting with members of Congress, a recovered Dulles emphasized "the importance of preventing the Soviet[s] from recouping [their global] position [after the Hungary fiasco] by a victory in the Middle East. [The secretary of state] stressed the importance of maintaining [U.S.] deterrent power, including a continued strengthening of local forces in various areas of the world." In a similar nod to Cold-War bipolarity, Eisenhower recalled "traditional Russian ambitions in the Middle East, the present impossibility of France and Britain acting as a counterweight, and the existing vacuum that must be filled by the United States before it is filled by Russia. [The president] cited Syrian developments as evidence of Russian intent." The Cold Warrior added that "the United States must put the entire world on notice that we are ready to move instantly if necessary."[65]

After Suez, Washington considered three options. It could join the Baghdad Pact, found a new organization "with somewhat broader Arab participants," or seek a declaration from Congress "somewhat similar to the Formosa Resolution." Such a statement could "support the Baghdad Pact and other activities in the area."[66]

Initially, the United States favored the Baghdad Pact. A December 14, 1956, Special National Intelligence Estimate (SNIE) noted that U.S. membership in the organization

> would have a considerable effect on dissipating the impression of U.S. indecision which, over the last two years, has discouraged the Baghdad Pact governments, weakened the will of friendly or uncommitted elements in other Arab states to stand up against Egyptian or Soviet-inspired anti-Western pressures, and encouraged greater boldness on the part of those seeking to undermine the Western position.

Yet Washington would benefit most by not joining the pact, a move that would uphold its anti-colonial credentials. "[B]y refusing to make a firm treaty commitment," the SNIE explained, America "would retain some extra room for maneuver in dealing with the Arab-Asian neutralists and with the USSR, and it might be in a better position to seek comprehensive accommodation with the forces of nationalism and anticolonialism in the Arab-Asian world."[67]

After careful evaluation, the Eisenhower administration passed on American membership in the Baghdad Pact. The State Department "does not favor the proposal, because the Pact has become so mixed up in Arab politics. Nasser opposes it, and more importantly [Saudi Arabia's] King Saud [America's most important Arab friend] does also," said Dulles. The secretary doubted the Senate would approve such a step anyway, since the United States would have to provide for Israel's defense.[68]

The Eisenhower Doctrine, announced in January 1957, thus resulted from a process of elimination. A necessary policy, it served as a "psychological" response to perceived Soviet gains in the Middle East. It provided a short-term answer until a detailed U.S. Near East strategy could be worked out. The Eisenhower Doctrine, notes scholar Ray Takeyh, "committed the United States to the conservative regimes in the ongoing inter-Arab struggle for hegemony. The new doctrine did not introduce any changes in America's objectives, but merely embraced a different set of local clients." As expected, pro-Western countries, such as Iraq and Iran, endorsed this "unilateral" policy, but some Arabs suspected a new round of Western imperialism despite American protests to the contrary.[69]

Imperial or not, the United States strove to deny its enemies, be they nationalists or Communists, oil from the Persian Gulf. After the Suez crisis, which paralyzed tanker traffic in the Suez Canal, newly constructed supertankers (initially built by the Japanese) carried vast quantities of Gulf crude on a safer journey around the Cape of Good Hope to Europe. To sustain this vital economic lifeline, Washington reconsidered NSC 5428. Via the Eisenhower Doctrine and NSC 5801, which in January 1958 confirmed the United States as a "status quo power" in the Middle East, Washington assured its allies in the region that it would not ignore potentially destabilizing Soviet incursions.[70]

While America established itself as a first-rate power in the Middle East, Ike's post-Suez policy floundered. Events in July 1958 (i.e., the coup d'état in Iraq, U.S. and UK intervention in Lebanon and Jordan, and concern over Kuwait's ability to prevent a Nasserite putsch and protect British- and American-owned oil reserves) rendered the Eisenhower Doctrine inoperative and irrelevant. Setbacks could not be blamed, moreover, on Soviet ruses. Arab nationalism, not Moscow-inspired communism, jeopardized American interests, a point Senator J. William Fulbright (D-Arkansas) harped on over and over during executive sessions of the Senate Foreign Relations committee. U.S. policy toward Iraq exemplified the White House's obsession with strategic concerns and insufficient attention to the roots of local unrest. American critics contended that such myopia exacerbated Middle Eastern tensions instead of alleviating them.[71]

Although very concerned about U.S. credibility, Washington recognized that its new Middle East policy would only further arouse Arabs determined to rid their lands of Western oppressors. Nasserism could not be minimized in the short term, despite President Eisenhower's belief that King Saud, the keeper of the Islamic holy cities Mecca and Medina, could serve as an alternative to the secular Egyptian president. Such thinking, albeit consistent with the administration's anti-communism, proved wishful, however, as Saud pursued an agenda, vis-à-vis Israel for example, incompatible with American policy. Thus, after July 1958, the White House preferred not to confront the immensely popular Nasser directly. A bellicose policy had only won America "the enmity of the Arab masses and played into the hands of the Soviets." Washington would henceforth stress cooperation with Egypt in lieu of provocation. If Cairo could not agree, then U.S.-Egyptian differences would be "stored in the icebox." The so-called icebox policy required no soldiers, quieted native anti-Americanism, and kept the United States out of inter-Arab rivalries.[72]

The turn toward an inconspicuous policy in 1958 brought a tumultuous era to an unspectacular close. As with most presidents, Eisenhower's international record proved mixed. His successes sparkled, none more than Suez. In that crisis, he exercised admirable restraint and statesmanship. The general's failures should not be dismissed, however, in a rush to celebrate what Eisenhower "revisionists" tout as sagacity. In their criticisms of Eisenhower's policies toward the Third World, various scholars refute the popular notion that the United States wisely propped up nationalistic anti-Soviet governments, thereby ensuring the preservation of U.S. regional and global interests. Ike's inability to differentiate between Middle Eastern nationalism and communism upset Iranians and many others ideologically inclined to side with the United States in the Cold War. Worst of all, the 1953 coup in Iran, and recourse elsewhere to similar oversimplification, initiated a nefarious reflex: the installation and heavy subsidization of repressive anti-Communist authoritarians whose murderous ways stained America's reputation in the all-important developing world, a prominent superpower battlefield, and led to a backlash.[73]

As independence movements continued to dismantle European empires, many Third-World nationalists evolved a virulent form of anti-Americanism whose origins stemmed, in part, from the implementation of the Eisenhower Doctrine. To his credit, the president recognized his mistake. Following the events of July 1958, he jettisoned the policy. The doctrine had remedied a short-term problem, perceived Soviet communism in the Middle East, but inspired revolutionaries to decry U.S. methods. Such thoughtlessness confirmed scholar Ronald Pruessen's contention that Ike's policies suffered from a common flaw: "short-run success and long-term disaster."[74]

Assessment

The *second* stage (1948–58) of U.S. expansion in the Persian Gulf witnessed a rigidifying of America's Cold-War policy and confirmed what historian Salim Yaqub calls the "radical transformation" of U.S. policy toward the Middle East since 1941. Events in Europe and Asia seemed to provide incontrovertible evidence of a Soviet assault upon Western values. Unfortunately for Washington, communism co-existed with indigenous nationalisms in many countries. This complication bewildered most especially the Eisenhower administration, whose intolerance of deviant (i.e., non-Western) political systems embroiled it in numerous situations where natives clamored for representation and sustenance, not Stalinism. In the Gulf, American responses to Saudi and Iranian demands for improved revenue, required so that these nations could modernize, varied. If the Cold War allowed flexibility, then the United States could show itself at least somewhat sympathetic to local needs (although on several occasions, in Algeria for example, it did not). Otherwise, the White House imposed its preference. Truman and Eisenhower even occasionally bullied their staunchest ally, the United Kingdom.[75]

U.S. behavior resulted in confrontations with fickle proxies (the Saudis over Buraimi), crotchety allies (the British over Iranian oil), and regional leaders suspicious of American motives (Nasser during Suez). In most cases, the United States increased its political and economic influence, if only because UK power plummeted. Although not directly affected by the Suez War, Gulf states, some of which (Saudi Arabia and Iran) feared an Egyptian build-up and loathed Nasser, acknowledged Washington's newly established prominence. Yet after that conflict, America's reputation declined somewhat.[76]

In examining this era (1948–58), the United States favored imperialism consistent with its budding informal empire in the Persian Gulf. American policies resembled those the British had relied on for decades. As Americans asserted themselves, they often purposely elbowed the region's long-time imperialists. Despite their professed aversion to imperialism, the Truman and Eisenhower administrations unashamedly took over various UK commitments in the Gulf and the Middle East. Whitehall grudgingly approved of the Americans inheriting their faltering position in Southwest Asia since Rule Britannia could not sustain it vigorously given UK financial difficulties and the recent "scuttle" of India, the so-called crown jewel of the Empire. To maintain their rump East of Suez imperium, the proud British resorted desperately to dubious measures, some of which the United States took part in, others it contested. This newfound ability to endorse or censor UK policy endowed the Americans with undeniable imperial power.

In removing Mossadeq, Washington and London interfered in Iranian politics so that someone more amenable to their interests, namely the Shah, could rule uncontested. These underhanded tactics, courtesy of the CIA, contravened Uncle Sam's repeated calls for liberty and U.S.-style democracy in the Third World. As such, the imposition of American will via Operation TPAJAX surely qualifies as an imperial gesture, even though it was covert and deniable. The same can be said of Washington's post-Suez policy, when it warned the Soviets off by way of the Eisenhower Doctrine. Before that, the United States countered the Soviet Union by pushing for the Baghdad Pact and supplying the Shah with extensive aid. These policies extended America's burgeoning client network.

Without explicitly aiming to do so, Washington behaved imperialistically. As historian John Lewis Gaddis argues, "[b]ecause of his tendency to *fret, hover, and meddle*—his inability to see when things were going well and need not be re-engineered—[Secretary of State] Dulles transformed his own country into the new imperial power in the Middle East in what he knew to be a post-imperial age." Cold-War imperatives mandated such conduct, or so Washington believed. While the Americans and Soviets accused one another of imperialism, they mimicked the insidious policies of past Great Powers rather well. Without question, Soviet brutality exceeded that of the United States, yet the case for U.S. imperialism, in the context of informal empire, seems irrefutable.[77]

In these years, America acquired new hegemonic interests in the Persian Gulf while safeguarding old ones. In 1950, Washington underwrote the Fifty-Fifty Agreement to please U.S. petroleum companies and the Saudis. During the Buraimi crisis, the White House sided with Riyadh so as not to jeopardize ARAMCO's concession. In 1954, the United States expanded its economic horizons when it secured access to Iranian oil. These deals and understandings exploited many local inhabitants, whose most valuable resource often brought them nothing while their leaders enriched themselves.

As U.S. influence in the Persian Gulf expanded, Washington often relied on contingent imperialism. In the case of the Fifty-Fifty Agreement, however, proposition P5 (The United States will not exercise any type of contingent imperialism if no threat to American hegemony and security exists) seems apropos. The Saudis only wanted what they considered equitable, as opposed to extravagant, royalties. They avoided talk of nationalization, a move that would have dramatically impacted U.S. economic and security interests in the region. Washington encouraged ARAMCO to grant Riyadh its wish and, in turn, absorbed the company's loss of profits. The satisfactory outcome kept America's de facto alliance with Saudi Arabia intact and preserved U.S. economic ascendancy.

American policymakers displayed no such charity when they authorized Operation TPAJAX. In that case, proposition P2 (The United States will exercise alliance contingent imperialism whenever a significant threat to American hegemony and security occurs, allies agree to join a U.S.-led venture or vice-versa, Washington can overcome any regional constraints, consensus exists within the executive, and no majority in Congress or critical segment of domestic opinion strongly opposes White House action) seems valid. The nationalization of Iranian oil set a precedent that others in the Persian Gulf might emulate. Mossadeq's flirtation with Communists only exacerbated this precarious situation for the West, which relied heavily on Gulf petroleum. The August 1953 coup thus relieved U.S.-UK anxieties. But their methods mirrored those of the Soviets, who ousted Czechoslovakia's democratic government in 1948 on account of its untrustworthiness. By endorsing the Shah unequivocally, America, contrary to its ideals, committed itself to dictatorship.

During the Buraimi crisis, the United States sided with another autocrat, the Saudi king, a move that satisfied ARAMCO and secured U.S. economic interests. According to historian Nathan Citino, Riyadh's oil ties to America, which dated to the 1930s, made Saudi Arabia "part of an informal American empire knitted together by private enterprise and corporate investment." But when London intervened in Buraimi, ending the Saudi-UK confrontation, the Eisenhower administration tacitly condoned British policy. Western European economic success demanded such a course given U.S. priorities in the Persian Gulf. As Washington supported, in turn, the Saudis and British, proposition P2 (i.e., alliance contingent imperialism) seems to explain American behavior. That the White House could maintain its beneficial position in the Gulf, while its Saudi partner and British ally bitterly feuded, confirms the advantageous role the United States played in the region in the 1950s and the "new kind of empire" it forged post-1945. This imperium emphasized an "American capitalist order," a more flexible system than Britain's protectionist sterling bloc. Such an order could accommodate both Saudi and British economic needs. Whitehall and the Saudi government upbraided the Americans, but neither gave up on them. Each knew it needed Uncle Sam, albeit for different reasons. Washington helped sustain the waxing British Empire while contributing to the enrichment of the Saudi monarchy.[78]

Although America assisted the British and Saudis, it declined to join the Baghdad Pact, an organization it fathered, even though the Soviets might overrun the U.S. economic and geostrategic position in the Middle East. In that case, proposition P3 (The United States will exercise proxy contingent imperialism whenever a significant or minor threat to American hegemony and security occurs, surrogates can preserve U.S. interests, Washington cannot overcome regional constraints, consensus may not exist within the executive, and a majority of Congress or critical segment of domestic opinion strongly opposes direct White House involvement) seems applicable. The White House left it up to the British to represent the West in an alliance repeatedly denounced by Nasser, whom the Americans courted in connection with the Arab-Israeli conflict. U.S. officials did participate in Baghdad Pact meetings but tried to keep as low a profile as possible.

Conversely, during the Suez crisis, President Eisenhower made sure the United States played a very visible role to prevent American association with Anglo-French imperialism. Yet, despite his denunciation of British-French policy, Ike utilized imperial methods, particularly economic coercion, along with assistance from the Canadians, to cow London and Paris. In that case, proposition P2 (i.e., alliance contingent imperialism) seems correct. With the British and French discredited in Arab eyes, America assumed the West's leadership mantle in the Middle East, which positioned Washington to exert greater influence in the Persian Gulf.

Without the events at Suez, the White House would likely have never proclaimed the Eisenhower Doctrine, an effort to shield Middle Eastern friends and protect U.S. economic interests by threatening intervention. In that case, proposition P1 (The United States will exercise unilateral contingent imperialism whenever a significant threat to American hegemony and security occurs, Washington can act alone or cannot rely on anyone else to secure its interests and can overcome any regional constraints, consensus exists within the executive, and no majority in Congress or critical segment of domestic opinion strongly opposes White House action) seems right. Despite Congressional approval, the doctrine proved a dud. But, notes historian Salim Yaqub, it "marked America's emergence as the dominant Western power in the Middle East, a role the United States continued to play long after the policy itself had been abandoned." The Eisenhower administration set a postwar precedent, moreover, with its Lebanon excursion. Unlike before, America did not hesitate to send soldiers to the Middle East to fulfil U.S. objectives.[79]

In this *second* stage (1948–58) of American expansion in the Persian Gulf, Washington alternated between alliance, proxy, and unilateral imperialism to preserve its hegemonic and security interests. Via these imperial policies, the United States established itself as a somewhat ruthless Great Power ready to oust whomever it disliked, whether friend or foe. Such perceived effrontery resulted in the kind of anti-Americanism that made Washington's position vulnerable to rhetorical and physical countermeasures in the following decades.

Notes

1. Donald Neff, *Fallen Pillars: U.S. Policy towards Palestine and Israel since 1945* (Washington, DC: Institute for Palestine Studies, 1995), 27–54, 196–99; George Lenczowski, *American Presidents and the Middle East* (Durham, NC: Duke University Press, 1990), 21–30; David E. Long, *The United States and Saudi Arabia: Ambivalent Allies* (Boulder, CO: Westview Press, 1985), 106; and Burton I. Kaufman, *The Arab Middle East and the United States: Inter-Arab Rivalry and Superpower Diplomacy* (New York: Twayne, 1996), 4–10. Quote can be found in Salim Yaqub, *Containing Arab Nationalism: The Eisenhower Doctrine and the Middle East* (Chapel Hill, NC: University of North Carolina Press, 2004), 25.

2. John Lewis Gaddis, *We Now Know: Rethinking Cold War History* (New York: Clarendon Press, 1997), 26–84; Thomas G. Paterson, *On Every Front: The Making and Unmaking of the Cold War*, rev. ed. (New York: W.W. Norton, 1992), 70–95; Melvyn P. Leffler, *The Specter of Communism: The United States and the Origins of the Cold War, 1917–1953* (New York: Hill & Wang, 1994); Michael J. Hogan, *The Marshall Plan: America, Britain, and the Reconstruction of Western Europe, 1947–1952* (Cambridge: Cambridge University Press, 1987); and Sergei N. Goncharov, John W. Lewis, and Xue Litai, *Uncertain Partners: Stalin, Mao, and the Korean War* (Stanford, CA: Stanford University Press, 1993). See also the 1998–99 Cable News Network (CNN) series, "Cold War": episode 3, "Marshall Plan"; episode 4, "Berlin Blockade"; and episode 5, "Korean War."

3. John Lewis Gaddis, *Strategies of Containment: A Critical Appraisal of Postwar American National Security Policy* (New York: Oxford University Press, 1982), 25–126, 352–53.

4. Lenczowski, *American Presidents and the Middle East*, 49; Gaddis, *Strategies of Containment*, 127–97, 353; and Gregory F. Treverton, *Covert Action: The Limits of Intervention in the Postwar World* (New York: Basic Books, 1987).

5. Thomas J. McCormick, *America's Half-Century: United States Foreign Policy during the Cold War* (Baltimore: Johns Hopkins University Press, 1989), 99 124.

6. Michael J. Cohen, *Fighting World War Three from the Middle East: Allied Contingency Plans, 1945–1954* (London: Frank Cass, 1997), 1–94. Quote can be found in Irene L. Gendzier, *Notes from the Minefield: United States Intervention in Lebanon and the Middle East, 1945–1958* (New York: Columbia University Press, 1997), 41–42.

7. Long, *The United States and Saudi Arabia*, 141–42; and Yong S. Lee, "Master and Servants: U.S.-East Asian Relations and the Tyranny of the Weak" (M.A. thesis, Ohio University, June 1995).

8. Long, *The United States and Saudi Arabia*, 5–8, 74–75; Parker T. Hart, *Saudi Arabia and the United States: Birth of a Security Partnership* (Bloomington, IN: Indiana University Press, 1998), 43–50; and Irvine H. Anderson, "The American Oil Industry and the Fifty-Fifty Agreement of 1950," in *Musaddiq, Iranian Nationalism, and Oil*, eds. James A. Bill and Wm. Roger Louis (Austin, TX: University of Texas Press, 1988), 145–46.

9. Michael A. Palmer, *Guardians of the Gulf: A History of America's Expanding Role in the Persian Gulf, 1833–1992* (New York: Free Press, 1992), 40–51.

10. Anderson, "The American Oil Industry and the Fifty-Fifty Agreement of 1950," 143–59; Long, *The United States and Saudi Arabia*, 15, 18–19; Daniel Yergin, *The Prize: The Epic Quest for Oil, Money & Power* (New York: Simon & Schuster, 1991), 431–33, 445–49; and Burton I. Kaufman, "Mideast Multinational Oil, U.S. Foreign Policy, and Antitrust: the 1950s," *Journal of American History* 63, no. 4 (March 1977): 945 46.

11. Yergin, *The Prize*, 447–48. Of the Fifty-Fifty deal, historian Nathan Citino notes that Washington "sought to assuage nationalist sentiment in producing countries [such as Saudi Arabia] through modest, judicious concessions administered privately by the oil corporations." Nathan J. Citino, *From Arab Nationalism to OPEC: Eisenhower, King Saud, and the Making of U.S.-Saudi Relations* (Bloomington, IN: Indiana University Press, 2002), 22. The Anglo-Persian Oil Company had renamed itself the Anglo-Iranian Oil Company.

12. Mary Ann Heiss, *Empire and Nationhood: The United States, Great Britain, and Iranian Oil, 1950–1954* (New York: Columbia University Press, 1997), 5–9.

13. Heiss, *Empire and Nationhood*, 15.

14. Heiss, *Empire and Nationhood*, 15; and Mark J. Gasiorowski, *U.S. Foreign Policy and the Shah: Building a Client State in Iran* (Ithaca, NY: Cornell University Press,

1991), 52–55. "In 1948," Gasiorowski writes (54), "the CIA began an operation code-named BEDAMN that was designed to undermine Soviet and Tudeh influence in Iran." See also James F. Goode, *The United States and Iran, 1946–51: The Diplomacy of Neglect* (New York: St. Martin's Press, 1989).

15. Heiss, *Empire and Nationhood*, 16–17.

16. Heiss, *Empire and Nationhood*, 17–19; and Gasiorowski, *U.S. Foreign Policy and the Shah*, 58–62.

17. Heiss, *Empire and Nationhood*, 18–19.

18. Heiss, *Empire and Nationhood*, 19–20.

19. Heiss, *Empire and Nationhood*, 38–44.

20. Heiss, *Empire and Nationhood*, 45–134; and Gasiorowski, *U.S. Foreign Policy and the Shah*, 62–67.

21. Heiss, *Empire and Nationhood*, 135–66; and Gasiorowski, *U.S. Foreign Policy and the Shah*, 67–71.

22. Heiss, *Empire and Nationhood*, 167–86. Contrary to the orthodox academic view, scholar Francis Gavin stresses the continuity between the policies of the Truman administration and those of his successor. He attributes this lack of change to balance-of-power—or structural—considerations that forced the United States to react a certain way regardless of who occupied the White House. See Francis J. Gavin, "Politics, Power, and U.S. Policy in Iran, 1950–1953," *Journal of Cold War Studies* 1, no. 1 (Winter 1999): 56–89.

23. Donald N. Wilber, "[CIA] Clandestine Service History: Overthrow of Premier Mossadeq of Iran, November 1952-August 1953," in *National Security Archive [Washington, D.C.] Electronic Briefing Book No. 28: The Secret CIA History of the Iran Coup*, ed. Malcolm Byrne (March 1954), iii–iv, http://www.gwu.edu/~nsarchiv/. As part of the same CIA history, see "Appendix A: Initial Operational Plan for TPAJAX as Cabled from Nicosia to Headquarters on 1 June 1953," "Appendix B: 'London' Draft of the TPAJAX Operational Plan," and "Appendix C: Foreign Office Memorandum of 23 July 1953 from British Ambassador [Roger] Makins to Assistant Under Secretary of State [Walter Bedell] Smith." Available through the *National Security Archive*. For more on the still classified CIA document, see "Secrets of History: The C.I.A. in Iran," *New York Times*, 16 April 2000, http://www.nytimes.com. For commentary on the document, see Mark Gasiorowski, "What's New on the Iran 1953 Coup in the New York Times Article (April 16, 2000, front page) and the Documents Posted on the Web," *National Security Archive Electronic Briefing Book No. 28*, 19 April 2000; and Reuel Marc Gerecht, "Blundering through History with the C.I.A.," *New York Times*, 23 April 2000, http://www.nytimes.com.

24. "Secrets of History." For a contemporary American assessment of the coup, see "Reversal in Iran," *New York Times*, 23 August 1953, in "Secrets of History." For an academic analysis of the coup, see Gasiorowski, *U.S. Foreign Policy and the Shah*, 72–84; Treverton, *Covert Action*, 44–83; and James A. Bill, *The Eagle and the Lion: The Tragedy of American-Iranian Relations* (New Haven, CT: Yale University Press, 1988), 51–97. For information on the post-coup period, see Bill, *The Eagle and the Lion*, 98–130; Gasiorowski, *U.S. Foreign Policy and the Shah*, 85–129; and Heiss, *Empire and Nationhood*, 187–220. For a concise overview of Anglo-Iranian-American relations in the 1950–54 period, see Heiss, *Empire and Nationhood*, 187–238.

25. Tore Tingvold Petersen, "Anglo-American Rivalry in the Middle East: The Struggle for the Buraimi Oasis, 1952–1957," *International History Review* 14, no. 1 (February 1992): 71; and Michael Donoghue, "The Buraimi Dispute and the Souring of Anglo-American-Saudi Relations, 1952–1956" (paper presented at the New England Historical Association's annual meeting, 17 October 1998), 1. For Oman's point of view on the crisis, see John C. Wilkinson, *The Imamate Tradition of Oman* (New York: Cam-

bridge University Press, 1987), 290–95. For the perspective of an American diplomat then stationed in Saudi Arabia, see Hart, *Saudi Arabia and the United States*, 56–67.

26. Petersen, "Anglo-American Rivalry in the Middle East," 71–74; and Donoghue, "The Buraimi Dispute," 1–6. First quote can be found in Long, *The United States and Saudi Arabia*, 105. Second and third quotes can be found in Citino, *From Arab Nationalism to OPEC*, 23, 27. On the Anglo-American rivalry in Saudi Arabia, see Long, *The United States and Saudi Arabia*, 103–5. Citino argues (22), however, that "[d]espite British suspicions of U.S. connivance with the Saudis, Anglo-American differences in Arabia and the Gulf were actually much narrower than naked economic competition, and instead involved a controversy over how best to preserve the postwar petroleum order." On the U.S. role in that order, see Robert Vitalis, "Black Gold, White Crude: An Essay on American Exceptionalism, Hierarchy, and Hegemony in the Gulf," *Diplomatic History* 26, no. 2 (Spring 2002): 185–213.

27. Petersen, "Anglo-American Rivalry in the Middle East," 74–75; Donoghue, "The Buraimi Dispute," 7–9; and Citino, *From Arab Nationalism to OPEC*, 27–36. According to Citino (31–32), "[t]he crisis over Buraymī erupted during a sensitive period in U.S.-Saudi relations. American policy makers had been debating whether the kingdom would receive military aid, which negotiators had held out as an inducement for the Saudis to renew the Dhahran air base agreement."

28. Petersen, "Anglo-American Rivalry in the Middle East," 75–76.

29. Petersen, "Anglo-American Rivalry in the Middle East," 77–78.

30. Petersen, "Anglo-American Rivalry in the Middle East," 78–80. For an analysis of U.S.-UK-Egyptian relations in the first decade of the Cold War, see Peter L. Hahn, *The United States, Great Britain, and Egypt, 1945–1956: Strategy and Diplomacy in the Early Cold War* (Chapel Hill, NC: University of North Carolina Press, 1991), 242–47.

31. Petersen, "Anglo-American Rivalry in the Middle East," 81–83.

32. Petersen, "Anglo-American Rivalry in the Middle East," 83.

33. Petersen, "Anglo-American Rivalry in the Middle East," 83–84; Donoghue, "The Buraimi Dispute," 10; and Long, *The United States and Saudi Arabia*, 36–37, 79–80. On America's difficulties with Cold-War clients, see Lee, "Master and Servants." For the nexus between cancellation of Point IV assistance and the renewal of the Dhahran lease, see Hart, *Saudi Arabia and the United States*, 64–65.

34. Petersen, "Anglo-American Rivalry in the Middle East," 84–86; and Donoghue, "The Buraimi Dispute," 10–13. For an analysis of the Buraimi crisis from 1953 until 1955, see Citino, *From Arab Nationalism to OPEC*, 39–87.

35. Frederick W. Axelgard, "U.S. Policy toward Iraq, 1946–1958" (Ph.D. dissertation, The Fletcher School of Law and Diplomacy, Tufts University, April 1988), 1–20; and Phebe Marr, *The Modern History of Iraq* (Boulder, CO: Westview Press, 1985), 95.

36. On Arab nationalism, see L. Carl Brown, *International Politics and the Middle East: Old Rules, Dangerous Game* (Princeton, NJ: Princeton University Press, 1984), 139–69; and Bernard Lewis, *The Shaping of the Modern Middle East* (New York: Oxford University Press, 1994), 71–98.

37. Marr, *The Modern History of Iraq*, 96–108.

38. Marr, *The Modern History of Iraq*, 102–6; Axelgard, "U.S. Policy toward Iraq, 1946–1958," 21–74. On U.S. policy regarding Egypt, see Hahn, *The United States, Great Britain, and Egypt, 1945–1956*, 243. On the American inability to cope with the region's internal dynamics, especially political change, see Charles A. Kupchan, "American Globalism in the Middle East: The Roots of Regional Security Policy," *Political Science Quarterly* 103, no. 4 (1988): 585–611.

39. Gaddis, *We Now Know*, 169–72; Michael Cohen, *Fighting World War Three from the Middle East*, 239–323; Axelgard, "U.S. Policy toward Iraq, 1946–1958," 107–20; Gendzier, *Notes from the Minefield*, 151–54; and Robert O. Freedman, *Moscow*

and the Middle East: Soviet Policy since the Invasion of Afghanistan (Cambridge: Cambridge University Press, 1991), 15–18.

40. Axelgard, "U.S. Policy toward Iraq, 1946–1958," 120–94; Marr, *The Modern History of Iraq*, 118–19; Keith Kyle, *Suez* (New York: St. Martin's Press, 1991), 57–60; Aysegül Sever, "The Compliant Ally? Turkey and the West in the Middle East 1954–58," *Middle Eastern Studies* 34, no. 2 (April 1998): 73–80; and Ara Sanjian, "The Formulation of the Baghdad Pact," *Middle Eastern Studies* 33, no. 2 (April 1997): 226–66.

41. Axelgard, "U.S. Policy toward Iraq, 1946–1958," 172–94. On project Alpha, see Kyle, *Suez*, 56–57.

42. Robert R. Bowie, "Eisenhower, Dulles, and the Suez Crisis," in *Suez 1956: The Crisis and Its Consequences*, eds. W.M. Roger Louis and Roger Owen (Oxford: Clarendon Press, 1989), 192–96; Louis L. Gerson, *John Foster Dulles* (New York: Cooper Square Publishers, 1967), 279–82; Gaddis, *We Now Know*, 171–72; Mohamed H. Heikal, *Cutting the Lion's Tail: Suez through Egyptian Eyes* (London: Andre Deutsch, 1986), xiii; Michael Brecher and Patrick James, *Crisis and Change in World Politics* (Boulder, CO: Westview Press, 1986), 77; and Gendzier, *Notes from the Minefield*, 157. Quote can be found in Robert Dallek, *The American Style of Foreign Policy: Cultural Politics and Foreign Affairs* (New York: Oxford University Press, 1983), 201. In a December 23, 1929, speech at the British House of Commons, Anthony Eden said: "If the Suez Canal is our back door to the East, it is the front door to Europe of Australia, New Zealand and India. If you like to mix your metaphors it is, in fact, the swing-door of the British Empire, which has got to keep continually revolving if our communications are to be what they should." The canal held similar strategic importance for the French. Quoted in Kyle, *Suez*, 7.

43. Albert Hourani, *A History of the Arab Peoples* (Cambridge, MA: Belknap Press, 1991), 365–67; Amin Hewedy, "Nasser and the Crisis of 1956," in *Suez 1956*, 161–72; and Keith Kyle, "Britain and the Crisis, 1955–1956," in *Suez 1956*, 103–30. French and UK antipathy for and suspicion of Nasser intensified in the months previous to Egyptian nationalization of the Suez Canal. This trend continued once Cairo decided to deny Paris and London any control over the waterway. See Maurice Vaïsse, "France and the Suez Crisis," in *Suez 1956*, 131–43. Scholar Keith Kyle notes that Middle Eastern oil "was shipped to Europe through the Suez Canal which, though popularly thought of in terms of passenger liners and general commerce, was in the course of becoming a virtual adjunct of the oil industry." Kyle, *Suez*, 7.

44. Mordechai Bar-On, "David Ben-Gurion and the Sèvres Collusion," in *Suez 1956*, 145–60. Engaging in "pseudo diplomacy," the Western powers unsuccessfully tried to wrest control of the canal from Nasser, whose political astuteness trumped them. See Gerson, *John Foster Dulles*, 282–94.

45. Bar-On, "David Ben-Gurion and the Sèvres Collusion," 155–56; and Heikal, *Cutting the Lion's Tail*, 177–78.

46. Kyle, *Suez*, 36; Douglas Little, "Gideon's Band: America and the Middle East since 1945," *Diplomatic History* 18, no. 4 (Fall 1994): 518; John C. Campbell, "The Soviet Union, the United States, and the Twin Crises of Hungary and Suez," in *Suez 1956*, 245; and Bowie, "Eisenhower, Dulles, and the Suez Crisis," 208.

47. Quotes can be found in Edwin L. Dale, Jr., "Americans May Leave," *New York Times*, 29 October 1956, 1. See also Stephen E. Ambrose, *Eisenhower: Soldier and President* (New York: Simon and Schuster, 1990), 424; and Moshe Brilliant, "Tel Aviv Declares Aim Is to Smash Egyptian Commando Bases," *New York Times*, 30 October 1956, 1.

48. First and second quotes can be found in "President to Continue to Seek World Peace," *New York Times*, 30 October 1956, 5. Third quote can be found in "Israel and Egypt," *New York Times*, 30 October 1956, 36.

49. Quote can be found in "2 Statements Explain West's Mideast Policy," *New York Times*, 30 October 1956, 3.

50. Quotes can be found in C. Burke Elbrick, Memorandum, 30 October 1956, *Foreign Relations of the United States* [hereafter *FRUS*], 1955–1957, 16, *Suez Crisis 26 July-31 December 1956* (Washington, DC: Government Printing Office, 1990), 867. According to historian Stephen Ambrose, Secretary of State Dulles "speculated that [the British and French] must have convinced themselves that in the end the United States would have to give its grudging approval, and support." Ambrose, *Eisenhower*, 424. On the consistency of U.S. policy regarding the United Kingdom and the Middle East from 1953 to 1956, see Steven Z. Freiberger, *Dawn Over Suez: The Rise of American Power in the Middle East, 1953–1957* (Chicago: Ivan R. Dee, 1992), 160. American policy could be traced back to National Security Council (NSC) Document Number 155/1 (NSC 155/1), approved on July 9, 1953, and later restated in NSC 5428 in 1954. See Freiberger, *Dawn Over Suez*, 53–54, 93–94. On NSC 5428, see *FRUS*, 1952–1954, 9, Part 1, *The Near and Middle East* (Washington, DC: Government Printing Office, 1986), 525–36.

51. First and third quotes can be found in Ambrose, *Eisenhower*, 424, 425. Second quote can be found in James Reston, "President in Plea: Bids Allies Hold Back Troops—Halt in Aid to Israel Planned," *New York Times*, 31 October 1956, 1. Fourth quote can be found in Message From President Eisenhower to Prime Minister Eden and Prime Minister Mollet, 30 October 1956, *FRUS*, 1955–1957, 16: 866. Fifth quote can be found in Message From Prime Minister Eden to President Eisenhower, 30 October 1956, *FRUS*, 1955–1957, 16: 872. According to scholar Wm. Roger Louis, Eisenhower "controlled" U.S. policy throughout the Suez crisis. Dulles followed the president's directives, though the secretary of state "agreed in principle and in detail with Eisenhower." Wm. Roger Louis, "Dulles, Suez, and the British," in *John Foster Dulles and the Diplomacy of the Cold War*, ed. Richard H. Immerman (Princeton, NJ: Princeton University Press, 1990), 135. That Ike exercised full control over U.S. foreign policy during the crisis should not surprise since he acted in similar fashion on numerous other occasions. See, for example, Richard H. Immerman, "Confessions of an Eisenhower Revisionist: An Agonizing Reappraisal," *Diplomatic History* 14, no. 3 (Summer 1990): 319–42; Fred I. Greenstein, "The Hidden-Hand Presidency: Eisenhower as Leader: A 1994 Perspective," *Presidential Studies Quarterly* 24, no. 2 (Spring 1994): 233–41; and Anna Kasten Nelson, "The 'Top of Policy Hill': President Eisenhower and the National Security Council," *Diplomatic History* 7, no. 4 (Fall 1983): 307–26. On Ike's "principled approach" to the crisis, see Cole C. Kingseed, *Eisenhower and the Suez Crisis of 1956* (Baton Rouge, LA: Louisiana State University Press, 1995), 90–91.

52. Quote can be found in Elbrick Memorandum, 30 October 1956, 868. See also Elbrick Memorandum of a Conversation, October 30, 1956, *FRUS*, 1955–1957, 16: 876. Studies of U.S.-Hungarian relations indicate that the United States never intended to use force to pry Hungary from the Soviet sphere of influence. See Jason George, "The U.S. and the Hungarian Revolution of 1956" (seminar paper, Ohio University, March 1994). According to scholar John Campbell, each superpower respected the other's interest in rectifying a serious and potentially dangerous intra-bloc breach. Campbell, "The Soviet Union, the United States, and the Twin Crises of Hungary and Suez."

53. Memorandum of a Telephone Conversation [transcribed by Phyllis D. Bernau] Between the Secretary of State in Washington and the Representative at the United Nations (Lodge) in New York, 31 October 1956, *FRUS*, 1955–1957, 16: 887. Quote can be found in Anthony Eden, *Full Circle* (Boston: Houghton Mifflin, 1960), 594–95.

54. First quote can be found in Letter From President Eisenhower to Swede Hazlett, 2 November 1956, *FRUS*, 1955–1957, 16: 944. Second quote can be found in Andrew J. Goodpaster Memorandum of a Conference With the President, 31 July 1956, *FRUS*,

1955–1957, 16: 64. See also Kingseed, *Eisenhower and the Suez Crisis of 1956*, 100–101. In historian Lawrence Kaplan's opinion, "[t]here was an element of hypocrisy in the American posture that was almost as obvious as the atavistic gunboat diplomacy of the French and British. While President Eisenhower summoned familiar isolationist and anticolonial sentiments to denounce the allies, the administration's concern was more over the damage that the abortive Anglo-French invasion did to anticommunist [i.e., NATO] unity than over the integrity of Third World territory." Lawrence S. Kaplan, *NATO and the United States, Updated Edition: The Enduring Alliance* (New York: Twayne, 1994), 66. According to one U.S. participant, "[a]nti-colonialism was rampant in post-World War II American official and private thinking." Hermann Frederick Eilts, "Reflections on the Suez Crisis: Security in the Middle East," in *Suez 1956*, 355.

55. Campbell, "The Soviet Union, the United States, and the Twin Crises of Hungary and Suez," 233–43; and Gaddis, *We Now Know*, 208–11.

56. Campbell, "The Soviet Union, the United States, and the Twin Crises of Hungary and Suez," 245; Bowie, "Eisenhower, Dulles, and the Suez Crisis," 207–14; and Frank Ninkovich, *Modernity and Power: A History of the Domino Theory in the Twentieth Century* (Chicago: University of Chicago Press, 1994), 221. On that day, Dulles said: "For many years we [the United States] have been in the awkward position of trying to ride two horses—our Western allies with their colonial policy, and the nationalism of southeastern Asia. For the first time, we stand apart from British imperialism." Quoted in Ninkovich, *Modernity and Power*, 221, n40. But the Joint Chiefs of Staff "urged the United States to support British military action to prevent Egyptian control of the Suez Canal." Anna Kasten Nelson, "History as a Period Piece?" *Diplomatic History* 18, no. 4 (Fall 1994): 613. See also Kingseed, *Eisenhower and the Suez Crisis of 1956*, 108–9. Historian Robert McMahon notes that every U.S. administration in the post-World War II era has been concerned with the credibility of American power. See Robert J. McMahon, "Credibility and World Power: Exploring the Psychological Dimension in Postwar American Diplomacy," *Diplomatic History* 15, no. 4 (Fall 1991): 455–71.

57. Goodpaster Memorandum, *FRUS*, 1955–1957, 16: 873; and S. Everett Gleason Memorandum, 302d Meeting of the National Security Council, 1 November 1956, *FRUS*, 1955–1957, 16: 914–16. It is more than likely that Eisenhower and Dulles dreaded a public backlash that surely would have accompanied any executive authorization for U.S. GIs to wage war on America's allies. One political scientist explains how the two were "pragmatists," who shunned public input into foreign-policymaking but kept careful tabs on public opinion's support or lack thereof for administration policies. He also points out that in another high profile crisis, the first Quemoy-Matsu crisis (1954–55), the president and his secretary of state favored an initial recourse to the United Nations so that political momentum could be built up if ever the United States chose to fight. See Douglas C. Foyle, "Public Opinion and Foreign Policy: Elite Beliefs as a Mediating Variable," *International Studies Quarterly* 41, no. 1 (March 1997): 141–69.

58. Terence Robertson, *Crisis: The Inside Story of the Suez Conspiracy* (New York: Atheneum, 1965), 171–72; and Memorandum of a Telephone Conversation [transcribed by Bernau] Between the Secretary of State in Washington and the Representative at the United Nations (Lodge) in New York, 31 October 1956, *FRUS*, 1955–1957, 16: 896–97.

59. First quote can be found in Dwight D. Eisenhower, *Waging Peace (1956–1961)* (New York: Doubleday, 1965), 81. Lodge informed Eisenhower that "never has there been such a tremendous acclaim [in the United Nations] for the President's policy." Eisenhower, *Waging Peace*, 81. Second quote can be found in Ambrose, *Eisenhower*, 427.

60. Quotes can be found in Memorandum by the President, 1 November 1956, *FRUS*, 1955–1957, 16: 924, 924n. For an analysis of the NSC meeting that preceded

Ike's memorandum and the president's use of the NSC as a tool of crisis management, see Kingseed, *Eisenhower and the Suez Crisis of 1956*, 103–7, 109.

61. Diane B. Kunz, "The Importance of Having Money: The Economic Diplomacy of the Suez Crisis," in *Suez 1956*, 215–32; Diane B. Kunz, "When Money Counts and Doesn't: Economic Power and Diplomatic Objectives," *Diplomatic History* 18, no. 4 (Fall 1994): 457–58; and Kyle, *Suez*, 464–68. On how states make use of economics, see David A. Baldwin, *Economic Statecraft* (Princeton, NJ: Princeton University Press, 1985). The Canadians, under the leadership of Foreign Minister Lester B. Pearson, and the Americans drew upon their respective "political comparative advantage" to resolve the crisis. See Marc J. O'Reilly, "Following Ike? Explaining Canadian-US Co-operation during the 1956 Suez Crisis," *Journal of Commonwealth & Comparative Politics* 35, no. 3 (November 1997): 75–107. See also Marc James O'Reilly, "Dudley Do-Right and Friends: Lester B. Pearson, Canada, and the 1956 Suez Crisis" (M.A. thesis, Ohio University, August 1995).

62. Yergin, *The Prize*, 479–98; Kyle, *Suez*, 466–67, 469–70; Kingseed, *Eisenhower and the Suez Crisis of 1956*, 122–23; Kunz, "The Importance of Having Money," 226–27; Freiberger, *Dawn Over Suez*, 190–91; and D.R. Thorpe, *Selwyn Lloyd* (London: Jonathan Cape, 1989), 251. Eden pressured Mollet to accept a cease-fire as well, which the Frenchman reluctantly did.

63. Citino writes that "[f]rom the reoccupation of Buraymī through the Suez crisis, the U.S. and Britain attempted to preserve the postwar petroleum order in sharply different ways. While the Eisenhower administration relied on private diplomacy to pacify oil-producing governments, Great Britain reinforced its colonial relationships in the Gulf and resorted to collusion and war to defend its economic interests. During the Suez crisis, these divergent approaches threatened to break the Anglo-American partnership, but Eisenhower's aggressive actions to restore Europe's oil supplies revealed his priorities in the Middle East and reflected the allies' common stake in the postwar petroleum order." Citino, *From Arab Nationalism to OPEC*, 110.

64. First quote can be found in Gaddis, *We Now Know*, 173–76. Second quote can be found in Deputy Under Secretary Murphy, "U.S. Views on Problems of Hungary and the Middle East," *Department of State Bulletin* 35, no. 911 (10 December 1956), 911.

65. Quotes can be found in L. Arthur Minnich, Jr., Memorandum of a Meeting, 1 January 1957, *FRUS*, 1955–1957, 12, *Near East Region; Iran; Iraq* (Washington, DC: Government Printing Office, 1991), 432–34. On bipolarity, see John Lewis Gaddis, *The Long Peace: Inquiries into the History of the Cold War* (New York: Oxford University Press, 1987), 215–45. On Cold Warriors, see H.W. Brands, *The Devil We Knew: Americans and the Cold War* (New York: Oxford University Press, 1993).

66. U.S. Delegation to the North Atlantic Council Ministerial Meeting Memorandum of a Conversation, 10 December 1956, *FRUS*, 1955–1957, 12: 399–400.

67. Quotes can be found in "Probable Consequences of US Adherence or Non-Adherence to the Baghdad Pact," Special National Intelligence Estimate–SNIE 30-7-56, 14 December 1956, *FRUS*, 1955–1957, 12: 404, 408–9. See also "U.S. Support for Baghdad Pact," *Department of State Bulletin*, 10 December 1956, 918.

68. Andrew J. Goodpaster Memorandum of a Conference with the President, 20 December 1956, *FRUS*, 1955–1957, 12: 415. Quote can be found in that document. For U.S. views on King Saud, see Citino, *From Arab Nationalism to OPEC*, 120.

69. Memorandum From the Director of the National Security Council Secretariat ([Marion W.] Boggs) to the National Security Council Planning Board, 5 September 1957, *FRUS*, 1955–1957, 12: 577–82; Thomas G. Paterson, *Meeting the Communist Threat: Truman to Reagan* (New York: Oxford University Press, 1988), 159–90; and Cecil V. Crabb, Jr., *The Doctrines of American Foreign Policy: Their Meaning, Role, and Future* (Baton Rouge, LA: Louisiana State University Press, 1982), 153–76. First

and third quotes can be found in Crabb, *The Doctrines of American Foreign Policy*, 165, 175. Crabb refers to the Ike Doctrine as an "extension" of the Truman Doctrine to the Middle East. Second quote can be found in Ray Takeyh, *The Origins of the Eisenhower Doctrine: The US, Britain and Nasser's Egypt, 1953–57* (New York: St. Martin's Press, 2000), 152. Robert Bowie, the director of the State Department's Policy Planning Staff, criticized the Eisenhower Doctrine as hypocritical. Kyle, *Suez*, 528. For an analysis of the Eisenhower Doctrine, see Takeyh, *The Origins of the Eisenhower Doctrine*, 142–59.

70. Yergin, *The Prize*, 496–97. Quote can be found in Gendzier, *Notes from the Minefield*, 366. In the advent of another world war, Eisenhower believed Washington and Moscow would be "determined that the other side not have access to the [Middle East's] oil and riches." Quote can be found in Douglas MacArthur, II, Memorandum to the Acting Secretary of State, 14 November 1956, *FRUS*, 1955–1957, 12: 322–23. According to Citino, America "would either have to adjust its policies to the reality of Arab nationalism and get behind development plans proposed by Arabs and non-Arabs for sharing the region's oil wealth, or assume the British mantle as enforcer of the postwar petroleum order. Eisenhower opted for the second alternative, and this decision proved much more important for defining the future U.S. role in the Middle East than his earlier one to halt the aggressors at Suez." Citino, *From Arab Nationalism to OPEC*, 119.

71. Gendzier, *Notes from the Minefield*, 367–70; Donald Neff, *Warriors at Suez: Eisenhower Takes America into the Middle East in 1956* (Brattleboro, VT: Amana Books, 1988), 438–43; Crabb, *The Doctrines of American Foreign Policy*, 186–92; Douglas Little, "His Finest Hour? Eisenhower, Lebanon, and the 1958 Middle East Crisis," *Diplomatic History* 20, no. 1 (Winter 1996): 27–54; and N.J. Ashton, "'A Great New Venture'?–Anglo-American Cooperation in the Middle East and the Response to the Iraqi Revolution July 1958," *Diplomacy & Statecraft* 4, no. 1 (March 1993): 59–89.

72. Yaqub, *Containing Arab Nationalism*, 237–38. Quotes can be found in Chester J. Pach, Jr., and Elmo Richardson, *The Presidency of Dwight D. Eisenhower* (Lawrence, KS: University Press of Kansas, 1991), 194–95. Historian Salim Yaqub argues (22) that "[t]he struggle over the Eisenhower Doctrine was largely a moral conflict, but one that occurred within a shared moral framework. The United States and the Nasserist movement each proclaimed the virtues of national liberation, political independence, economic empowerment, and international harmony, but they disagreed over when and where those values were at stake. . . . Theirs was a clash of interests and priorities, not of civilizations." On U.S.-Saudi relations, see Citino, *From Arab Nationalism to OPEC*, 122–28. According to Citino (128), "For Eisenhower, courting Sa'ūd was not just a strategy for containing communism, but was also a way to render palatable to Arab and Muslim countries the Anglo-American rapprochement that was essential to restoring the postwar petroleum order."

73. Robert A. Divine, *Eisenhower and the Cold War* (New York: Oxford University Press, 1981); Ambrose, *Eisenhower*; Robert J. McMahon, "Eisenhower's Failure in the Third World," in *Major Problems in American Foreign Policy, Volume II: Since 1914*, 3rd ed., edited by Thomas G. Paterson (Lexington, MA: D.C. Heath, 1989), 480–96; Stephen G. Rabe, "Eisenhower Revisionism: A Decade of Scholarship," *Diplomatic History* 17, no. 1 (Winter 1993): 97–115; and Paterson, *Meeting the Communist Threat*, 159–90.

74. According to historian Douglas Little, Eisenhower recognized that U.S. policy could open a Pandora's Box. See Little, "His Finest Hour?" 46. Ronald Pruessen's quote can be found in Robert A. Divine, "John Foster Dulles: What You See Is What You Get," *Diplomatic History* 15, no. 2 (Spring 1991): 285.

75. Lenczowski, *American Presidents and the Middle East*, 7–66; and Palmer, *Guardians of the Gulf*, 52–81. Quote can be found in Yaqub, *Containing Arab Nationalism*, 23. Yaqub writes (23) that "[i]n 1941 the United States had minimal political contact

with Middle Eastern countries; by late 1956 American officials believed that only the United States could keep the region from falling under Soviet domination."

76. For an analysis of U.S.-UK-Egyptian relations in this era, see Hahn, *The United States, Great Britain, and Egypt, 1945–1956*, 240–47. Yaqub notes that "[t]he Americans wanted the Arabs to be conciliatory toward Zionism and European imperialism but partisan in the Cold War. The Nasserists insisted on their right to make deals with the communist bloc even as they demanded U.S. support for the Arab positions against Zionism and imperialism." Yaqub, *Containing Arab Nationalism*, 20.

77. Gaddis, *We Now Know*, 176. Italics in original.

78. Quotes can be found in Citino, *From Arab Nationalism to OPEC*, 4.

79. Yaqub, *Containing Arab Nationalism*, 1.

Chapter 4

Assists and Reformulations: 1959–72

In the third stage (1959–72) of its postwar involvement in the Persian Gulf, the United States generally kept a low profile. Washington either opted for diplomacy or relied on friends to advance U.S. interests in the region. The country's priorities lay elsewhere.

In the previous stage (1948–58), America mixed acquiescence with temerity. It followed Whitehall's lead in Iran, for example, but upstaged the British during the Suez War. In a post-colonial age, London struggled to maintain its imperial preferences. Overburdened and underfunded, Her Majesty's Government desperately tried to postpone, if not reverse, an ignoble retreat from empire. Washington seemed torn. It encouraged self-determination in the so-called Third World, yet expressed dismay at some of its consequences. Events in Iran, Egypt, Iraq, and Lebanon confused the White House. President Dwight D. Eisenhower and his advisors criticized Great Britain's anachronistic methods, but could not offer an effective alternative to UK heavy-handedness. The Baghdad Pact and the Eisenhower Doctrine proved woefully inadequate. Neither could overcome Egyptian President Gamal Abdel Nasser's political-cultural appeal to Arabs everywhere.

As the Eisenhower administration entered its twilight years, the Middle East underwent ideological convulsions that polarized the entire region. In 1958, a politically fragile Syria united with Egypt, the vanguard of a reincarnated Arab nationalism. The United Arab Republic (UAR) stirred passions, but could not extricate most Arabs from their poverty. Unlike Damascus, Baghdad, in a renewal of its historic competition with Cairo, eschewed Nasserist fervor. Abd al-Karim Qasim, who overthrew Iraq's Hashemite monarchy in July 1958, infuriated Nasserites when he repressed the country's Arab nationalists and Ba'thists in a bid to consolidate his power. As a result of antipathy between Baghdad and Cairo, an Arab Cold War evolved. This clash corroded area politics.[1]

In the following decade, Egypt tried to stamp its will upon the region. While Syria (which seceded from the UAR in 1961) and even Iraq approved of Nasser's pan-Arabism, they mistrusted the Egyptian president's intentions. Quarrels among Arab secular republicans hardly reassured the Middle East's prominent monarchs, whose conservatism Cairo, Damascus, and Baghdad detested. The royal families of Saudi Arabia, Iran, and Jordan sought to forge a common front to counter their ideological opponents and thus preserve their rule. Each confrontation between the Egyptian-inspired radicals, who preached Arab socialism, and the Saudi-led moderates, who preferred their brand of conservative authoritarianism, could reward one camp with a potentially decisive propaganda victory.[2]

In 1961, Qasim threatened the newly independent Gulf emirate Kuwait with invasion. The next year, Nasser sided with the republicans in the Yemeni civil war. Events in June 1967 quelled inter-Arab rivalries, however. Israel's preemptive strike into Arab lands threw Nasserites, Ba'thists, and royalists together. In a series of audacious maneuvers, their common enemy seized the West Bank from Jordan, the Golan Heights from Syria, and Gaza and the Sinai from Egypt. Israeli military prowess outraged Arabs, who clamored for an immediate redress of the situation. While Nasser and his newfound allies plotted their revenge, in 1968 the British announced their impending withdrawal from the Persian Gulf. London's exit prompted Washington to devise a measured response that preserved American geopolitical and commercial assets at a time when the Vietnam War raged.

While the balance of power in the Middle East shifted in the 1958–72 period, the Cold War entered a most dangerous phase. In 1959, Fidel Castro ousted Fulgencio Batista, an unpopular and corrupt U.S. proxy. Due to American resistance and provocation (to wit, the failed 1961 Bay of Pigs invasion), this nationalist revolution in Cuba metamorphosed into a Marxist regime that unsettled the Americas. In October 1962, President John F. Kennedy jolted his fellow citizens when he announced the discovery of Soviet missiles on the Caribbean island where another American risk taker, Theodore Roosevelt, had famously charged up San Juan Hill in 1898. The ensuing Cuban Missile crisis terrified Communists and capitalists alike until Soviet Premier Nikita Khrushchev called a halt to the confrontation he precipitated. For the second time in two years, Moscow admitted defeat—the Berlin Wall, constructed in August 1961, symbolized the unfulfilled promise of Marxism-Leninism.[3]

Washington's joy dissipated quickly, however, as it dispatched advisors and soldiers to South Vietnam to snuff out a perceived Communist threat to U.S. interests. Kennedy's New Frontier collided with the aspirations of post-colonial societies tired of Western injustice. Indigenous peoples from Southeast Asia to Africa clamored for self-rule, a claim that some Americans interpreted as a call for Stalinism or Maoism.[4]

Lyndon B. Johnson emulated JFK's activism, convinced that an LBJ presidency could meet every challenge, both abroad and at home. Yet America's involvement in the Vietnam War cast the country as an imperial power bent on propping up an undemocratic regime in Saigon and provoked an intense domestic reaction. Other controversies, mainly over civil rights, complicated Johnson's twin tasks—to win the war and implement Great-Society legislation. Once the American public abandoned him, LBJ quit.[5]

His successor, Richard M. Nixon, promised "peace with honor" in the 1968 campaign, but once elected ordered renewed attacks upon the Vietcong and the North Vietnamese Army, all the while gradually withdrawing U.S. forces from

South Vietnam. In 1970, Nixon authorized a controversial incursion into Cambodia. The following year, to ease America's fiscal imbalances, he devalued the U.S. dollar and took his country off the gold standard. In the aftermath of the bloody Kent State riot, an event that reinforced public cynicism, the commander-in-chief continually recalled soldiers from Southeast Asia.[6]

To restore his nation's international credibility, Nixon issued a statement in 1969—while transiting in Guam—that would redefine America's role in Asia as well as the Persian Gulf. The Nixon Doctrine epitomized Washington's rededication to "asymmetrical containment," a strategy that culminated in the president's visit to the People's Republic of China in 1972 and détente with the Soviet Union. Under this eponymous doctrine, which, in the words of historian John Lewis Gaddis, "reflected a determination to apply strengths against weaknesses while leaving to allies forms of military activity uncongenial to the United States," regional powers monitored and protected U.S. assets. Ironically, unlike Operation Desert Storm in 1991, the White House relied on a similar policy in 1961, when Iraq seemed poised to invade its neighbor, Kuwait.[7]

Quiet Diplomacy: The Kuwaiti Crisis of 1961

In June 1961, the British relinquished their sixty-two-year old Kuwaiti protectorate, a decision that overjoyed the nationalistic al-Sabah rulers. London promised to aid the Kuwaitis, moreover, should any country imperil their sovereignty. This guarantee satisfied the emirate, whose people reveled in their newly independent status.[8]

While Kuwaitis rejoiced, Iraq's General Qasim spied an opportunity to annex the wealthy monarchy. His impoverished country could enrich itself considerably by appropriating its neighbor's oil fields. Perhaps such a grab could reverse his domestic and foreign-policy woes. Internal problems included failure to unify the country, reform Iraqi society, resuscitate the economy, defeat a Kurdish insurrection, and distance himself from the Communists, the only political organization that staunchly supported him during most of his dictatorship. Tense relations emerged with Iran and Turkey, a result of the March 1959 Iraqi withdrawal from the Baghdad Pact and Qasim's growing ties to the Soviet Union. Isolated and thus unable to repair the instability that racked Iraq, Qasim thought seizing Kuwait could erase his troubles. At the very least, a grievance directed at a rich and ungrateful neighbor would provide a reprieve. Better yet, this classic ploy might rally Iraqi public opinion and bestow renewed prestige upon the former elementary school teacher.[9]

Understandably, Emir Abdalla Salim rebuffed Qasim's June 25 claim that Kuwait constituted an Iraqi province. When the strongman nevertheless persisted, the Kuwaiti leader asked for Whitehall's help. London answered affirmatively. Qasim's recent hard-nosed dealings with the Iraq Petroleum Company had alienated the British, who resented his impudence and considered him unstable.

The standoff between Iraq and Kuwait galvanized the Arab world. Nasser approved of Kuwaiti independence, but objected to British interference in inter-

Arab disputes. Cairo thus called for London to back off. Unfortunately for the hero of Suez, the emir mistrusted his Egyptian brethren.

Qasim's irredentism struck U.S. representatives in Baghdad as a "desperate and ill-conceived move fraught with dangers both to him and to [the] West." They ascribed his bombast to miscalculation and reported that most Iraqis scoffed at his inflated audacity. He could renege on his pledge to incorporate Kuwait into Iraq, but the "[p]ossibility exists . . . that if faced with [the] prospect of becoming [a] laughing stock[,] Qassim [sic] may decide on [a] military move against Kuwait even in [the] face of opposition which such [a] move seems bound [to] provoke in other Arab states, particularly [the] UAR and Saudi Arabia." Embassy staff also warned that the Soviet Union could "stiffen Qassim's [sic] spine" to distract the United States and Great Britain from priorities in Laos and Berlin.[10]

News of the Iraqi prime minister's assertion "stunned and infuriated" Kuwaitis. They could dismiss his earlier snub—in a previous message, he omitted any reference to the emirate's June 19 declaration of independence—as uncouth. His predatory rhetoric, they could not tolerate. Still, Kuwaiti leaders hoped to avoid a confrontation. To deter the Iraqis, they implored "peace-loving states" to uphold Kuwaiti sovereignty. The al-Sabahs especially urged President Kennedy to bless their country's independence with a public declaration of support.[11]

From his post in Baghdad, U.S. Ambassador John Jernegan advised on June 27 that Washington refrain from any such pledge. Qasim would claim an "imperialist plot." Jernegan recommended that the Arab community settle this issue. American silence would rob Qasim of an easy scapegoat. The ambassador's UK counterpart agreed. While the British and Americans talked, Kuwaitis cheered the arrival of the Saudi chief of staff—King Saud had promised he would aid the emirate. Meanwhile, the emir worried about Qasim's plans.[12]

The State Department concluded that the dispute constituted "basically [an] inter-Arab controversy." It agreed with Jernegan's assessment that the United States should not expose itself to needless criticism. Any American statement could "(a) shift [the] focus of the problem[,] (b) be detrimental to [the] recent favorable trend in Iraq[,] and (c) goad Qasim to new intemperance which will exacerbate [the] problem." The department noted that the Kuwaitis were staying "in close touch" with London, with Whitehall "advising them how [to] handle [the] matter." With the British more deeply involved, Washington could sit back and observe. In the complacent view of Foggy Bottom (i.e., the State Department), the crisis would end "if Kuwaiti reaction to Qasim['s] statement[,] though firm[,] remains dignified, calm and low key."[13]

The Iraqi foreign minister, Hashim Jawad, insisted that his country would not attack Kuwait. He informed Jernegan that Qasim lacked diplomatic sophistication. While excusing his boss, Jawad nonetheless questioned Kuwait's legitimate status. He considered the country an "anomaly in [the] modern world," deriding the al-Sabahs and criticizing the emirate's lack of democratic institutions. If Kuwait could possess its own state, he mused, what would become of the sheikdoms in the Lower Gulf? Jernegan replied that "M[iddle] E[astern] territories had lost their military significance in the atomic age and that [the] only outside interests at stake were economic. Arabs recognized [the] legitimacy of such interests and [the United States] could be assured [that] [W]estern interests would be respected if there were changes in [the] area." To underline his point, the American informed Jawad that the United States endorsed Kuwaiti statehood. The Iraqi "expressed regret," claiming Washington had misjudged the situation.[14]

On June 29, the British conveyed to Foreign Minister Jawad their intention to protect Kuwait from any Iraqi assault. In Baghdad, UK Ambassador Sir Humphrey Trevelyan informed Jernegan that "it would be desirable if Saudi forces should enter Kuwait, so that Iraqis would be faced with other Arabs if they attacked." With British-Saudi relations suspended since the face-off over the Buraimi Oasis, Washington would have to persuade Riyadh to aid the Kuwaitis, should the Saudis not take the initiative. At the United Nations (UN), the Americans agreed with the British that Kuwait should argue its own case, if the Security Council asked to hear it. Both delegations realized that such recourse would prompt the Iraqis to hold the United Kingdom responsible and the United States complicit, resulting in injury to Anglo-American oil interests in Iraq.[15]

Notwithstanding such concerns, UK Foreign Secretary Lord Home believed that the emir should invite Britain immediately to defend Kuwait lest the Iraqis gain a quick, decisive advantage. Home pleaded for Washington's "full political support," noting that U.S. approval "would be absolutely essential." His country would not enter the emirate without cause and vacate it upon resolution of the crisis. He highlighted the critical importance of Kuwait to the West. Echoing Trevelyan, he asked that the United States "urge King Saud to throw his weight . . . in favour of restraint." Finally, mindful of his country's post-Suez policy of "interdependence" with the United States, Home assured American Secretary of State Dean Rusk that U.S.-UK consultation would continue.[16]

Rusk assured his British counterpart, "Your thinking coincides with ours. We understand the depth of your obligation, we agree that the independence of Kuwait must not be destroyed by force and we are prepared to render the full political support you request." The United States would continue to consult with the Saudis as well as study the ramifications of a Security Council démarche. Rusk nonetheless hoped that, "given time to work[,] political forces among the Arabs will dissuade Qasim from committing himself to an unfortunate course of action with unpredictable consequences."[17]

U.S. policy called for bolstering the British. Although Home fondly referred to previous Anglo-American military collaboration in Lebanon and Jordan, Washington rejected comparisons to the events of July 1958. Any assistance provided to London would not imply "direct [American] responsibility" for Kuwait's defense. UK-U.S. military intervention could once again taint the United States as a neo-imperial state bent on perpetually interfering in Arab affairs. To avoid such a risk, the National Security Council, when briefed by Rusk, approved the Foreign Office's desire for two types of American cooperation: political and logistical. Mindful of its own preference for a peaceful resolution to the crisis, Washington emphasized stealth, presuming that careful diplomacy would serve the national interest better than mobilization. It continued to dissuade the Iraqis from carrying out any invasion and gently urged the Saudis to intercede on Kuwait's behalf.[18]

On June 30, the emir requested that Great Britain fulfil its treaty obligation to his country. The British gladly acquiesced, knowing that their economy would slump without oil from Kuwait. To ward off Arab criticism, Whitehall kept its decision private. It asked Washington not to divulge the secret until a formal announcement came from London. The entry of UK armed forces into the emirate contravened the American wish for an Arab solution. Nevertheless, the U.S. military would consider any British plea for American assistance. Fortunately for the White House, the Soviets made no protest.[19]

Gulf Oil Company representatives feared that the United Kingdom could not repel an Iraqi assault upon Kuwait. If Baghdad annexed its neighbor, then Gulf's investment in the Kuwait Oil Company, which it co-owned with the Anglo-Iranian Oil Company, could be lost. The American "major" therefore pleaded with Washington to backstop the British. The United States recognized Kuwaiti independence, but State Department officials informed Gulf they would not impede upon UK primacy in this matter. They would assist their ally, but believed London could effect a satisfactory outcome.[20]

On July 1, UK military preparations continued. As British soldiers and firepower arrived in Kuwait, Whitehall announced *Operation Vantage* to the Arab world and beyond. Nasser seethed. The UAR would not tolerate such UK effrontery, he said. Although the Americans preached restraint, the U.S. Joint Chiefs of Staff ordered "Solant Amity" naval units to speed toward the Persian Gulf. This squadron expected to enter the Gulf on July 5. The Eastern Mediterranean command responsible for American forces in the area—Commander in Chief, North Atlantic and Mediterranean (CINCNELM)—expressed concern, however, regarding this deployment. CINCNELM's anxiety may have subsided somewhat when, on July 2, Secretary of State Rusk assigned "[n]o special significance" to Solant Amity and stated that "[n]o decision [has] yet [been] made whether vessels will move to [the] Persian Gulf but they may refuel at Aden." Though grateful for American involvement, the British worried that U.S. movements might give the Soviets cause to malign the Anglo-Americans as "imperialists ganging up on Kassem [sic]." London asked that Washington wait before it deployed its force. The Kennedy administration obliged.[21]

Starting on July 2, the matter of whether and when the U.S. Navy should patrol northern Gulf waters to reinforce British flanks receded into the political background, as the diplomatic confrontation opposing Kuwait and Iraq commenced at the United Nations. Initially, the Kuwaitis presented a complaint before the Security Council. They accused Baghdad of coveting their territory, in violation of the international law safeguarding national boundaries. Iraq denied any wrongdoing. In turn, it charged the United Kingdom with an illegal occupation of the emirate. Washington sided with Kuwait, while urging a peaceful resolution to the dispute. Simultaneously, the Americans remained skeptical of British and Kuwaiti claims of an imminent Iraqi threat, which seemed more trumped up than real.[22]

On July 5, Ambassador Jernegan reported from Baghdad that he and his UK counterpart considered an Iraqi assault on Kuwait unlikely. With London's deterrence a success, attention turned to the removal of the British military from the emirate. The League of Arab States (LAS) inherited the issue from the Security Council. After much contentious debate, the LAS, minus Iraq, agreed to send a multinational force (made up of soldiers from Saudi Arabia, the United Arab Republic, Jordan, and the Sudan) to Kuwait to prevent any recurrence of trouble. Diplomacy thus ended the crisis in the Kuwaitis' favor.[23]

In 1963, with Qasim ousted and the Ba'th Party installed, Baghdad admitted defeat, at least temporarily, by recognizing its neighbor's independence in return for Kuwaiti financial aid. Such generosity would not prevent future Iraqi rapacity, however. Three decades later, Saddam Hussein was to study Qasim's mistakes and employ a different strategy.[24]

In 1961, Whitehall's assertiveness deterred Iraq and safeguarded British, Kuwaiti, and American commercial interests. A hesitant Washington preferred "quiet" diplomacy while following London's lead. This reliance on an ally willing to balance the Iraqi threat (and with extensive ties to Kuwait) conveniently enabled the White House to avoid Nasser's wrath and participate in regional contests without recourse to military might, which could tar the United States with the brush of imperialism. U.S. influence extended especially to Saudi Arabia, whose clout within the LAS in July 1961 ensured an outcome favorable to American interests. When civil war broke out in Yemen the following year, U.S. officials expected their views to carry weight in Riyadh once more.[25]

Countering Nasser: The Yemeni Civil War

After the Suez crisis, Washington had failed to intimidate Nasser with the Eisenhower Doctrine and gained nothing by shunning him, so it eventually tried to coax Egypt into friendlier relations with the United States. White House conflation of Arab nationalism with Soviet communism ceased. This unexpected tack allayed America's obsession with Middle Eastern neutralism. Contrary to many accounts of this period, and unbeknownst to U.S. diplomats such as Parker Hart, who later wrote of "six years of chill," Ike extended a hand to the Egyptian president in the expectation that a rapprochement, no matter how tentative, would fortify the American position in the region. In the view of scholar Fawaz Gerges, "[a]ccommodation and cooperation replaced suspicion and hostility." As a result, National Security Council (NSC) Document 5820/1 and NSC 6011 highlighted local and regional needs. Under these new directives, attention to Arab economic wants and cultural frustrations complemented the U.S. fixation with Cold-War bipolarity.[26]

Eisenhower's successor endorsed similar tactics, although President Kennedy envisioned different objectives when he pushed for a policy of "selective cooperation" with Cairo. According to White House aide Arthur Schlesinger, Jr., JFK "wished to preserve an entrée to Nasser in order both to restrain Egyptian policy toward Israel and to try to work more closely with the modernizing forces in the Arab world." To add substance to the New Frontier's rhetoric, the president pressed some of America's most vital partners, such as the Saudis, to abandon their feudal ways—slavery, in Riyadh's case. Yet a moralizing Kennedy could not admonish Saudi Arabia and other medieval polities at the cost of U.S. influence. During the Yemeni civil war, which started with a coup d'état in 1962, this need to reconcile ethical imperatives with geopolitical necessity addled Washington's relations with the House of Saud.[27]

The royals in Yemen (especially the rulers from the House of Hamid al-Din) incarnated everything that Kennedy abhorred. They rejected modernity and kept their traditional country mired in political incompetence and economic venality. Within this closed society, tribal animosities festered. In September 1962, a week after the Imam, the Yemeni head of state, died, army officials led by Brigadier Abd Allah al-Sallal overthrew Prince Badr's royalist clique in San'a, the capital. State Department Director of Intelligence and Research Roger Hilsman acknowledged the rebels' reformist tendencies and the expected widespread approval for this political revolution, but noted that this victory for Arab nationalism would incite a conservative counterattack. Hilsman prophesied, moreover, that UAR involvement in Yemen on behalf of Sallal would only exacerbate tensions within the country and the region.[28]

The White House's subdued reaction to Yemeni events underlined its displeasure with Hamid al-Din authoritarianism and cautious disposition toward manifestations of Arab nationalism. American officials endorsed neither side. They would not partake in any restoration and refused to condone the coup. The United States cared not if the UAR befriended Sallal and his coterie unless such a policy jeopardized U.S. security interests in the area. The viability of America's position in the Persian Gulf hinged on continued UK mastery over Aden. This protectorate enabled London to deny countries access to the Strait of Hormuz or punish states that threatened Anglo-American oil supplies and other regional assets. Washington insisted that, in league with the British, it would oppose any hostile maneuver against Aden originating in Yemen. To prevent such an ill-advised move, the State Department expected the Egyptians to restrain the Yemeni republicans, who, in Foggy Bottom's opinion, should be encouraged to reform their economy rather than pursue "external adventures."[29]

Nasser applauded Sallal and his followers, who professed fealty to Arab nationalism. With Syria recently divorced from the UAR, the Egyptian president needed some kind of victory, symbolic or otherwise, to break out of his regional isolation. A Yemen Arab Republic (YAR) subservient to Egypt could enable him to upstage rivals and silence detractors. U.S. Ambassador to Egypt John Badeau predicted that the UAR "will provide some support to [the] Yemen[i] regime, but not commit itself so deeply as to precipitate [an] all-out British-Saudi-UAR struggle or run [an] overly grave risk of backing [a] losing horse." To reach his pot of gold, Nasser sent his soldiers into a jagged land he barely knew to assist his Yemeni companions-in-arms.[30]

Riyadh and Amman impugned the Egyptian president's motives, as they denounced Egypt's intervention. King Hussein of Jordan excoriated his fellow Arab head of state, suspecting that Cairo continued to plot his overthrow. The Saudis accused Nasser of wanting to conquer their country via Yemen. To prevent such a calamity, they resolved to arm Prince Badr, who had escaped assassination and retreated to the safety of northern Yemen. This aid would allow the Yemeni royalists to recover lost territory and authority. Prince Faisal (who, substituting for the spendthrift and ill King Saud, now formally governed Saudi Arabia) preferred to oppose Egypt on Yemeni, rather than Saudi, soil. With their oil wealth and proximity to the battlefield, the Saudis could bleed Nasser's troops in a war of attrition that Riyadh could afford indefinitely.[31]

Washington worried that this duel between conservative and socialist Arabs could result in long-lived acrimony, thereby jeopardizing American relations with all the participants and undermining President Kennedy's desire for a regional strategy. JFK favored inclusiveness in the Middle East; he ascribed a positive role to every country and sought to align the United States with reformist trends in the area. While committed to Saudi Arabia's and Jordan's safety, he tried to coddle Egypt, recognizing Nasser's appeal to the downtrodden and outraged, who resented the sway of corrupt Muslim elites within their societies. Kennedy wanted to harness Nasser's fury and ambition, or so it seemed, to forge a new American reputation in the Near East, one more in tune with recent developments in the region.[32]

Utopian thoughts of pleasing everyone in such a conflict-ridden part of the world may have warmed the U.S. president's liberal heart, but the region's messy reality forced him to make unsentimental, tactical adjustments. Initially, he urged the Saudis to refrain from involvement in Yemen. His government proposed a Yemeni solution. When Egyptian pilots bombed Saudi border towns early in the crisis, however, he reiterated the American commitment to Saudi Arabian independence (despite Riyadh's cancellation of U.S. base rights at Dhahran in 1961) while stressing that Faisal pursue his modernization program. At the same time, consistent with his preference for enlightened leadership, the president wished to recognize Yemen's step forward. Preferably, though, U.S. recognition of the YAR should not occur while a civil war raged.[33]

While a self-described neutral White House watched and waited, Faisal fretted. He needed American help. In his October 1962 meeting with President Kennedy, the prince reaffirmed his country's solidarity with the United States. But wary of Nasser's reckless Yemen policy, the Saudi autocrat objected to U.S. aid to Egypt, a policy unwittingly underwriting Cairo's audacious and unsettling foray into the Arabian Peninsula.[34]

Despite Faisal's dissent, the United States recognized the YAR in December 1962. The controversial decision elicited strong Saudi-Jordanian disapproval and vexed the British, privately irritated that Washington could disregard its ally's interests in such a cavalier manner. Whitehall's continued stake in Yemen explained UK disappointment. With its border colony at Aden exposed to republican infiltration, London's vulnerable position in the Middle East risked collapse in yet another humiliating setback for the waning British Empire.[35]

Washington's views evolved once Nasser's refusal to evacuate Yemen precipitated a more intransigent Saudi riposte. Washington sought to "terminate foreign military intervention in Yemen and permit Yemenis [to] determine [their] own future," as well as "prevent escalation and [the] spread of conflict"; "protect US interests in [the] entire Arabian Peninsula"; and "prevent [the] enhancement of Soviet influence and position in Yemen which likely [will] occur if [the] conflict continues." While Kennedy aide Robert Komer justified White House policy "on [the] grounds of realpolitik," Secretary of State Rusk emphasized that his country "[m]ust remain [a] friend of both [the] UAR and Saudi Arabia." This conciliatory approach upset American oil companies, which pressed the Kennedy administration to oppose Nasser.[36]

Hardly naïve, Rusk recognized the vulnerabilities of America's position. Without a Yemeni truce, critics could harp on Faisal's reliance upon U.S. military insurance. The Egyptians incorrectly assumed, moreover, that the Americans could order the Saudis to cease their aid to Yemeni royalists. Similarly, Riyadh seemed to think Washington could tame Cairo's impetuousness. To satisfy its desire for a peaceful resolution and dodge brickbats, the White House pursued a malleable policy, in contrast with British intransigence. Whitehall's tart policy denied the YAR formal recognition. Such recalcitrance prompted Komer to predict: "this peanut war will be with us a long time yet."[37]

To break a military stalemate, in March 1963 Kennedy sent Ambassador Ellsworth Bunker as a personal emissary to explore possibilities for a cease-fire. In Cairo, Ambassador John Badeau informed Nasser advisor Ali Sabri that an American intermediary raised the specter of excessive U.S. interference: "I pointed out [the] possible dangers of [a] US representative, particularly laying us [i.e., the United States] open to [the] accusation [that] we might be trying to revive great power imperialistic control of [the] Middle East and enforce a pax-Americana [sic]." Sabri obligingly replied that Egypt did not object to Bunker. Meanwhile, Komer stressed that the "President wanted Bunker to say to Faysal [sic] that we [i.e., Americans] were trying to help him but felt that [the prince] must suspend aid to the royalists and let the [Saudi-UAR] disengagement process go forward." If Riyadh indulged JFK, then the United States "would offer the politico-military reassurance of a 'plate glass fighter squadron.'" With Washington convinced that Nasser wished for a "graceful withdrawal," a compromise now seemed possible, Kennedy's pessimism notwithstanding.[38]

The Bunker Mission proved successful, if contentious, as Faisal and Nasser haggled over concessions and promises. Neither man trusted the other. Still, they came to an agreement that allowed, after several delays, the United Nations to send an observer group to Yemen. The United Nations Yemen Observer Mission (UNYOM) thereupon monitored the removal of Egyptian soldiers and cessation of Saudi supplies to the royalists. Nasser soon violated terms by rotating his armed forces in and out of Yemen. Faisal honored his pledge, but could not prevent clandestine shipments of weapons and other essentials to Badr loyalists.[39]

As a reward for Riyadh's endorsement of the Bunker formula, Washington assigned a U.S. Air Force (USAF) squadron to Saudi Arabia. Operation Hardsurface aimed to reassure Faisal of benevolent American intentions. A USAF presence (albeit far from the Saudi-Yemeni border to avoid a clash with Egyptian fighters) would remind Cairo, moreover, to respect Saudi sovereignty.[40]

Despite the American show of force and his avowed intention to "avoid any clash with [the] USAF," Nasser kept his infantry in Yemen. As a result, the conflict festered. Washington persuaded Riyadh and Cairo to renew UNYOM, but the UN monitors left in 1965. Nevertheless, Egypt and Saudi Arabia pushed for a diplomatic solution. Despite the 1965 Jeddah Agreement, animosity between Yemeni republicans and royalists, combined with Saudi and Egyptian hesitation, precluded any armistice. The same result ensued in 1966, when Cairo and Riyadh resorted to secret talks in Kuwait. Eventually, the crisis petered out, as more important events rocked the Arab world. At the 1967 Khartoum summit following the disastrous Six-Day War, Faisal and Nasser finally terminated their respective involvement in southwestern Arabia—in sum, a bloody proxy flare-up of the Arab Cold War. With the Israelis freshly entrenched in various Arab lands, the Egyptian president needed a united Arab front to rehabilitate his battered image. A futile sideshow in Yemen could not win back Jerusalem or the Sinai.[41]

President Johnson welcomed this dénouement after six years of intermittent and inconclusive warfare. After Kennedy was assassinated in November 1963, LBJ remained aloof from the Yemeni conflict. Still, the United States achieved its objective of limiting the hostilities, with Ambassador Parker Hart asserting that his nation "had played an essential role in preventing a direct trial of military strength between the parties." As an interested arbiter, Washington had tried to curtail Nasser's adventurism in a bid to reassure the nervous Saudis, without whom Americans could not secure their substantial economic interests in the Persian Gulf. This favoritism poisoned U.S.-Egyptian relations, which had improved markedly from Fall 1958 to September 1962.[42]

In June 1967, America's reputation sank as Arabs dwelled on the present, not the past. Israel bewildered its foes with stunning victories that shocked Muslims throughout the Middle East and North Africa. Washington's unabashed support of Tel Aviv insulted Arabs everywhere and strained America's ties with its Gulf friends.

Playing Favorites: The Six-Day War

As the Yemeni War smoldered in the years 1964–66, Arabs enjoyed a brief period of regional reconciliation. But in 1966–67 events rekindled intense rivalries. The Ba'th Party usurped power in yet another Syrian coup. Immediately, it tried to rally the Arab world behind an ideological platform inimical to Israel and skeptical of Nasser's pan-Arab credentials. Though he had reasserted his dominant status within the region at the 1964 Cairo summit, the Egyptian president could not dismiss the Syrians. They could win over area opinion and discredit Cairo as uninterested in the plight of the Palestinians, rhetorically the Arabs' foremost concern. The Saudis irritated Nasser as well, as they sought a Muslim alignment with the Iranians, fellow conservatives, to counterbalance Egyptian sway over the League of Arab States.[43]

Nasser answered these provocations with anti-Israeli barbs. Tel Aviv fumed. It warned of reprisals should Cairo threaten Israeli interests. When Egypt closed the Strait of Tiran on May 22, 1967, Israel waited and waited, then on June 5 replied with a pre-emptive assault on Arab positions in the Sinai, East Jerusalem, Gaza, and the Golan Heights. Israeli prowess humbled Nasser, who underestimated his enemy's military dexterity. In reaction to this debacle, Arabs everywhere remonstrated against the so-called Zionists. In Saudi Arabia, Kuwait, and Bahrain, Muslims vociferously condemned American favoritism toward the Jewish state. But, in contrast to Baghdad and the region's radical governments, Riyadh and Kuwait City refused to break off relations with Washington.[44]

To appease the Arab masses and perpetuate the "propaganda war," the Saudis, Kuwaitis, and other Gulf oil producers ordered an embargo. Targeted at the United States, United Kingdom, and the Federal Republic of Germany (countries friendly to Israel), economic sanctions foundered when American and British petroleum officials rerouted international deliveries so that no shortages occurred in America, Great Britain, or West Germany. Publicly infuriated by this circumvention, Gulf Arabs vowed not to repeat the same mistake. In the aftermath of the Six-Day War, they and their Organization of Petroleum Exporting Countries (OPEC) partners bullied Occidental and other independents, as well as the "majors," into agreements that rewarded producer states far more than previously. Spurred on by Libya's Mohamar Qaddafi, OPEC members soon tilted the industry balance of power in their favor. By 1973, this oligopoly could inflict severe economic pain on developed countries and others addicted to oil, a situation Washington could not countenance since U.S. global hegemony hinged on Western access to plentiful and affordable "black gold."[45]

In June 1967, however, the Johnson administration concentrated on Israel. As the latter's soldiers battered the Egyptians, Jordanians, and Syrians, LBJ winked. Yet some uneasiness accompanied this presidential assent. With Moscow already involved in the region via arms sales to radical Arab countries, Washington dreaded any excuse, such as an Israeli rout, that might ensure increased Soviet participation in Middle Eastern affairs. The spectacular Arab defeat emboldened the Kremlin, which rushed to replenish Cairo's and Damascus' supply of weapons and matériel.[46]

Although the Soviet toehold in the region turned into a foothold and the U.S. position seemed to weaken, the Six-Day War enlightened Washington. Henceforth, the United States would count on Israel as an anti-Communist power capable of thwarting Arab nationalism. While the Israelis joined the Saudis and Iranians as American bulwarks in a volatile region, the British prepared to pull out of the Persian Gulf. Their withdrawal coincided with the White House's effort to extricate the United States from the Vietnam War.[47]

The Anointed Ones: The Twin Pillars Policy

London's farewell to over a century's worth of Pax Britannica in the Middle East commenced in November 1967, when Her Majesty's Government relinquished its Aden protectorate. The British retreat from South Arabia paved the way for Marxists to found the People's Democratic Republic of Yemen (i.e., South Yemen). These zealots who despised monarchical rule soon harangued and harassed their ideological adversaries in the Arabian Peninsula. They attacked Saudi Arabia and fomented insurrection in the Sultanate of Muscat and Oman. This type of radicalism could draw the Kremlin further into the region, Washington believed. With the Soviet Navy present in the Red Sea and Indian Ocean, and with Moscow supplying weapons and military expertise to Egyptian and Syrian nationalists, revolutionary socialism in Southern Arabia threatened the Anglo-American oil imperium in the Persian Gulf and, therefore, the economies of Western Europe. To sustain its hegemony, the United States needed to exercise constant vigilance. Any encroachment could spell the demise of the American position in the region.[48]

The United States could tolerate South Arabia's independence, even though The *Washington Post* reported U.S. worries about a "volatile and strategic triangle stretching from Iran in the Middle East to Morocco on the Atlantic and south in Black Africa." A State Department paper noted that America's "most important concern is not with respect to South Arabia itself but with the implications of the transition for neighboring regimes friendly to us [i.e., the United States], notably Saudi Arabia, Iran and Ethiopia." Washington sought to stay out of messy South Arabian internal disputes. It aimed instead "to discourage adventures by external powers, notably the UAR and the USSR."[49]

Suspicion of Egyptian and Soviet motives extended to the Persian Gulf. To counter Moscow and Cairo, Washington wanted London to remain involved in the Lower Gulf. A May 1967 U.S. National Intelligence Estimate pointed out that should the United Kingdom refuse, the United States "will be urged to take over some of the British responsibility in the Gulf. If it did so, it would become the principal target of Arab revolutionary propaganda and subversion and would become involved in a variety of dynastic rivalries and troublesome political disputes." To avoid such a distasteful scenario, in mid-1967 the U.S. government's Special State-Defense Study Group issued the Holmes Report, which, according to the Foreign Office, "raised questions such as whether the United States should revert to a policy of supporting the 'northern tier' and the allocation of defence responsibilities between the Western Powers."[50]

Although a UK withdrawal would allegedly "seriously undermine the Western position in the Gulf," British Prime Minister Harold Wilson and his cabinet could not grant the Johnson administration its wish that Whitehall continue ensuring the region's security. To cut overseas expenses and honor domestic commitments, the Labour Government opted in January 1968 to sever imperial connections with Great Britain's Gulf protectorates (i.e., Bahrain, Qatar, the Trucial States, and the Sultanate of Muscat and Oman). The United Kingdom would resign its obligations starting in 1971, a controversial step that dismayed the ruler of Dubai, Sheik Rashid, and other area monarchs, who preferred that the British not leave and offered to pay UK expenses. Edward Heath's Conservative government—elected in June 1970—would dash any hope, however, of a British volte-face.[51]

A January 1968 Foreign Office Planning Staff brief, prepared for Prime Minister Wilson's White House visit the following month, exemplified UK thinking. According to that document, Wilson would tell President Johnson that the British Government has "been of the view that the security and stability [of the Persian Gulf], on which the interests of our two countries in that part of the world depend, would have to rest in the long run on some local balance of power, not on the presence of extraneous forces." While noting that "[t]he Gulf is at present more stable than it has been for many years," Wilson would observe that "[t]he presence of the Shah and King Faisal at the helm provides a unique opportunity for the exercise of responsible leadership in Iran and Saudi Arabia in order to establish a local basis for security in the future."[52]

The prime minister would add that "[t]here are reasons for hoping that withdrawal by the end of 1971 will offer us [i.e., the United Kingdom] a reasonable chance of leaving arrangements which will preserve an adequate degree of security in the Gulf." He would concede, though, that "[i]t is of course an unpredictable area and our plans may go awry." "But," he would opine, "I do not believe that the risks are as great as you and Dean Rusk have suggested; they are risks which in my and my colleagues' view we can and should accept." Finally, Wilson would impress upon LBJ that "[British] influence is limited in the Gulf; we cannot control events there. But I hope that from what I have said you will see why I believe that our policy has a reasonable chance of success and that, if successful, it will bring about a more lasting security system in the Gulf than could be achieved by the indefinite presence of foreign forces."[53]

Although London considered Iran and Saudi Arabia apt successors to Her Majesty's Government, the British recognized potential difficulties that might hamper the preservation of Western interests in the Persian Gulf. "The Shah," Whitehall noted, "conscious of Iran's greater wealth and population and her cultural superiority over Saudi Arabia, will find it difficult to give King Faisal the equal treatment the latter will expect. Nor will he easily disguise his ambition to succeed to our [i.e., Britain's] position of dominance." "Equally," the Foreign Office continued, "the long tradition of Arab-Persian hostility in the Gulf, together with current Arab suspicion of the Shah's intentions, will make King Faisal reluctant to be seen to be arranging the Gulf's affairs with him."[54]

The pace of events "deeply disturbed" Secretary of State Rusk and startled the U.S. government, which wanted no new burdens but nevertheless promised "discreet assistance" to the British government as it withdrew from the Persian Gulf, a region where American businesses had made substantial investments whose value exceeded that of UK assets. A convenient Great-Power arrangement, whereby Washington oversaw the Greater Levant (i.e., Middle Eastern states adjacent to the Mediterranean as well as Saudi Arabia) while London supervised East of Suez, suddenly expired after twelve years of countering Communist and nationalist threats to Western economic and other strategic interests. As Whitehall prepared to abandon this critical sphere of influence, the West's position in the Arabian Peninsula now seemed precarious. The Soviets or Arab radicals could press Gulf states for concessions or else try to oust their reactionary sheiks. When the rabidly anti-Western Iraqi Ba'th Party seized power once more in 1968, it joined a worrisome list—topped by Egypt and Syria—of regimes inimical to the United States. Yet psychological setbacks in Vietnam, especially the Tet offensive and its consequences, ruled out an American countermove.[55]

As American influence in the Middle East ebbed, Washington considered its limited options. Following Wilson's announcement, U.S. Undersecretary of State for Economic Affairs Eugene V. Rostow clumsily stated at a January 19, 1968, press conference in Tehran, broadcast by Voice of America, that "hopefully" Iran, Turkey, Pakistan, Saudi Arabia, and Kuwait could evolve a "security arrangement" of some sort. An expanded "northern tier" defense system seemed unlikely, however, given strong regional disapproval of such a scheme and American disappointment with the Central Treaty Organization, the successor to the Baghdad Pact. The State Department recognized, moreover, that "[n]either containment nor [economic] development provides the key." For its part, the Interdepartmental Regional Group for Near East and South Asia proposed a "low-key policy approach" since "[i]t is neither politically feasible nor desirable for the US to 'replace' the British presence in the Persian Gulf." Based on these assessments, the United States needed proxies, ideally Iran and Saudi Arabia, to preserve its regional interests.[56]

Richard Nixon tried to remedy this potentially dire situation. Without prompt rectification, Arab nationalists might further imperil an already faltering American "containment" grand strategy. The Nixon Doctrine shifted responsibility for regional stability to worthy surrogates. In selecting these proxies, the president and National Security Advisor Henry Kissinger evaluated the capacity of a state to resist and repel unwanted impingements in the Gulf area. The administration chose these guardians based on compatibility and trustworthiness. Their objectives mirrored White House goals and they would advance U.S. interests as well as their own. Nixon and Kissinger also wanted countries with a proven affinity for the United States.[57]

As the Kennedy and Johnson administrations, as well as the UK government, had done, Nixon and Kissinger anointed Iran and Saudi Arabia. Both monarchies thrived within a Western sphere of influence. Their wealth, mistrust of the Soviet Union, and regional clout endowed them with the requisite attributes. They would counter any foray into the Gulf and thus shore up America's geopolitical flank in Southwest Asia while Washington attempted to reinforce its crumbling stronghold in Southeast Asia.[58]

In Congressional testimony, Assistant Secretary of State for Near Eastern and South Asian Affairs Joseph Sisco explained America's new policy. He stressed to the House of Representatives Subcommittee on the Near East, chaired by Lee Hamilton (D-Indiana), that, from a geostrategic standpoint, the Gulf region "ought to be an area of peaceful competition between the Soviet Union and the United States." Sisco alluded to the vast oil resources available in Saudi Arabia, Kuwait, and Iran; to his country's projected reliance on Gulf petroleum in coming decades; and to private U.S. commercial opportunities that Washington should promote. He denied, however, that the White House sought to appropriate Whitehall's former informal empire. Instead of reflexively fulfilling a "protective role," the Nixon administration would proffer advice and extend assistance only when asked by local authorities. Or so he said. Washington really intended to create bulwarks that could defend American interests.[59]

This official preference for a secondary role in the Gulf correlated with the U.S. military posture in the area. "We have maintained a small American naval contingent at Bahrain [i.e., Middle East Force (MIDEASTFOR)]," Sisco noted, "which has for a quarter century carried out the mission of visiting friendly ports in the region to symbolize American interest." He emphasized that "it is not our intention to expand this presence or to alter its role nor indeed to undertake an operational American military role in any state in the area. There is no need for the United States to assume responsibilities for security that the British exercised in the [G]ulf in a different era." Sisco pointed out, moreover, that the Gulf states rejected extra-regional interference.[60]

This inclination suited the Nixon administration. Consonant with the White House's attempt to reduce America's responsibilities worldwide, Sisco informed the House subcommittee that "[w]e [i.e., the Nixon administration] are making no new military commitments in the region but will support as we can the endeavors of the new states [Bahrain, Qatar, and the United Arab Emirates (UAE)] to consolidate their independence through economic and social progress and improvement of their means of self-defense and internal security." The United States wanted pillars and proxies, not formal empire.[61]

In remarks before Lee Hamilton's subcommittee, Deputy Assistant Secretary of Defense for Near Eastern, African, and South Asian Affairs James Noyes insisted that MIDEASTFOR occupied a "facility" rather than a "base" in Bahrain, from which it could not carry out serious missions. Similarly, the Department of State contended that the American naval posture in the Gulf "makes a symbolic but psychologically significant contribution to the continuation of an atmosphere of tranquility in the area." It added that "[t]his longstanding [sic] presence is not intended to represent a commitment to, or threat to intervene in, the area, nor is it intended as a provocation to any state." This rationalization sought to refute what James Timberlake of the Department of Defense dubbed "the usual charges of imperialist interference" leveled by "some Middle East papers."[62]

In the same vein, Noyes corrected the erroneous presumption that Great Britain would completely vanish from the region. "The United Kingdom continues [to fulfil] an important role in the [G]ulf," he opined, "obviously political and commercial but also military." Following this clarification, Noyes evaluated London's replacements, Iran and Saudi Arabia, the Gulf's newest sentinels. He stated that the Shah, Mohammed Reza Pahlavi, "views Iranian military power as a stabilizing factor which can guarantee the area against possible turmoil." He added that Saudi Arabia, "as the most powerful state on the peninsula and as a fellow Arab state, has a political entree to the [G]ulf Sheikhdoms that Iran, for all its superior strength and sophistication, cannot match." "Most important," he said, "the conservative states of the [L]ower [G]ulf regard the survival of the Saudi regime as crucial to their security." He concluded that Tehran and Riyadh "expect to play major roles in maintaining the stability of the [G]ulf in the future."[63]

The Nixon-Kissinger "Twin Pillars" policy, which built upon the Johnson administration's end-of-term Gulf strategy, hinged on a risky, even dubious, calculus: that local substitutes could maintain a regional equilibrium acceptable to the White House with an increasing number of hostile forces arrayed against them. To offset any military disadvantage, real or perceived, the United States intended to sell vast quantities of sophisticated arms to Tehran and Riyadh. In a reprise of World War II, America designated itself an arsenal—then of democracy, now of conservative autocracy.[64]

Despite America's confidence in them, the Saudis could not deliver much in the way of regional security. Their best intentions could not compensate for their small population and inferior military. They bought U.S. arms and upgraded their defensive capabilities, but left the Iranians to provide the vigilance and muscle the Americans desired.[65]

Unlike the reserved King Faisal, the ambitious Shah lobbied Nixon for an enhanced Iranian role in the Gulf. He aspired to return his country, via the White Revolution, to the glory days of Cyrus the Great. An avid reader of arms trade magazines, he requested that Washington deliver every piece of high-tech equipment Iran could afford. Once the Nixon administration acquiesced in Pahlavi's various schemes to increase oil prices—the 1971 Tehran Agreement empowered OPEC countries and ushered in the decline of the Anglo-American petroleum cartel, hegemonic since the discovery of black gold—vast Iranian sums could be spent on weapons purchases. President Nixon confirmed this policy of expediency when he visited the Shah in May 1972.[66]

With U.S. approval, Pahlavi established himself as the Gulf's newest eminence. His navy invaded three islands (Abu Musa and the Greater and Lesser Tunbs, all property of the UAE) in the Strait of Hormuz. He sent Iranian reinforcements to the Sultanate of Oman, whose Dhofari province South Yemen tried to subvert. He also covertly aided the Kurds in their civil war with Tehran's archenemy Baghdad, which in 1972 signed a treaty of friendship with the Soviet Union.[67]

Nixon and his national security advisor endorsed the Shah with almost no reservation. Kissinger knew of Pahlavi's flaws—his vanity and autocratic manner—yet celebrated the Shah's achievements as an economic reformer and touted his ability as a statesman. Without Pahlavi, the United States simply could not implement its Gulf strategy. In his memoirs, Kissinger wrote:

> The Shah sought to shape his country's destiny and make Iran a major partner in the West. He believed in assuming the burden of his own defense, at least to the point where he balanced the strength of his radical neighbors, like Iraq, and where he would force Moscow, if it ever sought to subdue Iran, to launch a direct invasion of a magnitude that the United States could not ignore. And he tried to earn our [i.e., U.S.] support not only by taking seriously the defense of his country—which was, after all, of crucial strategic importance—but also by displaying his friendship to us [i.e., America] at times when he might well have stood aside. . . . Under the Shah's leadership, the land bridge between Asia and Europe . . . was pro-American beyond any challenge.

Not everyone endorsed the national security advisor's rationale. The U.S. Department of Defense thought Pahlavi more reckless than Bismarckian. The Pentagon pointed out consistently that Iran could not make proper use of advanced American weaponry without adequate training, which the Iranians sorely lacked. The Shah dismissed such criticisms while Nixon and Kissinger (with help from the Iranian lobby, whose membership included the powerful Rockefeller family and others with extensive commercial interests in Iran) outmaneuvered the Defense Department in various bureaucratic tugs of war.[68]

The president and his major foreign-policy advisor thus responded to a "strategic disruption" within the Persian Gulf region (i.e., the British pullout in 1971) by evaluating the "balance of risk" implicit in any reorientation of American policy. Nixon and Kissinger concluded that, in the short term, a Twin Pillars policy presented the United States with the best opportunity to achieve its regional and global objectives. They could not foresee that within a year the Yom

Kippur/October War would severely test America's Gulf strategy. During and after the Watergate investigation, numerous critics would assail Nixon and Kissinger's faulty geostrategic premises, in particular their misplaced confidence in, and overreliance on, the Shah. More worrisome from Washington's standpoint, the pillars themselves would start to erode.[69]

Assessment

The third stage (1959–72) of U.S. expansion in the Persian Gulf defies easy explanation. In this period, Washington arrogated different roles for itself: interested bystander, mediator, cheerleader, and supplier. During the Kuwaiti crisis, it seconded UK policy. With respect to the Yemeni War, it tried to devise a diplomatic solution. In June 1967, it endorsed Israel without apology. When the British renounced their Gulf commitments in 1971, the White House entrusted Iran and Saudi Arabia with the arduous task of preserving U.S. political, economic, and military interests in the region.

At first glance, to designate American behavior imperialistic in this stage would seem inaccurate. Washington refrained from any coups d'état or other military reprisals. It even failed to support American oil companies in their efforts to ensure price stability. This assent to decartelization soon allowed OPEC to impose its own cartel upon a frazzled but dependent world. Notwithstanding these arguments, the continued existence of an informal U.S. empire seems hard to refute. London's withdrawal from the Gulf left the United States as the most likely Great Power to step into the region's strategic vacuum. Washington could have begged off. Instead, it encouraged Tehran and Riyadh to assume extra political and military responsibilities. To facilitate Iran's and Saudi Arabia's transition to area watchmen, the White House agreed to send billions of dollars worth of arms to these countries so that they could thwart any challenge to the U.S.-sanctioned Gulf security system.

Soviet communism and Arab radicalism constituted equal threats to the American geostrategic position in the Gulf. Washington sought therefore to counter any country or alliance trying to overturn the regional equilibrium. Kennedy opposed Qasim and Nasser when they threatened U.S. interests in the Arabian Peninsula; LBJ favored Israel in the Six-Day War to counterbalance an Arab coalition bent on destroying the Jewish state; and, finally, Nixon and Kissinger offset growing Soviet power in the area with their Twin Pillars policy. They sought as well to check Iraq, South Yemen, and other radical states.

To preserve its position in the Persian Gulf, the United States engaged in two-way, or reciprocal, guardianship. It elected Iran and Saudi Arabia proxies and armed them so they could protect U.S. hegemonic and security interests. With the Vietnam War consuming a disproportionate amount of American funds, personnel, and matériel, Washington could not afford a significant presence in the Gulf. But without U.S. weapons, Tehran and Riyadh could not defend themselves particularly well.

From an economic perspective, Washington and several American businesses collected handsome profits as a result of sales concluded with the Saudis and

Iranians. Still, if the White House sought to extend U.S. hegemony in this era, it apparently stumbled quite purposely. In 1971, for example, it favored Middle Eastern countries over American oil majors and independents. Although these companies undeniably exploited Arabs and Iranians, the so-called excesses of capitalism also enabled Gulf societies to enjoy unprecedented standards of living via increased oil rents. In the decade that followed, most Arabian Peninsula countries transformed themselves into exceedingly wealthy "oil monarchies." They used their petrodollars to overcome scarcity, build impressive infrastructures, and evolve the world's most comprehensive welfare states.[70]

If Washington treaded gingerly while upholding its hegemony and informal empire, then what about contingent imperialism? In the case of the Kuwaiti crisis, proposition P2 (The United States will exercise alliance contingent imperialism whenever a significant threat to American hegemony and security occurs, allies agree to join a U.S.-led venture or vice-versa, Washington can overcome any regional constraints, consensus exists within the executive, and no majority in Congress or critical segment of domestic opinion strongly opposes White House action) seems valid. The Kennedy administration offered the British and Kuwaitis important diplomatic support, but overall displayed more hesitancy than assuredness. London took charge and Baghdad took notice. Qasim wanted an easy victory to distract his disgruntled population, but Her Majesty's Government denied him a potential triumph. The Americans benefited from UK intransigence since it safeguarded their oil interests in Kuwait.

Washington acquitted itself better during the Yemeni civil war when it earnestly tried to resolve the conflict in what it considered a just manner. President Kennedy monitored developments in Yemen until his untimely death in November 1963. Neither the Egyptians nor the Saudis made it easy for him. Their recalcitrance prevented a U.S.-brokered resolution to the crisis and extended its duration several years. As president, LBJ let the protagonists work out their own solution, which they did in 1967. Because the Saudis could hold their own with minimal American assistance, proposition P3 (The United States will exercise proxy contingent imperialism whenever a significant or minor threat to American hegemony and security occurs, surrogates can preserve U.S. interests, Washington cannot overcome regional constraints, consensus may not exist within the executive, and a majority of Congress or critical segment of domestic opinion strongly opposes direct White House involvement) seems to apply.

Since the Six-Day War did not involve any Gulf states, Washington never seriously pondered the conflict's impact on its economic position in the Arabian Peninsula. Thus, proposition P5 (The United States will not exercise any type of contingent imperialism if no threat to American hegemony and security exists) seems correct. After the war, Gulf Arab states tried to impose an oil embargo, but without success. It would take another six years for America's strong commitment to Israel to hurt its Gulf ties significantly.

In the meantime, Washington grappled with London's exit from East of Suez. Busy with the Vietnam War, the Nixon administration desperately turned to the Iranians and Saudis, who were offended by the United States' pro-Israeli bias and therefore not predisposed to cater to U.S. needs. Riyadh nevertheless signed on to the Twin Pillars policy because it offered the Saudis weaponry, something they very much wanted. Tehran also readily bought into Washington's plan, as it aspired to dominate the Persian Gulf. As a result, proposition P3 (i.e., proxy contingent imperialism) seems apropos once more.

In this third stage (1959–72), the United States relied on alliance and proxy imperialism. This should not have surprised anyone since, in these years, America mostly tried to stem calamities instead of preventing or ending them. In December 1967, Undersecretary of State for Political Affairs Eugene V. Rostow stated: "We [i.e., Americans] believe in reaching [our] goal [to 'promote a system of peace'] through political means, and on the indispensable basis of the responsible decisions of the people of the region themselves." He added ironically (given his country's involvement in Vietnam) yet accurately that "[w]e cannot solve these problems [in the Middle East and elsewhere] alone. We do not have the wealth, the power, the wisdom, or the imperial will to build a world after the manner of the Romans." Washington's twin pursuits in this era—to balance enemies and export weapons to area partners—belied weakness rather than strength. Perhaps sensing this ebb in U.S. power, America's rivals sought henceforth to knock it from its precarious regional perch.[71]

Notes

1. Malcolm Kerr, *The Arab Cold War 1958–1967: A Study of Ideology in Politics* (London: Oxford University Press, 1967); and Phebe Marr, *The Modern History of Iraq* (Boulder, CO: Westview Press, 1985), 153–64.

2. Kerr, *The Arab Cold War*.

3. Thomas G. Paterson, *Contesting Castro: The United States and the Triumph of the Cuban Revolution* (New York: Oxford University Press, 1994); James G. Blight and David A. Welch, *On The Brink: Americans and Soviets Reexamine the Cuban Missile Crisis* (New York: Noonday Press, 1990); John Lewis Gaddis, *We Now Know: Rethinking Cold War History* (New York: Clarendon Press, 1997), 143–49, 260–80; and Philip Nash, *The Other Missiles of October: Eisenhower, Kennedy, and the Jupiters 1957–1963* (Chapel Hill, NC: University of North Carolina Press, 1997). See also the 1998–99 Cable News Network (CNN) series, "Cold War": episode 9, "The Wall"; and episode 10, "Cuba."

4. John Lewis Gaddis, *Strategies of Containment: A Critical Assessment of Postwar American National Security Policy* (New York: Oxford University Press, 1982), 198–236; and Robert Dallek, *The American Style of Foreign Policy: Cultural Politics and Foreign Affairs* (New York: Oxford University Press, 1983), 221–51.

5. Gaddis, *Strategies of Containment*, 237–73; Thomas J. McCormick, *America's Half-Century: United States Foreign Policy in the Cold War* (Baltimore: Johns Hopkins University Press, 1989), 125–54; George C. Herring, *America's Longest War: The United States and Vietnam 1950–1975* (New York: Alfred A. Knopf, 1986); David L. Anderson, ed., *Shadow on the White House: Presidents and the Vietnam War 1945–1975* (Lawrence, KS: University Press of Kansas, 1993); Marilyn B. Young, *The Vietnam Wars 1945–1990* (New York: Harper Perennial, 1991); and Yuen Foong Khong, *Analogies at War: Korea, Munich, Dien Bien Phu, and the Vietnam Decisions of 1965* (Princeton, NJ: Princeton University Press, 1992). See also CNN's "Cold War" series: episode 11, "Vietnam"; episode 12, "MAD"; and episode 13, "Make Love Not War: The 60s."

6. Gaddis, *Strategies of Containment*, 274–344; Raymond L. Garthoff, *Détente and Confrontation: American-Soviet Relations from Nixon to Reagan* (Washington, DC:

Brookings Institution, 1985), 1–105; McCormick, *America's Half-Century*, 155–67; and Dallek, *The American Style of Foreign Policy*, 252–82.

7. Robert J. McMahon, "Credibility and World Power: Exploring the Psychological Dimension in Postwar American Diplomacy," *Diplomatic History* 15, no. 4 (Fall 1991): 467–68; Cecil V. Crabb, *The Doctrines of American Foreign Policy: Their Meaning, Role, and Future* (Baton Rouge, LA: Louisiana State University Press, 1982), 278–324; Henry Kissinger, *White House Years* (Boston: Little, Brown, 1979), 222–25; and Gaddis, *Strategies of Containment*, 298–99, 304–6. Quote can be found in Gaddis, *Strategies of Containment*, 304. See also CNN's "Cold War" series: episode 15, "Red China 1949–72"; episode 16, "Détente 1969–75"; and episode 17, "Good Guys, Bad Guys 1967–78."

8. The United Kingdom signed a treaty in 1899 making it responsible for Kuwait's foreign policy. On this event and other background to the 1961 crisis, see Miriam Joyce, *Kuwait 1945–1996: An Anglo-American Perspective* (London: Frank Cass, 1998), 1–92. On the UK-Ottoman rivalry in Kuwait in the late nineteenth and early twentieth century, see Frederick F. Anscombe, *The Ottoman Gulf: The Creation of Kuwait, Saudi Arabia, and Qatar* (New York: Columbia University Press, 1997), 91–142.

9. Marr, *The Modern History of Iraq*, 159–80.

10. Telegram from U.S. Embassy in Iraq to Dean Rusk (U.S. Secretary of State), no. 912, 26 June 1961, John F. Kennedy (JFK) National Security Files (NSF), Box 129A, Folder A, John F. Kennedy Library (JFKL), Boston, MA. Quotes can be found in this document.

11. Telegram from Mak (U.S. Consulate in Kuwait) to Rusk, no. 215, 26 June 1961, JFK NSF, Box 129A, Folder A, JFKL. First quote can be found in this document. Telegram from Mak to Rusk, no. 216, 26 June 1961, JFK NSF, Box 129A, Folder A, JFKL; and Telegram from Mak to Rusk, no. 219, 26 June 1961, JFK NSF, Box 129A, Folder A, JFKL. Second quote can be found in this document.

12. Telegram from John Jernegan (U.S. Ambassador to Iraq) to Rusk, no. 914, 27 June 1961, JFK NSF, Box 129A, Folder A, JFKL, quote can be found in this document; Telegram from Jernegan to Rusk, no. 917, 27 June 1961, JFK NSF, Box 129A, Folder A, JFKL; and Telegram from Mak to Rusk, no. 223, 27 June 1961, JFK NSF, Box 129A, Folder A, JFKL.

13. Telegram from Rusk to the American Consulate in Kuwait, no. 257, 27 June 1961, JFK NSF, Box 129A, Folder A, JFKL. Quotes can be found in this document. See also Parker T. Hart, *Saudi Arabia and the United States: Birth of a Security Partnership* (Bloomington, IN: Indiana University Press, 1998), 78. Former Ambassador to Saudi Arabia and Kuwait Parker Hart characterizes U.S. policy toward Iraq at the time as "ambiguous." Hart, *Saudi Arabia and the United States*. On UK policy and behavior, see Nigel Ashton, "Britain and the Kuwaiti Crisis, 1961," *Diplomacy & Statecraft* 9, no. 1 (March 1998): 163–81; and W. Taylor Fain, "John F. Kennedy and Harold Macmillan: Managing the 'Special Relationship' in the Persian Gulf Region, 1961–63," *Middle Eastern Studies* 38, no. 4 (October 2002): 102–6.

14. Telegram from Jernegan to Rusk, no. 922, 28 June 1961, JFK NSF, Box 129A, Folder A, JFKL. In 1969, John S. Badeau, the U.S. Ambassador to Egypt in 1961, recalled a conversation with Nasser during the crisis where they discussed Qasim's decision making with respect to Kuwait. Badeau suggested that the Iraqi prime minister sought to nationalize the Iraq Petroleum Company. If Qasim could annex Kuwait, he would control much of the Near East's oil market. Nasser responded that Badeau might be correct, but he believed in a simpler explanation. The American offered the following "almost . . . exact quote" from Nasser: "I think Kassem [sic] and his chief of staff went to the men's room one morning. And one said to the other, 'Why don't we take Kuwait?' And the other one said, 'Well, Mufti by god, it's a good idea. Let's do it.'" Nasser added,

"That is the way many of our decisions are made." In his 1969 interview, Badeau pointed out, "Now of course, this is oversimplified, but there is a certain pragmatic element that he [Nasser] was picking out that I thought was very interesting. And, as a matter of fact, we [i.e., the United States] learned afterwards that there was a measure of truth to this. That there were certain circumstances that kind of threw this problem up suddenly to Kassem [sic] and he picked it up." Interview with John S. Badeau, 25 February 1969, John S. Badeau Oral History, JFKL.

15. Telegram from Jernegan to Rusk, no. 931, 29 June 1961, JFK NSF, Box 129A, Folder A, JFKL, quote can be found in this document; and Telegram from Adlai Stevenson (U.S. Ambassador to the United Nations) to Rusk, no. 3448, 29 June 1961, JFK NSF, Box 129A, Folder A, JFKL.

16. Message from Lord Home (U.K. Foreign Secretary) to Rusk, 29 June 1961, in Memorandum from Lucius D. Battle (Executive Secretary at the U.S. Department of State) to McGeorge Bundy (U.S. National Security Advisor), 29 June 1961, JFK NSF, Box 129A, Folder A, JFKL. Quotes can be found in this document. The UK policy of "interdependence," developed by the Foreign Office, "was designed," notes scholar Taylor Fain, "to redress the imbalance of power within the Anglo-American alliance by making British expertise in arcane areas [such as the Persian Gulf] indispensable to American policy makers." Fain, "John F. Kennedy and Harold Macmillan," 97. See also 101–2. On U.S.-UK relations in the early 1960s pertaining to the Persian Gulf, see 95–102.

17. Telegram from Rusk to the U.S. Embassy in the United Kingdom, no. 6138, 29 June 1961, JFK NSF, Box 129A, Folder A, JFKL, quotes can be found in this document.

18. Telegram from Rusk to U.S. Embassy in Cairo, no. 2220, 29 June 1961, JFK NSF, Box 129A, Folder A, JFKL, quote can be found in this document; Memorandum for Record, 486th Meeting of the National Security Council, 29 June 1961, JFK NSF, Box 313, Folder 13, JFKL; and Telegram from Rusk to U.S. Embassy in Saudi Arabia, no. 478, 29 June 1961, JFK NSF, Box 129A, Folder A, JFKL. On the importance of U.S. support for UK policy, see Ashton, "Britain and the Kuwaiti Crisis," 171, 173. See also Miriam Joyce, "Preserving the Sheikhdom: London, Washington, Iraq and Kuwait, 1958–61," *Middle Eastern Studies* 31, no. 2 (April 1995): 281–92; and Fain, "John F. Kennedy and Harold Macmillan," 105. According to Fain, American policy toward Kuwait "derived primarily from [Washington's] interest in general Gulf stability and in the value of [Kuwaiti] oil to its Western European allies." Fain, "John F. Kennedy and Harold Macmillan," 103.

19. Telegram from Bruce (U.S. Embassy in the United Kingdom) to Rusk, no. 5357, 30 June 1961, JFK NSF, Box 129A, Folder A, JFKL; Telegram from Bruce to Rusk, no. 5364, 30 June 1961, JFK NSF, Box 129A, Folder A, JFKL; Message from Mr. Smith (the White House) to General Clifton (U.S. Military), 30 June 1961, JFK NSF, Box 129A, Folder A, JFKL; and Telegram from Thompson (U.S. Embassy in the Soviet Union) to Rusk, no. 3268, 30 June 1961, JFK NSF, Box 129A, Folder A, JFKL.

20. Telegram from Rusk to the U.S. Consulate in Kuwait, no. 283, 30 June 1961, JFK NSF, Box 129A, Folder A, JFKL. On the official U.S. position, see also Circular Telegram from Rusk, no. 2142, 30 June 1961, JFK NSF, Box 129A, Folder A, JFKL.

21. Telegram from Mak to Rusk, no. 2, 1 July 1961, JFK NSF, Box 129A, Folder A, JFKL; Telegram from Bruce to Rusk, no. 3, 1 July 1961, JFK NSF, Box 129A, Folder A, JFKL; Telegram from Bruce to Rusk, no. 4, 1 July 1961, JFK NSF, Box 129A, Folder A, JFKL; Circular Telegram from Rusk, no. 6, 2 July 1961, JFK NSF, Box 129A, Folder A, JFKL. First two quotes can be found in this document. "U.S. Support for Kuwait and British Effort," Memorandum written by the Joint Chiefs of Staff, under the heading of "Operations/Military Policy Matters," 3 July 1961, JFK NSF, Box 129A, Folder A, JFKL. Final quote can be found in this document. On UK thinking, see

Message from Lord Home to Rusk, 2 July 1961, in Memorandum from Battle to Bundy, 3 July 1961, JFK NSF, Box 129A, Folder A, JFKL. On *Operation Vantage*, see Fain, "John F. Kennedy and Harold Macmillan," 104. The U.S. military also authorized TF-88 (presumably Task Force 88) to sail for Bahrain "as a precautionary move and in order to position a potential reinforcing naval force accessible to the Kuwait trouble area[.]" See Message from Commander Shepard (the White House) to General Clifton (Hyannisport), no date (but either 1 or 2 July 1961), JFK NSF, Box 129A, Folder A, JFKL. John Jernegan, the U.S. Ambassador to Iraq, counseled that the United States not send reinforcements to the Persian Gulf since the British commitment seemed substantial. He cabled that "addition[al] US naval force would seem to me to be superfluous and politically very disadvantageous." Telegram from Jernegan to Rusk, no. 10, 3 July 1961, JFK NSF, Box 129A, Folder A, JFKL. For Nasser's reaction to the British disembarkment as well as an overview of the entire crisis from both a regional and international perspective, see Benjamin Shwadran, "The Kuwait Incident," *Middle Eastern Affairs* 13, no. 1 (January 1962): 2–13. In his excellent contemporary article, Shwadran describes the U.S. role as "passive," an accurate assessment of U.S. policy, but one that fails to account for the American contribution to the denouement of the crisis. For other analyses of the 1961 episode, see Joyce, *Kuwait 1945–1996*, 93–108; and Hart, *Saudi Arabia and the United States*, 74–78.

22. Benjamin Shwadran, "The Kuwait Incident," *Middle Eastern Affairs* 13, no. 2 (February 1962): 43–46. For the Kuwaiti contention, see Statement by Abdul Aziz Hussein to the Security Council, 5 July 1961, in JFK White House Central Subject Files (WHCSF), Box 63, JFKL. For the U.S. statement before the same body, see *American Foreign Policy: Current Documents 1961* (Washington, DC: Government Printing Office, 1965), 693–94. On U.S. incredulity regarding the Iraqi menace, see Ashton, "Britain and the Kuwaiti Crisis," 172.

23. Telegram from Jernegan to Rusk, no. 15, 5 July 1961, JFK NSF, Box 129A, Folder A, JFKL. On the Arab League proceedings, see Shwadran, "The Kuwait Incident," 46–52; Telegram from John Badeau (U.S. Ambassador to Egypt) to Rusk, no. 94, 14 July 1961, JFK NSF, Box 129A, Folder B, JFKL; and Telegram from Badeau to Rusk, no. 148, 20 July 1961, JFK NSF, Box 129A, Folder B, JFKL. For the Kuwaiti reaction, see Telegram from Mak to Rusk, no. 32, 23 July 1961, JFK NSF, Box 129A, Folder B, JFKL. For the Iraqi reaction, see Jernegan to Rusk, no. 68, 29 July 1961, JFK NSF, Box 129A, Folder B, JFKL.

24. Joyce, *Kuwait 1945–1996*, 127–34.

25. In response to a Qasim query regarding the American endorsement of UK policy during the crisis, Jernegan opined that "it was not a question of support but that we did not oppose moves [the] British had made." Jernegan to Rusk, 29 July 1961. This American preference for comity contrasted markedly with President Eisenhower's angry repudiation of the UK course of action during the 1956 Suez crisis. For information on events in Kuwait following the 1961 incident (i.e., 1961–1968), see Joyce, *Kuwait 1945–1996*, 108–58.

26. Hart, *Saudi Arabia and the United States*, 234, first quote can be found on 234; and Fawaz A. Gerges, *The Superpowers and the Middle East: Regional and International Politics, 1955–1967* (Boulder, CO: Westview Press, 1994), 128–35. Second quote can be found on 131.

27. Arthur M. Schlesinger, Jr., *A Thousand Days: John F. Kennedy in the White House* (Boston: Houghton Mifflin, 1965), 566–67. Both quotes can be found on 566.

28. Hart, *Saudi Arabia and the United States*, 129–35; and "Turmoil in Prospect in the Yemen," Intelligence Note from Roger Hilsman (U.S. State Department Director of Intelligence and Research) to George Ball (Acting U.S. Secretary of State), 27 September 1962, JFK NSF, Box 207, Folder 8/61–9/62, JFKL.

29. Telegram from George Ball (U.S. Assistant Secretary of State) to USUN (U.S. Embassy at the United Nations), 27 September 1962, JFK NSF, Box 207, Folder 8/61–9/62, JFKL. Quote can be found in this document. See also Telegram from Badeau to Rusk, no. 538, 1 October 1962, JFK NSF, Box 207, Folder 10/1/62–10/8/62, JFKL; Circular Telegram from Rusk, no. 575, 2 October 1962, JFK NSF, Box 207, Folder 8/61–9/62, JFKL; and Circular Telegram from Rusk, no. 579, 3 October 1962, JFK NSF, Box 207, Folder 8/61–9/62, JFKL. In that document, Rusk pointed out that the presence of some one hundred and ten Americans in Yemen—hired to build roads and water projects—warranted special attention on Washington's part. He claimed, however, that the United States would consult with Whitehall previous to any "unilateral action." For an overview and analysis of the situation, see Memorandum from William H. Brubeck (Executive Secretary of the U.S. Department of State) to Bundy, 4 October 1962, JFK NSF, Box 207, Folder 10/1/62–10/8/62, JFKL. In that document, Brubeck refers to previous Soviet aid to the Yemenis and Moscow's recognition of the new regime. He also states that the Kremlin "would hope to expand its position of influence in Yemen." For U.S. and British interests at stake, see Fain, "John F. Kennedy and Harold Macmillan," 108–9.

30. Gerges, *The Superpowers and the Middle East*, 145–47, 149–50; and George Lenczowski, *American Presidents and the Middle East* (Durham, NC: Duke University Press, 1990), 79. Quote can be found in Telegram from Badeau to Rusk, no. 583, 6 October 1962, JFK NSF, Box 207, Folder 10/1/62–10/8/62, JFKL.

31. Lenczowski, *American Presidents and the Middle East*, 80; Gerges, *The Superpowers and the Middle East*, 151–53; Burton I. Kaufman, *The Arab Middle East and the United States: Inter-Arab Rivalry and Superpower Diplomacy* (New York: Twayne, 1996), 35; "Saudi Instability Sharpened by Yemen Coup," Intelligence Note from Hilsman to Rusk, 4 October 1962, JFK NSF, Box 207, Folder 10/1/62–10/8/62, JFKL; and Telegram from Lewis (U.S. Embassy in Jordan) to Rusk, no. 197, 6 October 1962, JFK NSF, Box 207, Folder 10/1/62–10/8/62, JFKL. On Faisal's ascension to power and his leadership style, see Hart, *Saudi Arabia and the United States*, 89.

32. Gerges, *The Superpowers and the Middle East*, 154–56.

33. Gerges, *The Superpowers and the Middle East*, 157; Lenczowski, *American Presidents and the Middle East*, 80–81; Circular Telegram from Ball, no. 612, 6 October 1962, JFK NSF, Box 207, Folder 10/1/62–10/8/62, JFKL; Circular Telegram from Ball, no. 615, 7 October 1962, JFK NSF, Box 207, Folder 10/1/62–10/8/62, JFKL; and Telegram from Ball to American Legation in Yemen, no. 121, 6 October 1962, JFK NSF, Box 207, Folder 10/1/62–10/8/62, JFKL. On King Saud's decision not to renew the Dhahran Airfield Agreement, see Hart, *Saudi Arabia and the United States*, 82–87. The U.S. Military Training Mission remained in Saudi Arabia, however. Hart, *Saudi Arabia and the United States*, 87–88.

34. Gerges, *The Superpowers and the Middle East*, 154; Rusk to U.S. Embassy in Egypt, no. 409, 13 October 1962, JFK NSF, Box 207, Folder 10/9/62–10/15/62, JFKL; "United States Position On Recognition of Yemen Arab Republic, 17 October 1962," JFK NSF, Box 207, Folder 10/16/62–10/31/62, JFKL; and Memorandum from Robert W. Komer (Special White House Assistant to JFK) to President Kennedy, 18 October 1962, JFK NSF, Box 207, Folder 10/16/62–10/31/62, JFKL. As the crisis intensified, Kennedy aide Robert Komer confided to Bundy: "I still agree with [the] State [Department] that we [i.e., United States] should stand aloof, while trying to get both sides not to over commit themselves. . . . All in all, we're in for a rough time in [the] Middle East over [the] next year or so. The Yemen revolt merely shows how fragile some of these [area] regimes are." Memorandum from Komer to Bundy, 11 October 1962, JFK NSF, Box 207, Folder 10/9/62–10/15/62, JFKL.

35. Lenczowski, *American Presidents and the Middle East*, 83; Memorandum on "United States Recognition of the Yemen Arab Republic" from Brubeck to Bundy, 6 December 1962, JFK NSF, Box 207A, Folder 12/62, JFKL; Telegram from Ball to U.S. Embassy in Egypt, no. 628, 14 December 1962, JFK NSF, Box 207A, Folder 12/62, JFKL; and Memorandum from Komer to Bundy, 18 December 1962, JFK NSF, Box 207A, Folder 12/62, JFKL.

36. Telegram from the U.S. Department of State to the U.S. Embassy in Egypt, No. 686, 4 January 1963, JFK NSF, Box 208, Folder 1/63, JFKL; Circular Telegram from Rusk, No. 1227, 11 January 1963, JFK NSF, Box 208, Folder 1/63, JFKL. First four quotes can be found in that document; Komer Memorandum for the Record, 25 January 1963, JFK WHCSF, Box 75, Folder CO 320, JFKL. "Realpolitik" quote can be found in this document. Underline in original. Telegram from Rusk to U.S. Embassy in Saudi Arabia, No. 415, 16 January 1963, JFK NSF, Box 208, Folder 1/63, JFKL; Telegram from Rusk to U.S. Embassy in Egypt, No. 908, 18 January 1963, JFK NSF, Box 208, Folder 1/63, JFKL; Badeau to Rusk, No. 1040, 21 January 1963, JFK NSF, Box 208, Folder 1/63, JFKL; Telegram from Rusk to the U.S. Embassy in the United Kingdom, No. 3959, 27 January 1963, JFK NSF, Box 208, Folder 1/63, JFKL; Telegram from Ball to U.S. Embassy in the United Kingdom, No. 4299, 12 February 1963, JFK NSF, Box 208, Folder 2/63, JFKL; Airgram from Rusk to U.S. Embassies in Addis Ababa, etc., No. CA-9409, 2 March 1963, JFK NSF, Box 208, Folder 3/63–4/63, JFKL, last quote can be found in that document; and Komer Memorandum for Record, 26 February 1963, JFK NSF, Box 208, Folder 2/63, JFKL.

37. Airgram from Rusk to U.S. Embassies in Addis Ababa, etc., 2 March 1963; Telegram from Badeau to Rusk, no. 951, 9 January 1963, JFK NSF, Box 208, Folder UAR Cables 1/63–3/63, JFKL; Telegram from Horner (Dhahran) to Rusk, no. 215, 13 February 1963, JFK NSF, Box 208, Folder Saudi Arabian Cables 1/63–3/63, JFKL; Ball to U.S. Embassy in Saudi Arabia, no. 481, 14 February 1963, JFK NSF, Folder Saudi Arabian Cables 1/63–3/63, JFKL; Horner to Rusk, no. 236, 2 March 1963, JFK NSF, Folder Saudi Arabian Cables 1/63–3/63, JFKL; Message from Rusk to Lord Home, 7 March 1963, JFK NSF, Box 208, Folder 3/63–4/63, JFKL; Message from Lord Home to Rusk, 16 March 1963, JFK NSF, Box 208, Folder 3/63–4/63, JFKL; and Memorandum from Komer to Bundy, 7 February 1963, JFK NSF, Box 208, Folder 2/63, JFKL. Quote can be found in that document.

38. Telegram from Rusk to USUN, no. 2028, 28 January 1963, JFK NSF, Box 208, Folder 1/63, JFKL; Telegram from Rusk to the U.S. Embassy in Yemen, no. 502, 25 February 1963, JFK NSF, Box 208, Folder 2/63, JFKL; Telegram from Badeau to Rusk, no. 1034, 19 January 1963, JFK NSF, Box 208, Folder UAR Cables 1/63–3/63, JFKL, first quote can be found in that document; Komer Memorandum for Record, 26 February 1963, next two quotes can be found in that document; Telegram from Rusk to the U.S. Embassy in the United Kingdom, no. 4592, 28 February 1963, JFK NSF, Box 208, Folder 2/63, JFKL, last quote can be found in that document; Telegram from Horner (Dhahran) to Rusk, no. 252, 8 March 1963, JFK President's Office Files (POF), Box 128A, Folder 8, JFKL; Memorandum from Phillips Talbot (Near Eastern Affairs Department, U.S. Department of State) to Rusk, 11 March 1963, JFK POF, Box 128A, Folder 8, JFKL; Memorandum from Komer to President Kennedy, 11 March 1963, JFK POF, Box 128A, Folder 8, JFKL; Telegram from Rusk to U.S. Embassy in Egypt, no. 2403, 13 April 1963, JFK NSF, Box 208, Folder 3/63–4/63, JFKL; and Telegram from Rusk to U.S. Embassy in Saudi Arabia, no. 655, 18 April 1963, JFK NSF, Box 208, Folder 3/63–4/63, JFKL. In March 1963, the U.S. Joint Chiefs of Staff ordered CINCNELM to "maintain two ships off Jidda until further notice." See Rusk to U.S. Embassy in Saudi Arabia, no. 577, 14 March 1963, JFK NSF, Box 208, Folder Saudi Arabian Cables 1/63–3/63, JFKL.

39. Hart, *Saudi Arabia and the United States*, 165–201; Memorandum from Komer to Bundy, 1 May 1963, JFK NSF, Box 208, Folder 5/63, JFKL; Telegram from Meyer (U.S. Embassy in Lebanon) to Rusk, no. 1044, 9 May 1963, JFK NSF, Box 208, Folder 5/63, JFKL; Telegram from Rusk to the American Consul General in Jerusalem, no. 168, 9 May 1963, JFK NSF, Box 208, Folder 5/63, JFKL; Rusk to USUN, no. 2889, 16 May 1963, JFK NSF, Box 208, Folder 5/63, JFKL; Memorandum from Komer to President Kennedy, 24 May 1963, JFK NSF, Box 208, Folder 5/63, JFKL; Memorandum from Komer to President Kennedy, 27 May 1963, JFK NSF, Box 208, Folder 5/63, JFKL; Memorandum from Komer to Bundy, 28 May 1963, JFK NSF, Box 208, Folder 5/63, JFKL; Memorandum from Komer to Bundy, 31 May 1963, JFK NSF, Box 208, Folder 5/63, JFKL; Memorandum from Komer to President Kennedy, 7 June 1963, JFK NSF, Box 208, Folder 6/63, JFKL; and Memorandum from HHS [Harold H. Saunders, Middle East expert at the NSC] to CK [Carl Kaysen, NSC], 26 June 1963, JFK NSF, Box 208, Folder 6/63, JFKL.

40. Hart, *Saudi Arabia and the United States*, 202–36; and Michael A. Palmer, *Guardians of the Gulf: A History of America's Expanding Role in the Persian Gulf, 1833–1992* (New York: Free Press, 1992), 81.

41. Memorandum from Sherman Kent (Chairman of the Central Intelligence Agency [CIA] Board of National Estimates) to the CIA Director, 2 July 1963, JFK NSF, Box 208A, Folder 7/63, JFKL; Telegram from Badeau to Rusk, no. 121, 11 July 1963, JFK POF, Box 128A, Folder 8, JFKL, quote can be found in that document; Telegram from Rusk to U.S. Embassy in Egypt, no. 184, 11 July 1963, JFK NSF, Box 208A, Folder 7/63, JFKL; Memorandum from Komer to President Kennedy, 12 July 1963, JFK NSF, Box 208A, Folder 7/63, JFKL; Hart, *Saudi Arabia and the United States*, 248–51; and Kerr, *The Arab Cold War*, 141–51. President Kennedy referred to the Yemeni War as "Komer's war." See Memorandum from Komer to Bundy, 12 July 1963, JFK NSF, Box 208A, Folder 7/63, JFKL.

42. Hart, *Saudi Arabia and the United States*, 218–36. Quote can be found on 232.

43. Kerr, *The Arab Cold War*, 127–69; Gerges, *The Superpowers and the Middle East*, 179–80; and Kaufman, *The Arab Middle East and the United States*, 46, 50–53.

44. Kaufman, *The Arab Middle East and the United States*, 54–57; John G. Stoessinger, *Why Nations Go to War* (New York: St. Martin's Press, 1990), 160–67; Palmer, *Guardians of the Gulf*, 83; Telegram from the Embassy in Iraq to the Department of State, 8 June 1967, *Foreign Relations of the United States* [hereafter *FRUS*], 1964–1968, 21, *Near East Region; Arabian Peninsula* (Washington, DC: Government Printing Office, 2000), 381–83; Telegram from the Embassy in Kuwait to the Department of State, 7 June 1967, *FRUS*, 1964–1968, 21: 401–3; Telegram from the Embassy in Kuwait to the Department of State, 10 June 1967, *FRUS*, 1964–1968, 21: 403–5; and Telegram from the Embassy in Saudi Arabia to the Department of State, 23 June 1967, *FRUS*, 1964–1968, 21: 567–72.

45. Telegram from the Embassy in Kuwait to the Department of State, 10 June 1967, *FRUS*, 1964–1968, 21: 403; Palmer, *Guardians of the Gulf*, 83–84; and Daniel Yergin, *The Prize: The Epic Quest for Oil, Money & Power* (New York: Simon & Schuster, 1991), 554–58. On 1967–1973 OPEC policy and the transformation of the oil industry in these years, see Yergin, *The Prize*, 563–87.

46. Kaufman, *The Arab Middle East and the United States*, 55–61; William B. Quandt, *Peace Process: American Diplomacy and the Arab-Israeli Conflict since 1967* (Washington, DC, and Berkeley, CA: The Brookings Institution and University of California Press, 1993), 25–62; Richard B. Parker, *The Politics of Miscalculation in the Middle East* (Bloomington, IN: Indiana University Press, 1993), 3–122; Lenczowski, *American Presidents and the Middle East*, 105–15; and Douglas Little, *American Orientalism: The United States and the Middle East Since 1945* (Chapel Hill, NC: University of North

Carolina Press, 2004), 101. For an overview of 1945–1967 U.S.-Israeli relations, see Little, *American Orientalism*, 77–102.

47. Little, *American Orientalism*, 102; and "The Eastern Arab World In The Aftermath Of Defeat," National Intelligence Estimate (NIE 30-2-68), 19 December 1968, *FRUS*, 1964–1968, 21: 81–82.

48. Information Memorandum from the Assistant Secretary of State for Near Eastern and South Asian Affairs (Battle) to Acting Secretary of State Katzenbach, 19 June 1967, *FRUS*, 1964–1968, 21: 215–17; Information Memorandum from the President's Special Assistant (Rostow) to President Johnson, 29 November 1967, *FRUS*, 1964–1968, 21: 248; Memorandum from Secretary of State Rusk to President Johnson, 4 December 1967, *FRUS*, 1964–1968, 21: 249; and T.B. Millar, "Soviet Policies South and East of Suez," *Foreign Affairs* 49, no. 1 (October 1970): 70–80.

49. *Washington Post*, 9 April 1967, in Foreign and Commonwealth Office [hereafter FCO] 17/11, Public Record Office [hereafter PRO], Kew, Surrey, England. First quote can be found in that article. "Future of South Arabia," Paper Prepared in the Department of State, Undated but Prepared for NSC Meeting of 24 May 1967, *FRUS*, 1964–1968, 21: 211–15. Second and third quotes can be found on 213. The State Department noted that the Shah "regards Aden as the backdoor to the Gulf. He exaggerates but is quite right in regarding South Arabia as a major test of strength between Arab radicals and Arab moderates." Quoted on 214.

50. "The Persian Gulf States," National Intelligence Estimate (NIE 30-1-67), 18 May 1967, *FRUS*, 1964–1968, 21: 206–8. First quote can be found on 208. Information Memorandum from the Assistant Secretary of State for Near Eastern and South Asian Affairs (Battle) to Secretary of State Rusk, 20 November 1967, *FRUS*, 1964–1968, 21: 244–45; and Briefing Memorandum from the Assistant Secretary of State for Near Eastern and South Asian Affairs (Battle) to Secretary of State Rusk, 9 January 1968, *FRUS*, 1964–1968, 21: 256–58. Second quote can be found in A.R. Moore (Foreign Office) to J.E. Killick (U.K. Embassy in Washington), 29 September 1967, FCO 17/11, PRO. For the Holmes Report, see "Near East, North Africa and the Horn of Africa: A Recommended American Strategy," Report Prepared by the Special State-Defense Study Group, Undated (the Office of the Secretary of Defense received it on 17 July 1967), *FRUS*, 1964–1968, 21: 49–58. The Holmes Report noted (51) the following U.S. interests, *inter alia*: "to maintain the means of strategic access, particularly through the Mediterranean, that are required if Western strength is to be brought to bear in the Northern Tier of Greece, Turkey and Iran; and to hinder Soviet access to the [Near East] region by strengthening the Northern Tier countries themselves."

51. "Defence Adjustments: Persian Gulf," Foreign Office Brief, Planning Staff, 25 January 1968, Talking Points Prepared for Prime Minister's Visit to Washington & Canada, February 1968, FCO 49/153, PRO; "Background Note to Brief," FCO 49/153, PRO; Annex A, Background Paper, "Withdrawal from the Persian Gulf," FCO 49/153, PRO; "Her Majesty's Government's Policy in the Gulf: Summary of Despatch of 27 January 1968," in FCO 49/153, PRO; Stewart Crawford to the Right Honourable George Brown [UK Foreign Minister], "Her Majesty's Government's Policy in the Gulf," FCO 49/153, PRO; Record of a Conversation between Mr. Goronwy Roberts, M.P., Minister of State, Foreign Office, and T.H. The Rulers of Qatar and Dubai in Dubai, 8 January 1968, FCO 7/792, PRO; Mr. Arthur (U.K. Embassy in Kuwait) to Foreign Office, 17 January 1968, FCO 7/792, PRO; The Center for Strategic and International Studies (CSIS), *The Gulf: Implications of British Withdrawal*, Special Reports Series no. 8 (Washington, DC: Georgetown University, 1969); D.C. Watt, "The Decision to Withdraw from the Gulf," *Political Quarterly* 39, no. 3 (July-September 1968): 310–21; William D. Brewer, "Yesterday and Tomorrow in the Persian Gulf," *Middle East Journal* 23, no. 2 (Spring 1969): 149–58; David Holden, "The Persian Gulf: After

the British Raj," *Foreign Affairs* 49, no. 4 (July 1971): 721–35; F. Gregory Gause, "British and American Policies in the Persian Gulf, 1968–1973," *Review of International Studies* 11, no. 4 (October 1985): 249–58; Yergin, *The Prize*, 565–66; and Jeffrey Pickering, *Britain's Withdrawal from East of Suez: The Politics of Retrenchment* (New York: St. Martin's Press, 1998), 177–93. Quote can be found in Battle to Rusk, 9 January 1968, 257.

52. "Defence Adjustments: Persian Gulf." Quotes can be found in Battle to Rusk, 9 January 1968.

53. Battle to Rusk, 9 January 1968.

54. "Withdrawal from the Persian Gulf," Background Paper, 1968 [April?], FCO 49/153, PRO.

55. Dean Rusk to George Brown, 6 January 1968, FCO 8/36, PRO. First quote can be found in that document. "Withdrawal of the British Military Presence from the Persian Gulf," A.B. Urwick (U.K. Embassy in Washington) to A.J.D. Stirling (Arabian Department, Foreign Office), 18 January 1968, FCO 8/36, PRO; "The Persian Gulf," Urwick to M.S. Weir (Arabian Department), 5 February 1968, FCO 8/36, PRO; "The Persian Gulf," Urwick to Weir, 15 February 1968, FCO 8/36, PRO; "The Persian Gulf," Urwick to Weir, 26 February 1968, FCO 8/36, PRO; Urwick to D.J. McCarthy (Aden Department, Foreign Office), 17 June 1968, FCO 8/37, PRO. Second quote can be found in that document. "United States and British Foreign Policy," Minute by Hood, 30 September 1968, FCO 7/778, PRO; CSIS, *The Gulf*, 18; Marr, *The Modern History of Iraq*, 204–25; and Gause, "British and American Policies in the Persian Gulf," 258–62.

56. Warren Unna, "Trucial States May Test Nixon Doctrine," *International Herald Tribune*, 18 February 1970, in FCO 8/1304, PRO. First quote can be found in that article. "Press Interview with Mr. Eugene Rostow," Killick to R.A. Sykes (U.K. Defence Department), 25 January 1968, FCO 8/36, PRO. See also text of Rostow's interview in that document. In his interview, Rostow noted: "In many ways the whole of postwar history has been a process of American movement to take over positions of stability, positions of security, which Britain, France, the Netherlands, Belgium had previously held"; Richard Beeston, "U.S. Blunder Imperils Gulf Pact," *Daily Telegraph* (London), 23 January 1968, FCO 8/36, PRO; "The Persian Gulf," Urwick to Weir, 29 January 1968, FCO 8/36, PRO; "U.S. Policy in the Middle East," Paper Prepared in the Department of State, 19 July 1968, *FRUS*, 1964–1968, 21: 76–78. Second quote can be found on 77. Record of Meeting (Interdepartmental Regional Group For Near East And South Asia [IRG/NEA]), 1 February 1968, *FRUS*, 1964–1968, 21: 272–73. Third quote can be found on 272. Fourth quote can be found on 273. Background Paper Prepared in the Department of State, 2 February 1968, *FRUS*, 1964–1968, 21: 274–75; "Security And Subversion In The Persian Gulf," Intelligence Report, 1 March 1968, *FRUS*, 1964–1968, 21: 283–84; "The Politico-Military Problem For the US In the Arabian Sea Littoral," Paper Prepared in the Department of State, 15 April 1968, *FRUS*, 1964–1968, 21: 289–91; Memorandum From the Deputy Assistant Secretary of Defense for International Security Affairs (Schwartz) to the Assistant Secretary of Defense for International Security Affairs (Warnke), 22 April 1968, *FRUS*, 1964–1968, 21: 292; Memorandum From the Assistant Secretary of Defense for International Security Affairs (Warnke) to Secretary of Defense McNamara, 12 June 1968, *FRUS*, 1964–1968, 21: 296–97; Memorandum From the Joint Chiefs of Staff to Secretary of Defense McNamara, 19 June 1968, *FRUS*, 1964–1968, 21: 298–99; Record of Meeting (IRG/NEA), 10 July 1968, *FRUS*, 1964–1968, 21: 299–301; Memorandum of Conversation (US/UK Middle East Talks), 13 September 1968, *FRUS*, 1964–1968, 21: 313–22; and "Neo-Isolationism," Sir Patrick Dean to Michael Stewart (Foreign Office), 16 July 1968, FCO 7/778, PRO. In that document, Sir Patrick opined that "American disenchantment with [the Central Treaty Organization (CENTO)] is most unlikely to be reversed. However strongly the Americans feel about Turkey, Iran or Saudi

Arabia, the CENTO Treaty is in practice little more relevant to these cases than it is to that of Israel which seems bound to remain an outstanding exception to the general desire for [U.S.] disengagement. . . ." In October 1968, one UK official wrote to another: "[The Americans] are, without briefing from us [i.e., the British Government], doing exactly the right thing in emphasizing the importance of Saudi/Iranian understanding and of co-operation rather than territorial demands." The same individual acknowledged that "U.S. influence on the Shah may become important at some stage. But we [i.e., the UK Government] do not think that that stage is now. The Shah is pretty good, whatever the subject, at playing the Americans and British off against one another." D.J. McCarthy (Foreign Office) to Urwick, 4 October 1968, FCO 8/37, PRO.

57. Kissinger, *White House Years*, 1258–65. For an overview of Nixon's Middle East policy, see Donald Neff, "Nixon's Middle East Policy: From Balance to Bias," *Arab Studies Quarterly* 12, nos. 1 and 2 (Winter/Spring 1990): 121–52.

58. On Kennedy and Johnson policies vis-à-vis the Persian Gulf, see Little, *American Orientalism*, 137–43.

59. "U.S. Interests In and Policy Toward the Persian Gulf," *Hearings Before the Subcommittee on the Near East of the Committee on Foreign Affairs*, House of Representatives, 92nd Congress, 2nd Session, 2 February, 7 June, 8 and 15 August 1972 (Washington, DC: Government Printing Office, 1972), 75–106. Quotes can be found on 80, 85.

60. Quotes can be found in "U.S. Interests In and Policy Toward the Persian Gulf," 83.

61. Quote can be found in "U.S. Interests In and Policy Toward the Persian Gulf," 83. For more information on U.S. policy, see Record of Anglo-American Talks on the Middle East, State Department, Washington, D.C., 18 November 1970, FCO 8/1304, PRO; "US Future Role in Persian Gulf," *Times* (London), FCO 8/1304, PRO; and Unna, "Trucial States May Test Nixon Doctrine." According to a British memorandum, in December 1970, Washington "notified all the 'littoral' countries of [its] intention to maintain MIDEASTFOR at Bahrain. In doing so, [the Americans] said that their decision had been taken independently of any British decision about a future military presence in the Gulf." The memo added that, "[t]he Ruler of Bahrain had welcomed the decision and no other country had raised any objection." Memo from D.J. Hall (Defence Department) to Mr. Edes (Arabian Department), 29 December 1970, Re: COMIDEASTFOR, FCO 8/1304, PRO. Although the Shah objected to the presence of extraregional navies (Soviet, American, or otherwise) in the Persian Gulf, the Nixon administration considered MIDEASTFOR justified given that five Soviet vessels had visited the Gulf in 1969–70— the first such forays since 1905. A UK memo noted that "[t]he Americans had . . . decided that [F]ree World interests would be served by continuing Mideastfor as at present . . . . [T]his did not mean a base at Bahrain but only that the American ships had home port facilities there; . . . they would spend 2/3 of their time outside the Gulf." Memo from D.F. Murray to Mr. Breeze, 12 December 1970, Re: MIDEASTFOR, FCO 8/1304, PRO.

62. "U.S. Interests In and Policy Toward the Persian Gulf," 1–21, 139–47. Quotes can be found on 5, 20, 143.

63. Quotes can be found in "U.S. Interests In and Policy Toward the Persian Gulf," 6, 14–15.

64. Little, *American Orientalism*, 143–46; and Gause, "British and American Policies in the Persian Gulf," 262–66. On U.S. relations with Iran and Saudi Arabia during the Cold War, see John P. Miglietta, *American Alliance Policy in the Middle East, 1945–1992: Iran, Israel, and Saudi Arabia* (Lanham, MD: Lexington Books, 2002).

65. David E. Long, *The United States and Saudi Arabia: Ambivalent Allies* (Boulder, CO: Westview Press, 1985), 54–55.

66. Barry Rubin, *Paved with Good Intentions: The American Experience and Iran* (New York: Oxford University Press, 1980), 124–49; Gary Sick, *All Fall Down: America's Tragic Encounter with Iran* (New York: Random House, 1985), 13–21; Yergin, *The Prize*, 566, 580–83; Franz Schurmann, *The Foreign Politics of Richard Nixon: The Grand Design* (Berkeley, CA: Institute of International Studies University of California, 1987), 256–96; and James A. Bill, *The Eagle and the Lion: The Tragedy of American-Iranian Relations* (New Haven, CT: Yale University Press, 1988), 197–205. For information on the Shah's White Revolution and other internal as well as external policies from 1959 to 1970, see Bill, *The Eagle and the Lion*, 120–82.

67. Rubin, *Paved with Good Intentions*, 132–33; Joseph A. Kechichian, *Oman and the World: The Emergence of an Independent Foreign Policy* (Santa Monica, CA: RAND, 1995), 99–100; and Marr, *The Modern History of Iraq*, 220–25.

68. Kissinger, *White House Years*, 1258–65, quote can be found on 1261–62; and Henry Kissinger, *Years of Upheaval* (Boston: Little, Brown, 1982), 667–70.

69. Jeffrey A. Lefebvre, "The Transformation of U.S. Security Policy in the Gulf: Strategic Disruption and the Balance of Risk" (paper presented at the annual meeting of the New England Political Science Association, New London, CT, 2–3 May 1997), 1–4. See also Jeffrey A. Lefebvre, "The Transformation of U.S. Security Policy in the Gulf: Strategic Disruption and the Balance of Risk," *Middle East Affairs Journal* 5, nos. 1/2 (Winter/Spring 1999): 51–54.

70. See, for example, F. Gregory Gause, III, *Oil Monarchies: Domestic and Security Challenges in the Arab Gulf States* (New York: Council on Foreign Relations Press, 1994); and Ian Skeet, *Oman: Politics and Development* (New York: St. Martin's Press, 1992).

71. Quote can be found in "The Middle Eastern Crisis and Beyond," Eugene V. Rostow, Under Secretary of State for Political Affairs, Address to University of Mississippi Law School, 8 December 1967, FCO 17/11, PRO.

Chapter 5

Insults and Reorientations: 1973–89

In the *fourth* stage (1973–89) of its postwar expansion in the Persian Gulf, the United States experienced economic hardship and repeated humiliations. Events rendered Washington mostly impotent. For some dozen years, presidents could not reverse a political tide that threatened to wash America out of the region. Only in Ronald Reagan's second term did the White House discover what Gulf current it should steer to recover some of its lost influence.

In the prior stage (1959–72), the United States promoted diplomatic solutions whenever problems arose or else encouraged friends to take the initiative. Crises in Kuwait, Yemen, and elsewhere in the Gulf tested America's commitment to the region's security. Reliance on the United Kingdom, Iran, and Saudi Arabia enabled Washington to husband valuable resources and marshal them when necessary elsewhere, such as in Vietnam.

The Nixon administration's recruitment of the Iranians and Saudis as area gendarmes, charged with warding off threats to American interests, exposed the White House to their whims as well as those of regional bullies, such as Iraq. Whether Tehran and Riyadh would remain loyal to the United States could not be divined. Periodically, Shah Mohammed Reza Pahlavi and King Faisal conveyed to U.S. diplomats their irritation and impatience with facets of American policy. Washington's sometimes imprudent course of action therefore could harm its position, rather than entrench it. Yet, invariably, results hinged on developments in the Middle East that America could not anticipate.[1]

If the Arab-Israeli standoff stayed unresolved, for example, then the United States could expect its standing in the Gulf to diminish. Successful mediation could ameliorate the U.S. predicament, however, and earn the White House recognition as a benevolent intermediary. Reflexive endorsement of Israel would not improve Washington's infamous reputation within the Arab world as a biased broker, confirmed, if not forged, when Lyndon B. Johnson condoned Israeli policy in the 1967 Six-Day War.

The matter of oil also loomed. As a result of the 1971 Tehran and Tripoli agreements, the Organization of Petroleum Exporting Countries (OPEC) sought to fix prices and control distribution, confident that the Western "majors" and independents could not easily dismiss OPEC concerns. With worldwide as well as U.S. demand on the increase, and with supplies scarce, America could not alienate states such as Saudi Arabia and Kuwait lest they resort to drastic measures that could dislocate the American and international economy. Arab frustration could even result in Washington's ejection from the Persian Gulf, a reversal of fortune that would handicap U.S. foreign policy and undermine the White House's authority at a time when withdrawal from Southeast Asia signaled global retrenchment.

In the 1973–89 period, many developments provided the United States with unwanted distractions. In the first two years, President Richard M. Nixon obsessed over a Watergate scandal that climaxed when he resigned in August 1974. While Nixon coped with this maelstrom, his secretary of state, Henry Kissinger, extricated the country from its Indochina morass by signing the 1973 Paris Peace Accords. At the same time, Kissinger tried to sustain détente with the Soviet Union, just as critics started to call for revision, or even abolition, of the administration's Soviet policy. In 1975, neither Kissinger nor President Gerald R. Ford could convince an agitated Congress and a country exhausted by the Vietnam War (which ended in April with the fall of Saigon) that the Vladivostok Agreement, the second installment of the Strategic Arms Limitations Talks, and the Helsinki Accords would redound to U.S. advantage.[2]

Not surprisingly, given such public sentiment, Jimmy Carter entered 1600 Pennsylvania Avenue in 1977 intent on jettisoning Nixon-Kissinger grand strategy. Carter touted human rights, democratic institutions, and nonproliferation. He shunned Metternichian legerdemain and cared minimally for the global balance of power. He disdained covert actions that empowered Chile's Augusto Pinochet and others of that ilk. He wanted an American policy that promoted Western ideals and restored U.S. decency and selflessness. He worked toward normalization with the People's Republic of China and concluded the controversial Panama Canal Treaty. Alas, invidious events betrayed his post-Cold War vision: stagflation slowed his country's economic growth measurably, the revelation of the existence of a Soviet brigade in Cuba embarrassed him, and the Red Army's invasion of Afghanistan in December 1979 shocked him. His two-fold riposte to the Kremlin's perfidy, the boycott of the 1980 Summer Olympic Games in Moscow and the grain embargo, could not rid the United States of its sense of unease or compensate for his policy maladroitness. His belated conversion to defiant anti-communism only made him seem further removed from his nation's Manichean contest with the Soviet Union, a deficiency that Republican candidate Ronald Reagan consistently exploited in the presidential race of that year. While Carter's ill-timed "Malaise" speech depicted America's predicament quite accurately, his defeatist message insured a loss at the polls in November.[3]

The victor in that election promised a robust U.S. defense posture and bitter opposition to the Kremlin. President Reagan's Cold-Warrior instincts belied his sunny disposition. His 1983 "Evil Empire" speech and endorsement of a Strategic Defense Initiative (i.e., the "Star Wars" outer-space missile shield) scared many observers, including Americans who distrusted Reagan's zealous anti-communism. With the California Republican in office, the Cold War seemed rejuvenated, to the horror of Europeans and other potential casualties of a Soviet-American nuclear war. Soviet General Secretary Mikhail S. Gorbachev's heterodox policies (known in the West as *Glasnost, Perestroika*, and "New Thinking") soon puzzled the hard-line Reagan administration, however. Fortunately for "nuclear freeze" and other peace advocates, the president mellowed once he and his Soviet counterpart exchanged candid views at several high-profile summits—Geneva in 1985, Reykjavik in 1986, and Moscow and Washington in 1988. These superpower talks dramatically decreased tensions between the two governments. The leaders explored a "double zero option" in Iceland that would have dismantled the U.S. and Soviet nuclear arsenals. In 1987, they agreed to eliminate an entire class of nuclear weapons with the Intermediate Nuclear Forces Treaty. In short, they dreamed of a world beyond the Cold War.[4]

Reagan's ethereal vision faded into the political background when the Iran-Contra scandal visited misery upon his second term. The president's efforts to restore his country's self-confidence could not prevent a Congressional investigation into illicit, covert arms deals to Iran that profited the Contras, Nicaraguan rebels. When Reagan left office in early 1989, he bequeathed to George H.W. Bush an impressive foreign-policy legacy. With Moscow exiting Afghanistan in disgrace (partly as a result of the Reagan Doctrine, which called for the arming of anti-Soviet insurgents such as the Afghan *mujahedeen*) and the Soviet economy in disrepair, it seemed that the United States would enter a new decade with an erstwhile foe desperate to accommodate Washington's wishes. Still, the Bush administration never expected the Kremlin to surrender its East-European empire voluntarily. When joyful East and West Germans tore down the Berlin Wall in November 1989, an era ended. A world-view honed over four decades required revision. Bush and his advisors stumbled as they tried to make sense of the startling events. A different kind of world beckoned, one where Washington praised its former Communist enemies and apprehended ex-friends such as Panama's Manuel Noriega.[5]

In the Middle East, animosities boiled over at American expense in this mostly Republican era of the "imperial presidency." At the 1974 Rabat conference, the Arab League punished Jordanian impuissance in the Arab-Israeli deadlock when it proclaimed the belligerent and anti-American Palestinian Liberation Organization (PLO) the representative of Palestinian interests in the Israeli-occupied West Bank. The PLO and other terrorists sought to avenge various alleged Israeli and U.S. travesties inflicted upon the Arab nation. When Israel invaded Lebanon in 1982 to punish the PLO and carve out a security zone, Yasir Arafat's organization turned more violent. Along with Hezbollah, Islamic Jihad, and other anti-Israeli extremists, it carried out reprisals against its enemies. Members of these notorious groups kidnapped and executed several Americans and other Westerners in Lebanon. They hijacked airplanes and bombed airports. In 1983, suicide missions in Beirut significantly damaged the French and American military compounds. Two hundred and forty-one U.S. Marines perished in one of the explosions.[6]

Arabs even killed their brethren. In 1975, a deranged relative murdered Saudi Arabia's King Faisal. When Egyptian President Anwar Sadat's semi-friendly handshake to Israel begot the Camp David Accords and the Egyptian-Israeli Peace Treaty in 1978–79, many Arab Muslims rejected such deals with the worst of all infidels. The assassination of Sadat in 1981 may have eliminated a so-called traitor to the Arab nation, but it could not rehabilitate Egypt in the eyes of Syria, Iraq, and other hard-line states that refused to acknowledge Israel's de jure existence. Attitudes softened in the mid-1980s, as Iraq and Saudi Arabia sought to end Cairo's isolation within the Arab League.[7]

In the midst of this reconciliation, enraged and desperate Palestinian youths started an *intifada* in 1987. The impoverished residents of Israeli-occupied Gaza and the West Bank hurled insults and rocks at their oppressors, who fired automatic weapons in return. This spontaneous uprising polarized Israeli opinion. Many Jews recognized an obvious irony: a David versus Goliath in reverse. The world press sympathized with the Palestinians and pilloried Tel Aviv, which justified its response as self-defense, with minimal success. Every dead Palestinian only further infuriated the Arab community.

Arab disdain for Israel, the United States, and the West carried over to the Persian Gulf as well. In the aftermath of the 1973 October/Yom Kippur War, the Saudis and other OPEC states imposed an embargo that targeted advanced and lesser-developed economies alike. For the first time, Americans experienced a gasoline shortage and exorbitant prices at the pump. As a result, the U.S. economy slumped further. In 1978–79, revolution forced the Shah into exile and yielded a theocratic Iran that vilified America, known as the "Great Satan." To underline their hatred of the United States, Iranian revolutionaries stormed the American Embassy in the fall of 1979 and seized hostages.

With Tehran distracted, Iraq attacked the Islamic Republic in September 1980. The Iran-Iraq War and the threat it posed to American interests in the Gulf alarmed Washington, which sided with Baghdad. The rich but vulnerable Gulf monarchies also endorsed Saddam Hussein over Ayatollah Khomeini. Their dislike of Baghdad's strongman accounted, however, for their hurried formation of the Gulf Cooperation Council in 1981.[8]

Seven years before the start of the Iran-Iraq War, OPEC ushered in a new era of international politics. The developed world's insatiable need for hydrocarbons catapulted into the spotlight an upstart organization from the developing world. All it took was another Arab-Israeli war.

Power Play: The October War, the Oil Weapon, and Shuttle Diplomacy

The consequences of the 1967 Six-Day War reverberated throughout the Middle East and beyond. Israelis rejoiced as their army raised the Star of David in East Jerusalem, allowing Jews to recover the sacred Temple Mount and pray before the revered Western Wall. Impressive victories over the Egyptians, Jordanians, and Syrians added valuable territory—the Sinai Peninsula, West Bank, Gaza, and the Golan Heights—to a besieged country. Supplementary lands may have improved Israeli security; they could not prevent Arab retaliation.[9]

Armed with Soviet weapons, Egypt and Syria conspired to push Israel back into its former, pre-June 1967, borders. Sadat could not tolerate continued humiliation, so he shrewdly authorized a deliberate 1973 October offensive designed to exploit the Israeli religious calendar. The Yom Kippur War surprised Tel Aviv. It reacted helter-skelter, not proactively as in the previous encounter. Egyptian and Syrian units capitalized on Israel's tardy mobilization to register significant initial gains on every front.[10]

When army supplies dwindled, the panicky Israeli cabinet asked Washington for matériel. The American airlift restored its ally's capabilities and mended Israel's bruised psyche—to Arab dismay. The Nixon administration further antagonized the Arabs when it requested that Congress approve a $2.2 billion emergency grant for Israel. Replenished and confident, the latter battered Egypt's and Syria's military, hampered by inferior equipment and less capable commanders. Tel Aviv retook its previously held positions and prepared to administer the coup de grâce. Israeli infantry and artillery rumbled toward Damascus while Israeli tanks encircled the Egyptian Third Army in the vicinity of the Suez Canal. The Jewish state intended to keep and defend conquered Syrian territory and destroy, if possible, Sadat's Third Army.[11]

Nasser's successor asked for help in warding off the Israelis, whose pincer movement could score another victory for Tel Aviv in the Arab-Israeli conflict. When the Kremlin threatened to intervene, the White House ordered a nuclear alert (i.e., Defense Condition Three). This unambiguous message cowed the Soviets.[12]

The volatile situation presented Henry Kissinger with a rare opportunity. With skillful diplomacy, he could discredit the Soviets and alter the balance of power in the region in favor of the United States. "We must prove to the Arabs that they are better off dealing with us on a moderate program than dealing with the Russians on a radical program," he said. This tactic pleased Sadat, who had expelled Soviet advisors in 1972 and sought improved Egyptian-American relations. He trusted Kissinger's political instincts and believed that the secretary of state's "step-by-step" diplomacy could pry concessions from the recalcitrant Israelis.[13]

The Arab OPEC states complicated Kissinger's task, however, when they imposed an oil embargo. In contrast to 1956 and 1967, Saudi Arabia, Kuwait, and other petroleum exporters successfully restricted their supply in the fall of 1973. Buoyed by a seller's market, they singled out America for the worst punishment, since the White House had brazenly resupplied Israel during the Yom Kippur War. With Saudi Arabia as the key producer, in lieu of the United States, an angry King Faisal ordered harmful cutbacks, penalizing countries that contravened Arab wishes. In the past, Faisal had refrained from such drastic measures, fearful that they would draw U.S. ire. The al-Saud monarch valued his kingdom's American ties; they helped preserve Saudi wealth and fend off enemies. In this case, though, he abandoned his cautious ways in order to sting his ally. He wanted Washington to restore the 1967 *status quo ante bellum* in the Middle East.[14]

Reduced output enabled OPEC to raise unilaterally the cost of a barrel of Arabian light crude (the industry standard) on October 16, 1973, from $3.01 to $5.12, a 70 percent mark-up. The October War facilitated this remarkable imposition. According to scholar J.B. Kelly, the Arab-Israeli clash "afforded OPEC the most plausible pretext it had ever had to push up prices, with the absolute assurance . . . that the industrial nations would swallow any increase." Except for the United States and the Netherlands, no developed country (or oil company) stood up to the owners of much of the world's petroleum reserves, who demanded that consumer states make explicit their pro-Arab bias. Unless buyers contributed to an amelioration of the Arab position, their supply quotas would be diminished by 5 percent every month. Satisfying this criterion implied vociferous and sustained criticism of Washington and its pro-Israeli policy. Much to Kissinger's disappointment, America's key allies refused to join U.S. opposition to OPEC's challenge. Britain, France, West Germany, and Japan deferred to the oligopoly's wishes in their frantic scramble to secure the oil that would power their economies. Kelly writes that

> As Egyptian arms suffered progressively severe reverses from this point onwards, the measures taken by the Arab oil states to raise oil prices and restrict supplies came to appear less and less like bold and resolute strokes in the tumult of war, and more and more like peevish requitals for Arab defeats on the field of battle—even, perhaps, as an underhand attempt to exploit the fortuitous circumstance of war as an opportunity to fleece the West.

This analysis mirrored Kissinger's sulfurous sentiments in the fall of 1973. Yet absent European and Japanese approval of his defiant point of view, the U.S. secretary of state could only condemn OPEC's extortion. Without a settlement to the Yom Kippur War satisfactory to the Arabs, the Vienna-based organization would not lift its embargo.[15]

Nonetheless, American officials refused to jettison or alter their country's policy toward the Persian Gulf. In his November 28, 1973, Congressional testimony, Deputy Assistant Secretary of State for Near Eastern and South Asian Affairs Rodger Davies noted that

> it would be premature to apply countermeasures. We [i.e., the U.S. Department of State] believe [that] we should try to remove the embargo by negotiation. We have asked them [i.e., OPEC] to consider if it would be possible to lift the embargo particularly in view of the constructive role [that] the United States has played in these past months. Now if diplomatic efforts are not successful and the Arab countries' economic pressure is prolonged unreasonably, we may be required, most reluctantly, to react.

Davies emphasized steadfastness. "[W]e should proceed normally," he said, "keeping in close contact with Israel, Egypt, [and] the other Arab states[,] proving our bona fides in order to bring about a just peace. In the meantime, we are going to try to conduct business as usual in this area."[16]

The mundane intersected with the extraordinary, however, when Kissinger traveled to the Middle East in search of disengagement agreements. Without them, an Arab-Israeli truce could not occur. The former Harvard professor reasoned that if Washington expected Cairo, Damascus, and Tel Aviv to consider America the ultimate arbiter of any peace process, then U.S. officials could not simply referee the battle of words over who respected or violated cease-fire terms. The United States could opt for one of two scenarios: it could persuade Egypt, Syria, and Israel that they should negotiate a final peace based on the "Land for Peace" formula called for in United Nations (UN) Security Council Resolution 242 or prod those countries to acquiesce in a process that could offer successive, albeit small, rewards to each. According to Kissinger, the first option was impractical, since it required solution to several heretofore intractable issues: the Palestinian question, the West Bank, and Jerusalem. In his opinion, "[i]t was the contemplation of these alternative risks—of bogging down in niggling detail and of consuming our energies in the pursuit of comprehensive goals more yearned for than attainable—that induced us [i.e., the United States] to decide instead on a 'step-by-step' approach."[17]

Kissinger selected the second option. "We needed to set objectives within the psychological capacities of the parties," he opined, "goals that could not be vetoed by the intransigent or the fanatic. Each step had to show that we could achieve results. Thereby each advance would build confidence and make further steps easier." If the United States could initiate "step-by-step" diplomacy, then perhaps Arabs and Israelis could trust each other and devise solutions.[18]

Kissinger thought he could involve Egypt, Syria, and Israel in the process, knowing that the present situation dissatisfied them. Sadat's audacious war plan, executed in partnership with Syria, achieved only its minimal objective: Arabs proved that they could defend themselves, pushing the Israeli Army back and inflicting numerous casualties. Humiliated on the battlefield in 1967, the Egyptians and the Syrians achieved self-respect in the 1973 October War. Still, their Pyrrhic victory could not reestablish the boundaries that existed prior to the June 1967 War.

From a military standpoint, Sadat and Syria's leader, Hafez al-Assad, lost the 1973 War. The Israeli Army surrounded many of Egypt's best soldiers and occupied Syrian lands not far from Damascus, the capital. Regardless, Sadat and Assad expected to recover territory in the Sinai and Golan Heights. Otherwise, they could not justify their citizens' various sacrifices for the Arab nation. Although victory enabled it to preserve its gains from the Six-Day War, Tel Aviv recognized that protracted war on multiple fronts might exhaust its resources and anger its denizens. Yet it could not tolerate Syrian guns on the Golan Heights capable of shelling Israeli villages.

Kissinger tackled this Herculean task with equanimity and aplomb, yet also relied on deception. In his memoirs, he characterized his thorny predicament: "I was also aware that neither the domestic nor the international environment gave me much room for maneuver." In his view, "Nixon was growing restless; he knew that his critics would blame Watergate for any failure of my mission, accelerating both his demise and the decline of credibility that must in time erode our world position." Kissinger strove to master the diplomatic process so that he could overcome political constraints that might undermine, or even doom, these most complex and intricate negotiations. In search of a bold stroke that could checkmate the Kremlin in the Middle East, he decided "to avoid wasting our diplomatic capital on the cease-fire and to move instead straight to a broader disengagement of forces."[19]

The U.S. Six-Point Plan helped end the October War and establish demarcation lines between the foes. Egyptian-Israeli discussions continued in November 1973 at Kilometer 101 on the Cairo-Suez road in an effort to formalize the plan. With initial success, Kissinger exuded confidence: "We had been instrumental in all these negotiations. We were gradually getting into a position where our support was essential for progress while the Soviet capacity for mischief was being systematically reduced." The U.S. secretary of state's tactics won him admiration and created momentum for the next "step," the December 1973 Geneva conference, a fruitless event that provided Kissinger with diplomatic cover to pursue his Egypt-first strategy. Excited that his calculus promised further achievements, he prepared to push Arabs and Israelis further toward peace.[20]

As co-sponsors of the 1973 Geneva Conference, the United States and the Soviet Union invited Cairo, Damascus, Amman, and Tel Aviv to send delegations to Switzerland. The American secretary of state believed that the conference achieved its objective: Arab states (Egypt and Jordan, but not Syria) talked to Israel. A banal diplomatic practice in other contexts, in U.S.-Soviet relations for example, that act revolutionized the Middle East. Though formal negotiations did not yet occur, an Arab-Israeli dialogue commenced in Geneva. Kissinger's exploit satisfied him. His efforts had culminated in a triumph of symbolism, an intangible so important that it could alter the entire psychology of the countries in the region. He noted that "the exertions needed to arrange the conference—and the final success—emphasized [U.S.] indispensability to all the Arab states, even the radicals."[21]

The Soviet Union could only deliver weapons to the Middle East; it could not reconcile Arab-Israeli differences. Despite Watergate, the United States positioned itself as the redeemer of the Holy Land, the intersection of hate and hope, destruction and transcendence. Many Arabs (but not the Palestinians) and Israelis now trusted the Americans and expected Washington to deliver results. In Kissinger's words, "We were systematically creating the framework for bilateral diplomacy between the parties through our mediation *after* the conference." He added that "[t]he absence of a Soviet alternative caused even its clients, like Syria, to fall in with a procedure that was the only hope for progress."[22]

Syrian President Assad refused to participate in the process, however, unless his soldiers could take back the Golan Heights. If Sadat could reclaim Egyptian territory in the Sinai via a U.S.-brokered disengagement agreement, then he would reconsider his intransigent stance. "A rapid separation of forces along the Suez Canal was the key," Kissinger stated. "I was sure it would bring Syria in its wake, almost certainly result in an end to the oil embargo, and enable us to pursue the peace process with less danger of a blowup."[23]

While Kissinger considered his next deft move, OPEC ministers visited Tehran in December 1973 for important talks. Despite Saudi concern that expensive crude could push the world economy into recession or worse, the Shah urged a substantial price hike. The megalomaniacal host sought additional oil profits to pursue his regional hegemonic ambitions and fulfil the promise of the White Revolution. In the end, his views prevailed. A barrel of Arabian Light would soon sell for $11.65, a 400 percent increase since the start of the October War. An outraged Washington resented the Shah's betrayal, yet Mohammed Reza Pahlavi offered no apology when he summarily dismissed American recriminations. His lust for profits overtook any desire to appease U.S. sensitivities.[24]

Resolute, Kissinger set out to reverse the tide of events. His journeys to Jerusalem, Aswan (Egypt), and other Middle Eastern cities in January 1974 heralded the era of "shuttle diplomacy." Soon Kissinger pulled the rabbit out of the sand, as Egypt and Israel signed a disengagement of forces agreement. Confident that his strategy had persuaded (or perhaps exhausted) Arabs and Israelis to turn to the United States ever more, he dwelled on the geopolitical significance of his accomplishment: "The disengagement agreement, above all, would mark Egypt's passage from reliance on the Soviet Union to partnership (in Sadat's phrase) with the United States." As a result of shuttle diplomacy, Kissinger had minimized, if not muted, Soviet influence in the region. Amid his travails, an elated Nixon gratefully acknowledged his secretary of state's extraordinary accomplishment in the Middle East by opportunistically calling it a presidential triumph.[25]

Yet problems remained. Sadat's moderate position in Arab politics would soon expose him to vehement criticism if radical Syria could not achieve its own disengagement agreement with Israel. To prevent such a backlash and solidify America's reputation as the region's touchstone, Kissinger embarked upon a second shuttle. These unique negotiations proved both arduous and contentious; the Golan Heights defied easy division and thus a Sinai-type disengagement seemed impossible. The Golan's geography, topography, and population flummoxed the U.S. secretary of state: How could one establish a UN zone, a security zone, and a limitation of forces if officially the Heights covered only a few dozen kilometers (but in reality spread out over an area of some two hundred square kilometers), were endowed with strategic peaks from where bullets, grenades, rockets, and missiles could be fired at Israel or Syria, and were home to hundreds of Israelis and thousands of Syrians (not to mention the tens of thousands who fled the area in 1967)? In addition, the issue of the Golan Heights stirred intense passions in both countries.[26]

Prior to a second shuttle, Kissinger insisted that the Arabs discontinue their anti-American oil embargo. He would not discuss the Golan issue and Syrian-Israeli disengagement unless the petroleum question was resolved to Washington's satisfaction. The Arabs refused to curtail the embargo, however, without a second Arab-Israeli disengagement.[27]

Kissinger stood firm. He did not submit to sustained blackmail. Finally, the Arab members of OPEC bowed to the wishes of the only individual who could tame the Israelis and reward Syrian irredentism. The petroleum exporters agreed to end their economic warfare if Washington promised to solve the region's political problems. With this OPEC guarantee, Kissinger gleefully returned to the Middle East for a second round of frenetic diplomacy. In his memoirs, he explained the oil issue and its salience in connection with the diplomacy he had conducted since October 1973: "We had come through a difficult period without succumbing to pressure. With the imminent end of the embargo, we had demonstrated that we could resist the vaunted oil weapon." In March 1974, Saudi Arabia, Kuwait, and the other Arab oil nations removed the United States from their blacklist. They expected yet another Kissinger diplomatic miracle.[28]

It took several months to work out a painstaking agreement. Nevertheless, the United States achieved another victory, as Kissinger preserved his "ability to continue to shape events." In the aftermath of the May 1974 Syrian-Israeli disengagement agreement, the American secretary of state received accolades once more before returning home to re-enter the politics of Watergate. He summed up: "the Syrian shuttle seemed to us the watershed between the world of crisis ushered in by the October war and the world of peace toward which we were striving."[29]

"Step-by-step" diplomacy qualified as a remarkable achievement. Kissinger had excluded the Soviets and, in the words of biographer Walter Isaacson, "America's historic difficulty in forging ties with Arab nations had been overcome." The next step or steps toward an Arab-Israeli peace proved more difficult to conceptualize, plan, and carry out. The U.S. secretary of state had dealt only with the tractable issues. Still, the United States benefited. Its interests were served and its position in the global balance of power improved. As for Kissinger, his reputation soared in the short term.[30]

Despite his considerable efforts, Kissinger's 1973–74 "step-by-step" diplomacy failed to end the Arab-Israeli conflict. Not that he expected such an outcome. He sought instead to introduce a "grammar of co-existence" within a narrative of tit-for-tat violence. The secretary of state's strategy, to pursue objectives he thought Egypt, Syria, and Israel could fulfil with U.S. assistance, in lieu of a comprehensive settlement, rewarded the parties involved in the negotiation and augmented American prestige in the region. According to Isaacson, "[t]he magic about the step-by-step approach was that this outcome was implicit from the very start."[31]

Kissinger's marathon sessions resonated in Washington, which sought, in the words of Assistant Secretary of State for Near Eastern and Southern Asian Affairs Alfred Atherton, to underpin "a self-sufficient, self-reliant, self-confident community of countries in the [Persian] [G]ulf." Regional tensions prevented widespread comity, however. The Kuwaitis and Iraqis tangled once more; Baghdad and Tehran quarreled over the Shatt al-Arab and the Kurdish rebellion in Iraq; and Saudi Arabia and Iran vied for mastery of OPEC policy. America took sides, as its oil policy meshed with Riyadh's, for example. Notwithstanding such intra-Gulf animosity, Atherton summarized American objectives:

> We remain committed to, first, support of indigenous regional cooperative efforts and the collective security and orderly economic progress of the area. Second is the encouragement of peaceful resolution of territorial and other disputes among states and widening channels of communication and consultation between them. Third is expanding our diplomatic, cultural, technical, commercial, and financial presence and activities, and, fourth is, maintaining access to the area's oil supplies at reasonable prices.

The assistant secretary of state mentioned one other U.S. aim that underscored the country's linchpin role: "to recycle [OPEC] surplus revenues into the world economy in an orderly and nondisruptive manner."[32]

U.S. policymakers tackled area dissension with Kissinger's diplomatic triumph in mind. In that instance, the secretary of state's skill and perseverance restored American influence. Fortuitous circumstances facilitated his task as well. In 1975, however, as events in Vietnam, Portugal, and Turkey sapped U.S. power, Kissinger could not extract meaningful concessions from the Israelis. This failure tainted the second Egyptian-Israeli disengagement agreement and effectively halted "step-by-step" diplomacy. In previous negotiations Kissinger had skirted Palestinian issues, but with the PLO now center stage, his short-term, partial solutions to the Arab-Israeli conflict seemed wholly inadequate.[33]

Good fortune continued to elude Washington when events in Iran soon resulted in an unexpected revolution. As the Shah's power ebbed and his regime unraveled, President Carter and other American officials braced themselves for an important transition within Persian society from authoritarianism to expected pluralism. The velocity of change and the upheaval's ferocious consequences stunned the White House, whose paralysis left it without its foremost ally in the region and its "Twin Pillars" strategy in tatters. While the United States could not adapt to a tectonic shift in area politics and thus experienced classic Great-Power "adjustment failure," Ayatollah Ruhollah Khomeini stepped forward to become Iran's theocrat.[34]

Stupefaction & Revulsion:
The Shah's Demise & Khomeini's Revolution

Despite his ostentatious ways and key role in OPEC price hikes, Mohammed Reza Pahlavi inspired official U.S. confidence. Nixon's favorite gendarme impressed Washington with his steady leadership. His country supported American allies worldwide and featured important Central Intelligence Agency (CIA) listening posts bordering the Soviet Union. Much to U.S. relief, he zealously safeguarded Western interests in the Persian Gulf at a time when America could not exert itself militarily in the region. The Shah struck an omnipotent pose within Iran, an impression that lulled the Carter administration into complacency. This illusion inculcated within the White House an institutional mentality known as "groupthink." Most policymakers could not fathom an alternative Iranian reality; therefore, they invested unwavering support in an authoritarian not known for his resilience or decisiveness.[35]

In 1953, the young Shah had fled his country when the National Front under Mohammed Mossadeq seemed poised to thwart a pro-Pahlavi coup d'état. Although the son of Reza Pahlavi returned to the throne that August, the CIA-assisted restoration failed to cure him of his cowardice. Americans ignored this omen, however, convinced that a seasoned Shah would display nerve rather than self-doubt whenever events conspired against him.[36]

In the decades following his resumption of royal duties, Mohammed Reza Pahlavi transformed Iran into an archetypal dictatorship. He initiated a White Revolution to modernize his country's economy, albeit reluctantly and under American pressure; purchased billions worth of sophisticated U.S. military equipment; and terrorized his subjects via SAVAK, his ruthless security apparatus. This triad of modernization, procurement, and repression convulsed Iranian society. Traditional Persian xenophobia moderated under the Shah, who imported many Western cultural values. His brand of development favored economic reform without political participation. He worshipped oil; it funded his delusions of grandeur. Vain and insecure, he muzzled any opponent who dared criticize his infallible policies. Jail sentences, torture, and murder intimidated most opposition movements and silenced potential critics.[37]

In 1978, the man who imbued his nation with a new sense of identity spied incipient political unrest reminiscent of his country's 1962–63 protests. Ever the creature of habit, Pahlavi intended to quell these disturbances with tokenism, the same way he subdued the earlier affronts to his authority. Such recourse assumed that no opposition figure could embody the frustrated will of an entire people and marshal the resources necessary to overthrow an ensconced monarch. Besides, the Shah never expected that a majority of Iranians would come to venerate Ayatollah Khomeini.[38]

The fiery exiled cleric exuded charisma. He detested the Pahlavis and their perceived evil patron, the United States—the so-called Great Satan. He rejected the Shah's secularism; he envisioned Iran as a theocratic state and clamored for a reversion to an Islamic way of life. Unfortunately for the Pahlavi dynasty, Khomeini's invective inspired the pauper classes (i.e., the lower and lower middle classes), whose adoration translated into blind allegiance. Even though the Shah had banished him, the Ayatollah continued to assail the Shah's injustice from his quarters in Iraq and France, as aides smuggled audiocassettes of his sermons into Iran. Ineffective for years, the Ayatollah finally seemed on the cusp of a breakthrough in the late 1970s. Still, unless Mohammed Reza Pahlavi rescinded previous orders to suppress dissent, religious scorn for his arbitrary ways could not possibly topple him. His ability to punish fanatics and disgruntled alike provided him with a considerable advantage when dealing with opposition. If the United

States endorsed this repression, then the Shah could strike back more or less with impunity.[39]

The Carter administration carried on the Nixon-Kissinger policy toward Iran except that it denied its client carte blanche on arms sales. Carter insisted on a review of each item sold to the Iranians but never vetoed a purchase. Oddly, the president who preached respect for human rights never pressed the Shah to curtail his abuses, even though Pahlavi and his detractors expected Washington to convey its opprobrium whenever the Shah utilized excessive violence to discipline unruly demonstrators. The White House dared not alienate its long-standing ally lest it jeopardize its status in the Persian Gulf. The Persian monarch could sever his American ties and rely exclusively on the Soviets, who already traded heavily in arms and other items with Tehran and conveniently overlooked the Peacock Throne's excesses. Years of reliance on Pahlavi thus yielded a form of indenture; without the Shah, the United States risked forfeiting influence in a country of strategic import. This lack of leverage manifested itself when American feebleness intersected with the Iranian leader's insistence that his U.S. benefactor not court members of Iran's opposition. While not atypical during the Cold War, this inversion of the patron-client relationship prevented Washington, out of respect for the Shah's wishes, from familiarizing itself with groups that contested Pahlavi's rule. Such deference hamstrung the Carter administration throughout Khomeini's revolution.[40]

As the president celebrated New Year's 1978 with the Shah in Tehran, he saluted his host in a testimonial replete with hyperbole and flattery. Within twelve months, the statement would be ironic and risible. Of course, Carter could not predict the cataclysm that would soon befall his country and so could earnestly say: "Iran is an island of stability in one of the more troubled areas of the world." Bereft of contradictory information, which only Iranian dissidents could provide, the president clung to Pahlavi's point of view and therefore discounted any serious threat to the latter's continued rule. The Shah projected strength, not weakness. American officials worried that he wielded too much power. They were unaware, moreover, that he had contracted cancer and became gravely ill by 1979.[41]

The president's policy of "gentle persuasion" toward Pahlavi confirmed America's unflagging confidence in its partner. As with a favorite feline, Carter reflexively caressed this Persian over and over believing that this regional stalwart served U.S. interests very well. For example, Iranian oil deliveries to Israel enabled the area's pariah to circumvent the anti-Israeli Arab embargo. Tehran's benevolent relations with a critical American ally pleased an administration on the verge of brokering an Egyptian-Israeli agreement. The Shah mistrusted Washington, however, and Carter reminded him of John F. Kennedy, no friend of the Peacock Throne. Pahlavi thus half expected the Americans to unseat him. The Carter administration eschewed conspiracy, yet failed to allay its proxy's fears or grasp the subtleties of Iranian society. Culturally, then, Iran and the United States misunderstood one another, a shortcoming that eased Khomeini's task.[42]

Despite a monopoly on state resources, throughout 1978 Pahlavi hesitated to draw on assets at his disposal when enemies called for his resignation or removal. A suddenly reluctant Shah refused to order his own people slaughtered. This aversion to wanton violence emboldened the motley opposition, which consisted of secular liberals, Communists, religious moderates, as well as devotees of Khomeini's Islamic radicalism. Each faction sought to overthrow the Peacock Throne. Aspirations beyond that aim varied. The National Front dreamed of carrying on Mossadeq's democratic tradition. The Tudeh harbored thoughts of a socialist Iran in ideological harmony with the Soviet Union. Some men of faith who attracted followers yearned for a polity anchored in the Shari'a, Muslim law. They wanted a return to Iran's 1906 constitution, which provided for religious oversight of the political system. Khomeini thought this solution incomplete and unsatisfactory; he would establish an Islamic theocracy.[43]

Pahlavi dismissed the Ayatollah as a "benighted reactionary." In pro-regime newspapers, the monarch's retinue slandered Khomeini mercilessly. The Shah underestimated the political skills of this pious man and thus not only doubted that the elderly cleric could spearhead a mutiny, but scoffed at the notion that the Ayatollah could oust him. The expatriate firebrand ignored the defamatory editorials and continued to exhort Iranians in their revolt. The adverse public reaction to the September 1978 Jaleh Square massacre vindicated him while dismaying Pahlavi. The Iranian police's brutality galvanized Iranian opinion and intensified dislike for the royal family and its patriarch. After months of protests, the anti-Shah coalition seemed ready to kick America's gendarme out of Iran.[44]

Although aware of the crisis, the State Department restated its preference for American inertia. It reiterated U.S. partiality for its client, endorsed his steps to liberalize Iranian politics, and expressed its distaste for any military junta, an expedient that National Security Advisor (NSA) Zbigniew Brzezinski soon came to favor. According to National Security Council (NSC) member Gary Sick, an October 1978 review of American policy "explicitly recognized the limited ability of the United States to influence the course of events in Iran and conceded that the shah's fortunes might well continue to erode despite [America's] best efforts—or perhaps even as a result of [U.S.] actions." Regardless of this admission, Foggy Bottom (i.e., the State Department) refused to characterize events in Iran as an "emergency." Busy at Camp David devising an Egyptian-Israeli compromise, President Carter never read the report. The administration's priorities precluded any serious evaluation of America's "Big Pillar." Without the Iranian column, however, Washington's Twin Pillars strategy would topple into rubble.[45]

Oblivious to such a repugnant possibility, Carter and Brzezinski renewed their country's vows to Pahlavi. But the U.S. marriage to the Shah sundered throughout the fall. American policymakers remained powerless; they could not prevent an implosion of authority within Iran. Scarcity of information about the intensifying political insurgency denied them, moreover, a detailed account of the situation on the streets of Tehran, Tabriz, and elsewhere. When Ambassador William Sullivan informed his superiors that, without American reassurance, Pahlavi might quit his kingship, the White House could only shrug. Unwilling to intervene directly, it urged its ally to hold on. Maybe he would recover his nerve in time to preserve his rule. Otherwise, hopefully the protesters would exhaust themselves before they could remove him.

As the Shah wavered, Washington finally woke up to the seriousness of the crisis. It fractured into two camps. The White House wanted Pahlavi to exercise ruthlessness, if that would quell dissent. In Sick's view, Brzezinski "attempted to convey a sense of U.S. steadfastness and the need for the shah to exert tough leadership." This tolerance for possible, if not probable, bloodshed clashed with the State Department's pacifist inclinations.[46]

Ambassador Sullivan maligned the NSC for its parochial stance. Contrary to the obdurate Brzezinski, whose Cold-War mentality nurtured his obsession with the Shah as an anti-Soviet bulwark and precluded thoughts of a Shah-less Iran, the ambassador warned of Pahlavi's imminent downfall. Whereas Sick impugned Sullivan's professional judgment, criticizing the latter's tendency to ignore instructions from Washington, the envoy in Tehran denied receiving any guidance and blamed bureaucratic rivalries for his country's inept reaction to Iranian events.[47]

The Shah's autumn performance won him no plaudits from his Iranian critics, whom he considered insolent. Some U.S. officials thought he would either sanction coalition rule or else unleash the dreaded SAVAK upon the upstarts who dared challenge him. Instead, in a futile move, he installed a military government. Members of the Iranian opposition braced for a crackdown that never materialized. Emboldened by Pahlavi's refusal to use coercion, they stepped up their demonstrations.[48]

U.S. policymakers winced as their favorite autocrat displayed continued indecision and apathy. According to political scientist Richard Cottam, "The shah seemed to be following a policy of staged disintegration of the institutional base of his own regime." Washington could not rouse him from his lethargy nor could it infuse him with vigor and resilience. With few ships and planes in the area, the United States could not strike quickly and efficiently to prevent another Fall-of-Saigon scenario. A repeat of the CIA's successful 1953 coup therefore seemed improbable. In far more favorable political circumstances (i.e., with Shah enthusiasts ready to carry him back to the throne), that earlier mission had skirted disaster. With Pahlavi hated by a majority of Iranians, no deus ex machina would intervene this time, or so it seemed. As the Shah's despair heightened, the prospect of curtailed Iranian oil production traumatized Westerners not yet recovered from the events of 1973. Petroleum shortages promised higher OPEC prices, renewed economic hardship, and irate Western voters.[49]

Vaguely aware of this doomsday scenario, sanguine American decision-makers nevertheless could not wean themselves from their addiction to Pahlavism. In a dispatch titled "Thinking the Unthinkable," Ambassador Sullivan speculated that someone other than the Shah's young son could succeed him. Yet other U.S. officials continued their "total support" for Pahlavi. Unfortunately, they overestimated their client's political reflexes and resolve. In Sick's words, that misjudgment stemmed from "an expectation that . . . proved to be unfounded and based largely on wishful thinking." Banned for years by Iran's despot from fraternizing with the various Iranian opposition groups, Washington remained privy to only one version of events—the Shah's.[50]

The latter's fumbling exacerbated an already tenuous situation. His refusal to rely on the iron fist left him with few, if any, options other than fleeing the country in utter disgrace. Most everyone in Iran hated him. Pahlavi's cult of personality had molded the country into a replica of him: modern (in the Western sense), corrupt, and without compassion. Only the army could save him, yet in contrast to previous episodes of domestic upheaval, he would not order soldiers to repress civilians. He professed to abhor the very thought of killing his own citizens. As the Soviets encouraged Iran's clerics to unite with the Tudeh party, an alarmed Brzezinski urged the Shah to exert himself, advice the Iranian rejected once more.[51]

The holy month of Moharram (December 1978) stirred an Iranian populace already teeming with emotion. As demonstrators filled the streets, U.S. policymakers grappled with events utterly foreign to them. In an independent review, elder statesman George Ball reprised his gadfly role (he had opposed Lyndon Johnson's Vietnam policy) when he concluded that Pahlavi could not sustain himself even with American succor. The Carter administration thanked Ball for his December 1978 report without subscribing to his careful analysis. It instead scrutinized those individuals or groups responsible for the protests in Iran. Some officials suspected the National Front, others Khomeini. Cold-War veterans naturally spotlighted the Kremlin. As the Iranian Revolution reached a crescendo, the mullahs continued to proselytize in the mosques. Inspired by Khomeini, they disseminated information on when and where the next rally would occur. This religious network allowed the revolt to mobilize more and more dissatisfied citizens.[52]

Brzezinski, Ambassador Sullivan, and Secretary of Energy James Schlesinger, a former secretary of defense, all urged bold remedies to prevent a take-over by the extremists, whom the national security advisor considered Soviet-backed. On December 7, Carter committed a gaffe, however, that undermined the "hawkish" (i.e., pro-Shah) viewpoints within his administration. Asked to comment on the Shah's predicament, the president noted that "[t]his is something that is in the hands of the people of Iran." He followed that paean to self-determination with a précis of his country's policy: "We have never had any intention and don't have any intention of trying to intercede in the internal political affairs of Iran. We primarily want an absence of violence and bloodshed, and stability. We personally prefer that the shah maintain a major role in the government, but that is a decision for the Iranian people to make." Carter's Wilsonian invocations impressed some foreign-policy analysts as a refutation of Pahlavi. The president apologized for any misconception, but the impression that the United States might abandon its ally stuck. The U.S. public's affinity for Khomeini, moreover, complicated the administration's effort to prop up the authoritarian Shah. Most Americans expected the Ayatollah to evolve a democratic polity whose interests would converge with Washington's. They knew nothing of his penchant for totalitarianism, an ignorance shared by many academic experts.[53]

While Khomeini and his acolytes recruited thousands of disaffected Iranians, who recited anti-American slogans in the streets of Tehran and other cities, Pahlavi sulked. America could only provide him with words, he lamented. In truth, the Shah had sinned in the worst way: in betraying Niccolò Machiavelli's advice, the Iranian head of state had flouted the philosopher's inviolate rule whereby a ruler must always crush his opponents or else perish. In the words of scholar Richard Cottam, the Iranian Revolution "would not have taken the form it did had it not been for the regime's entirely avoidable failure to maintain coercive control."[54]

For some American officials, the Shah's ineptitude now seemed obvious. Independently of one another, Gary Sick of the NSC and Henry Precht of the State Department's Iran desk concluded that Pahlavi could no longer hold off his enemies. Sick argued that the United States should insist upon immediate reform. But Ambassador Sullivan frustrated any such démarche, an accusation he later vehemently denied. Discord of this sort hampered American policymaking through the end of the year. As the Shah pondered his next move, the U.S. Joint Chiefs of Staff instructed the USS *Constellation* and the Seventh Fleet Carrier Task Force to sail for Singapore. If needed, these warships could speed toward the Persian Gulf. Unfortunately for Washington, the press reported the deployment; the story not only embarrassed the administration, it anchored the fleet. While the White House tried to refute its reputation for incessant vacillation, Pahlavi refused to cede power. The NSC advocated a cautious policy; it would not pressure him to abdicate and/or leave Iran. The Carter administration emphasized precedents. If it helped to oust an erstwhile partner, then other American allies would consider U.S. commitments untrustworthy. Washington's credibility within Iran would plummet as well. Finally, the withdrawal of American influence might spark bitter civil war between moderate and radical factions.[55]

To avoid such a scenario and dispel rumors that the United States intended to abandon its ally, General Robert Huyser visited Tehran in January 1979. In his conversations with Iran's military leadership, the deputy commander of the Supreme Allied Command in Europe emphasized that any Iranian executive must seek comity with America, not enmity. This U.S. prerequisite impressed no one. While the White House awkwardly conveyed its concern, the Shah's newest prime ministerial appointee explored ways to extricate the regime from a thickening morass. Unfortunately for the Peacock Throne, Shapour Bakhtiar's quixotic attempts to refashion Iranian politics quickly fizzled out.[56]

With Pahlavi expected to leave his beloved country very shortly, Ambassador Sullivan contravened his own advice that Washington refrain from exploring alternative political arrangements with members of the Iranian opposition, including Ayatollah Khomeini. Sullivan secretly tried to broker a modus vivendi with various Iranian dissidents only to incur Brzezinski's and President Carter's disapproval. They vetoed his plans. At this point, unless Iran's military could assert its authority throughout the country, American influence would likely ebb.[57]

Although Sullivan's initiative testified to his sense of desperation and genuine search for a workable compromise that could ensure U.S. relevance within Iran, his unhelpful diplomacy weakened an already unpopular Bakhtiar. Still, the ambassador's faux-pas underlined the obvious: any Iranian government without the Shah would be preferable to one that included the discredited monarch. Many of America's Iran experts believed that. They could tolerate Khomeini; his political inexperience might allow moderates from the National Front to democratize Iran. Gary Sick and other officials dismissed such utopian talk. They predicted that the Ayatollah would exceed Pahlavi's abuses. Officially, though, Washington endorsed the Iranian Army. All three U.S. options, dubbed "A, B, and C," involved the segment of Iranian society most familiar with the United States—this intimacy between Iran's military and America derived from the Shah's voluminous arms purchases.[58]

After New Year's 1979, the probable became the inevitable. In January, Mohammed Reza Pahlavi succumbed to the constant chants for his removal. He left for Egypt. Maybe he would return to his homeland in a replay of the events of 1953. This analogy assumed that his supporters could frustrate Khomeini enthusiasts. The Shah's hopes faded, however, once the Ayatollah arrived in Tehran in February. Khomeini's presence electrified ecstatic crowds. The acclaimed cleric immediately manipulated the unbridled Iranian masses that worshipped him and surprised Westerners with his deftness and political acumen. The rest of the year he worked assiduously to effect an Islamic state true to his vision and worthy of his sanction. To fulfil his dream, he outwitted the secular and religious moderates. He ordered them either killed or incarcerated. By 1980, this Muslim Robespierre ruled Iran as an omnipotent theocrat.[59]

As for the Shah, the revolution's fury exhausted him. He started his career as an insecure autocrat who scared easily. He matured into a mostly competent dictator who built his nation into a wealthy, heavily armed regional power. After four decades as supreme leader of a reinvented Persia, he could not comprehend the political, economic, social, and cultural backlash that he provoked with policies he thought wise and magnanimous. Cancer weakened his body and impaired his judgment. In the end, he could not cope with Khomeini's undeniable popularity and charisma. This albatross froze him, and he dared not authorize a massacre. Iran's revolutionaries proceeded to uproot the once proud Pahlavi dynasty, snapping in half every reminder of its unwanted legacy.[60]

For Washington, humiliation turned into agony. First, with his Twin Pillars policy shattered, Kissinger reprised Republican Party canards of years past (regarding China, for example) when he accused the Carter administration of "losing" Iran. He along with other committed Pahlavites with long-standing political and financial ties to the Shah (i.e., Nelson and David Rockefeller as well as other conservative elites) had criticized the White House for an irresponsible policy. Their skepticism turned into disbelief and outrage when the president hesitated to allow the former American protégé into the United States for medical treatment. When pressed to grant the request, Carter relented. His tardy acquiescence spared him no grief, however, as cynics in the press and elsewhere resumed their inquisition of a presidency victimized by opportunistic Iranian mullahs and their fevered partisans. The disrespect accorded a former staunch ally reverberated throughout the world, and U.S. credibility eroded once more.[61]

Second, Washington witnessed Iranian youths kidnap U.S. Embassy personnel in Tehran in November 1979, an egregious violation of international law that convulsed the United States for over a year. This affront to American dignity overwhelmed the Carter administration, which dithered, much to the despair of Americans everywhere. NSA Brzezinski and Secretary of State Cyrus Vance repeatedly verbalized their distaste for one another's policy preferences, immortalizing the bureaucratic rivalry between the president's two most important foreign-policy advocates. Vance pleaded for negotiations and counseled patience, whereas his impatient nemesis touted military remedies that promised quick results. Consistent with his well-deserved workaholic reputation and desire to act, Carter-the-impresario considered every detail as he presided over a tragedy that surely cost him the 1980 presidential election. When diplomacy stalled, he certified America's inept response to the hostage crisis by authorizing a rescue mission that epitomized the popular perception of his tenure in office: futile. That April 1980 debacle resulted in the deaths of several U.S. servicemen and depressed furthermore a cursed executive that, nevertheless, redoubled its efforts to free the fifty-two American prisoners. An exhausted and angry Vance resigned as the ordeal continued. It ended with the Algiers Accord in January 1981, on the 444th day, when, ironically, Ronald Reagan celebrated his inaugural.[62]

As a result of Khomeini's revolution, not only did Carter suffer the ignominy of his successor garnering praise for the release of the hostages, the Georgian chafed under OPEC's renewed pressure as well. Iran's travails shut down its considerable oil output in December 1978, which, in turn, enabled the well-known cartel to more than double its price for a barrel of crude—from $13 to $34. Consumers panicked when the world's second most important petroleum exporter ceased operations. With memories of 1973 in mind, buyers of every kind spent vast sums on the hitherto neglected spot market to assure themselves of an inventory in case the shortage worsened. OPEC members indulged themselves; they demanded and received more money for their "black gold." The Saudis warned, however, that the organization's greed would provoke recession in Western economies, prompting energy conservation, investment in non-OPEC drilling in the North Sea and elsewhere, and the search for alternative fuels. These outcomes would lessen demand for OPEC oil. Riyadh's confrères derided such reasoning, as they proceeded with new hikes.[63]

Carter could only express dismay. Saudi admonitions could not prevent nor end the lines that formed at service stations throughout the United States. The president implored the al-Sauds to raise their production. The latter obliged in July 1979, but the increase, from 8.5 to 9.5 million barrels per day, served as a mere palliative. Meanwhile, Americans fumed. They blamed Carter, despite his pre-crisis sermons about the need to diversify America's energy resources and cut back on its oil consumption. Although not responsible for the country's increasing dependence on foreign supplies, the president had to resolve this thorny issue or else be content with a single term in office.[64]

Americans expected their leader to pressure OPEC. If he threatened a puni-tive mission whereby America seized Persian Gulf petroleum facilities, then he risked higher prices and possibly worse—terrorist attacks, renewed violence against Israel, and other forms of retaliation. Fortunately for the United States, the cartel's cocksure outlook at the December 1979 Caracas and June 1980 Al-giers meetings resulted in incredulity: OPEC could not fathom a drop in price and therefore never adjusted its supply when worldwide demand faltered. As the Saudis upped their output, a glut manifested itself by the summer of 1980. Sadly for Carter, prices did not tumble until the Reagan years. In a replay of the hos-tage crisis dénouement, Americans offered the Georgian no praise for his dogged efforts to end the oil crisis.[65]

The fiascoes that beset Washington humbled the Carter administration. When the Soviets invaded Afghanistan in December 1979, the president sought to avoid a repeat of past mistakes. He alerted the world that America would not comply with yet another infringement upon its interests.

Military Answers:
The Carter Doctrine and the Iran-Iraq War

After three years of mostly conciliatory foreign policies, setbacks in South-west Asia sobered Carter and called for American firmness. Vance's resignation facilitated this volte-face. Instead of relying primarily upon his secretary of state's recommendations, the president now solicited Brzezinski's counsel regu-larly and often heeded his advice. Whereas Vance stressed diplomacy and nego-tiation, Brzezinski preferred threats and the use of force. The national security advisor's world-view seemed more in sync with recent events. His talk of an "arc of crisis," imperiling pro-Western and neutral countries from eastern Africa to the Indian Subcontinent, persuaded Carter that the United States must respond to perceived Soviet machinations. Otherwise, the Kremlin might significantly at-tenuate Washington's influence within the region. Or so it seemed.[66]

Ayatollah Khomeini's revolt robbed America of its "strategic pivot" and pretense that it could defend its petroleum and other interests in the Persian Gulf via the Iranians, Saudis, or other proxies. In early 1979, according to NSC offi-cial Gary Sick, "[t]here was a growing awareness that the policy of the preceding decade had steadily placed more and more reliance on Iran, to the extent that when the shah's regime collapsed, the United States was left strategically naked, with no safety net." This mixed metaphor underscored the sorry U.S. predica-ment at the end of a tumultuous decade. In some thirty-six months, Ethiopia shunned its erstwhile American ally in favor of Moscow, Iran renounced its Washington and Central Treaty Organization (CENTO) connections (Turkey and Pakistan withdrew from CENTO as well), Marxist South Yemen reportedly in-tended to invade North Yemen, someone murdered U.S. Ambassador Adolph

Dubs in Kabul, and the Red Army occupied Afghanistan. By 1980, then, these ominous events threatened to downgrade Washington's status in the Horn of Africa, the Gulf, and elsewhere in the Greater Indian Ocean.[67]

This bleak scenario jolted the Carter administration and jeopardized the president's reelection. As a result, Washington revised its policy dramatically. Methodically, it crafted retorts that could rehabilitate America's reputation within the region. These replies highlighted the country's renewed preference for military responses. In February 1979, the U.S. Navy cruised into the Arabian Sea ready to intervene in case the People's Democratic Republic of Yemen assaulted its ethnic brethren to the north. The symbol of American sea power, the carrier unit monitored the Yemeni situation in a bid to reassure Riyadh of the U.S. commitment to Saudi security. The White House complemented this overt manifestation of American resolve with $390 million in military aid to North Yemen. The United States also warned the Soviet Union and Cuba (still involved in Angola and Ethiopia) not to meddle in the southwestern corner of the Arabian Peninsula.[68]

Brzezinski coordinated this gradual shift to a more assertive policy. Secretary of Defense Harold Brown traveled to Saudi Arabia in February 1979 with bilateral security on his mind, not bases, which the Saudis could not accommodate for political reasons. Saudi Arabia and the Gulf emirates, Kuwait most vociferously, professed disdain for Great-Power involvement in the area despite their long-time cooperation with the British and Americans. Riyadh and its conservative neighbors sought justice for the Palestinians, moreover, a ticklish matter for an administration that brokered an Egyptian-Israeli peace treaty in March 1979 at the expense of the Syrians and the Palestinians, the only Arabs in the Middle East without their own land. Although the Saudis resisted initial American entreaties, the White House considered several military steps (i.e., a rapid deployment force and permission to stockpile and preposition material in Oman, Kenya, and Somalia) that could improve America's regional defense and convey U.S. intentions to the Soviets.[69]

The failed effort in April 1980 to snatch the fifty-two Americans held in Tehran exposed the White House's inability to marshal sufficient resources in times of crisis, yet that debacle buoyed U.S. efforts to build up the country's military presence in the Indian Ocean. To counter provocative Soviet moves in the area, the United States evolved a "security framework" tailored to the realities of what Brzezinski called a "third strategic zone." He considered the three zones—Europe, Asia, and the Middle East–Persian Gulf—interdependent and advocated a firm American response to the Kremlin's recent encroachments in Southwest Asia.[70]

Ironically, the Soviets feared the Americans. With a significant Muslim population in the southern Soviet Union, Moscow intervened in Afghanistan in December 1979 to prevent what it considered an American-supported Islamist take-over spurred on by the Iranian Revolution. While initially optimistic that it could co-exist with the Islamic Republic, the Politburo soon considered Iran a serious threat to Soviet regional security. More importantly, the Kremlin foolishly sent the Red Army into Afghanistan without considering Washington's probable reaction.[71]

The end of détente and the return to Cold-War conformity prevented the Carter administration from empathizing with the Soviets' predicament. Washington instead sought ways to deter Moscow. In his January 23, 1980, State of the Union address, Carter outlined America's new commitment to the Gulf, whose voluminous oil exports provided Western economies with critical energy supplies. Inspired by Harry Truman's March 1947 speech (which established the Truman Doctrine), the Middle East peacemaker warned that "[a]n attempt by any outside force to gain control of the Persian Gulf region will be regarded as an assault on the vital interests of the United States of America, and such an assault will be repelled by any means necessary, including military force." Journalist Richard Burt reported that the president's pronouncement "represented a fundamental shift, not only in Mr. Carter's policy but in positions adopted by previous administrations." The White House would achieve its ambitious objective via "preponderant naval power," a Mahanian strategy.[72]

The Carter Doctrine spotlighted the alleged Soviet menace to the region, at best a secondary threat according to most Gulf countries. Publicly, Kuwait and Saudi Arabia dismissed U.S. concerns, but whereas the former belittled the Americans for their imperial pretensions, in private the latter welcomed Washington's increased naval presence in the Gulf and conveyed its intention to buy more American weapons. If widely known, such candor would only exacerbate an already tense regional situation. As Baghdad, in violation of the 1975 Algiers Agreement, tangled with Tehran over the Shatt al-Arab, the waterway separating them, the Gulf monarchies eyed revolutionary Iran with extreme wariness. Only the Palestinian issue united Arabs and Persians; they spoke with a single voice whenever they criticized Israel, America's so-called strategic asset.[73]

The pro-Israeli American public cared not for the Arab-Persian reaction to Carter's announcement. It approved of the president's speech. Unlike ordinary Americans and the Israelis, U.S. allies in Western Europe provided only lukewarm support for the Democrat's Monroesque declaration. A French official referred to Washington's international resurgence by noting that "America's post-Vietnam slough has ended, this is a turning point in U.S. policy." But the European Economic Community's reticence to endorse the White House's initiative tempered such exuberance. Western Europe's détente with the Soviet Union, epitomized by the Federal Republic of Germany's *Ostpolitik*, could not countenance military face-offs with the Kremlin. Moscow knew of Europe's preference and predictably pilloried Carter's version of the Brezhnev Doctrine. *Tass* disparaged the president's concerns and ridiculed "mythical threats" to Persian Gulf oil. These varied assessments of the Carter Doctrine followed the fault lines of world politics and reignited the region's Great Game. While some U.S. analysts attributed nefarious objectives to the Red Army's forays into Afghanistan, a sure harbinger of more adventurism to come, they argued, Soviet expert George F. Kennan dispelled such alarmist distillations. He deemed Moscow's expedition defensive.[74]

Exaggerated or not, Washington's verbal counterattack signified a modification of American policy in Southwest Asia—and prompted a renewed commitment to Pakistan, whose territory served as a base for anti-Soviet Afghan insurgents. When, early in its first term, the Reagan administration, with Secretary of State Alexander Haig in the forefront, tried to impose an anti-Soviet "strategic consensus" on Israel and the status quo Arabs (i.e., the so-called moderate regimes), the president endorsed the Carter Doctrine. Reagan said that America intended "to safeguard the West's oil lifeline in the Persian Gulf area." Although mutual suspicion and Arab politics prevented a rapprochement between Tel Aviv and the Arab moderates, the United States embarked upon a decade of military improvements. In 1981, America lacked resources and preparation; it could not prevent the Soviets from taking over Iran, a recurrent U.S. fear, and possibly incorporating the Gulf into its empire. Any such conquest could secure a warm-water port, both a Tsarist and Bolshevik objective. Although, paradoxically, Moscow feared an American intervention in Iran, the White House assumed throughout the 1980s that it had to build up its forces and augment its capabilities within the region.[75]

To do so, Washington strengthened its Indian Ocean Navy so that it could compete favorably with the Soviet fleet in the area. It expanded its facility at Diego Garcia—from this island in the center of the sea, the United States could send its Navy and Air Force anywhere in the region. It assigned another aircraft carrier and two more destroyers to its Bahrain-based Middle East Force. It concluded access agreements with Oman, Kenya, and Somalia in April, June, and August of 1980 so that it could preposition supplies needed for the Rapid Deployment Force (RDF), an inter-service emergency unit that could forestall a Soviet advance into the Persian Gulf. As part of the RDF initiative, Washington secured transit rights in Morocco and created Central Command (CENTCOM), headquartered at MacDill Air Force Base in Tampa, Florida, rather than in the Gulf. Also out of respect for emirate and Saudi political sensitivities, American forces in the region stayed "over the horizon."[76]

These unusual arrangements left the Gulf more vulnerable to Soviet penetration. But events in Afghanistan rendered such analysis moot. As a result of its own Vietnam scenario, the Soviet Union never threatened the Gulf countries. Muslims throughout the region condemned Moscow's policy. Ayatollah Khomeini not only indicted the Soviet Union for its invasion of a Muslim state, he deplored Soviet atheism.[77]

Iraq, one of the Kremlin's staunchest allies in the Middle East but also a critic of the Soviet move into Afghanistan, worried about the cleric's zeal. Secular Baghdad feared that the Islamic Republic would export its sectarian extremism to the Iraqi Shi'a, co-religionists of the Iranians who mostly lived in the south and outnumbered Iraq's Sunni. President Saddam Hussein seized upon the turmoil in Iran; he wanted to wound Khomeini, his nemesis, politically or possibly evict him from power. After numerous border clashes, Iraqi soldiers marched into Iran in September 1980. Although Baghdad achieved some early successes in the Iran-Iraq War, within a year or so the Iranians used their superior numbers, and the elixir of the revolution, to overwhelm the Iraqis and recover lost territory. Tehran then pushed into southern Iraq in July 1982.[78]

This shocking reversal alarmed the Gulf monarchies. Although supposedly neutral, they backed their fellow Arabs. Led by the Kuwaitis and Saudis, they funded Hussein's multi-billion dollar war effort. Still, they mistrusted the Iraqis, who had repeatedly tried to annex parts or all of Kuwait. To protect themselves, Saudi Arabia, Kuwait, Bahrain, Qatar, the United Arab Emirates, and Oman founded the Gulf Cooperation Council (GCC) in May 1981. The GCC could not by itself end the conflict between Iraq and Iran, so in November 1987, after seven years of war, it asked members of the Arab League to call for a cease-fire. Hussein desperately needed such relief with the Iranians on the offensive. His air force and artillery had bombed and shelled the Islamic Republic's cities, and his army had carried out gas attacks, yet the Ayatollah's so-called martyrs kept winning the war of attrition.[79]

Throughout the Iran-Iraq War, the United States viewed events pessimistically. It needed Iraq to stem Iran's revolutionary fervor. The alleged 1981 Iranian coup attempt in Bahrain, and before it the 1979 riots at the Grand Mosque in Saudi Arabia, presaged the possible collapse of the Gulf's conservative monarchies. To fend off unwanted Iranian encroachments, GCC states, which needed to "omnibalance" (i.e., balance internal and external threats) secretly allowed U.S. warships and planes to monitor area security, thereby preserving American assets in the region. Although the White House opted for neutrality in the war, unofficially it helped arm the Iraqis and provided intelligence on Iranian troop movements. The Reagan administration thus amended the Carter Doctrine: Washington would take on any state in the area that threatened U.S. interests. To counterbalance Iran, the United States also invested in its Gulf partners. In a controversial decision, it sold sophisticated air surveillance (AWACS) aircraft and fighter planes to the Saudis, to the consternation of the Israeli lobby on Capitol Hill. Furthermore, starting in 1984, the U.S. Navy escorted Kuwaiti and Saudi tankers plying hazardous Gulf waters.[80]

America's then positive reputation in the Arab Gulf seemed mostly assured until the 1986 Iran-Contra scandal dismayed the GCC. Sales in 1985–86 of TOW and HAWK missiles via Israel to the Iranians, in exchange for the release of U.S. hostages in Lebanon, offended the monarchies. They considered Washington's behavior prejudicial as well as hypocritical. Worse for the White House, Hezbollah terrorists freed few of their captives and abducted other Americans to make up for the temporary loss of leverage. Clearly, the Iranians duped the unknowing Americans. Yet the Reagan presidency teetered for a year or so while Congress investigated possible abuses of power and violations of U.S. law.[81]

When in 1987, during the four-year old "Tanker War," the Kuwaitis asked Washington to pilot eleven of their ships through the mine-strewn Persian Gulf, the Reagan administration recognized an opportunity to redeem itself and its tarnished credibility following Irangate, but only once Moscow agreed to a similar request for three tankers. Since the White House aimed to exclude the Soviets from the area, it replied affirmatively to Kuwait's surprising inquiry. Previously, the Kuwaitis had consistently asserted their independence from the superpowers.

Now, they were eager to internationalize the war. In *Operation Earnest Will*, the U.S. Navy escorted Kuwaiti vessels flying American colors. These convoys watched for Iranian speedboats that could lay mines surreptitiously. Throughout 1987, Iran and Iraq impeded local commerce with indiscriminate attacks upon Gulf shipping. They continued to ruin each other's economies despite the presence of U.S., British, French, and Italian warships in the region. At its peak, the American Navy kept twenty-seven men-of-war in the Gulf.[82]

While the Soviets tried to oust the Americans from the area by courting the Iranians, the Iraqis inadvertently crippled the USS *Stark* in May 1987 with a French-made Exocet missile. Baghdad apologized and offered compensation. Washington forgave Iraq and turned its attention back to the Islamic Republic's transgressions. When, in July 1987 and April 1988, Iran's World War I-type "contact" mines damaged the *Bridgeton*, a neutral ship exempt from hostilities under international law, and the USS *Samuel B. Roberts*, the United States carried out retaliatory strikes against Iranian oil platforms and other such facilities in the Gulf, which Iranian Revolutionary Guard units liked to use. Another facet of *Operation Praying Mantis* included the U.S. Navy's pursuit of Iranian boats suspected of laying mines (an important facet of Ayatollah Khomeini's *Operation Martyrdom*). The Navy spied several of them performing this task in international waters, yet another flagrant violation of a UN-sanctioned global norm. To avenge the disabling of the *Samuel B. Roberts*, American warships incapacitated six Iranian men-of-war, thus eliminating half of the Islamic Republic's Navy by the summer of 1988. In reaction to the decimation of its naval forces, Tehran immediately halted its attacks. The United States encountered its own ethical problems in July, however, when the USS *Vincennes* shot down an Iranian Airbus (Iran Air 655) flying through the combat zone on its way to Dubai. Nearly three hundred passengers and crew died.[83]

In August 1988, Iran accepted UN Security Council Resolution 598. Khomeini acknowledged the war's cost to himself and his people. After years of rejecting UN and other mediation, as well as the November 1987 Arab League call for peace, he reluctantly ended one of the twentieth century's bloodiest contests. "I repeat that accepting this [resolution] was more deadly for me than taking poison," the Ayatollah said. The acrimony between the Islamic Republic and Iraq remained, but mercifully the killing ceased. Hussein showed his appreciation in typically ruthless fashion. He continued his genocidal Anfal campaign against the Kurds, his adversaries in northern Iraq, who sided with the Iranians during the war. The Reagan administration belatedly condemned these atrocities, but reprehensibly Congress refrained from imposing sanctions. Washington did not want to anger its regional bulwark against Iranian expansion, nor did it want to harm America's significant business interests in Iraq.[84]

Iran raged. When Baghdad fired chemical weapons at the Islamic Republic's soldiers during the Iran-Iraq War, the Americans declined to protest Iraqi barbarism. As with the Kurds, wartime expediency explained U.S. silence. Necessity also accounted for *Operation Staunch*, Washington's bid to deny Iran arms. Once the war had ended and the crisis had passed, American affinity for Hussein lessened somewhat. Although the White House suspected Iranian complicity in the bombing of Pan Am 103 over Lockerbie, Scotland, in December

1988, and knew of the Islamic Republic's connection to pro-Iranian terrorists in Lebanon who continued to abduct Americans and repeatedly threatened to kill them, Tehran could not at that point export its revolution to area countries aligned with the United States. With Iran thus held in check, Washington could withdraw some of its tacit approval for Iraqi tactics.[85]

Unfortunately for the White House and the GCC, Saddam Hussein considered himself victorious in his confrontation with Khomeini. The Iraqi president took full credit for keeping the Iranian fundamentalists at bay. As a result, he expected the Gulf monarchies to forgive his country's substantial debts— approximately $70 billion. He also wanted OPEC to raise oil prices so that he could rebuild his devastated country. The White House expedited this renewal project, as President George H.W. Bush continued Reagan's generous aid policy despite Hussein's appalling human-rights record. Blessed with the Arab world's premier army and abundant U.S. agricultural and other credits, the Iraqi leader mulled over his next campaign. Ominously, he had hired Canadian ballistics expert Gerald Bull to assemble a "Super Gun" and ordered his scientists to develop a nuclear program that, if ever operational, could threaten the region's stability.[86]

These potential problems left Washington unfazed in 1989. It preferred to emphasize its resurgence in the Persian Gulf rather than dwell on the wisdom of its Iraq policy. After a sixteen-year period (1973–88) marked by numerous upheavals and political culs-de-sac, the United States, via the Carter Doctrine and its Reagan corollary, seemed poised to assert itself in a manner concordant with American interests in the Gulf. With an impressive military presence, albeit one "over the horizon" to assuage emirate and Saudi distaste for foreign soldiers, the United States stood ready to impose its will on the region, should that be required, while hoping intervention would not be necessary any time soon. In the aftermath of the Iran-Iraq War, the U.S. Navy relied on only ten warships (in contrast to twenty-seven at the height of the reflagging operation) to monitor an unstable area. But when Baghdad invaded Kuwait in August 1990, the Gulf's newest guardian, successor to the British and the Ottomans, could count on ten years of military build-up in the area. It would need that head start to defeat the Iraqis in the winter of 1991.[87]

Assessment

In the *fourth* stage (1973–89) of U.S. expansion in the Persian Gulf, Washington endured repeated insults. OPEC imposed a burdensome embargo; Ayatollah Khomeini spurred on anti-American Iranian revolutionaries, who swept away the Shah's decrepit regime; and Kuwait, Saudi Arabia, and most of the other Gulf emirates publicly disapproved of the Carter Doctrine. The White House partially recovered from these repudiations of U.S. power when Henry Kissinger dazzled the Middle East with his diplomatic wizardry and the Iran-Iraq War provided the United States with a new raison d'être—to help arm Baghdad, via agricultural credits and so-called dual use items, and defend the GCC states.

To call the American performance in this era imperialistic would seem rather preposterous. Yet informal empire, consistent with the history of Great Powers, allows for the contraction of interests and influence. America's dismissal from Iran came as a slap, but Washington never contemplated exiting the Gulf. When the GCC countries banded together in 1981, most of them privately asked the United States to stay involved in the region's security. Eager to counter the Iranians and convinced that the Soviets might move in otherwise, the Americans acquiesced in what became an unstated request for guardianship.

The stark improvement in U.S. defense posture during the Reagan years enabled Washington to take over Iran's previous area responsibilities—i.e., to police the Gulf and thereby safeguard American hegemonic and security interests. The United States accomplished this task while respecting emirate and Saudi wishes for an "over the horizon" U.S. presence. The American preference for a regional imperium that married both liberal and classical empire dovetailed nicely with GCC political and military necessities.

Although, as in the past, U.S. officials eschewed the vocabulary of empire, a lesson of decolonization and failed colonial experiments, American means and objectives mirrored those of past Gulf imperialists, such as the British. With its focus on semantics and ideas, constructivist analysis seems to explain Washington's penchant for rhetorical evasiveness—i.e., for words that reassure and do not offend. The White House spoke of defensive motivations, but its plans undeniably corresponded to imperial intentions. To wit, the Carter Doctrine sought to impose a distinctly American imprint upon the region. According to scholar Fouad Ajami, moreover, "[a]t the end of the day, when the Arab governments needed protection . . . they have turned to *Pax Americana*."[88]

Before the United States recovered some of its lost influence near the end of the Iran-Iraq War, U.S. hegemony weakened appreciably when OPEC revolutionized the business of oil. As the cartel swung the industry balance of power in its favor, it achieved a stunning political victory on behalf of developing countries everywhere (though the latter received no discount when buying petroleum). Instead of submitting to the imperatives of advanced economies, a normal practice for Third-World nations, OPEC dictated prices to consumers and manipulated supply. As a result, impressive oil rents enriched all of the Gulf states. Not everyone enjoyed the same luxury—with small populations, the Arabian monarchies benefited more on a per capita basis—but the region experienced an incredible economic upturn until the ruinous Iran-Iraq War and the oil glut of the 1980s dampened area spirits. The Americans contributed to OPEC's misfortunes by prodding the Saudis to pump more crude.

In the 1970s, OPEC's harsh policies crippled the world capitalist economy, forcing the developed world to conserve energy and search for new fields in the North Sea and elsewhere. When the petroleum market fizzled due mainly to oversupply, the U.S. economy recovered from acute recession and registered impressive growth, especially during Reagan's second term. The collapse of oil prices, which humbled OPEC and forced it to adopt a quota system in 1986, heartened the United States and its allies, both of which imported increasing amounts of Gulf crude, and derailed conservation efforts. By 1987, with the Cold War not yet over, Washington's stake in the Iran-Iraq War seemed obvious. If the Iranians sank too many Saudi and Kuwaiti tankers, then Western and Asian economies would suffer. America therefore needed to protect the world's most essential economic lifeline.

The United States slowly rebuilt its hegemonic position in the Gulf after a dozen or so years of steady decline. As the informal American empire struggled to survive a turbulent era, what became of contingent imperialism? The 1973–74 OPEC crisis dislocated the American economy and imperiled the Twin Pillars policy. When Secretary of State Kissinger forced OPEC to drop the oil embargo in return for continued shuttle diplomacy on the Israeli-Syrian track, he got the cartel to concede, something no one else at the time could do. In that case, proposition P1 (The United States will exercise unilateral contingent imperialism whenever a significant threat to American hegemony and security occurs, Washington can act alone or cannot rely on anyone else to secure its interests and can overcome any regional constraints, consensus exists within the executive, and no majority in Congress or critical segment of domestic opinion strongly opposes White House action) seems correct. The lifting of the embargo did not cure America of its economic ills, but the country recovered somewhat. More importantly, Washington showed itself indispensable when it came to resolving the Arab-Israeli conflict, a fact the OPEC Gulf states, which professed to care deeply about Palestinian issues, begrudgingly acknowledged.

Similarly, when the Iranian monarchy teetered in 1978–79, only the United States could save it. The Soviets expected as much. But President Carter chose not to prop up the Shah, one of America's most important, not to mention visible, allies. Content to see Iran fulfil its destiny without outside interference, the Georgia Democrat stood by as Iranians remade their country into a theocracy bitterly opposed to Uncle Sam. Carter's strong belief in the right to self-determination earned him Iranian enmity (via the hostage crisis, most obviously), not gratitude, and two years of political purgatory at home. In contrast, a Truman, Eisenhower, or Nixon might have ordered some kind of operation, covert or otherwise, to prevent the downfall of Mohammed Reza Pahlavi. Regardless, in that case proposition P4 (Even in the event of a significant threat to American hegemony and security, the United States will not exercise any type of contingent imperialism if it cannot overcome regional constraints, no consensus within the executive exists, and either a majority of Congress or critical segment of domestic opinion [or both] strongly opposes White House action or involvement) seems apropos. Deprived of decisive presidential leadership, the Carter administration could not agree on a course of action and thus could only dither until events in Iran overwhelmed it.[89]

After his terrible blunder, Carter tried to redeem himself. His 1980 doctrine enabled the United States to build up its forces in the vicinity of the Persian Gulf. Military assets in Oman, Bahrain, Kuwait, and the Indian Ocean meant nothing, however, until Washington began escorting Saudi and Kuwaiti tankers during the Iran-Iraq War. This assistance preserved U.S. hegemonic interests, signaled the country's return to regional relevance, and gained America some prominence within the Gulf. In that case, proposition P2 (The United States will exercise alliance contingent imperialism whenever a significant threat to American hegemony and security occurs, allies agree to join a U.S.-led venture or vice-versa, Washington can overcome any regional constraints, consensus exists within the executive, and no majority in Congress or critical segment of domestic opinion strongly opposes White House action) seems right. The White House proved reliable, a quality not lost on GCC leaders, who needed trustworthy partners to preserve their rule.

Despite its travails during this period (1973–89), the United States drew upon contingent imperialism twice. The first instance occurred in a time of decline, the other when the country's reputation in the Gulf was improving. America's resurgence, courtesy of Jimmy Carter and Ronald Reagan, followed the unexpected and dramatic demise of its Twin Pillars policy. Now poised to ameliorate its standing in the region, Washington prepared to counter any threat to its hegemonic and security interests.

Notes

1. Michael A. Palmer, *Guardians of the Gulf: A History of America's Expanding Role in the Persian Gulf, 1833–1992* (New York: Free Press, 1992), 85–97.

2. Carl Bernstein and Bob Woodward, *All the President's Men* (New York: Warner Books, 1975); John Lewis Gaddis, "Rescuing Choice from Circumstance: The Statecraft of Henry Kissinger," in *The Diplomats, 1939–1979*, eds. Gordon A. Craig and Francis L. Loewenheim (Princeton, NJ: Princeton University Press, 1994), 564–92; Robert L. Beisner, "History and Henry Kissinger," *Diplomatic History* 14, no. 4 (Fall 1990): 511–27; Raymond L. Garthoff, *Détente and Confrontation: American-Soviet Relations from Nixon to Reagan* (Washington, DC: Brookings Institution, 1985), 1–105; and Carol R. Saivetz, "Superpower Competition in the Middle East and the Collapse of Détente," in *The Fall of Détente: Soviet-American Relations during the Carter Years,* ed. Odd Arne Westad (Oslo: Scandinavian University Press, 1997), 72–76.

3. Jerel A. Rosati, "Jimmy Carter, A Man Before His Time? The Emergence and Collapse of the First Post-Cold War Presidency," *Presidential Studies Quarterly* 23, no. 3 (Summer 1993): 459–76; John Lewis Gaddis, *Strategies of Containment: A Critical Appraisal of Postwar American National Security Policy* (New York: Oxford University Press, 1982), 345–57; Zbigniew Brzezinski, *Power and Principle: Memoirs of the National Security Adviser 1977–1981* (New York: Farrar, Straus & Giroux, 1983), 426–37, 459–60; Gary Sick, *All Fall Down: America's Tragic Encounter with Iran* (New York: Random House, 1985), 290–92; Cecil V. Crabb, Jr., *The Doctrines of American Foreign Policy: Their Meaning, Role, and Future* (Baton Rouge, LA: Louisiana State University Press, 1982), 325–41; and Daniel Yergin, *The Prize: The Epic Quest for Oil, Money & Power* (New York: Simon & Schuster, 1991), 695–96.

4. Don Oberdorfer, *The Turn: From the Cold War to a New Era: The United States and the Soviet Union 1983–1990* (New York: Poseidon Press, 1991); John Lewis Gaddis, *The United States and the End of the Cold War: Implications, Reconsiderations, Provocations* (New York: Oxford University Press, 1992), 119–32; George P. Shultz, *Turmoil and Triumph: My Years as Secretary of State* (New York: Charles Scribner, 1993); and

Robert Dallek, *The American Style of Foreign Policy: Cultural Politics and Foreign Affairs* (New York: Oxford University Press, 1983), 283–90. See also the 1998–99 Cable News Network (CNN) series, "Cold War": episode 19, "Freeze 1977–81," and episode 22, "Star Wars 1981–88." Carter initiated the so-called Reagan military buildup when he issued Presidential Directive 59 toward the end of his presidency. See Brzezinski, *Power and Principle*, 454–59. From 1974 to 1986, however, U.S. national intelligence estimates "substantially" overstated the Soviet Union's capacity and intention to improve its strategic nuclear arsenal. See Jonathan S. Landay, "Document: CIA Exaggerated Soviet Plans for Nuclear Expansion," *Hartford Courant*, 10 March 2001, A6.

5. George Lenczowski, *American Presidents and the Middle East* (Durham, NC: Duke University Press, 1990), 226–33; James A. Baker, III, with Thomas M. DeFrank, *The Politics of Diplomacy: Revolution, War & Peace, 1989–1992* (New York: G.P. Putnam, 1995), 1–16, 37–46, 61–96, 133–76; John Newhouse, "Shunning the Losers," *New Yorker*, 26 October 1992, 40–52; Michael R. Beschloss and Strobe Talbott, *At the Highest Levels: The Inside Story of the End of the Cold War* (Boston: Little, Brown, 1993); Michael J. Hogan, ed., *The End of the Cold War: Its Meaning and Implications* (Cambridge: Cambridge University Press, 1992); Charles W. Kegley, Jr., "How Did the Cold War Die? Principles for an Autopsy," *Mershon International Studies Review* 38 (1994): 11–41; and Bob Woodward, *The Commanders* (New York: Simon & Schuster, 1991), 35–196. See also the CNN series, "Cold War": episode 20, "Soldiers of God 1975–88"; and episode 23, "The Wall Comes Down 1989."

6. Michael Beschloss, "The End of the Imperial Presidency," *New York Times*, 18 December 2000, http://www.nytimes.com; Arthur M. Schlesinger, Jr., *The Imperial Presidency* (Boston: Houghton Mifflin, 1973); Lenczowski, *American Presidents and the Middle East*, 212–26; Richard B. Parker, *The Politics of Miscalculation in the Middle East* (Bloomington, IN: Indiana University Press, 1993), 167–78; and William B. Quandt, *Peace Process: American Diplomacy and the Arab-Israeli Conflict since 1967* (Washington, DC, and Berkeley, CA: The Brookings Institution and University of California Press, 1993), 340–50.

7. Quandt, *Peace Process*, 255–331.

8. F. Gregory Gause, III, "Gulf Regional Politics: Revolution, War, and Rivalry," in *Dynamics of Regional Politics: Four Systems on the Indian Ocean Rim*, ed. W. Howard Wriggins (New York: Columbia University Press, 1992), 25–88; and F. Gregory Gause, III, *Oil Monarchies: Domestic and Security Challenges in the Arab Gulf States* (New York: Council on Foreign Relations Press, 1994).

9. Quandt, *Peace Process*, 25–62.

10. Yergin, *The Prize*, 592–93, 602–3; and Burton I. Kaufman, *The Arab Middle East and the United States: Inter-Arab Rivalry and Superpower Diplomacy* (New York: Twayne, 1996), 65–81.

11. Kaufman, *The Arab Middle East and the United States*, 81–83; and Yergin, *The Prize*, 604–5.

12. Saivetz, "Superpower Competition in the Middle East and the Collapse of Détente," 76–80.

13. Kaufman, *The Arab Middle East and the United States*, 84–85; Henry Kissinger, *Years of Upheaval* (Boston: Little, Brown, 1982), 616, quote can be found on 616; and Walter Isaacson, *Kissinger: A Biography* (New York: Simon & Schuster, 1992), 537. For information on "step-by-step" diplomacy, see Quandt, *Peace Process*, 148–82.

14. David E. Long, *The United States and Saudi Arabia: Ambivalent Allies* (Boulder, CO: Westview Press, 1985), 24–25; Kaufman, *The Arab Middle East and the United States*, 83–84; Kissinger, *Years of Upheaval*, 854–74; Miriam Joyce, *Kuwait 1945–1996: An Anglo-American Perspective* (London: Frank Cass, 1998), 159; and Yergin, *The Prize*, 588–602, 605–9. Yergin writes (591) that "[a]s demand worldwide bobbed up against the limit of available supply, market prices exceeded the official posted prices. It was a decisive change, truly underlining the end of the twenty-year surplus."

15. J.B. Kelly, *Arabia, the Gulf and the West* (New York: Basic Books, 1980), 395–424, quotes can be found on 396–97, 398; and Kissinger, *Years of Upheaval*, 872–74, 881. Kissinger argues (873) that "the Arab embargo was a symbolic gesture of limited practical impact. To be sure, Saudi and other Arab oil were not shipped to the United States. But since the oil companies were operating a common pool, they simply substituted non-embargoed non-Arab oil for embargoed Arab oil and shifted other allocations accordingly. The true impact of the embargo was psychological." For more on the U.S. position, see Congressional testimony from 28 November 1973, in "New Perspectives On the Persian Gulf," *Hearings Before the Subcommittee on the Near East of the Committee on Foreign Affairs*, House of Representatives, 93rd Congress, 1st Session, 6 June, 17, 23, 24 July, and 28 November 1973 (Washington, DC: Government Printing Office, 1973), 145–84. On the Arab-Israeli conflict–Persian Gulf nexus, see scholar John Duke Anthony's statements in "New Perspectives On the Persian Gulf," 204–7.

16. "New Perspectives On the Persian Gulf," 164, 171.

17. Kissinger, *Years of Upheaval*, 615.

18. Kissinger, *Years of Upheaval*, 615–16.

19. First quote can be found in Kissinger, *Years of Upheaval*, 634. Second quote can be found on 631.

20. Kissinger, *Years of Upheaval*, 666.

21. Kissinger, *Years of Upheaval*, 794.

22. Kissinger, *Years of Upheaval*, 794.

23. Kissinger, *Years of Upheaval*, 799.

24. Long, *The United States and Saudi Arabia*, 24–27; James A. Bill, *The Eagle and the Lion: The Tragedy of American-Iranian Relations* (New Haven, CT: Yale University Press, 1988), 202–3; and Yergin, *The Prize*, 625–26.

25. Quote can be found in Yergin, *The Prize*, 825. According to Kissinger, the United States had a strategy of "demonstrating the limits of Soviet influence." See Yergin, *The Prize*, 863. The secretary of state pointed out that U.S. strategy "sought to reduce the Soviet role in the Middle East because our respective interests in the area . . . could not be reconciled, at least as long as the Soviet Union identified itself only with a maximum Arab program and did nothing to induce compromise on the part of its clients . . . . [I]t was détente [though] that enabled the United States to bring about a diplomatic revolution in the Middle East." See Yergin, *The Prize*, 943. On the significance of this diplomatic coup de théâtre, see Garthoff, *Détente and Confrontation*, 413–14; Isaacson, *Kissinger*, 549–50; and Saivetz, "Superpower Competition in the Middle East and the Collapse of Détente," 79. For a journalist's account of this first Egyptian-Israeli disengagement agreement, see Edward R.F. Sheehan, "Step by Step in the Middle East," *Foreign Policy*, no. 22 (Spring 1976): 4–34.

26. Kissinger, *Years of Upheaval*, 846.

27. Kaufman, *The Arab Middle East and the United States*, 91.

28. Kaufman, *The Arab Middle East and the United States*, 91; Yergin, *The Prize*, 630–32; Sheehan, "Step by Step in the Middle East," 35–36; and Kissinger, *Years of Upheaval*, 894.

29. First quote can be found in Kissinger, *Years of Upheaval*, 1087. Second quote can be found on 1110. On the Syrian-Israeli disengagement agreement, see Sheehan, "Step by Step in the Middle East," 34–44.

30. Isaacson, *Kissinger*, 537.

31. In the aftermath of the November 1995 assassination of Israeli Prime Minister Yitzak Rabin, Kissinger used the expression "grammar of co-existence" to describe the Arab-Israeli peace process. "Remarks by Henry A. Kissinger," CNN, 5 November 1995. Second quote can be found in Isaacson, *Kissinger*, 551.

32. "The Persian Gulf, 1974: Money, Politics, Arms, and Power," *Hearings Before the Subcommittee on the Near East and South Asia of the Committee on Foreign Affairs*, House of Representatives, 93rd Congress, 2nd Session, 30 July, 5, 7, and 12 August 1974 (Washington, DC: Government Printing Office, 1975), 62–100. Quotes can be found on 64–65, 91. Atherton spoke on 7 August 1974.

33. Sheehan, "Step by Step in the Middle East," 44–70.

34. On Great-Power adjustment failure, see Charles A. Kupchan, *The Vulnerability of Empire* (Ithaca, NY: Cornell University Press, 1994), 3.

35. Sick, *All Fall Down*, 22–23; and Irving Janis, *Groupthink* (Boston: Houghton Mifflin, 1982), 2–13.

36. Palmer, *Guardians of the Gulf*, 92; and Bill, *The Eagle and the Lion*, 51–97.

37. Bill, *The Eagle and the Lion*, 154–233. On the United States, Iran, and the White Revolution, see April R. Summitt, "For a White Revolution: John F. Kennedy and the Shah of Iran," *Middle East Journal* 58, no. 4 (Autumn 2004): 560–75. Summitt writes (574) that President Kennedy, "faced with conflicting advice from the NSC and State Department, attempted to walk a middle road. . . . He hoped that this approach would quietly encourage reform while avoiding accusations of imperialism." Summitt adds (575) that "the Shah used superpower rivalries to bolster his regime. In the long term, however, he became entangled in his attempts to keep his support flowing and failed to address a growing Islamic movement inside Iran. Inevitably, this failure would lead directly to the 1978 revolution."

38. Richard W. Cottam, *Iran and the United States: A Cold War Case Study* (Pittsburgh, PA: University of Pittsburgh Press, 1988), 169–72.

39. Cottam, *Iran and the United States*, 163–69.

40. Cottam, *Iran and the United States*, 156–69; Bill, *The Eagle and the Lion*, 226–33; and Saivetz, "Superpower Competition in the Middle East and the Collapse of Détente," 85. Saivetz writes (85) that the Soviets followed a "double-track policy of criticizing the Shah's close military ties with the United States, while establishing cordial and mutually beneficial economic relations with Iran." On reverse donor dependency, see Jeffrey A. Lefebvre, *Arms for the Horn: U.S. Security Policy in Ethiopia and Somalia 1953–1991* (Pittsburgh, PA: University of Pittsburgh Press, 1991), 3–10.

41. Barry Rubin, *Paved with Good Intentions: The American Experience and Iran* (New York: Oxford University Press, 1980), 190–201. Quote can be found on 201.

42. Sick, *All Fall Down*, 32–34. Quote can be found on 28.

43. Cottam, *Iran and the United States,* 165–69.

44. Sick, *All Fall Down*, 50–51. Quote can be found on 58.

45. Sick, *All Fall Down*, 58–60. Quote can be found on 59.

46. Sick, *All Fall Down*, 61–74. Quote can be found on 72.

47. William H. Sullivan, "Dateline Iran: The Road Not Taken," *Foreign Policy*, no. 40 (Fall 1980): 177–78; and Sick, *All Fall Down*, 60.

48. Sick, *All Fall Down*, 75–77, 79–80.

49. Sick, *All Fall Down*, 78–79. Quote can be found in Cottam, *Iran and the United States*, 177.

50. Sick, *All Fall Down*, 81–87, 89–91. Quotes can be found on 86.

51. Sick, *All Fall Down*, 93–100; Sullivan, "Dateline Iran," 176, 178; and Saivetz, "Superpower Competition in the Middle East and the Collapse of Détente," 87.

52. Sick, *All Fall Down*, 101–6, 115–16.

53. Sick, *All Fall Down*, 107–13.

54. Niccolò Machiavelli, *The Prince*, translated by George Bull (New York: Penguin Books, 1986). Quote can be found in Cottam, *Iran and the United States*, 186.

55. Sick, *All Fall Down*, 118–31; and Sullivan, "Dateline Iran," 177–78.

56. Sick, *All Fall Down*, 131–32.

57. Sick, *All Fall Down*, 132–38; and Sullivan, "Dateline Iran," 178–86.

58. Sick, *All Fall Down*, 138–39.

59. Sick, *All Fall Down*, 150–51; Cottam, *Iran and the United States*, 189–206; and Bill, *The Eagle and the Lion*, 233–43.

60. Rubin, *Paved with Good Intentions*, 204–5.

61. Rubin, *Paved with Good Intentions*, 206–16; Sick, *All Fall Down*, 148–94; and Bill, *The Eagle and the Lion*, 319–23, 337–40. For an excellent overview of U.S. policy during the 1978–79 crisis, see Bill, *The Eagle and the Lion*, 243–60.

62. Sick, *All Fall Down*, 195–342. For an explanation of the bureaucratic rivalry between the national security advisor and the secretary of state, see John Spanier and Eric M. Uslaner, *American Foreign Policy Making and the Democratic Dilemmas* (Pacific Grove, CA: Brooks/Cole, 1989), 49–61.

63. Yergin, *The Prize*, 678–91.

64. Yergin, *The Prize*, 691–98.

65. Yergin, *The Prize*, 703–6; and Joseph Wright Twinam, *The Gulf, Cooperation and the Council: An American Perspective* (Washington, DC: Middle East Policy Council, 1992), 166. For an overview of Saudi policy during this second "oil shock," see Long, *The United States and Saudi Arabia*, 27–30.

66. Gary Sick, "The Evolution of U.S. Strategy Toward the Indian Ocean and Persian Gulf Regions" [hereafter referred to as "The Evolution of U.S. Strategy"], in *The Great Game: Rivalry in the Persian Gulf and South Asia*, ed. Alvin Z. Rubinstein (New York: Praeger, 1983), 68–73; and Brzezinski, *Power and Principle*, 437–47.

67. Brzezinski, *Power and Principle*, 446–47, first quote can be found on 447; Sick, "The Evolution of U.S. Strategy," 69–71, second quote can be found on 70; "The Persian Gulf Region: Source of Two-Thirds of the West's Oil," *New York Times*, 25 January 1980, A8; and Anthony J. Parisi, "Hormuz: America's Economic Interest," *New York Times*, 27 January 1980, Section 3, 1, 4. Parisi wrote (1) that "[e]very 21 minutes, on average, a tanker exits [the Strait of Hormuz (the waterway linking the Persian Gulf to the Indian Ocean)] on its way to some distant country. Two thirds of all the oil [OPEC] sells—more than half the oil involved in international trade—flows through this narrow passageway, including perhaps a third of what the United States imports." In the Horn of Africa, Washington embraced former Soviet client Somalia, Addis Ababa's major rival, once the Ethiopians turned to Moscow.

68. Sick, "The Evolution of U.S. Strategy," 71; and Bernard Weinraub, "Reagan Blames Carter 'Failure' for Soviet Move," *New York Times*, 25 January 1980, A12.

69. Brzezinski, *Power and Principle*, 446–47; and Sick, "The Evolution of U.S. Strategy," 71–75.

70. Sick, "The Evolution of U.S. Strategy," 72–75; and Brzezinski, *Power and Principle*, 443–44.

71. Odd Arne Westad, "The Road to Kabul: Soviet Policy on Afghanistan, 1978–1979," in *The Fall of Détente*, 136–42; and Saivetz, "Superpower Competition in the Middle East and the Collapse of Détente," 87–90.

72. Westad, "The Road to Kabul," 443–54; Crabb, *The Doctrines of American Foreign Policy,* 325–41, first quote can be found on 329; Drew Middleton, "The President Draws the Line: In Persian Gulf and for Kennedy," *New York Times*, 25 January 1980, A1, A7; Richard Burt, "How U.S. Strategy Toward Persian Gulf Evolved," *New York Times*, 25 January 1980, A6, second and third quotes can be found in that article; "Clear and Present Dangers," *New York Times*, 25 January 1980, A22; Stanley Hoffmann, "Toward a Foreign Policy," *New York Times*, 25 January 1980, A23; James Reston, "Carter's Poker Game," *New York Times*, 25 January 1980, A23. Reston wrote of the Carter speech: "He said quite clearly that the United States was now drawing a sharp line [in the Persian Gulf]"; and Hedrick Smith, "Tough Talk," *New York Times*, 27 January 1980, Section 4, 1. Smith opined that "President Carter has seized the moment to formally ring down the curtain on the hesitant American neo-isolationism of the post-Vietnam period: Now American flotillas are steaming in the Indian Ocean, a region Mr. Carter once sought to demilitarize." In the late nineteenth century, U.S. Navy icon Alfred T. Mahan advocated an invigorated American naval presence worldwide.

73. John Kifner, "Arabs React Coolly to Carter's Address," *New York Times,* 25 January 1980, A9; John Kifner, "Arabs Are Critical of Carter's Stand," *New York Times*, 26 January 1980, A6; Crabb, *The Doctrines of American Foreign Policy*, 356–60; Brzezinski, *Power and Principle*, 449–50; Phebe Marr, *The Modern History of Iraq* (Boulder, CO: Westview Press, 1985), 232–34, 291–94; Adeed Dawisha, "The Stability of the Gulf: Domestic Sources and External Threats," in *The Great Game*, 3–21; and David D. Newsom, "America Engulfed," *Foreign Policy*, no. 43 (Summer 1981): 17–32. Newsom wrote (21) that "[t]he Persian Gulf states welcome a U.S. military presence in the area, but they prefer it to be distant and unobtrusive. They believe that such a presence would provide security from both the Soviets and unpredictable neighbors. But the desire of local regimes for an outside presence is counterbalanced by fears that such a presence will increase their own political and military vulnerability."

74. Kifner, "Arabs React Coolly to Carter's Address"; Flora Lewis, "Carter Step Seems to Please Europeans," *New York Times*, 25 January 1980, A8, first quote can be found in that article; Craig R. Whitney, "Soviet Terms Carter's Warning on Gulf an 'Absurdity,'" *New York Times*, 25 January 1980, A8, second quote can be found in that article; "Carter Comes On Strong; Allies Like What They Hear," *New York Times*, 27 January 1980, Section 4, 1; Brzezinski, *Power and Principle*, 460–62; and Crabb, *The Doctrines of American Foreign Policy*, 341–60. Historically, the Russians and the British had engaged in the Great Game, a contest for geopolitical mastery of Southwest Asia. In the 19th century and into the 20th, Moscow and London had considered Afghanistan a buffer zone between their respective empires.

75. Crabb, *The Doctrines of American Foreign Policy*, 348–52, quote can be found on 349; Saivetz, "Superpower Competition in the Middle East and the Collapse of Détente," 89–90; Sick, "The Evolution of U.S. Strategy," 73–78; Lenczowski, *American Presidents and the Middle East*, 213; and Brzezinski, *Power and Principle*, 445, 448–49. The national security advisor argues (445) that, similar to the Truman Doctrine, the Carter Doctrine aimed "to make the Soviet Union aware of the fact that the intrusion of Soviet armed forces into an area of vital importance to the United States would precipitate an engagement *with* the United States, and that the United States would then

be free to choose the manner in which it would respond." Italics in original. But as Carter delivered his January 1980 speech that reoriented American policy toward the Persian Gulf, Washington recalled five of its twenty-six Indian Ocean ships. Concurrently, Moscow added men-of-war to the region, raising its total to twenty-six. United Press International, "U.S. Cuts, Soviet Builds Forces in Indian Ocean," *New York Times*, 25 January 1980, A7.

76. Larry W. Bowman and Jeffrey A. Lefebvre, "The Indian Ocean: U.S. Military and Strategic Perspectives," in *The Indian Ocean: Perspectives on a Strategic Arena*, eds. William L. Dowdy and Russell B. Trood (Durham, NC: Duke University Press, 1985), 413–35; Jeffrey A. Lefebvre, "The Transformation of U.S. Security Policy in the Gulf: Strategic Disruption and the Balance of Risk" (paper presented at the annual meeting of the New England Political Science Association, New London, CT, 2–3 May 1997), 4–8; Crabb, *The Doctrines of American Foreign Policy*, 360–70; Palmer, *Guardians of the Gulf*, 101–17; Joseph A. Kechichian, *Oman and the World: The Emergence of an Independent Foreign Policy* (Santa Monica, CA: Rand, 1995), 147–50; Brzezinski, *Power and Principle*, 447, 454–59; and Sick, "The Evolution of U.S. Strategy," 77. Washington had agreed to sell fifty aircraft to Morocco in early 1980, likely facilitating a quid pro quo—i.e., U.S. helicopters, jets, and reconnaissance planes for transit rights. Reuters, "U.S. Will Sell Planes to Morocco to Encourage Peace in Sahara," *New York Times*, 25 January 1980, A7.

77. Oles M. Smolansky, "Soviet Interests in the Persian/Arabian Gulf," in *The Indian Ocean*, 458–77.

78. Dilip Hiro, *The Longest War: The Iran-Iraq Military Conflict* (New York: Routledge, 1991); Marr, *The Modern History of Iraq*, 292–94; and Lenczowski, *American Presidents in the Middle East*, 243–44.

79. Twinam, *The Gulf, Cooperation and the Council*, 131–44; R.K. Ramazani, "The Gulf Cooperation Council: A Search for Security," in *The Indian Ocean*, 170–89; and Hiro, *The Longest War*, 134–35.

80. Bruce W. Jentleson, *With Friends Like These: Reagan, Bush, and Saddam, 1982–1990* (New York: W.W. Norton, 1994), 31–67; Sick, "The Evolution of U.S. Strategy," 76–78; Twinam, *The Gulf, Cooperation and the Council*, 145–70; Palmer, *Guardians of the Gulf*, 118–21; Lenczowski, *American Presidents and the Middle East*, 258–61; and Hiro, *The Longest War*, 131. On "omnibalancing," see Stephen R. David, "Explaining Third World Alignment," *World Politics* 63, no. 2 (January 1991): 233–56.

81. Lenczowski, *American Presidents and the Middle East*, 233–42; and Palmer, *Guardians of the Gulf*, 121–22. For an analysis of the Reagan administration's difficulties with Iran and lack of policy vis-à-vis that country, see Kenneth M. Pollack, *The Persian Puzzle: The Conflict Between Iran and America* (New York: Random House, 2004), 233–35.

82. Pollack, *The Persian Puzzle*, 223–27; Palmer, *Guardians of the Gulf*, 122–49; Hiro, *The Longest War*, 129–33, 213–40; Lenczowski, *American Presidents and the Middle East*, 243–46; and Shultz, *Turmoil and Triumph*, 925–35.

83. Pollack, *The Persian Puzzle*, 227–32; Lenczowski, *American Presidents and the Middle East*, 246–52; Palmer, *Guardians of the Gulf*, 123–49; and Robert O. Freedman, *Moscow and the Middle East: Soviet Policy since the Invasion of Afghanistan* (Cambridge: Cambridge University Press, 1991), 227–29, 267–90. The Moscow-Baghdad axis underwent considerable strain during the war as the Soviets tilted toward Iran. Freedman, *Moscow and the Middle East*, 227. The United States went without minesweepers in the Gulf until October 1987. Palmer, *Guardians of the Gulf*, 135.

84. Pollack, *The Persian Puzzle*, 232–33; Lenczowski, *American Presidents and the Middle East*, 252–54; Hiro, *The Longest War*, 241–53, quote can be found on 241; and Jentleson, *With Friends Like These*, 68–93. The November 1987 Amman summit re-

turned Egypt to the Arab fold after a decade of ostracism following the 1978 Camp David Accords and the 1979 Egyptian-Israeli peace treaty. When Cairo rejoined the Arab League, the Gulf monarchies welcomed the opportunity to make use of Cairo as a "geopolitical counterweight" to both Iran and Iraq. Twinam, *The Gulf, Cooperation and the Council*, 140–41. Quote can be found on 141. On the U.S. response to the murderous 1988 Anfal campaign, which saw Iraqi forces infamously use chemical weapons in Halabja in March, see Samantha Power, *"A Problem from Hell:" America and the Age of Genocide* (New York: Basic Books, 2002), 170–231.

85. Jentleson, *With Friends Like These*, 68–93; and Marc Jay Selverstone, "Planes, Causal Chains, and Terrorist Zeal: Chaos and the Bombing of Pan Am Flight 103," *Ohio University Contemporary History Institute Think Piece Series*, no. 26, February 1994.

86. Jentleson, *With Friends Like These*, 94–138; and Power, *"A Problem from Hell,"* 223, 231–34. See also Kenneth I. Juster, "The Myth of Iraqgate," *Foreign Policy*, no. 94 (Spring 1994): 105–19.

87. Twinam, *The Gulf, Cooperation and the Council*, 169–70. The Bush administration's National Security Directive 26 (approved by the president on October 2, 1989) called for "normal relations between the United States and Iraq." Quote can be found in Jentleson, *With Friends Like These*, 94.

88. Cottam, *Iran and the United States*, 4. On constructivism, see Jack Snyder, "One World, Rival Theories," *Foreign Policy*, no. 145 (November/December 2004): 59–61; and Stephen M. Walt, "International Relations: One World, Many Theories," *Foreign Policy*, no. 110 (Spring 1998): 38, 40–41. Fouad Ajami's quote is from The History Channel's 1999 presentation of the "20th Century with Mike Wallace: Guardians of the Gulf."

89. On the importance of beliefs and leadership, see Margaret G. Hermann, "Assessing Leadership Style: Trait Analysis," in *The Psychological Assessment of Political Leaders*, ed. Jerrold M. Post (Ann Arbor, MI: University of Michigan Press, 2003), 178–214; Margaret G. Hermann, Thomas Preston, Baghat Korany, and Timothy M. Shaw, "Who Leads Matters: The Effects of Powerful Individuals," *International Studies Review* 3, no. 2 (Summer 2001): 86–95; and Margaret G. Hermann and Joe D. Hagan, "International Decision Making: Leadership Matters," *Foreign Policy*, no. 110 (Spring 1998): 124–37.

Chapter 6

Victory and Quarantine: 1990–2000

During the *fifth* stage (1990–2000) of U.S. expansion in the Persian Gulf, the White House assembled a multinational coalition to expel the Iraqi Army from Kuwait, established a new fleet for the region, and tried to isolate Iran and Iraq politically, economically, and militarily. Washington's bid for Gulf mastery hinged on naval and aerial supremacy. Without it, the United States could not have secured unimpeded access to the area's critical oil resources. According to experts, denial of Gulf crude would have severely injured Western economies tethered to Saudi, Kuwaiti, and other Organization for Petroleum Exporting Countries (OPEC) derricks.

Operation Desert Shield/Storm prevented such a cataclysm and made up for several bitter setbacks incurred in the previous stage (1973–89). Consecutive humiliations (i.e., steep increases in world oil prices in 1973–74 and 1979–80, the deposition of the Shah of Iran in 1979, the Iranian hostage crisis in 1979–81, and Irangate in 1986) underscored American weakness and undermined Washington's ability to mold regional events. The announcement of the Carter Doctrine in January 1980 symbolized America's renewed commitment to the Gulf, yet two presidents waited seven years before one of them formally involved his country in area disputes. Ronald Reagan's successful 1987–88 foray into the Iran-Iraq War enabled the U.S. Navy to shepherd Kuwaiti vessels, flying the Stars and Stripes, in and out of treacherous Gulf waters. This gesture demonstrated American indispensability; without a weighty U.S. military presence in the region, the Gulf Cooperation Council (GCC) states would likely have struggled to assert their independence vis-à-vis Baghdad and Tehran. The Reagan administration's decision to assume primary responsibility for the safe passage of Kuwaiti tankers also allowed the United States to display its renewed self-confidence a dozen years after the climax of Washington's Vietnam trauma.

America's newfound relevance in the Gulf coincided with the end of the Cold War, Washington's epic forty-year ideological dual with Soviet communism. George H.W. Bush presided over this transition from political-military bipolarity to unipolarity. As the world's "only superpower," the United States watched in amazement as events vindicated its postwar strategy of "containment." Germany's reunification in October 1990 and its North Atlantic Treaty Organization (NATO) membership epitomized the West's triumph over the East. While Germans celebrated, Soviet President Mikhail S. Gorbachev vainly tried to reform his country's sclerotic economy, but to no avail. The failed coup of

August 1991 only hastened the demise of the Soviet Union, which ceased to exist in December of that year. The implosion of the Union of Soviet Socialist Republics cost Gorbachev his job, yielded fifteen new countries (with Russia designated as the Soviet Union's successor for international law purposes), and left East-Central Europe outside of Moscow's empire for the first time since 1945. Russian President Boris N. Yeltsin informed Washington and the world that he intended to democratize his country. He invited Western economists to join his team of reformers in devising a blueprint that could extricate Russia from its economic morass. Russians experienced much hardship, however, as they transitioned from communism to market democracy. Their bitterness and despair worried some U.S. national-security experts, who feared a renewed threat from the Russian Bear if its political experiment foundered.[1]

Despite this concern over Russia, when Bill Clinton entered office in January 1993, Washington half expected a Kantian world of "perpetual peace" to emerge. Consistent with this benign outlook, the White House evolved a foreign policy that stressed, above all else, international commercial opportunities for U.S. companies. Events quickly reminded President Clinton and his advisors, however, that "zones of conflict" would not disappear with the burial of the Soviet state. Ethnic wars in Africa and the Balkans and a military coup in the Caribbean tempered U.S. enthusiasm for President Bush's "New World Order." In the "failed state" of Somalia, several Americans died trying to apprehend a nasty warlord with no fear of U.S. firepower. In the Bosnian civil war, Serbs, and to a lesser extent Croats, either killed or drove out Muslims, thereby implementing a policy of ethnic removal reminiscent of the Holocaust. In Haïti, a junta ousted Jean-Bertrand Aristide, the country's first ever democratically elected leader. These affronts to so-called Western values contradicted Francis Fukayama's congratulatory "end of history" essay and sobered American officials. The Clinton administration and its humanitarian proclivities ran into a wall of nationalist discrimination, patriotism without scruples, and hyper violence. In Bosnia, the Serbs even used rape, a tactic of war particularly appalling to Westerners, who thought Europeans cured of such barbarism. The 1994 carnage in Rwanda further shocked Americans, yet unlike in Somalia and Haïti, the White House neglected Tutsis from Central Africa, whose plight the United States considered peripheral to its national interests and therefore unimportant.[2]

Somewhat remorseful that America and the global community had ignored the Rwandan genocide, a hitherto timid White House prodded its European allies to endorse military solutions to stop Serbian atrocities in Bosnia. As a result, NATO planes bombed Serb positions in 1995, prompting Belgrade to sign the Dayton Accords in December and Washington to send peacekeepers to the Balkans. In 1999, with the Atlantic Alliance extended to Poland, Hungary, and the Czech Republic, the Clinton administration punished Yugoslav President Slobodan Milosevic for yet another war crime. NATO pulverized his country to end Serb repression of ethnic Albanians in Kosovo, Yugoslavia's renegade province. Clinton's liberal instincts (his preference for spotlighting environmental, health, and financial threats such as global warming, the HIV/AIDS pandemic, and the 1997–98 Asian panic), and possible need for personal redemption after a sex scandal nearly ended his presidency, also led him to facilitate peace talks in Northern Ireland and the Middle East.[3]

Arguably the world's most volatile region, the Middle East certainly needed Washington's aid, diplomatic and otherwise. After the Persian Gulf War, America used its political clout to organize a conference in Madrid where Israel met with its enemies—the Palestinians, Jordanians, Syrians, and Lebanese. That track yielded no agreements, however. The Arab-Israeli conflict seemed destined to intensify once more until the Israelis and Palestinians revealed the Oslo I Accords in 1993 to a stunned world, as Palestinian Liberation Organization Chairman Yasir Arafat's handshake with Israeli Prime Minister Yitzhak Rabin on the White House lawn in September consummated a most unlikely deal. Secret diplomacy, courtesy of Norway, gave way to more conventional negotiation when Amman and Tel Aviv signed a peace treaty the following year. In November 1995, after Oslo II provided the Palestinians with more land and autonomy and promised *shalom* for the Israelis, a Jewish religious extremist who opposed Arab-Israeli peace assassinated Rabin.[4]

After Rabin's death, events threatened to obliterate the tenuous peace process. As prime minister, Benjamin Netanyahu provoked the Palestinians with his belligerent tone and delay tactics. He stalled whenever Israel owed the Palestinians additional territory. Scheduled withdrawals consistently occurred past deadline. Yet Netanyahu agreed to the 1998 Wye Plantation Accords. His successor, Ehud Barak, withdrew Israeli soldiers from Lebanon and, at Camp David in the summer of 2000, offered Arafat land, a sovereign state, and partition of Jerusalem (with a suburb of the city serving as the Palestinian capital). Under pressure from his constituents, who wanted the right of return for those Arabs evicted from Palestine in 1948–49, the president of the Palestinian National Authority turned Barak down. In the aftermath of this rejection, the Palestinians initiated a second *intifada*, known as al-Aqsa. Israel responded with a swift crackdown. Scores of Arabs died, as did several Israelis.[5]

As the Arab-Israeli conflict redefined itself from 1991 on and iconic leaders such as Jordan's King Hussein and Syria's Hafez al-Assad passed away, the Middle East experienced Islamic calls for political reform. Most area leaders resisted, repressed, or placated extremist movements that threatened their power. These autocrats continued to stifle democracy, restrict economic liberalization, and shamelessly promote nepotism. As a result, many societies teemed with dissent and dissatisfaction. Continued Palestinian outrage represented a vivid example of the region's unmet needs and unfulfilled expectations. Although destructive, violence seemed to offer a psychological palliative.[6]

Concern with this kind of collective frustration occupied the minds of George H.W. Bush and his administration in 1990. The first *intifada*, which started in 1987, explained yet another Middle East impasse. When Saddam Hussein invaded Kuwait in early August, Palestinians believed he would stand up for them and fulfil their aspirations. The United States decided otherwise; it needed continued access to Gulf oil.

George H.W. Bush's War: Operation Desert Shield/Storm

Baghdad harbored many frustrations in the summer of 1990. Inexpensive crude slowed Iraq's recovery after nine years of ruinous conflict with Ayatollah Khomeini's Islamic Republic. Saddam Hussein wanted increased petroleum revenues to finance myriad reconstruction projects. While the GCC and Western countries considered such development both harmless and beneficial to their economies, Iraqi oil rents also paid for military procurement—i.e., conventional, biological, chemical, and nuclear arms. Iraq's rearmament threatened every state in the region and emboldened Hussein, whose tendency to misjudge repercussions whenever he embarked upon reckless ventures promised a reprise of earlier Iraqi disasters. Ever the bully, the Iraqi president demanded that Kuwait City absolve Baghdad of debts incurred during the Iran-Iraq War; from 1980 to 1988, the Kuwaitis sold billions worth of their "black gold" for Iraq's benefit. Kuwait refused to forgive some $20 billion in loans and turned to the Arab world for protection. The petulant Hussein reacted with customary bluster. He disparaged Kuwaiti overproduction that kept OPEC prices too low for his expensive plans; accused the emirate of stealing Iraqi oil while drilling in the disputed Rumaila field; and even asked that Kuwait surrender Warba and Bubiyan, islands that could provide Baghdad with access to the Persian Gulf.[7]

The dictator vented his displeasure by massing soldiers at the Kuwaiti border in late July 1990. Yet he assured Arab leaders he would not invade the territory referred to as Iraq's "nineteenth province." With the exception of a few U.S. intelligence experts, most Western and Arab officials expected Saddam to pressure the Kuwaitis into concessions. On August 2, however, blackmail turned into blitzkrieg, as Iraqi armor rumbled into Kuwait City. Most of the Kuwaiti royal family fled to Saudi Arabia. Another crisis convulsed the Gulf, courtesy of Hussein. For the second time in a decade, he audaciously declared war on a neighbor.[8]

President Bush disapproved of Hussein's lawlessness. In the previous months, U.S. disenchantment with Iraq had intensified. The partnership of convenience that bought Baghdad much needed American assistance in the 1980s—when the Iraqis fought the Iranians—had dissipated. With Iran appreciably weakened, Washington would not tolerate encroachments upon its geostrategic position in the region. Whether or not U.S. Ambassador April Glaspie misinformed Saddam in July 1990 about American views regarding inter-Arab disputes in the Gulf, the Iraqi autocrat flouted U.S. warnings not to violate international law, which forbade interstate aggression. Bush would not accept Iraq's annexation of Kuwait, an event that reminded the World War II veteran of Nazi Germany's depredations. The White House could not tolerate, moreover, Iraqi threats to the area's vast petroleum reserves, America's primary interest in the area. If Iraq's troops went on to seize Saudi Arabia's lucrative oil fields, then surely Baghdad would inherit Riyadh's status as OPEC's most influential member. In the short term, Hussein would be in position to command exorbitant prices for Gulf crude. Dramatic increases in the cost of gasoline, diesel, heating oil, and other fuels would strain the world economy and slow U.S. economic growth.[9]

The White House dreaded such a dismal scenario, which could sink a presidency. To prevent a cataclysm, it needed to compel an Iraqi exit from Kuwait. Following Baghdad's surprise move, President Bush uttered his famous, "This will not stand," to the international press. Unlike when Indonesia annexed oil-less East Timor in 1975, the United States refused to acquiesce in this latest brutal takeover of one country by another. Oblivious to his country's hypocrisy, Bush urged the world community to overturn Iraq's mockery of the so-called law of nations. Fortuitously, U.S. allies and other states that begrudged Iraq its rapacity rallied to his point of view. Although the anti-Saddam coalition spoke in righteous terms, *Realpolitik* explained the formation of this alliance. Every country involved in *Operation Desert Shield* stood to benefit, whether economically, politically, or militarily, if and when the Iraqis left Kuwait as defeated soldiers. North Americans, Europeans, and Asians could avoid a lengthy economic calamity, while many Middle Easterners would celebrate Hussein's setback since it would allow them a respite from the Iraqi menace to the region. Palestinians would not rejoice, however, as their support of the Iraqis would probably earn them much of the world's enmity, at least temporarily. Saddam's other supporters—Jordan, Yemen, Libya, Algeria, and Cuba, for example—would likely suffer as well. The Bush administration would see to it.[10]

As members of their country's so-called Greatest Generation, the president and his secretary of state, James A. Baker III, "embraced wholeheartedly," in the latter's words, "the concept of Pax Americana, an America engaged as a force for creative and constructive change around the world." To this end, in the summer of 1990 they assembled a coalition that translated what they perceived as the will of the international community into a policy. Once the United Nations (UN) condemned Iraqi transgressions in a series of Security Council resolutions (starting with Resolution 660), the Bush administration set out to establish a credible deterrent force, via Operations Plan 90-1002, that could defend Saudi Arabia, America's most important regional ally and the linchpin of its Gulf strategy. The U.S. commander-in-chief asked for and received permission from Riyadh (which adhered to Wahhabism, a strict, patriarchal version of Islam) to station infidel American servicemen and women on sacred Saudi soil. With the Iraqi Army in Kuwait, Saudi King Fahd acknowledged that only the United States could ensure his country's safety. Without U.S. infantry and air power, his family's reign could not be assured. Fahd's decision contradicted the typical Saudi practice of not allowing foreign soldiers into the Kingdom; the monarch and his advisors always worried that Islamists inside and outside Saudi Arabia would spotlight the al-Sauds' association with the Christian West and label Saudi leaders traitors to the Muslim nation. With the Saudi authorization, Washington could upgrade its presence in the Gulf from "over the horizon" to "in country." President Bush promised, however, that American troops would leave Saudi Arabia as soon as feasible.[11]

The U.S. timetable hinged on Saddam Hussein's disposition. The sooner his soldiers evacuated Kuwait, the shorter the American stay in the Arabian Peninsula would be. Iraqi refusal to quit the emirate would effect the opposite outcome and possibly result in a war of unknown duration and fury. In the fall of 1990, the consequences of such a conflict seemed very uncertain. Each side eschewed compromise. Iraq resisted international pressure to rescind its conquest and reiterated its right to occupy Kuwaiti land. President Bush rejected Baghdad's dubious claim to its wealthy neighbor's territory and steeled himself for a military showdown. A clash would likely occur unless UN sanctions altered Hussein's thinking, the anti-Iraq coalition unraveled, or U.S. public opinion prevented Washington from driving the Iraqi Army out of Kuwait.[12]

Democrats in Congress not only applauded the imposition of economic sanctions on Iraq, they also believed that these punitive measures would compel Baghdad to vacate Kuwait. Senators and representatives rekindled the specter of the Vietnam War when they warned of thousands of American casualties, should the White House use force to free Kuwait from Iraqi oppression. Federal politicians spotlighted the purported strength of Hussein's divisions, the fourth largest army in the world, and predicted that disaster would befall the United States if war broke out.[13]

To avert a debacle, the Bush administration crafted a unique alliance that, in the event of hostilities, could overwhelm Iraq with superior cohesion, morale, resources, equipment, tactics, and execution. Washington persuaded Moscow, its erstwhile enemy, to rebuke Baghdad, a long-time beneficiary of Soviet largesse. Similarly, President Bush cajoled NATO countries to join in the campaign to oust the Iraqis from Kuwait. The White House even enlisted Syria, another Cold-War Soviet proxy, in the U.S.-led confrontation with Saddam Hussein. Syrian President Assad detested Hussein, his Ba'th rival, and sought American aid to offset the loss of Soviet economic and military assistance.[14]

While impressive, the coalition remained susceptible to myriad twists that could render it ineffective. If Iraq attacked Israel and Tel Aviv retaliated, would the Arab members of *Operation Desert Shield* honor their commitment to expel the Iraqis from Kuwait or would they join Baghdad in another Arab-Israeli war? Should an offensive require an incursion into Iraq, would Egyptians and Syrians fight their Arab brethren? If the Iraqi Army partially withdrew from Kuwaiti soil, would the coalition consider the crisis over or would it answer a U.S. call to push the Iraqis out completely? Lastly, if the standoff could not be resolved within a few months, would this ad hoc alliance hold? Unlike NATO, *Desert Shield* lacked an institutional structure that could sustain it for years. The Bush administration worried that the international solidarity and purpose it worked so assiduously to cultivate in the weeks after Iraq's August 1990 invasion would dissipate beyond a certain deadline, thought to be months. Sanctions would not suffice since Iraq could survive their effects for several years to come. Historically, this type of coercion almost never proved very effective. Only a short-term solution could ensure the cohesion necessary to defeat Saddam Hussein.[15]

Americans would not necessarily approve of the use of force in the Persian Gulf, however, if it resulted in many dead U.S. soldiers. Every post-Vietnam commander-in-chief knew that Americans would not sacrifice countless lives unless a country attacked the United States or an event jeopardized U.S. national security in an obvious, tangible way. The president and his advisors could explain the rationale for intervention in Kuwait—economic prosperity and strategic imperative—yet many constituents would not consider the restoration of a feudal regime a noble or worthwhile endeavor. Despite concerted efforts to educate the populace as to the severity of the geopolitical problem and "frame" the issue in as palatable a way as possible, George Bush convinced only part of the electorate to endorse his *Desert-Shield* policy in the fall of 1990. The president lacked rhetorical expertise.[16]

This public-relations conundrum hindered Washington's policy in other ways. The American aversion to casualties had revolutionized Pentagon thinking. The Department of Defense now shied away from conflict whenever significant losses of personnel seemed probable. The Weinberger checklist, recast as the Powell Doctrine, called for well-defined objectives, extraordinary firepower, public support, and a precise time frame that allowed for an expeditious pullout (i.e., "exit strategy") once the United States had achieved its mission. Satisfying these criteria would be most difficult in the Persian Gulf and entail extensive coordination with America's coalition partners.[17]

Fortunately for the Bush administration, *Desert Shield* evolved into a formidable defensive force. Within months, it developed offensive capability. The president authorized the U.S. Armed Forces to send approximately five hundred thousand soldiers and their equipment to the Gulf, the most significant build-up since the Vietnam War. The United Kingdom sent an appreciable contingent of its own, and many countries followed suit. Japan and Germany, whose constitutions forbade the assignment of troops abroad, contributed money and matériel. Saudi Arabia and Kuwait agreed to pay for much of the coalition's expenses, estimated in the billions for every month of *Desert Shield*'s existence. While these preparations preoccupied Washington, Iraq prepared for war. Baghdad tried to marry its occupation of Kuwait to the Palestinian cause, but to no avail. The Bush administration rebuffed such "linkage," although the French and Soviets urged the White House to couple justice for Kuwaitis with similar promises for the Palestinians. The Americans preferred that a new round of Arab-Israeli talks occur only upon conclusion of the crisis in Kuwait, and their point of view prevailed.[18]

On November 29, 1990, the Security Council voted 12-2 (with one abstention) in favor of Resolution 678, which authorized "all necessary means" to evict the Iraqi Army from Kuwait as of January 15, 1991. With the imprimatur of the world's premier forum secured, the Bush administration lobbied Congress to bless American policy with a joint resolution so that, if war came, the country would be united. Even though by now most Americans supported *Desert Shield*, House and Senate Democrats remained skeptical. Most of them favored continued sanctions. They would not allow a president to prosecute a war for oil—"No Blood for Oil," protesters inside and outside the Capitol chanted.[19]

Before he dared order American servicemen and women into combat, President Bush sought to convince his critics, whose recalcitrance bewildered him, that the Arab dictator with the Hitleresque streak would not leave Kuwait unless forcefully removed. Bush asked Secretary of State Baker to meet with Iraqi Foreign Minister Tariq Aziz in Geneva on January 9, 1991, to dispel any notion that diplomacy could avert a clash between the U.S.-led coalition and Baghdad. As Bush expected, Aziz repeated his country's stance: Iraq would not withdraw unconditionally from Kuwait, as stipulated in the various Security Council resolutions approved since August 1990. Saddam wanted recompense for any evacuation, whereas the American president refused to reward the pillage of a sovereign country. Iraqi brutality in the emirate, documented in a scathing Amnesty International report, infuriated Bush. In Switzerland, Baker told journalists Baghdad would not revise the status quo. The secretary of state's message conveyed his own as well as his superior's sentiment: the United States would not appease Iraq.[20]

Congress ratified presidential will on January 12, 1991, but without a comfortable majority in either chamber (the resolution passed 250-183 in the House of Representatives, 52-47 in the Senate). Although President Bush intended to use force in the Persian Gulf with or without congressional approval, he and his advisors believed that a mandate from Capitol Hill would facilitate the White House's task. From a political standpoint, the executive branch could ill afford an acrimonious confrontation with a balky legislature over the 1973 War Powers Resolution, which circumscribed a president's ability to commit American soldiers abroad. Bush considered the law unconstitutional, yet preferred to avoid a public dispute that could weaken the international coalition and hearten Saddam Hussein. Luckily for the commander-in-chief, Congressional assent rendered such a nightmarish scenario moot.[21]

Bush's political victory failed to dissuade Hussein, however. The Sunni, who murdered rivals and friends alike, refused to believe that the genial Texan could best him on the battlefield. The Iraqi despot wagered that the United States could not stomach the heavy casualties a drawn out ground war (the "Mother of All Battles," so Hussein predicted) would surely yield. In short, he assumed that America's Vietnam experience would repeat itself. The Bush administration kept that analogy in mind as it prepared for a possible war. Although casualty estimates varied from a few thousand dead and wounded Americans to twenty thousand, the president authorized U.S. soldiers to roll back Iraq's Army. While confident that the coalition would win, Bush pondered a stark question: Could Saddam be humbled without killing too many innocent Iraqi civilians?[22]

On January 17, 1991, after six months of intensive preparations and with U.S. coercive diplomacy a failure, *Operation Desert Storm* commenced. The coalition's war plan initially called for a sustained air campaign that would smash Iraqi infrastructure and decimate the country's command and control capability. American General H. Norman Schwarzkopf commanded a remarkable multinational force that made effective use of new U.S. technologies (such as stealth bombers and precision-guided munitions) and imaginative military doctrines that stressed mobility and coordinated assaults. The results proved mostly one-sided: bombs and missiles battered Iraq. Eight of Saddam's SCUD missiles exploded in Israel, an alarming development that could provoke an Israeli entry into the conflict. Tel Aviv displayed unprecedented restraint, however, when it declined to retaliate. To prevent such a potentially calamitous move, Washington coaxed the Israelis; it would search for and destroy the SCUD launch sites. The White House also sent Patriot missile batteries to protect the Jewish state.[23]

With Hussein's preferred ploy (i.e., to provoke an intolerable Israeli reprisal that forced Arab members to quit the anti-Iraq coalition) neutralized, the Bush administration watched as the air war ravaged Iraqi military assets. Baghdad could only muster a raid on Khafji, an empty Saudi border town. Saddam's apparent effort to lure his enemy into a bloody land contest that could traumatize Western public opinion, backfired. To avoid the continued demolition of his country and forces, Hussein needed someone to extricate him from his knotty predicament. Fortunately for him, a horrified Kremlin desperately tried to terminate the hostilities. Moscow clamored for an immediate cease-fire, a measure that would allow Iraq to reevaluate its strategy and perhaps withdraw from Kuwait with its army still intact. On January 29, Secretary of State Baker issued a joint statement with his Soviet counterpart Alexander Bessmertnykh that could redound to Iraq's advantage if it agreed to leave Kuwaiti territory. A vexed President Bush braced for the worst, which never materialized. The Iraqi Army remained entrenched, its leader unresponsive to Soviet-brokered overtures.[24]

While a frantic Soviet Union searched for an agreement that could shield its long-time Arab client, America's military men haggled over *Desert Storm* tactics. Although Air Force officials believed air power alone could pry the Iraqis from Kuwait, Schwarzkopf disagreed. Commander-in-Chief Bush sided with the general: "I did not believe that Iraq's army had the ability to inflict as much damage as Saddam, or our critics, seemed to think it could. Briefing after briefing had convinced me that we could do the job fast and with minimum coalition casualties.... Air power could do only so much." As a result, on February 24 Schwarzkopf ordered a "left hook" maneuver; his armored and mechanized divisions would seek to envelop Iraq's Army. If U.S. VII Corps, normally on NATO duty in Germany and trained to fight the Soviets in Europe, and XVIII Corps could prevent an Iraqi escape into the area north of Basra, then Hussein's forces would be boxed in.[25]

Schwarzkopf's intricate plan worked to near perfection. Arab soldiers quickly liberated Kuwait City, as the coalition routed its foe. To end the carnage, Saddam enlisted the Soviets. When he insisted that his demands be met, however, hopes for an immediate cease-fire evaporated, and the devastation continued. Iraq contributed to the latter by setting Kuwaiti oil wells ablaze, yet such defiance could not salvage the shattered Iraqi war machine. Iraq's soldiers surrendered by the thousands, as the coalition destroyed Iraqi matériel and killed countless personnel on the so-called highway of death, the road that connected Kuwait City to Basra. To avoid overkill, President Bush halted the ground phase of the war on February 28, 1991, after a mere one hundred hours. Overall, *Desert Storm* inflicted terrible destruction. The alliance rendered Hussein's armed forces impotent except for his elite Republican Guard units, which barely escaped the coalition's pincer movement.[26]

Although it easily defeated Iraq, Washington never intended to occupy the country or remove Saddam Hussein. The Bush administration lacked such a mandate from the United Nations and recoiled at direct occupation. Furthermore, members of the coalition, especially the Arab ones (but not the Saudis), opposed such a step. As President Bush and his national security advisor, Brent Scowcroft, explained: "Trying to eliminate Saddam, extending the ground war into an occupation of Iraq, would have violated our guideline about not changing objectives in midstream, engaging in 'mission creep,' and would have incurred incalculable human and political costs." In a March 1991 interview, Schwarzkopf mentioned that he would have pushed on rather than end the war, yet his statement contradicted previous ones. When corrected by Bush, who said the general concurred with the presidential decision to terminate the conflict, Schwarzkopf retracted his dissent.[27]

Unwilling to resort to *formal* imperialism, the White House urged Iraqis to rid themselves of their cruel dictator, but disapproved of postwar efforts by Kurds in the north and Shi'a in the south to dismember the country. Disintegration could invite intervention from Iran, Syria, as well as Turkey, and thus destabilize the entire region. The White House condemned the brutal tactics Saddam used to reassert his arbitrary rule, yet could only blame itself for this unpleasant development. At the Safwan cease-fire talks that formally ended the Persian Gulf War, Schwarzkopf informed the Iraqis they could fly their helicopters throughout the country with impunity—Iraqi officials claimed they needed them to ferry goods and personnel. Inadvertently, then, he buoyed Saddam's spirits by allowing Baghdad to carry out its vicious repression. Directed at the Kurds and Shi'a, whose separatist aspirations he despised, Hussein's vengeance yielded a humanitarian disaster in the mountains that straddle the Turkish-Iraqi border and the swamps of the Basra district. Global television broadcast the Kurdish cataclysm and, in the West, revulsed viewers clamored for an intervention that could stem this most despicable form of retribution. As *Operation Provide Comfort* awaited the Bush administration, the United States realized that it could not trust Iraq or its neighbor, Iran. Either or both could menace American interests in the Gulf.[28]

With *Operation Desert Shield/Storm*, Washington rallied world opinion so that it could preserve its hegemonic and security interests. Grateful allies, mainly the Kuwaitis and Saudis, even paid for most of George H.W. Bush's war. Once the coalition ejected the Iraqi Army from Kuwait, the United States refrained from colonialism in Iraq proper. Unfettered Western access to Gulf oil supplies, the major objective of America's *informal* empire in the region, did not require an occupation.[29]

Fencing in the Rogues: Dual Containment

Iraq: Public Enemy Number One

Reluctantly, the Bush administration stepped in to deny Saddam Hussein the full measure of his post-Gulf War revenge. Although it hardly served the U.S. national interest and irritated Arab allies who wanted a unified Iraq, the White House and a couple of its European allies devised "no-fly" zones in northern and southern Iraq in 1991 and 1992, so that Kurds and Shi'a could survive. American, British, and French planes enforced these decisions (made by Paris, London, and Washington, not the United Nations) so that Baghdad could not murder the ethnic and confessional communities living at opposite ends of the country. The results of *Operations Northern* and *Southern Watch* varied dramatically. In the north, the NATO threesome acted quickly and inserted soldiers into Kurdish lands, a policy it eschewed in Shi'ite territory. The most prominent members of the Gulf War coalition kept Hussein's divisions away from makeshift refugee camps and safeguarded the Kurds' return home. In the south, Saddam's troops massacred many Shi'a while the coalition pondered its strategy for a year—a costly delay. As a result, Hussein consolidated his rule in much of that area.[30]

Saddam salvaged his dictatorship, but the United Nations monitored his every move. The world body promised a stern riposte whenever Baghdad refused to carry out the will of the international community. After the Gulf War, the Security Council imposed draconian sanctions on Iraq to prevent renewed revanchism. The Iraqis could no longer sell their oil, the basis of their economy. Without these sales, Iraq could not easily rearm nor could it build a nuclear device that could threaten the Middle East. To dismantle Baghdad's weapons of mass destruction, be they biological, chemical, or nuclear, the United Nations created a special commission—UNSCOM.[31]

Washington intended to parlay UNSCOM into a prominent feature of its new Gulf policy, christened "dual containment" by Assistant Secretary of State for Near Eastern and South Asian Affairs Martin Indyk. This 1993 policy initiative sought to isolate both Iran and Iraq, the two most powerful and dangerous countries in the area. In previous decades, America had favored one state or the other to rectify any geopolitical imbalance. With the United States still bitter at Tehran for the seizure of the American Embassy in 1979 and Saddam Hussein Uncle Sam's newest enemy, the Clinton administration thought it should oppose both countries simultaneously. National Security Advisor Anthony Lake justified "dual containment" in a 1994 *Foreign Affairs* article. "As the sole superpower," he wrote, "the United States has a special responsibility for developing a strategy to neutralize, contain and, through selective pressure, perhaps eventually transform these backlash states [which also included Cuba, North Korea, and Libya] into constructive members of the international community." Lake explained that "'[d]ual containment' does not mean duplicate containment. The basic purpose is to counter the hostility of both Baghdad and Tehran, but the challenges posed by the two regimes are distinct and therefore require tailored approaches."[32]

According to Lake, the White House intended to rely on its considerable political, economic, and military assets in the Persian Gulf to "establish a favorable balance of power, one that will protect critical American interests in the security of our friends and in the free flow of oil at stable prices." To achieve its goal, Washington recruited the United Kingdom, France, and the GCC states. Without their assistance, America's multilateral pretensions could turn into unilateral acts. Unpopular moves might anger the Arab-Muslim world, a reaction the United States wished to avoid since it could endanger American economic assets in the Gulf.[33]

Domestic and foreign critics of the administration objected to and even ridiculed "dual containment," which they considered misinformed and ill-suited to the regional dynamic. While some analysts bemoaned this "geopolitical dead end," one scholar noted that the doctrine "explicitly disavows the need for any kind of political relationship with Iran and Iraq and rejects the idea that a rough military equivalence between them is an important element of gulf stability." The policy bestowed upon the United States a "much larger, unilateral role in managing gulf affairs than any previous administration has envisaged at a time that American influence over the two most important strategic actors in the gulf is practically nil." "Dual containment" thus elevated Washington onto a pedestal. "It is aimed," the same observer argued, "at preventing any power from supplanting the United States as the dominant force in the gulf." As the self-appointed "Guardian of the Gulf," America sought to impose its strategic preferences on the region. To keep Iraq and Iran at bay, GCC countries accepted this U.S. security framework. Explicit U.S. political-military collaboration with the Arabian states exposed Washington, however, to Arab-Muslim charges of neo-imperialism and possible Islamic or other violence.[34]

As a short-term solution to its Saddam problem, "dual containment" appeared sensible. Yet U.S. policymakers never expected Hussein to remain in power for more than a brief period. They misjudged his ability to survive politically, to attract international sympathy, and to provoke repeated clashes with the United States that eventually undermined the anti-Iraq coalition. The Iraqi leader snuffed out all plots; his extensive security measures exposed traitors, who were killed, or kept them away. He offered subordinates (mostly family members and Sunnis from his tribe and/or hometown of Tikrit) rewards—food and luxuries that most Iraqis could not buy or afford. This system ensured that those he favored remained beholden to him. His secret police infiltrated cells and disposed of any opposition to his rule. Ethnic and confessional rivals such as the Kurds and the Shi'a often quarreled among themselves, moreover, making his task even easier.[35]

While Saddam repressed his people, he exploited their suffering for political gain. He refused UN humanitarian aid until 1996, yet blamed international sanctions for his country's misery. As Iraq's children, elderly, and sick died at alarming rates, and as Iraqi infrastructure crashed, Arabs and others expressed dismay. When Hussein finally agreed to an oil-for-food arrangement, many countries blamed the United States for Iraq's health disaster. Washington refuted such charges, but appeased few skeptics when its retaliatory attacks further devastated Iraq.[36]

The White House moved punitively whenever Saddam misbehaved. In 1993, Baghdad tried to assassinate George H.W. Bush when the former president visited Kuwait. The next year, it threatened the sheikdom with invasion. In 1996, it violated the "no-drive" zone in northern Iraq to side with one Kurdish faction, the Kurdish Democratic Party, in its internecine rivalry with the Patriotic Union of Kurdistan. It misled UNSCOM inspectors, illegally acquired weapons from East-Central European countries, and failed to comply with other Security Council resolutions, such as those requiring the Iraqis to provide information on Kuwaiti and other prisoners from the Gulf War. The United States cited these transgressions whenever it punished Saddam with a barrage of cruise missiles, "smart" bombs, and other weapons. When a scathing UNSCOM report prompted the Clinton administration to order *Operation Desert Fox* in December 1998 at the height of the Monica Lewinsky sex scandal, Hussein banned the intrusive commission from reentering Iraq. Paradoxically, Saddam's defiance enabled him to subvert the coalition. Because the American reprisals hurt mostly innocent Iraqi citizens rather than the leadership, Russia, the People's Republic of China, and France, which disapproved of U.S.-British policy starting in the mid-1990s, started to criticize the vigorous Anglo-American enforcement of the "no-fly" zones. Beyond supposed concern for human rights, these three members of the Security Council sought trade with and investment in Iraq. Increasing Arab dissatisfaction with the White House's military policy must have pleased Hussein as well.[37]

In March 2000, Assistant Secretary of State for Near Eastern Affairs Edward Walker reaffirmed Washington's commitment to an anti-Hussein policy. In his Senate presentation, he noted that Hussein's Iraq "remains dangerous, unreconstructed, and defiant. Saddam's record makes clear that he will remain a threat to regional peace and security as long as he remains in power." Owing to Hussein's unrepentance and myriad treaty violations, Walker asserted that the United States "is committed to containing Saddam Hussein as long as he remains in power." The diplomat referred to Security Council Resolution 1284, approved in December 1999, which created the United Nations Monitoring, Inspection, and Verification Commission (UNMOVIC), UNSCOM's successor. According to Walker, that resolution underscored the international community's continued dissatisfaction with Baghdad. Yet America's wrath vis-à-vis Hussein in no way extended to Iraq's citizens. Walker therefore stressed his country's commitment to "helping alleviate the suffering of the Iraqi people and to supporting Iraqis who seek a new government and a better future for Iraq." Despite the assistant secretary's passable sincerity, senators expounded upon what they considered the numerous flaws in the Clinton administration's policy. Senators Sam Brownback (R-Kansas) and Joseph R. Biden, Jr., (D-Delaware) discounted UNMOVIC, which Hussein barred from Iraq and the United Nations would not impose on Baghdad. On the very serious matter of aid to destitute Iraqis, Senator Paul Wellstone (D-Minnesota) pointed to Anglo-American bureaucratic callousness retarding the delivery of essentials to Iraq. Walker acknowledged the criticisms, but offered no remedies. The White House refused to alter its basic strategy of economic and military coercion.[38]

Iran: Public Enemy Number Two

While the United States and Iraq clashed throughout the 1990s, U.S.-Iranian relations continued to alternate between stagnant and tense until 1997. Washington reprimanded Tehran for its sponsorship of terrorist organizations (such as Hezbollah in Lebanon), condemned Iran's weapons of mass destruction program, and criticized the Islamic Republic's sustained efforts to disrupt the Arab-Israeli peace process. Tehran replied in kind with its own list of grievances. It wanted America to release Iranian funds seized at the time of the hostage crisis, demanded an apology for past U.S. interference in Persian affairs (such as the 1953 Central Intelligence Agency-assisted coup), and resented the American military presence in the Persian Gulf. Consistent with much of its history, Iran continued to perceive itself as the area's foremost power and foreigners, such as the Americans, as usurpers.[39]

Following *Operation Desert Storm* and the Madrid peace conference, Tehran returned to its bold ways, which included the recruitment of countries and organizations inimical to U.S. interests, to thwart American efforts to make the

Middle East more Washington friendly. To counter Iran's antithetical policies, the Clinton administration added the Islamic Republic to its Gulf containment strategy. Whereas the Iraq component of "dual containment" emphasized offensive measures, the Iran variant called mostly for defensive ones. According to Kenneth Pollack, twice Clinton's director of Gulf affairs at the National Security Council (NSC), "[t]he central aim of the Iranian segment of Dual Containment was merely to constrain Iran's ability to make trouble in the Middle East through a rather modest series of measures—most of which were already in place—until Iran's behavior changed." The policy, moreover, was "designed to reassure Israel that the United States would keep Iran in check while Jerusalem embarked on the risky process of peacemaking and placed some limited constraints on Iran's freedom of action. But it was not the start of an aggressive new American action to cripple the Iranian economy or to weaken its political structure." While Washington preferred to punish Iran for its various misdeeds, unilaterally if need be, the Europeans opted to entice the Islamic Republic via a "Critical Dialogue." Neither approach succeeded in altering Iranian conduct. Much to American dissatisfaction, European businesses profited handsomely from their Persian ventures. Yet U.S. subsidiaries overseas bought more Iranian oil than anyone else following a Bush administration decision to lessen sanctions on Iran.[40]

As Washington and Tehran eyed each other warily, psychological predispositions exacerbated the mutual hostility. Warren Christopher, Clinton's first secretary of state, served under President Carter in 1979 and carried with him the unpleasant memories of trying to negotiate the release of the U.S. hostages. Meanwhile, the mullahs who governed the Islamic Republic hated the United States, particularly its secular culture, which they considered depraved. Only some kind of Iranian-American compromise could overcome such acrimony. Neither party seemed interested in resolving their quarrel diplomatically, however. While Iranian conservatives continued to defy the "Great Satan," American legislators passed the 1996 Iran-Libya Sanctions Act (ILSA), so-called secondary sanctions that in theory penalized countries whose companies invested more than $20 million in Iran's oil industry.[41]

The impasse persisted into 1997. That year's election of moderate reformer Mohammed Khatami to the presidency surprised Western analysts, who wondered whether his success presaged renewed U.S.-Iranian ties. In a January 1998 interview on the Cable News Network, the bearded cleric with the warm smile spoke of "crack[ing] the wall of mistrust" separating the two countries. He called for cultural and academic exchanges as a first step toward an improved modus vivendi. The Iranian president thus promoted interpersonal contacts rather than intergovernmental "dialogue," which the White House preferred. Secretary of State Madeleine Albright responded to Khatami's overtures in June 1998 by stating that her nation "can develop with the Islamic Republic, when it is ready, a road map leading to normal relations." Assistant Secretary of State Indyk informed U.S. senators, however, that the Clinton administration's "basic purpose is to persuade Iran that it cannot have it both ways." He stressed that the Islamic Republic "cannot benefit from participation in the international community while at the same time going around threatening the interests of its member states." Secondly, "it cannot improve its relations and standing in the West and in the

Middle East while at the same time pursuing policies that threaten the peace and stability of a vital region." Notwithstanding such concerns, in March 2000, courtesy of a dramatic speech by Albright to the Iranian-American Council, Washington confessed to its prominent role in the 1953 coup and allowed Iran, impoverished by years of economic mismanagement and corruption, to resume exporting Persian rugs, pistachios, and caviar to the United States. In her memoirs, Albright asserted that the administration "chose a course that, though incremental, helped to move [the U.S.-Iranian] relationship in the right direction, while opening the door to increased contacts." When reformers won a majority of seats in the *Majlis* that year, an eventual U.S.-Iranian rapprochement seemed at least plausible.[42]

For the conservatives in Iran, however, these events could have spelled their demise. To prevent such a scenario and preserve their revolution, they suppressed their opponents, many of them students, starting in the summer of 1999. Ayatollah Ali Khamanei, the supreme authority in the Islamic Republic, and his allies repressed, if not silenced, Khatami and his supporters, thereby ensuring a continued U.S.-Iranian antagonism and the perpetuation of the Iranian facet of "dual containment." If Khatami and his partisans could have somehow triumphed, then a genuine opening to Washington might have been possible, although both sides would have needed to address a variety of contentious issues, such as Iran's continuing support for anti-American terrorists and the development and transportation of Caspian Sea energy resources.[43]

While the White House tangled with Tehran, GCC states continued to mind their economic assets. After the Iraqi invasion of Kuwait threatened their revenues and very existence, they asked the United States to safeguard their substantial hydrocarbon reserves and their rule within the Arabian Peninsula. Washington did not need convincing.

Guarding the Gulf: The GCC States and Their Dilemmas

In March 1991, U.S. Undersecretary of Defense for Policy Paul Wolfowitz stated that his country "will stay [in the Gulf] as long as we are needed and leave when our hosts ask us to go. That is a firm commitment. And it is an important fact about the United States that makes others willing to ask for our help." Following the Gulf War, every member of the GCC forged explicit military ties (in the form of base agreements and arms sales) with the Americans except for Saudi Arabia, which preferred not to advertise its security relationship with the United States. To minimize domestic criticism and not admit to permanent foreign bases on its soil, a typical Saudi policy, Riyadh opted for informal arrangements with Washington. The White House honored Saudi wishes, as they did not hinder its plans to bolster America's regional presence. Despite Saudi sensitivities, U.S. aircraft regularly flew out of Saudi bases in the country's Eastern Province to enforce the southern "no-fly" zone in Iraq. Washington's use of Gulf facilities and the establishment of joint exercises with the Arabian Peninsula states solidified the U.S.-GCC partnership and warned Baghdad and Tehran not to meddle in Arabian affairs.[44]

The Bush administration's "GCC" strategy confirmed America's status as regional colossus. Never before had the country exercised so much influence in the Gulf. In twelve years, Washington had recovered remarkably from the humiliation of the Shah's expulsion and the hostage crisis. Whereas in 1979 U.S. policy drew ridicule, in 1991 it intimidated foes and reassured friends. Bush's strategy synthesized International Relations theory notions of offensive and defensive realism, resulting in a conspicuous American land and sea presence in the Gulf that transcended the "over the horizon" posture favored by Presidents Carter and Reagan. Since stealth had not precluded an Iraqi invasion of Kuwait, Bush and his advisors concluded that the United States had to station its military personnel much closer to potential battlefields than the Diego Garcia base in the Indian Ocean and the international waters of the Gulf. America's "empire of bases" displeased many Arabs and other Muslims, however, and prompted Osama bin Laden, the leader of al-Qaeda (i.e., the Base), a little-known Islamist organization that had fought the Soviets in Afghanistan, to declare war on the United States and its soldiers, whose every footstep on Saudi soil desecrated the Islamic Holy Land. Unbeknown to Americans, then, the White House's *tour de force* in 1991 portended America's 9/11 agony, as well as the War on Terror, *Operation Enduring Freedom* in Afghanistan and *Operation Iraqi Freedom*.[45]

This Achilles heel would not manifest itself until Bush's son gained the presidency, however. Before that fateful day in September 2001, the Clinton administration carried on oblivious to the vulnerability—Islamic rage—inherent in the "GCC" strategy, which it married to its own "dual containment" strategy. In his March 1995 Congressional testimony, Assistant Secretary of Defense for International Security Affairs Joseph Nye explained that America "pursues a three-tier cooperative approach" with the GCC countries. This framework, he said, "consists of strengthening local self-defense capabilities, promoting GCC and inter-Arab defense cooperation, and enhancing the ability of US and coalition forces to return and fight effectively alongside local forces in a crisis." So whenever Saddam Hussein misbehaved, Washington's response aimed to reassure Gulf allies. For example, when the United States deterred Iraq from attacking Kuwait in 1994, the Clinton administration, in Nye's words, "showed the states in the Gulf that we [i.e., Americans] can respond very quickly and with preponderant force." Without a demonstrated American commitment to GCC security, the so-called oil monarchies of the Arabian Peninsula might examine other options to ensure their safety, such as befriend Iran, Iraq, or both.[46]

To avoid such a catastrophe and enhance its credibility in the area, the U.S. Navy created the Fifth Fleet in July 1995. Stationed in Bahrain, this armada of twenty-one ships, sixty-six aircraft, and some ten thousand sailors and Marines could respond to any Iraqi or Iranian provocation with a carrier strike force, which included attack submarines and Aegis cruisers armed with Tomahawk cruise missiles. These capabilities enabled Washington to project its impressive power quickly into an area often beset with hostilities. In September 1996, Secretary of Defense William Perry underscored the Fifth Fleet's purpose when he remarked that Americans "are not in Saudi Arabia as a favor to any other country. We are there to protect our vital interest. We do have close cooperation with friends in the region...[and] they want us to remain, and that cooperation will continue." Two years later, Joseph Marty, the NSC's Director for Near East and South Asia, delivered an even more blunt assessment of the American purpose in the Arabian Peninsula. "On the Gulf States [sic]," he opined, "without a doubt we're the preeminent security partner of all the GCC States, and there is no sign that that will change. The other countries sell hardware. We sell security. We share with the Gulf States a view of Iran and Iraq, and we are clearly the region's 911 emergency service."[47]

Whenever Americans uttered such vivid, if indiscreet, words, they only annoyed the GCC countries, which cared not for U.S. bombast since it further irritated the Gulf's Islamists and nationalists and exacerbated Arab xenophobia vis-à-vis the United States. Yet GCC distaste for American cockiness, which betrayed the country's imperial outlook, never jeopardized the relationship. Arabian emirs, kings, and sultans needed U.S. military prowess to fend off perceived threats from Iraq and Iran, both of which possessed weapons of mass destruction (WMD). In 1998, Washington introduced the Cooperative Defense Initiative (CDI) to reaffirm its commitment to Gulf security. Essentially an updated version of the Baghdad Pact, CDI interconnected the GCC, Egypt, and Jordan in a strategic defense framework, provided the Gulf states with high-quality intelligence, and tutored them on how to respond to WMD attacks. CDI, noted one analyst, thus served as a "*military* response to the *political* complaints long heard from Arabs concerning America's favoritism toward Israel, lack of trust in regional Arab partners, and lack of vision for integrating Gulf policy into a larger regional strategy."[48]

CDI may have pleased GCC leaders, but they wanted increased U.S. consultation on security matters, disapproved of "dual containment," and disliked (but tolerated) the conspicuous American military presence in the area. They sought a protector invisible to their restless populations, whose economic prospects worsened as a result of fluctuations in the world oil market, governmental inability to diversify sources of revenue, demographic expansion, increased unemployment, educational shortcomings, budget deficits, overreliance on expatriate labor, bureaucratic incompetence, and corruption. GCC countries needed assistance in tackling these potentially devastating socio-economic problems. The United States passed, however, on this opportunity to help remedy Gulf ills. America's informal empire—an "empire by invitation" in this case—relied on military measures, not on so-called nation-building, which most members of the Republican Party abhored.[49]

Gulf monarchs coped not only with the aforementioned domestic woes, but also with unruly Islamists and nationalists who wanted the Americans to leave immediately. To convey their dissatisfaction, Islamic terrorists, such as the exiled Saudi Osama bin Laden and Iranian-supported Saudi Hezbollah, carried out various attacks. In 1995 and 1996, terrorist explosions occurred in Riyadh and at the Khobar Towers near Dhahran. Twenty-four Americans died. The zealotry displayed by fellow Muslims reminded Gulf leaders that they must counter internal as well external threats to their rule. In response to the bombings in Saudi Arabia, Secretary of Defense Perry told senators in Washington that those individuals who rely on terror "seek to drive a wedge between the U.S. security strategy in the Gulf and the American public, and between the United States and our regional allies." These unfortunate events prompted the Pentagon to relocate its personnel to remote facilities that could be more easily protected. In October 2000 these countermeasures proved insufficient, as suicide bombers crippled the USS *Cole* while it refueled in Yemen's Aden port. The blast killed seventeen sailors.[50]

Despite the loss of American life, Saudi and Iranian indignation over the Khobar Towers investigation, and the likelihood of more terrorist attacks, Washington professed its intention to remain in the Persian Gulf indefinitely, though some analysts speculated that its presence might become far less conspicuous. As the most voracious consumer of petroleum-based energy, the United States coveted the region's plentiful oil resources. The same could be said for America's Western and Asian allies.[51]

Assessment

In the *fifth* stage (1990–2000) of U.S. expansion in the Persian Gulf, Washington assembled and sustained an anti-Iraq coalition that expelled Saddam Hussein's army in the winter of 1991. The United States spent the rest of the decade thwarting Iraqi moves and mostly opposing Iran. "Dual containment" won the White House minimal admiration, although that policy preserved American interests adequately. As a result of its political, economic, and military policies, America established itself as the "Guardian of the Gulf."

Washington's increased militarization throughout the 1990s grated numerous Arab, U.S., and other critics who accused it of unilateralism. In meeting its security needs in such an uncompromising way, the United States resembled imperial powers of eras past. Via its so-called Tomahawk diplomacy, it imposed its will just as one would expect an empire to do so. Advances in technology enabled it to rely on an unmatched arsenal of aircraft carriers, submarines, and fighter planes instead of land-based garrisons, whose visibility and behavior often annoyed, if not infuriated, nationalistic local populations. This modern strategy, whether intended or not, underscored the adaptability of the U.S. informal empire in the Gulf to a post-colonial, twenty-first century reality.[52]

Able to rely consistently on its technological superiority, Washington sought to ensure unimpeded Western access to Gulf oil. This policy preserved the American position in the world economy. As suppliers of an indispensable commodity to core nations in North America, Western Europe, and Asia, GCC countries continued to play the role of cherished periphery.

As the United States pursued hegemonic and security interests, it continued to rely on contingent imperialism. In the case of the Gulf War, Washington intervened to protect its Arabian Peninsula friends and their precious oil, as well as return Kuwaiti land to its citizens. By organizing a UN coalition, President George H.W. Bush only made American goals easier to achieve. Thus, proposition **P2** (The United States will exercise alliance imperialism whenever a significant threat to American hegemony occurs, allies agree to join a U.S.-led venture or vice-versa, Washington can overcome any regional constraints, consensus exists within the executive, and no majority in Congress or critical segment of domestic opinion strongly opposes White House action) seems correct. The House of Representatives and Senate sanctioned the use of force, realizing that most Americans supported the commander-in-chief and U.S. troops in the Gulf.

Whereas the White House recruited many countries to evict the Iraqis from Kuwait, after the war only Paris (for a few years) and London assisted Uncle Sam in boxing in Saddam Hussein. Nevertheless, proposition **P2** (i.e., alliance imperialism) seems to apply once more. With respect to Iran, however, the United States carried out its policy unilaterally. In that case, proposition **P1** (The United States will exercise unilateral imperialism whenever a significant threat to American hegemony occurs, Washington cannot rely on anyone else to secure its interests and can overcome any regional constraints, consensus exists within the executive, and no majority in Congress or critical segment of domestic opinion strongly opposes White House action) seems valid.

Finally, in forging explicit and implicit (in the case of Saudi Arabia) military ties with the GCC states, America strengthened a relationship that started in earnest during the Iran-Iraq War. Publicly, the oil monarchies may not have welcomed this development, but privately they seemed pleased with the U.S. security guarantee. Washington approved of this de facto alliance, which made it far easier for the United States to project its power in an emergency. In that case, proposition **P2** (i.e., alliance imperialism) seems true yet again.

In this era (1990–2000), America utilized alliance and unilateral imperialism to fulfil its economic and security goals in the Persian Gulf. With its victory in the Gulf War, Washington strove for a *Pax Americana*. With its regional and worldwide reputation at an apex, it tried to browbeat Iraq and Iran. When Baghdad and Tehran resisted U.S. diktats, the White House meted out severe punishment in Iraq via air strikes and kept up its economic coercion of Iran. Former members of *Operation Desert Storm* (with the notable exception of the United Kingdom) criticized such ruthlessness, leaving the United States diplomatically isolated by the end of the millennium. Deprived of support for "dual containment," which evolved into "differentiated containment" once the Clinton administration pursued divergent policies vis-à-vis Iraq and Iran, Washington could only resort to an increasingly unilateralist policy in the Gulf.[53]

Notes

1. Don Oberdorfer, *The Turn: From the Cold War to a New Era: The United States and the Soviet Union 1983–1990* (New York: Poseidon Press, 1991); Nicholas X. Rizopoulos, ed., *Sea-Changes: American Foreign Policy in a World Transformed* (New York: Council on Foreign Relations Press, 1990), 163–292; John Lewis Gaddis, *The United States and the End of the Cold War: Implications, Reconsiderations, Provocations* (New York: Oxford University Press, 1992); James A. Baker, III, with Thomas M. DeFrank, *The Politics of Diplomacy: Revolution, War & Peace, 1989–1992* (New York: G.P. Putnam, 1995); John Newhouse, "Shunning the Losers," *New Yorker*, 26 October 1992, 40–52; Michael R. Beschloss and Strobe Talbott, *At the Highest Levels: The Inside Story of the End of the Cold War* (Boston: Little, Brown, 1993); Michael J. Hogan, ed.,

The End of the Cold War: Its Meaning and Implications (Cambridge: Cambridge University Press, 1992); Charles W. Kegley, Jr., "How Did the Cold War Die? Principles for an Autopsy," *Mershon International Studies Review* 38 (1994): 11–41; Bob Woodward, *The Commanders* (New York: Simon & Schuster, 1991), 35–196; Joseph S. Nye, Jr., *Bound to Lead: The Changing Nature of American Power* (New York: Basic Books, 1990); Terry L. Deibel, "Bush's Foreign Policy: Mastery and Inaction," *Foreign Policy*, no. 84 (Fall 1991): 3–23; "America and the World 1991/92," *Foreign Affairs* 71, no. 1 (1992); Mikhail Gorbachev, *The August Coup: The Truth and the Lessons* (New York: Harper-Collins, 1991); James Schlesinger, "New Instabilities, New Priorities," *Foreign Policy*, no. 85 (Winter 1991–92): 3–24; and Dimitri Simes, "Russia Reborn," *Foreign Policy*, no. 85 (Winter 1991–92): 41–62. See also the Cable News Network's 1998–99 series, "Cold War," episode 24, "Conclusions 1989–1991."

2. Lewis White Beck, ed., *Kant on History* (New York: Macmillan, 1963), 85–105; John Stremlau, "Clinton's Dollar Diplomacy," *Foreign Policy*, no. 97 (Winter 1994–95): 18–35; David E. Sanger, "Economic Engine for Foreign Policy," *New York Times*, 28 December 2000, <http://www.nytimes.com>; James M. Goldgeier and Michael McFaul, "A Tale of Two Worlds: Core and Periphery in the Post-Cold War Era," *International Organization* 46, no. 2 (Spring 1992): 467–91; Ted Galen Carpenter, "The New World Disorder," *Foreign Policy*, no. 84 (Fall 1991): 24–39; Lawrence Freedman, "Order and Disorder in the New World," *Foreign Affairs* 71, no. 1 (1992): 20–37; Gerald B. Helman and Steven R. Ratner, "Saving Failed States," *Foreign Policy*, no. 89 (Winter 1992–93): 3–20; Paul Kennedy, *Preparing for the Twenty-First Century* (New York: Random House, 1993); Michael J. O'Neill, *The Roar of the Crowd: How Television and People Power Are Changing the World* (New York: Random House, 1993); Michael Ignatieff, *Blood and Belonging: Journeys into the New Nationalism* (New York: Farrar, Straus & Giroux, 1993); Christopher Layne & Benjamin Schwartz, "American Hegemony— Without an Enemy," *Foreign Policy*, no. 92 (Fall 1993): 5–23; Michael Mandelbaum, "The Reluctance to Intervene," *Foreign Policy*, no. 95 (Summer 1994): 3–18; Owen Harries, "My So-Called Foreign Policy," *New Republic*, 10 October 1994, 24–31; Dusko Doder, "Yugoslavia: New War, Old Hatreds," *Foreign Policy*, no. 91 (Summer 1993): 3–23; Cvijeto Job, "Yugoslavia's Ethnic Furies," *Foreign Policy*, no. 92 (Fall 1993): 52–74; Peter Neckermann, "Forum: Serbs Hope to Realize Ancient Dream," *Columbus Dispatch*, 2 April 1994, 4A; Ronald Steel, "Beware the Superpower Syndrome," *New York Times*, 25 April 1994, A11; Evan Thomas, "Trial by Unfriendly Fire," *Newsweek*, 25 April 1994, 21–24; "The Nightmare Next Door," *Economist*, 24 September 1994, 19–21; Francis Fukuyama, "The End of History?" *National Interest*, no. 16 (Summer 1989): 3–18; Michael Mandelbaum, "Foreign Policy as Social Work," *Foreign Affairs* 75, no. 1 (January/February 1996): 16–32; William G. Hyland, "A Mediocre Record," *Foreign Policy*, no. 101 (Winter 1995–96): 69–74; Richard H. Ullman, "A Late Recovery," *Foreign Policy*, no. 101 (Winter 1995–96): 75–79; Stephen M. Walt, "Two Cheers for Clinton's Foreign Policy," *Foreign Affairs* 79, no. 2 (March/April 2000): 63–79; Richard N. Haass, "The Squandered Presidency," *Foreign Affairs* 79, no. 3 (May/June 2000): 136–140; and Lance Morrow, "Rwandan Tragedy, Lewinsky Farce," *Time*, 12 October 1998, 126. On the Rwandan genocide, see also the Frontline documentary, "The Triumph of Evil," aired on the Public Broadcasting Service on 26 January 1999.

3. Walter Russell Mead, "Foreign Policy: The Political Risks," *Hartford Courant*, 22 October 1995, C1, C4; Tony Snow, "Pray that the President Is Right about the Balkans," *Hartford Courant*, 30 November 1995, A21; Christopher Bassford, "Americans Always Balk at Sending Troops Afar," *Hartford Courant*, 10 December 1995, D1, D4; Roger Cohen, "Yes, Blood Stains the Balkans. No, It's Not Just Fate," *New York Times*, 4 October 1998, <http://www.nytimes.com>; David E. Sanger, "Clinton's Foreign Policy Lacks Coherence, but So Does the World," *New York Times*, 7 March 1999,

<http://www.nytimes.com>; James M. Goldgeier, *Not Whether But When: The U.S. Decision to Enlarge NATO* (Washington, D.C.: Brookings Institution Press, 1999); Leon Wieseltier, "Force without Force," *New Republic*, 26 April & 3 May 1999, 28–36; David E. Sanger, "America Finds It's Lonely at the Top," *New York Times*, 18 July 1999, <http://www.nytimes.com>; and Fouad Ajami, "Home Base," *New Republic*, 4 June 2001, 62. On Serb atrocities and the U.S. response, see Samantha Power, *"A Problem from Hell:" America and the Age of Genocide* (New York: Basic Books, 2002), 391–441.

4. Leon T. Hadar, *Quagmire: America in the Middle East* (Washington, DC: Cato Institute, 1992); Abba Eban, *Diplomacy for the Next Century* (New Haven, CT: Yale University Press, 1998), 141–53; Burton I. Kaufman, *The Arab Middle East and the United States: Inter-Arab Rivalry and Superpower Diplomacy* (New York: Twayne, 1996), 166–84; William B. Quandt, *Peace Process: American Diplomacy and the Arab-Israeli Conflict since 1967* (Washington, DC & Berkeley, CA: Brookings Institution & University of California Press, 1993), 383–412; Louise Lief, "A New Beginning," *U.S. News & World Report*, 13 September 1993, 24–32; Russell Watson, "Peace at Last?" *Newsweek*, 13 September 1993, 21–26; James Walsh, "Risking Peace," *Time*, 13 September 1993, 32–35; Bruce W. Nelan, "Can They Pass the Test?" *Time*, 13 September 1993, 36–49; Kevin Fedarko, "Swimming the Oslo Channel," *Time*, 13 September 1993, 50–51; Nancy Gibbs, "Yitzhak Rabin & Yasser Arafat," *Time*, 3 January 1994, 30–37; Steve Wulf, "Thou Shalt Not Kill," *Time*, 13 November 1995, 23–27; and Kevin Fedarko, "Man of Israel," *Time*, 13 November 1995, 29–31.

5. Thomas L. Friedman, "A Dangerous Peace," *New York Times,* 12 January 1999, <http://www.nytimes.com>; "Oslo and the Israeli Election," *New York Times*, 4 May 1999, <http://www.nytimes.com>; Thomas L. Friedman, "The Price of Admission," *New York Times*, 21 May 1999, <http://www.nytimes.com>; Deborah Sontag, "Israel's Next Leader Picks Up Rabin's Mantle and Alters It to Fit," *New York Times*, 23 May 1999, <http://www.nytimes.com>; "Mideast Peace Prospects," *New York Times*, 28 August 1999, <http://www.nytimes.com>; Deborah Sontag, "Peace. Period." *New York Times Magazine*, 19 December 1999, <http://www.nytimes.com>; Thomas L. Friedman, "All Fall Down," *New York Times*, 26 May 2000, <http://www.nytimes.com>; "Failure at Camp David," *New York Times*, 26 July 2000, <http://www.nytimes.com>; Thomas L. Friedman, "It Ain't Over Till It's Over," *New York Times*, 26 July 2000, <http://www.nytimes.com>; Deborah Sontag, "Eye for Eye Once Again," *New York Times*, 9 October 2000, <http://www.nytimes.com>; Jane Perlez, "News Analysis: Falling Short of Peace After Camp David Deadlock," *New York Times*, 15 October 2000, <http://www.nytimes.com>; Jane Perlez, "Can Arafat Turn It Off? U.S. Officials Debate Degree of His Control," *New York Times*, 17 October 2000, <http://www.nytimes.com>; Chas. W. Freeman, "A U.S. Role Is Crucial for Peace," *New York Times*, 18 October 2000, <http://www.nytimes.com>; Thomas L. Friedman, "Diplomacy by Other Means," *New York Times*, 3 November 2000, <http://www.nytimes.com>; Gershom Gorenberg, "Power of Myth," *New Republic*, 20 November 2000, 13–15; Thomas L. Friedman, "Senseless in Israel," *New York Times*, 24 November 2000, <http://www.nytimes.com>; Daniel Klaidman, "Walking Off a Cliff," *Newsweek*, 27 November 2000, 53–56; and "Mr. Clinton's Mideast Peace Plan," *New York Times*, 27 December 2000, <http://www.nytimes.com>.

6. Olivier Roy, *The Failure of Political Islam*, translated by Carol Volk (Cambridge, MA: Harvard University Press, 1994); John L. Esposito and James P. Piscatori, "Democratization and Islam," *Middle East Journal* 45, no. 3 (Summer 1991): 427–40; Jeffrey Goldberg, "Learning How To Be King," *New York Times Magazine*, 6 February 2000, <http://www.nytimes.com>; Neil MacFarquhar, "Hafez al-Assad, Who Turned Syria Into a Power in the Middle East, Dies at 69," *New York Times*, 10 June 2000,

<http://www.nytimes.com>; Trudy Rubin, "In Middle East, Passing the Torch," *Hartford Courant*, 14 June 2000, <http://www.courant.com>; Susan Sachs, "Unleashed, Anger Can Bite Its Master," *New York Times*, 22 October 2000, <http://www.nytimes.com>; and "Like Father, Like Son," *Economist*, 5 June 2001, <http://www.economist.com>.

7. Walid Khalidi, *The Gulf Crisis: Origins and Consequences* (Washington, DC: Institute for Palestine Studies, 1991), 1–14; Fouad Ajami, "The Summer of Arab Discontent," *Foreign Affairs* 69, no. 5 (Winter 1990/91): 1–20; Shafeeq Ghabra, "Kuwait and the United States: The Reluctant Ally and U.S. Policy Toward the Gulf," in *The Middle East and the United States: A Historical and Political Reassessment*, ed. David W. Lesch (Boulder, CO: Westview Press, 1999), 300–2; Woodward, *The Commanders*, 199–204; and Kaufman, *The Arab Middle East and the United States*, 152.

8. Kaufman, *The Arab Middle East and the United States*, 152–53; and Woodward, *The Commanders*, 205–24.

9. George Bush and Brent Scowcroft, *A World Transformed* (New York: Alfred A. Knopf, 1998), 302–14; Baker, *The Politics of Diplomacy*, 260–74; Bruce W. Jentleson, *With Friends Like These: Reagan, Bush, and Saddam, 1982–1990* (New York: W.W. Norton, 1994), 139–76; Amatzia Baram, "U.S. Input into Iraqi Decisionmaking, 1988–1990," in *The Middle East and the United States*, 313–40; Michael Dobbs, "When an Ally Becomes the Enemy," *Washington Post National Weekly Edition*, 6–12 January 2003, 9; and Edward L. Morse, "The Coming Oil Revolution," *Foreign Affairs* 69, no. 5 (Winter 1990/91): 36–56.

10. Khalidi, *The Gulf Crisis*, 14–31; and Stanley Reed, "Jordan and the Gulf," *Foreign Affairs* 69, no. 5 (Winter 1990/91): 21–35.

11. Bush and Scowcroft, *A World Transformed*, 314–87; Baker, *The Politics of Diplomacy*, 275–99. Quote can be found on 276; Woodward, *The Commanders*, 231–289; Kaufman, *The Arab Middle East and the United States*, 154–55; and F. Gregory Gause III, "From 'Over the Horizon' to 'Into the Backyard': The U.S.-Saudi Relationship and the Gulf War," in *The Middle East and the United States*, 341–53. On the "Greatest Generation," see Tom Brokaw, "A Generation's Trial by Fire," *Newsweek*, 14 May 2001, 58.

12. Bush and Scowcroft, *A World Transformed*, 388–415.

13. Bush and Scowcroft, *A World Transformed*, 416–29.

14. Bush and Scowcroft, *A World Transformed*, 388–415; and Baker, *The Politics of Diplomacy*, 275–99.

15. Bush and Scowcroft, *A World Transformed*, 412. On economic coercion, see David A. Baldwin, *Economic Statecraft* (Princeton, NJ: Princeton University Press, 1985).

16. Kaufman, *The Arab Middle East and the United States*, 159.

17. Woodward, *The Commanders*, 117. The Weinberger checklist refers to Ronald Reagan's defense secretary, Caspar Weinberger. The Powell Doctrine refers to Colin Powell, chairman of the Joint Chiefs of Staff under George H.W. Bush.

18. Michael A. Palmer, *Guardians of the Gulf: A History of America's Expanding Role in the Persian Gulf, 1833–1992* (New York: Free Press, 1992), 163–80; Baker, *The Politics of Diplomacy*, 275–99; and Bush and Scowcroft, *A World Transformed*, 375–76.

19. Bush and Scowcroft, *A World Transformed*, 438–39; and Baker, *The Politics of Diplomacy*, 300–28.

20. Baker, *The Politics of Diplomacy*, 345–65; and Bush and Scowcroft, *A World Transformed*, 441–43. On Bush's mindset throughout the Gulf crisis, see Stephen J. Wayne, "President Bush Goes to War: A Psychological Interpretation from a Distance," in *The Political Psychology of the Gulf War: Leaders, Publics, and the Process of Conflict*, ed. Stanley A. Renshon (Pittsburgh, PA: University of Pittsburgh Press, 1993), 29–48.

21. Bush and Scowcroft, *A World Transformed*, 443–46.

22. Palmer, *Guardians of the Gulf*, 180–192; and Bush and Scowcroft, *A World Transformed*, 446–49.

23. Bush and Scowcroft, *A World Transformed*, 450–59; Baker, *The Politics of Diplomacy*, 382–90; Palmer, *Guardians of the Gulf*, 193–224; and Yair Evron, "The Invasion of Kuwait and the Gulf War: Dilemmas Facing the Israeli-Iraqi-U.S. Relationship," in *The Middle East and the United States*, 354–64. On the failure of U.S. coercive diplomacy, see Alexander L. George, *Bridging the Gap: Theory & Practice in Foreign Policy* (Washington, DC: United States Institute of Peace Press, 1993).

24. Baker, *The Politics of Diplomacy*, 391–95; and Bush and Scowcroft, *A World Transformed*, 459–61.

25. Bush and Scowcroft, *A World Transformed*, 461–77. Quote can be found on 462; Baker, *The Politics of Diplomacy*, 396–408; and Palmer, *Guardians of the Gulf*, 224–27.

26. Palmer, *Guardians of the Gulf*, 228–42; Bush and Scowcroft, *A World Transformed*, 477–87; Baker, *The Politics of Diplomacy*, 408–10; Miriam Joyce, *Kuwait 1945–1996: An Anglo-American Perspective* (London: Frank Cass, 1998), 167; John G. Heidenrich, "The Gulf War: How Many Iraqis Died?" *Foreign Policy*, no. 90 (Spring 1993): 108–25; and Kaufman, *The Arab Middle East and the United States*, 162–64.

27. Kaufman, *The Arab Middle East and the United States*, 164–65; Palmer, *Guardians of the Gulf*, 238–42; Bush and Scowcroft, *A World Transformed*, 488–92. Quote can be found on 489; General H. Norman Schwarzkopf, with Peter Petre, *It Doesn't Take a Hero* (New York: Linda Grey Bantam Books, 1992), 497–98; and Baker, *The Politics of Diplomacy*, 411–15. On the Saudi desire for the United States to overthrow Saddam Hussein, see Kenneth M. Pollack, *The Persian Puzzle: The Conflict between Iran and America* (New York: Random House, 2004), 284.

28. Pollack, *The Persian Puzzle*, 430–42.

29. For an analysis of the Bush administration's Iraq and overall Gulf policy, see Robert J. Pauly, Jr., *US Foreign Policy and the Persian Gulf: Safeguarding American Interests through Selective Multilateralism* (Aldershot, England: Ashgate, 2005), 37–64. For a theoretical explanation of U.S. decision-making during the Persian Gulf War, see Steve A. Yetiv, *Explaining Foreign Policy: U.S. Decision-Making and the Persian Gulf War* (Baltimore: Johns Hopkins University Press, 2004).

30. Daniel L. Byman and Matthew C. Waxman, *Confronting Iraq: U.S. Policy and the Use of Force Since the Gulf War* (Santa Monica, CA: Rand, 2000), 1–52. For an eyewitness account of rebellion in southern Iraq, see Zainab Al-Suwaij, "The Fire Last Time," *New Republic*, 10 February 2003, 19–23.

31. Byman and Waxman, *Confronting Iraq*, 32–36, 39–43.

32. Pollack, *The Persian Puzzle*, 259–62; Gary G. Sick, "US Policy in the Gulf: Objectives and Prospects," in *Managing New Developments in the Gulf*, ed. Rosemary Hollis (London: Royal Institute of International Affairs, 2000), 36–37; Anthony Lake, "Confronting Backlash States," *Foreign Affairs* 73, no. 2 (March/April 1994): 45–55. Quotes can be found on 46, 49; and "U.S. Policy toward Iran and Iraq," *Hearings before the Subcommittee on Near Eastern and South Asian Affairs of the Committee on Foreign Relations of the United States Senate*, 104th Congress, 1st Session, 2 March and 3 August 1995 (Washington, DC: Government Printing Office, 1995), 14–19.

33. Lake, "Confronting Backlash States," 45–55. Quote can be found on 47–48; and Michael Collins Dunn, "Five Years after Desert Storm: Gulf Security, Stability and the U.S. Presence," *Middle East Policy* 4, no. 3 (March 1996): 30–38. Assistant Secretary of State for Near Eastern Affairs Robert Pelletreau told senators in 1995 that the "success of our [i.e., American] policies toward both [Iraq and Iran] requires not only firm US unilateral action, but the collaboration of other influential governments and a willingness to

stay the course of constant pressure on both regimes." "U.S. Policy toward Iran and Iraq," 18.

34. Graham E. Fuller and Ian O. Lesser, "Persian Gulf Myths," *Foreign Affairs* 76, no. 3 (May/June 1997): 42–52. First quote can be found on 47; F. Gregory Gause III, "The Illogic of Dual Containment," *Foreign Affairs* 73, no. 2 (March/April 1994): 56–66. Second, third, and fourth quotes can be found on 59–60; Alon Ben-Meir, "The Dual Containment Strategy Is No Longer Viable," *Middle East Policy* 4, no. 3 (March 1996): 58–71; and William A. Rugh, "Time to Modify Our Gulf Policy," *Middle East Policy* 5, no. 1 (January 1997): 46–57. See also Robert S. Deutsch, Anthony H. Cordesman, Hervé Magro, and William A. Rugh, "Symposium: The Challenge in the Gulf: Building a Bridge from Containment to Stability," *Middle East Policy* 5, no. 2 (May 1997): 1–21; Joseph Marty, Ivan Eland, Shibley Telhami, and Dov Zakheim, "Symposium: U.S. Gulf Policy: How Can It Be Fixed?" *Middle East Policy* 6, no. 1 (June 1998): 1–24; and Simon Serfaty, "Bridging the Gulf Across the Atlantic: Europe and the United States in the Persian Gulf," *The Middle East Journal* 52, no. 3 (Summer 1998): 337–50.

35. Byman and Waxman, *Confronting Iraq*, 14–21; and "Like Father, Like Son."

36. Rod Nordland, "Saddam's Long Shadow," *Newsweek*, 31 July 2000, 32–34; Amatzia Baram, "The Effect of Iraqi Sanctions: Statistical Pitfalls and Responsibility," *Middle East Journal* 54, no. 2 (Spring 2000): 194–223; Walid Khadduri, "U.N. Sanctions on Iraq: 10 Years Later," *Middle East Policy* 7, no. 4 (October 2000): 156–62; Daniel Byman, "Misunderstanding Sanctions," *Hartford Courant*, 5 November 2000, C1, C4; "Revisiting the Iraq Sanctions," *New York Times*, 11 February 2001, <http://www.nytimes.com>; and Michael Rubin, "Food Fight," *New Republic*, 18 June 2001, 18–19.

37. Byman and Waxman, *Confronting Iraq*, 37–76; "Bomb Attack in Saudi Arabia," *Hearings before the Committee on Armed Services of the United States Senate*, 104th Congress, 2nd Session, 9 July & 18 September 1996 (Washington, DC: Government Printing Office, 1997), 90–91; Romesh Ratnesar, "What Good Did It Do?" *Time*, 28 December 1998–4 January 1999, 68–73; and Barbara Crossette, "U.N. Sanctions Didn't Stop Iraq From Buying Weapons," *New York Times*, 18 June 2001, <http://www.nytimes.com>.

38. "Saddam's Iraq: Sanctions and U.S. Policy," *Hearing before the Subcommittee on Near Eastern and South Asian Affairs of the Committee on Foreign Relations of the United States Senate*, 106th Congress, 2nd Session, 22 March 2000 (Washington, DC: Government Printing Office, 2000), 3–23. Quotes can be found on 4.

39. Lake, "Confronting Backlash States," 52–53; Gause, "The Illogic of Dual Containment," 64–66; and Geoffrey Kemp, "Iran: Can the United States Do a Deal?" *Washington Quarterly* 24, no. 1 (Winter 2001): 109–24. On Iran's pre-1997 foreign policy, see R.K. Ramazani, "Iran's Foreign Policy: Both North and South," *Middle East Journal* 46, no. 3 (Summer 1992): 393–412; John Duke Anthony, "Iran in GCC Dynamics," *Middle East Policy* 2, no. 3 (1993): 107–20; and Dariush Zahedi and Ahmad Ghoreishi, "Iran's Security Concerns in the Persian Gulf," *Naval War College Review* 49, no. 3 (Summer 1996): 73–95.

40. Pollack, *The Persian Puzzle*, 253–65. Quotes can be found on 263. Pollack writes (263) that "at least initially, there was very little to the Iranian side of Dual Containment. The United States committed itself to maintaining its arms embargo on Iran and a variety of other sanctions, mostly related to Iran's inclusion on the annual State Department 'terrorism list.' The United States also stated that it would work to convince other countries likewise not to sell weapons and nuclear materials to Iran and to limit their economic contacts as well. The United States did not indicate that it would make any efforts to overthrow the Iranian regime. There was no stated willingness to use military force to make Iran comply with America's will. Indeed, there was not even a com-

prehensive set of economic sanctions in place and U.S. trade with Iran was actually quite substantial at this time."

41. Pollack, *The Persian Puzzle*, 265–89; Kemp, "Iran," 112–14. In 1998 testimony before the Senate, Assistant Secretary of State Indyk said that "[u]nilateral sanctions have proven costly to U.S. business. However, we believe that Iran poses threats so significant that we have no choice but [to] accept these costs. Economic pressure has an important role in our efforts to convince Iran to cease its efforts to acquire weapons of mass destruction and missiles and to support terrorism." "United States Policy toward Iran," *Hearing before the Subcommittee on Near Eastern and South Asian Affairs of the Committee on Foreign Relations of the United States Senate*, 105th Congress, 2nd Session, 14 May 1998 (Washington, DC: Government Printing Office, 1998), 7.

42. Kemp, "Iran," 110–12. First and second quotes can be found on 111; Third, fourth, and fifth quotes can be found in "United States Policy toward Iran," 7; Pollack, *The Persian Puzzle*, 289–342; Madeleine Albright, with Bill Woodward, *Madam Secretary* (New York: Miramax Books, 2003), 319–26. Final quote can be found on 325–26; Douglas Jehl, "Despite Iran's Overtures, U.S. Is Wary on Relations," *New York Times*, 26 May 1998, <http://www.nytimes.com>; Barbara Crossette, "Albright, in Overture to Iran, Seeks a 'Road Map' to Amity," *New York Times*, 18 June 1998, <http://www.nytimes.com>; Howard Schneider, "Iran Reaching Out to Arab Neighbors," *Hartford Courant*, 15 May 1999, <http://www.courant.com>; "Iran's Diplomatic Initiatives," *New York Times*, 23 May 1999, <http://www.nytimes.com>; Susan Sachs, "Turnout High in Iran Elections, a Referendum on Reform," *New York Times*, 18 February 2000, <http://www.nytimes.com>; "America's Relations with Iran," *New York Times*, 25 February 2000, <http://www.nytimes.com>; Thomas L. Friedman, "A Rogue Worth Knowing," *New York Times*, 25 February 2000, <http://www.nytimes.com>; and "More Than Nuts and Caviar," *Hartford Courant*, 19 March 2000, C2. On post-1997 Iranian foreign policy, see R.K. Ramazani, "The Shifting Premise of Iran's Foreign Policy: Towards a Democratic Peace?" *Middle East Journal* 52, no. 2 (Spring 1998): 177–87; R.K. Ramazani, "The Emerging Arab-Iranian Rapprochement: Towards an Integrated U.S. Policy in the Middle East?" *Middle East Policy* 6, no. 1 (June 1998): 45–62; and Charles Kurzman, "Soft on Satan: Challenges for Iranian-U.S. Relations," *Middle East Policy* 6, no. 1 (June 1998): 63–72.

43. Edmund Herzig, "Iran: Internal Developments and International Implications," in *Managing New Developments in the Gulf*, 50–69; Guy Taillefer, "Intifada Iranienne [Iranian Intifada]," *Le Devoir* (Montréal), 13 July 1999, <http://www.ledevoir.com>; Fen Montaigne, "Reform vs. Revolution, Iran's Perpetual Tug-of-War," *New York Times*, 14 July 1999, <http://www.nytimes.com>; Saeed Barzin, "The Student Revolt," *Middle East International*, 16 July 1999, 12–13; Elaine Sciolino, "For Once, the Veil That Hides Conflict Slips," *New York Times*, 18 July 1999, <http://www.nytimes.com>; Thomas L. Friedman, "Ayatollah Deng," *New York Times*, 20 July 1999, <http://www.nytimes.com>; and Anthony J. Dennis, "Could Tolerance Come to Tehran? Or Will Tanks Roll In?" *Hartford Courant*, 5 May 2000, <http://www.courant.com>. On the Caspian controversy, see Assistant Secretary for International Affairs, U.S. Department of Energy, David Goldwyn's remarks in David L. Goldwyn, Martha Brill Olcott, Julia Nanay, Thomas R. Stauffer, "Symposium: The Caspian Region and the New Great Powers," *Middle East Policy* 7, no. 4 (October 2000): 1–5. According to Goldwyn (4), "U.S. Caspian policy is not anti-Iran, it is pro-Central Asia. It is based on our interest in the prosperity, stability and progress of the countries in that region." See also "Caspian Hydrocarbons and the Iranian Connection," *Middle East Institute Newsletter* 51, no. 2 (March 2000): 5; and "Transporting Caspian Oil and Gas," *Middle East Institute Newsletter* 51, no. 3 (May 2000): 5, 11. Washington favored the construction of a complex East-West pipeline connecting Baku, Tblisi, and Ceyhan. Tehran preferred a North-South

scheme with Iran as the hub of a Central Asian-Persian Gulf transportation network. The think tank Stratfor reported, however, that "[t]he race to get oil from Central Asia to the Black Sea [the East-West route] is over, and Russia has won." See Christian Caryl, "Texas Tea, Anyone?" *Newsweek*, 30 July 2001, 24.

44. Paul D. Wolfowitz, "Remarks on the Conclusion of the Gulf War," *American-Arab Affairs*, no. 35 (Winter 1990–91): 1–10. Quote can be found on 6; Joseph Wright Twinam, *The Gulf, Cooperation and the Council: An American Perspective* (Washington, DC: Middle East Policy Council, 1992), 191–233; and Rachel Bronson, "Beyond Containment in the Persian Gulf," *Orbis* 45, no. 2 (Spring 2001): 195–96.

45. On the "GCC" strategy, see Marc J. O'Reilly and Wesley B. Renfro, "Evolving Empire: America's 'Emirates' Strategy in the Persian Gulf," *International Studies Perspectives* 8, no. 2 (May 2007): 137–51. On America's "empire of bases," see Chalmers Johnson, *The Sorrows of Empire: Militarism, Secrecy, and the End of the Republic* (New York: Owl Books, 2004), 237–53. On bin Laden's *jihad* against America, see Fawaz A. Gerges, *Journey of the Jihadist: Inside Muslim Militancy* (Orlando, FL: Harcourt, 2006), 178–79.

46. "U.S. Policy toward Iran and Iraq," 19–29. Quotes can be found on 23, 25; Jeffrey A. Lefebvre, "The Transformation of U.S. Security Policy in the Gulf: Strategic Disruption and the Balance of Risk," *Middle East Affairs Journal* 5, no. 1/2 (Winter/Spring 1999): 62–64; and Anthony H. Cordesman, *Bahrain, Oman, Qatar, and the UAE: Challenges of Security* (Boulder, CO: Westview Press, 1997), 1–32. According to one scholar, the GCC countries "have always exhibited a desire to duck direct confrontation if at all possible." F. Gregory Gause III, *Oil Monarchies: Domestic and Security Challenges in the Arab Gulf States* (New York: Council on Foreign Relations Press, 1994), 121.

47. Ian Brodie, "US Forms New Fleet to Police the Gulf," *Times* (London), 5 July 1995, accessed via Lexis-Nexis; "US Gulf Forces Come Under New Fleet," *Middle East Economic Digest*, 14 July 1995, accessed via Lexis-Nexis; Shibley Telhami and Michael O'Hanlon, "Europe's Oil, Our Troops," *New York Times*, 30 December 1995, accessed via Lexis-Nexis; and "Bomb Attack in Saudi Arabia," 81. First quote can be found in that source. Second quote can be found in "Symposium: U.S. Gulf Policy: How Can It Be Fixed?" 4. On the Fifth Fleet, see also "Vigilance and Volatility," <http://www.mediacen.navy.mil/pubs/allhands/feb99/febpg12.html>. On aircraft carriers, America's "big, mean war machine," and their strike forces, see Bruce B. Auster, "Diplomacy's Gunboat," *U.S. News & World Report*, 28 February 1994, 28–50. Figures for U.S. military assets in the Persian Gulf as of June 2001. In his April 1994 testimony before the Armed Services committee, Rear Admiral John Scott Redd explained the U.S. Navy's post-Gulf War "vision." "Instead of a Navy which is designed to conduct war at sea more or less independently against a global maritime power," he said, "it envisions a Navy which is focused on joint warfare in littoral coastal regions of the world, projecting high intensity power ashore from the sea." "That Navy," Redd added, "is embodied in a force structure which we call Force 2001.... It represents a force of about 330 ships which is shaped and sized for two purposes—forward presence and littoral warfare in two major regional contingencies." "Implementation of Lessons Learned from the Persian Gulf Conflict," *Joint Hearing before the Subcommittee on Coalition Defense and Reinforcing Forces and the Subcommittee on Military Readiness and Defense Infrastructure of the Committee on Armed Services of the United States Senate*, 103rd Congress, 2nd Session, 18 April 1994 (Washington, DC: Government Printing Office, 1994), 26.

48. Bronson, "Beyond Containment in the Persian Gulf," 204. Quote can be found on that page. Italics in original. Defense experts perceived CDI as a "strategic shift to a more land-based military presence in the region." See Peter Feuilherade, "US Seeks More Bases," *Middle East International*, 21 April 2000, 12–14. Quote can be found on 13.

49. Rugh, "Time to Modify Our Gulf Policy," 57; John Duke Anthony, "The U.S.-GCC Relationship: A Glass Half-Empty or Half-Full?" *Middle East Policy* 5, no. 2 (May 1997): 22–41; Abdullah Al-Shayeji, "Dangerous Perceptions: Gulf Views of the U.S. Role in the Region," *Middle East Policy* 5, no. 3 (September 1997): 1–13; "Bomb Attack in Saudi Arabia," 80–94; Ed Blanche, "New Challenges to the US in the Gulf," *Middle East International*, 27 October 2000, 22–24; F. Gregory Gause III, "The Political Economy of National Security," in *The Persian Gulf at the Millennium: Essays in Politics, Economy, Security, and Religion*, eds. Gary G. Sick and Lawrence G. Potter (New York: St. Martin's Press, 1997), 61–84; Marc J. O'Reilly, "Omanibalancing: Oman Confronts an Uncertain Future," *Middle East Journal* 52, no. 1 (Winter 1998): 70–84; Marc J. O'Reilly, "Oil Monarchies without Oil: Omani & Bahraini Security in a Post-Oil Era," *Middle East Policy* 6, no. 3 (February 1999): 78–92; Joseph A. Kechichian, "Saudi Arabia's Will to Power," *Middle East Policy* 7, no. 2 (February 2000): 47–60; F. Gregory Gause III, "Saudi Arabia Over a Barrel," *Foreign Affairs* 79, no. 3 (May/June 2000): 80–94; Ghanim Alnajjar, "The GCC and Iraq," *Middle East Policy* 7, no. 4 (October 2000): 92–99; and Bronson, "Beyond Containment in the Persian Gulf," 193–209. On "empire by invitation," see Geir Lundestad, *The American "Empire" and Other Studies of US Foreign Policy in a Comparative Perspective* (New York: Oxford University Press, 1990).

50. Pollack, *The Persian Puzzle*, 282–286; O'Reilly, "Omanibalancing;" O'Reilly, "Oil Monarchies without Oil;" Michael R. Gordon, "Military Analysis: Superpower Suddenly Finds Itself Threatened by Sophisticated Terrorists," *New York Times*, 14 October 2000, <http://www.nytimes.com>; "The Terrorist Threat at Sea," *New York Times*, 17 October 2000, <http://www.nytimes.com>; Fareed Zakaria, "The New Twilight Struggle," *Newsweek*, 23 October 2000, 37; Daniel Klaidman, "Bin Laden's Poetry of Terror," *Newsweek*, 26 March 2001, 39; Mary Matouk, "Yemen's Security Environment and the Bombing of the USS Cole," *Middle East Institute Newsletter* 52, no. 2 (April 2001): 8; and Timothy Phelps, "Terrorism Trail Leads to Shrine," *Hartford Courant*, 26 June 2001, A11. Quote can be found in "Bomb Attack in Saudi Arabia," 91. For Kenneth Pollack, with the Khobar bombing, which Tehran sponsored, "Iran crossed a momentous line. Through a thinly veiled proxy, it had mounted a direct attack on Americans." Pollack, *The Persian Puzzle*, 298.

51. "U.S. Troops Staying, Says Cohen," *Deutsche Presse-Agentur*, 16 November 2000, accessed via Lexis-Nexis; Blanche, "New Challenges to the US in the Gulf." On the military situation in the Gulf, see Anthony H. Cordesman, "The Changing Military Balance in the Gulf," *Middle East Policy* 6, no. 1 (June 1998): 25–44.

52. As U.S. Army and Marine Corps units could be exposed to an enemy's chemical or biological agents far more easily than Navy or Air Force personnel, Washington had every incentive to continue favoring naval and aerial warfare to minimize the risk of casualties and public-relations brouhahas such as Persian Gulf War syndrome. The latter afflicted several American veterans who fought in the 1991 war. They claim to have been exposed to depleted uranium found in artillery shells. The Pentagon denied any correlation between battlefield conditions in the Kuwaiti theatre of operations and subsequent illness. Still, in 2001, one study confirmed "the veterans have brain and nerve damage likely caused by low-level wartime exposures to combinations of nerve agents, including nerve gas, pesticides and anti-nerve gas pills." See Thomas D. Williams, "Study Links Chemical Exposure, Vets' Ills," *Hartford Courant*, 23 June 2001, A6.

53. On "differentiated containment," which occurred once the Clinton administration abandoned its "rogue state" policy, see Robert S. Litwak, "Iraq and Iran: From Dual to Differentiated Containment," in Robert J. Lieber, *Eagle Rules? Foreign Policy and American Primacy in the Twenty-First Century* (Upper Saddle River, NJ: Prentice Hall,

2002), 173–93. For an assessment of Clinton's overall Gulf policy, see Pauly, *US Foreign Policy and the Persian Gulf*, 65–90.

Chapter 7

In Search of Monsters to Destroy: 2001–07

During the *sixth* stage (2001–07) of American expansion in the Persian Gulf, Washington aimed to depose Iraqi President Saddam Hussein. Unlike previous, mostly covert, endeavors in the Middle East (and elsewhere) to remove an unde sirable leader, the White House touted this *overt* effort months in advance. With Hussein removed, President George W. Bush and his advisors (especially neo-conservatives such as Paul Wolfowitz, but nationalists like Dick Cheney as well) aspired to remake the Middle East into a more U.S. friendly region. Yet an oc-cupation of Iraq would draw charges of colonialism, a foreign-policy strategy the United States typically avoided. Such a development would also likely upset Iranian leaders, many of whom remained sworn enemies of the Americans, and agitate the Gulf Cooperation Council (GCC) countries, which, historically, fret-ted whenever events threatened to upset or overturn the status quo.

In striving for formal empire in Iraq, Washington intended to exploit mili-tary advantages acquired in the previous stage (1990–2000), when the United States consolidated its informal empire in the Persian Gulf. Following *Operation Desert Storm*, GCC states invited America to serve as a mercenary force that could shield these wealthy kingdoms and emirates from Iraqi and Iranian depre-dations. The White House gladly accepted and used the decade to build up an impressive military capability in the region. New air, sea, and land bases and the nascent Fifth Fleet enabled the Pentagon to carry out missions and respond to crises quickly. The administrations of George H.W. Bush and Bill Clinton did not attempt, however, to extend U.S. influence to Iraq (other than the Kurdish-held north) or Iran. While Bush and Clinton generally proceeded cautiously, George W. Bush, son of America's forty-first president, arrived in Washington in January 2001 with a very different agenda.[1]

Bush *fils*' tenure as president promised a "humble" America internationally, while returning the country to the kind of traditional foreign-policy concerns (U.S.-Russian and U.S.-Chinese relations, for example) which had preoccupied his father's administration. Like his elder, George W. Bush sought to overhaul the American military force structure and evolve a strategic doctrine more in sync with the post-Cold War world. But, unlike his dad, he made a national missile defense system an urgent priority despite the exorbitant cost and daunting technological challenges associated with such a venture. To pursue this dream of shielding the United States from enemy missile attacks, and to husband U.S. financial and other resources needed for significant tax cuts, his most important campaign promise, he and his administration thought it imperative for the country to avoid Clintonesque "social work" abroad—"nation-building" especially.[2]

Early Bush foreign policy irritated America's friends and enemies alike, as the White House eschewed the Clinton preference for multilateralism in favor of a series of unilateral measures that won the United States scant international admiration. In a cavalier manner reminiscent of the Reagan years, Bush rejected the 1997 Kyoto Protocol, which sought to curb alarming rates of greenhouse gas emissions harmful to Planet Earth's ecology; withdrew from (or "unsigned") the 1998 Rome Treaty that created the International Criminal Court (ICC), an institution that could try individuals, such as ex-Yugoslav President Slobodan Milosevic, accused of hideous crimes (i.e., so-called crimes against humanity); imposed onerous steel tariffs in violation of World Trade Organization stipulations forbidding such protectionism; and supported a Congressional farm bill that appealed shamelessly to agribusiness interests and Farm Belt politicians hungry for votes. The Texan with the Harvard MBA justified his controversial decisions by invoking American self-interest. In his mind, the United States had to seek self-sufficiency rather than global well-being, which required cooperation and compromise with other countries. Similarly, Bush maligned international norms, such as environmental stewardship, human rights, and fair trade, while promoting unchecked U.S. economic growth and exempting American soldiers and citizens from ever standing trial at The Hague should they commit atrocities on foreign soil and not be prosecuted in America—the only circumstances under which Americans could have appeared before the ICC.[3]

Conservatives may have applauded Bush's assertiveness, but his administration's realism—jingoism, said critics—clashed with increasingly assertive allies opposed to U.S. policy. Europeans, especially, expressed profound dismay when Washington substituted diktat for consultation, a reversal of Clinton policy. They preferred the forty-second president's dictum of "multilateralism when we can, unilateralism when we must" to the forty-third's "unilateralism when we can, multilateralism when we must." Bush may have reassured Americans that he would not sacrifice their best interests to the whims of the United Nations (UN) and the European Union, but White House selfishness promised much global acrimony at a time when U.S. plenty, the result of half-a-dozen or so years of spectacular economic expansion, contrasted dramatically with an international scene often racked by inequality, injustice, poverty, disease, strife, anger, and despair—a "world on fire," in scholar Amy Chua's words. Africa's agony—with genocide in Darfur, Sudan, and a devastating HIV/AIDS crisis—epitomized the despair felt by millions who waited for the global community to arrest their misery. Ironically, in many cases only the United States (with the assistance of various non-governmental organizations) could provide assistance, relief, and salvation—which it often did, though not to everyone's satisfaction.[4]

This charitable impulse served Americans well on September 11, 2001, as they unexpectedly experienced a trauma unlike any other in the country's history. As television cameras recorded hijacked commercial airliners tearing into the very symbols of U.S. prowess—the World Trade Center towers in New York City and the Pentagon in Washington, DC—a horrified audience struggled to comprehend why anyone would seek to carry out such an attack. As the burning twin towers imploded on live TV, extinguishing three thousand or so lives (mostly American, but dozens of countries lost citizens as well), the United States experienced a flashback to December 7, 1941—the attack at Pearl Harbor. Unlike many nations, America lacked experience when it came to war on its own soil. Although familiar with domestic and international terrorism, the events of 9/11 easily overshadowed the 1993 World Trade Center and 1995 Oklahoma City bombings, as well as the 2000 attack on the USS *Cole*.[5]

As New York City Mayor Rudy Giuliani tried to console a grief-striken nation, President Bush overcame his initial bewilderment to rally his countrymen and women. He vowed justice for those wantonly murdered and committed the country to a unique campaign—the defeat of international terrorism. He promised no quick victories, but spoke confidently of eventual victory in this Manichean contest. While some U.S. and other commentators reexamined America's supposed innocence abroad—they spotlighted foreigners' (Palestinian, for example) grievances stemming from decades of dubious, duplicitous, and destructive U.S. foreign policy—Bush dismissed any American culpability for the apocalyptic events of 9/11. Armed with the world's sympathy—Paris' *Le Monde* exclaimed "Nous sommes tous Américains" ("We Are All Americans")—the White House carefully and deliberately crafted a nuanced response that sought to punish culprits, mainly members of Osama bin Laden's al-Qaeda Islamic organization, while reassuring Muslims (in the United States and elsewhere) that Washington would not wage a civilizational war on the *umma* (i.e., the community of believers), the followers of Prophet Muhammad.[6]

Although fifteen of the nineteen September 11th hijackers hailed from Saudi Arabia, in the fall of 2001 the Bush administration targeted the Taliban, Afghanistan's medieval rulers, and their al-Qaeda terrorist guests for removal. Following a shaky start, *Operation Enduring Freedom* achieved its objective within a few months. Sustained U.S. bombing of Taliban positions enabled that organization's archrivals, the Washington-funded Northern Alliance and Eastern Alliance, to unseat the repressive and unpopular Islamist government. *Operation Enduring Freedom*'s success owed much to Pakistan's president, General Pervez Musharraf, who allowed American forces to use his country's air bases despite his countrymen's and women's strong anti-U.S., pro-Taliban sentiments. As a result of expeditious negotiations involving financial aid in return for military access, Washington also made excellent use of former Soviet bases in Central Asia, thereby increasing American influence in that region significantly.

Hamid Karzai, a moderate politician, assumed the Afghan presidency with White House blessing and support. His government may have allowed Afghan women to store or throw away their *burqas*—mandatory dress under the Taliban—but warlords continued to rule the country. Karzai could not immediately overcome two decades of strife—war with the Soviet Union (1979–89) followed by years of civil war—no matter how many billions of dollars the United States pledged to rebuild this fractured and "failed" state. Despite U.S. protection, Karzai barely escaped assassination in his first year as president. Afghan soldiers loyal to him, moreover, kept but a tenuous hold on the capital city, Kabul. A small North Atlantic Treaty Organization (NATO) contingent inserted in August 2003 to lead the International Security Assistance Force (ISAF) helped stabilize Afghanistan somewhat and allowed the Americans to reduce their financial and military commitments significantly. But serious problems (a thriving narco-economy, courtesy of opium and heroin exports, and continued widespread lawlessness, especially in the Afghan-Pakistani border area, where members of the Taliban and al-Qaeda, including possibly Osama bin Laden, remained) still prevailed on the eve of the October 2004 national election, won by Karzai, and persisted thereafter. In 2007, despite a stronger ISAF presence (some 35,000 soldiers) which included additional U.S. and British forces, Afghanistan struggled to improve, as the Taliban and its allies fought fiercely, especially in the essentially anarchic southern part of the country. Worrisome for ISAF, the Taliban applied techniques (i.e., suicide bombings and improvised explosive device attacks) borrowed from the insurgency in Iraq or learned there.[7]

Six years earlier, a Bush administration eager to claim a victory in its "War on Terror" had spotlighted the end of the Taliban's tyrannical rule and the routing of al-Qaeda forces. Yet, despite a concerted effort, U.S. Special Forces could not accomplish one of their chief tasks: to kill or capture Osama bin Laden and Taliban leader Mullah Omar. Although several top al-Qaeda organizers were nabbed, videotapes featuring bin Laden, shown on al-Jazeera, the Qatari-based Arab satellite television station, flustered the White House, which tried to counter its nemesis' propaganda with its own. The Bush administration continuously demonized the gangly scion of a wealthy Saudi family, who, much to the satisfaction of Carter and Reagan officials, had fought bravely with the *mujaheddin*, rebel fighters who received considerable U.S. military and financial assistance to push the Soviet infidels out of Afghanistan. Many of Washington's critics highlighted this irony—the creation of a U.S.-approved al-Qaeda Frankenstein that turned its wrath onto America once Uncle Sam's soldiers stepped onto sacred Muslim soil in Saudi Arabia in 1990. Denying any "blowback" or U.S. hypocrisy, President Bush continued to portray his policy as just and consistent with both American and global values. The U.S. public wholeheartedly concurred with its president, as any criticism of the Bush administration struck most Americans—who clamored "United We Stand"—as unpatriotic.

With dissent frowned upon following the 9/11-induced erosion of U.S. civil liberties, Bush sought to polarize the world further by alerting Americans and a worldwide audience, in his January 2002 State of the Union Address, to the existence of an "Axis of Evil" reminiscent of World War II's Axis Powers. The president substituted Iraq, Iran, and North Korea for Nazi Germany, Japan, and Italy. While consistent with the Texan's Evangelical Christianity, Bush's dichotomy between "Good and Evil" satisfied many Americans fearful of renewed attacks against the U.S. homeland. The White House's de facto emphasis on civilizational conflict (rhetorically, though, Bush praised Islam) alarmed many Europeans and Asians, who greeted a twenty-first century crusade with utmost trepidation. With imams in the Middle East calling for *jihad* (an Arabic word connoting the every day struggle for devoutness but which could also be interpreted as a call to holy war with non-Islamic peoples), Washington forged ahead with its plan to defend so-called Western civilization from enemies who either sought to undermine or destroy it.[8]

In a June 1, 2002, speech at West Point, President Bush previewed a transformation in American foreign policy. He spoke of his country's right to eliminate threats before they manifested themselves. A doctrine of prevention would call for an offensive rather than defensive military policy, in contravention of international law. Although the White House already considered the United States at war—the 9/11 attacks certainly allowed Washington to invoke Article 51 of the UN Charter, which authorized national self-defense—the discarding of the Cold War strategy of "containment" for a policy of selected aggression promised to set a dubious precedent and draw howls of disapproval from foreign leaders. Owing to its military without peer, America could behave capriciously, or so the international community feared. Bush dismissed such concerns, however, and reported to Congress in the fall that henceforth the United States would reserve the right to dispose of threats before they materialized. His national security strategy struck another blow for American primacy when it stated that the United States would oppose any country that tried to compete with it for political-military supremacy.[9]

The Bush Doctrine's imperial features forecast an America indefinitely trying to counter potential harm to U.S. national interests. As the administration proceeded with its missile defense project and continued to hunt down Osama bin Laden, it fixated upon its favorite *bête noire*, Saddam Hussein's Iraq. North Korea's fall 2002 confession to an illicit resumption of its nuclear program annoyed the White House, but President Bush and his advisors preferred diplomacy to a military campaign with Northeast Asia's impoverished, Stalinist member of the "Axis of Evil." Pyongyang's conventional and possible nuclear arsenal, as well as its army's proximity to Seoul, the capital of America's ally South Korea, dictated a cautious policy. To avoid a similar scenario in Iraq,

whereby a nuclear-armed Baghdad could deter the United States, early in 2003
Bush officials kept their eyes trained on Hussein and his purported weapons of
mass destruction (WMD).[10]

With the United States preparing to invade Iraq, a sovereign country, the
White House exhibited unmistakably imperial reflexes, a development that invigorated neo-conservatives such as Max Boot and William Kristol. As *The New
Yorker*'s Joshua Marshall would note in early 2004, nearly a year into *Operation
Iraqi Freedom*, "hard-liners who were frustrated by Clinton's bumbling and hesi-
tations saw no reason to deny that America was an imperial power, and a great
one[.]" *Operation Enduring Freedom* warranted such a designation. Opined
Marshall, "how else to describe a country that had so easily vanquished Afghanistan, once legendary as the graveyard of empires?" In March 2003, he concluded, "[t]he only question was whether America would start running its empire
with foresight and determination, rather than leaving it to chance, drift, and disaster." As Marshall and other journalists covering the war in Iraq soon found
out, the Bush administration thoroughly mismanaged the Iraqi component of the
U.S. empire in the Persian Gulf. Although President Bush won re-election in
2004 despite obvious travails in Iraq, the worsening debacle in that country thereafter undercut U.S. authority and power worldwide and resulted in bitter anti-
American sentiment most everywhere.[11]

To counter such attitudes, sway U.S. opinion, and restore hemorrhaging
American influence, Bush turned to Condoleezza Rice, who as secretary of state
vowed to implement a "practical idealism" that promised the kind of multilateralism conspicuously absent from the president's first term in office. As Washington coped with "strategic fatigue," following four years of antagonistic diplomacy, strenuous military exertion, and skyrocketing deficit spending (the budget
deficit stood at $412.5 billion in FY 2004, 3.6 percent of Gross Domestic Prod-
uct), Secretary of State Rice succeeded somewhat in rehabilitating U.S. foreign
policy, a task made easier by the departure of two prominent neo-conservatives,
Paul Wolfowitz and Douglas Feith, architects of *Operation Iraqi Freedom*. Despite their resignations, the imperious Donald Rumsfeld, who remained secretary
of defense, continued to dismiss his as well as administration critics, as did Vice
President Dick Cheney and U.S. Permanent Representative to the United Nations
John Bolton, a man rhetorically committed to the demise of that important,
though flawed, international organization. These unilateralists clung to the notion, seemingly so discredited, that the United States must rely primarily, if not
solely, on itself when confronting matters such as the North Korean and Iranian
nuclear programs, both of which preoccupied the global community in the summer of 2006.[12]

In August 2006, Cheney, Bush, and other Republicans, who worried about
fall Congressional elections that might yield majorities in the House of Representatives and Senate to the war-skeptic Democrats, spotlighted a major terrorist
plot in Britain and Pakistan that aimed to blow up airplanes flying from the Unit-

ed Kingdom to the United States, but which British and Pakistani intelligence foiled, as evidence that America had to remain vigilant in the War on Terror as well as firmly committed to the war in Iraq lest replays occur of al-Qaeda, or al-Qaeda-style, attacks à la 9/11, Bali in 2002, Casablanca in 2003, Madrid in 2004, and London in 2005. As the president consistently reminded his countrymen and women, it was better to fight terrorists overseas rather than on U.S. soil. Such an admonition may have persuaded most Americans in 2002, when the Bush administration adhered to the "One Percent Doctrine," whereby Washington took any and all WMD threats equally seriously, but in 2006 that kind of maxim infuriated many Americans following several years of dubious White House practices, such as violating the Geneva Conventions by holding so-called illegal enemy combatants at the U.S. Guantánamo Bay prison in Cuba without charging them; "extraordinary rendition," whereby the United States sent suspected terrorists to countries, such as Syria, that allowed the use of torture to exact information; and the surveillance program authorizing the National Security Agency to monitor phone calls and e-mails between the United States and other countries without a warrant in suspected cases of terrorism, in violation of the 1978 Foreign Intelligence Surveillance Act.[13]

In addition to renewed concern about international terrorism, the summer of 2006 saw oil exceed $75 per barrel based on strong demand, especially U.S., Chinese, and Indian, lack of spare capacity in the global petroleum market, and worries over the potential repercussions of Iran's defiant nuclear stance. Although earlier in the year, at his State of the Union address, President Bush had proclaimed the United States addicted to this fossil fuel, his administration, typically very friendly to energy corporations, did little to curtail voracious American consumption and assure U.S. energy security. While the White House remained complacent as the price of oil climbed and oil company profits surged, upsetting many Americans, the U.S. dollar continued to depreciate, making other imports more expensive as well.[14]

Within seventeen months, the American economy was ailing due to weak consumer spending and the subprime mortgage crisis, which engendered a so-called credit crunch. As a recession loomed, a barrel of crude sold for nearly $100, which especially benefited exporters such as Russia and Venezuela, whose leaders, Vladimir Putin and Hugo Chavez, dominated their countries' politics and continued asserting themselves internationally. Despite the exorbitant price of oil, consumers kept pumping this precious refined liquid into their gas tanks now well aware of the ravages this and other fossil fuels had visited upon Planet Earth in previous decades thanks to destructive industrialization—which the People's Republic of China, the newest superpower, seemed intent on perpetuating in order to achieve its ambitious economic objectives. With Arctic ice melting at record pace in summer 2007, former U.S. Vice President Al Gore and the UN Intergovernmental Panel on Climate Change, co-winners in October of the Nobel Peace Prize, pointed to that bellwether as they urged nations at the December Bali conference to adopt eco-friendly policies in the hope such measures could stave off an environmental cataclysm. A calamity of a different sort ended the year: the assassination of Benazir Bhutto, the former prime minister of Pakistan who was seeking a third term. Her death, two weeks before a critical election, jarred that nuclear-armed South Asian country anew and exposed America's flawed policy, which depended on the ability of an illegitimate and unpopular autocrat, President Pervez Musharraf, to prevent Pakistani and Afghan Islamists associated with al-Qaeda and the Taliban from wreaking national, regional, and global havoc.[15]

Despair in Pakistan contrasted with the hope, however tenuous, that stirred the dormant Palestinian-Israeli peace process in November 2007. The Annapolis conference, the best attended meeting on this contentious, hitherto insoluble subject, committed the antagonists to a treaty by the end of 2008. Yet cynicism pervaded the conference's aftermath, as skeptical analysts spotlighted the main impediment to a successful conclusion to this acrimonious sixty-year dispute. Hamas (i.e., the Islamic Resistance Movement), a terrorist organization inveterately opposed to Israel's existence, held sway in the Gaza Strip following its defeat and expulsion of Fatah, its rival Palestinian faction, from the territory in June 2007. Fatah's Mahmoud Abbas, Israeli Prime Minister Ehud Olmert's interlocutor at Annapolis, remained in charge in the West Bank, but his party's future seemed very much in doubt. Nevertheless, the lame duck Bush administration wagered on Abbas as the man who could provide a historic signature on a document Bush could claim as his own, thereby assuring him some kind of positive foreign-policy legacy in the Middle East. With barely one year for U.S. Secretary of State Condoleezza Rice to secure a seminal agreement, which had eluded a fully engaged Bill Clinton seven years earlier, the odds seemed nearly impossible.[16]

Previous to Annapolis, the Bush administration, undoubtedly the most pro-Israeli in U.S. history, had contented itself with mostly half-hearted mediation efforts. Following Likud Party candidate Ariel Sharon's decisive electoral defeat of incumbent Ehud Barak in February 2001, the White House had rarely reprimanded the Israeli government. Early on, Prime Minister Sharon and his unity government vowed to ensure Israeli security, but acknowledged that they would have to work out a modus vivendi with the Palestinians lest Israel revert to a garrison state, a situation sure to hamper impressive Israeli economic growth and fray Israeli nerves. By the spring of that year, however, Israeli-Palestinian violence had increased many-fold. With several hundred dead Palestinians and a hundred or so Israelis killed, a war in all but name inflamed the Holy Land despite a U.S.-brokered cease-fire.[17]

The terrorist attacks in New York and Washington enabled Prime Minister Sharon to equate Israeli policy with America's "War on Terror." Busy with al-Qaeda, the Bush administration made no proposals to end the Israeli-Palestinian deadlock, offered no serious diplomatic mediation, and typically refused to chastise the Sharon government when it authorized new settlements in the Occupied Territories. Bush called for the creation of a Palestinian state by 2005, the first American president to do so, but also demanded that the Palestinian Authority democratize—thus tying Palestinian aspirations to Yasir Arafat's resignation as leader of that organization.

In January 2003, Israeli voters rewarded Sharon for his hard-line foreign policy with an easy electoral victory, although the country continued to experience acute insecurity and regular terrorist attacks. Obsessed with Saddam Hussein and Iraq, the White House, despite blueprints (i.e., the Mitchell Plan and the Abdullah Plan) to resolve the Palestinian-Israeli conflict, left it to the so-called Quartet—the United Nations, European Union, Russia, and the U.S. State Department—to sustain some kind of diplomatic pretense. Finally in May 2003, in the aftermath of the Second Persian Gulf War, the Bush administration reentered the diplomatic fray when it issued its "Road Map," a series of steps that would end the al-Aqsa *intifada*, create a Palestinian state within two years, provide Israel with security, and establish a Palestinian-Israeli peace. While many critics considered the Quartet-endorsed Road Map unachievable—either Sharon or Palestinian extremists, or both, would undermine it, many experts predicted—no better alternative existed. As evidence of the Road Map's early success, Washington could point to Mahmoud Abbas' election as Palestinian prime minister (and the concurrent marginalization of Arafat), Sharon's acknowledgment to his Likud Party that Israel could not sustain indefinitely its occupation (a term Likud usually avoided) of the West Bank and Gaza, and Hamas' and Islamic Jihad's acceptance of a three-month Palestinian-Israeli cease-fire.[18]

The Road Map's achievements proved ephemeral, however. Abbas resigned in September 2003. Tel Aviv erected a security fence, parts of which encroached upon Palestinian land—a trespass even Israel's Supreme Court would deem illegal in June 2004. The barrier symbolized the victory of division and separateness over conciliation and co-existence, yet most Israelis believed the wall would keep out suicide-homicide bombers. Despite the fence, Palestinian bombings continued, though less frequently than before, while the Israeli Army assassinated Sheik Ahmed Yassin, Hamas' spiritual head, and other terrorist leaders. Like boxers, each protagonist staggered whenever struck by a mighty blow, but kept throwing punches. With no winner, Israelis and Palestinians started to tire. After four years of *intifada*, the Israeli-Palestinian dispute remained unresolved, though the unofficial "Geneva Accord" of December 2003 provided yet another potential starting point. As a result of renewed stalemate, both Sharon and Arafat struggled politically. The former's effort to withdraw from Gaza stalled as Likud hardliners balked, while the latter refused to liberalize the Palestinian Authority even when his Arab brethren urged him to do so.[19]

With Iraq seeming to unravel, an obviously distracted Washington did nothing to halt Tel Aviv's settlements policy, which violated the provisions of the Road Map, other than express U.S. disapproval. Mild rebuke gave way to support for the beleaguered Sharon; in August 2004, the White House condoned restricted (i.e., "natural growth") settlement expansion in a transparent effort to garner votes for President Bush from American supporters of Israel. Such commission, following the April U.S. endorsement of the Israeli right to annex sections of the West Bank while denying Palestinians the "right of return," only embittered Arabs, most of whom considered the United States a dishonest broker incapable of ending the protracted Palestinian-Israeli conflict, which had intensified rather than abated since the 1993 Oslo Accords. Due to these setbacks, Arab hopes for a Palestinian state seemed dashed once more until, ironically, Arafat's death in November 2004 restored a semblance of hope to the moribund peace process. Arafat's successor, Abbas, pleased the Bush administration, which praised the new leader's January 2005 election as president of the Palestinian Authority, but kept the onus on him and other Palestinian leaders when it came to peace with Israel. Sharon also much preferred Abbas to Arafat. With Abbas in charge, Sharon could more easily withdraw Israeli settlers from Gaza (and a few West Bank settlements), which he did in August 2005—though only a bare majority of Israelis, 52 percent according to one poll, supported this most controversial of decisions.[20]

Despite these developments in Israel/Palestine, which Washington perceived as positive, the region failed to achieve peaceful co-existence. Once Hamas won the January 2006 parliamentary elections, moreover, Israel resumed its implacable policy toward the Palestinians. With Sharon in a coma following a stroke earlier that month, Prime Minister Ehud Olmert, who led Sharon's Kadima party to electoral victory in March, refused to interact with Hamas given its hostility toward Israel and terrorist standing. For similar reasons, the Bush administration ostracized Hamas via its "Three No's" policy (i.e., "no recognition, no dialogue, and no financial aid"), which contradicted the White House's Middle East democracy initiative, while favoring Abbas, who nevertheless could not overcome the Islamist party's popularity among Palestinians.[21]

In June 2006, Hamas kidnapped an Israeli soldier, which prompted Tel Aviv to retaliate with force. Hezbollah (i.e., the Party of God), a major Shi'ite party in Lebanon whose members served in Parliament and the Lebanese cabinet but whose militia, armed by Iran and Syria, existed in violation of UN Security Council Resolution 1559, then killed some Israeli troops and took two as hostages. This audacious cross-border raid by another terrorist organization and sworn enemy of Israel boomeranged into an Israeli invasion of southern Lebanon on July 12 that convulsed that country only a year after its so-called Cedar Revolution resulted in Syria's withdrawal after many years of occupation. Five weeks of nearly relentless fighting between Hezbollah and the Israeli Defense Forces shattered Lebanon's infrastructure, especially Shi'ite areas such as south Beirut. Meanwhile, northern Israel endured waves of Hezbollah-fired Katyusha rocket attacks. Eager to preserve the Lebanese government, which President Bush supported wholeheartedly, Washington tried to end the hostilities diplomatically, but not before encouraging Tel Aviv to "degrade" Hezbollah's capabilities. In a controversial move, especially considering Arab leaders' initial condemnation of Hezbollah, the United States sent weapons to Israel, a step that only antagonized ordinary Arabs, many of them already stridently anti-American. Arming Israel also isolated Arab reformers in the Middle East, the very individuals who could fulfil the Bush administration's fervent wish for democracy in that region. Most seriously, the White House's pro-Israeli policy threatened to complicate U.S. efforts to rehabilitate Iraq. Thankfully for the United States, the war finally ended on August 14 with Security Council Resolution 1701, which called for a cease-fire and 15,000 UN peacekeepers. Yet, with neither Israel nor Hezbollah admitting defeat, a war of attrition seemed to await the Levant, not at all the road map the Quartet had envisaged.[22]

As conflict in the Holy Land flared once more in the summer of 2006, Arab humiliation and frustration persisted, likely ensuring continued success for Hezbollah and other Islamic groups that promised the restoration of Arab pride, honor, and dignity, as well as delivery of health, education, and other essential services. Such promises, emanating from a political Islam considered moribund in the 1990s, but now clearly rejuvenated, presaged more violence since their fulfillment would likely require further confrontation with Israel and the West. Despite Hezbollah's psychological victory, which strengthened its position within the fragile Lebanese state and brought it acclaim throughout the region, the Middle East remained beset with political and economic shortcomings, as evidenced by the Arab Human Development Report, which in 2002 identified three "deficits"—freedom, women's rights, and knowledge. That same year, the Bush administration thought it could transform what it considered a fossilized Arab world—with its anachronistic authoritarians, sclerotic economies, and apparent abundance of suicidal-homicidal terrorists ready to murder scores of Israeli Jews and Americans in return for Islamic salvation—into a progressive, thriving, and, most importantly, friendlier area for both the United States and Israel, by toppling the man who incarnated the worst political, economic, and military trends in the Middle East: Saddam Hussein.[23]

Overthrowing Saddam

Ten years after *Operation Desert Storm*, Saddam Hussein struck many observers as untouchable and the Iraqi component of "dual containment" a political failure. In February 2001, President George W. Bush could only imitate his predecessor, Bill Clinton, when Hussein threatened U.S. interests once more. Bush ordered another round of attacks on Iraqi military targets. The president justified the reprisals by claiming that Iraq's improved anti-aircraft capabilities and aggressive tactics endangered British and American pilots patrolling the "no-fly" zones. But the raid may have only encouraged Baghdad to redouble its efforts to shoot down U.S. and UK aircraft over Iraq.[24]

Not content to rely simply on military strikes, the Bush administration revisited sanctions as a way to discipline the insolent Hussein regime. Secretary of State Colin Powell spoke of "smart" sanctions that targeted Saddam and his entourage instead of desperate Iraqi civilians. This tactic hardly impressed anyone, especially Arabs, and confirmed the bankruptcy and irrelevance of American policy. Making matters worse, Baghdad sold discounted oil to Turkey and Syria. These revenues contravened the UN Oil-for-Food program, but provided the Turks, Syrians, and Iraqi Kurds with much needed trade. Jordan benefited from similar, albeit UN-approved, commerce. While Hussein schemed to circumvent sanctions and in June 2001 withdrew from the Oil-for-Food program (whose mismanagement and corruption had advantaged him), in early July of that year the Russians helped Baghdad's cause by blocking a British-sponsored resolution designed to curb Iraqi suffering and endorsed by the Security Council's fourteen other members.[25]

Tired of Saddam's duplicity, many Republicans on Capitol Hill clamored for his removal via the 1998 Iraq Liberation Act, authorizing the White House to fund Iraqi dissidents. The Clinton administration had only half-heartedly endorsed the so-called rollback option, which many qualified analysts considered risible anyway. Disunity within the ranks of the Iraqi National Congress and other groups, in conjunction with Hussein's Stalinist tactics, made an overthrow a very unlikely possibility. Despite such odds, Bush officials did not rule out actively promoting regime change.[26]

The White House's opportunity to dislodge Hussein arose once al-Qaeda terrorists utilized three hijacked planes to fell New York City's Twin Towers and tear into the Pentagon. Within a week of the 9/11 attacks, President Bush ordered that something be done about the Hussein government. Secretary of Defense Donald Rumsfeld obliged the commander-in-chief by instructing General Tommy Franks, head of U.S. Central Command, to devise an invasion plan for Iraq. Although the interdiction of much illegal Iraqi commerce by the U.S. and Australian navies restricted Hussein's ability to import military items, the White House pressed on with its agenda to remove the Iraqi autocrat. Consistent with his nascent doctrine of preventive war, formally announced in September 2002, President Bush invoked Baghdad's WMD threat as a sufficient reason for America to attack Iraq. Secretary of State Powell insisted, however, that the United States seek international approval for its policy. Members of the president's inner circle—Vice President Dick Cheney, Rumsfeld, and Deputy Secretary of Defense Paul Wolfowitz—disparaged such a tactic, asserting that the United Nations would only impede the United States as it sought to achieve its foreign-policy objectives. Powell considered such thinking shortsighted and potentially very harmful to U.S. relations with its allies. Better to build up American credibility, the retired general argued, than waste it needlessly via some unpopular, unilateral U.S. venture.[27]

President Bush sided with Powell, who favored renewed inspections rather than a hasty invasion. In fall 2002 at the UN General Assembly, Bush urged member states to tackle the Iraq issue to ensure that the world's premier international organization carried out its obligation to uphold global peace. Following the president's speech, Security Council members worked feverishly to craft a resolution that allowed the United Nations Monitoring, Inspection, and Verification Commission (UNMOVIC), still barred by Hussein from entering Iraq, to inspect Iraqi facilities suspected of WMD activity. On November 8, the Security Council voted unanimously to approve Resolution 1441, which promised "serious consequences" should Iraq not fully comply. President Bush and British Prime Minister Tony Blair, whose solidarity with the U.S. position ingratiated him to the White House and thus earned him input into American policy, wanted explicit authorization to wage war on Iraq, should Hussein thwart UN will. France, Russia, and the People's Republic of China strenuously objected, however. As a result, the permanent, veto-wielding members of the Security Council bickered over whether a second resolution would be necessary to sanction a military campaign to disarm Iraq. Washington and London said no; Paris, Moscow, and Beijing took a contrary view. Previous to the approval of Resolution 1441, members of the U.S. Congress expressed confidence in the president's policy by authorizing him to use whatever means he considered appropriate to enforce Iraq's compliance with UN resolutions. The timing of the vote, just before the Congressional election, hamstrung many Democrats, who risked alienating constituents if they opposed the measure.[28]

With only minimal dissent from Democrats and rousing support from fellow Republicans (who in November took back the Senate and increased their advantage in the House of Representatives), President Bush used his January 2003 State of the Union Address to deliver an ultimatum: either the Security Council honored its commitment to disarm Iraq or the world's most exclusive political club risked forfeiting its relevance. The commander-in-chief also informed ordinary Iraqis that the United States intended to emancipate them from Saddam Hussein's slavery. That day's initial UN inspectors' report confirmed Bush's impatience with the Iraqi government. UNMOVIC head Hans Blix reproached Baghdad for its unwillingness to account for, or disclose the whereabouts of, certain weapons components and quantities of various chemical and biological agents.[29]

Bolstered by Blix's remarks, Bush promised that Secretary of State Powell would unveil damning evidence at the Security Council to convince skeptics, especially France and Germany, of Baghdad's duplicitous ways and connect Hussein to al-Qaeda, an administration contention that most terrorism, intelligence, and Middle East experts doubted or disbelieved. Powell's presentation swayed many Americans, yet Paris and Berlin still opposed the proposed American remedy to Iraqi deceit. French Foreign Minister Dominique de Villepin, who reportedly so irritated Powell when he hinted that France would never approve an attack on Iraq that the secretary of state joined the so-called hawks in the Bush administration in pushing for an invasion, advocated instead that the number of inspectors be doubled or tripled.[30]

Despite Blix's apparent validation of its assertions, the Bush administration struggled to present a coherent rationale for intervention in Iraq—it would advocate twenty-three justifications for war, according to one researcher. Oddly, Bush officials refused publicly to invoke the precedents of Bosnia and Kosovo to justify their call for Saddam Hussein's removal. Perhaps these Republicans considered "humanitarian intervention," Bill Clinton's reason for sending U.S. forces overseas, impolitic. To avoid any comparisons to their detested predecessor, the president and his Reaganite advisors emulated their political hero (who promoted democracy in Central America while U.S. surrogates such as the Contras trampled upon the rights of ordinary Latin Americans) when they announced that the United States would seek to democratize Iraq, whose example hopefully would spur neighbors to imitate it. Cynics blew raspberries at this idea of occupation à la Germany and Japan circa 1945, which they considered preposterous given the near absence of any democratic tradition in the Arab world. Furthermore, they doubted Washington would want to spend years inculcating Iraqi society with democratic theory and habits and to invest the billions of dollars necessary to fashion a successful liberal economy.[31]

When confronted with such derision, the White House conjured up the specter of a WMD attack upon the United States in an attempt to quell criticism of its policy. This appeal to fear of a possible, rather than probable, calamity likely convinced many Americans, a majority of whom consented to a war whether or not the Security Council approved one. As long as some U.S. allies endorsed American policy, nearly 60 percent favored intervention, according to a *Washington Post-ABC News* poll. Americans only expressed lukewarm support (44 percent), however, for a lengthy and costly U.S. occupation.[32]

With scarce knowledge of what could transpire in postwar Iraq, Defense and State Department officials hardly reassured U.S. senators when they testified before the Foreign Relations Committee. Under Secretary of Defense for Policy Douglas Feith conceded that American forces would occupy Iraq for two years at a cost of at least $15 billion per year. This minimum sum contrasted with those analysts who believed that a war and its aftermath would tally in the hundreds of billions of dollars. In an era of spiraling budget deficits, due to Bush tax cuts and exorbitant expenses for homeland as well as national security, additional fiscal burdens courtesy of an invasion and occupation potentially promised bruising economic times.[33]

Notwithstanding the uncertainty sure to result from any invasion, the momentum toward warfare seemed inexorable. An audiotape of Osama bin Laden, urging Muslims to stand shoulder to shoulder with their Iraqi brethren to repel any American incursion, seemed to link al-Qaeda to Saddam Hussein. Yet bin Laden expressed personal disdain for the secular leader, whom Islamists still sought to overthrow. Excited to spotlight Hussein's complicity with al-Qaeda, the Bush administration seemed to overlook the possibility that bin Laden and his cohorts could benefit immensely from a U.S. intervention. With Hussein eliminated, al-Qaeda could infiltrate Iraq and eventually establish a power base within the country. An American attack would also probably facilitate recruitment of new members.[34]

Primarily concerned with its public-relations effort to convince recalcitrant Americans and allies to sign on to U.S. policy, the Bush administration awaited the February 14 weapons inspectors' report to the Security Council. An indictment of Iraq would enable the White House to press its case for an immediate invasion—the preferred military timetable called for an early to mid-March start date, when 250,000 or so U.S. soldiers would be ready for combat in the Persian Gulf. With the United States poised to present a pro-invasion resolution co-sponsored with the British, and with a majority of Americans in favor of war without UN authorization, Blix dashed U.S. hopes for further confirmation of Iraqi obstruction when he reported to the Security Council some improvement in Baghdad's cooperation with UNMOVIC. To Powell's indignation, Blix even questioned the secretary of state's conclusions from the previous week regarding videotapes and intercepted communications that supposedly underscored Iraqi violations of Resolution 1441. Mohamed ElBaradei, the head of the International Atomic Energy Agency, stated, moreover, that his team could find no evidence of either Iraqi nuclear weapons or an active Iraqi nuclear program.[35]

The Bush administration disputed Blix's and ElBaradei's findings and opinions. As it defended itself, several million anti-war protesters in cities and towns worldwide vocalized their displeasure with Washington's rush to war. They refuted the White House's various rationales for intervention and offered alternative explanations for, and thoughts on, the Bush administration's haste—summarized in pithy and irreverent placard slogans such as "Sacrifice Our SUVs, Not Our Children," "Let's Bomb Texas, They Have Oil Too," "Empires Fall," "Let Exxon Send Their Troops," "9-11-01: 15 Saudis, 0 Iraqis," "America's Problems Won't Be Solved in Iraq," "War Is Expensive, Peace Is Priceless," and "How Many Lives Per Gallon." In Washington, London, Rome, and many other venues, dissenters of various political, religious, and ideological stripes—pacifists, Marxists, Christians, Jews, Muslims, mothers, veterans, critics of globalization, and many others—chanted "No Blood for Oil," reprising the cliché bandied on the eve of the previous war in the Persian Gulf.[36]

A determined President Bush seemed convinced, however, of his policy's correctness and sure of his own righteousness. He and his advisors dismissed the claims, which they considered spurious, of critics who suspected a U.S.-ExxonMobil conspiracy to seize Iraq's oil resources. With Baghdad apparently intending to torch Iraqi oil fields should an invasion occur, the White House denial seemed credible, especially when coupled with administration assurances that it would instruct American occupation officials to use Iraqi crude to pay for the rebuilding of the country's infrastructure—already shattered after years of war, international sanctions, and misrule. Such promises underwhelmed many opponents of Bush's policy, who could recite numerous occasions when the U.S. government reneged on its word or plain lied. Passionate opposition to Washington's proposed course of action confirmed that the memory of Vietnam, a searing experience and a seminal event in the country's recent history, remained vivid for many skeptical Americans, whether inexperienced students, veteran protesters, or simply concerned citizens.[37]

Elites in western Europe added their doubts to those of the U.S. and their continent's masses. Disagreement over how to deal with Iraq exposed a deep rift within NATO. France, Germany, and Belgium opposed arming Turkey so that it could defend itself, should Iraq attack it. British Prime Minister Blair and his Spanish counterpart, Jose Maria Aznar, zealously supported Bush, a stance which earned both leaders continued brickbats at home. Eventually, the allies resolved the issue to American satisfaction, but this victory threatened to turn Pyrrhic when Ankara informed Washington it would not approve American use of its bases unless the United States awarded Turkey $32 billion in loans, loan guarantees, and grants. Ankara's revised demands incensed the Bush administration, which considered its previous offer of a $26 billion package exceedingly generous. Finally, the two sides settled on $15 billion in assistance. With Turkey in mind, some U.S. observers bemoaned the prohibitive cost of recruiting partners—what Secretary of Defense Rumsfeld referred to as a "coalition of the willing" and editorialist Paul Krugman called the "coalition of the bought off"—in this potentially risky Middle East endeavor.[38]

As the White House struggled to persuade non-permanent Security Council members (such as Guinea, Cameroon, and Angola) and other governments whose populations vociferously opposed war in the Middle East, irate U.S. officials issued ultimata in a concerted effort to dragoon states reluctant to endorse American policy despite the promise of significant financial rewards. U.S. heavy-handedness and arrogance on the part of some American decision-makers—to wit, Rumsfeld's caustic reference to France and Germany as "Old Europe"—corroded America's ties with its traditional partners and friends, some of which, notably the French and Germans, sought to rein in or even corral U.S. power. Still, the White House seemed either not to care or simply expected the Europeans, Australians, Japanese, and Canadians, whose compromise UN resolution proved futile, to follow the American lead or risk irrelevance.[39]

U.S. intransigence only frustrated friends and embittered enemies. But on February 21, with Americans weary after weeks of endless discussions regarding Iraq's fate, Hans Blix unexpectedly buoyed Bush administration spirits when he called on Baghdad to dispose expeditiously of its al-Samoud 2 missiles and rocket technology, specifically foreign-made engines. When fired, the al-Samoud

2s could strike targets over one hundred miles away, surpassing the UN-imposed limit of ninety-two. According to U.S. intelligence, such missiles could transport weapons of mass destruction, making Israel, Kuwait, and Saudi Arabia—and U.S. forces in these Arab countries—vulnerable to an Iraqi chemical or biological attack.[40]

Though the Iraqis started to dismantle the al-Samoud 2s, the Bush administration relentlessly pressed its case for intervention. Turkish legislators dismayed the White House, however, when they denied the U.S. military access to their country's bases for the purpose of invading adjacent Iraqi territory. This refusal, which mirrored majority public sentiment in Turkey, complicated American war plans; deprived of a two-front strategy, U.S. and British infantry could only enter Iraq via Kuwait.[41]

At the Security Council, Washington continued to clash with the French, Germans, Russians, Chinese, and Secretary-General Kofi Annan, who opposed any non-UN-sanctioned use of force in Iraq. Despite this opposition, the United States, United Kingdom, and Spain submitted a resolution asking for exactly that. American diplomats lobbied the other Security Council countries intensely in a Sisyphean effort to recruit them to the U.S.-UK-Spanish position. The Bush administration hoped to persuade nine members; even if a permanent member vetoed the proposal, support from a Council majority would have satisfied the White House. With an unsuccessful vote likely to embarrass Washington and London, the pro-invasion threesome withdrew its proposal in mid-March.[42]

Although British Prime Minister Blair's Labour Party clamored for a UN mandate, President Bush ignored—presumably unintentionally—his partner's political needs to satisfy his own. Having accused Saddam Hussein of ruthless and unpardonable crimes, and of harboring weapons of mass destruction with the intent to strike U.S. targets or arm anti-American terrorists, the self-assured Texan could not back down without forfeiting his own as well as his country's credibility and disappointing the 71 percent of Americans, according to an *ABC News/Washington Post* poll, who approved of war in Iraq. Bush thus issued an ultimatum on March 17. If Hussein did not disarm to U.S. satisfaction within forty-eight hours, then Washington would attack Iraq and depose Hussein. Unlike *Operation Desert Storm*, General Franks' Op Plan 1003 V, codenamed "Cobra II," emphasized speed, versatility, joint service operations, and extensive use of Special Operations Forces—utilized so successfully in Afghanistan. To carry out this blitzkrieg, Franks, at Rumsfeld's urging, would rely on technological prowess, a featured component of the so-called Revolution in Military Affairs, and on far fewer soldiers than General Norman Schwarzkopf had twelve years before.[43]

Predictably, the unsavvy Hussein, who apparently thought war improbable or, if unleashed, confined to an air campaign his regime could survive, rejected Bush's demand. On March 19, when seemingly reliable intelligence—courtesy of the U.S. DB/ROCKSTARS spy network in Iraq—persuaded the president to authorize a "decapitation strike" aimed at Hussein and his sons, American missiles and heavy bombs crashed into an Iraqi government facility, thereby initiating *Operation Iraqi Freedom*. While Iraq's despot seemed to have survived this opening salvo, his regime endured a relentless barrage of U.S. high-tech weaponry, courtesy of the Pentagon's "Shock and Awe" strategy, in the first week of this second Persian Gulf war. Unlike *Operation Desert Storm*, American and British ground forces proceeded into Iraq while the air assault continued.[44]

Taking southern Iraqi Shi'ite towns such as Basra proved far more difficult than expected, however, as some Iraqi units fought fiercely. Perhaps more worrisome to the Bush administration, which seemed to believe pre-war claims by Iraqi exiles that their brethren would acclaim coalition soldiers, most inhabitants did not cheer the arriving Westerners—with Hussein presumed alive, Iraqis likely worried that he would suppress them bitterly should the Americans abandon them once more. Despite these setbacks, which the White House considered minor, tanks and armored personnel carriers from the Third Infantry Division dashed toward Baghdad. This maneuver created an extended supply line vulnerable to repeated attacks by the Fedayeen Saddam, whose members wreaked temporary havoc on U.S. forces by relying on guerilla tactics. Ambushes of American convoys resulted in casualties and prisoners of war paraded on al-Jazeera. Sand storms, which halted the U.S. Army, compounded early American setbacks, turning the second week of the war into a public-relations disaster for the Bush administration. Based on these distressing events, most print and electronic media worldwide forecast a difficult and lengthy campaign to depose Saddam Hussein.[45]

As the weather improved, so did U.S. and UK prospects for victory. The British surrounded Basra, the key city in southern Iraq. Meanwhile, from the air and on land, the Americans battled Republican Guard units, considered Hussein's finest, as well as Iraqi regulars and irregulars in An Nasiriyah, Najaf, Al Kut, Al Hillah, and Karbala. U.S. soldiers also joined Kurdish *peshmergas* fighting Saddam's army in northern Iraq. To the relief of British and U.S. commanders, the Iraqis never fired chemical or biological weapons. Without these attacks, the branches of the American military (Army, Air Force, Marines, Navy, and their Special Forces) worked in unison—as called for in the Pentagon's revised modus operandi—to pummel the ineffective and disorganized Iraqi Army. On April 4, with the Republican Guard in disarray, the Third Infantry Division seized the Baghdad airport.[46]

The American advance on the Iraqi capital inflicted heavy damage and yielded mounting enemy casualties. Iraqi civilian deaths and injuries increased as well. International opinion of the war wavered as the Arab media consistently spotlighted this facet of the war while glossing over Saddam Hussein's past persecution of Iraqi citizens. The U.S. television networks, on the other hand, parroted the Bush administration's interpretation of events while mostly shielding the American public from scenes of death and destruction, the gruesome yet unavoidable consequences of warfare.[47]

Arab and U.S. media may have reported the conflict differently, but their cameras could not distort its swift conclusion. Third Infantry Division soldiers and Marines maneuvered their tanks and vehicles toward downtown Baghdad. They overcame Iraqi resistance easily and quickly. On April 9, with no government or Ba'th Party officials to defend Saddam Hussein's regime, the Americans assisted jubilant Iraqis as they tore down statues of Hussein and other despised symbols of their oppressor's decades of tyrannical rule. One Marine even briefly covered a replica of Saddam's face with a U.S. flag, a gesture that must have horrified White House and Pentagon officials eager to characterize this American invasion as one of liberation, not imperial conquest.[48]

Postwar Iraq fell into mayhem as Washington and London prepared to occupy a country of some twenty-seven million mostly embittered residents. While Iraqis ransacked their homeland, the Pentagon dithered—U.S. soldiers merely watched as Iraqis looted presidential palaces, museums, shops, and government buildings and facilities. When Shi'ite clergy returned from exile in Iran to claim positions of authority and organize their followers, Secretary of Defense Rumsfeld thundered that the United States would never allow an Iranian-style theocracy in Iraq. As the U.S. Army worked to feed a hungry population and restore potable water and electricity, Iraqis grumbled. The slow return of basic services stoked anti-American sentiment—not the scenario the Bush administration had hoped for when it drew up plans for the reconstruction of Iraq.[49]

Although the State Department had developed many of those plans, courtesy of the "Future of Iraq" project, the Pentagon, via Retired Lieutenant General Jay Garner, oversaw initial U.S. efforts to rebuild Iraqi institutions and infrastructure—while mostly ignoring Foggy Bottom's recommendations. To help Garner succeed, the White House convinced the Security Council to rescind decade-old sanctions, designed to penalize the Hussein regime, and phase out within six months the Oil-for-Food program. In Resolution 1483, the Security Council also agreed to entrust the Americans and British with the reconstruction of Iraq. L. Paul Bremer III soon replaced Garner, whose managerial efforts presaged a woeful U.S. administration of Iraq. As head of the Coalition Provisional Authority (CPA), the more resolute Bremer sought to reestablish as expeditiously as possible internal security as well as some sort of rule of law. The transition to an interim Iraqi government made up of Iraqi exiles, Shi'ite clergy, and Kurds would thus have to wait, a decision that left some of those Iraqis eager to govern seething. To achieve his objective, Bremer needed more American soldiers, not less, especially once he disbanded the Iraqi Army, an ill-considered move that left hundreds of thousands of disgruntled Iraqis unemployed and thus susceptible to recruitment by various anti-American militias. Realizing its manpower shortage, the Pentagon, which had previously wanted to withdraw most of its personnel by the fall of 2003, extended many units' tours of duty in Iraq and assigned the

Fourth Infantry Division, which would have invaded Iraq from Turkey had Ankara given permission, to help out as well.[50]

As the Bush administration girded itself for a lengthy and probably difficult occupation—with Arabs stunned and humiliated once more by yet another Western-inflicted defeat, with a democratic, prosperous, and U.S.-allied Iraqi federation only a dream, and with Washington's record of democratization less than stellar—critics wondered why the American military could not find Saddam Hussein, dead or alive, or any weapons of mass destruction, one of the rationales for invading Iraq and ousting its tyrant. Disenchanted members of the intelligence community accused the Pentagon, specifically the Office of the Secretary of Defense, of manipulating information so that it meshed with White House policy. Whether President Bush and his advisors overstated the Iraqi WMD threat would not alter the outcome of the Second Persian Gulf War, however. One hundred and fifty thousand or so U.S. soldiers now occupied Iraq, the heartland of the Middle East—far fewer than Army General Eric Shinseki's preinvasion recommendation to Congress of several hundred thousand, which Paul Wolfowitz dismissed as "wildly off the mark."[51]

As the supreme authority in a country with vast oil resources and significant geopolitical importance, the Bush administration hoped to transform its victory in Iraq into a revamped Middle East more compatible with American interests—i.e., a region more friendly to Israel and safe from threats to petroleum supplies and crude prices. While the Pentagon planned to add strategically important bases in Iraq to its Middle Eastern network, many Iraqis resented the American presence. Some of them, probably Ba'th Party members and others associated with the deposed Hussein regime, attacked and killed U.S. servicemen regularly. Most American military personnel lacked adequate training for their post-combat mission and could not look forward to an early withdrawal from Iraq, yet by May 1 the White House considered the military facet of *Operation Iraqi Freedom* concluded. President Bush's "Mission Accomplished" speech-cum-2004 reelection advertisement aboard the aircraft carrier USS *Abraham Lincoln* allowed the commander-in-chief to celebrate American martial prowess and his administration's policy.[52]

Unfortunately for Bush, his celebration proved premature as events in Iraq in the months that followed bore out the prewar contention of several analysts that many conquered Iraqis would resist the Western invaders. Given America's historic aversion to colonialism, Washington should have been eager to allow Iraqis to govern themselves. The Bush administration yearned for just such a scenario, yet instability in Iraq precluded an early withdrawal of U.S. soldiers and bureaucrats. To stem Iraqi resentment of the American-led occupation, in July 2003 CPA head Paul Bremer approved a "governing council," made up of some twenty-five Iraqis representing different secular and religious political factions—Kurdish, Sunni, Shi'ite, Turkmen, and Christian. While the council's efficacy could not be predicted, at least Bremer responded to majority Iraqi sentiment.[53]

The same could not be said, however, for the Bush administration's answer to others who wanted to help the Iraqis. The White House could have made efficient use of the United Nations, non-governmental organizations (NGOs), and allies such as France, Germany, and Canada, to rebuild and "resocialize" Iraq into a so-called model country—by Western and 2002 Arab Human Development Report standards—that other states in the Middle East could emulate. Instead, a spiteful Washington mostly refused assistance except from states that supported its war policy (i.e., the United Kingdom, Australia, Poland, and a host of countries, such as Colombia, that received U.S. military and economic aid). Ironically, a significant multilateral effort—complete with multinational peacekeeping force, development experts from various UN agencies and NGOs, and substantial financial contributions from UN members—could have reinforced the U.S. role in the Persian Gulf. In such a context, Iraqis could have blamed many nationalities and organizations—not just the Americans—for the inevitable societal woes that follow war. Conversely, a concerted international push to rehabilitate Iraq could have ensured quicker success, added much needed legitimacy to such an effort, and allowed the United States to revert to its preferred role in the region—that of guardian and "offshore balancer."[54]

By mid-summer 2003, U.S. officials finally seemed to have awoken to the occupation's perils. Although substantial UN assistance could have helped remedy a variety of military, political, and administrative problems, the Bush administration, which had previously scorned the United Nations, welcomed only those contributions (such as the August 14 Security Council resolution that condoned the Iraqi Governing Council and created the United Nations Assistance Mission for Iraq) that did not undermine American authority under Resolution 1483. Without an additional Security Council resolution, however, India and other countries prepared to rebuild Iraq under an expanded international mandate refused to aid the Americans (and the British) as they tried to restore within a year or so what would presumably be pro-U.S. Iraqi civilian rule. If Washington could somehow have satisfied the Security Council, or vice-versa, then the United States could have striven to dissolve its *formal* empire in Iraq while incorporating that country into its expanding *informal* empire in the Persian Gulf. As fall beckoned, such a possibility seemed remote as the Bush administration continued to spurn most multilateral solutions. U.S. colonialism would thus continue indefinitely—not what one would expect in a post-colonial era, but maybe entirely understandable in a post–September 11 context.[55]

The August 19 truck bomb that tore into UN headquarters in Baghdad and killed Sergio Vieira de Mello, a most capable and seasoned diplomat whom the White House had wanted appointed as Kofi Annan's special envoy in post-Saddam Iraq, made the Bush administration rethink its approach once more. Increased sabotage (e.g., the cutting of oil and water pipelines), the bombing of the

Jordanian Embassy in the Iraqi capital earlier in the month, the August 29 assassination of a prominent pro-American Shi'ite cleric, and continued attacks on U.S. soldiers belied optimistic statements by Bush officials. With American deaths since May 1 exceeding the total from the combat phase of *Operation Iraqi Freedom*, Washington could not deny that Baghdad and other cities remained unsafe and that a guerilla war, likely involving al-Qaeda and other Islamists, was well underway. To improve U.S. political fortunes, administration critics counseled that either a NATO (perhaps under Norwegian leadership) or UN multinational force (possibly under American command) be sent to Iraq to assist the U.S. military and the Coalition Provisional Authority as well as to protect UN and NGO personnel. Whether the Pentagon could acquiesce to such a scenario (which would resemble missions in Somalia, Bosnia, Kosovo, and Afghanistan) remained unclear, however, on the eve of the second anniversary of 9/11. Yet a unified American command, the Department of Defense's preferred modus operandi, might seem less critical to the occupation's success should France, Germany, and other wealthy countries agree to invest billions of dollars in Iraqi reconstruction in exchange for some, probably limited, UN political and military authority. A Donors conference, scheduled for October, promised continued diplomatic wrangling as the White House tried to lessen its financial burden in Iraq while not weakening America's central role as principal occupying power.[56]

At the Donors conference in Madrid, several countries, as well as the World Bank and International Monetary Fund, pledged millions of dollars (totaling some $9 billion in loans and $4 billion in grants) to rebuild Iraq, but other than Japan, no state offered a substantial amount that could be added to U.S. assistance. France and Germany, vociferous opponents of the war, refused to commit financial resources other than the small sum the European Union promised. Russia and the People's Republic of China, two other prominent critics of *Operation Iraqi Freedom*, made no contribution.[57]

UN Security Council Resolution 1511, adopted on October 16, authorized America to rehabilitate Iraq via a U.S.-led occupation, yet forced Washington to shoulder much of the financial burden for Iraqi reconstruction. As a result, the White House asked Congress that fall to appropriate $87 billion: $68.4 billion to pay for U.S. military expenditures in Iraq and Afghanistan and $18.6 billion for myriad Iraqi infrastructure and other projects. Angry Democrats on Capitol Hill pressed U.S. officials for clarifications. Senators asked, for example, how the Bush administration could saddle American taxpayers with this kind of financial responsibility without explaining how the United States intended to proceed with its occupation of Iraq. Ill-conceived postwar planning and mounting American casualties in the so-called Sunni Triangle, the area north and west of Baghdad, did not stop Republican majorities, however, from approving President Bush's $87 billion request.[58]

Although the White House secured funds for Iraq's rehabilitation, it could not hide increasing insurgent or terrorist attacks—exactly what the invasion sought to prevent—from ordinary Americans, many of whom would vote in the following year's presidential election. Having seized supervision for *Operation Iraqi Freedom* from Secretary of Defense Rumsfeld following the creation of the Iraq Stabilization Group, National Security Advisor Condoleezza Rice grappled with an increasingly worrisome situation. Despite President Bush's impassioned talk of democratizing the Islamic Middle East, starting with Iraq, a two-year occupation, which the U.S. military had committed to originally, now seemed politically unfeasible given the unrest in that country. To remedy this problem, the White House instructed CPA head Paul Bremer to negotiate with the Iraqi Governing Council a transfer of authority. The November 15 agreement provided for a restoration of Iraq's sovereignty on June 30, 2004. The multi-step process and complicated formula that would result in renewed Iraqi self-government seemed ambitious. Iraqis would have to craft an interim constitution, or Basic Law, and grasp the intricacies of a convoluted caucus system that eventually would yield a transitional national assembly. Critics doubted that the Iraqis, inexperienced in the ways of Western representative democracy, could pull off such a Herculean feat in seven or so months. Apparently more concerned with President Bush's political difficulties and the potential boon that an early withdrawal could provide to his reelection bid, the White House dismissed initial critiques of its plan, calling them unfounded. Persistent criticisms, however, prompted U.S. officials to consider alternatives.[59]

In December, the Bush administration annoyed its war critics—Canada, France, Germany, Russia, and the People's Republic of China—once more when it barred them from bidding on U.S. reconstruction contracts in Iraq. At the same time, Washington called on these same countries, as well as others, to forgive Iraqi debts owed to them. With the Americans seemingly ensnared in Iraq, yet indelicate in their demands, Saddam Hussein's former creditors did not care to help out an ungrateful White House.[60]

As the Iraqi occupation continued to infuriate many in the United States and the international community, American soldiers discovered Saddam Hussein on December 13 hiding in a spider hole near his hometown of Tikrit. A jubilant Bush administration hoped that the deposed dictator would reveal the locations of his regime's weapons of mass destruction, which David Kay's Iraq Survey Group could not find. Following Hussein's capture, U.S. Special Envoy and former Secretary of State James A. Baker III garnered several important pledges: formerly recalcitrant countries such as France and Germany promised to forgive significant amounts of Iraqi debt.[61]

After a brief period of euphoria, the new year delivered only glum Iraq news. U.S. soldiers continued to die in attacks, as did scores of Iraqis. Insurgents also killed foreign servicemen from other *Operation Iraqi Freedom* countries. Compounding American difficulties, the Kurds insisted on retaining their autonomy within a federal Iraq, thereby jeopardizing the U.S. preference for an ethnically united state—a segregated country could yield civil war, Middle East experts believed. Most worrisome for the Bush administration, Grand Ayatollah Ali al-Sistani, the most prominent Iraqi Shi'ite cleric, objected to the November 15 agreement. Rather than endorse regional caucuses that would result in appointments to a transitional assembly, Sistani called for national elections. To impress his point upon Washington, he ordered demonstrations in favor of his preferred solution. The Bush administration contended that elections could not be held before the June 30 transfer-of-authority deadline due to inadequate voter registration lists and other problems, such as inadequate security in some areas of Iraq. Analyst Dilip Hiro and Iraqi Shi'a, who constituted 60 or so percent of the country's population and thus ought to possess a majority of seats in any Iraqi legislature, disputed the U.S. assertion. To satisfy Sistani, a reclusive individual with whom American officials found it difficult to communicate, the White House asked UN Secretary-General Kofi Annan to send a team to assess the viability of short-term elections. Annan considered the task appropriate for his organization to tackle, but wanted to ensure the safety of his personnel. After the horrific bombing of August 19, 2003, that destroyed UN headquarters in Baghdad, the secretary-general did not want his employees in harm's way. In early February 2004, with the White House reconsidering its Iraqi blueprint, Annan agreed to the U.S. request. This initial step presaged perhaps an eventual UN administrative takeover of Iraq following the scheduled end of the American occupation on June 30.[62]

As the Bush administration struggled to recruit a recalcitrant United Nations, a partner it would most certainly need to usher in Iraqi self-rule, David Kay resigned as head of the Iraq Survey Group. The former chief weapons inspector ignited a political firestorm, fanned by Democrats in Congress and journalists (several of whom had not dared criticize the prewar U.S. rationale for removing Saddam Hussein's regime), by asserting that Iraq did not possess any weapons of mass destruction—confirming the assessments of the United Nations and the International Atomic Energy Agency, which the Bush administration had ridiculed in the weeks before *Operation Iraqi Freedom*. With the White House's principal casus belli seemingly invalidated, critics of the Second Persian Gulf War called for an investigation of pre-war U.S. intelligence. President Bush soon ordered an inquiry (with a report due in March 2005, four months after the presidential election), which he surely believed would exonerate him just as the Hutton Report had absolved UK Prime Minister Tony Blair of any responsibility for faulty information regarding Hussein's WMD arsenal. To ensure that outcome, Bush's executive order directed commission members, only one of whom had served as a member of the intelligence community, to examine how the Central Intelligence Agency (CIA) could have overestimated so egregiously Iraq's WMD capability while underestimating that of other countries, such as North Korea, Iran, Afghanistan, and Libya. Interestingly, Bush's list omitted Pakistan, a valued ally in the War on Terror, which for years had exported nuclear technology to U.S. enemies. Unlike his friend Blair, who allowed a similar British investigation to examine how the Labour government utilized UK intelligence to advocate military intervention in Iraq, Bush precluded investigators from assessing how his administration used CIA estimates to trumpet war in the Middle East.[63]

The White House's political expediency may have temporarily sheltered it from the slings of its increasingly emboldened critics—and, more importantly, soothed undecided Americans who might otherwise vote for Democrat John Kerry in the fall presidential election—but events in Iraq belied administration optimism that the country would reinvent itself quickly as an economically successful liberal democracy. Despite some noteworthy achievements, such as the March 8, 2004, signing of an interim Iraqi constitution that, according to *The Washington Post*, would "create the most progressive, democratic government in the Arab world," grim accounts from Iraq failed to reassure most Americans that their government could win the War on Terror—not when al-Qaeda terrorist bombings in Madrid on March 11, just days before a national election, only heightened U.S. insecurity and prompted Spaniards to vote in the Socialists, who were committed to Spain's withdrawal from Iraq.[64]

For the Bush administration, however, losing Jose Maria Aznar's unwavering support for U.S. policy—despite the White House's postwar blunders, refusal to admit to any mistakes, and inability to explicate who would succeed the Coalition Provisional Authority on June 30 (supposedly a UN matter)—paled in comparison with American loss of life on the battlefield. Every month, dozens of U.S. soldiers died trying to extinguish a raging two-front Iraqi insurgency. The American military tangled with Sunni militiamen (which likely included Ba'thists and non-Iraqi members of al-Qaeda) in Fallujah as well as other cities and towns in the Sunni Triangle. In Najaf and other Shi'ite strongholds, the U.S. Army and Marine Corps fought Muqtada al-Sadr's Mahdi Army. Repeated clashes yielded scores of Iraqi deaths and injuries, not the kind of result, President Bush acknowledged, likely to ingratiate natives to their occupiers. Making matters worse for Washington, insurgents abducted foreigners working in Iraq and executed some of them—with gruesome videos of decapitations testifying to the captors' ruthlessness.[65]

Lest Americans gain comfort that their soldiers eschewed the barbaric ways of the enemy, in April photographs taken months earlier at the Abu Ghraib prison near Baghdad stripped the United States of its claim to moral superiority. Though the Bush administration dismissed U.S. abuses of Iraqi prisoners as confined to the misjudgment of just a few guards and interrogators, world opinion did not discriminate. Subsequent U.S. investigations, such as the August 2004 Schlesinger Report, reprimanded both military and civilian leaders, including Secretary of Defense Rumsfeld, who did not resign following the scandal, for fostering a sadistic interrogation climate in Iraq (as well as Afghanistan and Guantánamo Bay, Cuba) that enabled Americans to flout the anti-torture provisions of the Geneva Conventions. Instead of upholding human rights in Iraq,

America had betrayed its prewar rhetoric in, ironically, the most notorious of Saddam Hussein's torture chambers. No matter how clever its public relations, the Bush White House could not efface such misdeeds. They reverberated throughout the world, especially in Muslim countries eager to pillory American efforts in Iraq.[66]

To deny insurgents an opportunity to disrupt the June 30 transition, as well as to rehabilitate its reputation and evidently improve the president's odds for reelection, the Bush administration transferred authority in Iraq, the country it had occupied since April 2003, two days early. On June 28, 2004, having repeatedly revised in the previous months America's woeful occupation policy (which relied on too few soldiers and military police and spent too little—only $600 million of the $18.4 billion available—on reconstruction projects that could benefit ordinary Iraqis), CPA head Paul Bremer, with UN assistance (especially that of Lakhdar Brahimi, special adviser to Secretary-General Kofi Annan), returned Iraqi sovereignty to a Security Council–approved (via Resolution 1546, adopted on June 8) interim government led by Prime Minister Ayad Allawi, a prewar Shi'ite exile and former Ba'th Party member under Hussein known more for his forceful manner than his commitment to democracy. American and coalition forces remained, however, thereby circumscribing Iraq's self-determination. Their main task, to which NATO agreed to contribute, consisted of assisting Iraqi authorities in the pacification and rebuilding of their battered state. When the Americans might exit Iraq, no one knew. Would they eventually withdraw to remote bases and adopt a stealthier profile, thus reprising the preferred U.S. modus operandi in the Persian Gulf, or would they imitate the British, who occupied Iraq from 1917 until 1932 (when their League of Nations mandate expired) but remained very influential in that country until the July 1958 coup overthrew the UK-backed monarchy? Whitehall also repeatedly promised to vacate Egypt following the invasion of 1882, but did not leave until the 1954 Anglo-Egyptian Treaty forced Her Majesty's Government out and the Suez debacle two years later kept the British from returning.[67]

Regardless of how the United States might proceed, President Bush, with a job approval rating of 42 percent, the lowest of his term, could now claim that henceforth Prime Minister Allawi would bear sole responsibility for Iraq's political destiny, even though observers knew the president could never disassociate himself from the war he started. Fortunately for Bush, as a result of Iraqi self-determination, nominal though it might have been, fewer Americans were likely to fixate on U.S. travails in Iraq given reduced mainstream media coverage. Better still, most Republican voters continued to support the president's Iraq policy, saying it strengthened the War on Terror. Most Democrats and many undecided voters severely criticized Bush, however, on those two issues. As of August 2004, moreover, a majority of Americans (52 percent according to a Pew poll) thought the president's performance unsatisfactory when it came to Iraq. More worrisome for the commander-in-chief, 65 percent considered the interim Iraqi government's achievement "only fair" or "poor." Only 19 percent answered "excellent" or "good" when asked the same question.[68]

President Bush likely discounted or simply mistrusted these poll results. Having staked his presidency on the U.S. venture in Iraq, his administration sought to ensure continued pervasive American influence within that country. To that end, the White House sent former UN Ambassador John Negroponte to Baghdad to head up the largest American embassy in the world. Negroponte would try to ensure that Iraqis achieved various milestones: a summer 2004 national conference that would select an interim assembly, legislative elections in January 2005, followed shortly thereafter by the writing and ratification of a constitution guaranteeing ethnic and religious rights, a federal state, representative government, and a liberal economy. Another round of voting in December of that year would result in fully representative government for the first time in Iraq's history.[69]

The unprecedented August 2004 convention constituted a veritable mosaic of Iraqi political society, as individuals representing various religious, ethnic, and secular traditions met in Baghdad to decide who would serve in the legislature until election day five months hence. Prewar parties, many of whose members had lived in exile or, in the case of the Kurds, in the "no-fly" zone guarded by the Americans and British, banded together so that several of their own could fill the eighty-one seats available—the other nineteen went to former members of the Iraqi Governing Council without portfolio in the Allawi cabinet. This cabal prevented independents from joining the interim assembly, which also excluded Sunni and Shi'ite radicals as well as Ahmad Chalabi, a Pentagon darling before and after the war who lost favor in Washington when he distanced himself from the Bush administration, befriended the Iranians, and stood accused of wrongdoing by the interim Iraqi government.[70]

Regardless of the dubious tactics used to select legislators, the prospect of procedural and substantive democracy (i.e., fair elections, uncorrupt as well as responsive government, and a vigorous civil society) seemed remote in August 2004 as rampant violence, sustained by the likes of Muqtada al-Sadr, continued throughout much of Iraq. Grand Ayatollah al-Sistani may have brokered an end to the U.S.-Mahdi Army stand-off at the Imam Ali mosque in Najaf, one of the holiest shrines in Shi'ite Islam, but this cease-fire seemed no more than a respite. Truce or not, violence continued in Fallujah, Sadr City (a Shi'ite slum in Baghdad), and elsewhere, prompting American withdrawals—some temporary, others likely permanent—from insurgent strongholds, as Sunni and Shi'ite spokesmen urged U.S. soldiers to stay away lest they further enrage local inhabitants.[71]

With so much at stake for all participants in the post–Saddam Hussein scramble for power, additional interference on the part of Iraq's neighbors only compounded an already volatile situation. Despite Bush administration warnings, Iran, Turkey, and Syria meddled in Iraqi politics, each trying to effect a different outcome. Tehran hoped for a Shi'ite Iraq. Ankara sought to prevent the creation of an independent Kurdistan. Finally, Damascus, by serving as a conduit for foreign fighters, wanted to keep the Americans preoccupied so that Washington would rule out invading Syria.

As the U.S. death toll neared one thousand (many thousands, in the case of Iraqis), as the White House struggled to keep its coalition together and the United Nations sufficiently involved, as Americans and Europeans continued to cope with the bitter legacy of the war, and as many Arab leaders remained unenthused about democratic reforms, the Bush administration continued to dismiss its critics. Yet its Elysian dream of a liberated and reformed Iraq congruent with American political and economic preferences—the prototype of the president's Greater Middle East Initiative—seemed wishful and fanciful at best, naive and utopian at worse, unless a liberal, rather than Islamist, revolution occurred. Though some Arab and other Muslim countries, such as Qatar and Bahrain, seemed committed to empowering their citizens, others, such as Egypt and Iran, seemed dedicated to perpetuating autocratic rule. Given conflicts over modernity and tradition, pitting moderate, conservative, and radical secularists and fundamentalists, the Muslim world seemed at odds with itself as well as the West, a tug of war whose rope seemed to slip through U.S. hands whenever Washington tried to join this epic ideological contest, whose outcome would likely set the Middle East on a specific course for decades to come.[72]

The summer and fall of 2004 witnessed an incumbent president fending off John Kerry's pointed criticisms of the Bush administration's Iraq policy. Even though Kerry spotlighted several deficiencies—most seriously, the lack of allies, insufficient U.S. soldiers to ensure security within Iraq, and the absence of a so-called exit strategy—Americans reelected Bush, their "war president," on November 2. The Texan's plainspoken, sanguine explications emphasizing inevitable success in Iraq seemed to reassure many voters, who disliked Kerry's more nuanced, but less resolute, views on Iraq. Bush's reelection did not quell Iraqi insurgent violence, however, as improvised explosive devices and other deadly weapons continued to kill and maim American servicemen and women, as well as scores of Iraqis.[73]

Just as those losses imperiled the White House's yearning for a united, democratic Iraq, historic elections in that country temporarily reversed American fortunes. On January 30, 2005, a mere ten days after Bush's second Inaugural Address and its clarion call for worldwide democratization, millions of Iraqis defied insurgent death threats to cast ballots for a transitional national assembly, whose primary task would be to author a constitution by mid-August. Proudly displaying their ink-stained fingers, voters seemed to vindicate the administration's decision to overthrow Saddam Hussein and usher in democracy. Yet, with Iraq considered a single electoral district, Sunni politicians knew that proportional representation rules would disadvantage their sect, which constituted only 20 percent or so of the population— Shi'a made up approximately 60 percent, Kurds 15 percent or so. Certain to lose the election badly, many Sunni leaders urged their supporters not to vote, so as to undermine the legitimacy of the elections. Fear of election-day attacks would also confine many Sunnis to their homes.[74]

While Sunnis braced for a smashing Shi'ite electoral victory, the Bush administration worried that Shi'ite religious parties closely aligned with the Iranian government, such as the Supreme Council for the Islamic Revolution in Iraq (SCIRI) and the Dawa Party, would win two-thirds or more of the 275 available seats and, as a result, derail American efforts to democratize Iraq. According to journalist Seymour Hersh, to counter SCIRI and Dawa (and their Iranian benefactors), the White House authorized the CIA to extend financial and other support to Prime Minister Allawi and other secular Shi'a whom the Bush administration favored. Washington's, as well as Tehran's, subversion may have tainted Iraq's electoral process, but few individuals or groups protested the outcome. Allawi's Iraqi List slate won nearly 14 percent of the vote (40 seats), depriving the United Iraqi Alliance (winner of 140 seats) of a two-thirds majority within the National Assembly, the *Majlis Watani*. This result ensured the creation of a coalition government with the Kurds, who, via the Democratic Patriotic Alliance of Kurdistan, secured 75 seats. Although well disposed toward the Americans, the Kurds could potentially jeopardize the creation of a federal Iraq; they wanted autonomous status for themselves to prevent unwanted encroachments from Baghdad.[75]

Whether the Kurds would seek to enshrine their separatist aspirations in the Iraqi constitution seemed less consequential, however, than the Sunnis' spectacular, albeit expected, loss of authority and influence within their own country. With the Sunnis, winners of only 17 seats, deprived of supreme political power for the first time in Iraq's history, newly selected interim Prime Minister Ibrahim al-Jaafari, a Shi'a from the Dawa Party, formed a transitional government, which succeeded the Iraqi interim government in April after months of haggling among the victorious parties. His cabinet included eight Sunnis, nearly one-fifth of the membership, even though that sect won only 6.2 percent of the *Majlis Watani* seats. By including a disproportionate number of Sunnis in his cabinet, al-Jaafari hoped to coax that community into embracing Iraq's new government, rather than rejecting it by assassinating its members, a favorite insurgent tactic, or simply not supporting it. For an acceptable Iraqi constitution to emerge, moreover, Sunnis would have to contribute to it significantly, a fact the Bush administration readily acknowledged.[76]

Despite the Iraqi election, White House elation dissipated quickly. The so-called Downing Street Memo, revealed in May 2005, convicted the administration of wanting war in summer 2002 and culling intelligence to justify its policy of regime change. This brouhaha proved short-lived given that the Republican majority in Congress refused to investigate the matter and Bush, unlike Tony Blair, disallowed his commission on intelligence from examining it. The president could cloak his pre-war decision-making, but he could not hide mounting

U.S. military fatalities (1,862 by mid-August), a sobering fact that explained increasing American pessimism about the war. As insurgents (al-Qaeda–linked foreign terrorists waging their anti-American *jihad* and ex-Sunni Ba'thists fighting the Americans, Shi'a, and Kurds in the name of Iraqi nationalism) continued their reign of death and destruction, civil war seemed likely unless the U.S.-led coalition and Iraqi security forces could somehow stem the disorder still afflicting many parts of the country. With the insurgency seemingly intensifying, rather than in "its last throes" as Vice President Cheney asserted, the Bush administration recognized, privately at least, that Iraq would not likely evolve into a safe, stable, and prosperous democracy. To prevent the country from imploding, a potentially disastrous development for American policy in the Persian Gulf and Middle East, Washington would need to keep its soldiers in Iraq indefinitely. Pentagon talk of withdrawing tens of thousands of military personnel starting in 2006 cast doubt on U.S. resolve, however. Although President Bush continued to dismiss such a possibility despite an unimpressive approval rating (44 percent in late July 2005), Senator Chuck Hagel (R-Nebraska) and other critics within his own party warned of a possible foreign-policy debacle. As Hagel disparaged Bush's drifting Iraq policy, jittery Congressional Republicans no doubt wondered whether an increasingly unpopular war might lead to a comeuppance during the November 2006 mid-term elections.[77]

In late August 2005, ten or so days behind the original deadline, Iraqis charged with drafting a constitution completed their work following weeks of disagreement over issues such as federalism, Islam, and women's rights. Sunnis complained about the content of the constitution, accusing Shi'a and Kurds of exploiting their majority in the *Majlis Watani* to impose their preferences. American conservatives, especially those from the Christian Right, assailed the White House for allowing Islam to serve as Iraq's official religion and a "main source" of law-making. Other critics objected to federal arrangements that, in effect, would divide Iraq into three parts—Kurdish in the north, Shi'ite in the south, and Sunni in the center. These Iraqi decisions, arrived at following an arduous negotiation process, diverged from Washington's original wish for a secular and united Iraqi state, but seemed the only way the country could function with the consent of its major ethnic and confessional groups. With Iraq experts such as Peter Galbraith, a staunch Bush critic, and Reuel Marc Gerecht approving of the constitution, columnist David Brooks exclaimed that the document "exposes the canard that America is some imperial power trying to impose its values on the world. There are many parts of this constitution any American would love. There are other parts that are strange to us." Such exuberance seemed hasty and somewhat odd, especially given that Iraq never could have adopted such an inclusive document without an imperial intervention by the United States.[78]

A year after Brooks' optimistic editorial, Iraq seemed utterly broken politically, despite the narrow approval of the constitution in October 2005, another successful round of parliamentary elections in December, in which the United

Iraqi Alliance and the Kurdistan Alliance secured 128 and 53 seats respectively out of 275, and the June 2006 death of Abu Musab al-Zarqawi, the notorious leader of the terrorist group al-Qaeda in Iraq. The Shi'ite-led government of Prime Minister Nuri al-Maliki, months in the making following the end-of-year vote, could not stem or overcome the sectarian strife that threatened to plunge the country into full-scale civil war. With Sunni insurgents and Shi'ite militias, such as the Mahdi Army, murdering each other as well as countless civilians, the prospect of a unified Iraqi state seemed risible. With bombs exploding in mosques (e.g., in Samarra) and other crowded areas regularly, extremists continued to demonize other groups and call for further violence. Life in Baghdad in the summer of 2006 took on an especially harrowing quality, as numerous daily killings reminded inhabitants that no refuge, not even in the heavily fortified Green Zone, home to the Iraqi government and U.S. Embassy, could shelter them from attacks. Unfortunately, survival elsewhere seemed nearly as tenuous, as bloodshed racked Mosul, Basra, and other Iraqi cities.[79]

Despite mounting, some critics said overwhelming, evidence that his Iraq policy had delivered both fiasco and quagmire, President Bush refused to despair, at least publicly. Even conservatives urged him to modify American strategy. Yet, as Washington struggled politically and militarily, Bush continued to advocate patience and emphasize the positive. Although his country's counterinsurgency strategy yielded very uneven results, he promised that U.S. soldiers would still be in Iraq upon his departure from the White House in January 2009. While in 2006 Democrats called for a withdrawal timetable and Republicans increasingly worried about their re-election chances in November, Bush reiterated his "stay the course" mantra even though in August 60 percent of Americans opposed his war and only 47 percent thought the United States would "definitely win" or "probably win," no matter how one defined victory in Iraq. With 2,606 U.S. servicemen and women killed in the conflict as of August 17, and with nearly 20,000 injured, bleak news belied the president's confident assessments that the United States would achieve its goals in Mesopotamia, which satirist Jon Stewart repeatedly referred to as "Mess'opotamia" on his much watched *Daily Show* program.[80]

The fall provided no reprieve, as violence in Iraq raged thanks to the continued ill effects of the Bush administration's "nation busting." That audacious strategy revolutionized the country but unleashed vicious ethno-sectarian terror and yielded only "illiberal" democracy. Bewildered and enraged Americans vented their frustration with President Bush's policy when they voted on November 7. Democrats won a majority in both the Senate and House of Representatives, an outcome that would likely restrict what the commander-in-chief could do. Bowing to public dissatisfaction, Bush quickly replaced the much vilified Secretary of Defense Rumsfeld with Robert Gates, who served the president's father—the man who chose not to invade Iraq in 1991 for fear it would only produce a quagmire. At his confirmation, Gates informed senators that, contrary to

Bush's assessment, the United States was not winning in Iraq. A further rebuke occurred in early December when the Iraq Study Group, led by James Baker III and Lee Hamilton, issued its report, which thoroughly criticized the president's policy and advocated a withdrawal of American combat forces by 2008, discussions with Iran and Syria, and serious efforts to resolve the Israeli-Palestinian conflict. All recommendations Bush disliked. As the president awaited reviews from the Pentagon and White House probably more to his liking, he promised to unveil his revamped Iraq strategy in early 2007. Yet good solutions seemed unachievable, as $38 billion in U.S. tax dollars could not rebuild the country, Iraqis perished by the tens of thousands, and the American death toll passed three thousand. Given the grim news, not even Saddam Hussein's execution on December 30 could lift Bush's spirits. The murder of the man responsible for so many murders only fractured Iraq more and, to add insult to America's injury, Sunni Arabs considered him a martyr, a victim of Shi'ite injustice. In 2003, Bush thought his removal would heal Iraq and usher in a democratic revolution throughout the Middle East. As 2006 ended, that mirage had evaporated, thanks to the relentless, blistering heat of Iraqi ethno-sectarian conflict.[81]

Bush's dashed expectations enervated his administration and seriously undermined American credibility worldwide. Still, he soldiered on. Despite vehement Congressional and popular opposition (only 17 percent of Americans approved of his Iraq policy), in January 2007 he authorized a "surge" of 21,500 soldiers (in fact, some 30,000 would deploy) that would be added to the 132,000 already serving. The new strategy also called for $1.1 billion in additional aid. Reportedly, Prince Bandar, the Saudi national security advisor and long-time Bush family friend, convinced the president to pursue this controversial course, which *The Economist* dubbed "Baghdad or Bust." Bush hoped such an escalatory step, which he deemed critical despite the risk involved, would sufficiently reduce Iraq's rampant violence so that its frightened citizens (especially in the capital, scene of such carnage) and beleaguered government could attend to the country's myriad political and socio-economic problems. Due to ethno-sectarian cleansing, for example, millions of Iraqis experienced internal displacement or else lived as refugees in adjacent and other countries. Even though many Shi'a doubted that a Sunni-Kurd-Shi'ite coalition—Bush's preference—could govern the country, Prime Minister al-Maliki agreed to a "Baghdad security plan," whose aim dovetailed with the president's strategy. Skeptics thought Bush's "way forward" quixotic. Conservative pundit David Brooks argued, for example, that without "flexible decentralization" in Iraq, a military surge would fail. Most worrisome for the president, the newly empowered Democrats, many of whom advocated immediate withdrawal or some kind of timetable, vigorously contested his policy, as did disaffected Republicans. In May, Bush successfully vetoed a troop funding bill mandating a withdrawal deadline. The successor bill, which he signed, specified no timetable. Repeating such a legislative victory would likely prove more difficult, however, as his authority waned in the final twenty months of his now very unpopular presidency. To invigorate his flagging policy, which proved contentious even within his own administration, others more credible than him would have to justify America's role in Iraq.[82]

In September, General David Petraeus, the man tasked with implementing the "surge," informed Congress that U.S. efforts since the spring had improved security in Iraq. He thus recommended that the United States maintain its significant military presence in that ravaged country. As part of his assessment, Petraeus announced that five brigades (out of twenty) were scheduled to return home by July 2008. This troop reduction may have pleased some Americans, but the remaining force in Iraq (130,000 or so soldiers) would approximate the pre-"surge" total. Luckily for the drifting Bush, the generally upbeat Petraeus Report (unlike the mostly pessimistic evaluations found in the August National Intelligence Estimate and September reports by the Government Accountability Office and Jones Commission) offered him a reed. He shamelessly grabbed it in the expectation that his Iraq policy could henceforth survive until Inauguration Day in January 2009. His unlucky successor would then inherit the Iraqi imbroglio, a mess Bush initiated and exacerbated, all too aware that no panacea existed. Staying would ensure more American casualties, whereas exiting would probably assure an Iraqi bloodbath. Several Iraqis recognized this likelihood despite their stated preference for an immediate U.S. withdrawal. While some Iraqis wanted American soldiers to remain in their country, few publicly applauded the "surge."[83]

The ameliorated military situation in Iraq (especially in Anbar province, once an al-Qaeda in Mesopotamia stronghold) drew praise mainly from Republicans. Yet the country remained politically dysfunctional, a fact U.S. Ambassador Ryan Crocker readily acknowledged in his September 2007 Congressional testimony. Given that the "surge" aimed to provide the Iraqi government with an opportunity to remedy a host of divisive issues, the continued futility of Iraqi politicians only augured more strife rather than reconciliation. Democrats and other critics, including some conservatives, underscored this shortcoming of the "surge" and thereby deemed the strategy a failure. Unfortunately for Democrats, they lacked the votes in Congress to alter Bush's policy in a meaningful way. Only Republicans could override the president, an unlikely development unless the war were to worsen appreciably.[84]

As Bush coped with the shocking reality of his "war of the imagination," a $450 billion debacle (as of September 2007) that called to mind the U.S. failure in Vietnam, Iran found itself the subject of intense international scrutiny once more. When American forces overthrew Saddam Hussein in April 2003, the Bush administration briefly thought it could turn its attention to this other sworn enemy in the War on Terror. The problems of occupation, not uncommon for imperialists, distracted Washington, however. Instead of possibly intervening in Iran, America would remain, for the most part, merely a very interested observer of Iranian domestic politics and foreign policy.[85]

Monitoring Another Enemy

Iranian President Mohammed Khatami's smashing re-election in June 2001 augured well for U.S.-Iranian relations, but a conservative backlash within Iran ensured that ties remained unfriendly. President Bush's renewal of so-called primary sanctions, which dated from the 1979–81 hostage crisis, did not effect a thaw either. The White House considered the Islamic Republic a "rogue state," a distinction the latter shared with Iraq, and treated Iran as an enemy. The week of the Iranian presidential election, moreover, members of Congress initiated legislation extending the Iran-Libya Sanctions Act (ILSA) to 2006. This reconsideration of ILSA occurred as a distinguished panel of former U.S. officials advocated the lifting of sanctions, deeming them counterproductive and hurtful to the American economy. With Congress and the Bush administration wary of his country, Khatami simply continued to woo Russia and the Gulf monarchies, where anti-Americanism often thrived and governments regularly reassessed their relations with the United States.[86]

As Tehran and Washington vied for supremacy in the Persian Gulf, Iran's Supreme Leader Ayatollah Khamanei and his conservative associates within the Council of Guardians denied President Khatami full discretion over domestic and foreign policy. Consequently, mullahs that favored the Iranian status quo (i.e., a theocratic state that remained mired in economic stagnation and offered only bleak employment prospects to a population with a majority under the age of twenty-five) continued to oppress a citizenry eager for cultural plurality and substantive democracy—as opposed to simply electoral democracy, which clerics manipulated anyway via the review of candidate lists. Three-fourths of Iranians, moreover, approved of a resumption of U.S.-Iranian relations, which must have appalled Ayatollah Khamanei and other revolutionaries who had spent years denouncing supposed American evils. In a gesture that presumably further infuriated Khamanei and his clique, President Bush indicated his satisfaction with Iranian reformers, students particularly, when he cheered them on in his 2003 State of the Union Address.[87]

Even though the Islamic Republic had proven very helpful to Washington in overcoming the Taliban and rehabilitating Afghanistan, Tehran resumed its mischievous ways once Bush fixated on the removal of Saddam Hussein and his Ba'th Party associates. Iran expanded its nuclear program and watched with keen interest as its Iraqi adversary clumsily tried to avert a U.S.-led invasion, which could divide the country into three distinct, possibly autonomous, sections—Kurd, Sunni, Shi'ite. The Iranians knew that the Turks vigorously opposed such a development and that Washington had promised Ankara it would preserve Iraq's territorial integrity. Still, the Islamic Republic had to contemplate a possible future whereby American soldiers could be on Iran's western border. With

U.S. forces already in Afghanistan, the country on Iran's eastern border, and Central Asia, immediately to Persia's north, the Iranian government, as a charter member of the "Axis of Evil," feared American strategic encirclement. This possibility disturbed conservative clerics, who came to power opposing the United States, the "Great Satan." To add insult to potential injury, Washington imperiously urged Tehran to refrain from any involvement in Iraq, should the United States invade, and requested that the Iranians assist Iraqi refugees. Asking an avowed enemy to help secure American interests seemed cavalier, to say the least, especially given that U.S.-Iranian relations had not improved much since Ayatollah Khomeini's death in 1989. Not surprisingly, when America initiated war in Iraq, the Iranians expressed their official opposition by opting for a policy of "active neutrality." Unlike Ba'thist Syria, Iran refrained from assisting Baghdad, its long-time political, ideological, and military rival.[88]

The overthrow of Saddam Hussein may have pleased the Islamic Republic—during the Iran-Iraq War, it called for his death—but America's occupation of Iraq alarmed conservative Iranian leaders, who must have wondered if Washington would attack their country next. Ironically, Iran's pursuit of nuclear weapons, sensical given that such a capability could deter an American attack à la Iraq (or an Israeli nuclear strike), worried the Bush administration. Unlike with the Iraqi dictator and despite majority U.S. public approval for a strike against Iran, the White House proceeded cautiously. It preferred to work with the International Atomic Energy Agency (IAEA), the European Union, Russia, and the People's Republic of China to monitor Iranian behavior. This emphasis on concert rather than self-righteousness resembled American policy vis-à-vis North Korea, another country eager to join the nuclear club. To counter the expansion of American influence in the Persian Gulf, Tehran could exploit the Iraqi Ba'th Party's demise by reshaping that country's politics more to its liking via support for the Shi'ite majority. As exiled Iraqi clerics left Iran and returned to the holy Shi'ite cities of Najaf and Karbala, Washington emphatically warned that it would not countenance a Shi'ite theocracy in Iraq sympathetic to the Islamic Republic of Iran. Nor would the Bush administration condone Tehran's hosting of al-Qaeda members, who may have assisted in the May 12, 2003, bombings in Saudi Arabia. Iran refuted the American accusation (the terrorists inhabited an area possibly beyond Tehran's authority), but recent U.S.-Iranian comity ended—Tehran had delivered al-Qaeda suspects to the governments of Saudi Arabia and Afghanistan, which helped Washington in its War on Terror.[89]

From Washington's standpoint, if Iran's student protesters could somehow seize power, then the White House might not have to care so much about complicity among Iraqi and Iranian Shi'a. Similarly, such a development could result in the eviction of al-Qaeda from Iran. Reformers touted Iranian nationalism, however; they would not simply seek to satisfy the United States.

Despite Iranian pride, Washington achieved an important political victory in fall 2003 courtesy of European diplomacy, specifically that of France, Germany, and the United Kingdom, countries eager to head off further confrontation in the Middle East involving the United States. Exposed in August 2002 by the National Council of Resistance, the political wing of the Mujahideen-e Khalq (MEK), an organization committed to the overthrow of the Islamic regime, Tehran eventually admitted to the existence of a long-standing illicit nuclear program and agreed to IAEA inspections. Iran tried to mislead the nuclear watchdog, but when the latter threatened to refer the country to the Security Council for violating the Nuclear Non-Proliferation Treaty (NPT), the Europeans intervened. Iran signed an additional IAEA protocol, which Washington insisted on since it could hamper the Islamic Republic's efforts to manufacture nuclear weapons.[90]

Washington did not merely gloat following this unexpected counterproliferation success. The December 2003 earthquake that devastated the historic Iranian city of Bam enabled the Bush administration to offer assistance, which Tehran accepted. As U.S. relief workers entered Iran, the first Americans allowed into the country since the 1979 revolution, the White House offered to send an official delegation to the Islamic Republic. Although Tehran declined, in late January 2004 it agreed to host Congressional aides.[91]

Thoughts of a U.S.-Iranian rapprochement, whose mutual benefits several foreign-policy experts touted, co-existed uneasily, however, with the ugly political reality within Iran. In advance of February 20 parliamentary elections, the Council of Guardians ruled thousands of reformist candidates ineligible, prompting scores of liberal members of the *Majlis* to resign in protest. As Iran braced for another round of internal upheaval, the Bush administration equivocated. It applauded reformers who yearned for representative democracy, while realizing that Khamenei and the Council of Guardians seemed likely to prevail in the short term. The White House worried, moreover, that staunch support for Khatami and the reformers might lead to a reversal of Tehran's helpful policies—Washington valued the pragmatism displayed by conservatives such as Supreme National Council Chief Hassan Rohani on important matters such as Afghanistan and Iraq.[92]

U.S. and Iranian interests diverged once more in the following months, as the Islamic Republic sought to influence events in Iraq and refused to discontinue its controversial nuclear program. To Washington's displeasure, Tehran offered financial and other support to Ahmad Chalabi and other Iraqi Shi'a vying for power in Sadr City in Baghdad as well as Najaf, Karbala, Basra, and other Shi'ite cities and towns in southern Iraq. While the Bush administration could tolerate some Iranian interference in Iraqi affairs, it could not condone Iran's pursuit of weapons of mass destruction. Though Tehran continued to insist that an increasingly populated Iran needed nuclear power to meet its burgeoning demand for energy, this contention underwhelmed Washington, which continually spotlighted the Islamic Republic's ample reserves of oil and gas while excluding the possibility that Tehran preferred to sell its vast stocks to foreigners, especially Asians, at attractive world prices rather than subsidize Iranian hydrocarbon consumption. IAEA reports documented, however, an extensive covert Iranian program that seemed to confirm U.S. suspicions. These revelations discredited European diplomatic efforts to ensure Iran only developed a civilian nuclear capability. Worse, this embarrassing news prompted an irate Tehran to resume assembling centrifuges that could be used to enrich uranium, a central ingredient in a nuclear weapon.

The Bush administration may have hoped that Iran would heed the example of Libya, which in December 2003 announced that it would dismantle its WMD programs following extensive discussions with the United Kingdom and United States. Whereas Mohamar Qaddafi sought much needed economic relief after years of harsh sanctions, Iranian hardliners preferred to continue defying the will of the international community, perhaps not an unreasonable or surprising way to proceed given the country's distressing geopolitical circumstances. Surrounded by nuclear armed countries—Russia, Pakistan, Israel, India, the People's Republic of China, America, and Great Britain—Tehran most likely thought it prudent and wise to build weapons that could deter an attack on Iran.

Alarmed by the Iranian push for weapons of mass destruction, the IAEA ordered the Iranian government in September 2004 to cease its pursuit of uranium enrichment, a process that, if successful, could yield several nuclear weapons which could be delivered to targets 810 miles away via Shahab 3 missiles. Such a scientific exploit would render Israel and U.S. bases in the Middle East vulnerable to an Iranian offensive. While Tel Aviv considered destroying Iranian nuclear facilities thirteen years after the Israeli Air Force turned Iraq's Osirak complex to rubble, the American military concluded that such a pre-emptive strike—which the United States could carry out more successfully than Israel given Iran's scattered, subterranean facilities—would merely exacerbate tensions and risk war. Not everyone in Washington agreed with that assessment, but bureaucratic wrangling and Beltway disputes over America's Iran policy did not translate into air attacks, never mind an invasion, which analysts warned would be much more difficult than "Cobra II"—the Iraq plan.[93]

The Islamic Republic may have avoided a fate similar to that of Iraq under Saddam Hussein, but its most conservative leaders, led by Ayatollah Khamenei, vehemently continued to assert its prerogative, as a party to the NPT, to develop nuclear energy. In June 2005, Mahmoud Ahmadinejad, Tehran's uncompromising mayor, scored an unlikely victory in the presidential election. His inflammatory remarks, replete with Holocaust denials and other anti-Israeli pronouncements, ushered in a return to firebrand rhetoric and the audacious, often reckless, foreign policy of the Khomeini era. Molded in those tumultuous years, especially on the battlefields of the Iran-Iraq War, he sought to purge his country's complex society and politics, with its overlapping and often opposing institutions of elected and non-elected officials, of their heretical ways and return Iran to a position of prominence within the Persian Gulf and Middle East. To achieve his goal, he and his hard-line allies, as well as Khamenei, continued to defy the IAEA, which kept pressing Tehran for more information on its nuclear program. In May 2006, Ahmadinejad wrote to President Bush, the first correspondence between Iranian and American leaders since the 1979 Iranian Revolution. The contents and condescending tone of the letter failed to impress Bush, however, ensuring that the president would not drastically modify his administration's Iran policy.[94]

Since the United States still lacked attractive military options, especially with Iran so influential with Shi'ite politicians, clerics, and militiamen in Iraq, Washington continued to favor multilateral diplomacy, just as it did with North Korea, the other "Axis of Evil" country whose nuclear proliferation ambitions worried the White House. But in a reversal of its policy, the Bush administration agreed to discuss issues of bilateral and international concern directly with the Iranian government as part of a June 1, 2006, package of incentives, sponsored by the permanent members of the Security Council (United States, United Kingdom, France, Russia, and the People's Republic of China) and Germany, that aimed to ensure Tehran could only develop civilian nuclear energy, not nuclear weapons that could strike Israel or U.S. targets in the Middle East, for example, and thus threaten regional as well as international security. A July 2006 Security Council resolution threatened Iran, however, with economic and diplomatic sanctions, should it not suspend its uranium enrichment by August 31.[95]

Before officially responding to the offer and the Security Council's ultimatum, Iran benefited from another round of Arab-Israeli violence as Hamas and Hezbollah, both recipients of Iranian assistance, battled with Israel in the summer of 2006. Iranian weaponry enabled Hezbollah, in particular, to inflict significant Israeli civilian and military casualties as well as serious damage upon towns and cities in northern Israel via barrages of Katyusha rockets. Washington responded to the June-August crisis by fingering Iran, as well as Syria, for its interference in Lebanon and the Palestinian territories while attempting to draw global attention away from its illicit nuclear activities.[96]

Whether Tehran provoked or exacerbated conflict in the Levant seemed only to confirm the Islamic Republic's waxing influence in the Middle East. As Western analysts highlighted a nascent "Shi'ite crescent" in the region, the Bush administration expected Tehran to rebuff the Security Council and turn down the assistance offer, which included help with Iran's civilian nuclear program. As expected, Tehran defied the Security Council's wishes. But Iran reaffirmed its willingness to discuss its atomic program, albeit via a "new formula," which it failed to explicate. Washington considered the Iranian response inadequate and called for sanctions, which Russia considered hasty and likely to fail. UN Secretary-General Kofi Annan's September 2 meeting with Ahmadinejad and other Iranian officials confirmed the Iranian leadership's intransigence and self-assurance, traits that presaged continued antipathy between Washington and Tehran despite their shared interest in opposing radical Sunni Islamists in both

Iraq and Afghanistan. President Bush's refusal to meet with his Iranian counterpart, who offered to debate the Texan, ruled out any "Nixon Goes to China" scenario and therefore any short-term U.S.-Iranian peaceful co-existence, even though Iranians spoke of their fondness for Americans and their consumer products and thought it possible for the two countries to work together despite their obvious differences. Ahmadinejad and other hard-liners no doubt rejected such a possibility since it would undermine their Shi'ite Islamist credentials.[97]

As world leaders met in New York in September for the opening session of the UN General Assembly, Bush used his speech to underscore Tehran's failings while exhorting Iranians to reclaim their government, which he considered unrepresentative of their wishes. Ahmadinejad replied in kind by deploring U.S. and Western hypocrisy on the matter of nuclear energy. If Western countries could develop such a resource, the Iranian president noted, then why should Iran, an NPT signatory, deprive itself of such a sovereign right? Before Ahmadinejad's address to the United Nations, over one hundred states had approved of this Iranian entitlement at a Non-Aligned Movement conference in Havana, Cuba. Ahmadinejad's self-confidence worried Western experts, who thought he and Iran's other conservative leaders, including Ayatollah Khamenei, might underestimate American resolve and proceed recklessly within the Middle East. To cope with such a possibility, Washington updated its military strategy, which prompted talk of another preventive strike against a U.S. enemy. A reprise of *Operation Iraqi Freedom* seemed unlikely in the short term, however, as the Bush administration privileged diplomacy over force, a course several analysts favored. A resort to negotiation might prove successful, especially if, as asserted in an August 2006 Chatham House report, Ayatollah Khamenei mistrusted Ahmadinejad's confrontational foreign policy. But Iran continued to enrich uranium throughout the fall, prompting the Security Council in December to impose sanctions.[98]

Resolution 1737, which Russia softened to protect its investments in Iran, did not seem to faze Tehran. With Moscow, in partnership with Beijing, intent on shielding the Islamic Republic from America's diplomatic wrath, Iran, flush with hydrocarbon wealth thanks to high energy prices, boldly continued to exert its growing influence in the Middle East, especially in Iraq, where Shi'ite parties and militias benefited from Iranian largesse and expertise—in explosives, for example. Likewise, Tehran invested in border security and infrastructure in Afghanistan, where the Karzai government struggled to cope with a resurgent Taliban and flourishing drug trade. The brash Ahmadinejad lost support internally, but his fiery rhetoric helped return his country to regional and international prominence. His allies, domestic and abroad, cheered his bombast, while Washington sought to counter his verbal assaults upon the United States and Israel. Unwilling and unable to strike a deal with Iran, "the world's most dangerous nation" (the title of Ted Koppel's November 19, 2006, Discovery Channel documentary), an exasperated Bush administration worked to isolate its nemesis, contra the Iraq Study Group recommendation that it do the opposite.[99]

In January 2007, as the Bulletin of the Atomic Scientists moved its "Doomsday Clock" forward two minutes (to 11:55 p.m.) in response to the Iranian and North Korean nuclear deadlocks, President Bush sent a second carrier task force to the Persian Gulf to underscore his menacing rhetoric just as American forces arrested Iranian agents in Iraq. Such bellicose measures once more precluded talks between the Gulf's imperial power and the region's aspiring hegemon that could repair the badly damaged U.S.-Iranian relationship. Even though Iran experts Vali Nasr and Ray Takeyh opined that "the United States would do better to shelve its containment strategy and embark on a policy of unconditional dialogue and sanctions relief," Bush resisted the kind of diplomacy that yielded a February nuclear agreement with North Korea, which had carried out an atomic test four months earlier.[100]

While Iranian scientists worked to master the nuclear fuel cycle, the White House pressed the Europeans to extend sanctions and refused to give up on its objective of regime change. In March, Security Council Resolution 1747 imposed additional sanctions on the Islamic Republic only hours after Iranian Revolutionary Guards seized fifteen British sailors and marines from HMS *Cornwall*, on patrol in the Persian Gulf near the disputed Iraq-Iran maritime border. Although Iranian officials, including Ahmadinejad, roared their displeasure with the UN Chapter VII measures and retaliated by curbing IAEA access to Iran's nuclear program, they had lost Russian support in the days that preceded the unanimous vote. Moscow accused Tehran of not paying for Russian work at the Bushehr nuclear facility, a charge the Iranians vigorously denied. As well, Russia told Iran it would not deliver fuel to that plant unless it ceased enriching uranium. This Russian-Iranian rift no doubt pleased the White House, which could continue eschewing détente with Iran, the policy Takeyh urged it to pursue with so-called Iranian pragmatists—younger conservatives who supposedly thought it better for Iran to work *with* the United States. Within the Bush administration, Secretary of State Rice and Vice President Cheney espoused opposing views on how to cope with Iran, which expanded its nuclear program in the summer of 2007. Rice touted diplomacy in an effort to engage the Islamic Republic, whereas Cheney and his advisors sought to "isolate and contain" Iran, via force if necessary. Unlike his predecessor, France's new president, Nicolas Sarkozy, echoed some of these militant views. This French volte-face, combined with American intransigence, promised tense months ahead as IAEA Director General Mohamed ElBaradei tried to broker a permanent nuclear deal with Iranian leaders busy tamping down internal dissent. The confrontation between Washington and Tehran threatened to escalate into hostilities that could involve Israel. (In September, Tel Aviv seemed to signal Iran by encroaching upon Syrian airspace. Israel also designated Iranian-allied Gaza under Hamas a "hostile entity.") The prospect of another American war in the Middle East seemed particularly worrisome, especially given U.S. vulnerabilities in the region, most obvious of all its numerous personnel in the Greater Middle East that could be targeted for bombings and assassinations.[101]

In the fall, President Bush and his advisors demonized Iran, warned of a possible "World War III" should the Islamic Republic develop nuclear weapons, and sanctioned the Revolutionary Guard Corps—which patrolled Persian Gulf waters adjacent to U.S. warships and whose elite Quds division stood accused of terrorism. In this inflamed context, a startling U.S. National Intelligence Estimate (NIE), issued in early December 2007, asserted that Tehran had suspended its nuclear weapons program in the fall of 2003—perhaps in response to *Operation Iraqi Freedom*. The revelation, which corrected a 2005 estimate, undercut the Bush administration's rationale for its uncompromising Iran policy, vindicated ElBaradei, and delivered an unexpected propaganda victory to a gloating Iranian regime. The NIE, which politicized the nominally apolitical intelligence bureaucracy, embarrassed Bush. Nevertheless, he insisted that Iran remained a serious threat to the Middle East and the world, a mantra Stephen Hadley and Robert Gates, his national security advisor and secretary of defense, repeated in various speeches. While conservatives such as John Bolton, the former U.S. ambassador to the United Nations, assailed the NIE, Democrats invoked it as they renewed their call for negotiations with the Iranian government, a tack even neoconservative Robert Kagan favored. Although previous American intelligence blunders left the incredulous Israelis and other critics skeptical of the NIE, a U.S. attack on Iranian nuclear installations now seemed highly unlikely in the short term, as did a third Security Council sanctions resolution. Still, the matter of Iranian nuclear weapons appeared merely postponed, given that Tehran persisted in refusing to curtail its uranium enrichment program.[102]

Despite America's repeated clashes with a defiant Islamic Republic, President Bush seemed no less committed to a reformed Middle East. His preference for a liberal revolution within Iran and an externally imposed overthrow of a sovereign government in Iraq had signaled his exasperation with "dual containment" and his willingness to effect a new order in the two countries outside the U.S. sphere of influence in the Persian Gulf. Under Bill Clinton, "dual containment" had enabled Washington to keep Iran and Iraq away from Western oil supplies in the Arabian Peninsula for a decade. The White House preferred this strategy since it meshed with America's *informal* empire in the Gulf. Many critics disparaged U.S. tactics, yet the Clinton administration could think of no better way to preserve American interests. George W. Bush believed otherwise. He used his bully pulpit to advocate a reformed Greater Gulf region in sync with U.S. interests. His proposed invasion of Iraq threatened American colonialism, a scenario that prompted journalists and scholars to admit to the existence of a U.S. empire. Leaders in the Arabian Peninsula knew, however, that an American imperium already existed.[103]

Nervous Allies

In early 2001, with several oil men, including the president, occupying top U.S. government posts, the White House promised to champion energy supply, both domestic and foreign. At the same time, it seemed content to uphold "dual containment." The policy satisfied almost no one (despite its rhetorical appeal), yet the Bush administration could not implement a better alternative. As Saddam Hussein's military and other mischief continued and Tehran resumed its ardent support for Middle Eastern extremists/terrorists opposed to Palestinian-Israeli peace, Washington kept the Iraqi leader in his "box" and the Islamic Republic isolated. Unfortunately for President Bush and his advisors, Hussein sidestepped U.S. trade restrictions while Khatami made friends worldwide.[104]

The attacks of September 11, 2001, effected a tectonic shift in international politics, allowing the Bush administration to discard the Iraqi part of "dual containment," which it perceived as wholly inappropriate even though critics such as the University of Chicago's John Mearsheimer and Harvard's Stephen Walt, two fervent International Relations realists, thought such a defensive strategy effective and preferable to any invasion of Iraq. Bush officials preferred to rely on Kenneth Pollack's analysis, which touted the necessity of U.S. violence to rid Iraq of its WMD capability. As the White House haltingly prepared for war with Saddam Hussein, it ignored Pollack's inconvenient priorities—the War on Terrorism should supersede any Iraq campaign, the former CIA analyst opined.[105]

In response to American haste, GCC countries displayed initial nervousness. Washington expected its Arabian Peninsula allies to conform to U.S. wishes regardless of public sentiment in the Persian Gulf. Unable to deny or hide their cozy ties to America, royal families worried that their subjects, many of them very dissatisfied with the lack of political participation, economic opportunity, and pervasive governmental corruption within their states, might protest the ubiquitous U.S. military presence in the Gulf and possibly carry out terrorist attacks against American personnel.[106]

Reactions to a possible U.S. intervention varied. Qatar invited the Bush administration to station American soldiers at a new air base, Al-Udeid, and command center, As Sayliyah, both built at great expense in the hope of attracting the U.S. Air Force. Pentagon planners urged the White House to sign an agreement with Doha since this facility resembled in capacity Prince Sultan Air Base in Saudi Arabia, a country eager for American servicemen and women to leave its sacred Muslim soil. Riyadh convinced the Organization of Petroleum Exporting Countries (OPEC) to keep oil affordable—between $22 and $28 per barrel—but Saudi Crown Prince Abdullah balked initially at providing Washington with the assistance it needed to prosecute a war in Iraq. To stave off conflict, his government tried to foment a coup within Iraq while Ankara sought to remove Saddam Hussein via exile. Neither effort succeeded. Eventually, with the White House insisting that Saudi Arabia agree to U.S. wishes, Abdullah relented.[107]

Saudi acquiescence came with a caveat, however. Various Saudi princes informed the U.S. government that, once the invasion completed, Riyadh would ask America to withdraw its soldiers from the Kingdom. Such an outcome would probably redound to U.S. advantage: al-Qaeda would stop hectoring the Saudis for hosting infidels, the Bush administration could distance itself from a country that contributed, presumably unknowingly, fifteen 9/11 hijackers, and Washington would not have to seek Saudi permission every time it wanted to use military facilities to carry out attacks in the Persian Gulf or Central Asia. With U.S.-Saudi ties tense since September 2001—Bush advisor Richard Perle's Defense Policy Board heard a presentation that named Saudi Arabia, a mostly staunch U.S. ally for many decades, America's number one enemy—Abdullah's postwar intentions offered the United States a way to adjust its imperial presence without having to exit the region. If an Islamic takeover by al-Qaeda or some other fundamentalist organization inimical to America threatened the Kingdom, Washington could always quickly intervene by relying on its twenty-eight bases in or close to the Persian Gulf.[108]

The U.S.-led invasion of Iraq in March-April 2003 resulted in American and British soldiers (and other infidels) occupying a Muslim country. GCC states despised Saddam Hussein and his secular tyranny and thus welcomed his downfall, yet they wondered how such an event would transform their region. (Before the American war to democratize Iraq, the leaders of Qatar and Bahrain may have already ushered in a new era when they started to liberalize their countries.) U.S. military personnel could now leave Saudi Arabia, but deadly May 12 bombings in Riyadh, purportedly carried out by al-Qaeda, that killed thirty-four Americans, Saudis, and others, reminded Washington that the War on Terror would continue and that its Saudi ally somehow had to cope—via autocracy, democracy, or otherwise—with terrorists funded and encouraged by its own citizens. The U.S. strategic position may have improved following the Second Persian Gulf War, but the American victory might well prove bittersweet should democratization in the Arabian Peninsula result in the overthrow of royal governments by anti-American Arabs intent on severing political-military ties with Washington.[109]

Dramatic political revolution did not ensue, however, as GCC monarchs liberalized somewhat and each country's *mukhabarat* (i.e., security service) stood ready to quash any upheaval. But even Saudi leaders, ultra conservative by any standard, introduced competitive elections, albeit tentatively and only at the municipal level. The 2003 U.S. departure from the Kingdom surely facilitated that decision. President Bush's call for democratization in the region thus yielded some positive results, as Arab governments in the Gulf became, at least theoretically, more accountable to their citizens. Yet, as the occupation of Iraq metastasized into quagmire following three years (2004–06) of insurgency and sectarian violence, Washington endorsed wholeheartedly the GCC dictatorships, which analyst Simon Henderson referred to as the "new pillar" of U.S. strategy in the Persian Gulf. Together with Egypt and Jordan, two other autocracies, the GCC states constituted a "six plus two" conservative Sunni bloc opposed to Shi'ite Iran. The White House's rhetoric-versus-reality paradox did not apparently bother the Bush administration, whose "emirates" strategy, with Qatar as its hub, sought to preserve America's informal empire in the Gulf.[110]

With Bush's effort at formal empire in Iraq unrewarded (Saudi King Abdullah called the American occupation "illegal" at a March 2007 Arab League summit), the United States needed its GCC "empire of bases" to secure its substantial interests in the region and project power into the Greater Middle East. Fortunately for Washington, GCC governments remained amenable to the decades-old "oil-for-security" quid pro quo, even though they and their populations continued to oppose America's Middle East policy, especially vis-à-vis the Arab-Israeli conflict. GCC monarchs may have lost confidence in U.S. competence thanks to the debacle in Iraq, but they continued to buy U.S. weapons and refused to dispense with American protection—a potentially ruinous course for both the patron and its clients. Additionally, Riyadh resumed an oil policy favorable to the United States. Despite the steep increase in hydrocarbon prices in 2005–06, Saudi Arabia sought to stabilize the cost of crude at $50–55 per barrel. As the industry's "swing producer," it continued to hold sway over OPEC even as it tried to marginalize fellow member Iran, a beneficiary of high oil prices and competitor of the Saudis in Iraq, where Tehran supported Shi'ite militias opposed to Sunni groups, including al-Qaeda in Mesopotamia.[111]

In spite of Saudi efforts, crude sold for nearly $100 per barrel in late 2007. This fall price spike further enriched Gulf countries, while Americans wrestled with the seemingly inevitable advent of $4 per gallon gasoline. To show their gratitude, GCC governments criticized the Bush administration's nuclear policy in the Middle East. They asked how Washington could condone Israel's undeclared possession of nuclear weapons while thwarting Iran's attempts to develop the same technology. U.S. Secretary of Defense Robert Gates denied a double standard. In his opinion, Iran threatened the Middle East with destruction; Israel did not. Gulf leaders objected. For them, Israel constituted the major threat to the region. This typical disagreement once more underscored the strains in this marriage of convenience. Still, each partner needed the other; commercial and security imperatives kept them joined. Whether this fifteen-year-old partnership, which *Operation Desert Shield/Storm* initiated, could withstand various temptations would prove crucial to its durability. In one scenario, GCC countries, like Iran, would sell vast quantities of hydrocarbons to the People's Republic of China, India, and other voracious fossil fuel importers in euros, yen, yuan, and rupee, instead of dollars—whose value steadily declined during George W. Bush's presidency, prompting the Gulf oil monarchies to ponder their currencies' peg to the dollar. Another possibility would be America fully embracing a "green" economy powered by alternative fuels. In either case, the GCC-U.S. union could dissolve. The amicability of such a divorce would surely reverberate throughout the Greater Middle East and beyond. Yet, in 2007, those hypothetical scenarios easily gave way to the sober reality of U.S.-GCC relations. Despite dissatisfaction on each side, their fates in the region remained very much intertwined.[112]

Although critics of American policy in the Gulf called for regional collaboration with allies and enemies alike, Iraq's civil war and Iran's defiance precluded any kind of condominium in the near term. Such anti-American trends made the "emirates" strategy the least-worst option. This sub-optimal policy displeased Arabs and Persians, as well as many Americans, yet Gulf dynamics left Washington stuck in a classic imperial bind. It could not forfeit its position, so it clung to an unpopular policy—gunboat diplomacy—that empires have always pursued, no matter the cost in lives and treasure.[113]

Assessment

Six years before America's various Persian Gulf conundrums would alarm and dismay the U.S. body politic, the 2001-07 phase of the American empire in the Gulf started out inauspiciously. George W. Bush ascended the presidency rhetorically committed to returning the United States to the kind of foreign-policy realism associated with his father's administration. His abrasive style irritated friends and foes alike, but his unilateralism remained tethered to what best served American interests. The 9/11 attacks traumatized Americans and their leaders, however, prompting the Bush administration to revamp U.S. foreign policy so that Washington would seize the initiative rather than respond to the salvos of its enemies. The Bush Doctrine armed the commander-in-chief with the rationale to subject the world to America's wrath and whim. The president's fevered post-9/11 policy, which sought "monsters to destroy" (contra John Quincy Adams' 1821 admonition), witnessed the U.S. war machine first descend upon Afghanistan, the so-called graveyard of empires, to expel al-Qaeda and its sponsor, the Taliban, from that rugged, tragic land. Washington's quick victory emboldened the White House, which then zeroed in on Saddam Hussein and his repugnant regime in Iraq. In March-April 2003, *Operation Iraqi Freedom* seemed to signal yet another blow struck on behalf of "freedom," as the United States toppled the next domino in its quest to rid the globe of "evil."[114]

The Bush administration insisted on the U.S. right to carry out such a policy, but, thanks to Secretary of State Powell, wisely sought UN support for it. Unlike in bygone eras, an intervention that smacked of imperial ambition needed international sanction. The Security Council approved Resolution 1441, which called Iraq to account, but refused to ratify a U.S.-led invasion. Unfazed, the White House assembled its "coalition of the willing," an ad hoc alliance of convenience whose prominent members included the United Kingdom, Australia, Spain, Italy, and Poland. Many participants officially acquiesced, but contributed minimally. Still, the Bush administration touted their membership, which enabled it to refute charges of unilateralism. U.S. strategy therefore seems to confirm proposition P2 (The United States will exercise alliance contingent imperialism whenever a significant threat to American hegemony and security occurs, allies agree to join a U.S.-led venture or vice-versa, Washington can overcome any regional constraints, consensus exists within the executive, and no majority in Congress or critical segment of domestic opinion strongly opposes White House action). But the stark asymmetry of motivation, commitment, and capability between the United States and its allies potentially invalidates that proposition while confirming P1 (The United States will exercise unilateral contingent imperialism whenever a significant threat to American hegemony and security occurs, Washington can act alone or cannot rely on anyone else to secure its interests and can overcome any regional constraints, consensus exists within the executive, and no majority in Congress or critical segment of domestic opinion strongly opposes White House action). British involvement in *Operation Iraqi Freedom* cannot be credited to American coercion, however. Prime Minister Tony Blair willingly signed on to George W. Bush's crusade to disarm Saddam Hussein's regime. The Australians, as well, went to Iraq committed to the same objective. Despite Washington's uncouth pre-war diplomacy, then, alliance imperialism succeeded in overthrowing Hussein.

Bush's mission may have seemed accomplished in May 2003, but soon a bitter wind swept up the United States and carried it into forbidding territory. This new geography punished and exhausted the country both physically and emotionally. Whereas initially American hubris promised to transform the Greater Middle East into a nirvana, unfulfilled promises, missed opportunities, incompetence (both U.S. and Iraqi), and developments within Iraq and elsewhere conjoined to dash Bush's plans to democratize, if not Americanize, a region only angered and humiliated by U.S. policy. Commenting on the Abu Ghraib prisoner abuse scandal, columnist George Will wrote: "Americans must not flinch from absorbing the photographs of what some Americans did in that prison. And they should not flinch from this fact: That pornography is, inevitably, part of what empire looks like. . . . [E]mpire is always about domination. Domination for self-defense, perhaps. Domination for the good of the dominated, arguably. But domination."[115]

The Bush administration rejected such a characterization of its policy, but Americans, many flummoxed and bewildered by the tempest stalking their well-meaning soldiers and administrators, progressively lost confidence in their commander-in-chief's refrain that life in Iraq for Americans, as well as Iraqis, would improve. President Bush tried, half-heartedly his critics claimed, to refashion a totalitarian country into a Western-style democracy. To facilitate that daunting transition, U.S. colonial efforts emphasized "unite and rule" instead of "divide and rule," an imperial strategy with often unseemly consequences. Unfortunately for Washington, its heterodox method encountered much Iraqi ingratitude as Sunnis tried to recoup their lost privileges, Shi'a attempted to govern their country for the first time, and Kurds sought to preserve their hard-earned self-determination. Insurgency and ethno-sectarian conflict overwhelmed the notable democratic gains made at the ballot box in 2005. Although American forces captured or killed countless terrorists and other wanted individuals, including Saddam Hussein and his sons, trends kept working against the U.S. occupation. President Bush remained stubbornly optimistic until the mid-term elections in 2006. By then, however, the American venture had veered toward "noble failure" at best, unprecedented catastrophe at worst. The 2007 "surge" may have improved U.S. fortunes temporarily and restored Bush's sunny outlook, but Iraq's prospects remained inauspicious.[116]

As it coped with spiraling events in Iraq, the Bush administration pondered how to deal with Iran. The unilateralism of sanctions and "dual containment" gave way to an alliance contingent imperialism (P2) whereby France, Germany, and the United Kingdom (the EU-3) worked to allay U.S. fears of an Iranian nuclear weapons program by enticing Tehran to forgo its atomic pursuits in exchange for substantial commercial benefits, some of which the United States would provide. When Iran balked, the White House pressed for additional alliance imperialism via a Security Council resolution in December 2006. Before and after EU-3/Security Council diplomacy, Washington threatened Iran with military intervention should it continue to flout international will. Such coercive diplomacy only emboldened Iranian conservatives, however, especially President Mahmoud Ahmadinejad, whose insolence vis-à-vis the "Great Satan" nevertheless proved controversial within his own country. Iran's regional ambitions, befitting its imperial past, clashed with America's Iraq and "emirates" strategies. Despite some common interests, Tehran and Washington diverged on how to achieve important objectives such as stability in Iraq and Afghanistan. Each supported the al-Maliki government in Baghdad, but Iran wanted a Shi'ite Iraq, whereas the United States preferred a shared Iraq. While the Americans accused the Iranians, specifically the Revolutionary Guards' Quds Force, of assisting Shi'ite militias in Iraq, the Persians labeled their archenemies nefarious imperialists who had destabilized the Middle East thanks to their Iraqi and pro-Israeli policies. On May 28, 2007, U.S. and Iranian diplomats met officially for the first time since 1979, but talks on Iraq merely confirmed their countries' disagreement.[117]

As Washington and Tehran traded barbs and warned of dire consequences should the other try to impose its way, the GCC countries worried that events in the Gulf (and elsewhere in the Middle East) could jeopardize their safety as well as their political and financial interests. As a result, they strengthened their ties with the United States except for Saudi Arabia, which asked Washington to remove its soldiers from its sacred Islamic soil following the March-April 2003 invasion of Iraq, which Riyadh tacitly endorsed. The Bush administration honored the request, since it suited American interests and U.S.-Saudi relations would benefit—as would the GCC as a whole. The White House thus opted for alliance contingent imperialism (P2) once more. From 2001 until 2003, it pursued this variant via a "GCC" strategy inaugurated by President George H.W. Bush in 1991. Once American servicemen and women exited the Saudi Kingdom, his son adopted an "emirates" strategy.[118]

According to Middle East expert Gregory Gause, this modus operandi aped that of its imperial predecessor in the region. "Whether consciously or not," he noted, "the United States [was] falling into the historic position of Great Britain in the Gulf, and seem[ed] set to replicate the general outlines of British Gulf strategy: a strong presence on the coast, with a general aversion to become too involved in inland Arabia." This geographic emphasis on littoral bases accorded with the air-naval quality of America's empire in the Gulf and the political dynamic within the emirate countries, who, opined Gause, "are better able to manage the political consequences of an American military presence than is Saudi Arabia." While America's "emirates" strategy may have seemed innovative, Gause asserted that it merely reprised British thinking: "[t]he same logic that made them [i.e., the emirate states] the centerpiece of British Gulf strategy for 150 years still remains today." He warned, however, that Washington "must avoid the fallacy that it can simply recreate the British role in the Gulf of a past colonial age. . . . With better-educated and more politically aware populations," he added, "these smaller states cannot be viewed simply as protectorates." Given that, he urged any U.S. administration to "avoid the temptation to play an overtly imperial role of direct intervention in local politics, such as in ruling family factional squabbles. Changes imposed from the outside, no matter how well intentioned, are likely to misread local realities and to engender a local backlash." The Bush administration heeded Gause's advice, proffered in spring 2003. Paradoxically, it proceeded inversely in Iraq, a choice that yielded many disastrous consequences for both Americans and Iraqis.[119]

Washington's imperial manner in Iraq (i.e., *formal* empire), which recalled McKinley-era imperialism, differed markedly from its efforts at *informal* empire in the GCC states. The advantages of a twenty-first century empire (i.e., cooptation of economic and political elites combined with military projection emphasizing isolated bases, speed, mobility, and the potential for awesome and precise destruction of enemy targets via coordinated air-land-sea attacks) surely seemed comparable, if not preferable, to the strengths of a nineteenth-centuryesque imperium (i.e., bureaucratic management and policymaking in harmony with the metropole's grand strategy). Informal empire in the Gulf may not have assured America complete mastery of its sphere of influence, but its disadvantages (e.g., independent-minded proxies whose decisions occasionally undermined the imperium) were much more acceptable than the shortcomings of its formal empire (e.g., thousands of soldiers and officials visible to restless and infuriated armed locals, who did not want invaders to rule over them).[120]

If Washington could have installed a pro-U.S. leader in Iraq in 2003, then maybe it could have retired to bases scattered throughout the country. In such a scenario, formal empire would have evolved into informal imperium, as Iraq would have joined the GCC states in forming America's sphere of influence in the Persian Gulf. Rather than try for such an outcome, the Bush administration assured itself an archetypal imperial dilemma. If 130,000 or so U.S. soldiers remained in Iraq, the population would continue to resent them—and suicide bombers, insurgents, and militias would continue to target them. If they left, however, Iraq would likely turn into a "failed state" that could some day sponsor terrorist attacks against the United States in the Gulf and elsewhere. To cope with such a predicament, in 2005–06 the White House touted its "as Iraqi forces stand up, U.S. forces will stand down" plan. The Pentagon drew lessons from U.S. policy in El Salvador during the Reagan years as it developed a "fallback strategy" of incremental withdrawal and intensified advising of the Iraqi military and police. That Washington would look to a controversial Latin American counterinsurgency policy that yielded countless human-rights abuses, many perpetrated by Salvadoran government death squads, inspired trepidation rather than confidence.[121]

In 2007, the American odyssey in Iraq seemed without end despite its prohibitive cost in U.S. and Iraqi lives as well as American treasure—$2 billion or so per week. As the U.S. military "surged" in Baghdad, the British withdrew from the key southern city of Basra, and the Iraqi government sought political and economic reforms via the UN-sanctioned Iraq Compact, Sunni and Shi'ite militants exploded increasingly sophisticated bombs to great effect as they sought *sahel*—i.e., total victory, including the humiliation of the enemy "by dragging his corpse through the streets." This Iraqi mentality explained the country's perpetual ethno-sectarian violence, which only exacerbated Iraqi despair and jeopardized American and Iraqi government plans. In response to U.S. travails, politicians, analysts, and pundits proposed solutions such as partition (particularly of the "soft" kind), power- and resource-sharing (especially oil, which Sunni areas lacked), and the use of additional State Department bureaucrats to help rehabilitate the still dysfunctional Iraqi state. Although countless observers discussed whether a hobbled United States should quit Iraq, the White House and Pentagon professed commitment to a lengthy American stay, but with a significantly reduced force. In duration and mission, this "post-occupation" plan would be akin to the U.S. role in the Korean Peninsula, where America had served as a buffer between North Korea and South Korea, its long-time ally, since 1953. Regardless of the Bush administration's intentions, whereby some 40,000 or so U.S. soldiers would be garrisoned in three or four bases, a U.S. National Intelligence Estimate only confirmed Iraq's grim outlook whether America stayed or left. Hence, the notion of a U.S. "way forward" in Iraq seemed oxymoronic and thus impossible to realize.[122]

The Bush administration never envisaged a Gordian knot of its own making that it could not cut, especially not in 2003, when it authorized an invasion of Iraq. Following a convincing victory in April that Alexander the Great would have likely admired for its speed and execution, the U.S. empire in the Persian Gulf exuded strength and confidence as it achieved its post–World War II apogee. After six decades of fitful expansion in the region, a U.S. colossus oversaw the Gulf, dominating it just as the British, Ottomans, Persian Safavids, Portuguese, and other imperia had decades and centuries earlier. Its inflated sense of power, so typical of empires, seemed to presage an era of uncontested American primacy. *Pax Americana* proved fleeting in Iraq, however, as the country quickly devolved into dystopia, a murderous zone of conflict where even the Green Zone in Baghdad (Iraqi government and U.S. administrative headquarters) could not keep out suicide bombers bent on destroying the nascent Iraqi state and humiliating its sponsor. Similar to many previous imperia, the United States struggled to assert its authority. Opinion-editorialist David Brooks noted that "it is now clear that the light-footprint approach has been a disaster." America's understandable unwillingness to treat Iraqis brutally on a consistent basis (which likely would have horrified Roman emperors) only compounded its increasing impotence. Its benevolence won few converts and minimal gratitude, while its malevolence only earned it enmity from a population accustomed to Saddam Hussein's injustice.[123]

With its regional, as well as global, reputation tarnished, courtesy of its incompetence in Iraq, Washington strove to shield the GCC countries, home to the U.S. informal empire in the Gulf, from the mayhem convulsing Mesopotamia. Part of the "emirates" strategy involved warning Iran not to meddle in those states. But "petrodollars" reinvigorated the sagging Iranian economy, and "petro politics" catapulted Tehran into regional and international prominence once more. With events seemingly conspiring against it, the Bush administration, very unpopular at home as well as abroad, continued to stagger in fall 2007 even though General Petraeus reported notable security gains in Iraq in the wake of the so-called Anbar Awakening, whereby Sunni tribes, with American assistance, turned their guns on al-Qaeda in Iraq. Given U.S. military success, America's formal empire in that country stood less in shambles after nearly five years of bitter occupation and approximately 4,000 U.S. military fatalities. The months ahead promised much uncertainty, however, as American troop strength returned to its pre-"surge" level, Iraqi ethno-sectarian violence persisted, and Iraq's government seemed incapable or unwilling to achieve U.S. "benchmarks." Washington's informal imperium in the Gulf fared much better, due in no small measure to impressive GCC economic success, but its future very much hinged on the outcome of the U.S. misadventure in Iraq.[124]

Notes

1. Scholar Robert Pauly writes that "[t]hose half-measures Clinton did choose to take only emboldened Saddam and allowed Al Qaeda to continue planning the 9/11 attacks that George W. Bush would have to deal with." Robert J. Pauly, Jr., *US Foreign Policy and the Persian Gulf: Safeguarding American Interests through Selective Multilateralism* (Aldershot, England: Ashgate, 2005), 87.

2. See Ivo H. Daalder and James M. Lindsay, *America Unbound: The Bush Revolution in Foreign Policy* (Washington, DC: Brookings Institution Press, 2003).

3. See Clyde Prestowitz, *Rogue Nation: American Unilateralism and the Failure of Good Intentions* (New York: Basic Books, 2003).

4. Amy Chua, *World on Fire: How Exporting Free Market Democracy Breeds Ethnic Hatred and Global Instability* (New York: Doubleday, 2003); and Jeffrey D. Sachs, "How Aid Can Work," *New York Review of Books*, 21 December 2006, 97. On Darfur, see "Keep Crying Out," *Economist*, 9 December 2006, 14.

5. For a sample of elite opinion regarding the events of 9/11, see the issue titled "It Happened Here," *New Republic*, 24 September 2001. For America's historic response to surprise attacks, see John Lewis Gaddis, *Surprise, Security, and the American Experience* (Cambridge, MA: Harvard University Press, 2004).

6. For information on the immediate aftermath of 9/11, see the special report titled "God Bless America," *Newsweek*, 24 September 2001. For assessments of the impact of 9/11 on U.S. foreign policy, see Thomas L. Friedman, *Longitudes and Attitudes: The World in the Age of Terrorism* (New York: Anchor Books, 2003); and Strobe Talbott and Nayan Chanda, eds., *The Age of Terror: America and the World After September 11* (New York: Basic Books, 2001).

7. Peter Bergen, "Afghan Spring," *New Republic*, 18 June 2007, 22–26; Carlotta Gall and David E. Sanger, "Civilian Deaths Undermine Allies' War on Taliban," *New York Times*, 13 May 2007, http://www.nytimes.com; Reuters, "Bomb Kills 6 Canadian Troops in Afghanistan," *CNN.com*, 8 April 2007, http://www.cnn.com; "NATO in Afghanistan," http://www.nato.int (21 August 2006); "Winning in Afghanistan Means Telling Home Truths," *Observer* (London), 9 July 2006, http://observer.guardian.co.uk; "NATO in Afghanistan," http://www.nato.int (2 September 2004); Fareed Zakaria, "Warlords, Drugs and Votes," *Newsweek*, 9 August 2004, 39; Christina Lamb, "Old Fears in the New Afghanistan," *New York Times*, 8 December 2002, http://www.nytimes.com; and Evan Thomas, "In The War Room," *Newsweek*, 25 November 2002, 30–33.

8. Gwynne Dyer, "Terrorism Deforms American Foreign Policy," *Blade* (Toledo, OH), 5 July 2002, A9. For an examination of differing U.S. and European world views, see Robert Kagan, *Of Paradise and Power: America and Europe in the New World Order* (New York: Alfred A. Knopf, 2003).

9. Daalder and Lindsay, *America Unbound*; Philip Zelikow, "The Transformation of National Security: Five Redefinitions," *National Interest*, no. 71 (Spring 2003): 17–28; John Lewis Gaddis, "A Grand Strategy of Transformation," *Foreign Policy*, no. 133 (November-December 2002), http://www.foreignpolicy.com; George W. Bush, "The National Security Strategy of the United States of America," September 2002, http://www.whitehouse.gov/nsc/nss.pdf; and James Dao, "One Nation Plays the Great Game Alone," *New York Times*, 6 July 2002, http://www.nytimes.com. For foreign reaction to the Bush Doctrine, see Glenn Frankel, "New U.S. Doctrine Worries Europe-

ans," *Washington Post*, 30 September 2002, http://www.washingtonpost.com; and Jefferson Morley, "Bush Doctrine Leaves Allies Feeling Left Out," *Washington Post*, 27 September 2002, http://www.washingtonpost.com. By expanding its global commitments and intimidating allies and foes alike, the Bush administration contravened the advice scholar Stephen Walt proffered—a recipe for long-term foreign-policy disaster, in Walt's opinion. See Stephen M. Walt, "Beyond bin Laden: Reshaping U.S. Foreign Policy," *International Security* 26, no. 3 (Winter 2001/02): 56–78.

10. "Fractured Foreign Policy," *Blade*, 5 January 2003, B4; Don Gregg, "Kim Jong Il: The Truth Behind the Caricature," *Newsweek*, 3 February 2003, 13; Mary McGory, "Fuzzy-Headed on North Korea," *Washington Post*, 9 February 2003, http://www.washingtonpost.com; Nancy E. Soderberg, "Escaping North Korea's Nuclear Trap," *New York Times*, 12 February 2003, http://www.nytimes.com; Richard Wolffe, "Who Is the Bigger Threat?" *Newsweek*, 13 February 2003, 20–23; Michael Hirsh, "Kim Is the Key Danger," *Newsweek*, 13 February 2003, 30; and Christopher Dickey, ". . . No, Saddam Is Worse," *Newsweek*, 13 February 2003, 31.

11. Max Boot, "Neither New nor Nefarious: The Liberal Empire Strikes Back," *Current History* (November 2003): 361–66; Max Boot, "The Sun Never Sets . . . ," *Weekly Standard*, 4 November 2002, 26–29; Max Boot, "The Case for American Empire," *Weekly Standard*, 15 October 2001, 27–30; Lawrence F. Kaplan and William Kristol, *The War Over Iraq: Saddam's Tyranny and America's Mission* (San Francisco, CA: Encounter Books, 2003); Joshua Micah Marshall, "Power Rangers: Did the Bush Administration Create a New American Empire—or Weaken the Old One?" *New Yorker*, 2 February 2004, http://www.newyorker.com; Philip H. Gordon, "The End of the Bush Revolution," *Foreign Affairs* 85, no. 4 (July/August 2006): 76–81; and Pew Research Center for the People & the Press, "Pew Global Attitudes Project: March 16, 2004, Survey: A Year After Iraq War," http://people-press.org/reports.

12. Robin Wright and Glenn Kessler, "At State, Rice Takes Control of Diplomacy," *Washington Post*, 31 July 2005, http://www.washingtonpost.com; Graham E. Fuller, "Strategic Fatigue," *National Interest*, no. 84 (Summer 2006): 37–42; Thomas L. Friedman, "Condi and Rummy," *New York Times*, 7 April 2006, http://www.nytimes.com; Reuters, "U.S. Budget Deficit Expands to $412.5 Billion," *MSNBC.com*, 14 October 2004, http://www.msnbc.msn.com; Gordon, "The End of the Bush Revolution," 81–86; Mike Allen and Romesh Ratnesar, "The End of Cowboy Diplomacy," *Time*, 9 July 2006, http://www.time.com; David E. Sanger, "Few Good Choices in North Korean Standoff," *New York Times*, 6 July 2006, http://www.nytimes.com; and David E. Sanger, "North Korean Diplomatic Strategy Mirrors Iran's," *New York Times*, 24 June 2006, http://www.nytimes.com.

13. "Special Report: Five Years of Terror," *Newsweek*, 21 & 28 August 2006, 38–56; Jim Rutenberg, "In Election Push, Bush Faults Talk of Iraq Pullout," *New York Times*, 22 August 2006, http://www.nytimes.com; Dan Eggen and Dafna Linzer, "Judge Rules Against Wiretaps," *Washington Post*, 18 August 2006, http://www.washingtonpost.com; Michiko Kakutani, "Personality, Ideology and Bush's Terror Wars," *New York Times*, 20 June 2006, http://www.nytimes.com; "The Trust Gap," *New York Times*, 12 February 2006, http://www.nytimes.com; and Jane Mayer, "Outsourcing Torture," *New Yorker*, 14 February 2005, http://www.newyorker.com.

14. John B. Judis, "Crude Joke," *New Republic*, 12 February 2007, 16–19; "The State of Energy," *New York Times*, 1 February 2006, http://www.nytimes.com; Thomas L. Friedman, "Will Pigs Fly?" *New York Times*, 3 February 2006,

http://www.nytimes.com; Paul Krugman, "State of Delusion," *New York Times*, 3 February 2006, http://www.nytimes.com; and Reuters, "Oil Closes at Record above $75," *CNNMoney.com*, 5 July 2006, http://money.cnn.com.

15. Gwynne Dyer, "2007 Was Year of Political Change, Conflict, and Occasional Hope," *Blade*, 1 January 2008, A11; S. Amjad Hussain, "Bhutto's Moderate Message Resonated with Pakistan's Masses," *Blade*, 31 December 2007, A7; Fareed Zakaria, "The Rise of a Fierce Yet Fragile Superpower," *Newsweek*, 31 December 2007/7 January 2008, 38–39; Adi Ignatius, "A Tsar Is Born," *Time*, 4 December 2007, http://www.time.com; "The US Sub-prime Crisis in Graphics," *BBC News*, 21 November 2007, http://news.bbc.co.uk; Ron Moreau and Michael Hirsh, "Where the Jihad Lives Now," *Newsweek*, 29 October 2007, 27–34; Robert J. Samuelson, "Globalization to the Rescue?" *Newsweek*, 29 October 2007, 41; and "Al Gore Wins Nobel Peace Prize," *MSNBC.com*, 12 October 2007, http://www.msnbc.com.

16. Steven Lee Myers and Helene Cooper, "Israel and Palestinians Set Goal of a Treaty in 2008," *New York Times*, 28 November 2007, http://www.nytimes.com; Steven Erlanger, "A Large Shadow Cast by an Absent Country," *New York Times*, 28 November 2007, http://www.nytimes.com; and Thomas L. Friedman, "Oasis or Mirage?" *New York Times*, 28 November 2007, http://www.nytimes.com. On Bush's legacy issues, see Ed Henry, "With One Year to Go, Bush's Legacy a Mixed Bag," *CNN.com*, 23 December 2007, http://www.cnn.com. On Rice's diplomatic record, see Fred Kaplan, "Why Her Dreams Crashed," *Washington Post*, 4 November 2007, http://www.washingtonpost.com.

17. Deborah Sontag, "Mixed Metaphor in the Mideast," *New York Times*, 5 January 2001, http://www.nytimes.com; John J. Mearsheimer, "The Impossible Partition," *New York Times*, 11 January 2001, http://www.nytimes.com; Shlomo Gazit and Edward Abington, "The Palestinian-Israeli Conflict," *Middle East Policy* 8, no. 1 (March 2001): 58–72; Alon Ben-Meir, "Behind the Palestinian-Israeli Violence and Beyond," *Middle East Policy* 8, no. 1 (March 2001): 81–88; Deborah Sontag, "News Analysis: For Israelis, Endless War and Sharon Put Peace Off Agenda," *New York Times*, 14 April 2001, http://www.nytimes.com; Thomas L. Friedman, "To Tell the Truth," *New York Times*, 20 April 2001, http://www.nytimes.com; Jane Perlez, "The Peacemaker Takes Up Another Line of Work," *New York Times*, 22 April 2001, http://www.nytimes.com; Jane Perlez, "U.S. Gingerly Considers More Active Role in Mideast," *New York Times*, 17 May 2001, http://www.nytimes.com; Thomas L. Friedman, "It Only Gets Worse," *New York Times*, 22 May 2001, http://www.nytimes.com; Ronald C. Kiener, "The Cease-Fire That Never Was," *Hartford Courant*, 17 June 2001, C1, C4; Jane Perlez, "Bush and Sharon Differ on Ending Violence," *New York Times*, 27 June 2001, http://www.nytimes.com; and Robert Malley, "Fictions About the Failure at Camp David," *New York Times*, 8 July 2001, http://www.nytimes.com.

18. Robert G. Kaiser, "Bush and Sharon Nearly Identical On Mideast Policy," *Washington Post*, 9 February 2003, http://www.washingtonpost.com; and Stephen S. Rosenfeld, "Beyond Slogans," *Washington Post*, 18 February 2003, http://www.washingtonpost.com. For the Road Map, see "Quartet Roadmap to Israeli-Palestinian Peace," http://www.mideastweb.org/quartetrm3.htm (30 April 2003).

19. Greg Myre, "Despite His Troubles, Arafat Endures as Leader and Symbol," *New York Times*, 27 July 2004, http://www.nytimes.com; Roger Cohen, "Building for Calm by Giving Up on Peace," *New York Times*, 18 July 2004, http://www.nytimes.com; Steven Erlanger, "Despite Setback, Sharon to Proceed With Withdrawal," *New York Times*, 19 August 2004, http://www.nytimes.com; "A Big Man on a Tightrope," *Economist*, 19

August 2004, http://www.economist.com; Associated Press, "Israel Must Shift W. Bank Wall," *Blade*, 1 July 2004, A2; Elaine Sciolino, "Self-Appointed Israeli and Palestinian Negotiators Offer a Plan for Middle East Peace," *New York Times*, 2 December 2003, http://www.nytimes.com; and Thomas L. Friedman, "The Wailing Wall?" *New York Times*, 7 September 2003, http://www.nytimes.com. The Israelis killed Yassin in March 2004. See "Death in Gaza," *New York Times*, 23 March 2004, http://www.nytimes.com.

20. Daoud Kuttab, "The Long Perspective from Gaza," *Washington Post*, 21 August 2005, http://www.washingtonpost.com; Daoud Kuttab, "Live from Gaza: A New View of Israel," *New York Times*, 21 August 2005, http://www.nytimes.com; James Bennet, "The New Occupation: Trying to Govern Gaza," *New York Times*, 21 August 2005, http://www.nytimes.com; Kevin Peraino, "The End of a Dream," *Newsweek*, 22 August 2005, 26–33; Ethan Bronner, "Why 'Greater Israel' Never Came to Be," *New York Times*, 14 August 2005, http://www.nytimes.com; Ibrahim Barzak, "Palestinians Cheer Upcoming Gaza Pullout," *Washington Post*, 12 August 2005, http://www.washingtonpost.com; Jackson Diehl, "A Golden Opportunity Squandered," *Washington Post*, 1 August 2005, http://www.washingtonpost.com; Dana Milbank, "President Outlines Foreign Policy," *Washington Post*, 2 December 2004, http://www.washingtonpost.com; "Betting on Mr. Sharon," *Washington Post*, 25 August 2004, http://www.washingtonpost.com; "Folly in the West Bank," *New York Times*, 24 August 2004, http://www.nytimes.com; Steven R. Weisman, "U.S. Now Said to Support Growth for Some West Bank Settlements," *New York Times*, 21 August 2004, http://www.nytimes.com; "The America-Israeli Settlements Dance Cannot Continue," *Daily Star* (Beirut), 18 August, 2004, http://www.dailystar.com.lb; Joshua Hammer, "'The End of Dreams,'" *Newsweek*, 26 April 2004, 36–37; "Mr. Sharon's Coup," *Washington Post*, 16 April 2004, http://www.washingtonpost.com; and Dana Milbank, "Bush Endorses Sharon's Withdrawal Plan," *Washington Post*, 14 April 2004, http://www.washingtonpost.com.

21. Steven Erlanger and Greg Myre, "Anticipating Hamas Victory, Palestinian Cabinet Resigns," *New York Times*, 26 January 2006, http://www.nytimes.com; James Glanz, "A Little Democracy or a Genie Unbottled," *New York Times*, 29 January 2006, http://www.nytimes.com; Steven R. Weisman, "Rice Admits U.S. Underestimated Hamas Strength," *New York Times*, 30 January 2006, http://www.nytimes.com; Steven Erlanger, "Sharon Has 'Significant' Stroke; Undergoes Surgery," *New York Times*, 5 January 2006, http://www.nytimes.com; Thomas L. Friedman, "Wanted: An Arab Sharon," *New York Times*, 11 January 2006, http://www.nytimes.com; Steven Erlanger, "Israel, in Slap at Hamas, Freezes Money for Palestinians," *New York Times*, 19 February 2006, http://www.nytimes.com; Steven Erlanger, "Not With a Bang but a Pop," *New York Times*, 30 March 2006, http://www.nytimes.com; and Robert Satloff, "Hobbling Hamas: Moving beyond the U.S. Policy of Three No's," *Weekly Standard*, 3 April 2006, http://www.washingtoninstitute.org.

22. Steven Erlanger, "Testing How Long the Mideast Cease-Fire Can Last," *New York Times*, 15 August 2006, http://www.nytimes.com; Helene Cooper, "Rice's Hurdles on Middle East Begin at Home," *New York Times*, 10 August 2006, http://www.nytimes.com; Neil MacFarquhar, "Anti-U.S. Feeling Leaves Arab Reformers Isolated," *New York Times*, 9 August 2006, http://www.nytimes.com; "Back to the Past," *New Republic*, 7 August 2006, 7; Lawrence F. Kaplan, "Other Means," *New Republic*, 31 July 2006, 12–13; Christopher Dickey, Kevin Peraino, and Babak Dehghanpisheh, "The Hand That Feeds the Fire," *Newsweek*, 24 July 2006, 22–30; "Attacked," *New Republic*,

24 July 2006, 7; "Assault on Lebanon," *Blade*, 15 July 2006, A6; Scott Wilson, "Dual Crises Test Olmert as Leader," *Washington Post*, 15 July 2006, http://www.washingtonpost.com; Hassan M. Fattah and Steven Erlanger, "Lebanon Seeks Cease-Fire; Bush Refuses to Press Israel," *New York Times*, 14 July 2006, http://www.nytimes.com; Robin Wright, "Options for U.S. Limited As Mideast Crises Spread," *Washington Post*, 13 July 2006, http://www.washingtonpost.com; and Ian Fisher and Steven Erlanger, "Israelis Batter Gaza and Seize Hamas Officials," *New York Times*, 29 June 2006, http://www.nytimes.com.

23. Michael Slackman, "And Now, Islamism Trumps Arabism," *New York Times*, 20 August 2006, http://www.nytimes.com; Michael Young, "Hezbollah's Other War," *New York Times Magazine*, 4 August 2006, http://www.nytimes.com; Michael Slackman, "Voices of Peace Muffled by Rising Mideast Strife," *New York Times*, 14 July 2006, http://www.nytimes.com; Thomas L. Friedman, "Empty Pockets, Angry Minds," *New York Times*, 22 February 2006, http://www.nytimes.com; and Charlene Barshefsky, "The Middle East Belongs in the World Economy," *New York Times*, 22 February 2003, http://www.nytimes.com. On the United Nations Development Programme's Arab Human Development Report, see http://www.undp.org/rbas/ahdr/english.html. For overviews of the Middle East and its problems, see Raymond Hinnebusch, "The Middle East Regional System," in *The Foreign Policies of Middle East States*, eds. Raymond Hinnebusch and Anoushiravan Ehteshami (Boulder, CO: Lynne Rienner, 2002), 29–53; B.A. Roberson, "The Impact of the International System on the Middle East," in *The Foreign Policies of Middle East States*, 55–69; and Nadia El-Shazly and Raymond Hinnebusch, "The Challenge of Security in the Post-Gulf War Middle East System," in *The Foreign Policies of Middle East States*, 71–90.

24. Gary G. Sick, "US Policy in the Gulf: Objectives and Prospects," in *Managing New Developments in the Gulf*, ed. Rosemary Hollis (London: Royal Institute of International Affairs, 2000), 37–41; Raad Alkadiri, "Iraq: The Dilemma of Sanctions and Confrontation," in *Managing New Developments in the Gulf*, 70–90; Judith S. Yaphe, "Iraq: The Exception to the Rule," *Washington Quarterly* 24, no. 1 (Winter 2001): 125–37; Serge Truffaut, "Dix Ans après la Guerre du Golfe, les Irakiens Sont sous le Joug de Hussein et des Etats-Unis [Ten Years after the Gulf War, the Iraqis Are under Hussein's and the United States' Juggernaut]," *Le Devoir* (Montréal), 17 January 2001, http://www.ledevoir.com; Robin Wright, "Bush May Find His Father's Foe a Formidable Adversary," *Los Angeles Times*, 17 January 2001, http://www.latimes.com; Robin Wright, "Bush's Foreign Policy Team Is Split on How to Handle Hussein," *Los Angeles Times*, 14 February 2001, http://www.latimes.com; Michael R. Gordon, "Military Analysis: U.S. Strikes Leave Plan for Iraq Fuzzy," *New York Times*, 18 February 2001, http://www.nytimes.com; Robin Wright, "Iraq May Have Gained from U.S. Airstrike," *Los Angeles Times*, 18 February 2001, http://www.latimes.com; Robin Wright, "Arab World Undermined by Crisis, Confusion," *Los Angeles Times*, 24 February 2001, http://www.latimes.com; "Middle East Dilemmas," *Economist*, 25 February, 2001, http://www.economist.com; Russell Watson and Roy Gutman, "Bush vs. Iraq: The Rematch," *Newsweek*, 26 February 2001, 38–40; Fareed Zakaria, "Let's Get Real about Iraq," *Newsweek*, 26 February 2001, 41; John F. Burns, "10 Years Later, Hussein Is Firmly in Control," *New York Times*, 26 February 2001, http://www.nytimes.com; Robin Wright, "With Iraq Unbowed, Powell Vows Indefinite Support for Kuwait," *Los Angeles Times*, 27 February, 2001, http://www.latimes.com; Jane Perlez, "Capitol Hawks Seek Tougher Line on Iraq," *New York Times*, 7 March 2001, http://www.nytimes.com; Mi-

chael Ignatieff, "Bush's First Strike," *New York Review of Books*, 29 March 2001, 6–10; and James Dao, "Rumsfeld Says Air Patrols Over Iraq Are in Peril," *New York Times*, 5 June 2001, http://www.nytimes.com.

25. Susan Sachs and Judith Miller, "U.N. Tainted by Oil-Food Scandal," *Blade*, 22 August 2004, B1–B2; Judith Miller, "Bribery Inquiry Needs a Year, Its Chief Says," *New York Times*, 10 August 2004, http://www.nytimes.com; Barbara Crossette, "U.N. Aides Cite Payoff Racket in Iraqi 'Oil for Food' Plan," *New York Times*, 7 March 2001, http://www.nytimes.com; Douglas Frantz, "At Iraq's Backdoor, Turkey Flouts Sanctions," *New York Times*, 30 March 2001, http://www.nytimes.com; Alan Sipress, "U.S. Tries to Strike a Balance on Iraq," *Hartford Courant*, 24 May 2001, A17; "Can Sanctions Be Smarter?" *Economist*, 29 May 2001, http://www.economist.com; "Making Sense of Sanctions," *Economist*, 29 May 2001, http://www.economist.com; Maggie Farley and Robin Wright, "Deal Extends Debate on Iraq Sanctions," *Los Angeles Times*, 1 June 2001, http://www.latimes.com; Louis Meixler, "Iraqi Oil Trade Thrives despite U.N. Sanctions," *Hartford Courant*, 9 June 2001, A9; Robin Wright, "New U.S. Strategy on Iraq Falters," *Los Angeles Times*, 2 July 2001, http://www.latimes.com; "Unwise Council," *Economist*, 3 July 2001, http://www.economist.com; Maggie Farley and Robin Wright, "Iraq Wins at U.N. but Loses Pair of Envoys," *Los Angeles Times*, 4 July 2001, http://www.latimes.com; and "Smart Exit," *Economist*, 7 July 2001, http://www.economist.com.

26. Daniel Byman, Kenneth Pollack, and Gideon Rose, "The Rollback Fantasy," *Foreign Affairs* 78, no. 1 (January/February 1999): 24–41; Lawrence F. Kaplan, "Rollback," *New Republic*, 30 October 2000, 28–30; and Robin Wright, "Hapless Hussein Opposition Has U.S. Looking Elsewhere," *Los Angeles Times*, 19 March 2001, http://www.latimes.com. For a solid overview of the Clinton administration's policy vis-à-vis Iraq, see Daniel Byman, "After the Storm: U.S. Policy Toward Iraq Since 1991," *Political Science Quarterly* 115, no. 4 (2000–2001): 493–516. Byman wrote (513) that "[o]n its own terms, U.S. policy in Iraq is generally successful, though hardly perfect. Most obviously, Iraq has been contained. A robust U.S. regional presence, a rapid surge capacity, and a willingness to use limited force probably have convinced Saddam that regional aggression will not succeed. Moreover, as a result of sanctions and the devastation of the Gulf War, Saddam's Iraq is far weaker than it was in 1990, both in relative and absolute terms." Byman warned (516), however, that "[t]he long-term resolution of the Iraq problem will not come even if the United States meets its most ambitious objective with Saddam's death. Rather, stability (and perhaps better governance) will only come to the region when Iraq is integrated into a regional structure that provides security. . . . Although a long-term solution remains far-off today [in 2000], the United States needs a blueprint for the region that goes beyond the removal of a particular leader. Only then, can its current short-term strategy serve long-term objectives."

27. Bob Woodward, *Plan of Attack* (New York: Simon & Schuster, 2004), 1–153; Glenn Kessler, "U.S. Decision On Iraq Has Puzzling Past," *Washington Post*, 12 January 2003, http://www.washingtonpost.com; Thom Shanker and David E. Sanger, "U.S. Envisions Blueprint on Iraq Including Big Invasion Next Year," *New York Times*, 28 April 2002, http://www.nytimes.com; and Michael R. Gordon, "With Allies Likely and Unlikely, U.S. Navy Stems Flow of Iraqi Oil," *New York Times*, 29 October 2002, http://www.nytimes.com. Without fanfare whatsoever, the Iranians assisted the Americans and Australians in preventing Iraqis from illegally exporting or importing goods via Persian Gulf waters. For a neo-conservative overview of U.S. policy vis-à-vis Iraq under

Bush *père*, Clinton, and Bush *fils*, see Kaplan and Kristol, *The War Over Iraq*. In their book, published before hostilities commenced, Kaplan and Kristol advocated war to remove Saddam Hussein.

28. Woodward, *Plan of Attack*, 154–227. For a succinct overview of Saddam Hussein's political career and the run-up to Resolution 1441, see Serge Schmemann, "Many Encounters Set Today's Stage," *New York Times*, 8 December 2002, http://www.nytimes.com. See also Christopher Dickey and Evan Thomas, "How Saddam Happened," *Newsweek*, 23 September 2002, 34–41.

29. Woodward, *Plan of Attack*, 228–295. On what could transpire in Iraq, much of it negative, once Saddam Hussein's government fell, see Nicholas D. Kristof, "The Day After," *New York Times*, 24 September 2002, http://www.nytimes.com. See also Walter Pincus, "Before War, CIA Warned of Negative Outcomes," *Washington Post*, 3 June 2007, http://www.washingtonpost.com. Despite the ritualistic ovations for President Bush as he delivered the State of the Union, not everyone praised the speech, especially its discussion of Iraq. See "The Nation, the President, the War," *New York Times*, 29 January 2003, http://www.nytimes.com; David S. Broder, "Echoes of 1991," *Washington Post*, 30 January 2003, http://www.washingtonpost.com; "Show Us the Evidence," *Blade*, 31 January 2003, A10; and Bill Bradley, "Bush Has Not Made the Case," *Washington Post*, 2 February 2003, http://www.washingtonpost.com. Some foreigners liked the speech, however. See "The Face of Leadership," *National Post* (Toronto), 29 January 2003, http://www.nationalpost.com. Others found much to fault. Abdel Monem Said, director of the Al Ahram Center for Political and Strategic Studies in Cairo, Egypt, wrote that "the American government seems to have divided the Middle East into a set of separate problems, each in its own little box: Iraq, Iran, the Palestinians and the Israelis, Fundamentalism, Terrorism. To an Arab, these are all related issues." In contrast to President Bush's "rosy view of an invasion of Iraq," Said argued, "Arabs have a drastically different view. Some Iraqis will look at Americans as new colonialists. The various Iraqi factions and ethnic groups will take the opportunity to settle old scores. Iraq will descend into chaos. Turkey and Iran will interfere. The fragile countries of the eastern Mediterranean and the Gulf will suffer. The Arab-Israeli conflict will become increasingly volatile as the flames of violence and fundamentalism cross national borders." Abdel Monem Said, "The Wrong Words," *New York Times*, 30 January 2003, http://www.nytimes.com. The speech and its reception seemed only to confirm the polarization within America regarding what to do about Saddam Hussein and his despicable regime. For criticism of the Bush administration's policy, see "Improvised March to War," *New York Times*, 2 February 2003, http://www.nytimes.com. For an endorsement of the White House, see George F. Will, "Luck and Leadership," *Washington Post*, 2 February 2003, http://www.washingtonpost.com. President Bush's treatment of Saddam Hussein resembled somewhat that of the Athenians vis-à-vis the Melians during the Peloponnesian War. Whatever Hussein decided, he would likely either plunge his country into war or else be forced into exile. Neither possibility must have pleased him, obviously. Unlike the Athenians, however, President Bush sought to avoid a draconian peace. The Texan may have behaved vindictively toward Hussein and his acolytes, but he sought to spare as best he could average Iraqis from the scourge of war. Bush's mercy may have contrasted with Athens' bloodlust, but many Arabs worried that the United States sought to enslave the Iraqis—enslavement corresponding to an imposed political and economic system agreeable to Washington first and foremost. On the "Melian Dia-

logue," see Thucydides, *History of the Peloponnesian War*, translated by Rex Warner (New York: Penguin Books, 1972), 400–408.

30. Woodward, *Plan of Attack*, 296–315; Martin Indyk and Kenneth M. Pollack, "How Bush Can Avoid the Inspections Trap," *New York Times*, 27 January 2003, http://www.nytimes.com; "Making the Case for War," *National Post* (Toronto), 30 January 2003, http://www.nationalpost.com; and Rex Murphy, "9/11 Was the Smoking Gun, Boys," *Globe and Mail* (Toronto), 8 February 2003, http://www.theglobeandmail.com. For information on Powell's migration to the "hawk" camp, see "The Powell Doctrine Revisited," *Economist*, 30 January 2003, http://www.economist.com. According to a *Washington Post-ABC News* poll, Bush's January 28 speech apparently convinced many Americans of war's appropriateness in this case, increasing the percentage of those who favored hostilities to 66 percent, up from 57 percent two weeks previous. See Richard Morin and Claudia Deane, "Support for a War With Iraq Grows After Bush's Speech," *Washington Post*, 2 February 2003, http://www.washingtonpost.com. Typically, support for presidential policies increases following the State of the Union Address. Whether the president could sustain voter approval seemed unclear at the end of January 2003. On how the Bush administration sold the Iraq War using select, biased intelligence, see "The Build-a-War Workshop," *New York Times*, 10 February 2007, http://www.nytimes.com.

31. David E. Sanger and James Dao, "U.S. Is Completing Plan to Promote a Democratic Iraq," *New York Times*, 6 January 2003, http://www.nytimes.com; Richard Wolffe and Michael Hirsh, "War and Consequences," *Newsweek*, 3 February 2003, 22–28; Jonathan Alter, "'Trust Me' Isn't Good Enough," *Newsweek*, 3 February 2003, 29; Christopher Dickey, "Perils of Victory," *Newsweek*, 3 February 2003, 30–32; Gwynne Dyer, "Iraqi Dictator Is Nasty, Not Mad," *Blade*, 8 February 2003, A7; Ann McFeatters, "The Great Debate: Is War Justified?" *Blade*, 9 February 2003, B5; "More to Do," *Washington Post*, 9 February 2003, http://www.washingtonpost.com; Thomas L. Friedman, "Present at . . . What?" *New York Times*, 12 February 2003, http://www.nytimes.com; Paul Krugman, "Behind the Great Divide," *New York Times*, 18 February 2003, http://www.nytimes.com; Nicholas D. Kristof, "Mr. Bush's Liberal Problem," *New York Times*, 18 February 2003, http://www.nytimes.com; E.J. Dionne, Jr., "Listen To the Doubters," *Washington Post*, 18 February 2003, http://www.washingtonpost.com; and Bill Keller, "Fear on the Home Front," *New York Times*, 22 February 2003, http://www.nytimes.com. Columnist Thomas Friedman noted that Bush officials "are gearing up for the rebuilding of Iraq, along the lines of the rebuilding of Germany and Japan after World War II, and the nation is geared up, at best, for the quick and dirty invasion of Grenada." See Thomas L. Friedman, "Will the Neighbors Approve?" *New York Times*, 5 February 2003, http://www.nytimes.com. That the Bush administration would tout democratization in the Middle East came as a surprise. One observer wrote in June 2002 that the Bush White House resisted the logic of democratizing the Middle East. See Lawrence F. Kaplan, "Return Address," *New Republic*, 10 June 2002, 16–19. Historian John Dower cautioned that a postwar Iraq would in no way resemble U.S.-occupied Japan. See John Dower, "Lessons From Japan About War's Aftermath," *New York Times*, 27 October 2002, http://www.nytimes.com. On the problems of nation-building, see Marina Ottaway, "Nation Building," *Foreign Policy*, no. 132 (September-October 2002), http://www.foreignpolicy.com. Unlike many commentators, Friedman and Fareed Zakaria noted the Middle East's twentieth-century shortcomings and the possible benefits of a U.S. invasion. See Thomas L. Friedman, "Thinking About Iraq (I),"

New York Times, 22 January 2003, http://www.nytimes.com; and Fareed Zakaria, "Looking on the Bright Side," *Newsweek*, 3 February 2003, 33. Kurds in northern Iraq, for example, very much wanted the United States to occupy their country. See Mary Ann Smothers Bruni, "Cowboys Welcome in Kurdistan," *Washington Post*, 29 January 2003, http://www.washingtonpost.com. U.S. liberals agonized over what to do, realizing that a case for humanitarian intervention could be made. See, for example, Michael Massing, "The Moral Quandary," *Nation*, 6 January 2003, http://www.thenation.com. Devon Largio wrote a University of Illinois undergraduate honors thesis examining the various rationales for war. See William Raspberry, "Tracking Why We Went to War," *Washington Post*, 31 May 2004, http://www.washingtonpost.com.

32. Richard Morin and Claudia Deane, "Most Support Attack On Iraq, With Allies," *Washington Post*, 11 February 2003, http://www.washingtonpost.com. In May 2003, Sam Tannenhaus of *Vanity Fair* quoted Deputy Secretary of Defense Paul Wolfowitz as saying in an interview that "[f]or bureaucratic reasons we [the Bush administration] settled on one issue, weapons of mass destruction, because it was the one reason everyone could agree on." The Pentagon later claimed, however, that Wolfowitz said, "[t]he truth is that for reasons that have a lot to do with the U.S. government bureaucracy we settled on the one issue that everyone could agree on, which was weapons of mass destruction, as the core reason." But Wolfowitz added that "[t]here have always been three fundamental concerns. One is weapons of mass destruction, the second is support for terrorism, the third is the criminal treatment of the Iraqi people. Actually, I guess you could say there's a fourth overriding one, which is the connection between the first two." See Jamie McIntyre, "Pentagon Challenges Vanity Fair Report," *CNN.com*, 30 May 2003, http://www.cnn.com.

33. Thomas L. Friedman, "Thinking About Iraq (II)," *New York Times*, 26 January 2003, http://www.nytimes.com; Jonathan Wright, "U.S. Plans for Two-Year Occupation of Iraq," *Washington Post*, 11 February 2003, http://www.washingtonpost.com; Molly Ivins, "Paying the Price for Bush's War," *Blade*, 14 February 2003, A15; "The Post-War Muddle," *Blade*, 15 February 2003, A10; Gordon Adams and Steve Kosiak, "The Price We Pay," *New York Times*, 15 February 2003, http://www.nytimes.com; Michael Hirsh and Melinda Liu, "Imagining the Day After," *Newsweek*, 17 February 2003, 44–45; and Judith Miller, "U.S. Officials Review Plan to Rebuild Iraq After a War," *New York Times*, 23 February 2003, http://www.nytimes.com. Obviously, no one could divine what exactly would transpire in the Middle East should war visit the region once more, but many experts thought that a second Persian Gulf war would spark a political earthquake whose aftershocks could very well result in the reconfiguration of this all important geopolitical area. See, for example, Paul Koring, "Liberate Iraq, Free the People," *Globe and Mail* (Toronto), 27 December 2002, A15. Some analysts criticized the allocation of U.S. federal monies for defense, believing too much expended on soldiers, procurement, and "traditional military investments" and too little on means to combat international terrorism. See Daniel Benjamin and Steven Simon, "The Worst Defense," *New York Times*, 20 February 2003, http://www.nytimes.com. The Defense Department's budget soared to $380 billion for FY 2003–04, a sum that excluded expenses incurred in any war with Iraq and postwar occupation costs. By spending in excess of $400 billion on defense, the United States threatened to outspend the rest of the world combined. See "Spending Spree at the Pentagon," *New York Times*, 10 February 2003, http://www.nytimes.com.

34. Richard Cohen, "The Hanging Gun," *Washington Post*, 30 January 2003, http://www.washingtonpost.com; Bill Keller, "The I-Can't-Believe-I'm-a-Hawk Club,"

New York Times, 8 February 2003, http://www.nytimes.com; and Gwynne Dyer, "The Evil Alliance Expands," *Blade*, 14 February 2003, A15.

35. Woodward, *Plan of Attack*, 315–18; "Disarming Iraq," *New York Times*, 15 February 2003, http://www.nytimes.com; "Sound and Fury," *Washington Post*, 15 February 2003, http://www.washingtonpost.com; and Karen DeYoung and Walter Pincus, "Shifting Sands at the U.N.," *Washington Post*, 15 February 2003, http://www.washingtonpost.com. On the problem with inspections, which provided opponents of U.S. policy with an opportunity to deny Washington its preferred outcome, see Lawrence F. Kaplan, "End Game," *New Republic*, 10 February 2003, 16–18. The U.S. military plan, dubbed "Shock and Awe," emphasized speed, maneuverability, coordinated attacks, and reliance on high-tech weapons. American war planners envisaged simultaneous U.S.-led breaches into Iraq's north and south. To facilitate postwar reconstruction, the U.S. military intended to avoid as much as possible damaging or destroying essential Iraqi infrastructure. To ensure maximum national and international support for its campaign to eliminate Saddam Hussein and his accomplices, and to thwart their propaganda efforts, Washington planned to minimize civilian casualties—which the Pentagon euphemistically referred to as "collateral damage." On U.S. military strategy, see Eric Schmitt and Thom Shanker, "War Plan Calls for Precision Bombing Wave to Break Iraqi Army," *New York Times*, 2 February 2003, http://www.nytimes.com; "Bound for Battle," *Newsweek*, 3 February 2003, 26–27; John Barry and Evan Thomas, "Boots, Bytes and Bombs," *Newsweek*, 17 February 2003, 38–43; James Dao, "U.S. Plan: Spare Iraq's Civilians," *New York Times*, 23 February 2003, http://www.nytimes.com; and "Preparing For the Worst," *Economist*, 30 January 2003. http://www.economist.com. For an assessment of proposed U.S. strategy and its potential ramifications for American foreign policy in the Middle East, see General Anthony Zinni's October 2002 keynote speech, titled "Strategic Implications of a War on Iraq," at the Middle East Institute's 56th annual conference in Washington, DC, http://www.mideasti.org. To slow any U.S.-led advance into Iraq and minimize America's high-tech advantage, Saddam Hussein reportedly instructed his generals to effect simultaneous refugee and environmental catastrophes while withdrawing Republican Guard units as well as Special Republican Guard soldiers into the vicinity of Baghdad. Using a double ring (i.e., staggered or defense-in-depth) formation to defend the city, the Iraqis hoped that from entrenched positions they could inflict substantial damage on approaching U.S., UK, and Australian infantry and armored columns. Eventually, the Iraqis would retreat into the city per se to engage in urban warfare, the kind of tactical fighting U.S. Army Rangers (18 of whom died) experienced in Mogadishu, Somalia, in 1993—which led to an American pull-out of Somalia. On Iraqi military strategy, see Michael R. Gordon, "Iraq Said to Plan Strategy of Delay and Urban Battle," *New York Times*, 16 February 2003, http://www.nytimes.com; and Barry and Thomas, "Boots, Bytes and Bombs." Knowing Baghdad's intended modus operandi, the Pentagon crafted an invasion plan similar to that implemented in Panama in December 1989. See Barry and Thomas, "Boots, Bytes and Bombs." Also, the United States promised to provide succor to destitute Iraqis once hostilities broke out. See Eric Schmitt and Thom Shanker, "U.S. Military Set to Provide Aid to Iraqi People in the Event of War," *New York Times*, 11 February 2003, http://www.nytimes.com. On the timing of an initial American attack, see Michael R. Gordon, "Timing Is Everything," *New York Times*, 4 February 2003, http://www.nytimes.com.

36. The slogans appeared on signs carried at the February 15, 2003, peace march in Washington, DC. Thank you to Gloria Pizana of Bowling Green State University for

forwarding these slogans by e-mail. On the issues of oil and war in Iraq and the postwar prospects of the Iraqi oil industry, see Thomas L. Friedman, "A War for Oil?" *New York Times*, 5 January 2003, http://www.nytimes.com; and John B. Judis, "Over a Barrel," *New Republic*, 20 January 2003, 20–23.

37. Richard W. Stevenson, "Antiwar Protests Fail to Sway Bush on Plans for Iraq," *New York Times*, 19 February 2003, http://www.nytimes.com; Paul Krugman, "The Martial Plan," *New York Times*, 21 February 2003, http://www.nytimes.com; and Colbert I. King, "A 21st-Century Tet?" *Washington Post*, 22 February 2003, http://www.washingtonpost.com. On Bush's cocksureness and Manichean world view, see Richard Cohen, "The Crude Crusader," *Washington Post*, 11 February 2003, http://www.washingtonpost.com. On the importance of having Iraqis administer their postwar oil resources, see J. Robinson West, "The Pipeline To Iraq's Future," *Washington Post*, 11 February 2003, http://www.washingtonpost.com.

38. Warren Hoge, "Blair's Stand on Iraq Costs Him Popularity at Home," *New York Times*, 26 January 2003, http://www.nytimes.com; "NATO Will Protect Turkey," *Blade*, 17 February 2003, A1, A8; Joel Brinkley, "Turkey and U.S. Remain at Impasse Over Invasion of Iraq," *New York Times*, 20 February 2003, http://www.nytimes.com; "Dollar Diplomacy," *New York Times*, 20 February 2003, http://www.nytimes.com; Krugman, "The Martial Plan"; and Steven R. Weisman and Judith Miller, "U.S. and Turkey Reach Accord to Let G.I.'s Establish a Base," *New York Times*, 22 February 2003, http://www.nytimes.com. According to one journalist, the Turkish government, led by the recently elected Justice and Development Party (AKP)—whose Islamic credentials no doubt worried the military, Turkey's de facto ruling class—stood to gain politically by backing Washington and its war. See Hassan Fattah, "Trade Partners," *New Republic*, 20 January 2003, 15–16.

39. Fareed Zakaria, "It's Time to Talk To the World," *Newsweek*, 27 January 2003, 49; "Ever Awkward, Sometimes Risky," *Economist*, 30 January 2003, http://www.economist.com; Nicholas D. Kristof, "Flogging the French," *New York Times*, 31 January 2003, http://www.nytimes.com; Serge Schmemann, "America's War Train Is Leaving the Station," *New York Times*, 2 February 2003, http://www.nytimes.com; Thomas L. Friedman, "Ah, Those Principled Europeans," *New York Times*, 2 February 2003, http://www.nytimes.com; Thomas E. Ricks, "NATO Allies Trade Barbs Over Iraq," *Washington Post*, 9 February 2003, http://www.washingtonpost.com; Fred Hiatt, "Herr Rumsfeld's Warning," *Washington Post*, 9 February 2003, http://www.washingtonpost.com; Josef Joffe, "Round 1 Goes to Mr. Big," *New York Times*, 10 February 2003, http://www.nytimes.com; "Standing With Saddam," *Washington Post*, 11 February 2003, http://www.washingtonpost.com; and Régis DeBray, "The French Lesson," *New York Times*, 23 February 2003, http://www.nytimes.com. Columnist Jim Hoagland wrote that "[i]t is possible to imagine today that America's most important alliance in the future will be built not along Europe's historical and geographical fault lines, as NATO was and is, but along a confluence of democracy and vulnerability to religious-based terrorism and state-sponsored hostility." See Jim Hoagland, "Allies in a New Era," *Washington Post*, 30 January 2003, http://www.washingtonpost.com. On Canada's failed effort to reprise its 1956 Suez crisis diplomacy, which earned its foreign minister, Lester B. Pearson, a Nobel Peace Prize, see Marc J. O'Reilly, "Canadian Foreign Policy in the Middle East: Reflexive Multilateralism in an Evolving World," in *Handbook of Canadian Foreign Policy*, eds. Patrick

James, Nelson Michaud, and Marc J. O'Reilly (Lanham, MD: Lexington Books, 2006), 337–363.

40. Felicity Barringer with Michael R. Gordon, "Inspector Orders Iraq to Dismantle Disputed Missiles," *New York Times*, 22 February 2003, http://www.nytimes.com; and "Power and Leadership: The Real Meaning of Iraq," *New York Times*, 23 February 2003, http://www.nytimes.com.

41. Woodward, *Plan of Attack*, 324–25; "In Need of Resolution," *Economist*, 25 February 2003, http://www.economist.com; and Philip P. Pan, "Turkey Rejects U.S. Use of Bases," *Washington Post*, 2 March 2003, http://www.washingtonpost.com.

42. Woodward, *Plan of Attack*, 339–47; Michael Elliott, "Who's with Him?" *Time*, 3 March 2003, 28–32; Felicity Barringer, "U.N. Split Widens as Allies Dismiss Deadline on Iraq," *New York Times*, 8 March 2003, http://www.nytimes.com; "Moment of Decision," *Washington Post*, 9 March 2003, http://www.washingtonpost.com; Dana Milbank, "For Bush, War Defines Presidency," *Washington Post*, 9 March 2003, http://www.washingtonpost.com; Richard Brookhiser, "The Mind of George W. Bush," *Atlantic Monthly*, April 2003, 55–69; Patrick E. Tyler and Felicity Barringer, "Annan Says U.S. Will Violate Charter if It Acts Without Approval," *New York Times*, 11 March 2003, http://www.nytimes.com; Jefferson Morley, "In Security Council Countries, the Diplomatic Crunch Hits Home," *Washington Post*, 12 March 2003, http://www.washingtonpost.com; Warren Hoge, "U.S., Britain and Spain to Make Final Push for U.N. Support," *New York Times*, 16 March 2003, http://www.nytimes.com; "The Summit of Isolation," *New York Times*, 16 March 2003, http://www.nytimes.com; and Glenn Kessler and Mike Allen, "U.S. Missteps Led to Failed Diplomacy," *Washington Post*, 16 March 2003, http://www.washingtonpost.com. For some thought-provoking analyses of American policy on the eve of war in Iraq, see, for example, George Packer, "Dreaming of Democracy," *New York Times Magazine*, 2 March 2003, http://www.nytimes.com; Michael T. Klare, "For Oil and Empire? Rethinking War with Iraq," *Current History* (March 2003): 129–35; Johanna McGeary, "Looking Beyond Saddam," *Time*, 10 March 2003, 26–33; David Shribman, "Slow March to War Will Reshape the World," *Blade*, 12 March 2003, A9; and Fareed Zakaria, "The Arrogant Empire," *Newsweek*, 24 March 2003, 18–33.

43. Woodward, *Plan of Attack*, 357–72; Jacob Heilbrunn, "The Rumsfeld Doctrine," *New York Times*, 30 April 2006, http://www.nytimes.com; Boris Johnson, "Bush's War, Blair's Gamble," *New York Times*, 16 March 2003, http://www.nytimes.com; Thomas L. Friedman, "Repairing the World," *New York Times*, 16 March 2003, http://www.nytimes.com; Rick Atkinson and Thomas E. Ricks, "Audacious Mission, Awesome Risks," *Washington Post*, 16 March 2003, http://www.washingtonpost.com; Bob Herbert, "With Ears and Eyes Closed," *New York Times*, 17 March 2003, http://www.nytimes.com; David S. Broder, "Step by Step to War," *Washington Post*, 18 March 2003, http://www.washingtonpost.com; Richard Morin and Claudia Deane, "71% of Americans Support War, Poll Shows," *Washington Post*, 19 March 2003, http://www.washingtonpost.com and "Waiting to Exhale," *Blade*, 19 March 2003, A6. For details on the various incarnations of the U.S. war plan for Iraq from fall 2001 until the commencement of hostilities in March 2003 (i.e., Op Plan 1003, Generated Start Plan, Hybrid Plan, and Op Plan 1003 V), see Woodward, *Plan of Attack*, 8, 36–38, 40–44, 53–66, 80–84, 96–103, 113–15, 117–26, 130, 133–38, 145–49, 153, 157–59, 173–74, 205–8, 231–34, 236–37, 257–58, 287–88, 365.

44. Michael R. Gordon and Bernard E. Trainor, "Even as U.S. Invaded, Hussein Saw Iraqi Unrest as Top Threat," *New York Times*, 12 March 2006, http://www.nytimes.com; Woodward, *Plan of Attack*, 364–405; Thom Shanker, "Regime Thought War Unlikely, Iraqis Tell U.S.," *New York Times*, 12 February 2004, http://www.nytimes.com; and "The Blitz Over Baghdad," *New York Times*, 22 March 2003, http://www.nytimes.com. On the DB/ROCKSTARS network, see Woodward, *Plan of Attack*, 301–5.

45. Woodward, *Plan of Attack*, 403–6; Michael R. Gordon, "Allies Adapt to Setbacks," *New York Times*, 27 March 2003, http://www.nytimes.com; Mary Suh, "Strategy, With the Benefit of Hindsight," *New York Times*, 30 March 2003, http://www.nytimes.com; James Webb, "The War in Iraq Turns Ugly. That's What Wars Do." *New York Times*, 30 March 2003, http://www.nytimes.com; Glenn Kessler and Walter Pincus, "Advisers Split as War Unfolds," *Washington Post*, 31 March 2003, http://www.washingtonpost.com; Michael R. Gordon, "The Test for Rumsfeld: Will Strategy Work?" *New York Times*, 1 April 2003, http://www.nytimes.com; and Rick Atkinson, Peter Baker, and Thomas E. Ricks, "Confused Start, Decisive End," *Washington Post*, 13 April 2003, http://www.washingtonpost.com.

46. Atkinson, Baker, and Ricks, "Confused Start, Decisive End"; Thomas E. Ricks, "What Counted: People, Plan, Inept Enemy," *Washington Post*, 10 April 2003, http://www.washingtonpost.com; and Evan Thomas and Martha Brant, "The Secret War," *Newsweek*, 21 April 2003, 24–32.

47. Alessandra Stanley, "TV Watch: Showing 'Shock and Awe,' but No Blood," *New York Times*, 23 March 2003, http://www.nytimes.com; Daoud Kuttab, "The Arab TV Wars," *New York Times*, 6 April 2003, http://www.nytimes.com; Frank Rich, "The Spoils of War Coverage," *New York Times*, 13 April 2003, http://www.nytimes.com; Thomas L. Friedman, "The Sand Wall," *New York Times*, 13 April 2003, http://www.nytimes.com; Tom Masland and Christopher Dickey, "The Rage Next Time," *Newsweek*, 14 April 2003, 49; and Michael Massing, "The Unseen War," *New York Review of Books*, 29 May 2003, 16–19.

48. Woodward, *Plan of Attack*, 407–08; Atkinson, Baker, and Ricks, "Confused Start, Decisive End"; Thomas and Brant, "The Secret War"; and David E. Sanger and Thom Shanker, "Bush Says Regime in Iraq Is No More; Victory 'Certain,'" *New York Times*, 16 April 2003, http://www.nytimes.com.

49. Antony Beevor, "Nobody Loves a Liberator," *New York Times*, 13 April 2003, http://www.nytimes.com; Marc Santora with Patrick E. Tyler, "Pledge Made to Democracy by Exiles, Sheiks and Clerics," *New York Times*, 16 April 2003, http://www.nytimes.com; David K. Shipler, "When Freedom Leads to Anarchy," *New York Times*, 18 April 2003, http://www.nytimes.com; Dilip Hiro, "Why the Mullahs Love a Revolution," *New York Times*, 23 April 2003, http://www.nytimes.com; Reuel Marc Gerecht, "How to Mix Politics With Religion," *New York Times*, 29 April 2003, A31; Steve Negus, "The Shi'ite Clergy Steps Into the Gap," *Middle East International*, 2 May 2003, 4–6; Dexter Filkins and Ian Fisher, "U.S. Is Now in Battle for Peace After Winning the War in Iraq," *New York Times*, 3 May 2003, http://www.nytimes.com; "What Is the Plan?" *Washington Post*, 7 May 2003, http://www.washingtonpost.com; and Peter Slevin and Dana Priest, "Wolfowitz Concedes Iraq Errors," *Washington Post*, 24 July 2003, http://www.washingtonpost.com.

50. Bradley Graham, "Prewar Memo Warned of Gaps in Iraq Plans," *Washington Post*, 18 August 2005, http://www.washingtonpost.com; "The Hard Path to New Nation-

hood," *Economist*, 19 April 2003, 17–19; Tom Zeller, "Building Democracy Is Not a Science," *New York Times*, 27 April 2003, http://www.nytimes.com; Maureen Dowd, "Hypocrisy & Apple Pie," *New York Times*, 30 April 2003, http://www.nytimes.com; Thomas L. Friedman, "Dear President Bush," *New York Times*, 30 April 2003, http://www.nytimes.com; Michael R. Gordon with Eric Schmitt, "U.S. Plans to Reduce Forces in Iraq, With Help of Allies," *New York Times*, 3 May 2003, http://www.nytimes.com; Thomas L. Friedman, "Our New Baby," *New York Times*, 4 May 2003, http://www.nytimes.com; Rajiv Chandrasekaran and Peter Slevin, "Bush Shakes Up Iraq Administration," *Washington Post*, 11 May 2003, http://www.washingtonpost.com; "Iraq's Untidy Postwar," *Washington Post*, 13 May 2003, http://www.washingtonpost.com; Thomas L. Friedman, "Bored With Baghdad— Already," *New York Times*, 18 May 2003, http://www.nytimes.com; Peter Slevin and Vernon Loeb, "Plan to Secure Postwar Iraq Faulted," *Washington Post*, 19 May 2003, http://www.washingtonpost.com; Ian Williams, "The UN Caves In," *Middle East International*, 30 May 2003, 14–16; Rajiv Chandrasekaran, "The Final Word on Iraq's Future," *Washington Post*, 18 June 2003, http://www.washingtonpost.com; Colum Lynch, "Security Council Votes to Lift Iraq Sanctions," *Washington Post*, 22 May 2003, http://www.washingtonpost.com; "Mission Incomplete," *New Republic*, 26 May 2003, 7; Scott Wilson, "U.S. Commander Says War Not Over in Iraq," *Washington Post*, 29 May 2003, http://www.washingtonpost.com; "Adjusting to Iraq," *Washington Post*, 1 June 2003, http://www.washingtonpost.com; Fareed Zakaria, "Giving Peace a Real Chance," *Newsweek*, 2 June 2003, 39; Rajiv Chandrasekaran, "U.S. Sidelines Exiles Who Were to Govern Iraq," *Washington Post*, 8 June 2003, http://www.washingtonpost.com; and Thomas L. Friedman, "Bad Planning," *New York Times*, 25 June 2003, http://www.nytimes.com.

51. Minxin Pei and Sara Kasper, "The 'Morning After' Regime Change: Should US Force Democracy Again?" *Christian Science Monitor*, 15 January 2003, http://www.csmonitor.com; Daniel W. Drezner, "Democracy by America," *New Republic*, 12 March 2003, http://www.tnr.com; Shibley Telhami, "History and Humiliation," *Washington Post*, 28 March 2003, http://www.washingtonpost.com; Ethan Bonner, "Iraq and the Lessons of Lebanon: 'Don't Forget to Leave,'" *New York Times*, 30 March 2003, http://www.nytimes.com; Neil MacFarquhar, "Arabs Shocked, Relieved at Baghdad's Fall," *New York Times*, 9 April 2003, http://www.nytimes.com; Neil MacFarquhar, "Humiliation and Rage Stalk the Arab World," *New York Times*, 13 April 2003, http://www.nytimes.com; Jefferson Morley, "Fear and Rethinking in the Middle East," *Washington Post*, 14 April 2003, http://www.washingtonpost.com; Barton Gellman, "Frustrated, U.S. Arms Team to Leave Iraq," *Washington Post*, 11 May 2003, http://www.washingtonpost.com; Dana Priest and Walter Pincus, "Bush Certainty On Iraq Went Beyond Analysts' Views," *Washington Post*, 7 June 2003, http://www.washingtonpost.com; Steven R. Weisman, "Truth Is the First Casualty. Is Credibility the Second?" *New York Times*, 8 June 2003, http://www.nytimes.com; George Joffé, "Things Fall Apart," *Middle East International*, 13 June 2003, 10–13; Kenneth M. Pollack, "Saddam's Bombs? We'll Find Them," *New York Times*, 20 June 2003, http://www.nytimes.com; Spencer Ackerman and John B. Judis, "The First Casualty," *New Republic*, 30 June 2003, 14–18, 23–25; Rajiv Chandrasekaran, "Many Iraqis Fear Hussein Is Plotting Return to Power," *Washington Post*, 7 July 2003, http://www.washingtonpost.com; and Thomas L. Friedman, "Shaking Up the Neighbors," *New York Times*, 6 August 2003, http://www.nytimes.com. For the Shinseki estimate and

Wolfowitz rebuttal, see Eric Schmitt, "Pentagon Contradicts General on Iraq Occupation Force's Size," *New York Times*, 28 February 2003, http://www.nytimes.com.

52. Woodward, *Plan of Attack*, 412; Thom Shanker and Eric Schmitt, "Pentagon Expects Long-Term Access to Four Key Bases in Iraq," *New York Times*, 20 April 2003, http://www.nytimes.com; David E. Sanger, "In Speech, Bush Focuses on Conflicts Beyond Iraq," *New York Times*, 1 May 2003, http://www.nytimes.com; and Nicholas D. Kristof, "Missing in Action: Truth," *New York Times*, 6 May 2003, http://www.nytimes.com. On the issue of Israel, the Israeli lobby in the United States, and the Iraq War, see John J. Mearsheimer and Stephen M. Walt, "The Israel Lobby and U.S. Foreign Policy," *Middle East Policy* 13, no. 3 (Fall 2006): 53–9.

53. David Rieff, "Blueprint for a Mess," *New York Times Magazine*, 2 November 2003, http://www.nytimes.com; Jim Hoagland, "The War Isn't Over," *Washington Post*, 22 May 2003, http://www.washingtonpost.com; Thomas E. Ricks, "U.S. Alters Stance in Baghdad Occupation," *Washington Post*, 25 May 2003, http://www.washingtonpost.com; Karen DeYoung and Walter Pincus, "U.S. Hedges on Finding Iraqi Weapons," *Washington Post*, 29 May 2003, http://www.washingtonpost.com; Patrick E. Tyler, "There's a New Enemy in Iraq: The Nasty Surprise," *New York Times*, 1 June 2003, http://www.nytimes.com; Thomas L. Friedman, "Because We Could," *New York Times*, 4 June 2003, http://www.nytimes.com; Michael Slackman, "Iraqi Attacks Imperil U.S. Rule," *Los Angeles Times*, 6 June 2003, http://www.latimes.com; Timothy L. O'Brien, "Just What Does America Want to Do With Iraq's Oil?" *New York Times*, 8 June 2003, http://www.nytimes.com; Evan Thomas, Richard Wolffe, and Michael Isikoff, "(Over)selling the World on War," *Newsweek*, 9 June 2003, 24–30; Elizabeth Drew, "The Neocons in Power," *New York Review of Books*, 12 June 2003, 20–22; George Ward, "In Iraq, Things Really Aren't That Bad," *New York Times*, 13 June 2003, http://www.nytimes.com; Jefferson Morley, "Bremer Catches Flak as Occupation Viceroy," *Washington Post*, 18 June 2003, http://www.washingtonpost.com; Douglas Jehl and David Johnston, "Hussein Is Probably Alive in Iraq, U.S. Experts Say," *New York Times*, 20 June 2003, http://www.nytimes.com; Daniel Williams and Rajiv Chandrasekaran, "U.S. Troops Frustrated With Role in Iraq," *Washington Post*, 20 June 2003, http://www.washingtonpost.com; Daniel Williams, "Attacks In Iraq Traced to Network," *Washington Post*, 22 June 2003, http://www.washingtonpost.com; Edmund L. Andrews, "Once Hailed, Soldiers in Iraq Now Feel Blame at Each Step," *New York Times*, 29 June 2003, http://www.nytimes.com; Peter Beinart, "Be Unprepared," *New Republic*, 7 and 14 July 2003, 6; Thomas E. Ricks and Rajiv Chandrasekaran, "In Postwar Iraq, the Battle Widens," *Washington Post*, 7 July 2003, http://www.washingtonpost.com; Thomas E. Ricks and Helen Dewar, "Senators Grill Rumsfeld About U.S. Future in Iraq," *Washington Post*, 10 July 2003, http://www.washingtonpost.com; Patrick E. Tyler, "Iraqis Will Join Governing Council U.S. Is Setting Up," *New York Times*, 8 July 2003, http://www.nytimes.com; Patrick E. Tyler, "Iraqis Set to Form an Interim Council With Wide Power," *New York Times*, 11 July 2003, http://www.nytimes.com; and Rajiv Chandrasekaran, "Plan Gives Iraqi Council Governing Role," *Washington Post*, 11 July 2003, http://www.washingtonpost.com.

54. "A New World Order," *Economist*, 17 April 2003, http://www.economist.com; Richard W. Stevenson, "Bush Sees Limited Role for U.N. in Postwar Iraq," *New York Times*, 8 April 2003, http://www.nytimes.com; Fareed Zakaria, "How to Make Friends in Iraq," *Newsweek*, 23 June 2003, 37; Jim Hoagland, "If Bush Asks, Who Will Help?" *Washington Post*, 3 July 2003, http://www.washingtonpost.com; "Facing Reality in

Iraq," *Washington Post*, 8 July 2003, http://www.washingtonpost.com; "A Troubled Occupation in Iraq," *New York Times*, 10 July 2003, http://www.nytimes.com; and Fareed Zakaria, "Iraq Policy Is Broken. Fix It." *Newsweek*, 14 July 2003, 35. Zakaria wrote that "[t]he Bush administration chose not to make Iraq an international project. There are advantages to this approach. It will allow for greater efficiency and clarity of decision-making. But nation-building is ultimately not a managerial challenge; it's a political one. To stay in Iraq, the United States will need not just power and efficiency, but legitimacy." Zakaria, "How to Make Friends in Iraq." "Resocialization," a Comparative Politics concept, involves the recasting of a country's political culture so as to minimize ethnic, sectarian, and other societal conflicts that previously resulted in discrimination, oppression, acrimony, and violence. From Iraq's foundation in the early twentieth century until 2003, Sunnis had continuously dominated the country's politics, thereby alienating Shi'a, Kurds, and other Iraqis. On offshore balancing, see John J. Mearsheimer, Christopher A. Preble, and Stephen Walt, "Correspondence: Real World," *New Republic*, 9 August 2004, 4; and Christopher Layne, "Offshore Balancing Revisited," *Washington Quarterly* 15, no. 2 (Spring 2002): 233–48.

55. "A Reluctant Enlightenment?" *Middle East International*, 25 July 2003, 3; Vernon Loeb and Colum Lynch, "U.S. Cool to New U.N. Vote," *Washington Post*, 2 August 2003, http://www.washingtonpost.com; "Time for Another UN Resolution?" *Economist*, 31 July 2003, http://www.economist.com; Steven R. Weisman with Felicity Barringer, "U.S. Abandons Idea of Bigger U.N. Role in Iraq Occupation," *New York Times*, 14 August 2003, http://www.nytimes.com; and Edith M. Lederer, "Iraq Wins a 14-0 Welcome," *Portland Press Herald* (Portland, ME), 15 August 2003, 2A.

56. Douglas Jehl, "Needing Help in Iraq, U.S. Weighs How to Get It From U.N.," *New York Times*, 28 August 2003, http://www.nytimes.com; Evan Thomas, "Groping in the Dark," *Newsweek*, 1 September 2003, 27–33; Richard Holbrooke, "After the U.N.'s Own 9/11 Crisis," *Newsweek*, 1 September 2003, 32–33; Fareed Zakaria, "What We Should Do Now," *Newsweek*, 1 September 2003, 23–25; and Peter Slevin, "Reluctance to Share Control in Iraq Leaves U.S. on Its Own," *Washington Post*, 28 September 2003, http://www.washingtonpost.com.

57. Keith B. Richburg and Glenn Kessler, "Iraq Donations Fall Short," *Washington Post*, 24 October 2003, http://www.washingtonpost.com; and Steven R. Weisman, "U.S. Set to Cede Part of Control Over Aid to Iraq," *New York Times*, 20 October 2003, http://www.nytimes.com.

58. Todd S. Purdum, "U.N. Vote Lifts the President, but Pressure to Deliver Remains," *New York Times*, 17 October 2003, http://www.nytimes.com; "The U.N. Vote on Iraq," *New York Times*, 17 October 2003, http://www.nytimes.com; Dana Milbank and Mike Allen, "Bush Urges Commitment To Transform Mideast," *Washington Post*, 7 November 2003, http://www.washingtonpost.com; David Firestone, "Defying Bush, Senate Votes to Make Iraq Pay Back Loan," *New York Times*, 17 October 2003, http://www.nytimes.com; Colum Lynch, "U.S. Gets Backing for More U.N. Aid in Iraq," *Washington Post*, 16 October 2003, http://www.washingtonpost.com; Felicity Barringer and Kirk Semple, "Security Council Adopts U.S. Plan for Iraq in 15-0 Vote," *New York Times*, 16 October 2003, http://www.nytimes.com; and Associated Press, "Bremer Urges Senate to Approve Iraq Funds," *Washington Post*, 22 September 2003, http://www.washingtonpost.com.

59. Rajiv Chandrasekaran, "Plan to End Occupation Could Trim U.S. Force," *Washington Post*, 16 November 2003, http://www.washingtonpost.com; Robin Wright and

Walter Pincus, "U.S. Plan May Be in Flux as Iraqis Jockey for Postwar Leverage," *Washington Post*, 30 November 2003, http://www.washingtonpost.com; "Iraq Goes Sour," *New York Times*, 16 November 2003, http://www.nytimes.com; Robin Wright and Thomas E. Ricks, "New Urgency, New Risks in 'Iraqification,'" *Washington Post*, 14 November 2003, http://www.washingtonpost.com; Fareed Zakaria, "Iraqification: A Losing Strategy," *Newsweek*, 10 November 2003, 32; Milbank and Allen, "Bush Urges Commitment To Transform Mideast"; Robin Wright, "Idealism in the Face Of a Troubled Reality," *Washington Post*, 7 November 2003, http://www.washingtonpost.com; and David E. Sanger, "White House to Overhaul Iraq and Afghan Missions," *New York Times*, 6 October 2003, http://www.nytimes.com.

60. Craig S. Smith, "France and Germany Join U.S. in Effort to Reduce Iraq's Debt," *New York Times*, 17 December 2003, http://www.nytimes.com.

61. Dana Milbank, "The 'Bush Doctrine' Experiences Shining Moments," *Washington Post*, 21 December 2003, http://www.washingtonpost.com; Thomas L. Friedman, "Moment of Truth," *New York Times*, 18 December 2003, http://www.nytimes.com; Smith, "France and Germany Join U.S. in Effort to Reduce Iraq's Debt"; Gwynne Dyer, "Will Saddam's Capture Make Any Difference?" *Blade*, 16 December 2003, A13; and Phebe Marr, "Saddam's Past, Iraq's Future," *New York Times*, 15 December 2003, http://www.nytimes.com.

62. Fareed Zakaria, "In Iraq, It's Time for Some Smarts," *Newsweek*, 1 March 2004, 39; Robin Wright and Rajiv Chandrasekaran, "U.S., U.N. Play 'After You' Game in Iraq," *Washington Post*, 23 February 2004, http://www.washingtonpost.com; "Panic Room," *New Republic*, 9 February 2004, 7; Colum Lynch and Robin Wright, "U.S. Plan to Transfer Power In Iraq May Shift Drastically," *Washington Post*, 6 February 2004, http://www.washingtonpost.com; Anthony Shadid, "Cleric Denies Reports of an Attempt on Life," *Washington Post*, 7 February 2004, http://www.washingtonpost.com; Robin Wright, "Annan: U.N. To Help End Iraq Impasse," *Washington Post*, 4 February 2004, http://www.washingtonpost.com; Steven R. Weisman, "Bush Presses U.N. to Mediate Iraqi Clash on Rule," *New York Times*, 4 February 2004, http://www.nytimes.com; Rajiv Chandrasekaran, "Attacks Force Retreat From Wide-Ranging Plans for Iraq," *Washington Post*, 28 December 2003, http://www.washingtonpost.com; Dilip Hiro, "One Iraqi, One Vote?" *New York Times*, 27 January 2004, http://www.nytimes.com; Edward Wong, "Delays and Split on Iraqi Council Imperil U.S. Plan," *New York Times*, 26 January 2004, http://www.nytimes.com; "Iraq's Undemocratic Transition," *New York Times*, 26 January 2004, http://www.nytimes.com; Edward Wong, "New Pressures Over U.S. Plan for Iraqi Rule," *New York Times*, 24 January 2004, http://www.nytimes.com; Robin Wright, "U.S., Britain Detail Iraq Plan at U.N.," *Washington Post*, 22 January 2004, http://www.washingtonpost.com; Warren Hoge, "Annan Signals He'll Agree to Send U.N. Experts to Iraq," *New York Times*, 20 January 2004, http://www.nytimes.com; "In Search of Rescue," *Washington Post*, 18 January 2004, http://www.washingtonpost.com Richard W. Stevenson, "U.S. Willing to Alter Steps to Iraqi Self-Rule, Bremer Says," *New York Times*, 17 January 2004, http://www.nytimes.com; Robin Wright and Daniel Williams, "U.S. Moves To Salvage Transition," *Washington Post*, 16 January 2004, http://www.washingtonpost.com; Peter Maass, "Professor Nagl's War," *New York Times Magazine*, 11 January 2004, http://www.nytimes.com; Edward Wong, "Governing Council Parties Are Said to Back Broad Autonomy for Kurds," *New York Times*, 10 January 2004, http://www.nytimes.com; Colum Lynch, "U.S. Is Trying to Coax U.N. to Return to Iraq," *Washington Post*, 9 January 2004, http://www.washingtonpost.com;

Steven R. Weisman, "The Shape of a Future Iraq: U.S. Entangled in Disputes," *New York Times*, 9 January 2004, http://www.nytimes.com; Warren Hoge, "Annan Resists Calls to Send U.N. Staff Back to Baghdad," *New York Times*, 28 December 2003, http://www.nytimes.com; and Robin Wright and Rajiv Chandrasekaran, "U.S. Seeks Compromise Plan for Iraqi Political Transition," *Washington Post*, 16 December 2003, http://www.washingtonpost.com.

63. Michael Massing, "Now They Tell Us," *New York Review of Books*, 26 February 2004, 43–49; John Barry and Mark Hosenball, "What Went Wrong," *Newsweek*, 9 February 2004, 24–31; Fareed Zakaria, "We Had Good Intel—The U.N.'s," *Newsweek*, 9 February 2004, 39; Douglas Jehl, "Bush Sets Panel on Intelligence Before Iraq War," *New York Times*, 7 February 2004, http://www.nytimes.com; Nicholas D. Kristof, "Secret Obsessions at the Top," *New York Times*, 7 February 2004, http://www.nytimes.com; Mike Allen, "Bush Stands Firmly Behind His Decisions to Invade Iraq," *Washington Post*, 6 February 2004, http://www.washingtonpost.com; "Another Week, Another War Inquiry," *Economist*, 5 February 2004, http://www.economist.com; Glenn Kessler, "Powell: Arms Doubts Might Have Affected View on War," *Washington Post*, 3 February 2004, http://www.washingtonpost.com; Dana Milbank, "For Bush, a Tactical Retreat on Iraq," *Washington Post*, 2 February 2004, http://www.washingtonpost.com; Douglas Jehl and David E. Sanger, "Powell's Case, a Year Later: Gaps in Picture of Iraq Arms," *New York Times*, 1 February 2004, http://www.nytimes.com; Patrick E. Tyler, "Leaders Sought a Threat. Spies Get the Blame," *New York Times*, 1 February 2004, http://www.nytimes.com; Richard W. Stevenson and Thom Shanker, "Ex-Arms Monitor Urges an Inquiry on Iraqi Threat," *New York Times*, 29 January 2004, http://www.nytimes.com; Walter Pincus and Dana Milbank, "Kay Says Evidence Shows Iraq Disarmed," *Washington Post*, 28 January 2004, http://www.washingtonpost.com; and James Risen, "Ex-Inspector Says C.I.A. Missed Disarray in Iraqi Arms Program," *New York Times*, 26 January 2004, http://www.nytimes.com. Despite being Bush's more articulate Siamese twin, Blair incurred the ridicule of the British press and populace for his "Made in the USA" Iraq policy. See Reuters, "Blair: May Not Find Iraq WMD, Defends Bush Ties," *New York Times*, 6 July 2004, http://www.nytimes.com; and Patrick E. Tyler, "Blair Confronts Political Burdens of Iraq," *New York Times*, 20 June 2004, http://www.nytimes.com.

64. Christopher Dickey, "From 9/11 to 3/11," *Newsweek*, 22 March 2004, 23–29; Michael Hirsh, "Terror's Next Stop," *Newsweek*, 22 March 2004, 30–36; and Fareed Zakaria, "Cruelty Is All They Have Left," *Newsweek*, 22 March 2004, 37; Scott Atran, "A Leaner, Meaner Jihad," *New York Times*, 16 March 2004, http://www.nytimes.com; Dexter Filkins, "Iraqi Council Signs Interim Constitution," *New York Times*, 8 March 2004, http://www.nytimes.com; and Rajiv Chandrasekaran, "Iraqis Hail Compromise On Interim Constitution," *Washington Post*, 2 March 2004, http://www.washingtonpost.com. Quote can be found in that article.

65. Sandra Mackey, "A City That Lives for Revenge," *New York Times*, 29 April 2004, http://www.nytimes.com; Edward Wong, "Iraqi Nationalism Takes Root, Sort Of," *New York Times*, 25 April 2004, http://www.nytimes.com; Babak Dehghanpisheh, Melinda Liu, and Rod Nordland, "'We Are Your Martyrs!'" *Newsweek*, 19 April 2004, 36–41; Dan Balz, "President Is Long On Resolve but Short on Details," *Washington Post*, 14 April 2004, http://www.washingtonpost.com; David E. Sanger, "President Makes a Case for Freedom in the Middle East," *New York Times*, 14 April 2004, http://www.nytimes.com; "Mr. Bush's Press Conference," *New York Times*, 14 April

2004, http://www.nytimes.com; Tom Shales, "A Prime Time to Ask The President Questions," *Washington Post*, 14 April 2004, http://www.washingtonpost.com; John F. Burns and Kirk Semple, "U.N. Envoy Suggests Initial Caretaker Government in Iraq," *New York Times*, 14 April 2004, http://www.nytimes.com; Robin Wright, "Series of U.S. Fumbles Blamed for Turmoil in Postwar Iraq," *Washington Post*, 11 April 2004, http://www.washingtonpost.com; Thom Shanker, "U.S. Prepares a Prolonged Drive to Suppress the Uprisings in Iraq," *New York Times*, 11 April 2004, http://www.nytimes.com; "The Story Line in Iraq," *New York Times*, 11 April 2004, http://www.nytimes.com; Thomas L. Friedman, "Nasty, Brutish and Short," *New York Times*, 11 April 2004, http://www.nytimes.com; "Is Iraq Becoming a Quagmire?" *Economist*, 9 April 2004, http://www.economist.com; Thomas L. Friedman, "Are There Any Iraqis in Iraq?" *New York Times*, 8 April 2004, http://www.nytimes.com; "In Deep Trouble," *Arab News* (Jeddah), 8 April 2004, http://www.arabnews.com; "The Challenge in Iraq," *Economist*, 7 April 2004, http://www.economist.com; George F. Will, "A War President's Job," *Washington Post*, 7 April 2004, http://www.washingtonpost.com; and Vali Nasr, "Iraq's Real Holy War," *New York Times*, 6 March 2004, http://www.nytimes.com.

66. Bradley Graham, "A Failure in Leadership, All the Way Up the Ranks," *Washington Post*, 26 August 2004, http://www.washingtonpost.com; "Closer to the Truth," *Washington Post*, 26 August 2004, http://www.washingtonpost.com; "Holding the Pentagon Accountable: For Abu Ghraib," *New York Times*, 26 August 2004, http://www.nytimes.com; Dahlia Lithwick, "No Smoking Gun," *New York Times*, 26 August 2004, http://www.nytimes.com; Thomas E. Ricks, "Rumsfeld's Status Taken Down a Notch," *Washington Post*, 25 August 2004, http://www.washingtonpost.com; Douglas Jehl, "A Trail of 'Major Failures' Leads to Defense Secretary's Office," *New York Times*, 25 August 2004, http://www.nytimes.com; Eric Schmitt, "Defense Leaders Faulted by Panel in Prison Abuse," *New York Times*, 24 August 2004, http://www.nytimes.com; Paul Krugman, "Just Trust Us," *New York Times*, 11 May 2004, http://www.nytimes.com; Seymour M. Hersh, "Torture at Abu Ghraib," *New Yorker*, 10 May 2004, http://www.newyorker.com; David Brooks, "Crisis of Confidence," *New York Times*, 8 May 2004, http://www.nytimes.com; and Thomas L. Friedman, "Restoring Our Honor," *New York Times*, 6 May 2004, http://www.nytimes.com.

67. "The Iraq Reconstruction Fiasco," *New York Times*, 9 August 2004, http://www.nytimes.com; "'After' the War," *Blade*, 21 July 2004, A10; "United States of Amnesia," *Mail & Guardian* (Johannesburg), 1 July 2004, http://www.mg.co.za; Scott Wilson, "From Occupation to 'Partnership,'" *Washington Post*, 29 June 2004, http://www.washingtonpost.com; "A Secretive Transfer in Iraq," *New York Times*, 29 June 2004, http://www.nytimes.com; "An Early Handover," *Blade*, 29 June 2004, A6; "Iraq's Sovereignty Restored, Up to a Point," *Economist*, 28 June 2004, http://www.economist.com; Ayad Allawi, "A New Beginning," *Washington Post*, 27 June 2004, http://www.washingtonpost.com; Mike Allen, "NATO Agrees to Help Train Iraq Government," *Washington Post*, 27 June 2004, http://www.washingtonpost.com; Rajiv Chandrasekaran, "As Handover Nears, U.S. Mistakes Loom Large," *Washington Post*, 20 June 2004, http://www.washingtonpost.com; Fareed Zakaria, "A Return to Sanity, Finally," *Newsweek*, 7 June 2004, 33; "A Positive First Step," *Blade*, 4 June 2004, A10; "Still Taking on the World?" *Economist*, 3 July 2004, 11–12; Robin Wright and Mike Allen, "Many Hurdles Ahead for U.S.," *Washington Post*, 2 June 2004, http://www.washingtonpost.com; "Iraq's Interim Government," *New York Times*, 2 June

2004, http://www.nytimes.com; Thom Shanker, "U.S. Shifts Focus in Iraq to Aiding New Government," *New York Times*, 1 June 2004, http://www.nytimes.com; Dexter Filkins and Kirk Semple, "Iraqi Governing Council Is Dissolved; Green Zone Attacked," *New York Times*, 1 June 2004, http://www.nytimes.com; Robin Wright and Mike Allen, "A Speech Meant to Rally Public Support Doesn't Answer Key Questions," *Washington Post*, 25 May 2004, http://www.washingtonpost.com; "Handing Off Power—But to Whom?" *Economist*, 24 May 2004, http://www.economist.com; "The U.N.'s Revenge," *New Republic*, 10 May 2004, 9; Richard W. Stevenson and David E. Sanger, "For White House, Reversed Iraq Tactics Are Billed as Bumps on Road to Peace," *New York Times*, 2 May 2004, http://www.nytimes.com; and Fareed Zakaria, "Our Last Real Chance," *Newsweek*, 19 April 2004, 44–49. On the British in Iraq and Egypt and possible lessons for the United States, see Judith S. Yaphe, "War and Occupation in Iraq: What Went Right? What Could Go Wrong?" *Middle East Journal* 57, no. 3 (Summer 2003): 381–99; and Niall Ferguson, *Colossus: The Price of America's Empire* (New York: Penguin Press, 2004), 217–25.

68. Pew Research Center for the People & the Press, "August 18, 2004, Survey: Foreign Policy Attitudes Now Driven by 9/11 and Iraq—Part Two: America's Place in the World," http://people-press.org/reports; Paul Krugman, "What About Iraq?" *New York Times*, 6 August 2004, http://www.nytimes.com; Mike Allen, "Bush: 'We Have Kept Our Word,'" *Washington Post*, 29 June 2004, http://www.washingtonpost.com; David E. Sanger, "Fresh Starts: One for Iraq, One for Bush," *New York Times*, 29 June 2004, http://www.nytimes.com; and Adam Nagourney and Janet Elder, "Bush's Rating Falls to Its Lowest Point, New Survey Finds," *New York Times*, 29 June 2004, http://www.nytimes.com.

69. Somini Sengupta, "U.S. Diplomat Starts New Job by Deferring to Iraq Rulers," *New York Times*, 18 July 2004, http://www.nytimes.com; and Steven R. Weisman, "U.S. Has Leverage, but Wants to Show Iraqis Are in Charge," *New York Times*, 29 June 2004, http://www.nytimes.com.

70. John F. Burns, "Two Power Brokers Collide in Iraq," *New York Times*, 22 August 2004, http://www.nytimes.com "Politics of Exclusion in Iraq," *New York Times*, 22 August 2004, http://www.nytimes.com; "A Step Back from the Brink," *Economist*, 19 August 2004, http://www.economist.com; Sabrina Tavernise, "Chalabi, Claiming Exoneration, Plans Another Comeback," *New York Times*, 2 September 2004, http://www.nytimes.com; Associated Press, "Iraqi Authorities Say They Will Not Arrest Chalabi," *MSNBC.com*, 12 August 2004, http://www.msnbc.msn.com; and Mark Hosenball, "Intelligence: A Double Game," *Newsweek*, 10 May 2004, http://msnbc.msn.com.

71. Dexter Filkins, "One by One, Iraqi Cities Become No-Go Zones," *New York Times*, 5 September 2004, http://www.nytimes.com; Robin Shulman, "Sadr Reportedly Forgoing Attacks for Political Role," *Washington Post*, 31 August 2004, http://www.washingtonpost.com; Dexter Filkins, "After 3 Weeks of Fighting in Najaf, 1 Riddle: Who Won?" *New York Times*, 29 August 2004, http://www.nytimes.com; and Jim Hoagland, "Ayatollah to the Rescue?" *Washington Post*, 29 August 2004, http://www.washingtonpost.com. Cairo's *Al-Ahram Weekly* blamed the violence in Najaf and elsewhere on "the continuation of US policies that seek to perpetuate the occupation and weaken any Iraqi government, even if loyal to the Americans." "It Is Because Nothing Changed," *Al-Ahram Weekly* (Cairo), 19–25 August 2004, http://weekly.ahram.org.eg.

72. "The U.N. Plays Catch-Up in Iraq," *New York Times*, 20 July 2004, http://www.nytimes.com; Robin Wright and Bradley Graham, "U.S. Works to Sustain Iraq Coalition," *Washington Post*, 15 July 2004, http://www.washingtonpost.com; Susan Sachs, "Bush Urges All Autocrats to Yield Now to Democracy," *New York Times*, 30 June 2004, http://www.nytimes.com; "A Creaking Partnership," *Economist*, 4 June 2004, http://www.economist.com; "Sixty Years On," *Economist*, 3 June 2004, http://www.economist.com; Neil MacFarquhar, "Arab Leaders Back Modest Reforms at Annual Summit," *New York Times*, 23 May 2004, http://www.nytimes.com; Shibley Telhami, "Double Blow To Mideast Democracy," *Washington Post*, 1 May 2004, http://www.washingtonpost.com; Jackson Diehl, "Undercutting Mideast Democracy," *Washington Post*, 10 May 2004, http://www.washingtonpost.com; Zbigniew Brzezinski, "The Wrong Way to Sell Democracy to the Arab World," *New York Times*, 8 March 2004, http://www.nytimes.com; Glenn Kessler and Robin Wright, "Arabs and Europeans Question 'Greater Middle East' Plan," *Washington Post*, 22 February 2004, http://www.washingtonpost.com; and "Democracy Needs More Work, Less Rhetoric by All," *Daily Star* (Beirut), 20 February 2004, http://www.dailystar.com.lb.

73. David Broder, "Bush Vulnerable—and It's His Own Fault," *Blade*, 17 August 2004, A11; Adriana Lins de Albuquerque, Michael O'Hanlon, and Amy Unikewicz, "The State of Iraq: An Update," *New York Times*, 10 August 2004, http://www.nytimes.com; and Roger Cohen, "Kerry's Must-Sell: Tough Foreign Policy Emphasizing Steadiness," *New York Times*, 28 June 2004, http://www.nytimes.com. The first presidential debate, held on September 30, 2004, at the University of Miami, spotlighted foreign-policy issues, especially Iraq. For a transcript of the debate, see http://www.debates.org/pages/trans2004a.html.

74. Anthony Shadid, "Iraqis Defy Threats as Millions Vote," *Washington Post*, 31 January 2005, http://www.washingtonpost.com; Fareed Zakaria, "High Hopes, Hard Facts," *Newsweek*, 31 January 2005, 22–26; and George W. Bush, "Second Inaugural Address," delivered in Washington, DC, 20 January 2005, http://www.whitehouse.gov. For Iraqi election results, see http://www.electionworld.org/iraq.htm. For the ethnic and sectarian composition of Iraq, see http://www.cia.gov/cia/publications/factbook. Democracy expert Larry Diamond criticized the U.S. government's approval, however reluctant, of Iraq's election rules. Unless Iraqi officials divided their country into multiple voting districts, allowing Sunnis to elect more of their own, Iraqi elections would continuously favor Shi'a, thereby alienating Sunnis. For analysis of this and other U.S. occupation issues, see Phebe Marr, "Occupational Hazards: Washington's Record in Iraq," *Foreign Affairs* 84, no. 4 (July/August 2005): 180–86.

75. Seymour M. Hersh, "Get Out the Vote," *New Yorker*, 25 July 2005, http://www.newyorker.com.

76. For information on the Iraqi cabinet, see Council on Foreign Relations, "Iraq: Cabinet Ministers," 12 May 2005, http://www.cfr.org/publication.php?id=8061.

77. Howard Fineman, "Hunting Big Game," *Newsweek*, 29 August/5 September 2005, 37; Associated Press, "Hagel: Iraq War Has Destabilized Mideast, Resembles Vietnam," *CNN.com*, 21 August 2005, http://www.cnn.com; Robin Wright and Ellen Knickmeyer, "U.S. Lowers Sights On What Can Be Achieved in Iraq," *Washington Post*, 14 August 2005, http://www.washingtonpost.com; David Stout, "Bush Says Troop Levels in Iraq Will Stay Unchanged for Now," *New York Times*, 11 August 2005, http://www.nytimes.com; Bob Herbert, "No End in Sight in Iraq," *New York Times*, 10 August 2005, http://www.nytimes.com; CNN, "Poll: Bush Approval Rating Still Low,"

CNN.com, 8 August 2005, http://www.cnn.com; "Does He Know Where It's Leading?" *Economist*, 30 July 2005, 22–24; "The Iraq Mess," *Blade*, 27 July 2005, A6; Ann Scott Tyson and Ellen Knickmeyer, "U.S. Signals Spring Start for Pullout," *Washington Post*, 28 July 2005, http://www.washingtonpost.com; John F. Burns, "If It's Civil War, Do We Know It?" *New York Times*, 24 July 2005, http://www.nytimes.com; and Walter Pincus, "British Intelligence Warned of Iraq War," *Washington Post*, 13 May 2005, http://www.washingtonpost.com. For statistics on U.S. military fatalities in Iraq, see http://icasualties.org. Some 56 percent of those queried in an 8 August 2005, CNN/USA Today/Gallup poll "thought things were going badly for the United States in Iraq," whereas 43 percent "said things were going well." See CNN, "Poll."

78. Fineman, "Hunting Big Game"; CNN, "One-Day Extension for Iraq Constitution," *CNN.com*, 25 August 2005, http://www.cnn.com. First quote can be found in that article. Zuhair al-Naher, a spokesman for the Dawa Party, told CNN that Islam would be a "main source" for Iraqi law; and David Brooks, "Divided They Stand," *New York Times*, 25 August 2005, http://www.nytimes.com. Second quote can be found in that article.

79. Dexter Filkins, "A Leader Is Eliminated, but Insurgency Is Likely to Carry On," *New York Times*, 8 June 2006, http://www.nytimes.com; Robert F. Worth, "Blast at Shiite Shrine Sets Off Sectarian Fury in Iraq," *New York Times*, 23 February 2006, http://www.nytimes.com; Babak Dehghanpisheh, Michael Hastings, and Michael Hirsh, "War of the Mosques," *Newsweek*, 6 March 2006, 24–28; "Meanwhile, in Baghdad . . . ," *New York Times*, 16 August 2006, http://www.nytimes.com; and Jeffrey Bartholet, "Sword of the Shia," *Newsweek*, 4 December 2006, 26–36. The February 2006 bombing of the Golden Mosque in Samarra, revered by Shi'a, led to a noticeable intensification of sectarian violence.

80. Peter W. Galbraith, "Mindless in Iraq," *New York Review of Books*, 10 August 2006, 28–31; Thomas L. Friedman, "Time for Plan B," *New York Times*, 4 August 2006, http://www.nytimes.com; Larry Diamond, James Dobbins, Chaim Kaufmann, Leslie Gelb, and Stephen Biddle, "What to Do in Iraq: A Roundtable," *Foreign Affairs* 85, no. 4 (July/August 2006): 150–69; Max Boot, "Radical Ideas for Iraq," *Los Angeles Times*, 9 August 2006, http://www.latimes.com; CNN, "Poll: 60 Percent of Americans Oppose Iraq War," *CNN.com*, 9 August 2006, http://www.cnn.com; and Richard H. Schultz Jr. and Andrea J. Dew, "Counterinsurgency, by the Book," *New York Times*, 7 August 2006, http://www.nytimes.com. On U.S. casualties, see http://icasualties.org.

81. Fareed Zakaria, "Vengeance of the Victors," *Newsweek*, 8 January 2007, 25. First quote can be found in that article; Fareed Zakaria, "Beyond Bush," *Newsweek*, 11 June 2007, 22–29. Second quote can be found on 28; Marc J. O'Reilly and Wesley B. Renfro, "Like Father, Like Son? A Comparison of the Foreign Policies of George H.W. Bush and George W. Bush," *Historia Actual Online*, no. 10 (Spring 2006): 17–36, http://www.historia-actual.com; Fareed Zakaria, "Rethinking Iraq: The Way Forward," *Newsweek*, 6 November 2006, 26–33; Griff Witte, "Despite Billions Spent, Rebuilding Incomplete," *Washington Post*, 12 November 2006, http://www.washingtonpost.com; "Special Issue: Iraq: What Next?" *New Republic*, 27 November & 4 December 2006; Thomas L. Friedman, "Ten Months or Ten Years," *New York Times*, 29 November 2006, http://www.nytimes.com; Thomas E. Ricks and Robin Wright, "As Iraq Deteriorates, Iraqis Get More Blame," *Washington Post*, 29 November 2006, http://www.washingtonpost.com; "Blood, Tears and Still No Victory," *Economist*, 30 November 2006, http://www.economist.com; Fareed Zakaria, "The Next Step? Think

Vietnam," *Newsweek*, 4 December 2006, 37; Glenn Kessler and Thomas E. Ricks, "The Realists' Repudiation of Policies for a War, Region," *Washington Post*, 7 December 2006, http://www.washingtonpost.com; John O'Neil and Brian Knowlton, "Panel Backs Overhaul of Iraq Policy," *New York Times*, 6 December 2006, http://www.nytimes.com; CNN, "U.S. Deaths in Iraq Reach 3,000," *CNN.com*, 1 January 2007, http://www.cnn.com; Michael R. Gordon, "Will Iraq Study Group's Plan Work on the Battlefield," *New York Times*, 7 December 2006, http://www.nytimes.com; Sheryl Gay Stolberg, "Will It Work in the White House," *New York Times*, 7 December 2006, http://www.nytimes.com; "Welcome Political Cover," *New York Times*, 7 December 2006, http://www.nytimes.com; David Ignatius, "Baker-Hamilton Does Its Job," *Washington Post*, 7 December 2006, http://www.washingtonpost.com; Thomas L. Friedman, "Set a Date and Buy Some Leverage," *New York Times*, 8 December 2006, http://www.nytimes.com; George F. Will, "A Report Overtaken by Reality," *Washington Post*, 7 December 2006, http://www.washingtonpost.com; Evan Thomas, "So Now What, Mr. President?" *Newsweek*, 11 December 2006, 30–40; Glenn Kessler and Robin Wright, "Rice Rejects Overture to Iran and Syria," *Washington Post*, 15 December 2006, http://www.washingtonpost.com; Charles Krauthammer, "In Baker's Blunder, A Chance for Bush," *Washington Post*, 15 December 2006, http://www.washingtonpost.com; Fred Hiatt, "A New Mideast, or Wishful Thinking?" *Washington Post*, 18 December 2006, http://www.washingtonpost.com; "The Rush to Hang Saddam Hussein," *New York Times*, 29 December 2006, http://www.nytimes.com; Christopher Dickey, "Death of a Tyrant," *Newsweek*, 8 January 2007, 18–24; Sabrina Tavernise, "Hussein Divides Iraq in His Death as He Did in Life," *New York Times*, 31 December 2006, http://www.nytimes.com; "After Saddam," *Economist*, 31 December 2006, http://www.economist.com; Associated Press, "Angry Protests in Iraq Suggest Sunni Arab Shift to Militants," *New York Times*, 2 January 2007, http://www.nytimes.com; Hassan M. Fattah, "Images of Hanging Make Hussein a Martyr to Many," *New York Times*, 7 January 2007, http://www.nytimes.com; and Nina Kamp, Michael O'Hanlon, and Amy Unikewicz, "The State of Iraq: An Update," *New York Times*, 20 December 2006, http://www.nytimes.com.

82. James Glanz and Alissa J. Rubin, "Migration Reshapes Iraq's Sectarian Landscape," *New York Times*, 19 September 2007, http://www.nytimes.com; Sabrina Tavernise, "Sectarian Toll Includes Scars to Iraq Psyche," *New York Times*, 17 September 2007, http://www.nytimes.com; Peter Baker, Karen DeYoung, Thomas E. Ricks, Ann Scott Tyson, Joby Warrick, and Robin Wright, "Among Top Officials, 'Surge' Has Sparked Dissent, Infighting," *Washington Post*, 9 September 2007, http://www.washingtonpost.com; Jim Rutenberg, "As Senate Deal Sinks, So Does Bush's Power," *New York Times*, 9 June 2007, http://www.nytimes.com; CNN, "House, Senate Pass War Funding Bill," *CNN.com*, 24 May 2007, http://www.cnn.com; David Stout and Sheryl Gay Stolberg, "Citing 'Rigid' Deadline, Bush Vetoes Iraq Bill," *New York Times*, 1 May 2007, http://www.nytimes.com; Judis, "Crude Joke," 19; Peter Beinart, "Binge and Surge," *New Republic*, 22 January 2007, 6; Brian Knowlton, "Bush and Cheney Rebuff Critics of Iraq Troop Increase," *New York Times*, 14 January 2007, http://www.nytimes.com; Helene Cooper, "The Best We Can Hope For," *New York Times*, 14 January 2007, http://www.nytimes.com; "Picking Up the Pieces," *New York Times*, 14 January 2007, http://www.nytimes.com; Frank Rich, "He's in the Bunker Now," *New York Times*, 14 January 2007, http://www.nytimes.com; "Baghdad or Bust," *Economist*, 13 January 2007, 11–12; Anthony H. Cordesman, "Bush's Iraq Plan, Be-

tween the Lines," *New York Times*, 12 January 2007, http://www.nytimes.com; Thomas L. Friedman, "Make Them Fight All of Us," *New York Times*, 12 January 2007, http://www.nytimes.com; Thom Shanker and David S. Cloud, "Bush's Plan for Iraq Runs Into Opposition in Congress," *New York Times*, 12 January 2007, http://www.nytimes.com; David E. Sanger, "Bush Adds Troops in Bid to Secure Iraq," *New York Times*, 11 January 2007, http://www.nytimes.com; Michael Abramowitz and Robin Wright, "Bush to Add 20,000 Troops In an Effort to Stabilize Iraq," *Washington Post*, 11 January 2007, http://www.washingtonpost.com; Michael R. Gordon, "Bid to Secure Baghdad Relies on Troops and Iraqi Leaders," *New York Times*, 11 January 2007, http://www.nytimes.com; Sabrina Tavernise and John F. Burns, "Promising Troops Where They Aren't Really Wanted," *New York Times*, 11 January 2007, http://www.nytimes.com; Sheryl Gay Stolberg, "Inviting a Battle on Capitol Hill," *New York Times*, 11 January 2007, http://www.nytimes.com; David Brooks, "The Fog Over Iraq," *New York Times*, 11 January 2007, http://www.nytimes.com; "The Real Disaster," *New York Times*, 11 January 2007, http://www.nytimes.com; David Brooks, "Making the Surge Work," *New York Times*, 7 January 2007, http://www.nytimes.com. Quote can be found in that article; Michael R. Gordon, "A New Commander, in Step With the White House on Iraq," *New York Times*, 6 January 2007, http://www.nytimes.com; Joshua Partlow, "Iraq Announces New Security Plan," *Washington Post*, 6 January 2007, http://www.washingtonpost.com; David E. Sanger and Jeff Zeleny, "Bush Facing Deep Divide Over More Troops for Iraq," *New York Times*, 6 January 2007, http://www.nytimes.com; and David Broder, "Bush's Hands Are Tied at Home and Abroad," *Blade*, 4 January 2007, A13. On Bush's and the world's 2006 *annus horribilis*, see Dan Simpson, "2006 Was Bad Year for Foreign Affairs," *Blade*, 3 January 2007, A7.

83. Jason Campbell, Michael O'Hanlon, and Amy Unikewicz, "The State of Iraq: An Update," *New York Times*, 4 September 2007, http://www.nytimes.com; David E. Sanger, "Bush Shifts Terms for Measuring Progress in Iraq," *New York Times*, 5 September 2007, http://www.nytimes.com; "The Iraq Prognosis," *Blade*, 7 September 2007, A14; Jon Cohen and Jennifer Agiesta, "Wide Skepticism Ahead of Assessment," *Washington Post*, 9 September 2007, http://www.washingtonpost.com; David E. Sanger, "Redefining Goals: Less Talk of Victory Now," *New York Times*, 10 September 2007, http://www.nytimes.com; William Branigin and Robin Wright, "Petraeus Says Objectives in Iraq Are Largely Being Met," *Washington Post*, 10 September 2007, http://www.washingtonpost.com; Michael R. Gordon, "Petraeus Sees Bigger Role in Protecting Iraqi Civilians," *New York Times*, 11 September 2007, http://www.nytimes.com; Eugene Robinson, "'Six Months' Without End," *Washington Post*, 11 September 2007, http://www.washingtonpost.com; David E. Sanger, "Officials Cite Long-Term Need for U.S. in Iraq," *New York Times*, 12 September 2007, http://www.nytimes.com; Alissa J. Rubin, "For Iraqis, General's Report Offers Bitter Truth," *New York Times*, 12 September 2007, http://www.nytimes.com; "The General Speaks," *Economist*, 13 September 2007, http://www.economist.com; "Why They Should Stay," *Economist*, 13 September 2007, http://www.economist.com; "In Bush's Words: Assessing the War Today, and the Risks to Avoid Tomorrow," *New York Times*, 13 September 2007, http://www.nytimes.com; David E. Sanger, "Multiple Messages and Audiences," *New York Times*, 14 September 2007, http://www.nytimes.com; David M. Herszenhorn, "A New Report on Iraq Lends Ammunition to Both Parties," *New York Times*,

7 September 2007, http://www.nytimes.com; and "Waiting for the General (and a Miracle)," *Economist*, 6 September 2007, http://www.economist.com.

84. Thomas L. Friedman, "Letter From Baghdad," *New York Times*, 5 September 2007, http://www.nytimes.com; Thomas L. Friedman, "What's Missing in Baghdad," *New York Times*, 9 September 2007, http://www.nytimes.com; Alissa J. Rubin and Damien Cave, "Envoy's Upbeat Tone Glosses Over Baghdad's Turmoil," *New York Times*, 11 September 2007, http://www.nytimes.com; Sanger, "Officials Cite Long-Term Need for U.S. in Iraq"; "The General Speaks"; George F. Will, "A War Still Seeking a Mission," *Washington Post*, 11 September 2007, http://www.washingtonpost.com; "No Exit, No Strategy," *New York Times*, 14 September 2007, http://www.nytimes.com; David M. Herszenhorn and Carl Huse, "Effort to Shift Course in Iraq Fails in Senate," *New York Times*, 20 September 2007, http://www.nytimes.com; and David Ignatius, "How This Ends," *Washington Post*, 13 September 2007, http://www.washingtonpost.com.

85. Robert G. Kaiser, "Trapped by Hubris, Again," *Washington Post*, 14 January 2007, http://www.washingtonpost.com; Mark Danner, "Iraq: The War of the Imagination," *New York Review of Books*, 21 December 2006, 81–96; Lawrence F. Kaplan, "Quiet American II," *New Republic*, 1 August 2005, 34; and Evan Thomas, "The Vietnam Question," *Newsweek*, 19 April 2004, 28–35. On the costs of the war, see http://www.nationalpriorities.org/Cost-of-War/Cost-of-War-3.html (16 September 2007). See also Joel Havemann, "Iraq War's Price Tag Close to Vietnam's," *Baltimore Sun*, 15 January 2007, http://www.baltimoresun.com.

86. Tamara Cofman Wittes, "Domestic Sources of Iranian Foreign Policy," *The Middle East Institute Newsletter* 52, no. 2 (April 2001): 3, 11; Elaine Sciolino with Nazila Fathi, "Iranian Elections: Where the Victor May Not Win," *New York Times*, 3 June 2001, http://www.nytimes.com; John Ward Anderson, "Iran Faces Dogmatic Divide," *Hartford Courant*, 4 June 2001, A7; Neil MacFarquhar with Nazila Fahti, "Iran's President Wins Mandate to Push Reform," *New York Times*, 10 June 2001, http://www.nytimes.com; Elaine Sciolino, "News Analysis: Iranians Back Their Leaders' Volatile Experiment," *New York Times*, 10 June 2001, http://www.nytimes.com; Neil MacFarquhar, "Conservatives in Iran Face Reassessment of Reforms," *New York Times*, 11 June 2001, http://www.nytimes.com; George Gedda, "Iran Tops State Department Terrorism List," Hartford Courant, 1 May 2001, A8; "Justice for Khobar Towers," *New York Times*, 22 June 2001, http://www.nytimes.com; James Risen and Jane Perlez, "News Analysis: Terror, Iran and the U.S.," *New York Times*, 23 June 2001, http://www.nytimes.com; Richard Allan Roth, Suzanne Maloney, Ray Takeyh, and Geoffrey Kemp, "U.S. Policy Toward Iran: Time for a Change?" *Middle East Policy* 8, no. 1 (March 2001): 1–24; R.K. Ramazani, "The Role of Iran in the New Millennium: A View from the Outside," *Middle East Policy* 8, no. 1 (March 2001): 43–47; Michael Wines, "Iran and Russia Sign Oil and Weapons Pact," *New York Times*, 12 March 2001, http://www.nytimes.com; John Ward Anderson, "Iran's Overtures Put U.S. on Spot," *Hartford Courant*, 2 April 2001, A5; "Sanctions Remain on Iran, Libya," *Hartford Courant*, 20 April 2001, A2; Robin Wright, "U.S. Blocks a Key Iran Arms Route," *Los Angeles Times*, 6 May 2001, http://www.latimes.com; and Robin Wright, "U.S. Panel Backs New Policy on Iran," *Los Angeles Times*, 8 June 2001, http://www.latimes.com.

87. James A. Bill, "The Politics of Hegemony: The United States and Iran," *Middle East Policy* 8, no. 3 (September 2001): 89–100; John Grimond, "God's Rule, or Man's? A Survey of Iran," *Economist*, 18 January 2003, 3–16; and Elizabeth Rubin, "The Milli-

meter Revolution," *New York Times Magazine*, 6 April 2003, http://www.nytimes.com. On life in Iran, see Azar Nafisi, *Reading Lolita in Tehran: A Memoir in Books* (New York: Random House, 2003).

88. Kenneth M. Pollack, *The Persian Puzzle: The Conflict between Iran and America* (New York: Random House, 2004), 343–58; Fareed Zakaria, "Time to Expose the Mullahs," *Newsweek*, 23 December 2002, 45; Peter Slevin, "U.S. Met With Iranians On War," *Washington Post*, 8 February 2003, http://www.washingtonpost.com; Peter Slevin and Joby Warrick, "U.S. Wary of Iranian Nuclear Aims," *Washington Post*, 11 February 2003, http://www.washingtonpost.com; and Reuel Marc Gerecht, "Iran Plays the Waiting Game," *New York Times*, 13 March 2003, http://www.nytimes.com.

89. Pollack, *The Persian Puzzle*, 358–61; K.L. Afrasiabi, "Iranian Diplomacy," *Middle East Insight* 17, no. 1 (January-February 2002): 15–17; Elaine Sciolino, "Iran Warily Confronts New Neighbors: Americans," *New York Times*, 13 April 2003, http://www.nytimes.com; Karl Vick, "Iranians Assert Right To Nuclear Weapons," *Washington Post*, 11 March 2003, http://www.washingtonpost.com; Anoushiravan Ehteshami, "Iran and the US Occupation of Iraq," *Middle East International*, 2 May 2003, 32–34; Angus McDowall, "Khatami's Dilemma," *Middle East International*, 2 May 2003, 11–13; Glenn Kessler, "Contacts With Tehran Ended," *Washington Post*, 25 May 2003, http://www.washingtonpost.com; "Please Sir, We Really Didn't," *Economist*, 29 May 2003, http://www.economist.com; "The Iranian Challenge," *Washington Post*, 29 May 2003, http://www.washingtonpost.com; "Why Go After Iran?" *Blade*, 5 June 2003, A10; Terence Hunt, "U.S., Russia Warn Iran, N. Korea on Nuclear Arms," *Washington Post*, 1 June 2003, http://www.washingtonpost.com; Felicity Barringer, "Plans by Iran for a Reactor Pose Concerns About Arms," *New York Times*, 7 June 2003, http://www.nytimes.com; Christopher Dickey and Maziar Bahari, "Scaring the Ayatollahs," *Newsweek*, 9 June 2003, 31; Lawrence F. Kaplan, "Iranamok," *New Republic*, 9 June 2003, 14–15; Jim Muir, "The American Threat," *Middle East International*, 13 June 2003, 22–24; "A Growing Fury in Iran," *New York Times*, 14 June 2003, http://www.nytimes.com; Scott Lindlaw, "Bush Takes Strong Stand Against Iran Nuclear Plans," *Washington Post*, 18 June 2003, http://www.washingtonpost.com; Joby Warrick, "Iran Urged To Explain Nuclear Plan," *Washington Post*, 20 June 2003, http://www.washingtonpost.com; Elaine Sciolino, "Nuclear Ambitions Aren't New for Iran," *New York Times*, 22 June 2003, http://www.nytimes.com; Ann McFeatters, "Next Up for the Bush Administration: Iran," *Blade*, 22 June 2003, B5; Richard Morin and Claudia Deane, "Poll: Majority Backs Use of Force in Iran," *Washington Post*, 24 June 2003, http://www.washingtonpost.com; Nazila Fathi, "British Minister Presses Iran to Allow Nuclear Inspections," *New York Times*, 30 June 2003, http://www.nytimes.com; Scott Lindlaw, "Bush, E.U. Leaders Warn Iran on Nuclear Weapons," *Washington Post*, 25 June, 2003, http://www.washingtonpost.com; "Long Shots in Iran," *Washington Post*, 9 July 2003, http://www.washingtonpost.com; Nazila Fathi, "Iran Confirms Test of Missile That Is Able to Hit Israel," *New York Times*, 8 July 2003, http://www.nytimes.com; and Douglas Frantz, "Iran Closes In on Ability to Build a Nuclear Bomb," *Los Angeles Times*, 4 August 2003, http://www.latimes.com. For doubts about Iran's nuclear program, see Thomas Stauffer, "Iran's Nuclear Programme," *Middle East International*, 13 June 2003, 29–31.

90. Pollack, *The Persian Puzzle*, 361–69; Christopher de Bellaigue, "Big Deal in Iran," *New York Review of Books*, 26 February 2004, 30–33; Steven R. Weisman, "That Continual Matter of Iran," *New York Times*, 8 February 2004, http://www.nytimes.com;

Karim Sadjadpour, "Iranians Don't Want To Go Nuclear," *Washington Post*, 3 February 2004, http://www.washingtonpost.com; Associated Press, "U.N. Agency Scolds Iran for Nuclear Cover-Ups," *Blade*, 27 November 2003, A2; David E. Sanger and William J. Broad, "Surprise Word on Nuclear Gains by North Korea and Iran," *New York Times*, 12 November 2003, http://www.nytimes.com; Nazila Fathi, "Iran Dismisses Criticism of Nuclear Program by U.N. Agency," *New York Times*, 11 November 2003, http://www.nytimes.com; and Nazila Fathi, "Under Pressure, Iran Agrees to Constraints on Nuclear Program," *New York Times*, 21 October 2003, http://www.nytimes.com.

91. Robin Wright, "Activity Heats Up as U.S. and Iran Flirt With Closer Ties," *Washington Post*, 1 February 2004, http://www.washingtonpost.com; Robin Wright, "Hold Off on Visit, Iran Advises U.S.," *Washington Post*, 3 January 2004, http://www.washingtonpost.com; Robin Wright, "U.S. Makes Overture to Iran," *Washington Post*, 2 January 2004, http://www.washingtonpost.com; Neil MacFarquhar, "Iran's President Thanks U.S. for Aid Following Earthquake," *New York Times*, 30 December 2003, http://www.nytimes.com; and Ray Takeyh, "Iranian Options," *National Interest*, no.73 (Fall 2003): 49–56.

92. Pollack, *The Persian Puzzle*, 369–74; Wright, "Activity Heats Up as U.S. and Iran Flirt With Closer Ties"; Karl Vick, "U.S. Talks Possible, Iranian Aide Says," *Washington Post*, 9 January 2004, http://www.washingtonpost.com; Bagher Asadi, "The Battle for Iran's Future," *New York Times*, 7 January 2004, http://www.nytimes.com; "The Iranian Seesaw," *Washington Post*, 6 January 2004, http://www.washingtonpost.com; Robin Wright, "U.S. Warms to Prospect Of New Talks With Iran," *Washington Post*, 30 December 2003, http://www.washingtonpost.com; David E. Sanger and Neil MacFarquhar, "After Depicting 'Axis of Evil': Gains and Problems," *New York Times*, 20 January 2004, http://www.nytimes.com; Nazila Fahti, "One-Third of Iranian Parliament Quits in Protest," *New York Times*, 2 February 2004, http://www.nytimes.com; "Showdown or Backdown?" *Economist*, 6 February 2004, http://www.economist.com; and Weisman, "The Continual Matter of Iran."

93. W. Patrick Lang and Larry C. Johnson, "Contemplating the Ifs," *National Interest*, no. 83 (Spring 2006): 26–30; and Pollack, *The Persian Puzzle*, 382–86.

94. Ray Takeyh, "A Profile in Defiance," *National Interest*, no. 83 (Spring 2006): 16–21; and "Of God and Men," *Economist*, 11 May 2006, http://www.economist.com.

95. Helene Cooper and David E. Sanger, "A Talk at Lunch That Shifted the Stance on Iran," *New York Times*, 4 June 2006, http://www.nytimes.com; "Breakthrough or Stalemate?" *Economist*, 1 June 2006, http://www.economist.com; "Make or Break?" *Economist*, 15 June 2006, http://www.economist.com; "The Axis Powers," *Economist*, 12 July 2006, http://www.economist.com; "Another Piece of the Puzzle," *Economist*, 1 August 2006, http://www.economist.com; Lang and Johnson, "Contemplating the Ifs"; and Kenneth Pollack and Ray Takeyh, "Taking on Tehran," *Foreign Affairs* 74, no. 2 (March/April 2005): 20–34.

96. Mark Mazzetti, "Some in G.O.P. Say Iran Threat Is Played Down," *New York Times*, 24 August 2006, http://www.nytimes.com; "Still Spinning," *New York Times*, 14 August 2006, http://www.nytimes.com; and Lawrence F. Kaplan, "Other Means," *New Republic*, 31 July 2006, 12–13.

97. Warren Hoge, "Iran Tells Annan It Won't Suspend Nuclear Efforts," *New York Times*, 3 September 2006, http://www.nytimes.com; Michael Slackman, "If America Wanted to Talk, Iran Would . . . ," *New York Times*, 3 September 2006, http://www.nytimes.com; "Mr. Bush's Nuclear Legacy," *New York Times*, 2 September

2006, http://www.nytimes.com; Steven Lee Myers, "Russia Says It Opposes U.N. Sanctions on Iran," *New York Times*, 26 August 2006, http://www.nytimes.com; "The Extraordinary Revival of the Islamic Republic," *Economist*, 24 August 2006, http://www.economist.com; Helene Cooper, "U.S. Says Iranian Nuclear Proposal Is Inadequate," *New York Times*, 24 August 2006, http://www.nytimes.com; Helene Cooper, "Iran Sanctions Could Fracture Coalition," *New York Times*, 23 August 2006, http://www.nytimes.com; Michael Slackman, "Iran Defiant as Nuclear Program Deadline Nears," *New York Times*, 22 August 2006, http://www.nytimes.com; Michael Slackman, "Iran Presents 'New Formula' for Talks," *New York Times*, 22 August 2006, http://www.nytimes.com; Fred Barbash and Dafna Linzer, "Iran Reportedly Rejects Demands to Halt Nuclear Efforts," *Washington Post*, 22 August 2006, http://www.washingtonpost.com; "No, but Yes," *Economist*, 22 August 2006, http://www.economist.com; Chatham House (The Royal Institute of International Affairs), "Iran, Its Neighbours and the Regional Crises: A Middle East Programme Report" (August 2006): 5–17; Henry A. Kissinger, "The Next Steps With Iran," *Washington Post*, 31 July 2006, http://www.washingtonpost.com; Juan Cole, Kenneth Katzman, Karim Sadjadpour, and Ray Takeyh, "Symposium: A Shia Crescent: What Fallout for the United States?" *Middle East Policy* 12, no. 4 (Winter 2005): 1–27; and Mark N. Katz, "Iran and America: Is Rapprochement Finally Possible?" *Middle East Policy* 12, no. 4 (Winter 2005): 58–65.

98. Elissa Gootman, "Security Council Approves Sanctions Against Iran Over Nuclear Program," *New York Times*, 24 December 2006, http://www.nytimes.com; Lawrence F. Kaplan, "Peace Now," *New Republic*, 2 October 2006, 14–15; Jim Rutenberg and Helene Cooper, "Leaders Spar Over Iran's Aims and U.S. Power," *New York Times*, 20 September 2006, http://www.nytimes.com; David Ignatius, "Ahmadinejad's Gauntlet," *Washington Post*, 24 September 2006, http://www.washingtonpost.com; Glenn Kessler, "U.S. Policy on Iran Evolves Toward Diplomacy," *Washington Post*, 20 September 2006, http://www.washingtonpost.com; Jim Rutenberg and Helene Cooper, "Bush Makes Direct Appeal to Iranians in U.N. Speech," *New York Times*, 19 September 2006, http://www.nytimes.com; Michael Duffy, "What Would War Look Like?" *Time*, 17 September 2006, http://www.time.com; Radio Free Europe/Radio Liberty, "Iran Wins Backing From Nonaligned Bloc," 17 September 2006, http://www.rferl.org; Scott D. Sagan, "How to Keep the Bomb From Iran," *Foreign Affairs* 85, no. 5 (September/October 2006): 45–59; and Chatham House, "Iran, Its Neighbours and the Regional Crises," 10–11.

99. Laura Secor, "Whose Iran?" *New York Times*, 28 January 2007, http://www.nytimes.com; "Iran Isn't Bothered," *Economist*, 28 December 2006, http://www.economist.com; Gootman, "Security Council Approves Sanctions Against Iran Over Nuclear Program"; Christine Hauser, "Iran Vows to Continue Nuclear Program," *New York Times*, 24 December 2006, http://www.nytimes.com; "'Nyet' on Iran," *Washington Post*, 23 December 2007, http://www.washingtonpost.com; Sudarsan Raghavan and Robin Wright, "Iraq Expels 2 Iranians Detained by U.S.," *Washington Post*, 30 December 2006, http://www.washingtonpost.com; Kenneth M. Pollack, "Don't Count on Iran to Pick Up the Pieces," *New York Times*, 8 December 2006, http://www.nytimes.com; David Rohde, "Iran Is Seeking More Influence in Afghanistan," *New York Times*, 27 December 2006, http://www.nytimes.com; Neil MacFarquhar, "How Iran's Leader Keeps the West Off Balance," *New York Times*, 17 December 2006, http://www.nytimes.com; Maziar Bahari, "A Brewing Battle of Heavyweights in Tehran,"

Newsweek, 8 January 2007, 8; "Saner Voices in Iran," *New York Times*, 22 December 2006, http://www.nytimes.com; "What Hope of a Grand Bargain?" *Economist*, 30 November 2006, http://www.economist.com; and Vali Nasr, "The New Hegemon," *New Republic*, 18 December 2006, 32–37.

100. Glenn Kessler and Edward Cody, "U.S. Flexibility Credited in Nuclear Deal With N. Korea," *Washington Post*, 14 February 2007, http://www.washingtonpost.com; David E. Sanger, "Outside Pressures Snapped Korean Deadlock," *New York Times*, 14 February 2007, http://www.nytimes.com; "The Lesson of North Korea," *New York Times*, 14 February 2007, http://www.nytimes.com; Vali Nasr and Ray Takeyh, "The Iran Option That Isn't on the Table," *Washington Post*, 8 February 2007, http://www.washingtonpost.com, quote can be found in that article; "Next Stop Iran?" *Economist*, 8 February 2007, http://www.economist.com; "A Countdown to Confrontation," *Economist*, 8 February 2007, http://www.economist.com; "Puzzling over Iran," *Economist*, 5 February 2007, http://www.economist.com; William J. Broad and David E. Sanger, "Iranian Boast Is Put to Test," *New York Times*, 4 February 2007, http://www.nytimes.com; Thomas L. Friedman, "Not-So-Strange Bedfellow," *New York Times*, 31 January 2007, http://www.nytimes.com; David E. Sanger, "On Iran, Bush Faces Haunting Echoes of Iraq," *New York Times*, 28 January 2007, http://www.nytimes.com; Associated Press, "'Doomsday Clock' Moved Forward," *CNN.com*, 17 January 2007, http://www.cnn.com; David E. Sanger, "U.S. Opens Up a New Front in Iraq War—Against Iran," *International Herald Tribune*, 15 January 2007, http://www.iht.com; John Kifner, "Gunboat Diplomacy: The Watch on the Gulf," *New York Times*, 14 January 2007, http://www.nytimes.com; CNN, "White House: Can't Rule Out Attack on Iran," *CNN.com*, 14 January 2007, http://www.cnn.com; and David E. Sanger and Michael R. Gordon, "Bush Authorized Iranians' Arrest in Iraq, Rice Says," *New York Times*, 13 January 2007, http://www.nytimes.com. On how the United States could improve its relationship with Iran, see Flynt Leverett, "The Gulf Between Us," *New York Times*, 24 January 2006, http://www.nytimes.com; and Pollack, *The Persian Puzzle*, 375–424. Leverett proposed a Gulf Security Council (modeled on the UN Security Council), Pollack a "triple track:" "Grand Bargain," "True Carrot-and-Stick Approach" or "New Containment Regime." On Iran's "Grand Bargain," proposed in May 2003 but rejected by Bush administration "hard-liners," see Nicholas D. Kristof, "Diplomacy at Its Worst," *New York Times*, 29 April 2007, http://www.nytimes.com.

101. "The 'Crazies' and Iran," *New York Times*, 27 September 2007, http://www.nytimes.com; Peter Baker and Robin Wright, "At U.N., Iranian Leader is Defiant on Nuclear Efforts," 26 September 2007, http://www.washingtonpost.com; Michael Slackman, "U.S. Focus on Ahmadinejad Puzzles Iranians," *New York Times*, 24 September 2007, http://www.nytimes.com; Associated Press, "General Says Iran Prepared to Bomb Israel If Attacked," *Blade*, 20 September 2007, A8; Washington Post, "Israel Slaps Gaza Strip with 'Hostile' Designation," *Blade*, 20 September 2007, A8; "Squeezing Harder," *Economist*, 19 September 2007, http://www.economist.com; Elaine Sciolino and William J. Broad, "An Indispensable Irritant to Iran and Its Foes," *New York Times*, 17 September 2007, http://www.nytimes.com; Helene Cooper, "In Bush Speech, Signs of Split on Iran Policy," *New York Times*, 16 September 2007, http://www.nytimes.com, quote can be found in that article; Peter Beaumont, "Was Israeli Raid a Dry Run for Attack on Iran?" *Observer*, 16 September 2007, http://observer.guardian.co.uk; David Ignatius, "Cooling The Clash With Iran," *Washington Post*, 16 September 2007, http://www.washingtonpost.com; Michael Slackman,

"Hard Times Help Leaders in Iran Tighten Their Grip," *New York Times*, 5 September 2007, http://www.nytimes.com; Elaine Sciolino and William J. Broad, "Iran Expanding Its Nuclear Program, Agency Reports," *New York Times*, 30 August 2007, http://www.nytimes.com; Ray Takeyh, "Time for Détente With Iran," *Foreign Affairs* 86, no. 2 (March/April 2007): 17–32; "Stand-Off in the Persian Gulf," *Economist*, 27 March 2007, http://www.economist.com; Thom Shanker and William J. Broad, "Iran to Limit Cooperation With Nuclear Inspectors," *New York Times*, 26 March 2007, http://www.nytimes.com; Thom Shanker, "Security Council Raises Sanctions on Nuclear Iran," *New York Times*, 25 March 2007, http://www.nytimes.com; Colum Lynch, "U.N. Backs Broader Sanctions On Tehran," *Washington Post*, 25 March 2007, http://www.washingtonpost.com; "Russia, Iran and the Bottom Line," *New York Times*, 21 March 2007, http://www.nytimes.com; Elaine Sciolino, "Russia Gives Iran Ultimatum on Enrichment," *New York Times*, 20 March 2007, http://www.nytimes.com; and Steven R. Weisman, "European Officials Agree to Widen Economic Sanctions Against Iran Over Nuclear Program," *New York Times*, 13 February 2007, http://www.nytimes.com. Iran released its British captives in early April. See "Sailing into Troubled Waters," *Economist*, 4 April 2007, http://www.economist.com. On the impact of that crisis within Iran, see Michael Slackman, "Seizure of Britons Underlines Iran's Political Split," *New York Times*, 4 April 2007, http://www.nytimes.com. On the Israeli-Iranian conflict, see Trita Parsi, "Iran and Israel: The Avoidable War," *Middle East Policy* 14, no. 3 (Fall 2007): 79–85.

102. Jim Hoagland, "The Spies Strike Back," *Washington Post*, 9 December 2007, http://www.washingtonpost.com; Thom Shanker, "Secretary Calls Iran a Threat to Regional Security," *New York Times*, 8 December 2007, http://www.nytimes.com; John R. Bolton, "The Flaws in the Iran Report," *Washington Post*, 6 December 2007, http://www.washingtonpost.com; Valerie Lincy and Gary Milhollin, "In Iran We Trust?" *New York Times*, 6 December 2007, http://www.nytimes.com; "Intelligence on Iran," *Washington Post*, 5 December 2007, http://www.washingtonpost.com; Graham Bowley, "Bush Says Iran Still a Danger Despite Report on Weapons," *New York Times*, 5 December 2007, http://www.nytimes.com; Gareth Evans, "The Right Nuclear Red Line," *Washington Post*, 5 December 2007, http://www.washingtonpost.com; Robert Kagan, "Time to Talk to Iran," *Washington Post*, 5 December 2007, http://www.washingtonpost.com; William J. Broad and David E. Sanger, "How Did a 2005 Estimate on Iran Go Awry," *New York Times*, 4 December 2007, http://www.nytimes.com; Steven Lee Myers, "An Assessment Jars a Foreign Policy Debate About Iran," *New York Times*, 4 December 2007, http://www.nytimes.com; Peter Baker and Robin Wright, "A Blow to Bush's Tehran Policy," *Washington Post*, 4 December 2007, http://www.washingtonpost.com; CNN, "Iran's Revolutionary Guards Patrol Persian Gulf, U.S. Says," *CNN.com*, 29 November 2007, http://www.cnn.com; and Helene Cooper and John H. Cushman, Jr., "U.S. Levels Sanctions Against Iran Military Unit," *New York Times*, 25 October 2007, http://www.nytimes.com.

103. For further criticism of "dual containment," see Kenneth Katzman, Richard Murphy, Fraser Cameron, Robert Litwak, Gary Sick, and Thomas Stauffer, "Symposium: The End of Dual Containment: Iraq, Iran and Smart Sanctions," *Middle East Policy* 8, no. 3 (September 2001): 71–88.

104. Judis, "Crude Joke"; Gregg Easterbrook, "The Producers," *New Republic*, 4 June 2001, 27–31; and Anthony H. Cordesman, "The One True U.S. Strategic Interest in the Middle East: Energy," *Middle East Policy* 8, no. 1 (March 2001): 117–27. Cordes-

man wrote (118) that estimates showed "Gulf oil production capacity ris[ing] from 30 percent of total world capacity in 1998 to 39 percent in 2020, and that the Gulf is projected to be virtually the only region in the world that will be able to keep oil production capacity substantially above actual production." As of 2001, Gulf states provided the United States with twenty-five percent of its oil imports (119). On the pre-9/11 threat of international terrorism, see "Terrorism Threat Puts U.S. Troops on Peak Alert," *CNN.com*, 22 June 2001, http://www.cnn.com.

105. John J. Mearsheimer and Stephen M. Walt, "Keeping Saddam Hussein in a Box," *New York Times*, 2 February 2003, http://www.nytimes.com; Kenneth M. Pollack, "Next Stop Baghdad?" *Foreign Affairs* 81, no. 2 (March/April 2002): 32–47; Kenneth M. Pollack, "A Last Chance to Stop Iraq," *New York Times*, 21 February 2003, http://www.nytimes.com. See also Brian Urquhart's "The Prospect of War," *New York Review of Books*, 19 December 2002, 16–22. In this article, Urquhart reviews Pollack's book *The Threatening Storm: The Case for Invading Iraq* (New York: Random House, 2002). Morton Halperin, another well-known analyst from the scholarly community, as well as Nicholas Kristof, a *New York Times* editorialist, also advocated continued U.S. containment of Iraq. See Morton H. Halperin, "A Case for Containment," *Washington Post*, 11 February 2003, http://www.washingtonpost.com; and Nicholas D. Kristof, "War and Wisdom," *New York Times*, 7 February 2003, http://www.nytimes.com.

106. Chas W. Freeman, Jr., "Even a Superpower Needs Help," *New York Times*, 26 February 2003, http://www.nytimes.com.

107. Michael R. Gordon, "U.S. Is Preparing Base in Gulf State to Run Iraq War," *New York Times*, 1 December 2002, http://www.nytimes.com; "Qatar Gives U.S. Broad Access to Air Base," *Blade*, 12 December 2002, A4; Patrick E. Tyler, "Fearful Saudi Leaders Seek a Way to Budge Saddam Hussein," *New York Times*, 19 January 2003, http://www.nytimes.com; and "The Axis of Oil," *New York Times*, 21 January 2003, http://www.nytimes.com. For insight into the contradictions of Saudi society, see Jonathan Alter, "The End of the Double Game," *Newsweek*, 13 January 2003, 34–35.

108. Thomas E. Ricks, "Briefing Depicted Saudis as Enemies," *Washington Post*, 6 August 2002, http://www.washingtonpost.com; and Patrick E. Tyler, "Saudis Plan to End U.S. Presence," *New York Times*, 9 February 2003, http://www.nytimes.com. On U.S.-Saudi relations following 9/11, see Todd S. Purdum, "Breaking Up Would Be Hard To Do," *New York Times*, 28 April 2002, http://www.nytimes.com; "The Saudis and Us," *Blade*, 5 September 2002, http://www.toledoblade.com; and Nicholas D. Kristof, "Are the Saudis the Enemy?" *New York Times*, 22 October 2002, http://www.nytimes.com. Washington certainly wanted Saudis to stop supplying terrorists with cash and ideological support. See "The Saudi Connection," *Blade*, 7 December 2002, A10. On U.S.-Saudi relations since World War II, see F. Gregory Gause, III, "The Approaching Turning Point: The Future of U.S. Relations with the Gulf States," *Brookings Project on U.S. Policy Towards the Islamic World*, Analysis Paper Number Two (May 2003), 6–13. On societal contradictions in contemporary Saudi Arabia, see Michael Slackman, "The (Not So) Eagerly Modern Saudi," *New York Times*, 6 May 2007, http://www.nytimes.com.

109. David Ignatius, "Regime Change's Regional Ripples," *Washington Post*, 15 April 2003, http://www.washingtonpost.com; Eric Schmitt, "U.S. to Withdraw All Combat Units from Saudi Arabia," *New York Times*, 30 April 2003, http://www.nytimes.com; "Sunset in Saudi Arabia," *New York Times*, 1 May 2003, http://www.nytimes.com; Glenn Kessler, "Saudis Link Al Qaeda to Bombings," *Washington Post*, 14 May 2003, http://www.washingtonpost.com; Neil MacFarquhar, "A Bombing Shatters the Saudi Art

of Denial," *New York Times*, 18 May 2003, http://www.nytimes.com; Thomas L. Friedman, "Hummers Here, Hummers There," *New York Times*, 25 May 2003, http://www.nytimes.com; Mark Hosenball and Michael Isikoff, "Al Qaeda Strikes Again," *Newsweek*, 26 May 2003, 24–30; Fareed Zakaria, "Now, Saudis See the Enemy," *Newsweek*, 26 May 2003, 31; Jackson Diehl, "Sheikdom Democracy," *Washington Post*, 2 June 2003, http://www.washingtonpost.com; Syed Rashid Husain, "Letter from Saudi Arabia: Dramatic Change in Landscape," *Gulf News* (Dubai), 6 June 2003, http://www.gulf-news.com; Vernon Loeb, "New Bases Reflect Shift in Military," *Washington Post*, 9 June 2003, http://www.washingtonpost.com; David Ignatius, "Mending the Marriage With Saudi Arabia," *Washington Post*, 29 July 2003, http://www.washingtonpost.com; and Jeffrey A. Lefebvre, "U.S. Military Hegemony in the Arabian/Persian Gulf: How Long Can It Last?" *International Studies Perspectives* 4, no. 2 (May 2003): 186–190.

110. Simon Henderson, *The New Pillar: Conservative Arab Gulf States and U.S. Strategy* (Washington, DC: Washington Institute for Near East Policy, 2003); and Marc J. O'Reilly and Wesley B. Renfro, "Evolving Empire: America's 'Emirates' Strategy in the Persian Gulf," *International Studies Perspectives* 8, no. 2 (May 2007): 137–51. On U.S. policy vis-à-vis Saudi Arabia since 9/11, see Rachel Bronson, *Thicker Than Oil: America's Uneasy Partnership with Saudi Arabia* (New York: Oxford University Press, 2006), 232–62. For an overview of Saudi Arabia, see Max Rodenbeck, "A Long Walk," *Economist*, 5 January 2006, http://www.economist.com. On the "six plus two" bloc, see Abramowitz and Wright, "Bush to Add 20,000 Troops In an Effort to Stabilize Iraq."

111. David S. Cloud, "Gates Assures Israel on Plan to Sell Arms to Saudis," *New York Times*, 20 April 2007, http://www.nytimes.com; Hassan M. Fattah, "Saudi King Condemns U.S. Occupation of Iraq," *New York Times*, 28 March 2007, http://www.nytimes.com; Judis, "Crude Joke"; Jad Mouawad, "Saudi Officials Seek to Temper the Price of Oil," *New York Times*, 28 January 2007, http://www.nytimes.com; and Marc J. O'Reilly, Sarah J. Lippitt, and Greg Trumble, "The United States and the Arab Gulf Monarchies: The Oil-for-Security Dynamic Revisited" (paper presented at the annual conference of the International Studies Association–Midwest, St. Louis, MO, 3 November 2006). On the U.S. "empire of bases," see Chalmers Johnson, *The Sorrows of Empire: Militarism, Secrecy, and the End of the Republic* (New York: Owl Books, 2004). Pierre Noël states that the United States has aimed to "sanctuarize" the Gulf oil monarchies. See Pierre Noël, "The New US Middle East Policy and Energy Security Challenges," *International Journal* 62, no. 1 (Winter 2006–2007): 43. Ray Takeyh argues that "the Bush administration's impetuous behavior and its inability to pacify Iraq have shattered local confidence in U.S. capabilities. Widespread anti-Americanism has made it harder for governments in the region to cooperate with Washington or to allow U.S. forces on their soil. The United States may be able to keep offshore naval forces and modest bases in reliable states such as Kuwait, but it is unlikely to have a significant presence in the region, as it is too unpopular with the masses and seems too erratic to the elites." Takeyh, "Time for Détente With Iran," 20. On GCC concerns, see Joseph A. Ké-chichian, "Can Conservative Arab Gulf Monarchies Endure a Fourth War in the Persian Gulf?" *Middle East Journal* 61, no. 2 (Spring 2007): 283–306.

112. Sebastian Abbot, "Gulf Challenges US on Iran, Israel," *Washington Post*, 8 December 2007, http://www.washingtonpost.com; Reuters, "Iran Stops Selling Oil in U.S. Dollars," 8 December 2007, http://uk.reuters.com; "Countdown to Lift-off,"

Economist, 22 November 2007, http://www.economist.com; and "Shock Treatment," *Economist*, 15 November 2007, http://www.economist.com.

113. On criticisms of U.S. strategy in the Gulf and calls for regional collaboration, see Michael Ryan Kraig, "Forging a New Security Order for the Persian Gulf," *Middle East Policy* 13, no. 1 (Spring 2006): 84–101; Riad Kahwaji "U.S.-Arab Cooperation in the Gulf: Are Both Sides Working From the Same Script?" *Middle East Policy* 11, no. 3 (Fall 2004): 52–62; Michael D. Yaffe, "The Gulf and a New Middle East Security System," *Middle East Policy* 11, no. 3 (Fall 2004): 118–30; Michael Kraig, "Assessing Alternative Security Frameworks for the Persian Gulf," *Middle East Policy* 11, no. 3 (Fall 2004): 139–56; and Kenneth M. Pollack, "Securing the Gulf," *Foreign Affairs* 82, no. 4 (July/August 2003): 2–16. For a critique of regional collaboration, see Richard L. Russell, "The Persian Gulf's Collective-Security Mirage," *Middle East Policy* 12, no. 4 (Winter 2005): 77–88. On America's imperial dilemma, see Charles W. Kegley and Gregory A. Raymond, *After Iraq: The Imperiled American Imperium* (New York: Oxford University Press, 2007).

114. Adams' famous warning can be found in his July 4, 1821, speech to the U.S. House of Representatives.

115. George F. Will, "No Flinching From the Facts," *Washington Post*, 11 May 2004, http://www.washingtonpost.com.

116. On "unite and rule," see Daniel H. Nexon and Thomas Wright, "What's at Stake in the American Empire Debate," *American Political Science Review* 101, no. 2 (May 2007): 267. On America's "noble failure," see Fouad Ajami, *The Foreigner's Gift: The Americans, the Arabs, and the Iraqis in Iraq* (New York: Free Press, 2006). On "ethnic cleansing," see Edward Wong, "Strife in North Iraq as Sunni Arabs Drive Out Kurds," *New York Times*, 30 May 2007, http://www.nytimes.com. Interestingly, author Ralph Peters notes that "[t]wo bipartisan failings in Washington hinder our [U.S.] efforts to help others achieve democracy: first, our blind acceptance of the world order left behind by collapsed European empires, and second, our prompt default to oppressive regimes in the name of maintaining stability." Ralph Peters, "An Errant Push for Democracy First," *USA Today*, 18 April 2007, http://blogs.usatoday.com/oped/2007/04/post (8 June 2007).

117. John Ward Anderson, "U.S., Iran Meet to Discuss Iraq Security," *Washington Post*, 28 May 2007, http://www.washingtonpost.com; and Kirk Semple, "In Rare Talks, U.S. and Iran Discuss Iraq," *New York Times*, 28 May 2007, http://www.nytimes.com. For an assessment of Iranian policy, see Peter Galbraith, "The Victor?" *New York Review of Books*, 11 October 2007, 6–9.

118. Regarding the U.S.-Saudi relationship and its future, see Gause, "The Approaching Turning Point," 13–19. He argues (13) that "[i]t is more accurate to think of [the United States and Saudi Arabia] as strategic partners on a number of vitally important issues, including oil, regional stability in the Gulf, Arab-Israeli peace, and the global debate in the Muslim world about radicalism and terrorism. [U.S.-Saudi] interests overlap, but are not identical. Where they do overlap, [they] can work together. Where they do not, [they] will go [their] separate ways." He adds (19) that "Washington should be aiming for a 'normal' relationship with Riyadh" rather than a "special relationship." With respect to terrorism, interests overlapped, as the Saudis coped in April 2007 with yet another terror plot on their soil. See Michael Slackman, "Saudis Round Up 172, Citing Plot Against Oil Rigs," *New York Times*, 28 April 2007, http://www.nytimes.com.

119. Gause, "The Approaching Turning Point." First quote is on 5, the other quotes on 3.

120. For commentary on and analysis of U.S. empire, see Tamer Nagy Mahmoud, "Arab Rationalism," *Weghat Nazar—Points of View* (Cairo) 5, no. 49 (February 2003), reprinted in *Foreign Policy*, http://www.foreignpolicy.com; William D. Hartung, "The New Imperialism," *Nation*, 17 February 2003, 5–6; David Shribman, "American Empire or American Enigma?" *Blade*, 23 April 2003, A9; Michael Elliott, "Why Empires Strike Out," *Time*, 12 May 2003, 45; John O'Sullivan, "The Reluctant Empire," *National Review*, 19 May 2003, 43–45; John B. Judis, "History Lesson," *New Republic*, 9 June 2003, 19–23; Jack Snyder, "Imperial Temptations," *National Interest*, no. 71 (Spring 2003): 29–40; Stephen Peter Rosen, "An Empire, If You Can Keep It." *National Interest*, no. 71 (Spring 2003): 51–61; and Issa Khalaf, "The Rebirth of Colonialism in Iraq," *Middle East International*, 13 June 2003, 31–33. For a comparison of Bush and McKinley imperialism, see Carlos L. Yordan, "The Imperial Turn: Analyzing Post-9/11 American Foreign Policy Through the Prism of 1898," *Revista de Historia Actual* 4, no. 4 (2006): 27–44.

121. On the "stand up, stand down" plan, see Thomas E. Ricks, "Military Envisions Longer Stay in Iraq," *Washington Post*, 10 June 2007, http://www.washingtonpost.com. On the Salvadoran analogy, see Michael Hirsh and John Barry, "Special Forces May Train Assassins, Kidnappers in Iraq," *Newsweek*, 14 January 2005, http://www.msnbc.com/id/6802629/site/newsweek. The "fallback strategy" quote can be found in that article. Regarding the U.S. occupation of Iraq, scholar Niall Ferguson suggested that Washington study how the British ruled Egypt from the 1880s to the 1950s. See Niall Ferguson, "True Lies," *New Republic*, 2 June 2003, 16–19. Ferguson wrote (16) that "[m]ost important, the Bush administration—and the American people—need to understand that successful imperialism (sorry, 'nation-building') requires a kind of willful hypocrisy: The United States must stay in Iraq for a long time, but never stop promising to leave." In a post-colonial era, however, it seemed unlikely that the United States could occupy Iraq for some seventy years.

122. Fareed Zakaria, "Go Down in Iraq, But Go Long," *Newsweek*, 24 September 2007, 38; Ricks, "Military Envisions Longer Stay in Iraq." The "post-occupation" quote can be found in that article; Jason Campbell, Michael O'Hanlon, and Amy Unikewicz, "The State of Iraq: An Update," *New York Times*, 10 June 2007, http://www.nytimes.com; David Brooks, "A Million Little Pieces," *New York Times*, 5 June 2007, http://www.nytimes.com; Ann Scott Tyson and John Ward Anderson, "Attacks on U.S. Troops in Iraq Grow in Lethality, Complexity," *Washington Post*, 3 June 2007, http://www.washingtonpost.com; Edward Wong, "Iraq's Curse: A Thirst for Final, Crushing Victory," *New York Times*, 3 June 2007, http://www.nytimes.com. The "dragging his corpse" quote can be found in that article; David E. Sanger, "With Korea as Model, U.S. Ponders Long Role in Iraq," *New York Times*, 3 June 2007, http://www.nytimes.com; Kenneth M. Pollack, "Civil Defense," *New Republic*, 21 May 2007, 24–25; Michael R. Gordon, "Sunni Militants Disrupt Plan to Calm Baghdad," *New York Times*, 18 March 2007, http://www.nytimes.com; Los Angeles Times, "U.S. Begins Work on Withdrawal Plan in Case Troop Surge in Iraq Fails," *Blade*, 12 March 2007, A1, A4; Sarah DiLorenzo, "Iraq Presents Economic Plan at U.N.," *Washington Post*, 16 March 2007, http://www.washingtonpost.com; and Mark Mazzetti, "Analysis Is Bleak on Iraq's Future," *New York Times*, 3 February 2007, http://www.nytimes.com. For an assessment of the occupation, see Sabrina Tavernise, "It Has Unraveled So Quickly,"

New York Times, 28 January 2007, http://www.nytimes.com; and David Ignatius, "Expect the Worst in Iraq," *Washington Post*, 7 February 2007, http://www.washingtonpost.com. For what the United States should do in Iraq, see, for example, David Brooks, "Parting Ways in Iraq," *New York Times*, 28 January 2007, http://www.nytimes.com; Edward N. Luttwak, "To Help Iraq, Let It Fend for Itself," *New York Times*, 6 February 2007, http://www.nytimes.com; Thomas L. Friedman, "Yes, We Can Find the Exit," *New York Times*, 7 February 2007, http://www.nytimes.com; and Nicholas D. Kristof, "Iraqis Show Us the Door," *New York Times*, 13 February 2007, http://www.nytimes.com. On "soft partition," an idea originated by Senator Joe Biden (D-Delaware) and Leslie Gelb of the Council on Foreign Relations, see David Brooks, "The Road to Partition," *New York Times*, 11 September 2007, http://www.nytimes.com; and "Long Division," *New Republic*, 24 September 2007, 1–2. For the UN role in Iraq, see Associated Press, "U.N. Would Consider Expanded Role in Iraq but First Needs a Building to Withstand Rockets," *International Herald Tribune*, 11 June 2007, http://www.iht.com. On U.S. policymakers and the use of faulty analogies, see Yuen Foong Khong, *Analogies at War: Korea, Munich, Dien Bien Phu, and the Vietnam Decisions of 1965* (Princeton, NJ: Princeton University Press, 1992). The Bush administration exhibited quite the propensity for analogical thinking given various comparisons of the U.S. predicament in Iraq to, for example, postwar Germany and Japan, El Salvador, and Korea. On the cost of the wars in Iraq and Afghanistan (approximately $800 billion since 9/11), see Josh White and Ann Scott Tyson, "Increase In War Funding Sought," *Washington Post*, 27 September 2007, http://www.washingtonpost.com. On the British withdrawal from Basra, see Reuters, "Brown Announces Troop Withdrawal," *New York Times*, 2 October 2007, http://www.nytimes.com.

123. Brooks, "Making the Surge Work." Cullen Murphy, author of *Are We Rome?: The Fall of an Empire and the Fate of America* (Boston: Houghton Mifflin, 2007), discussed the issue of U.S. versus Roman brutality in his interview with Stephen Colbert on *The Colbert Report*, which aired on the Comedy Central television network on 7 June 2007. For an analysis of life in the Green Zone, see Rajiv Chandrasekaran, *Imperial Life in the Emerald City: Inside Iraq's Green Zone* (New York: Alfred A. Knopf, 2006). For an assessment of the U.S. invasion and occupation of Iraq, see Thomas E. Ricks, *Fiasco: The American Military Adventure in Iraq* (New York: Penguin Press, 2006); James Fallows, *Blind Into Baghdad: America's War in Iraq* (New York: Vintage Books, 2006); and George Packer, *The Assassins' Gate: America in Iraq* (New York: Farrar, Straus & Giroux, 2005). For a synopsis and succinct analysis of *Operation Iraqi Freedom* and its immediate aftermath, see Douglas Little, *American Orientalism: The United States and the Middle East Since 1945* (Chapel Hill, NC: University of North Carolina Press, 2004), 319–28.

124. On "petro politics," see "Petrodollar Power," *Economist*, 9 December 2006, 14–16. For late 2007 assessments of the Iraq situation, see Kenneth M. Pollack, "Après-Surge," *New Republic*, 31 December 2007, 12–14; Jason Campbell, Michael O'Hanlon, and Amy Unikewicz, "The State of Iraq: An Update," *New York Times*, 22 December 2007, http://www.nytimes.com; Alissa J. Rubin, "A Calmer Iraq: Fragile, and Possibly Fleeting," *New York Times*, 5 December 2007, http://www.nytimes.com; Charles Peters, "The Case for Facing Facts," *Newsweek*, 3 December 2007, 41; Steven Lee Myers and Alissa J. Rubin, "U.S. Scales Back Political Goals for Iraqi Unity," *New York Times*, 25 November 2007, http://www.nytimes.com; "Iraq's Narrow Window," *Washington Post*, 18 November 2007, http://www.washingtonpost.com; and Jack Kelly, "The Real Story in

Iraq," *Blade*, 17 November 2007, A6. For casualty statistics, see http://icasualties.org. As of 3 January 2008, 3,908 U.S. soldiers had died. On GCC economic success, see F. Gregory Gause, III, Fareed Mohamedi, Afshin Molavi, Wayne White, and Anthony H. Cordesman, "The Future of the Middle East: Strategic Implications for the United States," *Middle East Policy* 14, no. 3 (Fall 2007): 5–8.

Chapter 8

Conclusion:
An Unexceptional Empire

America is a Nation with a mission—and that mission comes from our most basic beliefs. We have no desire to dominate, no ambitions of empire. Our aim is a democratic peace—a peace founded upon the dignity and rights of every man and woman. America acts in this cause with friends and allies at our side, yet we understand our special calling: This great Republic will lead the cause of freedom.

—George W. Bush (2004)[1]

[I]t is certain that the rest of the world will continue to think of us [the United States] as an empire. Foreigners pay little attention to what we say. They observe what we do. We on the other hand think of what we feel. And the result is that we go on creating what mankind calls an empire while we continue to believe quite sincerely that it is not an empire because it does not feel to us the way we imagine an empire ought to feel.

—Walter Lippmann (1927)[2]

In September 2004, scholar Ronald Steel wrote: "The United States today is what it is, and has been at least since 1945: a great imperial power with global interests to protect and advance." Three additional years of bloody conflict in Iraq and Afghanistan have only reinforced Steel's blunt assessment, yet many Americans still do not acknowledge this sobering reality. For them, a U.S. empire, whether in the Persian Gulf or anywhere else, does not exist. They consider their country an exceptional Great Power, whose anti-imperialist values foreigners should admire and assimilate.[3]

Faithful to this Wilsonian credo, George W. Bush, son of a president who promoted multilateral internationalism, sought to perpetuate this national philosophy upon entering the Oval Office in January 2001. Staffed with veterans of the Ford, Reagan, and his father's administrations, his presidency promised a "hum-

279

ble" stewardship that could inspire the world. But rather than lead, Bush dictated. Aided by neo-conservative advisors who favored an assertive foreign policy, he abrasively tried to maximize American geopolitical advantage, a strategy that alienated friends and stunned many in the international community. Such arrogance allowed Senate Majority Leader Tom Daschle (D-South Dakota) and other critics to chastise the White House for its isolationism and unilateralism.[4]

The appalling events of September 11, 2001, muted Congressional criticism of the Bush administration's foreign policy and prompted the president to forge an international anti-terrorism coalition. As a result of the horror visited upon the World Trade Center and the Pentagon, the White House continued to impose its pre-9/11 preferences. Bush underscored this stratagem whenever he repeated his "You're either with us or against us" ultimatum to the world.[5]

Washington's refusal to consult meaningfully with other governments in the months before 9/11, and its pro forma consultations afterward, flowed from the administration's intoxication with America's redoubtable global standing, which had improved steadily from 1776 until World War II. Following that conflict, U.S. power increased exponentially until the Vietnam War halted its expansion. After an era of "relative decline," the United States recovered spectacularly once the Cold War ended. During the 1990s, the Pentagon married new technologies to revised military doctrine, the nation's economy boomed thanks to improved efficiencies and electronic commerce, and countries everywhere embraced American market capitalism. Although the U.S. economy stalled in 2001 following the "dot com" bust amidst criticism at home and abroad of the inequities of American liberalism, no nation could rival the United States. With immense reserves of "soft power" to complement its wealth and martial prowess, Washington achieved a lofty status on par with, if not surpassing, Pericles' Athens, Rome under the Caesars, Napoleonic France, and Victorian England.

Unlike those self-proclaimed empires, however, America rarely portrayed itself as an imperium while evolving into a twentieth century "hyperpower." As a liberal state, it usually disdained British and French atavism. In a post-1945 era of worldwide emancipation, Americans considered empire vulgar and anachronistic, even though their country remained legally segregated until the 1960s. The United States cloaked its considerable geopolitical ambition in words that reassured rather than threatened. It called itself a superpower or hegemon, terms that inspired neither the hatred nor trepidation associated with empire. Sanguine presidents spoke of a world community that America would gratify, not plunder. With generosity as their mantra, Americans conceived of themselves as citizens of a selfless country that could endear itself to everyone who recognized the universality of its national values. Washington would lead out of duty to the international community; others would follow willingly. This legitimization of its world role positioned the United States as an anti-imperialist Great Power. To reinforce this notion, Americans invented and promoted terminology that connoted improvement for all rather than simply self-promotion.

Abroad, however, the juxtaposition of its paternalistic intentions with certain infelicitous acts since the 1898 Spanish-American War earned Washington the title of "liberal imperialist," especially in the so-called developing world. The foreign perception of the United States as a hypocritical bully eagerly imposing its wishes on other nations, while refusing any checks on its power, continued to pervade many countries in the early twenty-first century. Leaders such as Venezuela's Hugo Chavez and Iran's Mahmoud Ahmadinejad underscored America's eroding legitimacy internationally when they decried what they perceived as the U.S. imperium's various injustices. As well, Harvard's Stephen Walt detailed the many ways countries sought to "tame" the United States. Still, despite a multitude of foreign-policy transgressions throughout American history, the U.S. imperial style did not typically humiliate friends and foes alike. *The New Yorker*'s Joshua Marshall epitomized this judgment when he wrote: "[i]f America, militarily unchallenged and economically dominant, indeed took on the functions of imperial governance, its empire was, for the most part, loose and consensual."[6]

As the United States found itself in many respects *between empire and post-empire*, its foreign policy, especially following the end of the Cold War, took on an amalgamated quality. Yet efforts to blend liberalism and realism typically resulted in policy incoherence. Nonetheless, George W. Bush's administration, which faulted its predecessor for its indecisiveness, pursued so-called maximalist policies, which American presidents, including Bill Clinton, had advocated since the Reagan years, even though those policies often irritated allies. The White House's tendency, under the younger Bush, to offend other countries, whether pro- or anti-American, earned it sustained foreign enmity, more so than any administration in U.S. history. Neo-conservatives, who combined Wilsonian and Reaganesque idealism with a penchant for militarism, dismissed criticism of U.S. foreign policy, especially that emanating from the French, Germans, and other so-called old Europeans, as petty envy of American power. As proponents of an internationalized, twenty-first century U.S. manifest destiny, neo-conservatives touted overt imperialism in lieu of the "covert empire" painstakingly constructed by Bush's predecessors.[7]

America's global imperium, a product of twentieth century capitalism and military exertion, reconfigured the world. Commerce and bases created an "American Century," a designation that connoted achievement and awe as well as bewilderment and destruction. Nowhere have these outcomes co-existed more tenuously than in the Middle East, a region frequently pregnant with despair and fury due to imperial doings and failed indigenous ideologies. Unfortunately for Washington, it entered the area without comprehending the Near East's political and social-cultural dynamic. Despite lacking such critical information, U.S. policymakers understood that Persian Gulf oil—ample as well as easily and affordably extractable—rendered that part of the Middle East invaluable both geopolitically and economically.

To secure that prize, the United States, recklessly or not, fashioned an *informal* empire in the Persian Gulf starting in 1941. As scholar Bernard Porter points out, that variant, unlike formal empire, implies "*judgements*." Still, despite such a caveat, America's imperium qualified as neo-classical and/or liberal-classical. Similar to empires such as Athens and Rome, it relied on economic and military prowess to achieve its geopolitical, economic, and strategic objectives. Like those imperia, it coerced as well as co-opted its friends and enemies in the region. Unlike those empires, however, it refrained from occupying Gulf territory, other than via bases, until *Operation Iraqi Freedom* in 2003. It thus never even tried to colonize or occupy the states within its Gulf sphere of influence.[8]

Seeking imperial influence in the era of decolonization that followed World War II, the United States eschewed the modalities of traditional empire in favor of a post-colonial imperium in the Gulf that, quickly or belatedly, adjusted to various regional upheavals. Accordingly, the boundaries of America's Gulf imperium shifted over the years and decades—a very common characteristic of empires, which usually expand and contract based on military, economic, diplomatic, and administrative performance as well as in response to events within and without the imperium. Middle East expert Fouad Ajami noted that America's "imperial acquisition came through the usual mix of default and design, by the push of [U.S.] interests, and by the furtive invitations extended to distant powers by worlds in need of an outside arbiter." In 1997, several years before George W. Bush ordered an invasion of Iraq and spoke of a Wilsonian project to democratize the Greater Middle East, analyst Adam Garfinkle observed that "what the United States is doing in [the Middle East], particularly in the Persian Gulf, is best described as imperial: Washington aims to stabilize the region even if it must use force to do so (as it has proven in the past). And the confessed reasons are neither transcendent nor sentimental, but cold-bloodedly strategic."[9]

To build and sustain its empire in the Persian Gulf, the United States relied on various forms of contingent imperialism: alliance, proxy, and unilateral. These strategies of imperialism typically allowed Washington to respond intermittently, rather than continuously or reflexively, to events in the region; usually permitted calibration of ends and means; and facilitated policy innovation whenever U.S. influence waned in the region. These flexible, situational strategies rarely ensured optimal outcomes—informal empires should not expect such results given their minimal attention to daily events within their imperia—but they assured America's continued relevance within the Gulf. As Washington became more aware of the area's geoeconomic and strategic importance during the Cold War, U.S. policymakers made countless decisions—spanning several decades and involving important corporate leaders—that eventually resulted in the establishment of an American empire in the Gulf. While neither President Franklin D. Roosevelt in 1941, nor his successors, aimed to create such an imperium, absence of purpose does not make that empire inexistent. America may claim a lack of imperial zeal—a dubious assertion given the country's various expansionist phases—but its actions in the Gulf, and elsewhere, rival those of past imperialists.

Before it entered the Second World War, the United States, heeding its corporate interests, cared mostly for the Persian Gulf's oil. On political and military issues, it remained essentially a spectator. The war and its aftermath, which constituted the *first* stage (1941–47) of U.S. expansion in the Gulf, transformed America into an interested Great Power. Washington relied on alliance and proxy imperialism, as it followed the British lead in supplying the Soviets with war matériel and encouraged Iran to resist postwar Soviet pressure. In the *second* stage (1948–58), the White House eschewed contingent imperialism when it came to the Fifty-Fifty Agreement. It reverted to alliance imperialism when it helped overthrow Iranian leader Mohammed Mossadeq. It pursued that same strategy when it sided in turn with the Saudis and British during the Buraimi crisis. Regarding the Baghdad Pact, it turned to proxy imperialism. It invoked alliance imperialism when it thwarted Anglo-French revanchism during the Suez crisis. With the Eisenhower Doctrine, it exercised unilateral imperialism. In the *third* stage (1959–72), Washington preferred alliance imperialism in the Kuwaiti crisis, while opting for the proxy variant during the Yemeni War. It avoided contingent imperialism during the Six-Day War, but the Nixon administration's Twin Pillars policy constituted more proxy imperialism. In the *fourth* stage (1973–89), the United States turned to unilateral imperialism during the initial Organization of Petroleum Exporting Countries (OPEC) crisis. Surprisingly, the country refrained from any contingent imperialism during the ensuing Iran crisis, but returned to alliance imperialism during the Iran-Iraq War. In the *fifth* stage (1990–2000), America selected the alliance variant on three occasions: to prosecute the Gulf War, contain Iraq after *Operation Desert Storm*, and aid the Gulf Cooperation Council (GCC) states with their security. Washington also reprised unilateral imperialism to punish Iran. In the *sixth* stage (2001–07), the United States opted for alliance imperialism, as it orchestrated and led an invasion of Iraq that ousted Saddam Hussein and his cronies. To prevent Iranian nuclear proliferation, the White House drew once more upon alliance imperialism. In that case, however, George W. Bush's administration fulfilled a secondary, albeit critical supportive role, as it watched the United Kingdom, France, and Germany vigorously pursue a diplomatic solution. In the Arab Gulf, Washington implemented alliance imperialism via its "emirates" strategy. Thus, GCC countries continued to provide America with oil and bases, while the United States continued to guarantee GCC security. This "oil-for-security" policy upheld the Carter Doctrine, the 1980 presidential pronouncement that henceforth wedded Washington to events in the Gulf. (For a summary of U.S. responses to events in the region since 1941, see Table 8.1.)

America's occupation of Iraq added a *formal* component to the U.S. empire in the Persian Gulf, blatantly belying Uncle Sam's self-proclaimed anti-imperialism. President Bush, the not-so-quiet American, insisted, however, that the United States merely sought to liberate Iraqis from a despotic leader, Saddam Hussein, rather than dominate and exploit Iraq, as a true imperium would. As the epigraphs at the outset of the chapter make plain, President Bush, in Walter Lippmann's words, did not know how empire should "feel." But the objects of American policy—the Iraqis—surely did, thus rendering the U.S. endeavor, no matter how nobly conceived, imperial. Disseminating "freedom," however a president defines such a malleable concept, may seem selfless and righteous to Americans, but such a *mission civilisatrice*, like others before it (French or otherwise), smacks of self-righteousness—a proud tradition of imperialists for millennia, not something George W. Bush invented. As editorialist Fareed Zakaria bitterly noted, the Bush administration "thoughtlessly engineered a political and social revolution as intense as the French or Iranian one and then seemed surprised that Iraq could not digest it happily, peaceably and quickly. We [the United States] did not give them a republic. We gave them a civil war."[10]

Table 8.1

Types of Contingent Imperialism (CI) and
Other U.S. Responses in the Persian Gulf, 1941–2007

Event	U (P1)	A (P2)	P (P3)	No CI (P4)	No CI (P5)
Stage I (1941–47)					
World War II Supply of Soviets		X			
Soviet-Iran Crisis			X		
Stage II (1948–58)					
Fifty-Fifty Agreement					X
Overthrow of Mossadeq		X			
Buraimi Crisis		X			
Baghdad Pact			X		
Suez Crisis		X			
Eisenhower Doctrine	X				
Stage III (1959–72)					
Kuwaiti Crisis		X			
Yemeni War			X		
Six-Day War					X
Twin Pillars Policy			X		
Stage IV (1973–89)					
OPEC Crisis	X				
Iranian Revolution				X	
Iran-Iraq War		X			
Stage V (1990–2000)					
Operation Desert Shield/Storm		X			
Containment of Iraq		X			
Partnerships with GCC States		X			
Containment of Iran	X				
Stage VI (2001–07)					
Invasion of Iraq		X			
Prevention of Iranian Nuclear Proliferation		X			
Emirates Strategy		X			
N = 22	3/22 (13.6%)	12/22 (54.5%)	4/22 (18.2%)	1/22 (4.5%)	2/22 (9.1%)

Key:
U (P1) = Unilateral CI
A (P2) = Alliance CI
P (P3) = Proxy CI
No CI (P4) = No CI, with Threat to U.S. Interests in the Persian Gulf
No CI (P5) = No CI, without Threat to U.S. Interests in the Gulf

Before the American-led invasion of Iraq, the Bush administration envisaged an ephemeral occupation. According to this plan, Washington would sanction a pro-American government that would approve of a dozen or so U.S. bases within Iraq as well as support American policy in the Gulf. But events and U.S. incompetence merged to thwart the White House's fervent wish, thus making it impossible for the United States to exercise *informal* empire in Iraq, the administration's preferred modus operandi, unless Washington were to overthrow the current Iraqi government, which it helped create, and replace it with a favored authoritarian who could serve as pawn. Such a maneuver would likely remind Middle Easterners of the 1953 Iran coup d'état and other perceived U.S. misdeeds. Most worrisome for Washington, such illegalities would surely exacerbate the rampant anti-Americanism permeating the Greater Middle East. Regardless of how the United States will seek to eliminate threats to U.S. interests in the Persian Gulf, American policy, dubbed "democratic globalism" by commentator Charles Krauthammer, will undoubtedly continue to dissatisfy many Arabs and Persians, while satisfying some groups and individuals, such as the Kurds and various elites in the Gulf monarchies, who *have* benefited from U.S. imperialism, to say nothing of the political, bureaucratic, and commercial gains made by an assortment of American politicians, institutions, and companies (many of them in the oil and defense business) over several decades.[11]

As the Bush administration considers how best to secure U.S. goals in Iraq and elsewhere in the Persian Gulf, it will surely draw upon past American policies—as will its successor starting in January 2009. Since 1941, the United States has alternated strategies of imperialism while evolving its empire in the Gulf. Initially, in the 1940s and '50s, Washington favored alliance imperialism. In the 1960s and '70s, presidents touted the proxy variant. In the 1980s and '90s, they typically opted for alliance imperialism. In its first term, the current administration rhetorically preferred unilateral imperialism, since ideologically it accorded with both its pre-9/11 worldview and the 2002 Bush Doctrine of preemption/prevention. Despite such a proclivity, the White House considered alliance imperialism more apropos when deciding American policy in the Gulf. Many cynics scoffed at this decision, however, considering it merely an exercise in public relations rather than a serious effort to recruit partners. For critics, the United States exercised unilateral imperialism when it invaded Iraq in March 2003: Washington made a decision and a few other countries followed, especially Great Britain. Calling that alliance imperialism distorted the fundamental inequality of decision-making input between America and its "coalition of the willing," whose members, except for the British, contributed little to *Operation Iraqi Freedom*. Notwithstanding such taxonomy issues, U.S. policy in the Gulf will remain controversial and continue to exercise partisans, pundits, scholars, and analysts, whether the White House seeks multilateral solutions to improve its global reputation, downplay its imperial doings, or assuage Americans, especially Democrats, who strongly disapprove of their country's brash unilateralism.[12]

Whatever the partisan fervor and administration motives may have been in any of the six stages of U.S. expansion in the Persian Gulf, Washington's choice of imperial strategy typically reflected American strength, the regional context, and the opportunity afforded the country to effect its preferred outcome. This progression/regression from alliance, to proxy, to alliance, to unilateral/alliance imperialism correlated with increasing U.S. influence worldwide and within the Gulf in the 1940s and '50s, waning American influence in the 1960s and '70s, resurgent U.S. power in the 1980s, and the country's development into an "über-power" following the end of the Cold War. Fortuitously for the United States, most Gulf countries welcomed an American presence. Some (e.g., Iraq) invited the Soviet Union into their countries, but Moscow never gained the confidence of area regimes the way Washington did. The smaller Gulf states, moreover, very much perceived America as the rightful heir to the United Kingdom.[13]

Due in part to that attitude, the U.S. empire in the Persian Gulf matured in ways reminiscent of imperial Britain, which oversaw the region for two-thirds of the twentieth century. When British power in the Middle East started to ebb in the late 1940s, London mostly abandoned its penchant for unilateralism in favor of partnerships with the United States. As UK influence in the area receded, the American stamp on Gulf events became unmistakable. The Iranian Revolution threatened to wreck the U.S. empire in the Gulf, but the Iran-Iraq War brought renewed American relevance to the region as Baghdad and the GCC countries worked to fend off the common Iranian enemy. To do so, they sought U.S. backing. America happily obliged, a decision that allowed it to reassert itself within the Gulf as the Cold War waned. Saddam Hussein's fateful decision to invade Kuwait in August 1990 then enabled Washington to entrench itself further within the region. By 1991, following *Operation Desert Storm* and partnership agreements with various GCC states, the U.S. empire in the Gulf seemed not only undeniable, but unassailable.[14]

In the aftermath of the 9/11 attacks, al-Qaeda's belligerent response to America's Gulf and global empire, the United States seized an unexpected opportunity to dispose of Hussein, in the expectation that his ouster would usher in a true era of *Pax Americana*, whose establishment throughout the Greater Middle East would redound to Israel's advantage as well as to its own. Or so neoconservatives believed. Yet, given similarities between post-invasion Iraq and Yugoslavia in the 1990s, Iraqi economic and political problems, especially vicious sectarian strife between Sunni and Shi'ite militias in Baghdad and some other cities, presaged full-fledged civil war. Ironically, Iraq's constitution could have facilitated the country's fracture into three entities—Kurdish, Shi'ite, and Sunni. Undoubtedly, however, adjacent states (particularly Turkey, Iran, and Syria) would have sought to influence and manipulate any partitioned Iraq. Compounding these difficulties, a virulent insurgency, made up of Iraqi Sunnis and foreign (especially al-Qaeda) terrorists, tried to expel U.S. soldiers from the Arab heartland. To stymie its foes, the American military evolved a "counterinsurgency doctrine" in 2006 following three years of bitter lessons in "asymmetrical" urban warfare. Despite various setbacks, the insurgents still threatened to succeed, an outcome that would have rendered the U.S. position in Iraq untenable. With American public opinion skeptical of the White House's Iraq policy, the Democrats holding the majority in Congress following the November 2006 elections, and U.S. forces seemingly overburdened, the Bush administration endured relentless criticism in the first nine months of 2007 as it coped with another quagmire on America's imperial periphery. Fortunately for President Bush, the "surge" he authorized in January 2007 yielded unequivocal military success by the end of the year. Although still politically dysfunctional, Iraq finally witnessed endurable levels of violence, which allowed many refugees, whether living in exile or internally displaced, to return to their country and homes. The White House touted these long-awaited U.S. achievements, which averted a worst-case scenario. Yet even if American geopolitical clout in the region were to weaken substantially due to a debacle in Iraq, the U.S. empire in the Persian Gulf would likely survive unless a wider war or revolution swept away the Arab Gulf regimes—an unlikely event given their unflagging rule and despite their tendency to overestimate internal and external threats.[15]

Even if the United States were to withdraw ignominiously from Iraq à la South Vietnam, Washington would almost certainly retain considerable sway over the emirate countries of the Arab Gulf. Thanks to its "emirates" strategy, evolved since *Operation Desert Shield*, America possesses substantial military, political, and economic assets in the region that could compensate for any loss of U.S. influence in Iraq. Should any country, such as Iran, or stateless entity, such as al-Qaeda, threaten American interests in the Gulf, the White House could reply in kind by ordering U.S. servicemen and women stationed in Kuwait, Qatar, and other emirates to strike enemy targets. Unless and until America's enemies possess weapons of mass destruction, especially nuclear weapons, this ability to exert significant force quickly and effectively within the Greater Middle East should ensure that the United States will not give up its preponderant position within the Persian Gulf any time soon. Yet, to achieve its policy objectives in the Gulf, America may have to resort continuously to unilateral imperialism, even though it might prefer to proceed otherwise. Alliance imperialism has served the United States better historically (Washington relied on that strategy in 55 percent of the cases examined in this book), but such a strategy may not be possible if the Bush administration and its successors prefer to dismiss the opinions of their friends while self-righteously promoting an infallible U.S. exceptionalism that yields repeated "exemptionalism." Taking exception to global norms may be the current American way, but every empire does what it can and must, sovereignty and morality be damned. Although such a hypocritical, Realist attitude, should it persist, will likely undermine the U.S. empire in the Gulf at some point, American hubris need not set the country on a path of inexorable imperial decline. Like a ship off course, the United States will likely have many opportunities to correct its position and avert a wreck. Analyst James Russell warns, however, that Gulf politics, characterized by "strategic insecurity" since the 2003 invasion of Iraq, invalidate the recently augmented U.S. military capacity in the region, which remains best suited to conventional warfare rather than insurgency and other intra-state conflict.[16]

Regardless of what type of contingent imperialism it may opt for in the coming years, Washington will have to determine whether it can achieve stability *and* democracy within the Persian Gulf and indeed throughout the Greater Middle East. Upon the release of the Iraq Study Group report, Secretary of State Condoleezza Rice believed that democracy would ensure stability, whereas James Baker III, who occupied her position under Bush *père*, thought stability could only occur *without* democracy. Although Rice eventually converted to

Baker's view, President Bush continued to advocate democratization. Yet the disparity between American and Arab definitions of democracy, unacknowledged by the current administration, may prove especially problematic for the United States. As scholar Reza Aslan points out, "[w]hen [U.S.] politicians speak of bringing democracy to the Middle East, they mean specifically an American secular democracy, not an indigenous Islamic one." More worrisome than American parochialism, newly enfranchised Arabs may very well vote for intensely anti-American parties (e.g., Hamas and Hezbollah), thereby potentially jeopardizing U.S. interests in the Gulf and elsewhere in the Greater Middle East. Such a possibility, and its likely adverse consequences, preoccupies U.S. policymakers. President Bush may have committed his country to "ending tyranny in the world" in his Second Inaugural Address, but he and his predecessors have tacitly or explicitly tolerated, if not endorsed, Arab and Iranian authoritarians, contradicting America's worldwide promotion of democracy but suiting its geopolitical and economic goals. The United States may have lost a critical part of its informal Gulf empire in 1979 thanks to its unabashed support of the Shah, but it rebounded by assisting other dictators and adopting new tactics, something every imperium must do.[17]

Just as evolutionary biology informs its students that species must adapt to unfamiliar environments or else die, history tells the story of empires that could not adjust to modified political circumstances. Hence, formal empires that relied consistently on imposed rule may have disappeared forever with the fall of the Soviet Empire in 1989. In the coming decades, it may be that only "empire by invitation" and a refusal to meddle overtly in another country's domestic politics, unless authorized by the United Nations, can ensure imperial success. Until 9/11 and *Operation Iraqi Freedom*, Washington seemed mostly in sync with Great-Power necessity in an era of global communications and instant information. America's democratic ways—its respect for dissenting points of view and tendency toward compromise—usually meshed with international norms such as self-determination and freedom from oppression. The Bush Doctrine, however, with its emphasis on unilateralism as well as contempt for world opinion and international institutions, delivered isolation and global scorn, not results that served the U.S. interest well.[18]

Before it ordered an invasion of Iraq in March 2003 to overthrow Saddam Hussein, the Bush administration refuted charges that U.S. soldiers would occupy the country indefinitely. Secretary of Defense Donald Rumsfeld curtly stated that Americans "don't do empire" and would exit Mesopotamia quickly. With a friendly government in Baghdad, the Pentagon could secure military installations throughout Iraq, thereby extending its "empire of bases," the hallmark of its Gulf imperium. As such, Rumsfeld unintentionally sought to use the *tactic* of formal empire to achieve the *strategy* of informal imperium. But neo-conservative officials such as Paul Wolfowitz and Douglas Feith strove to democratize Iraq and the region, an aim President Bush embraced, especially once American soldiers and inspectors could not find the nominal casus belli, Hussein's weapons of mass destruction.[19]

Formal empire has not worked in Iraq due to several factors. First, occupying a country is unpopular and therefore counterproductive in a post-colonial era.

Despite Washington's self-proclaimed altruistic and noble intentions, the U.S. occupation confirmed Arab and global animus vis-à-vis the Bush administration. Second, military technology (e.g., improvised explosive devices and rocket-propelled grenades) married to zeal (e.g., suicide bombers and insurgents) has yielded potent attacks against American and Iraqi soldiers and civilians. Thousands of Americans and hundreds of thousands of Iraqis have died as a result. U.S. conventional power may be formidable in inter-state war, but much of its superiority vanishes when confined to intra-state counterinsurgency. Third, remaking Iraqi politics via "nation busting" only enraged the now dispossessed Sunnis while emboldening Shi'a and Kurds, the communities most victimized by Hussein's cruelty and megalomania. That reversal of power spurred vicious ethno-sectarian conflict, which the United States took years to dampen and could easily resume. With initially only 140,000 or so soldiers to oversee a restless country of approximately 27 million, Washington struggled mightily to tame the fury it unleashed—a task with much precedent in imperial history.[20]

Starting in 2003, then, the Bush administration showed the temerity to smash Saddam Hussein's regime, the first step in formal empire, but mostly shied away from occupying Iraq brutally, the all-important second step in establishing a colonial imperium. That reticence, inevitable once President Bush made Iraqi sovereignty his policy's sine qua non, ensured the failure of formal empire. Disastrously, that result also ruled out America adding Iraq to its informal Gulf imperium. With civil war having almost driven a bloody stake through the Iraqi nation, Washington could only hope its decisions would stave off an Iraqi or regional cataclysm. With more private U.S. contractors in Iraq (approximately 180,000) than American soldiers (160,000 or so), the soon to be completed "surge" seemed unlikely to stamp out all of the country's violence. Although the U.S. military had killed many al-Qaeda fighters and sectarian killings in Baghdad and elsewhere had declined dramatically, the Iraqi government's futility persisted. Political factions continued to squabble over the oil industry, the distribution of petroleum revenues, and other contentious issues. As a result, several Sunni ministers quit Prime Minister Nouri al-Maliki's cabinet in early August 2007. No American policy—whether immediate or phased withdrawal, redeployment, "sustainable security," "bottom up," or "overwatch"—could compensate for the Iraqi government's underachievement. Still, such a verdict did not absolve the United States of responsibility for Iraq's plight. The American invasion and occupation had razed the Iraqi state and its institutions. Albeit corrupt and ineffective under Hussein, in many ways they had provided services more effectively than their U.S.-sanctioned successors, which only embittered Iraqis who were promised a better life once rid of the dictator from Tikrit. Iraqi anger and disappointment did not seem to discourage President Bush, however, even though his legacy very much hinged on the outcome in Iraq. Unwilling to concede defeat or admit to misjudgment, he seemed content, if not eager, to burden his successor with the messy task of either extricating the United States from Mesopotamia or ensuring a more satisfactory status quo. While in Iraq General David Petraeus and Ambassador Ryan Crocker continued trying to salvage Bush's chimera, the 2008 U.S. elections promised yet another national referendum on Iraq policy. The result doubtfully would provide Petraeus with the decade he probably needed to prosecute a successful counterinsurgency. That said, voters should have remembered that President Richard Nixon expanded America's war in Vietnam and U.S. soldiers remained in Germany, Japan, and South Korea. Those precedents underscored how difficult it could be for the United States to exit a country—regardless of which party held the White House—even sixty or so years after entering it.[21]

America's mostly dismal performance in Iraq, which ranked as the world's second most "failed state" in June 2007, confirmed Washington's imperial predilection: inept at formal empire, adept at informal empire. (U.S. bullying, which often proved costly in lives lost, ruined, or altered in Latin America and other regions where the United States imposed its ideological orthodoxy, especially its brand of capitalism, did not undermine the second half of this axiom but rather underscored the notion that empire, no matter its incarnation, rewards the strong while penalizing the weak.) Recognizing America's skill, one consonant with global trends since 1945, eluded President Bush, whose commitment to democratization in Iraq and the Middle East, thus to "imperial liberalism," blinded him to his country's aptitude for informal imperium in the Gulf. The commander-in-chief excelled at regime change, yet, forgetting his own advice about forgoing nation-building, seemed overwhelmed by the task of rehabilitating the vassal he created. Half measures may sustain informal empire, but usually only wholehearted commitment can secure formal empire. Bush's refusal to invest his nation fully in the task of reinventing Iraq therefore doomed his naïve policy.[22]

As he tried to extricate his country from its Iraq morass, Bush invoked multilateralism, which he mostly shunned during his first term. Many critics thought such a pursuit imperative for the United States to achieve its many objectives, which, in a world replete with transnational problems that no single nation could remedy, often necessitated the cooperation of many countries. Although the president refrained from the kind of obnoxious unilateralism that defined his early years in office, he remained stubborn. Lucky for him, his country could still afford such a disposition despite the hundreds of billions of dollars spent on a thus far minimally successful war.[23]

Notwithstanding its bitter occupation of Iraq and the resultant chaos, the United States has retained the ability to intervene in the Persian Gulf when it needs to and hold back when it must. As the preeminent power in the region, it can defeat any area or extra-regional opponent in a conventional war. But, if major changes to the political, economic, military, or cultural environment continue to occur and favor Iran, for example, then the U.S. empire in the Gulf will have to adapt or else suffer the same fate—extinction—as many perfectly acclimated creatures that perished once their habitats underwent transformation. Success may require renewed American support for authoritarianism in Iraq and elsewhere in the Middle East lest Washington reap the proverbial whirlwind having pushed democratization upon a skeptical region via "electoral exercises" that, according to Arabs, delivered less substantive democracy rather than more. Reversing course, as the December 2006 Iraq Study Group report implied, would undo George W. Bush's so far underwhelming handiwork, but it might solidify his country's Gulf imperium. Conversely, a reversion to America's contemptible, yet serviceable doctrine of dictatorship might prove foolhardy should the region experience continuous, or even intermittent, upheaval and rabid anti-Americanism.[24]

Whether the United States adjusts, and thus retains its preponderance in the Persian Gulf, will depend on events elsewhere in the Middle East, especially those pertaining to the thus far intractable Arab-Israeli conflict. The same can be said for international developments, such as those associated with America's "War on Terror." Domestic factors, including the country's deficit spending ($400–500 billion "in the red" per year), $9 trillion debt, negative balance of trade, weak dollar, squeezed middle class, and underfunded entitlement programs such as Medicare, will also impact the U.S. ability to intervene in the Gulf. Already slowed by "strategic fatigue," Washington will have to cope with economic burdens that historically have undermined empires. In the short term, Democratic majorities in Congress ought to check administration adventurism. But, to avoid "imperial overstretch," the U.S. government will have to reevaluate its priorities, both national and global, especially in an era where China looms as the United States' foremost competitor. Like Washington, Beijing must secure fuel supplies so that its society can prosper. That members of a renewed "axis of oil," led by Venezuela, Russia, and Iran, seem intent on selling their valuable commodity to China and India, instead of Western countries, only presages a "resource war" sure to tax America economically and strategically.[25]

Unless China and the United States, as well as other advanced and developing economies, alter their consumption habits, the Persian Gulf will continue to supply a crucial percentage of the world's petroleum and natural gas. If Beijing continues to ink deals with Gulf energy exporters, then Washington could lose influence temporarily, if not permanently, within the region. Although worrisome, increased Chinese involvement in Gulf affairs need not imperil the U.S. position in the area. The Cold War proved that America can withstand and overcome competition from another Great Power. Although a clash may occur, the two countries could unite to achieve energy security. Or China might defer to and rely on its U.S. trade partner to assure a steady supply of Gulf hydrocarbons. If, however, the United States incurs serious defeat in what scholar Andrew Bacevich calls World War IV, a Gulf-centered conflict under way since 1980 now synonymous with the "War on Terror," then Washington may be kicked out of the Gulf. Possible scenarios that could effect such a sea-change include the familiar, Islamic revolutionaries overthrowing the conservative regimes in the Arabian Peninsula, as well as the obvious, but rarely acknowledged—Arab oil monarchies opting for a different security patron (e.g., China).[26]

Washington could very well accept such an outcome since OPEC must sell its petroleum at a price the rest of the world can afford. Otherwise, the United States and other countries dependent upon oil will invest heavily in energy conservation, alternative fuels, and fuel efficiency (issues Congress addressed in its December 2007 energy bill), a decision that could some day impoverish, if not bankrupt, the Persian Gulf states but provide Americans with some much needed energy security. If America moves away from a fossil fuel–based economy (President Bush acknowledged his country's "addiction" to oil in 2006 but took no meaningful steps to curtail U.S. consumption), then it may *voluntarily* withdraw from the Gulf. Given that such a scenario, though highly unlikely in the short term, is now plausible in the wake of recent gasoline prices (Americans paid in excess of $3 per gallon much of 2005–07), a very different U.S. Gulf policy could materialize at some point in the next decade. Of course, America's role in the region might instead intensify.[27]

Options other than withdrawal or occupation (of countries or bases) exist, however. Several prominent scholars, for example, have promoted "offshore balancing." Adopting this posture would return the United States "over the horizon," its policy of the early 1980s. Such a strategy may be better suited to the U.S. air-naval empire in the Gulf, but having American sailors, airmen, and Marines stationed at sea, rather than in Qatar, the current U.S. military hub in the region, and elsewhere in the GCC, will not make the United States invisible. Arabs and Iranians will know that Americans remain in the Gulf, as well as the nearby Indian Ocean, and thus will resent their presence, which they will continue to regard as imperial. Striking exclusively from the air and sea may save U.S. lives and ensure a degree of stealth in a region where Islamists seek to bomb as many American targets as they can. But a shallower "footprint" in the Gulf will not transform Washington's enemies into friends. Nor will it prevent foes such as Iran from defying it. In fact, it could embolden them, thereby necessitating renewed American intervention on land, via temporary military facilities known as "warm bases" or "lily pads," to protect U.S. political and economic interests, including friendly regimes. Lest the United States forget, GCC countries will no doubt remind their protector that "offshore balancing" did not deter Saddam Hussein's Iraq from invading Kuwait in August 1990. Hence, the "emirates" strategy, although flawed, remains America's best short-term modus operandi given U.S. goals in the Gulf. If Washington can scale back its presence in Iraq significantly yet retain bases in that country, then American strategy will likely evolve. But post-Saddam Iraq will remain volatile, thus necessitating the retention of the flexible "emirates" strategy.[28]

Hussein may now only be a memory, but American geopolitical ambition continues to convulse the Persian Gulf, which is experiencing yet another round of intrusive, pervasive foreign meddling—in addition to the regional upheaval that has recently made it the nexus of Middle East politics. Notes Bacevich: "From the Carter Doctrine came a new pattern of U.S. military actions, one that emerged through fits and starts. Although not fully apparent until the 1990s, changes in U.S. military posture and priorities gradually converted the Persian Gulf into the epicenter of American grand strategy and World War IV's principal theater of operations." This shift away from a Cold-War policy that spotlighted Europe and East Asia underscored the U.S. need for energy security. Securing scarce natural resources is something empires have sought for millennia. The White House may not conceive of America's policy in the Gulf that way, but many observers of U.S. foreign policy perceive no difference between American behavior in the region and that of previous imperia.[29]

The United States may not purposely seek to reprise the British, Ottomans, Persian Safavids, and Portuguese, all of which evolved empires in the Persian Gulf in recent centuries, but American rhetorical aversion to colonialism will not shelter it from Middle Eastern opprobrium (what The Economist calls the "axis of resistance"), nor will it make Washington's experience easy, especially given the current global "clash of ignorance" and what Reza Aslan calls the "Islamic Reformation," a deadly political and theological contest, analogous to the Christian Reformation, pitting Islamic radicals such Osama bin Laden versus moderates. Although America's Gulf empire combines classical features (e.g., a reliance on force) with modern ones (e.g., a commitment to self-determination), this hybrid, as Fouad Ajami opines, "will never be a happy imperium," especially given vociferous public objection in the Middle East to U.S. regional policies. The United States and its citizens may consider themselves exceptional (as most imperialists do), but historically most empires, both formal and informal, have not fared particularly well in the Middle East. Sadly for both Americans and inhabitants of the region, who know each other mostly via stereotypes, bittersweet U.S. relations with Gulf countries since World War II only presage more of the same in the coming years. Fearing an Islamic "totalitarian empire," an alternative President Bush considers far worse than American supremacy, Washington seeks, *ironically*, imperial success in the Middle East without ever admitting to such a purpose.[30]

Whether or not the rest of the world concurs with the White House's judgment that Islamic terrorism constitutes an existential threat will undoubtedly contribute to the near-term fate of America's empire in the Persian Gulf. With that critical issue in mind, supporters and opponents of that imperium continue to debate its benevolence and malevolence as well as compare it to the British Empire, the *Pax Romana*, and even to imperial Venice. Like journalist David Ignatius, analysts are asking: "How does a nation have the benefits of imperial reach without the ruinous costs of empire?"[31]

No matter how the United States copes with its imperial predicament, it will almost certainly emulate past Gulf empires. Yet, despite Secretary of Defense Robert Gates' reference in December 2006 to his country's "enduring presence" in the region, pinpointing when America's Gulf imperium will vanish remains unknowable. Its current informal nature (save Iraq) may be well suited to Thomas Friedman's non-hierarchical "flat world," but the Persian Gulf and the Greater Middle East continue to thrive on authoritarianism. Whether that trend persists will impact the U.S. empire's durability. As such, America's Gulf imperium could endure, possibly excel, for many decades, centuries even, especially if the United States can maximize its "smart" power—a synergy of "hard" (i.e., military-economic prowess) and "soft" power (i.e., the ability to co-opt). Alternatively, that empire could decline precipitously. Or it could do both—a common imperial experience. As mentioned in the preface, the U.S. imperial trajectory in the Gulf tends to be jagged. Apogees and nadirs have occurred throughout the stages of U.S. expansion described herein. High points include the 1956 Suez crisis, 1991's *Operation Desert Storm*, and the 2003 invasion of Iraq. Low points include the 1958 Iraq coup, the 1973 OPEC crisis, the 1979 Iranian Revolution, and the current occupation of Iraq. Such a "peak and valley" pattern will likely reoccur without the empire disintegrating. If American power and influence erode irrevocably, then some other Great Power could succeed the United States as regional Leviathan, just as America took over from the British during the Cold War. In an alternate scenario, a historic Middle Eastern power such as Iran could reestablish its own political as well as military hegemony within the region. For now, though, the U.S. empire in the Gulf continues a cen-turies-old habit—one that the Roman Caesars, Ottoman sultans, and "Rule Bri-tannia" policymakers would have easily recognized.[32]

Many Americans carry on oblivious to that reality. They continue to believe their country exceptional and therefore incapable of imperialism. Some Ameri-cans, like many foreigners, think otherwise. They know the United States pos-sesses an empire in the Gulf. Created and evolved since World War II, that im-perium's achievements as well as failures qualify as ordinary by imperial standards. As such, the U.S. empire in the Persian Gulf remains *unexceptional*—whether or not Americans acknowledge its existence.

Notes

1. "Text of Bush's [2004 State of the Union] Speech," *New York Times*, 20 January 2004, http://www.nytimes.com.

2. Walter Lippmann, *Men of Destiny* (New York: Macmillan, 1927), 217.

3. Ronald Steel, "Totem and Taboo," *Nation*, 20 September 2004, http://www.thenation.com. For an assessment of the war in Afghanistan, see David Rohde and David E. Sanger, "How the 'Good War' in Afghanistan Went Bad," *New York Times*, 12 August 2007, http://www.nytimes.com.

4. On the relationship between George H.W. Bush and George W. Bush, see Sheryl Gay Stolberg, "First Father: Tough Times on Sidelines," *New York Times*, 9 August 2007, http://www.nytimes.com.

5. On November 6, 2001, President Bush stated: "You're either with us or against us in the fight against terror." CNN, "You Are Either With Us or Against Us," *CNN.com*, 6 November 2001, http://www.cnn.com.

6. Stephen M. Walt, *Taming American Power: The Global Response to U.S. Prima-cy* (New York: W.W. Norton, 2005); and Joshua Micah Marshall, "Power Rangers: Did the Bush Administration Create a New American Empire—or Weaken the Old One?" *New Yorker*, 2 February 2004, http://www.newyorker.com. On foreign disdain for U.S. policies, see Glenn Kessler, "Anger at U.S. Policies More Strident at U.N.," *Washington Post*, 24 September 2006, http://www.washingtonpost.com. On U.S. problems with the developing world, see David D. Newsom, *The Imperial Mantle: The United States, Deco-lonization, and the Third World* (Bloomington, IN: Indiana University Press, 2001). In a column in *The New Republic* spotlighting Chavez's and Ahmadinejad's criticisms of American policy, Peter Beinart wrote that "unless freedom imposes restraints on the United States as well as other nations, it will sound to many in the postcolonial world like domination." See Peter Beinart, "Free For All," *New Republic*, 9 October 2006, 6.

7. Stephen Sestanovich, "American Maximalism," *National Interest*, no. 79 (Spring 2005): 13–23; Marshall, "Power Rangers." For foreigners' views of U.S. foreign policy, see Pew Research Center for the People & the Press, "Pew Global Attitudes Project: 23 June 2005 Survey: U.S. Image Up Slightly, But Still Negative," http://people-press.org/reports. For Americans' infatuation with militarism, see Andrew J. Bacevich, *The New American Militarism: How Americans Are Seduced by War* (New York: Oxford University Press, 2005). America's in-between foreign policy can be dubbed liminal.

8. On informal empire, Bernard Porter, *Empire and Superempire: Britain, America and the World* (New Haven, CT: Yale University Press, 2006), 2. Italics in original.

9. Fouad Ajami, "Where U.S. Power Is Beside the Point," *New York Times*, 17 October 2000, http://www.nytimes.com; and Adam Garfinkle, "The U.S. Imperial Postulate in the Mideast," *Orbis* 41, no. 1 (Winter 1997): 16.

10. Fareed Zakaria, "Vengeance of the Victors," *Newsweek*, 8 January 2007, 25. For the classic tale of American imperial *naïveté*, involving the U.S. role in Vietnam in the 1950s, see Graham Greene, *The Quiet American* (New York: Penguin Classics, 2004). For an application to the Iraq War, see Lawrence F. Kaplan, "Quiet American II," *New Republic*, 1 August 2005, http://www.tnr.com. In his book on American involvement in Iraq, *The Foreigner's Gift: The Americans, the Arabs, and the Iraqis in Iraq* (New York: Free Press, 2006), Fouad Ajami refers to the venture as possibly a "noble failure," a characterization consistent with his imperial analysis of U.S. policy in Iraq. For a review of the book, see L. Carl Brown, "The Dream Palace of the Empire," *Foreign Affairs* 85, no. 5 (September/October 2006): 144–48.

11. On the Bush administration's Iraq policy, see, for example, James Fallows, *Blind Into Baghdad: America's War in Iraq* (New York: Vintage Books, 2006). On U.S., especially Bush administration, incompetence in Iraq, see Mark Danner, "Iraq: The War of the Imagination," *New York Review of Books*, 21 December 2006, 81–96; Frank Rich, "So You Call This Breaking News?" *New York Times*, 1 October 2006, http://www.nytimes.com; and Michiko Kakutani, "A Portrait of Bush as a Victim of His Own Certitude," *New York Times*, 30 September 2006, http://www.nytimes.com. On America's quest for informal empire in Iraq, see Gwynne Dyer, "Iraqis Feeling the Referendum Blues," *Blade* (Toledo, OH), 10 October 2005, A9. On anti-Americanism, see S. Amjad Hussain, "Anti-American Views Easy to Understand," *Blade*, 10 October 2005, A9. On America's occupation of Iraq and its problems, see Phebe Marr, "Occupational Hazards: Washington's Record in Iraq," *Foreign Affairs* 84, no. 4 (July/August 2005): 180–86. On whether renewed authoritarianism could remedy Washington's Iraq policy, see John F. Burns, "Could a New Strongman Help?" *New York Times*, 12 November 2006, http://www.nytimes.com. On "democratic globalism," see Charles Krauthammer, "Democratic Realism: An American Foreign Policy for a Unipolar World" (2004 Irving Kristol Lecture at the American Enterprise Institute Annual Dinner, Washington, DC, 10 February 2004), http://www.aei.org. In his speech, Krauthammer advocated "democratic realism," which, unlike the Bush administration's expansive doctrine of liberty, "must be targeted, focused and limited."

12. For examples of academic and pundit disagreements over Iraq, see Larry Diamond, James Dobbins, Chaim Kaufmann, Leslie Gelb, and Stephen Biddle, "What to Do in Iraq: A Roundtable," *Foreign Affairs* 85, no. 4 (July/August 2006): 150–69; and the 27 November and 4 December 2006 special issue of *The New Republic*, titled "Iraq: What Next?" On U.S. public opinion and American foreign policy, see Daniel Yankelovich, "Poll Positions: What Americans Really Think About U.S. Foreign Policy," *Foreign Affairs* 84, no. 5 (September/October 2005): 2–16.

13. On America as "überpower," see Michael Hirsh, *At War with Ourselves: Why America Is Squandering Its Chance to Build a Better World* (New York: Oxford University Press, 2003), 1–25.

14. On the British Empire in the Persian Gulf, see Uzi Rabi, "Britain's 'Special Position' in the Gulf: Its Origins, Dynamics and Legacy," *Middle Eastern Studies* 42, no. 3 (May 2006): 351–64.

15. Two weeks before the U.S.-led invasion of Iraq, in a 6 March 2003 talk at Johns Hopkins University's School for Advanced International Studies, *New York Times* columnist Thomas Friedman spoke of two scenarios that could await the United States following the overthrow of Saddam Hussein's regime. In the first scenario, Washington would win the Arab version of postwar Germany. In the second scenario, which Friedman considered more probable, the White House would inherit the Arab version of Yugoslavia. C-SPAN aired Friedman's talk. On how the Iraqi government tried to cope with sectarian violence, see Richard A. Oppel, Jr., and Qais Mizher, "Iraqi Leader Unveils New Security Plan Amid Rising Violence," *New York Times*, 3 October 2006,

http://www.nytimes.com. For an analysis of the Iraqi constitution, see James Glanz, "Constitution or Divorce Agreement?" *New York Times*, 9 October 2005, http://www.nytimes.com. On the U.S. military "counterinsurgency doctrine," see Michael R. Gordon, "Military Hones a New Strategy on Insurgency," *New York Times*, 5 October 2006, http://www.nytimes.com. For an initial assessment of the "surge" and overall U.S. Iraq policy, see "Baghdad or Bust," *Economist*, 13 January 2007, 11–12. For contrasting mid-2007 analyses, see Jack Kelly, "Keep On Surging," *Blade*, 30 June 2007, A8; and Thomas L. Friedman, "Dog Paddling in the Tigris," *New York Times*, 1 July 2007, http://www.nytimes.com. See also David E. Sanger and Thom Shanker, "General's Iraq Progress Report Has Competition," *New York Times*, 24 June 2007, http://www.nytimes.com. On the situation in Iraq in July and August 2007, see "Iraq's Demise," *Blade*, 8 August 2007, A6; Andrew J. Bacevich, "Army of One," *New Republic*, 6 August 2007, 25–26; Bill Marsh, "Iraq Withdrawal: Five Difficult Questions," *New York Times*, 29 July 2007, http://www.nytimes.com; and Michael R. Gordon, "U.S. Seen in Iraq Until at Least '09," *New York Times*, 24 July 2007, http://www.nytimes.com. Even U.S. soldiers publicly weighed in on the war. See Buddhika Jayamaha, Wesley D. Smith, Jeremy Roebuck, Omar Mora, Edward Sandmeier, Yance T. Gray, Jeremy A. Murphy, "The War As We Saw It," *New York Times*, 19 August 2007, http://www.nytimes.com. On how the Iraq War only exacerbated America's terrorism problem, see Karen DeYoung, "Spy Agencies Say Iraq War Hurting U.S. Terror Fight," *Washington Post*, 24 September 2006, http://www.washingtonpost.com. Gregory Gause asserts that "[w]hile transborder ideological and political challenges in the Persian Gulf are real, the local states have developed relatively strong state structures to maintain their regimes in power. However, they continue to conduct their foreign policies on the assumption that such transborder challenges are major threats." See F. Gregory Gause, III, "Threats and Threat Perceptions in the Persian Gulf Region," *Middle East Policy* 14, no. 2 (Summer 2007): 119–24. Quote can be found on 123. See also Thomas R. Mattair, "Mutual Threat Perceptions in the Arab/Persian Gulf: GCC Perceptions," *Middle East Policy* 14, no. 2 (Summer 2007): 133–40. On what the U.S. military may have to confront in the coming years, see Wesley K. Clark, "The Next War," *Washington Post*, 16 September 2007, http://www.washingtonpost.com.

16. On Washington's "emirates" strategy, see Marc J. O'Reilly and Wesley B. Renfro, "Evolving Empire: America's 'Emirates' Strategy in the Persian Gulf," *International Studies Perspectives* 8, no. 2 (May 2007): 137–51. For U.S. policy vis-à-vis the Gulf as well as the rest of the Middle East as of August 2007, see "Arming Its Friends and Talking Peace," *Economist*, 2 August 2007, http://www.economist.com. For a recent analysis of American exceptionalism, see Anatol Lieven, *America Right or Wrong: An Anatomy of American Nationalism* (New York: Oxford University Press, 2004). Scholar John Ruggie has written on U.S. "exemptionalism" and "doctrinal unilateralism." See John G. Ruggie, "Doctrinal Unilateralism and Its Limits: America and Global Governance in the New Century," Corporate Social Responsibility Initiative Working Paper no. 16 (Cambridge, MA: John F. Kennedy School of Government, Harvard University, 2006). Political scientist Stephen Krasner argues that sovereignty is merely "organized hypocrisy." See Stephen D. Krasner, *Sovereignty: Organized Hypocrisy* (Princeton, NJ: Princeton University Press, 1999). On America's ability to recover from shortsighted decisions, see "Still No. 1," *Economist*, 28 June 2007, http://www.economist.com. On U.S. military capability and Gulf politics, see James A. Russell, "Whither Regional Security in a World Turned Upside Down?" *Middle East Policy* 14, no. 2 (Summer 2007): 141–48. He argues (147–48), moreover, that, "[i]f Iraq proves to be a precursor to a prolonged period of strategic instability as new actors vie for political power throughout the region, the facilities infrastructure established by the British and passed on to the United States may prove to be a casualty of war. Such an environment suggests that externally

applied military power via forward-based ground presence will decrease in importance and may well become politically untenable for the regional elites. . . . The end result of the coming regional upheavals and the pressure this will place on the ground-based military means that the U.S. Navy may once again reign supreme, projecting power and influence on an episodic basis from the sea." On al-Qaeda's comeback, see Bruce Riedel, "Al Qaeda Strikes Back," *Foreign Affairs* 86, no. 3 (May/June 2007): 24–40.

17. Reza Aslan, *No god but God: The Origins, Evolution, and Future of Islam* (New York: Random House, 2006), 260–61; and George W. Bush, "Second Inaugural Address" (delivered in Washington, D.C., 20 January 2005), http://www.whitehouse.gov. On the Rice-Baker rivalry, see David E. Sanger, "Dueling Views Pit Baker Against Rice," *New York Times*, 8 December 2006, http://www.nytimes.com. On Rice's conversion, see Helene Cooper, "As Her Star Wanes, Rice Tries to Reshape Legacy," *New York Times*, 1 September 2007, http://www.nytimes.com. Interestingly, Bahrain declared itself a constitutional monarchy in 2002, making it, in theory at least, the only democracy, or pseudo democracy, among the emirate states of the Persian Gulf, countries which the United States staunchly supports. See Gwynne Dyer, "Democracy for Bahrain," *Blade*, 25 February 2002, A7; and "Bahrain Turnout Hailed for 1st Vote in 30 Years," *Blade*, 25 October 2002, A2. Unfortunately for the Bush administration, officials in Bahrain may be reverting to their autocratic ways. See Hassan M. Fattah, "Report Cites Bid by Sunnis in Bahrain to Rig Elections," *New York Times*, 2 October 2006, http://www.nytimes.com. The penchant of Middle East leaders for "liberal autocracy" makes democratization that much more difficult to effect. See Ray Takeyh, "Close, But No Democracy," *National Interest*, no. 78 (Winter 2004/05): 57–64. For more on democratization in the Middle East and elsewhere, see "Does He Know Where It's Leading?" *Economist*, 30 July 2005, 22–24; "Democracy and the West," *Middle East International*, 1 October 1999, 3; and Tony Smith, *America's Mission: The United States and the Worldwide Struggle for Democracy in the Twentieth Century* (Princeton, NJ: Princeton University Press, 1994).

18. For discussions of "empire by invitation" versus "empire by imposition," see John Lewis Gaddis, *Strategies of Containment: A Critical Appraisal of American National Security Policy during the Cold War*, revised and expanded edition (New York: Oxford University Press, 2005), 384–85; and John Lewis Gaddis, *Surprise, Security, and the American Experience* (Cambridge, MA: Harvard University Press, 2004), 106–13. Historian Thomas Paterson notes that, with respect to "empire by invitation," "[t]he thesis becomes less workable elsewhere in the world [i.e., outside western Europe in the early Cold War] because so often no invitations whatsoever were tendered prior to U.S. interventions." See Thomas G. Paterson, "Cold War Revisionism: A Practitioner's Perspective," *Diplomatic History* 31, no. 3 (June 2007): 393. On America's "democratic empire," see John Lewis Gaddis, *We Now Know: Rethinking Cold War History* (New York: Clarendon Press, 1997), 288–89. On the Bush Doctrine, see Clyde Prestowitz, *Rogue Nation: American Unilateralism and the Failure of Good Intentions* (New York: Basic Books, 2003).

19. For the Rumsfeld quote, see Porter, *Empire and Superempire*, 1. On America's "empire of bases," see Chalmers Johnson, *The Sorrows of Empire: Militarism, Secrecy, and the End of the Republic* (New York: Owl Books, 2004).

20. On the limits or non-fungibility of American military prowess, see Russell, "Whither Regional Security in a World Turned Upside Down?" 146–47. Russell avers (147) that "the Bush administration's plans to achieve global military reach using forward-deployed forces operating from networks of bases appear mismatched to the region's threat environment, which is likely to be dominated by populist warlords and internal sectarian strife."

21. On the issue of sovereignty, see Helene Cooper, "Bush's Task: Thrusting New Strategy on 'a Sovereign Nation,'" *New York Times*, 9 January 2007,

http://www.nytimes.com. On private U.S. contractors, see T. Christian Miller, "Critics: Guns for Hire in Iraq," *Plain Dealer* (Cleveland, OH), 5 July 2007, A1, A10. On the problems of the Iraqi government, see Alissa J. Rubin, "Maliki Gains Time, but Faces a Daunting Task," *New York Times*, 25 September 2007, http://www.nytimes.com; and Tina Susman, "Iraqi Bill on Oil Industry Stalled," *Plain Dealer*, 5 July 2007, A8.

22. Reuters, "Iraq Ranks No. 2 of Failed States," *New York Times*, 19 June 2007, http://www.nytimes.com; and Robert Cooper, "Imperial Liberalism," *National Interest* 79 (Spring 2005): 25–34. On the advantages of informal empire via a U.S.-GCC-style alliance, see George Liska, *Imperial America: The International Politics of Primacy* (Baltimore: Johns Hopkins Press, 1967), 96. For a condemnation of America's imperialism in Iraq, see John B. Judis, "Bush's Neo-Imperialist War," *American Prospect*, 22 October 2007, http://www.prospect.org. On formal versus informal empire, see Daniel H. Nexon and Thomas Wright, "What's at Stake in the American Empire Debate," *American Political Science Review* 101, no. 2 (May 2007): 258–66.

23. For the fate of the Bush Doctrine and the need for renewed multilateralism, see Philip H. Gordon, "The End of the Bush Revolution," *Foreign Affairs* 85, no. 4 (September/October 2006): 75–86; and Richard N. Haass, *The Opportunity: America's Moment to Alter History's Course* (New York: PublicAffairs, 2005).

24. On comparisons to evolutionary biology, see Gaddis, *We Now Know*, 295. See also Stephen Jay Gould, "The Evolution of Life on the Earth," *Scientific American*, October 1994, 85–91. Using as a template Charles Darwin's emphasis on "local adaptation" (85) and paleontologist Gould's reminder of the importance of contingency in the development of organisms over time, students of world politics should understand that empires adapt to local circumstances, but not necessarily in predictable ways. Good fortune can ensure the perpetuation of empire, whereas bad luck can assure its destruction. Scholar Shibley Telhami referred to "electoral exercises" and discussed Arab public opinion regarding democracy. See Shibley Telhami, Brian Katulis, Jon B. Alterman, and Milton Viorst, "Symposium: Middle Eastern Views of the United States: What Do the Trends Indicate?" *Middle East Policy* 13, no. 3 (Fall 2006): 2.

25. For an assessment of the Middle East and its difficulties, see F. Gregory Gause, III, Fareed Mohamedi, Afshin Molavi, Wayne White, and Anthony H. Cordesman, "The Future of the Middle East: Strategic Implications for the United States," *Middle East Policy* 14, no. 3 (Fall 2007): 1–28; and Thomas L. Friedman, "Between Dust and Deliverance," *New York Times*, 13 June 2007, http://www.nytimes.com. On America's economic liabilities, see "Edging Away from the Dollar," *Blade*, 2 January 2007, A6; Associated Press, "U.S. Borrowing Putting Nation on Ruinous Course," *Blade*, 5 November 2006, B4; and Christopher Layne, "Impotent Power? Re-examining the Nature of America's Hegemonic Power," *National Interest*, no. 85 (Sept./Oct. 2006): 41–47. On U.S. strategic fatigue, see Graham E. Fuller, "Strategic Fatigue," *National Interest*, no. 84 (Summer 2006): 37–42. On the new "axis of oil," see Flynt Leverett and Pierre Noël, "The New Axis of Oil," *National Interest*, no. 84 (Summer 2006): 62–70. On the upcoming "resource war," see Joshua Kurlantzick, "Crude Awakening," *New Republic*, 2 October 2006, 19–27. On Chinese and Indian interests in the Persian Gulf, see Geoffrey Kemp, "The East Moves West," *National Interest*, no. 84 (Summer 2006): 71–77. For a scathing critique of the Bush administration's "War on Terror," see Zbigniew Brzezinski, "Terrorized by 'War on Terror,'" *Washington Post*, 25 March 2007, http://www.washingtonpost.com. See also "The President's Prison," *New York Times*, 25 March 2007, http://www.nytimes.com.

26. Bacevich, *The New American Militarism*, 175–204. Bacevich considers the Cold War World War III. On China and the Gulf, see Steve A. Yetiv and Chunlong Lu, "China, Global Energy, and the Middle East," *Middle East Journal* 61, no. 2 (Spring 2007): 199–218. On how China has helped the United States on a number of key diplo-

matic matters, see Steven Lee Myers, "Look Who's Mr. Fixit for a Fraught Age," *New York Times*, 7 October 2007, http://www.nytimes.com. On Asia's role in the twenty-first century, see Robert D. Kaplan, "Lost at Sea," *New York Times*, 21 September 2007, http://www.nytimes.com. On energy security, see Michael T. Klare, "Oil, Iraq, and American Foreign Policy," *International Journal* 62, no. 1 (Winter 2006–2007): 31–42; and Pierre Noël, "The New US Middle East Policy and Energy Security Challenges," *International Journal* 62, no. 1 (Winter 2006–2007): 43–54. Noël writes (53) that "by applying military force to try and democratize the Middle East from the outside, the United States is putting its national security at risk—including its energy security." On the GCC's predicament, see Joseph A. Kéchichian, "Can Conservative Arab Gulf Monarchies Endure a Fourth War in the Persian Gulf?" *The Middle East Journal* 61, no. 2 (Spring 2007): 283–306; and Mattair, "Mutual Threat Perceptions in the Arab/Persian Gulf."

27. On the need for U.S. energy independence, see Thomas L. Friedman, "The First Energy President," *New York Times*, 5 January 2007, http://www.nytimes.com; and Thomas L. Friedman, "The Energy Wall," *New York Times*, 1 December 2006, http://www.nytimes.com. On the energy bill, see John M. Broder, "U.S. Congress Passes Sweeping Energy Bill," *International Herald Tribune*, 19 December 2007, http://www.iht.com. The bill will increase the average fuel efficiency standard for U.S. bought cars and light trucks from 25 miles per gallon (mpg) to 35 mpg by 2020. On high gas prices, see CNNmoney.com, "One State Left with Gasoline Below $3," *CNNmoney.com*, 22 May 2007, http://money.cnn.com. See also Steve Hargreaves, "Get Ready for $4 Gasoline," *CNNmoney.com*, 7 May 2007, http://money.cnn.com. Despite their hydrocarbon wealth, Gulf states are interested in alternative energy. See Hassan M. Fattah, "Abu Dhabi Explores Energy Alternatives," *New York Times*, 18 March 2007, http://www.nytimes.com.

28. Eugene Gholz, Daryl G. Press, and Benjamin Valentino, "Time to Offshore Our Troops," *New York Times*, 12 December 2006, http://www.nytimes.com. Scholars that favor "offshore balancing" include Christopher Layne, John Mearsheimer, and Stephen Walt. See, for example, Christopher Layne, *The Peace of Illusions: American Grand Strategy from 1940 to the Present* (Ithaca, NY: Cornell University Press, 2006), 159–92. On "warm bases" and "lily pads," see Richard L. Russell, "The Persian Gulf's Collective-Security Mirage," *Middle East Policy* 12, no. 4 (Winter 2005): 82–83. Professor Russell opines (82) that "[a]n American over-the-horizon presence would be the instrument of statecraft to tend, mend and shape the struggle for power in the Gulf." He warns, though, that "Americans should not harbor any illusion that militant Islamic charges of American colonization that so powerfully resonate in the Arab world will be completely dampened with lower-profile warm bases or lily pads." For criticism of "lily pads" in Iraq, see "Forget the 'Lily Pads,'" *Blade*, 26 May 2007, A8. For more on base possibilities in Iraq, see Walter Posch, "Staying the Course: Permanent U.S. Bases in Iraq?" *Middle East Policy* 13, no. 3 (Fall 2006): 109–20.

29. Bacevich, *The New American Militarism*, 183. For more on the legacy and continued relevance of the Carter Doctrine for both U.S. policy in the Gulf and worldwide, see Klare, "Oil, Iraq, and American Foreign Policy." On the Gulf as the new nexus, as opposed to Egypt, Palestine, and the Levant, see Fouad Ajami, "Brothers to the Bitter End," *New York Times*, 19 June 2007, http://www.nytimes.com.

30. For analyses of the Middle East and of U.S.–Middle East relations, see "Coalitions of the Unwilling," *Economist*, 21 October 2006, 25–28; Shibley Telhami, *The Stakes: America and the Middle East: The Consequences of Power and the Choice for Peace* (Boulder, CO: Westview Press, 2002); Ian Lustick, "The Absence of Middle Eastern Great Powers: Political 'Backwardness' in Historical Perspective," *International Organization* 51, no. 4 (Fall 1997): 653–83; L. Carl Brown, *International Politics and*

the Middle East: Old Rules, Dangerous Game (Princeton, NJ: Princeton University Press, 1984); and Douglas Little, *American Orientalism: The United States and the Middle East Since 1945* (Chapel Hill, NC: University of North Carolina Press, 2004). Little notes (327–28) that, "[l]ike British empire-builders in the Middle East during an earlier era, U.S. policy-makers in Washington and U.S. foot soldiers in Baghdad gradually came to regard their Iraqi adversaries as wily orientals, ungrateful thugs, or religious fanatics." On America's inability to understand Iraq, see also Fouad Ajami, "Blind Liberation," *New Republic*, 23 April 2007, 42–49. French Foreign Minister Philippe Douste-Blazy referred to "a clash of ignorance." See Kessler, "Anger at U.S. Policies More Strident at U.N." For Aslan's discussion of an "Islamic Reformation," see his *No god but God*, 249–66. See also Anthony H. Cordesman, "Winning the 'War on Terrorism': A Fundamentally Different Strategy," *Middle East Policy* 13, no. 3 (Fall 2006): 101–8. Cordesman writes (106) that "[t]he real 'war on terrorism' can only be won if the religious, political and intellectual leaders of Islamic countries and communities actively confront and fight neo-Salafi Sunni Islamist extremism at the religious and ideological level." On bin Laden and jihadism, see Fawaz A. Gerges, *Journey of the Jihadist: Inside Muslim Militancy* (Orlando, FL: Harcourt, 2006). The Ajami quote can be found in his "Where U.S. Power Is Beside the Point." See also Fouad Ajami, "The Sentry's Solitude," *Foreign Affairs* 80, no. 6 (November/December 2001): 2–16. For public opinion in the Middle East vis-à-vis the United States, see Telhami et al., "Symposium: Middle Eastern Views of the United States," 1–28. For the "totalitarian empire" quote, see "President Bush's Speech," *New York Times*, 6 October 2005, http://www.nytimes.com. On alternatives "more frightening than your own hegemony," see Gaddis, *Surprise, Security, and the American Experience*. Quote is on 117. On irony in American history, see Reinhold Niebuhr, *The Irony of American History* (New York: Charles Scribner, 1952).

31. David Ignatius, "From Venice, a Lesson on Empire," *Washington Post*, 20 September 2006, http://www.washingtonpost.com.

32. Associated Press, "Gates Talks with Leaders of Iraq and U.S. Troops," *Blade*, 22 December 2006, A8; and Thomas L. Friedman, *The World Is Flat: A Brief History of The Twenty-First Century* (New York: Farrar, Straus & Giroux, 2005). For a critique of Friedman's book, see John Gray, "The World Is Round," *New York Review of Books*, 11 August 2005, 15. For more on "smart" power, see Richard L. Armitage and Joseph S. Nye, Jr., "Why So Angry, America?" *Washington Post*, 9 December 2007, http://www.washingtonpost.com. For a recent assessment of empires and America's imperial venture in the Greater Middle East, see Niall Ferguson, "Empires with Expiration Dates," *Foreign Policy* (September/October 2006), http://www.foreignpolicy.com. On the matter of British retrenchment, which could hold lessons for the United States, see Jeffrey Pickering, *Britain's Withdrawal from East of Suez: The Politics of Retrenchment* (New York: St. Martin's Press, 1998). For an assessment of Iran's ambition and capabilities, see Mark Gasiorowski, "The New Aggressiveness in Iran's Foreign Policy," *Middle East Policy* 14, no. 2 (Summer 2007): 125–32. Gasiorowski asserts (132) that "[i]n the longer term, the withdrawal of U.S. forces from Iraq, a reduction of U.S. forces in the Persian Gulf and elsewhere in the region, and efforts to forge a regional security framework that strengthens both Iran's security and that of its neighbors would reduce Iran's need for deterrence and therefore its need to pursue these aggressive activities." For a survey of Iran, see Peter David, "The Revolution Strikes Back: A Special Report on Iran," *Economist*, 21 July 2007, 1–16.

Selected Bibliography

Archival Materials

Badeau, John S. Oral History. John F. Kennedy Library (JFKL). Boston, MA.
Foreign and Commonwealth Office. Files. Public Record Office. Kew, Surrey, England.
Kennedy, John F. National Security Files. JFKL.
———— President's Office Files. JFKL.
————. White House Central Subject Files. JFKL.

Published Documents

American Foreign Policy: Current Documents 1961. Washington, DC: Government Printing Office, 1965.
Bush, George W. "The National Security Strategy of the United States of America," September 2002. http://www.whitehouse.gov/nsc/nss.pdf.
Department of State Bulletin. 1942, 1943, 1945, 1956.
U.S. Congress. "Saddam's Iraq: Sanctions and U.S. Policy." *Hearing before the Subcommittee on Near Eastern and South Asian Affairs of the Committee on Foreign Relations of the United States Senate*, 106th Congress, 2nd Session, 22 March 2000. Washington, DC: Government Printing Office, 2000.
————. "United States Policy toward Iran." *Hearing before the Subcommittee on Near Eastern and South Asian Affairs of the Committee on Foreign Relations of the United States Senate*, 105th Congress, 2nd Session, 14 May 1998. Washington, DC: Government Printing Office, 1998.
————. "Bomb Attack in Saudi Arabia." *Hearings before the Committee on Armed Services of the United States Senate*, 104th Congress, 2nd Session, 9 July and 18 September 1996. Washington, DC: Government Printing Office, 1997.
————. "U.S. Policy toward Iran and Iraq." *Hearings before the Subcommittee on Near Eastern and South Asian Affairs of the Committee on Foreign Relations of the United States Senate*, 104th Congress, 1st Session, 2 March and 3 August 1995. Washington, DC: Government Printing Office, 1995.
————. "Implementation of Lessons Learned from the Persian Gulf Conflict." *Joint Hearing before the Subcommittee on Coalition Defense and Reinforcing Forces and the Subcommittee on Military Readiness and Defense Infrastructure of the Committee on Armed Services of the United States Senate*, 103rd Congress, 2nd Session, 18 April 1994. Washington, DC: Government Printing Office, 1994.

————. "The Persian Gulf, 1974: Money, Politics, Arms, and Power." *Hearings Before the Subcommittee on the Near East and South Asia of the Committee on Foreign Affairs*, House of Representatives, 93rd Congress, 2nd Session, 30 July, 5, 7, and 12 August 1974. Washington, DC: Government Printing Office, 1975.

————. "New Perspectives On the Persian Gulf." *Hearings Before the Subcommittee on the Near East of the Committee on Foreign Affairs*, House of Representatives, 93rd Congress, 1st Session, 6 June, 17, 23, 24 July, and 28 November 1973. Washington, DC: Government Printing Office, 1973.

————. "U.S. Interests In and Policy Toward the Persian Gulf." *Hearings Before the Subcommittee on the Near East of the Committee on Foreign Affairs*, House of Representatives, 92nd Congress, 2nd Session, 2 February, 7 June, 8 and 15 August 1972. Washington, DC: Government Printing Office, 1972.

U.S. Department of State. *Foreign Relations of the United States (FRUS)*, 1964–1968, 21, *Near East Region; Arabian Peninsula*. Washington, DC: Government Printing Office, 2000.

————. *FRUS*, 1955–1957, 12, *Near East Region; Iran; Iraq*. Washington, DC: Government Printing Office, 1991.

————. *FRUS*, 1955–1957, 16, *Suez Crisis 26 July–31 December 1956*. Washington, DC: Government Printing Office, 1990.

————. *FRUS*, 1952–1954, 9, Part 1, *The Near and Middle East*. Washington, DC: Government Printing Office, 1986.

————. *FRUS*, 1947, 5, *The Near East and Africa*. Washington, DC: Government Printing Office, 1971.

————. *FRUS*, 1946, 7, *The Near East and Africa*. Washington, DC: Government Printing Office, 1969.

————. *FRUS*, 1945, 8, *The Near East and Africa*. Washington, DC: Government Printing Office, 1969.

————. *FRUS*, 1943, 4, *The Near East and Africa*. Washington, DC: Government Printing Office, 1964.

Wilber, Donald N. "[CIA] Clandestine Service History: Overthrow of Premier Mossadeq of Iran, November 1952–August 1953," March 1954. Available through the *National Security Archive [Washington, DC] Electronic Briefing Book No. 28: The Secret CIA History of the Iran Coup, 1953*, edited by Malcolm Byrne. http://www.gwu.edu/~nsarchiv/NSAEBB/NSAEBB28/01.

Survey Reports

Pew Research Center for the People & the Press. "Pew Global Attitudes Project: June 23, 2005, Survey: U.S. Image Up Slightly, But Still Negative." http://people-press.org/reports.

————. "August 18, 2004, Survey: Foreign Policy Attitudes Now Driven by 9/11 and Iraq." http://people-press.org/reports.

————. "Pew Global Attitudes Project: March 16, 2004 Survey: A Year After Iraq War." http://people-press.org/reports.

Books and Book Chapters

Acheson, Dean. *Present at the Creation: My Years in the State Department*. New York: W.W. Norton, 1969.

Ajami, Fouad. *The Foreigner's Gift: The Americans, the Arabs, and the Iraqis in Iraq.* New York: Free Press, 2006.

Albright, Madeleine, with Bill Woodward. *Madam Secretary.* New York: Miramax Books, 2003.

Alkadiri, Raad. "Iraq: The Dilemma of Sanctions and Confrontation." In *Managing New Developments in the Gulf,* edited by Rosemary Hollis. London: Royal Institute of International Affairs, 2000.

Ambrose, Stephen E. *Eisenhower: Soldier and President.* New York: Simon & Schuster, 1990.

Anderson, David L., ed. *Shadow on the White House: Presidents and the Vietnam War 1945–1975.* Lawrence, KS: University Press of Kansas, 1993.

Anderson, Irvine H. "The American Oil Industry and the Fifty-Fifty Agreement of 1950." In *Musaddiq, Iranian Nationalism, and Oil,* edited by James A. Bill and Wm. Roger Louis. Austin, TX: University of Texas Press, 1988.

Anscombe, Frederick F. *The Ottoman Gulf: The Creation of Kuwait, Saudi Arabia, and Qatar.* New York: Columbia University Press, 1997.

Aron, Raymond. *The Imperial Republic: The United States and the World 1945–1973.* Translated by Frank Jellinek. Cambridge, MA: Winthrop Publishers, 1974.

Aslan, Reza. *No god but God: The Origins, Evolution, and Future of Islam.* New York: Random House, 2006.

Bacevich, Andrew J. *The New American Militarism: How Americans Are Seduced by War.* New York: Oxford University Press, 2005.

———, ed. *The Imperial Tense: Prospects and Problems of American Empire.* Chicago: Ivan R. Dee, 2003.

———. "New Rome, New Jerusalem." In *The Imperial Tense: Prospects and Problems of American Empire,* edited by Andrew J. Bacevich. Chicago: Ivan R. Dee, 2003.

———. *American Empire: The Realities & Consequences of U.S. Diplomacy.* Cambridge, MA: Harvard University Press, 2002.

Baker, James A., III, with Thomas M. DeFrank. *The Politics of Diplomacy: Revolution, War & Peace, 1989–1992.* New York: G.P. Putnam, 1995.

Baldwin, David A. *Economic Statecraft.* Princeton: Princeton University Press, 1985.

Baram, Amatzia. "U.S. Input into Iraqi Decisionmaking, 1988–1990." In *The Middle East and the United States: A Historical and Political Reassessment,* edited by David W. Lesch. Boulder, CO: Westview Press, 1999.

Bar-On, Mordechai. "David Ben-Gurion and the Sèvres Collusion." In *Suez 1956: The Crisis and Its Consequences,* edited by W.M. Roger Louis and Roger Owen. Oxford: Clarendon Press, 1989.

Beck, Lewis White, ed. *Kant on History.* New York: Macmillan, 1963.

Bernstein, Carl, and Bob Woodward. *All the President's Men.* New York: Warner Books, 1975.

Beschloss, Michael R., and Strobe Talbott. *At the Highest Levels: The Inside Story of the End of the Cold War.* Boston: Little, Brown, 1993.

Bill, James A. *The Eagle and the Lion: The Tragedy of American-Iranian Relations.* New Haven, CT: Yale University Press, 1988.

Bills, Scott L. *Empire and Cold War: The Roots of U.S.-Third World Antagonism, 1945–47.* New York: St. Martin's Press, 1990.

Blight, James G., and David A. Welch. *On The Brink: Americans and Soviets Reexamine the Cuban Missile Crisis.* New York: Noonday Press, 1990.

Bowie, Robert R. "Eisenhower, Dulles, and the Suez Crisis." In *Suez 1956: The Crisis and Its Consequences,* edited by W.M. Roger Louis and Roger Owen. Oxford: Clarendon Press, 1989.

Bowman, Larry W., and Jeffrey A. Lefebvre. "The Indian Ocean: U.S. Military and Strategic Perspectives." In *The Indian Ocean: Perspectives on a Strategic Arena*, edited by William L. Dowdy and Russell B. Trood. Durham, NC: Duke University Press, 1985.

Brands, H.W. *The Devil We Knew: Americans and the Cold War*. New York: Oxford University Press, 1993.

Brecher, Michael, and Patrick James. *Crisis and Change in World Politics*. Boulder, CO: Westview Press, 1986.

Bronson, Rachel. *Thicker Than Oil: America's Uneasy Partnership with Saudi Arabia*. New York: Oxford University Press, 2006.

Brown, L. Carl. *International Politics and the Middle East: Old Rules, Dangerous Game*. Princeton, NJ: Princeton University Press, 1984.

Brzezinski, Zbigniew. *Power and Principle: Memoirs of the National Security Adviser 1977–1981*. New York: Farrar, Straus & Giroux, 1983.

Bush, George, and Brent Scowcroft. *A World Transformed*. New York: Alfred A. Knopf, 1998.

Byman, Daniel L., and Matthew C. Waxman. *Confronting Iraq: U.S. Policy and the Use of Force Since the Gulf War*. Santa Monica, CA: Rand, 2000.

Campbell, John C. "The Soviet Union, the United States, and the Twin Crises of Hungary and Suez." In *Suez 1956: The Crisis and Its Consequences*, edited by W.M. Roger Louis and Roger Owen. Oxford: Clarendon Press, 1989.

Carrière, Erin, Marc O'Reilly, and Richard Vengroff. "'In the Service of Peace': Reflexive Multilateralism and the Canadian Experience in Bosnia." In *International Public Opinion and the Bosnia Crisis*, edited by Richard Sobel and Eric Shiraev. Lanham, MD: Lexington Books, 2003.

Center for Strategic and International Studies. *The Gulf: Implications of British Withdrawal*, Special Reports Series No. 8. Washington, DC: Georgetown University, 1969.

Chace, James. "In Search of Absolute Security." In *The Imperial Tense: Prospects and Problems of American Empire*, edited by Andrew J. Bacevich. Chicago: Ivan R. Dee, 2003.

Chandrasekaran, Rajiv. *Imperial Life in the Emerald City: Inside Iraq's Green Zone*. New York: Alfred A. Knopf, 2006.

Chua, Amy. *World on Fire: How Exporting Free Market Democracy Breeds Ethnic Hatred and Global Instability*. New York: Doubleday, 2003.

Citino, Nathan J. *From Arab Nationalism to OPEC: Eisenhower, King Saud, and the Making of U.S.-Saudi Relations*. Bloomington, IN: Indiana University Press, 2002.

Cohen, Michael J. *Fighting World War Three from the Middle East: Allied Contingency Plans, 1945–1954*. London: Frank Cass, 1997.

Cohen, Warren I. *America in the Age of Soviet Power, 1945–1991*. In *Cambridge History of American Foreign Relations*, 4, edited by Warren I. Cohen. Cambridge: Cambridge University Press, 1993.

Cordesman, Anthony H. *Bahrain, Oman, Qatar, and the UAE: Challenges of Security*. Boulder, CO: Westview Press, 1997.

Cottam, Richard W. *Iran and the United States: A Cold War Case Study*. Pittsburgh, PA: University of Pittsburgh Press, 1988.

Crabb, Cecil V., Jr. *The Doctrines of American Foreign Policy: Their Meaning, Role, and Future*. Baton Rouge, LA: Louisiana State University Press, 1982.

Daalder, Ivo H., and James M. Lindsay, *America Unbound: The Bush Revolution in Foreign Policy*. Washington, DC: Brookings Institution Press, 2003.

Dallek, Robert. *The American Style of Foreign Policy: Cultural Politics and Foreign Affairs*. New York: Oxford University Press, 1983.

————. *Franklin D. Roosevelt and American Foreign Policy, 1932–1945.* New York: Oxford University Press, 1979.

Dawisha, Adeed. "The Stability of the Gulf: Domestic Sources and External Threats." In *The Great Game: Rivalry in the Persian Gulf and South Asia,* edited by Alvin Z. Rubinstein. New York: Praeger, 1983.

Divine, Robert A. *Eisenhower and the Cold War.* New York: Oxford University Press, 1981.

————. *Roosevelt & World War II.* New York: Penguin Books, 1969.

Dower, John W. *War without Mercy: Race & Power in the Pacific War.* New York: Pantheon Books, 1986.

Doyle, Michael W. *Empires.* Ithaca, NY: Cornell University Press, 1986.

Eban, Abba. *Diplomacy for the Next Century.* New Haven, CT: Yale University Press, 1998.

Eddy, William A. *F.D.R. Meets Ibn Saud.* New York: American Friends of the Middle East, 1954.

Eden, Anthony. *Full Circle.* Boston: Houghton Mifflin, 1960.

Eilts, Hermann Frederick. "Reflections on the Suez Crisis: Security in the Middle East." In *Suez 1956: The Crisis and Its Consequences,* edited by W.M. Roger Louis and Roger Owen. Oxford: Clarendon Press, 1989.

Eisenhower, Dwight D. *Waging Peace (1956–1961).* New York: Doubleday, 1965.

El-Shazly, Nadia, and Raymond Hinnebusch. "The Challenge of Security in the Post-Gulf War Middle East System. In *The Foreign Policies of Middle East States,* edited by Raymond Hinnebusch and Anoushiravan Ehteshami. Boulder, CO: Lynne Rienner, 2002.

Evron, Yair. "The Invasion of Kuwait and the Gulf War: Dilemmas Facing the Israeli-Iraqi-U.S. Relationship." In *The Middle East and the United States: A Historical and Political Reassessment,* edited by David W. Lesch. Boulder, CO: Westview Press, 1999.

Fallows, James. *Blind Into Baghdad: America's War in Iraq.* New York: Vintage Books, 2006.

Ferguson, Niall. *Colossus: The Price of America's Empire.* New York: Penguin Press, 2004.

————. *Empire: The Rise and Demise of the British World Order and the Lessons for Global Power.* New York: Basic Books, 2002.

Freedman, Robert O. *Moscow and the Middle East: Soviet Policy since the Invasion of Afghanistan.* Cambridge: Cambridge University Press, 1991.

Freiberger, Steven Z. *Dawn Over Suez: The Rise of American Power in the Middle East, 1953–1957.* Chicago: Ivan R. Dee, 1992.

Friedman, Thomas L. *The World Is Flat: A Brief History of The Twenty-First Century.* New York: Farrar, Straus & Giroux, 2005.

————. *Longitudes and Attitudes: The World in the Age of Terrorism.* New York: Anchor Books, 2003.

Gaddis, John Lewis. *Strategies of Containment: A Critical Appraisal of American National Security Policy during the Cold War,* rev. and exp. ed. New York: Oxford University Press, 2005.

————. *Surprise, Security, and the American Experience.* Cambridge, MA: Harvard University Press, 2004.

————. *The Landscape of History: How Historians Map the Past.* New York: Oxford University Press, 2002.

————. *We Now Know: Rethinking Cold War History.* New York: Clarendon Press, 1997.

————. "Rescuing Choice from Circumstance: The Statecraft of Henry Kissinger." In *The Diplomats, 1939–1979*, edited by Gordon A. Craig and Francis L. Loewenheim. Princeton, NJ: Princeton University Press, 1994.

————. *The United States and the End of the Cold War: Implications, Reconsiderations, Provocations*. New York: Oxford University Press, 1992.

————. *The Long Peace: Inquiries into the History of the Cold War*. New York: Oxford University Press, 1987.

————. *Strategies of Containment: A Critical Appraisal of Postwar American National Security Policy*. New York: Oxford University Press, 1982.

————. *The United States and the Origins of the Cold War, 1941–1947*. New York: Columbia University Press, 1972.

Galeano, Eduardo. *Upside Down: A Primer for the Looking-Glass World*. Translated by Mark Fried. New York: Picador USA, 2000.

Gardner, Lloyd C., and Marilyn B. Young, eds. *The New American Empire: A 21st Century Teach-In on U.S. Foreign Policy*. New York: New Press, 2005.

Garthoff, Raymond L. *Détente and Confrontation: American-Soviet Relations from Nixon to Reagan*. Washington, DC: Brookings Institution, 1985.

Gasiorowski, Mark J. *U.S. Foreign Policy and the Shah: Building a Client State in Iran*. Ithaca, NY: Cornell University Press, 1991.

Gause, F. Gregory, III. "From 'Over the Horizon' to 'Into the Backyard': The U.S.-Saudi Relationship and the Gulf War." In *The Middle East and the United States: A Historical and Political Reassessment*, edited by David W. Lesch. Boulder, CO: Westview Press, 1999.

————. "The Political Economy of National Security." In *The Persian Gulf at the Millennium: Essays in Politics, Economy, Security, and Religion*, edited by Gary G. Sick and Lawrence G. Potter. New York: St. Martin's Press, 1997.

————. *Oil Monarchies: Domestic and Security Challenges in the Arab Gulf States*. New York: Council on Foreign Relations Press, 1994.

————. "Gulf Regional Politics: Revolution, War, and Rivalry." In *Dynamics of Regional Politics: Four Systems on the Indian Ocean Rim*, edited by W. Howard Wriggins. New York: Columbia University Press, 1992.

Gendzier, Irene L. *Notes from the Minefield: United States Intervention in Lebanon and the Middle East, 1945–1958*. New York: Columbia University Press, 1997.

George, Alexander L. *Bridging the Gap: Theory & Practice in Foreign Policy*. Washington, DC: United States Institute of Peace Press, 1993.

————. "Case Studies and Theory Development: The Method of Structured, Focused Comparison." In *Diplomacy: New Approaches in History, Theory, and Policy*, edited by Paul Gordon Lauren. New York: Free Press, 1979.

Gerges, Fawaz A. *Journey of the Jihadist: Inside Muslim Militancy*. Orlando, FL: Harcourt, 2006.

————. *The Superpowers and the Middle East: Regional and International Politics, 1955–1967*. Boulder, CO: Westview Press, 1994.

Gerson, Louis L. *John Foster Dulles*. New York: Cooper Square Publishers, 1967.

Ghabra, Shafeeq. "Kuwait and the United States: The Reluctant Ally and U.S. Policy Toward the Gulf." In *The Middle East and the United States: A Historical and Political Reassessment*, edited by David W. Lesch. Boulder, CO: Westview Press, 1999.

Gilpin, Robert. *The Political Economy of International Relations*. Princeton, NJ: Princeton University Press, 1987.

————. *War and Change in World Politics*. Cambridge: Cambridge University Press, 1981.

Goldgeier, James M. *Not Whether But When: The U.S. Decision to Enlarge NATO.* Washington, DC: Brookings Institution Press, 1999.

Goncharov, Sergei N., John W. Lewis, and Xue Litai. *Uncertain Partners: Stalin, Mao, and the Korean War.* Stanford, CA: Stanford University Press, 1993.

Goode, James F. *The United States and Iran, 1946–51: The Diplomacy of Neglect.* New York: St. Martin's Press, 1989.

Gorbachev, Mikhail. *The August Coup: The Truth and the Lessons.* New York: Harper-Collins, 1991.

Greene, Graham. *The Quiet American.* New York: Penguin Classics, 2004.

Guppy, Shusha. *The Blindfold Horse: Memories of a Persian Childhood.* Boston: Beacon Press, 1988.

Haass, Richard N. *The Opportunity: America's Moment to Alter History's Course.* New York: PublicAffairs, 2005.

Hadar, Leon T. *Quagmire: America in the Middle East.* Washington, DC: Cato Institute, 1992.

Hahn, Peter L. *The United States, Great Britain, and Egypt, 1945–1956: Strategy and Diplomacy in the Early Cold War.* Chapel Hill, NC: University of North Carolina Press, 1991.

Hanson, Victor Davis. *A War Like No Other: How the Athenians and Spartans Fought the Peloponnesian War.* New York: Random House, 2005.

———. "What Empire?" In *The Imperial Tense: Prospects and Problems of American Empire*, edited by Andrew J. Bacevich. Chicago: Ivan R. Dee, 2003.

Hardt, Michael, and Antonio Negri. *Empire.* Cambridge, MA: Harvard University Press, 2000.

Hart, Parker T. *Saudi Arabia and the United States: Birth of a Security Partnership.* Bloomington, IN: Indiana University Press, 1998.

Heikal, Mohamed H. *Cutting the Lion's Tail: Suez through Egyptian Eyes.* London: Andre Deutsch, 1986.

Heilbroner, Robert L. *The Worldly Philosophers: The Lives, Times and Ideas of the Great Economic Thinkers.* New York: Simon & Schuster, 1992.

Heiss, Mary Ann. *Empire and Nationhood: The United States, Great Britain, and Iranian Oil, 1950–1954.* New York: Columbia University Press, 1997.

Henderson, Simon. *The New Pillar: Conservative Arab Gulf States and U.S. Strategy.* Washington, DC: Washington Institute for Near East Policy, 2003.

Hermann, Margaret G. "Assessing Leadership Style: Trait Analysis." In *The Psychological Assessment of Political Leaders*, edited by Jerrold M. Post. Ann Arbor, MI: University of Michigan Press, 2003.

Herring, George C. *America's Longest War: The United States and Vietnam 1950–1975.* New York: Alfred A. Knopf, 1986.

Hertsgaard, Mark. *The Eagle's Shadow: Why America Fascinates and Infuriates the World.* New York: Picador, 2002.

Herzig, Edmund. "Iran: Internal Developments and International Implications." In *Managing New Developments in the Gulf*, edited by Rosemary Hollis. London: Royal Institute of International Affairs, 2000.

Hewedy, Amin. "Nasser and the Crisis of 1956." In *Suez 1956: The Crisis and Its Consequences*, edited by W.M. Roger Louis and Roger Owen. Oxford: Clarendon Press, 1989.

Hinnebusch, Raymond. "The Middle East Regional System." In *The Foreign Policies of Middle East States*, edited by Raymond Hinnebusch and Anoushiravan Ehteshami. Boulder, CO: Lynne Rienner, 2002.

Hiro, Dilip. *The Longest War: The Iran-Iraq Military Conflict.* New York: Routledge, 1991.

Hirsh, Michael. *At War with Ourselves: Why America Is Squandering Its Chance to Build a Better World.* New York: Oxford University Press, 2003.

Hogan, Michael J., ed., *Hiroshima in History and Memory.* Cambridge: Cambridge University Press, 1996.

———, ed. *The End of the Cold War: Its Meaning and Implications.* Cambridge: Cambridge University Press, 1992.

———. *The Marshall Plan: America, Britain, and the Reconstruction of Western Europe, 1947–1952.* Cambridge: Cambridge University Press, 1987.

Hourani, Albert. *A History of the Arab Peoples.* Cambridge, MA: Belknap Press, 1991.

Howe, Stephen. *Empire: A Very Short Introduction.* Oxford: Oxford University Press, 2002.

Hull, Cordell. *Memoirs of Cordell Hull,* 2. New York: Macmillan, 1948.

Hunt, Michael H. *The American Ascendancy: How the United States Gained and Wielded Global Dominance.* Chapel Hill, NC: University of North Carolina Press, 2007.

———. *Ideology and U.S. Foreign Policy.* New Haven, CT: Yale University Press, 1987.

Ignatieff, Michael. *Blood and Belonging: Journeys into the New Nationalism.* New York: Farrar, Straus & Giroux, 1993.

Isaacson, Walter. *Kissinger: A Biography.* New York: Simon & Schuster, 1992.

James, Harold. *The Roman Predicament: How the Rules of International Order Create the Politics of Empire.* Princeton, NJ: Princeton University Press, 2006.

Janis, Irving. *Groupthink.* Boston: Houghton Mifflin, 1982.

Jentleson, Bruce W. *With Friends Like These: Reagan, Bush, and Saddam, 1982–1990.* New York: W.W. Norton, 1994.

Jervis, Robert. "Perceiving and Coping with Threat." In *Psychology and Deterrence,* edited by Robert Jervis, Richard Ned Lebow, and Janice Gross Stein. Baltimore: Johns Hopkins University Press, 1985.

Johnson, Chalmers. *The Sorrows of Empire: Militarism, Secrecy, and the End of the Republic.* New York: Owl Books, 2004.

Joyce, Miriam. *Kuwait 1945–1996: An Anglo-American Perspective.* London: Frank Cass, 1998.

Kagan, Robert. *Of Paradise and Power: America and Europe in the New World Order.* New York: Alfred A. Knopf, 2003.

Kaplan, Lawrence F., and William Kristol. *The War Over Iraq: Saddam's Tyranny and America's Mission.* San Francisco, CA: Encounter Books, 2003.

Kaplan, Lawrence S. *NATO and the United States, Updated Edition: The Enduring Alliance.* New York: Twayne, 1994.

Kaplan, Robert D. *Imperial Grunts: The American Military on the Ground.* New York: Random House, 2005.

———. *The Arabists: The Romance of an American Elite.* New York: Free Press, 1993.

Kaufman, Burton I. *The Arab Middle East and the United States: Inter-Arab Rivalry and Superpower Diplomacy.* New York: Twayne, 1996.

Kechichian, Joseph A. *Oman and the World: The Emergence of an Independent Foreign Policy.* Santa Monica, CA: RAND, 1995.

Kegley, Charles W., and Gregory A. Raymond. *After Iraq: The Imperiled American Imperium.* New York: Oxford University Press, 2007.

Kelly, J.B. *Arabia, the Gulf and the West.* New York: Basic Books, 1980.

Kennan, George F. *American Diplomacy.* Chicago: University of Chicago Press, 1984.

———. *Memoirs 1925–1950.* Boston: Little, Brown, 1967.

Kennedy, Paul. *Preparing for the Twenty-First Century.* New York: Random House, 1993.

———. *The Rise and Fall of the Great Powers: Economic Change and Military Conflict from 1500 to 2000*. London: Fontana Press, 1989.

Keohane, Robert O. *After Hegemony: Cooperation and Discord in the World Political Economy*. Princeton, NJ: Princeton University Press, 1984.

Kerr, Malcolm. *The Arab Cold War 1958–1967: A Study of Ideology in Politics*. London: Oxford University Press, 1967.

Khalidi, Rashid. *Resurrecting Empire: Western Footprints and America's Perilous Path in the Middle East*. Boston: Beacon Press, 2004.

Khalidi, Walid. *The Gulf Crisis: Origins and Consequences*. Washington, DC: Institute for Palestine Studies, 1991.

Khong, Yuen Foong. *Analogies at War: Korea, Munich, Dien Bien Phu, and the Vietnam Decisions of 1965*. Princeton, NJ: Princeton University Press, 1992.

Kimball, Warren F. *The Juggler: Franklin Roosevelt as Wartime Statesman*. Princeton, NJ: Princeton University Press, 1991.

Kingseed, Cole C. *Eisenhower and the Suez Crisis of 1956*. Baton Rouge, LA: Louisiana State University Press, 1995.

Kissinger, Henry. *Does America Need a Foreign Policy? Toward a Diplomacy for the 21st Century*. New York: Simon & Schuster, 2001.

———. *Years of Upheaval*. Boston: Little, Brown, 1982.

———.*White House Years*. Boston: Little, Brown, 1979.

Knorr, Klaus. *The Power of Nations: The Political Economy of International Relations*. New York: Basic Books, 1975.

Krasner, Stephen D. *Sovereignty: Organized Hypocrisy*. Princeton, NJ: Princeton University Press, 1999.

Kuniholm, Bruce Robellet. *The Origins of the Cold War in the Near East: Great Power Conflict and Diplomacy in Iran, Turkey, and Greece*. Princeton, NJ: Princeton University Press, 1980.

Kunz, Diane B. "The Importance of Having Money: The Economic Diplomacy of the Suez Crisis." In *Suez 1956: The Crisis and Its Consequences*, edited by W.M. Roger Louis and Roger Owen. Oxford: Clarendon Press, 1989.

Kupchan, Charles A. *The Vulnerability of Empire*. Ithaca, NY: Cornell University Press, 1994.

Kyle, Keith. *Suez*. New York: St. Martin's Press, 1991.

———. "Britain and the Crisis, 1955–1956." In *Suez 1956: The Crisis and Its Consequences*, edited by W.M. Roger Louis and Roger Owen. Oxford: Clarendon Press, 1989.

LaFeber, Walter. *The American Search for Opportunity, 1865–1913*. In *Cambridge History of American Foreign Relations*, 2, edited by Warren I. Cohen. Cambridge: Cambridge University Press, 1993.

Lal, Deepak. "In Defense of Empires." In *The Imperial Tense: Prospects and Problems of American Empire*, edited by Andrew J. Bacevich. Chicago: Ivan R. Dee, 2003.

Layne, Christopher. *The Peace of Illusions: American Grand Strategy from 1940 to the Present*. Ithaca, NY: Cornell University Press, 2006.

Layne, Christopher, and Bradley A. Thayer. *American Empire: A Debate*. New York: Routledge, 2007.

Lefebvre, Jeffrey A. *Arms for the Horn: U.S. Security Policy in Ethiopia and Somalia 1953–1991*. Pittsburgh, PA: University of Pittsburgh Press, 1991.

Leffler, Melvyn P. *The Specter of Communism: The United States and the Origins of the Cold War, 1917–1953*. New York: Hill & Wang, 1994.

———. *A Preponderance of Power: National Security, the Truman Administration, and the Cold War*. Stanford, CA: Stanford University Press, 1992.

Lenczowski, George. *American Presidents and the Middle East.* Durham, NC: Duke University Press, 1990.

Lerner, Daniel. *The Passing of Traditional Society: Modernizing the Middle East.* New York: Free Press, 1958.

Levin, N. Gordon, Jr. *Woodrow Wilson and World Politics: America's Response to War and Revolution.* New York: Oxford University Press, 1968.

Lewis, Bernard. *The Shaping of the Modern Middle East.* New York: Oxford University Press, 1994.

Lieven, Anatol. *America Right or Wrong: An Anatomy of American Nationalism.* New York: Oxford University Press, 2004.

Lieven, Dominic. *Empire: The Russian Empire and Its Rivals.* New Haven, CT: Yale University Press, 2000.

Link, Arthur S. *Woodrow Wilson: Revolution, War, and Peace.* Arlington Heights, IL: Harlan Davidson, 1979.

Lippmann, Walter. *Men of Destiny.* New York: Macmillan, 1927.

Liska, George. *Imperial America: The International Politics of Primacy.* Baltimore: Johns Hopkins Press, 1967.

Little, Douglas. *American Orientalism: The United States and the Middle East Since 1945.* Chapel Hill, NC: University of North Carolina Press, 2004.

Litwak, Robert S. "Iraq and Iran: From Dual to Differentiated Containment." In *Eagle Rules? Foreign Policy and American Primacy in the Twenty-First Century*, edited by Robert J. Lieber. Upper Saddle River, NJ: Prentice Hall, 2002.

Long, David E. *The United States and Saudi Arabia: Ambivalent Allies.* Boulder, CO: Westview Press, 1985.

Louis, Wm. Roger. "Dulles, Suez, and the British." In *John Foster Dulles and the Diplomacy of the Cold War*, edited by Richard H. Immerman. Princeton, NJ: Princeton University Press, 1990.

———. *The British Empire in the Middle East 1945–1951: Arab Nationalism, the United States, and Postwar Imperialism.* Oxford: Clarendon Press, 1984.

Lundestad, Geir. *The American "Empire" and Other Studies of US Foreign Policy in a Comparative Perspective.* New York: Oxford University Press, 1990.

Lytle, Mark Hamilton. *The Origins of the Iranian-American Alliance: 1941–1953.* New York: Holmes & Meier, 1987.

Macdonald, Douglas J. *Adventures in Chaos: American Intervention for Reform in the Third World.* Cambridge, MA: Harvard University Press, 1992.

Machiavelli, Niccolò. *The Prince.* Translated by George Bull. New York: Penguin Books, 1986.

Maier, Charles S. *Among Empires: American Ascendancy and Its Predecessors.* Cambridge, MA: Harvard University Press, 2006.

Marr, Phebe. *The Modern History of Iraq.* Boulder, CO: Westview Press, 1985.

McCormick, Thomas J. *America's Half-Century: United States Foreign Policy during the Cold War.* Baltimore: Johns Hopkins University Press, 1989.

McMahon, Robert J. *The Limits of Empire: The United States and Southeast Asia since World War II.* New York: Columbia University Press, 1999.

———. "Eisenhower's Failure in the Third World." In *Major Problems in American Foreign Policy, Volume II: Since 1914*, 3rd ed., edited by Thomas G. Paterson. Lexington, MA: D.C. Heath and Company, 1989.

Mead, Walter Russell. *Special Providence: American Foreign Policy and How It Changed the World.* New York: Knopf, 2001.

Miglietta, John P. *American Alliance Policy in the Middle East, 1945–1992: Iran, Israel, and Saudi Arabia.* Lanham, MD: Lexington Books, 2002.

Miscamble, Wilson D. *George F. Kennan and the Making of American Foreign Policy, 1947–1950,* Princeton, NJ: Princeton University Press, 1992.

Morgenthau, Hans J., and Kenneth W. Thompson. *Politics Among Nations: The Struggle for Power and Peace,* 6th ed. New York: Alfred A. Knopf, 1985.

Motyl, Alexander J. "Thinking about Empire." In *After Empire: Multiethnic Societies and Nation-Building,* edited by Karen Barkey and Mark von Hagen. Boulder, CO: Westview Press, 1997.

Murphy, Cullen. *Are We Rome?: The Fall of an Empire and the Fate of America.* Boston: Houghton Mifflin, 2007.

Nafisi, Azar. *Reading Lolita in Tehran: A Memoir in Books.* New York: Random House, 2003.

Nash, Philip. *The Other Missiles of October: Eisenhower, Kennedy, and the Jupiters 1957–1963.* Chapel Hill, NC: University of North Carolina Press, 1997.

Neff, Donald. *Fallen Pillars: U.S. Policy towards Palestine and Israel since 1945.* Washington, DC: Institute for Palestine Studies, 1995.

———. *Warriors at Suez: Eisenhower Takes America into the Middle East in 1956.* Brattleboro, VT: Amana Books, 1988.

Newsom, David D. *The Imperial Mantle: The United States, Decolonization, and the Third World.* Bloomington, IN: Indiana University Press, 2001.

Niebuhr, Reinhold. *The Irony of American History.* New York: Charles Scribner, 1952.

Ninkovich, Frank. *Modernity and Power: A History of the Domino Theory in the Twentieth Century.* Chicago: University of Chicago Press, 1994.

Nuechterlein, Donald E. *Defiant Superpower: The New American Hegemony.* Washington, DC: Potomac Books, 2005.

Nye, Joseph S., Jr. *The Paradox of American Power: Why the World's Only Superpower Can't Go It Alone.* New York: Oxford University Press, 2002.

———. *Bound to Lead: The Changing Nature of American Power.* New York: Basic Books, 1990.

Oberdorfer, Don. *The Turn: From the Cold War to a New Era: The United States and the Soviet Union 1983–1990.* New York: Poseidon Press, 1991.

Odom, William E., and Robert Dujarric. *America's Inadvertent Empire.* New Haven, CT: Yale University Press, 2004.

O'Neill, Michael J. *The Roar of the Crowd: How Television and People Power Are Changing the World.* New York: Random House, 1993.

O'Reilly, Marc J. "Canadian Foreign Policy in the Middle East: Reflexive Multilateralism in an Evolving World." In *Handbook of Canadian Foreign Policy,* edited by Patrick James, Nelson Michaud, and Marc J. O'Reilly. Lanham, MD: Lexington Books, 2006.

Oren, Michael B. *Power, Faith, and Fantasy: America in the Middle East, 1776 to the Present.* New York: W.W. Norton, 2007.

Ostrower, Gary B. *The United Nations and the United States.* New York: Twayne, 1998.

Overy, Richard. *Why the Allies Won.* New York: W.W. Norton, 1995.

Pach, Chester J., Jr., and Elmo Richardson. *The Presidency of Dwight D. Eisenhower.* Lawrence, KS: University Press of Kansas, 1991.

Packer, George. *The Assassins' Gate: America in Iraq.* New York: Farrar, Straus & Giroux, 2005.

Painter, David S. "Cold War." In *Encyclopedia of U.S. Foreign Relations,* 1, edited by Bruce W. Jentleson and Thomas G. Paterson. New York: Oxford University Press, 1997.

———. *Oil and the American Century: The Political Economy of U.S. Foreign Oil Policy, 1941–1954.* Baltimore: Johns Hopkins University Press, 1986.

Palmer, Michael A. *Guardians of the Gulf: A History of America's Expanding Role in the Persian Gulf, 1833–1992.* New York: Free Press, 1992.

Parker, Richard B. *The Politics of Miscalculation in the Middle East.* Bloomington, IN: Indiana University Press, 1993.

Paterson, Thomas G. *Contesting Castro: The United States and the Triumph of the Cuban Revolution.* New York: Oxford University Press, 1994.

———. *On Every Front: The Making and Unmaking of the Cold War,* rev. ed. New York: W.W. Norton, 1992.

———. *Meeting the Communist Threat: Truman to Reagan.* New York: Oxford University Press, 1988.

Paterson, Thomas G., J. Garry Clifford, and Kenneth J. Hagan. *American Foreign Relations: A History—since 1895.* Boston: Houghton Mifflin, 2000.

———. *American Foreign Relations: A History—To 1920.* Boston: Houghton Mifflin, 2000.

Pauly, Robert J., Jr. *US Foreign Policy and the Persian Gulf: Safeguarding American Interests through Selective Multilateralism.* Aldershot, England: Ashgate, 2005.

Pickering, Jeffrey. *Britain's Withdrawal from East of Suez: The Politics of Retrenchment.* New York: St. Martin's Press, 1998.

Pollack, Kenneth M. *The Persian Puzzle: The Conflict between Iran and America.* New York: Random House, 2004.

———. *The Threatening Storm: The Case for Invading Iraq.* New York: Random House, 2002.

Porter, Bernard. *Empire and Superempire: Britain, America and the World.* New Haven, CT: Yale University Press, 2006.

Power, Samantha. *"A Problem from Hell": America and the Age of Genocide.* New York: Basic Books, 2002.

Prestowitz, Clyde. *Rogue Nation: American Unilateralism and the Failure of Good Intentions.* New York: Basic Books, 2003.

Quandt, William B. *Peace Process: American Diplomacy and the Arab-Israeli Conflict since 1967.* Washington, DC, and Berkeley, CA: Brookings Institution and University of California Press, 1993.

Ramazani, Rouhollah K. "The Gulf Cooperation Council: A Search for Security." In *The Indian Ocean: Perspectives on a Strategic Arena,* edited by William L. Dowdy and Russell B. Trood. Durham, NC: Duke University Press, 1985.

———. *Iran's Foreign Policy 1941–1973: A Study of Foreign Policy in Modernizing Nations.* Charlottesville, VA: University Press of Virginia, 1975.

Ricks, Thomas E. *Fiasco: The American Military Adventure in Iraq.* New York: Penguin Press, 2006.

Rizopoulos, Nicholas X., ed. *Sea-Changes: American Foreign Policy in a World Transformed.* New York: Council on Foreign Relations Press, 1990.

Roberson, B.A. "The Impact of the International System on the Middle East." In *The Foreign Policies of Middle East States,* edited by Raymond Hinnebusch and Anou-shiravan Ehteshami. Boulder, CO: Lynne Rienner, 2002.

Robertson, Terence. *Crisis: The Inside Story of the Suez Conspiracy.* New York: Atheneum, 1965.

Rosecrance, Richard. *The Rise of the Trading State: Commerce and Conquest in the Modern World.* New York: Basic Books, 1986.

Rosenberg, Emily S. *Spreading the American Dream: American Economic and Cultural Expansion, 1890–1945.* New York: Hill & Wang, 1982.

Roy, Olivier. *The Failure of Political Islam.* Translated by Carol Volk. Cambridge, MA: Harvard University Press, 1994.

Rubin, Barry. *The Great Powers in the Middle East 1941–1947.* London: Frank Cass, 1980.

———. *Paved with Good Intentions: The American Experience and Iran.* New York: Oxford University Press, 1980.

Ruggie, John Gerard. "International Regimes, Transactions, and Change: Embedded Liberalism in the Postwar Economic Order." In *International Regimes*, edited by Stephen D. Krasner. Ithaca, NY: Cornell University Press, 1983.

Said, Edward W. "Preface to the Twenty-Fifth Anniversary Edition," *Orientalism.* New York: Vintage Books, 1979.

———. *Orientalism.* New York: Vintage Books, 1979.

Saivetz, Carol R. "Superpower Competition in the Middle East and the Collapse of Détente." In *The Fall of Détente: Soviet-American Relations during the Carter Years*, edited by Odd Arne Westad. Oslo: Scandinavian University Press, 1997.

Schlesinger, Arthur M., Jr. *The Imperial Presidency.* Boston: Houghton Mifflin, 1973.

———. *A Thousand Days: John F. Kennedy in the White House.* Boston: Houghton Mifflin, 1965.

Schurmann, Franz. *The Foreign Politics of Richard Nixon: The Grand Design.* Berkeley, CA: Institute of International Studies University of California, 1987.

Schwarzkopf, General H. Norman, with Peter Petre. *It Doesn't Take a Hero.* New York: Linda Grey Bantam Books, 1992.

Sherry, Michael S. *In the Shadow of War: The United States since the 1930s.* New Haven, CT: Yale University Press, 1995.

Shultz, George P. *Turmoil and Triumph: My Years as Secretary of State.* New York: Charles Scribner, 1993.

Sick, Gary G. "US Policy in the Gulf: Objectives and Prospects." In *Managing New Developments in the Gulf*, edited by Rosemary Hollis. London: Royal Institute of International Affairs, 2000.

———. *All Fall Down: America's Tragic Encounter with Iran.* New York: Random House, 1985.

———. "The Evolution of U.S. Strategy Toward the Indian Ocean and Persian Gulf Regions." In *The Great Game: Rivalry in the Persian Gulf and South Asia*, edited by Alvin Z. Rubinstein. New York: Praeger, 1983.

Skeet, Ian. *Oman: Politics and Development.* New York: St. Martin's Press, 1992.

Smith, Tony. *America's Mission: The United States and the Worldwide Struggle for Democracy in the Twentieth Century.* Princeton, NJ: Princeton University Press, 1994.

———. *The Pattern of Imperialism: The United States, Great Britain, and the Late Industrializing World since 1815.* New York: Cambridge University Press, 1981.

Smolansky, Oles M. "Soviet Interests in the Persian/Arabian Gulf." In *The Indian Ocean: Perspectives on a Strategic Arena*, edited by William L. Dowdy and Russell B. Trood. Durham, NC: Duke University Press, 1985.

Snyder, Jack. *Myths of Empire: Domestic Politics and International Ambition.* Ithaca, NY: Cornell University Press, 1991.

Spanier, John, and Eric M. Uslaner. *American Foreign Policy Making and the Democratic Dilemmas.* Pacific Grove, CA: Brooks/Cole, 1989.

Steel, Ronald. *Pax Americana.* New York: Viking Press, 1967.

Stoessinger, John G. *Why Nations Go to War.* New York: St. Martin's Press, 1990.

Takeyh, Ray. *The Origins of the Eisenhower Doctrine: The US, Britain and Nasser's Egypt, 1953–57.* New York: St. Martin's Press, 2000.

Talbott, Strobe, and Nayan Chanda, eds. *The Age of Terror: America and the World After September 11.* New York: Basic Books, 2001.

Tannen, Deborah. *The Argument Culture: Stopping America's War of Words.* New York: Ballantine Books, 1999.

Taylor, A.J.P. *The First World War: An Illustrated History.* London: Penguin Books, 1966.

Telhami, Shibley. *The Stakes: America and the Middle East: The Consequences of Power and the Choice for Peace.* Boulder, CO: Westview Press, 2002.

Thayer, Bradley A. "The Case for the American Empire." In *American Empire: A Debate,* edited by Christopher Layne and Bradley A. Thayer. New York: Routledge, 2007.

Thorpe, D.R. *Selwyn Lloyd.* London: Jonathan Cape, 1989.

Thucydides. *History of the Peloponnesian War.* Translated by Rex Warner. New York: Penguin Books, 1972.

Treverton, Gregory F. *Covert Action: The Limits of Intervention in the Postwar World.* New York: Basic Books, 1987.

Twain, Mark. *The Innocents Abroad.* New York: Signet Classic, 1966.

Twinam, Joseph Wright. *The Gulf, Cooperation and the Council: An American Perspective.* Washington, DC: Middle East Policy Council, 1992.

Vaïsse, Maurice. "France and the Suez Crisis." In *Suez 1956: The Crisis and Its Consequences,* edited by W.M. Roger Louis and Roger Owen. Oxford: Clarendon Press, 1989.

Vloyantes, John P. *Silk Glove Hegemony: Finnish-Soviet Relations, 1944–1974: A Case Study of the Theory of the Soft Sphere of Influence.* Kent, OH: Kent State University Press, 1975.

Walker, Martin. "An Empire Unlike Any Other." In *The Imperial Tense: Prospects and Problems of American Empire,* edited by Andrew J. Bacevich. Chicago: Ivan R. Dee, 2003.

Wallerstein, Immanuel. *The Capitalist World-Economy: Essays by Immanuel Wallerstein.* Cambridge: Cambridge University Press, 1979.

———. "The Three Instances of Hegemony in the History of the Capitalist World-Economy." In *The Theoretical Evolution of IPE: A Reader,* edited by George T. Crane and Abla Amawi. New York: Oxford University Press, 1991.

Walt, Stephen M. *Taming American Power: The Global Response to U.S. Primacy.* New York: W.W. Norton, 2005.

———. *The Origins of Alliances.* Ithaca, NY: Cornell University Press, 1987.

Waltz, Kenneth N. *Theory of International Politics.* New York: Random House, 1979.

———. *Man, the State and War: A Theoretical Analysis.* New York: Columbia University Press, 1954.

Wayne, Stephen J. "President Bush Goes to War: A Psychological Interpretation from a Distance." In *The Political Psychology of the Gulf War: Leaders, Publics, and the Process of Conflict,* edited by Stanley A. Renshon. Pittsburgh, PA: University of Pittsburgh Press, 1993.

Westad, Odd Arne. "The Road to Kabul: Soviet Policy on Afghanistan, 1978–1979." In *The Fall of Détente: Soviet-American Relations during the Carter Years,* edited by Odd Arne Westad. Oslo: Scandinavian University Press, 1997.

Wilkinson, John C. *The Imamate Tradition of Oman.* New York: Cambridge University Press, 1987.

Williams, William Appleman. *Empire As A Way of Life.* Brooklyn, NY: Ig Publishing, 2007.

Woodward, Bob. *Plan of Attack.* New York: Simon & Schuster, 2004.

———. *The Commanders.* New York: Simon & Schuster, 1991.

Yaqub, Salim. *Containing Arab Nationalism: The Eisenhower Doctrine and the Middle East.* Chapel Hill, NC: University of North Carolina Press, 2004.

Yergin, Daniel. *The Prize: The Epic Quest for Oil, Money & Power.* New York: Simon & Schuster, 1991.
Yetiv, Steve A. *Explaining Foreign Policy: U.S. Decision-Making and the Persian Gulf War.* Baltimore: Johns Hopkins University Press, 2004.
Young, Marilyn B. "Imperial Language." In *The New American Empire: A 21st Century Teach-In on U.S. Foreign Policy*, edited by Lloyd C. Gardner and Marilyn B. Young. New York: New Press, 2005.
———. *The Vietnam Wars 1945–1990.* New York: Harper Perennial, 1991.
Zakaria, Fareed. *From Wealth to Power: The Unusual Origins of America's World Role.* Princeton, NJ: Princeton University Press, 1998.
Zubok, Vladislav, and Constantine Pleshakov. *Inside the Kremlin's Cold War: From Stalin to Khrushchev.* Cambridge, MA: Harvard University Press, 1996.

Articles

Agnew, John. "American Hegemony Into American Empire? Lessons from the Invasion of Iraq." *Antipode* 35, no. 5 (November 2003): 871–85.
Ajami, Fouad. "The Sentry's Solitude." *Foreign Affairs* 80, no. 6 (November/December 2001): 2–16.
———. "The Summer of Arab Discontent." *Foreign Affairs* 69, no. 5 (Winter 1990/91): 1–20.
"America and the World 1991/92." *Foreign Affairs* 71, no. 1 (1992).
Alnajjar, Ghanim. "The GCC and Iraq." *Middle East Policy* 7, no. 4 (October 2000): 92–99.
Al-Shayeji, Abdullah. "Dangerous Perceptions: Gulf Views of the U.S. Role in the Region." *Middle East Policy* 5, no. 3 (September 1997): 1–13.
"Anglo-American Petroleum Agreement." *Department of State Bulletin*, 30 September 1945, 13, no. 327, 481–83.
Anthony, John Duke. "The U.S.–GCC Relationship: A Glass Half-Empty or Half-Full?" *Middle East Policy* 5, no. 2 (May 1997): 22–41.
———. "Iran in GCC Dynamics." *Middle East Policy* 2, no. 3 (1993): 107–20.
Ashton, Nigel. "Britain and the Kuwaiti Crisis, 1961." *Diplomacy & Statecraft* 9, no. 1 (March 1998): 163–81.
———. "'A Great New Venture'?—Anglo-American Cooperation in the Middle East and the Response to the Iraqi Revolution July 1958." *Diplomacy & Statecraft* 4, no. 1 (March 1993): 59–89.
Baram, Amatzia. "The Effect of Iraqi Sanctions: Statistical Pitfalls and Responsibility." *Middle East Journal* 54, no. 2 (Spring 2000): 194–223.
Beisner, Robert L. "History and Henry Kissinger." *Diplomatic History* 14, no. 4 (Fall 1990): 511–27.
Bender, Peter. "America: The New Roman Empire?" *Orbis* 47, no. 1 (Winter 2003): 145–59.
Ben-Meir, Alon. "Behind the Palestinian-Israeli Violence and Beyond." *Middle East Policy* 8, no. 1 (March 2001): 81–88.
———. "The Dual Containment Strategy Is No Longer Viable." *Middle East Policy* 4, no. 3 (March 1996): 58–71.
Binder, Leonard. "The Middle East as a Subordinate International System." *World Politics* 10, no. 3 (April 1958): 408–29.
Boot, Max. "Neither New nor Nefarious: The Liberal Empire Strikes Back." *Current History* (November 2003): 361–66.
———. "The Sun Never Sets . . . ." *Weekly Standard*, 4 November 2002, 26–29.

———. "The Case for American Empire." *Weekly Standard*, 15 October 2001, 27–30.

Brewer, William D. "Yesterday and Tomorrow in the Persian Gulf." *Middle East Journal* 23, no. 2 (Spring 1969): 149–58.

Bronson, Rachel. "Beyond Containment in the Persian Gulf." *Orbis* 45, no. 2 (Spring 2001): 193–209.

Brown, L. Carl. "The Dream Palace of the Empire." *Foreign Affairs* 85, no. 5 (September/October 2006): 144–48.

Byman, Daniel. "After the Storm: U.S. Policy Toward Iraq Since 1991." *Political Science Quarterly* 115, no. 4 (2000–01): 493–516.

Byman, Daniel, Kenneth Pollack, and Gideon Rose. "The Rollback Fantasy." *Foreign Affairs* 78, no. 1 (January/February 1999): 24–41.

Carpenter, Ted Galen. "The New World Disorder." *Foreign Policy*, no. 84 (Fall 1991): 24–39.

Clifford, J. Garry. "Both Ends of the Telescope: New Perspectives on FDR and American Entry into World War II." *Diplomatic History* 13, no. 2 (Spring 1989): 213–30.

Cole, Juan, Kenneth Katzman, Karim Sadjadpour, and Ray Takeyh. "Symposium: A Shia Crescent: What Fallout for the United States?" *Middle East Policy* 12, no. 4 (Winter 2005): 1–27.

Colley, Linda. "Imperial Trauma: The Powerlessness of the Powerful, Part 1," *Common Knowledge* 11, no. 2 (Spring 2005): 198–214.

Cooper, Robert. "Imperial Liberalism." *National Interest*, no. 79 (Spring 2005): 25–34.

Cordesman, Anthony H. "Winning the 'War on Terrorism': A Fundamentally Different Strategy." *Middle East Policy* 13, no. 3 (Fall 2006): 101–8.

———. "The One True U.S. Strategic Interest in the Middle East: Energy." *Middle East Policy* 8, no. 1 (March 2001): 117–27.

———. "The Changing Military Balance in the Gulf." *Middle East Policy* 6, no. 1 (June 1998): 25–44.

Cox, Michael. "Forum on the American Empire: Introduction: A New American Empire?" *Review of International Studies* 30, no. 4 (October 2004): 583.

———. "Empire, Imperialism, and the Bush Doctrine." *Review of International Studies* 30, no. 4 (October 2004): 585–608.

———. "September 11th and U.S. Hegemony—Or Will the 21st Century Be American Too?" *International Studies Perspectives* 3, no. 1 (February 2002): 53–70.

———. "The New Liberal Empire: US Power in the Twenty-First Century." *Irish Studies in International Affairs* 12 (2001): 39–56.

Cumings, Bruce. "Is America an Imperial Power?" *Current History* (November 2003): 355–60.

Danner, Mark. "Iraq: The War of the Imagination." *New York Review of Books*, 21 December 2006, 81–96.

David, Stephen R. "Explaining Third World Alignment." *World Politics* 63, no. 2 (January 1991): 233–56.

Davis, Simon. "Keeping the Americans in Line? Britain, the United States and Saudi Arabia, 1939–45: Inter-Allied Rivalry in the Middle East Revisited." *Diplomacy & Statecraft* 8, no. 1 (March 1997): 96–136.

Deibel, Terry L. "Bush's Foreign Policy: Mastery and Inaction." *Foreign Policy*, no. 84 (Fall 1991): 3–23.

Denemark, Robert A. "World System History: From Traditional International Politics to the Study of Global Relations." *International Studies Review* 1, no. 2 (Summer 1999): 43–75.

DeNovo, John A. "The Culbertson Economic Mission and Anglo-American Tensions in the Middle East, 1944–1945." *Journal of American History* 63, no. 4 (March 1977): 913–36.

————. "The Movement for an Aggressive American Oil Policy Abroad, 1918–1920." *American Historical Review* 61, no. 3 (April 1956): 854–76.

Deutsch, Robert S., Anthony H. Cordesman, Hervé Magro, and William A. Rugh. "Symposium: The Challenge in the Gulf: Building a Bridge from Containment to Stability." *Middle East Policy* 5, no. 2 (May 1997): 1–21.

Diamond, Larry, James Dobbins, Chaim Kaufmann, Leslie Gelb, and Stephen Biddle. "What to Do in Iraq: A Roundtable." *Foreign Affairs* 85, no. 4 (July/August 2006): 150–69.

Divine, Robert A. "John Foster Dulles: What You See Is What You Get." *Diplomatic History* 15, no. 2 (Spring 1991): 277–85.

Doder, Dusko. "Yugoslavia: New War, Old Hatreds." *Foreign Policy*, no. 91 (Summer 1993): 3–23.

dos Santos, Theotonio. "The Structure of Dependence." *American Economic Review* 60, no. 2 (May 1970): 231–36.

Drew, Elizabeth. "The Neocons in Power." *New York Review of Books*, 12 June 2003, 20–22.

Dunn, Michael Collins. "Five Years after Desert Storm: Gulf Security, Stability and the U.S. Presence." *Middle East Policy* 4, no. 3 (March 1996): 30–38.

Eckes, Alfred E., Jr. "Open Door Expansionism Reconsidered: The World War II Experience." *Journal of American History* 59, no. 4 (March 1973): 909–24.

Elliott, Michael. "Why Empires Strike Out." *Time*, 12 May 2003, 45.

————. "The Trouble with Saving the World." *Time*, 30 December 2002–6 January 2003, 90–93.

————. "The Lessons of Empire." *Time*, 29 September 2002, http://www.time.com.

Esposito, John L., and James P. Piscatori. "Democratization and Islam." *Middle East Journal* 45, no. 3 (Summer 1991): 427–40.

Fain, W. Taylor. "John F. Kennedy and Harold Macmillan: Managing the 'Special Relationship' in the Persian Gulf Region, 1961–63." *Middle Eastern Studies* 38, no. 4 (October 2002): 95-122.

Ferguson, Niall. "Empires with Expiration Dates." *Foreign Policy* (September/October 2006). http://www.foreignpolicy.com.

————. "Hegemony or Empire?" *Foreign Affairs* 82, no. 5 (September/October 2003): 154–61.

Foyle, Douglas C. "Public Opinion and Foreign Policy: Elite Beliefs as a Mediating Variable." *International Studies Quarterly* 41, no. 1 (March 1997): 141–69.

Freedman, Lawrence. "Order and Disorder in the New World." *Foreign Affairs* 71, no. 1 (1992): 20–37.

Fukuyama, Francis. "The End of History?" *National Interest*, no. 16 (Summer 1989): 3–18.

Fuller, Graham E. "Strategic Fatigue." *National Interest*, no. 84 (Summer 2006): 37–42.

Fuller, Graham E., and Ian O. Lesser. "Persian Gulf Myths." *Foreign Affairs* 76, no. 3 (May/June 1997): 42–52.

Gaddis, John Lewis. "A Grand Strategy of Transformation." *Foreign Policy*, no. 133 (November-December 2002): 50–57.

————. "International Relations Theory and the End of the Cold War." *International Security* 17, no. 3 (Winter 1992/93): 5–58.

Galbraith, Peter W. "Mindless in Iraq." *New York Review of Books*, 10 August 2006, 28–31.

Ganguly, Sumit. "Imperial Nostalgia." *Current History* (November 2003): 394–95.

Garfinkle, Adam. "The U.S. Imperial Postulate in the Mideast." *Orbis* 41, no. 1 (Winter 1997): 15–29.

Gasiorowski, Mark. "The New Aggressiveness in Iran's Foreign Policy." *Middle East Policy* 14, no. 2 (Summer 2007): 125–32.

Gause, F. Gregory, III. "Threats and Threat Perceptions in the Persian Gulf Region." *Middle East Policy* 14, no. 2 (Summer 2007): 119–24.

———. "Saudi Arabia Over a Barrel." *Foreign Affairs* 79, no. 3 (May/June 2000): 80–94.

———. "The Illogic of Dual Containment." *Foreign Affairs* 73, no. 2 (March/April 1994): 56–66.

———. "British and American Policies in the Persian Gulf, 1968–1973." *Review of International Studies* 11, no. 4 (October 1985): 247-73.

Gause, F. Gregory, III, Fareed Mohamedi, Afshin Molavi, Wayne White, and Anthony H. Cordesman. "The Future of the Middle East: Strategic Implications for the United States." *Middle East Policy* 14, no. 3 (Fall 2007): 1–28.

Gavin, Francis J. "Politics, Power, and U.S. Policy in Iran, 1950–1953." *Journal of Cold War Studies* 1, no. 1 (Winter 1999): 56–89.

Gazit, Shlomo, and Edward Abington. "The Palestinian-Israeli Conflict." *Middle East Policy* 8, no. 1 (March 2001): 58–72.

Godfried, Nathan. "Economic Development and Regionalism: United States Foreign Relations in the Middle East, 1942–5." *Journal of Contemporary History* 22, no. 3 (1987): 481–500.

Goldgeier, James M., and Michael McFaul. "A Tale of Two Worlds: Core and Periphery in the Post-Cold War Era." *International Organization* 46, no. 2 (Spring 1992): 467–91.

Goldwyn, David L., Martha Brill Olcott, Julia Nanay, Thomas R. Stauffer. "Symposium: The Caspian Region and the New Great Powers." *Middle East Policy* 7, no. 4 (October 2000): 1–21.

Golub, Philip S. "Westward the Course of Empire." *Le Monde Diplomatique* (September 2002). http://mondediplo.com.

Gordon, Philip H. "The End of the Bush Revolution." *Foreign Affairs* 85, no. 4 (July/August 2006): 75–86.

Gray, John. "The Mirage of Empire." *New York Review of Books*, 12 January 2006, 4–8.

Greenstein, Fred I. "The Hidden-Hand Presidency: Eisenhower as Leader: A 1994 Perspective." *Presidential Studies Quarterly* 24, no. 2 (Spring 1994): 233–41.

Haass, Richard N. "The Squandered Presidency." *Foreign Affairs* 79, no. 3 (May/June 2000): 136–40.

Heidenrich, John G. "The Gulf War: How Many Iraqis Died?" *Foreign Policy*, no. 90 (Spring 1993): 108–25.

Heiss, Mary Ann. "The Evolution of the Imperial Idea and U.S. National Identity." *Diplomatic History* 26, no. 4 (Fall 2002): 511–40.

Helman, Gerald B., and Steven R. Ratner. "Saving Failed States." *Foreign Policy*, no. 89 (Winter 1992–93): 3–20.

Hermann, Margaret G., and Joe D. Hagan. "International Decision Making: Leadership Matters." *Foreign Policy*, no. 110 (Spring 1998): 124–37.

Hermann, Margaret G., Thomas Preston, Baghat Korany, and Timothy M. Shaw. "Who Leads Matters: The Effects of Powerful Individuals." *International Studies Review* 3, no. 2 (Summer 2001): 86–95.

Hess, Gary R. "The Iranian Crisis of 1945–46 and the Cold War." *Political Science Quarterly* 89, no. 1 (March 1974): 117–46.

Hirsh, Michael. "Bush and the World." *Foreign Affairs* 81, no. 5 (September/October 2002): 18–43.

Hixson, Walter L. "Empire as a Way of Life." *Diplomatic History* 31, no. 2 (April 2007): 331–34.

Holden, David. "The Persian Gulf: After the British Raj." *Foreign Affairs* 49, no. 4 (July 1971): 721–35.

Hudson, Michael C. "Imperial Headaches: Managing Unruly Regions in an Age of Globalization." *Middle East Policy* 9, no. 4 (December 2002): 61–74.

———. "To Play the Hegemon: Fifty Years of US Policy Toward the Middle East." *Middle East Journal* 50, no. 3 (Summer 1996): 329–43.

Hunt, Michael H. "Conquest American Style." *Diplomatic History* 31, no. 2 (April 2007): 325–29.

Huntington, Samuel P. "The Lonely Superpower." *Foreign Affairs* 78, no. 2 (March/April 1999): 35–49.

———. "The Clash of Civilizations?" *Foreign Affairs* 72, no. 3 (Summer 1993): 22–49.

Hyland, William G. "A Mediocre Record." *Foreign Policy*, no. 101 (Winter 1995–96): 69–74.

Ignatieff, Michael. "The Burden." *New York Times Magazine*, 5 January 2003, http://www.nytimes.com.

———. "The Attack on Human Rights." *Foreign Affairs* 80, no. 6 (November-December 2001): 102–16.

Ikenberry, G. John. "Liberalism and Empire: Logics of Order in the American Unipolar Age." *Review of International Studies* 30, no. 4 (October 2004): 609–30.

———. "Illusions of Empire: Defining the New American Order." *Foreign Affairs* 83, no. 2 (March/April 2004): 144–54.

———. "America's Imperial Ambition." *Foreign Affairs* 81, no. 5 (September/October 2002): 44–60.

Immerman, Richard H. "Confessions of an Eisenhower Revisionist: An Agonizing Reappraisal." *Diplomatic History* 14, no. 3 (Summer 1990): 319–42.

Jervis, Robert. "Cooperation Under the Security Dilemma." *World Politics* 30, no. 2 (January 1978): 186–214.

Job, Cvijeto. "Yugoslavia's Ethnic Furies." *Foreign Policy*, no. 92 (Fall 1993): 52–74.

Joyce, Miriam. "Preserving the Sheikhdom: London, Washington, Iraq and Kuwait, 1958–61." *Middle Eastern Studies* 31, no. 2 (April 1995): 281–92.

Judt, Tony. "Dreams of Empire." *New York Review of Books*, 4 November 2004, 38–41.

Juster, Kenneth I. "The Myth of Iraqgate." *Foreign Policy*, no. 94 (Spring 1994): 105–19.

Kagan, Robert. "The Benevolent Empire." *Foreign Policy*, no. 111 (Summer 1998): 24–35.

Kahwaji, Riad. "U.S.-Arab Cooperation in the Gulf: Are Both Sides Working From the Same Script?" *Middle East Policy* 11, no. 3 (Fall 2004): 52–62.

Kaplan, Amy. "Violent Belongings and the Question of Empire Today: Presidential Address to the American Studies Association, October 17, 2003." *American Quarterly* 56, no. 1 (March 2004): 1–18.

Katz, Mark N. "Iran and America: Is Rapprochement Finally Possible?" *Middle East Policy* 12, no. 4 (Winter 2005): 58–65.

Kaufman, Burton I. "Mideast Multinational Oil, U.S. Foreign Policy, and Antitrust: the 1950s." *Journal of American History* 63, no. 4 (March 1977): 937–59.

Kéchichian, Joseph A. "Can Conservative Arab Gulf Monarchies Endure a Fourth War in the Persian Gulf?" *Middle East Journal* 61, no. 2 (Spring 2007): 283–306.

———. "Saudi Arabia's Will to Power." *Middle East Policy* 7, no. 2 (February 2000): 47–60.

Kegley, Charles W., Jr. "How Did the Cold War Die? Principles for an Autopsy." *Mershon International Studies Review* 38 (1994): 11–41.

Kemp, Geoffrey. "The East Moves West." *National Interest*, no. 84 (Summer 2006): 71–77.

———. "Iran: Can the United States Do a Deal?" *Washington Quarterly* 24, no. 1 (Winter 2001): 109–24.

Keohane, Robert O. "The United States and the Postwar Order: Empire or Hegemony?" *Journal of Peace Research* 28, no. 4 (1991): 435–39.

Khadduri, Walid. "U.N. Sanctions on Iraq: 10 Years Later." *Middle East Policy* 7, no. 4 (October 2000): 156–62.

Khanna, Parag. "The Counsel of Geopolitics." *Current History* (November 2003): 388–93.

Kindleberger, Charles P. "Dominance and Leadership in the International Economy." *International Studies Quarterly* 25, no. 2 (June 1981): 242–54.

Klare, Michael T. "Oil, Iraq, and American Foreign Policy." *International Journal* 62, no. 1 (Winter 2006–2007): 31–42.

———. "For Oil and Empire? Rethinking War with Iraq." *Current History* (March 2003): 129–35.

Krahmann, Elke. "American Hegemony or Global Governance? Competing Visions of International Security." *International Studies Review* 7, no. 4 (December 2005): 531–45.

Kraig, Michael Ryan. "Forging a New Security Order for the Persian Gulf." *Middle East Policy* 13, no. 1 (Spring 2006): 84–101.

———. "Assessing Alternative Security Frameworks for the Persian Gulf." *Middle East Policy* 11, no. 3 (Fall 2004): 139–56.

Kunz, Diane B. "When Money Counts and Doesn't: Economic Power and Diplomatic Objectives." *Diplomatic History* 18, no. 4 (Fall 1994): 451–62.

Kupchan, Charles A. "American Globalism in the Middle East: The Roots of Regional Security Policy." *Political Science Quarterly* 103, no. 4 (1988): 585–611.

Kurzman, Charles. "Soft on Satan: Challenges for Iranian-U.S. Relations." *Middle East Policy* 6, no. 1 (June 1998): 63–72.

Lake, Anthony. "Confronting Backlash States." *Foreign Affairs* 73, no. 2 (March/April 1994): 45–55.

Lang, Patrick W., and Larry C. Johnson. "Contemplating the Ifs." *National Interest*, no. 83 (Spring 2006): 26–30.

Layne, Christopher. "Impotent Power? Re-examining the Nature of America's Hegemonic Power." *National Interest*, no. 85 (Sept./Oct. 2006): 41–47.

———. "Offshore Balancing Revisited." *Washington Quarterly* 25, no. 2 (Spring 2002): 233–48.

Layne, Christopher, and Benjamin Schwartz. "American Hegemony—Without an Enemy." *Foreign Policy*, no. 92 (Fall 1993): 5–23.

Lefebvre, Jeffrey A. "U.S. Military Hegemony in the Arabian/Persian Gulf: How Long Can It Last?" *International Studies Perspectives* 4, no. 2 (May 2003): 186–90.

———. "The Transformation of U.S. Security Policy in the Gulf: Strategic Disruption and the Balance of Risk." *Middle East Affairs Journal* 5, nos. 1/2 (Winter/Spring 1999): 51–69.

Leverett, Flynt, and Pierre Noël. "The New Axis of Oil." *National Interest*, no. 84 (Summer 2006): 62–70.

Little, Douglas. "His Finest Hour? Eisenhower, Lebanon, and the 1958 Middle East Crisis." *Diplomatic History* 20, no. 1 (Winter 1996): 27–54.

———. "Gideon's Band: America and the Middle East since 1945." *Diplomatic History* 18, no. 4 (Fall 1994): 513–40.

Loftus, John A. "Petroleum in International Relations." *Department of State Bulletin*, 5 August 1945, 13, no. 319, 173–75.

Luce, Henry R. "The American Century." *Life*, 17 February 1941. Reprinted in "The American Century: A Roundtable (Part 1)," *Diplomatic History* 23, no. 2 (Spring 1999): 159–71.

Lustick, Ian S. "The Absence of Middle Eastern Great Powers: Political 'Backwardness' in Historical Perspective." *International Organization* 51, no. 4 (Autumn 1997): 653–83.

Lynn-Jones, Sean. "Realism and America's Rise." *International Security* 23, no. 2 (Fall 1998): 157–82.

Maier, Charles S. "An American Empire?" *Harvard Magazine*, November–December 2002, http://www.harvardmagazine.com.

Mallaby, Sebastian. "The Reluctant Imperialist." *Foreign Affairs* 81, no. 2 (March/April 2002): 2–7.

Mandelbaum, Michael. "David's Friend Goliath." *Foreign Policy*, no. 152 (January/February 2006): 50–56.

———. "Foreign Policy as Social Work." *Foreign Affairs* 75, no. 1 (January/February 1996): 16–32.

———. "The Reluctance to Intervene." *Foreign Policy*, no. 95 (Summer 1994): 3–18.

Mann, Michael. "The First Failed Empire of the 21st Century." *Review of International Studies* 30, no. 4 (October 2004): 631–53.

Mark, Eduard. "The War Scare of 1946 and Its Consequences." *Diplomatic History* 21, no. 3 (Summer 1997): 383–415.

Marr, Phebe. "Occupational Hazards: Washington's Record in Iraq." *Foreign Affairs* 84, no. 4 (July/August 2005): 180–86.

Marshall, Joshua Micah. "Power Rangers: Did the Bush Administration Create a New American Empire—or Weaken the Old One?" *New Yorker*, 2 February 2004, http://www.newyorker.com.

Marty, Joseph, Ivan Eland, Shibley Telhami, and Dov Zakheim. "Symposium: U.S. Gulf Policy: How Can It Be Fixed?" *Middle East Policy* 6, no. 1 (June 1998): 1–24.

Mattair, Thomas R. "Mutual Threat Perceptions in the Arab/Persian Gulf: GCC Perceptions." *Middle East Policy* 14, no. 2 (Summer 2007): 133–40.

McKeown, Timothy J. "Hegemonic Stability Theory and 19th Century Tariff Levels in Europe." *International Organization* 37, no. 1 (Winter 1983): 73–91.

McMahon, Robert J. "Credibility and World Power: Exploring the Psychological Dimension in Postwar American Diplomacy." *Diplomatic History* 15, no. 4 (Fall 1991): 455–71.

Mearsheimer, John J., and Stephen M. Walt. "The Israel Lobby and U.S. Foreign Policy." *Middle East Policy* 13, no. 3 (Fall 2006): 29–87.

Millar, T.B. "Soviet Policies South and East of Suez." *Foreign Affairs* 49, no. 1 (October 1970): 70–80.

Milner, Helen V. "International Political Economy: Beyond Hegemonic Stability." *Foreign Policy*, no. 110 (Spring 1998): 112–23.

Mohamedi, Fareed, and Yahya Sadowski. "The Decline (But Not Fall) of US Hegemony in the Middle East." *Middle East Report*, no. 220 (Fall 2001): 12–22.

Morse, Edward L. "The Coming Oil Revolution." *Foreign Affairs* 69, no. 5 (Winter 1990/91): 36–56.

Motyl, Alexander J. "Empire Falls: Washington May Be Imperious, but It Is Not Imperial," *Foreign Affairs* 85, no. 4 (July/August 2006): 190–94.

Neff, Donald. "Nixon's Middle East Policy: From Balance to Bias." *Arab Studies Quarterly* 12, nos. 1 and 2 (Winter/Spring 1990): 121–52.

Nelson, Anna Kasten. "History as a Period Piece?" *Diplomatic History* 18, no. 4 (Fall 1994): 611–14.

————. "The 'Top of Policy Hill': President Eisenhower and the National Security Council." *Diplomatic History* 7, no. 4 (Fall 1983): 307–26.

Newhouse, John. "Shunning the Losers." *New Yorker*, 26 October 1992, 40–52.

Newsom, David D. "America Engulfed." *Foreign Policy*, no. 43 (Summer 1981): 17–32.

Nexon, Daniel H., and Thomas Wright, "What's at Stake in the American Empire Debate," *American Political Science Review* 101, no. 2 (May 2007): 253–71.

Noël, Pierre. "The New US Middle East Policy and Energy Security Challenges." *International Journal* 62, no. 1 (Winter 2006–2007): 43–54.

O'Reilly, Marc J. "Oil Monarchies without Oil: Omani & Bahraini Security in a Post-Oil Era." *Middle East Policy* 6, no. 3 (February 1999): 78–92.

————. "Omanibalancing: Oman Confronts an Uncertain Future." *Middle East Journal* 52, no. 1 (Winter 1998): 70–84.

————. "Following Ike? Explaining Canadian-US Co-operation during the 1956 Suez Crisis." *The Journal of Commonwealth & Comparative Politics* 35, no. 3 (November 1997): 75–107.

O'Reilly, Marc J., and Wesley B. Renfro. "Evolving Empire: America's 'Emirates' Strategy in the Persian Gulf." *International Studies Perspectives* 8, no. 2 (May 2007): 137–51.

————. "Like Father, Like Son? A Comparison of the Foreign Policies of George H.W. Bush and George W. Bush." *Historia Actual Online*, no. 10 (Spring 2006): 17–36. http://www.historia-actual.com.

Ottaway, Marina. "Nation Building." *Foreign Policy*, no. 132 (September/October 2002). http://www.foreignpolicy.com.

Parsi, Trita. "Iran and Israel: The Avoidable War." *Middle East Policy* 14, no. 3 (Fall 2007): 79–85.

Paterson, Thomas G. "Cold War Revisionism: A Practitioner's Perspective." *Diplomatic History* 31, no. 3 (June 2007): 387–95.

Pérez, Louis A. "Intervention, Hegemony, and Dependency: The United States in the circum-Caribbean, 1898–1980." *Pacific Historical Review* 51, no. 2 (May 1982): 165–94.

Petersen, Tore Tingvold. "Anglo-American Rivalry in the Middle East: The Struggle for the Buraimi Oasis, 1952–1957." *International History Review* 14, no. 1 (February 1992): 71–91.

Peterson, J.E. "The Arabian Peninsula in Modern Times: A Historiographical Survey." *American Historical Review* 96, no. 5 (December 1991): 1435–49.

Pfau, Richard. "Containment in Iran, 1946: The Shift to an Active Policy." *Diplomatic History* 1, no. 4 (Fall 1977): 359–72.

Pollack, Kenneth M. "Securing the Gulf." *Foreign Affairs* 82, no. 4 (July/August 2003): 2–16.

Pollack, Kenneth, and Ray Takeyh. "Taking on Tehran." *Foreign Affairs* 84, no. 2 (March/April 2005): 20–34.

Posch, Walter. "Staying the Course: Permanent U.S. Bases in Iraq?" *Middle East Policy* 13, no. 3 (Fall 2006): 109–20.

Rabe, Stephen G. "Eisenhower Revisionism: A Decade of Scholarship." *Diplomatic History* 17, no. 1 (Winter 1993): 97–115.

Rabi, Uzi. "Britain's 'Special Position' in the Gulf: Its Origins, Dynamics and Legacy." *Middle Eastern Studies* 42, no. 3 (May 2006): 351–64.

Ramazani, R.K. "The Role of Iran in the New Millennium: A View from the Outside." *Middle East Policy* 8, no. 1 (March 2001): 43–47.

————. "The Emerging Arab-Iranian Rapprochement: Towards an Integrated U.S. Policy in the Middle East?" *Middle East Policy* 6, no. 1 (June 1998): 45–62.

————. "The Shifting Premise of Iran's Foreign Policy: Towards a Democratic Peace?" *Middle East Journal* 52, no. 2 (Spring 1998): 177–87.

————. "Iran's Foreign Policy: Both North and South." *Middle East Journal* 46, no. 3 (Summer 1992): 393–412.

Reed, Stanley. "Jordan and the Gulf." *Foreign Affairs* 69, no. 5 (Winter 1990/91): 21–35.

Riedel, Bruce. "Al Qaeda Strikes Back." *Foreign Affairs* 86, no. 3 (May/June 2007): 24–40.

Rosati, Jerel A. "Jimmy Carter, A Man Before His Time? The Emergence and Collapse of the First Post-Cold War Presidency." *Presidential Studies Quarterly* 23, no. 3 (Summer 1993): 459–76.

Rosen, Stephen Peter. "An Empire, If You Can Keep It." *National Interest*, no. 71 (Spring 2003): 51–61.

Roth, Richard Allan, Suzanne Maloney, Ray Takeyh, Geoffrey Kemp. "U.S. Policy Toward Iran: Time for a Change?" *Middle East Policy* 8, no. 1 (March 2001): 1–24.

Rubin, Barry. "Anglo-American Relations in Saudi Arabia, 1941–1945." *Journal of Contemporary History* 14, no. 2 (1979): 253–67.

Rugh, William A. "Time to Modify Our Gulf Policy." *Middle East Policy* 5, no. 1 (January 1997): 46–57.

Russell, James A. "Whither Regional Security in a World Turned Upside Down?" *Middle East Policy* 14, no. 2 (Summer 2007): 141–8.

Russell, Richard L. "The Persian Gulf's Collective-Security Mirage." *Middle East Policy* 12, no. 4 (Winter 2005): 77–88.

Sagan, Scott D. "How to Keep the Bomb From Iran," *Foreign Affairs* 85, no. 5 (September/October 2006): 45–59.

Sanjian, Ara. "The Formulation of the Baghdad Pact." *Middle Eastern Studies* 33, no. 2 (April 1997): 226–66.

Schlesinger, James. "New Instabilities, New Priorities." *Foreign Policy*, no. 85 (Winter 1991–92): 3–24.

Selverstone, Marc Jay. "Planes, Causal Chains, and Terrorist Zeal: Chaos and the Bombing of Pan Am Flight 103." *Ohio University Contemporary History Institute Think Piece Series*, no. 26 (February 1994).

Serfaty, Simon. "Bridging the Gulf Across the Atlantic: Europe and the United States in the Persian Gulf." *Middle East Journal* 52, no. 3 (Summer 1998): 337–50.

Sestanovich, Stephen. "American Maximalism." *National Interest*, no. 79 (Spring 2005): 13–23.

Sever, Aysegül. "The Compliant Ally? Turkey and the West in the Middle East 1954–58." *Middle Eastern Studies* 34, no. 2 (April 1998): 73–80.

Sheehan, Edward R.F. "Step by Step in the Middle East." *Foreign Policy*, no. 22 (Spring 1976): 4–34.

Shwadran, Benjamin. "The Kuwait Incident." *Middle Eastern Affairs* 13, no. 1 (January 1962): 2–13.

————. "The Kuwait Incident." *Middle Eastern Affairs* 13, no. 2 (February 1962): 43–46.

Simes, Dimitri K. "America's Imperial Dilemma." *Foreign Affairs* 82, no. 6 (November/December 2003): 91–102.

————. "Russia Reborn." *Foreign Policy*, no. 85 (Winter 1991–92): 41–62.

Skidelsky, Robert. "Hot, Cold & Imperial." *New York Review of Books*, 13 July 2006, 50–55.

Slater, Jerome. "Is United States Foreign Policy 'Imperialist' or 'Imperial'?" *Political Science Quarterly* 91, no. 1 (Spring 1976): 63–87.

Snyder, Jack. "One World, Rival Theories." *Foreign Policy*, no. 14 (November/December 2004): 52–62.

————. "Imperial Temptations." *National Interest*, no. 71 (Spring 2003): 29–40.

Snyder, Robert S. "The U.S. and Third World Revolutionary States: Understanding the Breakdown in Relations." *International Studies Quarterly* 43, no. 2 (June 1999): 265–90.

Stoler, Mark A. "A Half Century of Conflict: Interpretations of U.S. World War II Diplomacy." *Diplomatic History* 18, no. 3 (Summer 1994): 375–403.

Stremlau, John. "Clinton's Dollar Diplomacy." *Foreign Policy*, no. 97 (Winter 1994–95): 18–35.

Sullivan, William H. "Dateline Iran: The Road Not Taken." *Foreign Policy*, no. 40 (Fall 1980): 175–86.

Summitt, April R. "For a White Revolution: John F. Kennedy and the Shah of Iran." *Middle East Journal* 58, no. 4 (Autumn 2004): 560–75.

Takeyh, Ray. "Time for Détente With Iran," *Foreign Affairs* 86, no. 2 (March/April 2007): 17–32.

————. "A Profile in Defiance." *National Interest*, no. 83 (Spring 2006): 16–21.

————. "Close, But No Democracy." *National Interest*, no. 78 (Winter 2004/05): 57–64.

————. "Iranian Options." *National Interest*, no. 73 (Fall 2003): 49–56.

Telhami, Shibley, Brian Katulis, Jon B. Alterman, and Milton Viorst. "Symposium: Middle Eastern Views of the United States: What Do the Trends Indicate?" *Middle East Policy* 13, no. 3 (Fall 2006): 1–28.

"The American Century: A Roundtable (Part 1)." *Diplomatic History* 23, no. 2 (Spring 1999): 157–370.

Thorpe, James A. "The United States and the 1940–1941 Anglo-Iraqi Crisis: American Policy in Transition." *Middle East Journal* 25, no. 1 (Winter 1971): 79–89.

Tolson, Jay. "The New American Empire?" *U.S. News & World Report*, 13 January 2003, 35–40.

Ullman, Richard H. "A Late Recovery." *Foreign Policy*, no. 101 (Winter 1995–96): 75–79.

Vitalis, Robert. "Black Gold, White Crude: An Essay on American Exceptionalism, Hierarchy, and Hegemony in the Gulf." *Diplomatic History* 26, no. 2 (Spring 2002): 185–213.

Walt, Stephen M. "Beyond bin Laden: Reshaping U.S. Foreign Policy." *International Security* 26, no. 3 (Winter 2001/02): 56–78.

————. "Two Cheers for Clinton's Foreign Policy." *Foreign Affairs* 79, no. 2 (March/April 2000): 63–79.

————. "International Relations: One World, Many Theories." *Foreign Policy*, no. 110 (Spring 1998): 29–46.

Watt, D.C. "The Decision to Withdraw from the Gulf." *Political Quarterly* 39, no. 3 (July-September 1968): 310–21.

Wills, Garry. "Bully of the Free World." *Foreign Affairs* 78, no. 2 (March/April 1999): 50–59.

Wolfowitz, Paul D. "Remarks on the Conclusion of the Gulf War." *American-Arab Affairs*, no. 35 (Winter 1990–91): 1–10.

Yaffe, Michael D. "The Gulf and a New Middle East Security System." *Middle East Policy* 11, no. 3 (Fall 2004): 118–30.

Yankelovich, Daniel. "Poll Positions: What Americans Really Think About U.S. Foreign Policy." *Foreign Affairs* 84, no. 5 (September/October 2005): 2–16.

Yaphe, Judith S. "War and Occupation in Iraq: What Went Right? What Could Go Wrong?" *Middle East Journal* 57, no. 3 (Summer 2003): 381–99.

————. "Iraq: The Exception to the Rule." *Washington Quarterly* 24, no. 1 (Winter 2001): 125–37.

Yetiv, Steve A., and Chunlong Lu. "China, Global Energy, and the Middle East." *Middle East Journal* 61, no. 2 (Spring 2007): 199–218.

Yordan, Carlos L. "The Imperial Turn: Analyzing Post-9/11 American Foreign Policy Through the Prism of 1898." *Revista de Historia Actual* 4, no. 4 (2006): 27–44.

Zahedi, Dariush, and Ahmad Ghoreishi. "Iran's Security Concerns in the Persian Gulf." *Naval War College Review* 49, no. 3 (Summer 1996): 73–95.

Zakaria, Fareed. "Our Way." *New Yorker*, 14 October, 2002, http://www.newyorker.com.

Zelikow, Philip. "The Transformation of National Security: Five Redefinitions." *National Interest*, no. 71 (Spring 2003): 17–28.

Published Papers

Chatham House (The Royal Institute of International Affairs). "Iran, Its Neighbours and the Regional Crises: A Middle East Programme Report." (August 2006).

Gause, F. Gregory, III. "The Approaching Turning Point: The Future of U.S. Relations with the Gulf States." *Brookings Project on U.S. Policy Towards the Islamic World*, Analysis Paper Number Two (May 2003).

Pechatnov, Vladimir O. "'The Allies Are Pressing on You to Break Your Will . . .': Foreign Policy Correspondence between Stalin and Molotov and Other Politburo Members, September 1945–December 1946." *Cold War International History Project*, Working Paper no. 26 (September 1999).

———. "The Big Three after World War II: New Documents on Soviet Thinking about Post War Relations with the United States and Great Britain." *Cold War International History Project*, Working Paper no. 13 (July 1995).

Ruggie, John G. "Doctrinal Unilateralism and Its Limits: America and Global Governance in the New Century." Corporate Social Responsibility Initiative Working Paper no. 16 (Cambridge, MA: John F. Kennedy School of Government, Harvard University, 2006).

Yegorova, Natalia I. "The 'Iran Crisis' of 1945–1946: A View from the Russian Archives." *Cold War International History Project*, Working Paper no. 15 (May 1996).

Speeches

Friedman, Thomas L. "American Foreign Policy." Talk given at Johns Hopkins University's School for Advanced International Studies, Washington, DC, 6 March 2003. Seen on C-SPAN.

Hull, Cordell. "Our Foreign Policy in the Framework of Our National Interests." Address given on 12 September 1943. Reprinted in *Department of State Bulletin*, 18 September 1943, 9, no. 221, 173–79.

———. "The War and Human Freedom." Address given on 23 July 1942. Reprinted in *Department of State Bulletin*, 25 July 1942, 7, no. 161, 639–47.

Krauthammer, Charles. "Democratic Realism: An American Foreign Policy for a Unipolar World." 2004 Irving Kristol Lecture delivered at the American Enterprise Institute Annual Dinner, Washington, DC, 10 February 2004. http://www.aei.org.

Unpublished Papers

Cox, Michael. "The Empire's Back in Town: Or America's Imperial Temptation— Again." Paper presented at the annual conference of the International Studies Association, Montreal, Canada, 17–20 March 2004.

Donoghue, Michael. "The Buraimi Dispute and the Souring of Anglo-American-Saudi Relations, 1952–1956." Paper presented at the annual meeting of the New England Historical Association, 17 October 1998.

George, Jason. "The U.S. and the Hungarian Revolution of 1956." Seminar Paper, Ohio University, March 1994.

Lefebvre, Jeffrey A. "The Transformation of U.S. Security Policy in the Gulf: Strategic Disruption and the Balance of Risk." Paper presented at the annual meeting of the New England Political Science Association, New London, CT, 2–3 May 1997.

McNeill, William H. "The Fall of Great Powers: Peace, Stability and Legitimacy." April 1993.

O'Reilly, Marc J., Sarah J. Lippitt, and Greg Trumble. "The United States and the Arab Gulf Monarchies: The Oil-for-Security Dynamic Revisited." Paper presented at the annual conference of the International Studies Association–Midwest, St. Louis, MO, 3 November 2006.

Unpublished Theses

Lee, Yong S. "Master and Servants: U.S.-East Asian Relations and the Tyranny of the Weak." M.A. thesis, Ohio University (June 1995).

O'Reilly, Marc James. "Dudley Do-Right and Friends: Lester B. Pearson, Canada, and the 1956 Suez Crisis." M.A. thesis, Ohio University (August 1995).

Unpublished Dissertation

Axelgard, Frederick W. "U.S. Policy toward Iraq, 1946–1958." Ph.D. dissertation, The Fletcher School of Law and Diplomacy, Tufts University (April 1988).

Newspapers

Al-Ahram Weekly (Cairo).
Arab News (Jeddah).
Baltimore Sun.
Blade (Toledo, OH).
Chicago Tribune.
Columbus Dispatch (Columbus, OH).
Daily Star (Beirut).
Daily Telegraph (London).
Economist (London).
Globe and Mail (Toronto).
Gulf News (Dubai).
Hartford Courant (Hartford, CT).
International Herald Tribune.
Le Devoir (Montréal).
Le Monde (Paris).

Los Angeles Times.
Mail & Guardian (Johannesburg).
National Post (Toronto).
New York Times.
Observer (London).
Plain Dealer (Cleveland, OH).
Portland Press Herald (Portland, ME).
Times (London).
USA Today.
Washington Post.
Washington Post National Weekly Edition.

Newsmagazines

American Prospect.
Atlantic Monthly.
Christian Science Monitor.
Harvard Magazine.
Middle East Economic Digest.
Middle East Insight.
Middle East International.
Middle East Report.
Nation.
National Review.
New Republic.
New York Review of Books.
New York Times Magazine.
New Yorker.
Newsweek.
Scientific American.
Time.
U.S. News & World Report.
Weekly Standard.
Weghat Nazar—Points of View (Cairo).

Newsletter

Middle East Institute Newsletter.

Other News Sources

American Enterprise Institute. http://www.aei.org.
Associated Press.
BBC News. http://news.bbc.co.uk.
Central Intelligence Agency's Web Site. http://www.cia.gov.
CNN.com.
CNNMoney.com.
Council on Foreign Relations's Web Site. http://www.cfr.org.
Deutsche Presse-Agentur.

Electionworld.org.

Icasualties.org.

Middle East Institute. http://www.mideasti.org.

MidEastWeb.

MSNBC.com.

National Priorities Project. http://nationalpriorities.org.

North Atlantic Treaty Organization. http://www.nato.int.

Radio Free Europe/Radio Liberty. http://www.rferl.org.

Reuters.

United Press International.

Washington Institute for Near East Policy. http://www.washingtoninstitute.org.

White House Web Site. http://www.whitehouse.gov.

World Socialist Web Site. http://www.wsws.org.

Index

About the Author

Marc J. O'Reilly is an Assistant Professor of Political Science at Heidelberg College in Tiffin, OH, where he also serves as Director of International and Multicultural Academic Programs and Chair of the International Studies Committee. He teaches Political Science courses on global politics, U.S. foreign policy, Middle Eastern politics, European politics, human rights, and the United Nations. As part of that course, he annually takes a group of students to the Model United Nations Conference of the Far West in San Francisco, California. He teaches Honors courses on Québec and empires as well as the capstone seminar in International Studies. He also co-teaches a First-Year Experience course with his spouse, Dr. Julie O'Reilly. He co-edited, with Patrick James and Nelson Michaud, *Handbook of Canadian Foreign Policy* (Lexington Books, 2006). He has published articles in *International Studies Perspectives, The Middle East Journal, Middle East Policy, The Journal of Commonwealth & Comparative Politics, Revista de Historia Actual, Historia Actual Online*, and *the American Review of Canadian Studies*. He has lectured at Baylor University, Bowling Green State University, the University of Windsor, and Butler University. He regularly presents papers at the annual International Studies Association (ISA) conference as well as ISA-Midwest. He holds a Ph.D. in Political Science from the University of Connecticut, an M.A. in Political Science from Ohio University (where he studied at the Contemporary History Institute), and a B.A. in Political Science from McGill University. He is a member of Phi Beta Kappa, Phi Kappa Phi, and Pi Sigma Alpha. Originally from Montréal, Canada, he lives in Tiffin with Julie and their two cats, Cleopatra and Queen Elizabeth. He likes to play and watch golf, follow Connecticut Huskies basketball, travel, and garden. Since 2001, the year he started teaching at Heidelberg, he has taken students on trips to England, Canada, Italy, and Greece.